KNOX ACADEMY LIBRARY
Please return the book on or before the last date stamped below.

INCHMARNOCK

'A proper habitation for one in Love with a Hermetical Life'

The Headland Project Team who were involved with the fieldwork, post-excavation analysis, illustration, research, writing up and delivery of this project. *Back row*: Dan Atkinson, Dave Henderson, Stephen Carter, Magnar Dalland, Julie Franklin, Ross Murray and Richard Conolly. *Middle row*: Kirsty Dingwall, Linn Breslin, Tim Holden, Davie Masson, Chris Lowe, Anna Faraś-Pągowska and Sarah-Jane Haston. *Front row*: Liz Jones, Tom Small and Mike Middleton.

INCHMARNOCK

An early historic island monastery and its archaeological landscape

CHRISTOPHER LOWE

with specialist contributions by

Daniel Atkinson, Rachel Butter, Stephen Carter, Richard Conolly, Kirsty Dingwall,
Ian Fisher, Katherine Forsyth, Julie Franklin, Andrew Heald, David Henderson, Timothy Holden,
Fraser Hunter, Elizabeth Jones, Dawn McLaren, Mike Middleton, Richard Oram, Anna Ritchie,
Carlo Tedeschi and Bruce Walker

Illustrators

Craig Williams, Linn Breslin, Thomas Small and Mike Middleton

Edinburgh 2008
SOCIETY OF ANTIQUARIES OF SCOTLAND

Cover image, from Blaeu's mid-17th-century *Atlas Novus*, shows *Buthe Insula Vulgo The Yle of Boot*.
Reproduced by kind permission of the British Library, London.

Published in 2008 by the Society of Antiquaries of Scotland

Society of Antiquaries of Scotland
National Museum of Scotland
Chambers Street
Edinburgh EH1 1JF
Tel: 0131 247 4115
Fax: 0131 247 4163
Email: admin@socantscot.org
Website: www.socantscot.org

The Society of Antiquaries of Scotland is a registered Scottish charity no SC010440

British Library Cataloguing-in-Publication Data
A catalogue record for this book is available from the British Library.

ISBN 978 0 903903 37 0

The Society gratefully acknowledges grant-aid for the publication of this volume from Lord Smith of Kelvin Kt.

Typeset in Bembo by Waverley Typesetters, Fakenham
Design and production by Lawrie Law and Alison Rae
Manufactured in Slovenia

Contents

Foreword

In March 1999 I bought Inchmarnock, a small 660-acre island, two kilometres off the west coast of the Island of Bute in the estuary of the river Clyde. At the time I knew very little about the island, except that it had been uninhabited for 25 years, though in fairly recent history it had supported a population of 41 people. There had also been discovered on the island some 30 years earlier the remains of a woman in a stone cist dating back some 3,500 years. The remains of a chapel linked to St Marnock were also just visible on the east of the island, covered in vegetation. Inchmarnock was also reported to have the largest herring gull colony in the Clyde estuary.

Today the island, though still uninhabited in the strict sense, has been transformed. Fields overgrown with bracken, brambles and even mature trees have been reclaimed. More than 200 pedigree Highland cattle roam every inch of the island, clearing ground, opening up dense birch and hazel woods and encouraging new plant life. The numbers and variety of species of birds have increased. Potatoes, turnips and cereal crops thrive and the winter feeding for cattle is grown on the island.

The *Marnock*, a working boat, new built and launched on Bute in November 1999 and capable of carrying 30-ton cargoes is docked on the island and a RIB plies its way most days between the new concrete slipways at the Port House, Straad, and the island, which is fully equipped with tractors, diggers, quad bikes and a generator.

The efforts of many people have achieved this transformation. My brother-in-law, Jock Turner who, with his wife Elaine, now lives on Bute and his colleague Alistair 'Fram' Murray, a born and bred Buteman, can take the principal credit for what has been achieved. My colleague Irene Adams who looks after many of my business interests has guided the various projects, mostly uncomplainingly! One such project, the subject of this book, was embarked on in May 1999.

At the time, I was Chairman of the Board of Trustees of The National Museums Scotland. Being interested in, and wanting to research, the history of Inchmarnock I spoke to senior museum staff. Although very interested they did not have the time to undertake the project. We had just (30 November 1998) opened the new Museum of Scotland in Chambers Street, Edinburgh, and curators were still involved in settling down the displays and working on a new Museum of Scottish Country Life. They recommended Headland Archaeology and this led to agreement in May 1999 for a seven-year investigation covering prehistory, early Christian (including the arrival of St Marnock), medieval and modern times. At the end we hoped we might have enough material to publish a book.

The discoveries have exceeded all my expectations as has the quality of this scholarly work. I have learned a very great deal about the history of Inchmarnock and grown to love it and to respect it and its former inhabitants even more, if that is possible. The work Headland has done will be useful to historians and archaeologists throughout Scotland, and indeed the UK and Europe.

While my wife Alison and I can enjoy the island as it is and watch its continuing transformation, our daughters Jeanette and Diane, and grandchildren Byron, Jim, Bonnie and Robbie will have a greater understanding of the importance Inchmarnock had, have a better grasp of Scottish history and culture and a knowledge of the way people lived in years gone by. Generations to come will be able to build on the work done here and by applying new techniques learn even more about our ancestors.

This book is about the past. We have undertaken some small studies on the flora and fauna of the island over the last seven years and look forward to engaging in more research in these areas as the island continues its regeneration. Perhaps this will lead to a new book – but that would be another story!

I would like to give my grateful thanks to many people: my patient wife Alison, who has watched with some amusement as I have undertaken slightly eccentric projects here and in South Africa; Jock and Fram, who have restored the island as a dear green place; Irene, who has to deal with all the unpleasant bits while I enjoy the results; all who have helped us in this endeavour but especially Chris Lowe and his colleagues at Headland Archaeology whose wonderful book this is.

Lord Smith of Kelvin Kt
May 2008

Acknowledgements

Preliminary research and fieldwork for the *Archaeology of Inchmarnock Research Project* were undertaken over the period 1999 to 2004. The post-excavation analysis and preparation of the publication report and the site archive were undertaken between March 2005 and November 2006.

The project was initiated in late 1999 by the island's then new owner, Lord Smith. The entire project, from the initial documentary research and site surveys, through to the fieldwork, the post-excavation research and analysis, the preparation of the publication and archive reports and, indeed, publication of this book itself, has been solely funded by Lord Smith. A particular gratitude is therefore offered to Lord and Lady Smith, not only for their patience, but also for their serious contribution to the study of the island's past. Some of the results of this work, however, are of more than local interest; with the inscribed slate assemblage, for example, it is clear that we have a body of material that is of national significance. Indeed, if we are right, there are pieces of written text in this assemblage which go back to the very earliest days of post-Roman Christianity in these islands.

Thanks are due to Jock Turner for getting us safely to site every day in the inflatable, even if it meant carrying the entire team out to the boat at low tide, though obviously one at a time; also to John McKinley, 'captain' of the *Marnock*, Lord Smith's roll-on/roll-off vessel, for getting the larger equipment on and off the island; and to Fram Murray for moving our gear and sample buckets to and from the various excavation areas.

Thanks too to Andrew McLean in the Bute Estate archives at Mount Stuart for tracking down maps and rentals and for answering our various enquiries; to Dr Anna Ritchie and Dr Barbara Crawford who acted as academic consultants to the project and who took the trouble to read and comment upon the various interim reports and project designs (*Archaeology of Inchmarnock Reports* [*AIR*] 1–13). A particular thank-you is also due to Jessica Herriot (formerly Jessica Middleton), not only for sharing her knowledge of the island but also for joining in with the fieldwork. The project would have been the poorer without her.

Over a dozen talks and seminars have been given on the project over the course of the past few years and it has been extremely useful to have had the opportunity to discuss the project with so many friends and colleagues in various local societies and university departments. Although it would be invidious, as ever, to single out named individuals, it would only be fair to mention the February 2007 research seminar in the Department of Archaeology in Oxford, and the thanks that must go to Dr David Howlett (Director, Dictionary of Medieval Latin from British Sources, University of Oxford) for his identification of the source of the *adeptus* fragment; to finally nail this text and to see it in its wider context has been particularly exciting.

Thanks are also due not only to the many specialists whose reports follow, but also to the various excavation supervisors and the field team who battled on in all the extremes of weather (and minor wildlife) that Argyll and Bute can offer. Particular thanks must go to Richard Conolly, Liz Jones and Kirsty Dingwall for their work in bringing together the records of the various excavated areas.

Supervisors

Richard Conolly	Site 4 (2002 to 2004)
Liz Jones	Site 16 (2002) and Site 8 (2003)
Stuart Halliday	Evaluations (2000), Sites 4 and 5 (2001)

Field Team (2000 to 2004)

Joe Ansell	Dan Atkinson	Graeme Cavers	Kelly Clapperton
Richard Conolly	Jo Dawson	Kirsty Dingwall	Hamish Fulford
Sarah-Jane Haston	Sam Hatrick	David Henderson	Colin Hewat
Liz Jones	Elizabeth McDonald-Gibson	Jonathan Millar	Ross Murray
Tom Ullathorne			

Thanks too to Davie Masson and all those who were involved in the samples processing work, and to Mhairi Hastie and Susan Lyons for seed identifications. Also, a big thank-you to Mike Middleton for his work in developing the recording techniques used here to illustrate and to better understand the incised stone assemblage; to Anna Faraś-Pągowska for the cover design; to David Simon for the fine reconstruction painting which captures a day in the life of the island's young scholars; to Craig Williams, Linn Breslin and Thomas Small for their illustration work, and to Thomas Small and all in the Graphics Department for seeing to the inevitable minor edits, reformats and all the illustrative miscellanea involved in bringing this material together for publication.

Other contributions (not otherwise acknowledged in reporting)
Magnar Dalland (surveying, 2002 and 2003)
Scottish Conservation Studio, South Queensferry (artefact conservation)
Richard Tipping, Eileen Tisdall and Althea Davies, University of Stirling (palynological studies, 2000 and 2001)

Acknowledgements are also due to the Royal Commission on the Ancient and Historical Monuments of Scotland (www.rcahms.gov.uk) for permission to reproduce the text and drawings from the publication 'Early Medieval Sculpture in the West Highlands and Islands', by Ian Fisher (2001, 77–9). Images are Crown Copyright: RCAHMS.

Finally, I am extremely grateful to Anna Ritchie and Andrea Smith for their detailed comments and observations on the first full draft; and to Alison Rae and Lawrie Law, on behalf of the Society of Antiquaries of Scotland, for seeing this through the publication process. As ever, any errors, inconsistencies or idiosyncrasies that remain will, unfortunately, be mine.

Chris Lowe
Edinburgh, 2008

Specialists' acknowledgements
Katherine Forsyth and Carlo Tedeschi are most grateful to Dr Ewan Campbell and Professor Thomas Clancy for guidance on matters of geological and linguistic detail respectively, and to Gilbert Márkus for his advice on Latinity; also to Dr David Howlett for his inspired identification and subsequently for saving us from error with his helpful interventions.

Fraser Hunter is grateful to Steve Driscoll and Martin Carver for access to relevant material from their excavations in advance of publication, and to Mick Jones for readily accepting to study samples of the oil shale and related material.

Julie Franklin is grateful to Nicholas Holmes for his comments on the coins, to Dianne Dixon for lithological identifications, and to Tobias Capwell for discussions about armour and chain-mail.

List of figures

List of plates

List of tables

List of contributors

DR DANIEL ATKINSON	Headland Archaeology Ltd, 13 Jane Street, Edinburgh EH6 5HE
LINN BRESLIN	Headland Archaeology Ltd, 13 Jane Street, Edinburgh EH6 5HE
DR RACHEL BUTTER	Department of Celtic, University of Glasgow
DR STEPHEN CARTER	Headland Archaeology Ltd, 13 Jane Street, Edinburgh EH6 5HE
RICHARD CONOLLY	Headland Archaeology Ltd, 13 Jane Street, Edinburgh EH6 5HE
KIRSTY DINGWALL	Headland Archaeology Ltd, 13 Jane Street, Edinburgh EH6 5HE
IAN FISHER	33 Bellfield Street, Edinburgh EH15 2BR
DR KATHERINE FORSYTH	Department of Celtic, University of Glasgow
JULIE FRANKLIN	Headland Archaeology Ltd, 13 Jane Street, Edinburgh EH6 5HE
DR ANDREW HEALD	Department of Archaeology, National Museums Scotland, Chambers Street, Edinburgh EH1 1JF
DAVID HENDERSON	Flat 19, 1 Chapel Lane, Leith, Edinburgh EH6 6ST
DR TIMOTHY HOLDEN	Headland Archaeology Ltd, 13 Jane Street, Edinburgh EH6 5HE
DR FRASER HUNTER	Department of Archaeology, National Museums Scotland, Chambers Street, Edinburgh EH1 1JF
ELIZABETH JONES	Headland Archaeology Ltd, 13 Jane Street, Edinburgh EH6 5HE
DR CHRISTOPHER LOWE	Headland Archaeology Ltd, 13 Jane Street, Edinburgh EH6 5HE
DAWN McLAREN	Department of Archaeology, National Museums Scotland, Chambers Street, Edinburgh EH1 1JF
MIKE MIDDLETON	Headland Archaeology Ltd, 13 Jane Street, Edinburgh EH6 5HE
PROFESSOR RICHARD ORAM	Department of History, University of Stirling, Stirling, FK9 4LA
DR ANNA RITCHIE	11/13 Powderhall Rigg, Edinburgh EH7 4GG
THOMAS SMALL	Headland Archaeology Ltd, 13 Jane Street, Edinburgh EH6 5HE
DR CARLO TEDESCHI	Dipartimento di Studi storici, Università Ca' Foscari, Venezia
DR BRUCE WALKER	149 Strathearn Road, West Ferry, Dundee DD5 1BR
CRAIG WILLIAMS	Headland Archaeology Ltd, 13 Jane Street, Edinburgh EH6 5HE

Chapter 1

The Background to the Project

CHRISTOPHER LOWE

1.1 INTRODUCTION

Inchmarnock is a small, low-lying island off the west coast of Bute, in the outer reaches of the Firth of Clyde. Early writers commented on its 'pleasant aspect'. Sir Donald Monro, High Dean of the Bishopric of the Isles, writing in 1549, described it as 'weill inhabit and manurit' (Macleod 1934, 487). Meanwhile, John Foulis, surveyor to the Bute Estate around the middle of the 18th century, went on to note:

> This Isle is a delightful retirement, can supply all the necessarys of Life within it Self, and would be a proper habitation for one in Love with a Hermetical Life.

As we will see, there are good reasons to believe that this is a view that would have been shared by the early Irish saints and the early church founders as they journeyed through these waters in the 6th and 7th centuries. Among these, of course, may have been the eponymous Ernán, for whom the island is named, or his followers.

Ecclesiastical remains, in all their various guises, constitute the most distinctive and widespread type of field-monument associated with the Irish settlement of Scottish Dál Riata, the area that roughly corresponds to the former county of Argyll. This ecclesiastical legacy is marked by stone crosses and other inscribed stones, holy wells, cave and chapel sites and early enclosed cemeteries. Also among the field-remains are the sites of several documented monasteries, principal among which is Columba's monastery on Iona, founded in 563. Other documented monasteries include Moluag's roughly contemporary foundation on the island of Lismore, established some time before his death in 592; Donnan's monastery on the island of Eigg where he and his community were martyred in 617; Maelrubha's monastery at Applecross, founded in 673; and, in a more local context, the rather shadowy Bláán (Blane) whose foundation at Kingarth, on Bute, was already well-established by c 659 when the death of Daniel, its bishop, is recorded. To this select group of individuals and assignable to the period of the late

6th or early 7th century, we will suggest, can now be added Ernán and his foundation on Inchmarnock.

Inchmarnock is unlikely to have been an 'empty' island prior to its ecclesiastical settlement. Rather, it will have been a piece of prehistoric 'real estate' and absence of evidence for later prehistoric settlement on the island should not, of course, be confused with evidence of absence. Indeed, Stephen Carter's analysis of the island's prehistoric past (Chapter 4) provides an insight into where that pre-medieval, pre-ecclesiastical settlement may have been. The focus of this study, however, has been with the island's early medieval and later past. And the particular focus, on which four of the seven excavation seasons were concentrated, has been the site at and around the church itself, preserved in the old stack-yard at Midpark. This is a sorry setting for this most important element of medieval Inchmarnock but it is clearly the key site for understanding the island's medieval and more recent past. What the present study now brings into focus, however, is the extent to which the Midpark site represents a very real break with earlier settlement on the island. Far from being an old or long-established 'central place', what we see is that Ernán's foundation must have started out as a 'green-field' development that was marginal and peripheral to the settlement focus of the island's prehistoric past. The settlement shift that occurred then, in the period around AD 600, marks a very real turning point in the island's fortunes.

1.2 RESEARCH AIMS AND SUMMARY OF RESULTS

The *Archaeology of Inchmarnock Research Project*, initiated by the island's new owner, Lord Smith, was undertaken over the period 1999 to 2004 with the aim of providing as complete a record as possible of the island's archaeology; of identifying and understanding better what was there, precisely where it was, and how it might be preserved for future generations.

The project began simply by collating what was known already, accurately locating (or in some cases, relocating) those sites and then assessing their place in the wider research agenda. Given the nature of the surviving remains, the great potential that the corpus of early medieval carved stones already offered, as well as this writer's research background and interests, it was recognised from the outset that the study would be focused on the island's medieval and more recent past. Detailed site-specific objectives were set out in the Project Research Design (*AIR* 6.1, Appendix 5).

The overarching objectives of the project were to consider how Inchmarnock's inhabitants made use of their island landscape in the medieval and later period and how the island itself related to the wider world. It was recognised that Inchmarnock offers the opportunity, in microcosm, of exploring major ideas of continuity and change at a variety of different levels; changes in the stewardship of the island in the medieval and later period, for example, will have impacted to a greater or lesser degree upon the ecclesiastical, political, social or economic life of its inhabitants. Equally, for the earlier period, there is the vexed question of the relationship between the Early Christian and the later Norse

Church, particularly in light of the fact that down to the middle of the 13th century, Inchmarnock, along with Bute, was technically part of the Norse kingdom of Man and the Isles.

The preliminary results of each season's fieldwork, together with assessments of the artefacts and environmental remains recovered, were reported on an annual basis (Table 1.1). In tandem with this was an extensive radiocarbon-dating programme (Appendix 1), providing the chronological framework for the investigation.

Back in 2004, a number of questions were raised (Lowe 2004). What would a small island monastery of the 7th or 8th century off the west coast of Scotland look like? How would buildings and space within the site be organised, how would the settlement itself relate to its broader landscape and what light could archaeology throw on the day-to-day life of its inhabitants and its cultural origins? The results of the current project go some way towards answering some of these questions.

The various surveys and excavations summarised below in Table 1.1 have thrown considerable light on

Table 1.1 Summary of annual fieldwork and reporting (*AIR* – *Archaeology of Inchmarnock Report series*)

	Fieldwork	Research	Reports
1999	Walk-over survey	Desk-based assessment	*AIR* 1
2000	Landscape survey (Season 1) Evaluation (Sites 1, 3, 4, 5, 8, 9 and 16) Building Recording Survey Preliminary Pollen Survey		*AIR* 2.1 *AIR* 3 & 4 *AIR* 5 Tipping *et al* 2000
2001	Excavation: Site 5 Excavation: Site 4 (Season 1) Pollen cores	Project design	*AIR* 6 *AIR* 7 *AIR* 8 Tipping *et al* 2001
2002	Landscape survey (Season 2) Excavation: Site 4 (Season 2) Excavation: Site 16		*AIR* 2.2 *AIR* 9 *AIR* 10
2003	Excavation: Site 4 (Season 3) Excavation: Site 8 Geophysical Survey	Historical background	*AIR* 11 *AIR* 12 Webb 2003 Oram & Martin 2003
2004	Excavation: Site 4 (Season 4)		*AIR* 13

the island's past. The gains have been in terms both of 'breadth', in the sense that only a handful of sites was known prior to this project (Chapter 2), as well as 'depth', in that we now have a very detailed knowledge and understanding of what happened at some of these places in the past. The development of the church and graveyard (Site 4), the key medieval site on the island, is central to this story, and the excavations have not only identified what is probably an earlier stone-built church on the site but also the remains of a much earlier monastic settlement, specifically the detritus associated with a school-house where novices and oblates were taught how to read and write, as well as compass-work and instruction in elementary design and decoration. Radiocarbon dates clearly indicate activity on the site from around at least the third quarter of the first millennium AD.

The key artefact associated with this early settlement is the large collection of inscribed slate. This is the largest assemblage of such material from anywhere in the British Isles and it is of particular importance because of its implications for monastic schooling and design. Epigraphic evidence suggests that some of the inscriptions from the early monastic site could date to the early 7th century. Meanwhile, the same site also gives us our first evidence for the informal, non-monumental use of ogham alongside Latin, as well as what is clearly evidence of training and instruction in both. A late medieval literate presence, possibly associated with the regulation of pilgrimage activity on the island, is also clearly evidenced.

The leisure activities of the island's past inhabitants are indicated by the large assemblage of gaming boards that have been found. Meanwhile, further finds of cross-incised slabs and other examples of early medieval sculpture mean that, in Scotland, Inchmarnock now sits second only to Iona in terms of the size of its cross-marked stone assemblage.

In structural terms, the Early Christian settlement is represented by a series of post-built huts, at least one of which was associated with metalworking activity. The production of shale bracelets (formed on oil shale and related materials) has also been identified on or near the site. Meanwhile, contemporary, late first millennium activity has also been identified in one of the caves or rock shelters at the south end of the island (Site 16) and from below the excavated building (Site 5) near the quarry. This latter site has also produced a series of late-, or more likely, post-medieval dates, whilst the nearby corn-drying site (Site 8), with the remains of several heavily robbed corn-driers, has been radiocarbon-dated to the period spanning the 11th to 13th centuries. The same site also produced a fragment of a soapstone bowl, an artefact type usually associated with a Norse presence. Evidence for Norse activity in this area is slight, although not unexpected given the presence of the rune-inscribed slab that was discovered near the church in 1889.

Meanwhile, analysis of early maps, together with the results of field survey itself, has allowed us to reconstruct, at least in part, the nature and extent of the pre-Improvement landscape, elements of which can be recognised among the present-day field boundaries and other enclosures.

Knowledge of the island in the later, post-medieval period comes to us almost wholly through the cemetery population. Here we come face to face with the island's past inhabitants; the people who will have worshipped in the church, attended funerals in the burial ground and, in turn, have been received there themselves. They will have worked in the fields whose boundaries, in many cases, we can still see today. Among this group also are probably those who constructed the building at our Site 5, the turf-built structure on the hillside above the coastal quarry, which was built around 1600 and altered about a hundred years later. Also among this group will doubtless be those who toiled in the quarry itself.

Each and every one of the excavated burials from the graveyard is, of course, an anonymous individual whose life story is essentially unknown to us. However, three very personal accounts emerge. In two cases these have become known as a result of the analyses of the human remains (SK91 and SK97) themselves, in the third (Grave G106) as a result of the objects that were found in different years (2001 and 2004) on different excavation areas.

Among the human remains are two individuals, a teenage boy (SK91) and a middle-aged woman (SK97), who suffered particularly violent deaths. Extensive blade injuries have been preserved on their skeletons and the forensic analysis provides a chilling account of their final moments. In the third case (G106), none of the young child's bones were preserved but we do know that she was buried in a dress that had been embroidered with glass beads. Tellingly, from the earth floor of the early 18th century building at Site 5 where the little girl had almost certainly played in life, came a similar bead, presumably part of the same assemblage. The whole event, reflected by a handful of tiny glass beads, provides an insight to the personal tragedy that unfolded in that building.

1.3 ORGANISATION OF THIS REPORT

This report has been constructed as a series of discrete chapters. The middle section of the report (Chapters 5–8) is taken up with the presentation of the results of the various investigations that go to make up the Project. Around this are a series of introductory, baseline and synthetic or 'overview' chapters which set the scene and consider the wider archaeological and historical issues that emerge from this Project.

Chapter 2 – *Location, survey and setting* – is an introductory chapter concerned with setting the scene, both in terms of the island's topography and its archaeological background. It also provides an archaeological baseline of what was known prior to 1999 together with what has been identified during the course of the various surveys undertaken since.

Richard Oram's study in Chapter 3.2 provides a historical framework of the Clyde estuary region for the period from about the middle of the 6th century down to *c* 1600, in which Inchmarnock is considered as a microcosm of the wider events that affected this area in this period. The study also illustrates a series of key themes in Scottish history in general. This is then followed in Chapter 3.3 by Rachel Butter's work on the Inchmarnock and Kildavanach place-names, and the significance of the Ernán dedication.

Chapter 4, by Stephen Carter, provides a summary and overview of Inchmarnock in prehistory. This is based on the finds and sites previously known on the island, together with those elements of the story that have emerged as a result of the present investigation. This wide-ranging study covers the period from the early Holocene (10,000 BC) down to the time at which Ernán and/or his followers first stepped ashore on the island in or around AD 600.

Chapters 5 to 7 take up the results of the investigation at Site 4, the early ecclesiastical site preserved in the stack-yard at Midpark. Chapter 5 deals with the archaeological structures, sequences and phasing; Chapter 6 with the artefacts, whilst Chapter 7 comprises David Henderson's analysis of the human remains from the cemetery.

The results of the 'minor' site excavations, at Sites 5, 8 and 16, are presented in Chapter 8.

Finally, Chapter 9 takes up the island narrative from where it left off in Chapter 4, providing an overview and, where possible, a connected account of the island from Ernán down to the Improvement period in the late 18th and early 19th centuries and the conversion of the old burial ground into the stack-yard. Thereafter, the excavations at Site 4 (and, indeed, elsewhere on the island) in the 1970s by the Middleton family, the island's last tenants, bring the story full circle.

Technical reports on the radiocarbon dates, the faunal remains, the boat graffiti and the methodology of preparing the illustrations, together with a catalogue of the minor incised slate fragments, are presented as a series of Appendices.

Chapter 2

Location, Survey and Setting

STEPHEN CARTER AND CHRISTOPHER LOWE

2.1 THE PHYSICAL BACKGROUND

STEPHEN CARTER

2.1.1 Location (Figure 2.1)

Inchmarnock is an island in the Firth of Clyde that few people will be aware of, unless they live on Bute or have crewed one of the many yachts that take advantage of the excellent sailing conditions that the Firth offers.

It is located just off the west coast of Bute; 1.3km at the closest point and 2km between the regular landing places on the two islands. Inchmarnock is a small island: viewed from Bute (Plate 2.1) it is a simple low ridge of land running parallel to the shore, 3.1km long and up to 1.1km wide. It is therefore dwarfed by the two principal islands in the firth, Arran and Bute which, along with Great Cumbrae, retain substantial human populations. Inchmarnock is one of a scattering of small islands in the firth that have all supported resident human populations at one time (Haswell-Smith 2004): Sanda off the Mull of Kintyre, Ailsa Craig at the outer end of the firth, Holy Island close to Lamlash in Arran, and Little Cumbrae between Ayrshire and the southern end of Bute. With the exception of Holy Island's recently formed Buddhist community, none of these islands has more than a single occupied house. Inchmarnock has been unoccupied since 1986 when the last farming tenant left.

A vantage point on the ridge that runs down the centre of Inchmarnock provides an excellent 360-degree view of the upper part of the Firth of Clyde. The view to the east is closed off by the low hills of Bute; to the north is the narrow entrance to the Kyles of Bute, hemmed in by the mountains of Cowal (Plate 2.2). Westwards, there is the entrance to Loch Fyne, the sea-route into Argyll, with the hills of Kintyre beyond. Further south, the view of Kintyre is blocked by the mass of mountains that make up the northern end of Arran, only 10km from Inchmarnock by sea. Steep-sided Holy Island can be distinguished close to the east coast of Arran and then a long view opens up down the firth to the Ayrshire coast, a hazy line some 50km away to the south.

2.1.2 Geology and topography (Figure 2.2)

In terms of geology, Inchmarnock is a small fragment of the extensive belt of metamorphosed sedimentary rocks that extends from Kintyre in the south to the Banffshire coast in the north. More specifically, it is composed of pebbly psammites with some cleaved, phyllitic semi-pelites and pelites of the Innellan Group (BGS 2000). Psammites are coarse grained metamorphic rocks that produce a flaggy rubble, used for all of the buildings on the island. The cleaved phyllitic rocks produce slates, which have been exploited in quarries at various points around the island's coast. The cleavage planes of the metamorphic rocks dip at an angle of 20–25°

Plate 2.1
Inchmarnock from the boat-slip at Straad, facing west, with St Ninian's Point to the right and the outline of Kintyre and Arran to the left

5

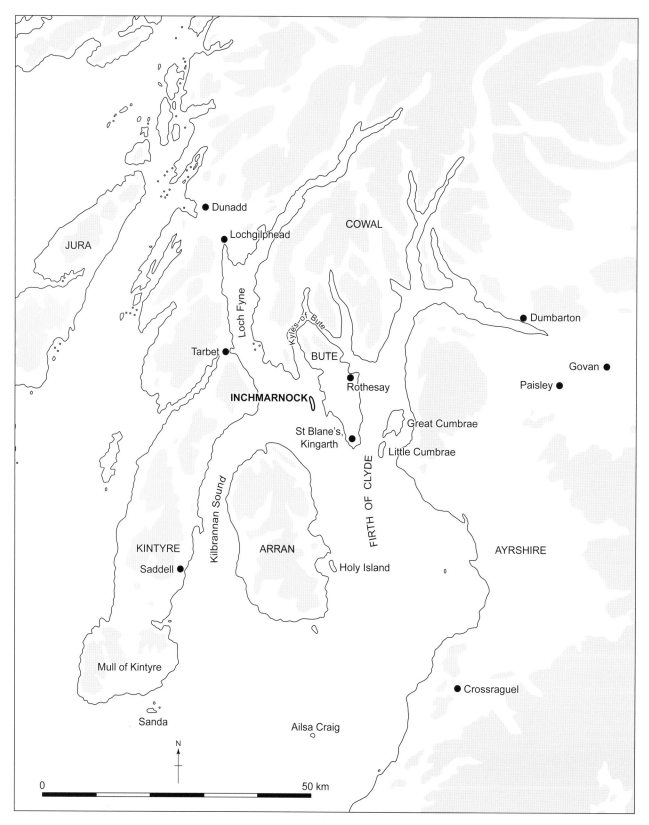

Figure 2.1
Inchmarnock in its regional context, Argyll and the Firth of Clyde

Plate 2.2
The Improvement-period landscape of the island, facing north from the hill above Site 5 with the steadings at Midpark and Southpark in the middle distance, and the Kyles of Bute beyond

to the south-east. This has led to the creation of many more rock outcrops on the west side of the island than the east, where the main slopes are generally parallel to the cleavage planes.

The current form of the island was only created during the most-recent glacial period (the Devensian, ending c 14,000 years ago). Ice moving from north to south from the mountains in Argyll produced a landscape of strongly pronounced north–south ridges and depressions. Inchmarnock is a minor example of this much larger landform, comprising a narrow north-south ridge that rises 60m above current sea level at its highest point.

The island is fringed by a low rocky and open coastline with no sheltered inlets or landing places. There is one small sand beach on the east coast at Midpark and areas of shingle beach further north at Northpark, and another near the south-east corner of the island; otherwise the shore is rocky and difficult to approach. The beach at Midpark has been the principal landing place for Inchmarnock in the historic past and probably for much longer.

The modern shoreline is formed from the mid-Holocene raised beach platform that emerged around 5,000 years ago following a fall in relative sea level. The platform is a well-defined but narrow feature running around the entire coastline, no more than 150m wide. It is generally rocky with little beach sediment but sections on the west and south-east coast

contain substantial deposits of 'shell marl' or 'maerl', accumulated fragments of cold-water calcareous corals. These deposits were exploited as a source of lime fertiliser from at least the 18th century onwards.

The raised beach is backed by a low cliff line, which marks the position of the coast in the late-Mesolithic period. On the sheltered east side of the island this old shoreline is now a steep overgrown bank but on the exposed west and south there are cliffs up to 30m high which contain a number of shallow sea caves. Exposures of slates on the shore and in the old cliffs have been widely exploited for roofing slates on a small scale with more extensive workings on the east coast, just to the south of Midpark.

Moving inland, gentle slopes rise to rounded ridges. There is a general contrast between the east and west side of the island in terms of rock outcrops, with more apparent on the west side. The principal topographic interest is provided by fragments of the late-glacial high-level raised beach. They have been mapped at various points on these slopes (BGS 2000) but only create significant landforms in the south-east of the island. The area of level and poorly drained ground immediately to the west and south of Midpark is interpreted as a beach platform up to 200m wide between 20–30m OD. To the south of this, the low-lying ground between two hills appears to have been an inlet of the late-glacial sea. Shingle ridges from a storm beach have blocked the inlet, creating a shallow basin

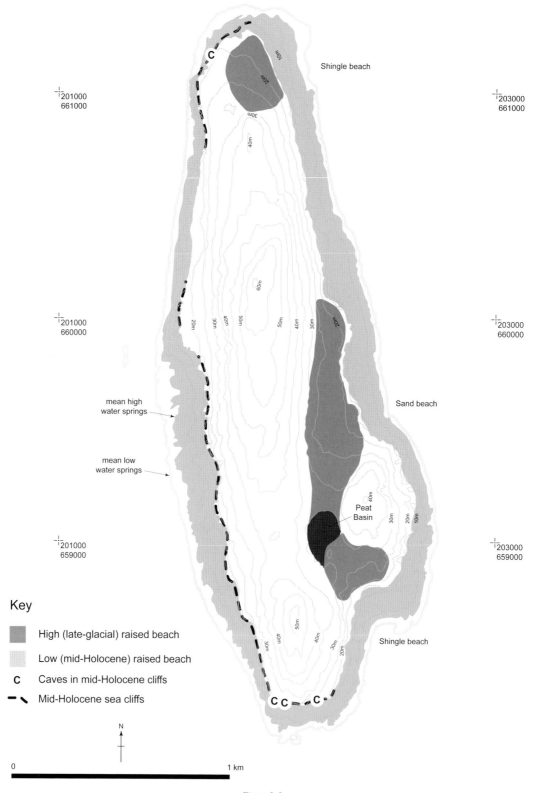

Figure 2.2
The geology and geomorphology of the island

behind that still retains peat deposits. These deposits are the only identified source of palaeoenvironmental data for the island and were investigated as part of the present project.

2.1.3 *The landscape of Inchmarnock (Figure 2.3)*

The current pattern of landuse in Inchmarnock can be traced back to the late 18th century, although elements of it are considerably earlier as will be explored later in this volume. In the 1780s, the Bute Estate (owners of Inchmarnock) reorganised the farming of the island into three single-tenant farms; a process typical of the agricultural improvements of this period. This landscape has largely survived to the present day, albeit with progressive amalgamation to the point where it is farmed as a single holding.

The three farms, logically named Northpark, Midpark and Southpark, divide the island into three holdings of approximately equal agricultural value if not equal size. Southpark is much larger than the other two but contains a large area of unimproved moorland and woodland. The boundaries between the farms are marked by two substantial stone dykes that cut across the full width of the island. The steadings of Midpark and Southpark (Plate 2.3) are sited together beside medieval St Marnock's Church and just above the traditional landing place for the island. The steading for Northpark was built away from the area of historic settlement at the northern end of the island, but close to the other useable landing place on the east shore.

Each of the three farms has its share of enclosed and improved arable land and open moorland grazings. The arable fields cover the summit of the main ridge and much of its east-facing slope; they are enclosed

Plate 2.3
Midpark and Southpark, from the photographic platform next to the church, facing south

either by drystone dykes or thorn hedges, which can be seen to replace earlier turf dykes in some areas. This is considered further in Chapter 2.3 below. The western slope and southern tip, fringing the raised beach platform, are unimproved except for small pockets and support rough grassy or heathy pasture and scrubby woodland. The woodland, a mixture of small birch, hazel and rowan trees, occurs in three main blocks on the east coast and appears to be of some antiquity. The earliest detailed map of the island (Foulis 1758–9: Figure 2.6) depicts trees in these same three areas, reinforcing the point that the woodland forms a third managed landuse type along with the arable and pasture.

The lack of active farming on the island between 1986 and 2000, when cattle were reintroduced, means that much of the detail of historic landuse has become obscured. During the period without grazing livestock there was some extension at the margins of the woods and bracken took over all of the arable land. All three steadings are now derelict and partially ruinous. However, the recent reintroduction of active management of the land has rapidly reversed these changes and the historic landscape of the island is becoming clear once more.

2.2 THE ARCHAEOLOGICAL BACKGROUND

CHRISTOPHER LOWE

2.2.1 *Archaeological base-line prior to 1999*

Only a handful of sites was known and recorded in the National Monuments Record of Scotland (NMRS) prior to the start of this investigation (Sites 1–5: Figure 2.5). The first sites on the island to be recognised, first recorded by the Ordnance Survey at the time of their mapping survey in 1863, were the cairn (Site 1) and the church itself (Site 4), though subsequent research would show that the location of the church was known to the Bute Estate surveyors roughly a century earlier (*Map Evidence & Landscape Reconstruction*, Chapter 2.3 below). Aside from sculpture finds from around the church in the late 19th century (Chapter 6.2.1), the next major site was not discovered until 1960 when three Bronze Age cists (Site 2) were unearthed during ploughing by Dan Boag, the then tenant at Northpark. Two of the cists had been disturbed in antiquity; in the third, however, were the well-preserved remains of a young woman (the so-called 'Queen of the Inch') together with her flint knife and an impressive jet bead

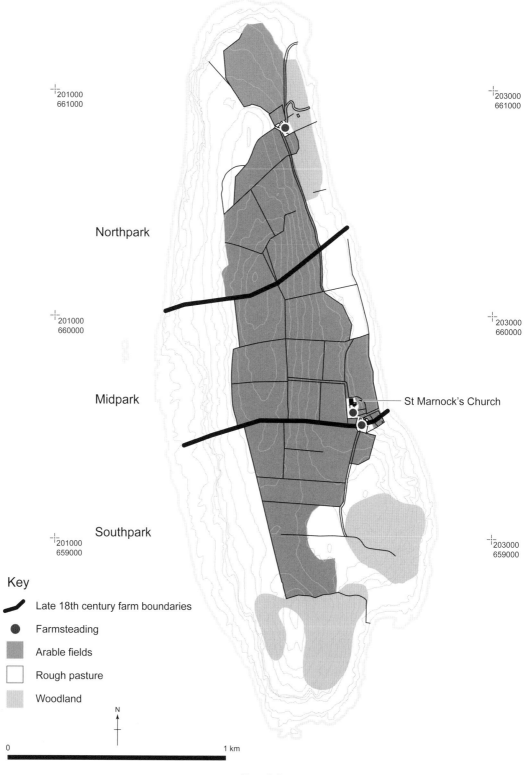

201000
661000

203000
661000

Northpark

201000
660000

203000
660000

Midpark

St Marnock's Church

201000
659000

203000
659000

Southpark

Key

Late 18th century farm boundaries

Farmsteading

Arable fields

Rough pasture

Woodland

N

0   1 km

Figure 2.3
The present-day landscape

necklace (Chapter 4.5). The other reported sites, a cup-and-ring-marked stone (Site 3) and a building (Site 5), together with notices of artefacts found during field-walking, were recorded in the 1970s by the Middleton family, the last tenants at Midpark.

Other sites, considered below, such as the quarry (Site 6), the upright stones nearby (Site 7) and the rock shelters (Sites 9, 15 and 16) at the south end of the island, were known to the Middletons but these would not be formally reported until the present survey was able to benefit from the local knowledge that Jessica Herriot (formerly, Jessica Middleton) was able to bring to the project. It was also clear that there had been some exploratory investigations at the post-medieval corn-drying kiln, at what would become our Site 8. In 1999, however, this was all for the future.

The pre-1999 base-line for the sites and monuments of Inchmarnock thus comprised these five sites and records of a few stray finds, plus an obscure reference to a possible sixth site, the so-called 'Devil's Cauldron', first recorded by Blain in 1818 but not published until 1880 (Ross 1880, 94). Its precise location, however,

was unknown; its very essence, moreover, was largely a matter of guesswork.

By analogy with the similarly known large sub-circular, drystone structure at St Blane's Church on Bute, the feature was identified in the NMRS record (NS05NW 7) as a probable dun. Duns are fortified homesteads and were circular or oval on plan with thick drystone walls, typically 3m to 6m wide, and up to 25m across overall. They were occupied from the late Iron Age to the Roman period (approximately 250 BC–AD 250). Their distribution extends from south-west Scotland to the Inner Hebrides and the northern Scottish mainland (eg Harding 1997, Figures 7.1–7.3). Clearly, Inchmarnock lies in 'dun country'. It is extremely difficult, however, to imagine how such a substantial structure could have been entirely removed or overlooked.

According to the published accounts, the Inchmarnock 'cauldron' was said to have been located near the 'south corner' of the island. It was not known, however, to the Middletons, nor to Dorothy Marshall, the local antiquarian who worked on the island with

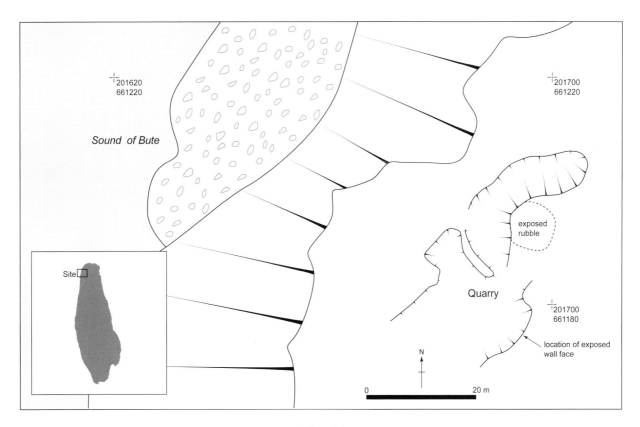

Figure 2.4
The quarry (Site 22) at the north end of the island – Blain's 'Devil's Cauldron'?

Plate 2.4
Blain's 'Devil's Cauldron'(?) (Site 22), from adjacent cliff-top
facing NNE

the family in the 1970s. At the time of the present base-line survey, it was assumed to perhaps refer to a natural rock formation (Jessica Herriot, pers comm).

Documentary research and fieldwork by the present investigation has almost certainly resolved this puzzle. It is not, however, a dun; nor is it located at the south end of the island. Blain's *History of the Island of Bute* was not published until some 60 years after his death in 1820 (Ross 1880). It was originally written as a commission for the earl of Bute and there are at least two manuscript fair copies with different pagination in the Bute Archive at Mount Stuart. Perhaps significantly, the second copy was evidently rewritten in a neater hand following comments by the Earl about Blain's handwriting in the first. It is clear from the second manuscript fair copy (p. 134) that the 'Devil's Cauldron' was not located at the south end of the island but, rather, at what Blain calls its 'north corner'. And, indeed, on the shore's edge, just below the old cliff-face, is where we were to find the remains of a curving drystone wall-face and a large area of disturbed ground, the south-west end of which is roughly 20m across (Figure 2.4; Plate 2.4). It is not, however, the remains of a large roundhouse but rather a stone retaining wall in an area that has previously been quarried for its stone (Site 22). Although it is impossible to date such a feature, the most likely historical context for its exploitation would be the opening up of the north end of the island in the late 18th century with the creation of the steading at Northpark and the enclosure of its various fields.

The pre-1999 archaeological base-line for the island thus comprised three prehistoric features (Sites 1–3), a medieval church (Site 4) and a building of medieval or later date (Site 5), some stray finds of various periods, and an obscure reference to a 'Devil's Cauldron' (Site 22).

The first tasks of the survey project would therefore be to visit and accurately locate those sites that were already recorded. Next, it would be a matter of tracing those which were known locally but which were essentially unrecorded; thereafter it would be a case of discovering what else may have survived, unrecognised (*Archaeological Survey*, Chapter 2.2.2 below). In all this work, we were fortunate enough to have two early pre-Improvement plans of the island. These would be important, not only for identifying individual sites but also for providing the basis on which we could start to see how the earlier, medieval landscape may have looked (*Map Evidence & Landscape Reconstruction*, Chapter 2.3 below).

2.2.2 Archaeological survey (2000–2) (Figure 2.5)

In all, a total of 35 sites were identified during the course of the archaeological survey (Table 2.1). This was undertaken over three seasons as the dense undergrowth that had engulfed the island since its abandonment in 1986 was gradually removed. All parts of the island were visited during the course of the survey. The densely wooded areas to the north-east, south-east and south, however, were only cursorily explored, as were areas along the western side of the island where rank vegetation still prevents easy access and impedes the visibility of any surface remains.

Two of the sites (Sites 12 and 21) known to Jessica Herriot could not be identified on the ground; another three (Sites 7, 10 and 20) are either definitely or very likely the remains of old field dykes and banks which, these examples aside, were not otherwise individually recorded in the Gazetteer. The remaining 30 sites are discussed below in terms of their probable chronology. Nine can probably be classified as prehistoric, twelve as medieval or post-medieval in date and another nine, specifically, can probably be dated to the 18th or 19th century.

Prehistoric sites (Table 2.2)

The prehistoric sites and stray finds of prehistoric artefacts, known to or reported by the Middleton children in the 1970s, make up a motley collection of

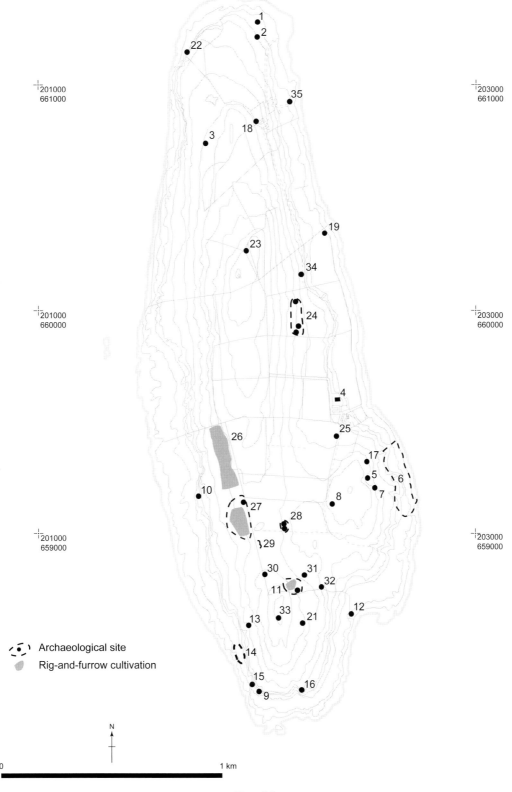

201000
661000

203000
661000

201000
660000

203000
660000

201000
659000

203000
659000

Archaeological site

Rig-and-furrow cultivation

N

0   1 km

Figure 2.5
Sites identified during archaeological survey (2000–2)

13

Table 2.1   Gazetteer of identified sites (Sites 1–35)

Site	NMRS no	NGR	Monument type	Description	References
1	NS06SW 6	NS 0202 6132	Burial cairn (kerbed)	Stone cairn 24.3 × 21.7m and up to 1.9m high, with a 0.5m deep central depression. Upright stones noted at NW edge of cairn, forming possible kerb. Marshall records undocumented excavation by Professor Bryce c 1903. Excavated trial trench in 2000 confirmed presence of kerb.	ONB 1863, v, 55; Marshall 1980, 15; AIR 3 & 4
2	NS06SW 11	NS 01998 61227	Bronze Age burial cists	Group of three cists discovered 1960 during ploughing. Two had been disturbed previously and were earth-filled, containing only a single jet-bead. Third cist was intact, containing female skeleton, flint knife and a necklace of 135 lignite beads (Marshall 1963). Cist constructed with rebated side-stones (Scott 1963).	Marshall 1963; Scott 1963; Sheridan et al forthcoming
3	NS06SW 17	NS 0176 6078	Cup- and ring-marked stone	Discovered 1976 by Jessica Middleton. Excavated trench around stone in 2000 clearly indicates this is a detached slab of schist, 1.5 × 1.3m and 0.10–0.17m thick. On its surface is a cup with a complete ring, 170mm diameter, and one cup mark, 120mm diameter. Three further cups, possibly with rings, previously reported but not identified.	Middleton, J 1977; AIR 3 & 4
4	NS05NW 2 & 23	NS 0237 5965	Medieval church/site of Early Christian monastery	Site of church recorded by Ordnance Survey 1863; foundations and disturbed floor of church (which contained burials) revealed during excavations by the Middletons and others in 1973–74 (Marshall 1973; 1974). Rune-inscribed slab discovered NW of site in 1889 (Hewison 1893, i, 223: Black 1890, 438: Fisher 2001, 77–79); others found since, mostly during 1970s investigations in and around the site of the church. Documentary references to robbing stones from the site in 1718 and again in 1829 (Hewison 1893, i, 133–4). Excavation Results: Chapters 5–7.	Marshall 1973; Marshall 1974; Hewison 1893; Fisher 2001
5	NS05NW 11	NS 0252 5930	Post-medieval building	Low footings of a rectangular building, located roughly 300m SE of Midpark, were investigated by the Middletons in the 1970s (Middleton, D 1977). Excavation reportedly revealed central hearth and among the finds was a cannon-ball (Jessica Herriot, pers comm). Finds also included sherds of 14th–16th-century pottery, and two coins reportedly dating to the 15th and late 17th century. The earlier coin has since been identified as an Alexander III silver penny (1280–c1286). Excavation results: Chapter 8.3	Middleton, D 1977
6		NS 0665 5931 (site centre)	Quarry	Traces of former slate quarries cover area of roughly 3ha on E coast of island, to S of Midpark landing place. Dumps of waste slate exposed for 300m along shore, up to 5m deep in places, and extending up to 100m inland. Remains of a round, stone-built powder house – 1m in diameter and 0.5m high – have been reported (Jessica Herriot, pers comm). Not located by this survey: the quarry is heavily overgrown and access is difficult. Quarry noted on Foulis plan of 1758/59, though apparently already then redundant; absent from Leslie's plan of 1769.	
7		NS 0256 5926	Upright stones	Group of 11 upright stones, probably the remains of what were otherwise turf dykes, located in the woodland south of Site 5. An open trench, 1m deep, around one of the stones (0.74m wide, 0.22m thick and >1.21m tall) indicates unrecorded antiquarian activity at the site.	

Table 2.1 Gazetteer of identified sites (Sites 1–35) (continued)

Site	NMRS no	NGR	Monument type	Description	References
8		NS 0235 5916	Post-medieval kiln; medieval kiln-site	Turf-covered stony remains of a post-medieval kiln, with a drystone-built bowl 2.5m diameter; partially excavated by the Middletons in the 1970s (Jessica Herriot, pers comm). Large oval mound, roughly 13 × 10.5m, lay a few metres to S. The robbed remains of further corn-drying kilns – medieval in date – were identified during excavation. Excavation results: Chapter 8.4.	
9		NS 0202 5834	Cave/rock shelter	Rock shelter, roughly 7.5m across and 5.5m wide, located in old cliff-face above raised beach near SW corner of island. Trial trench evaluation across mouth of cave revealed series of occupation deposits; environmental remains yielded large quantities of marine shell, bone, charcoal and small quantity of charred hazel nutshells. Basal deposit in cave radiocarbon-dated to the period cal 346–4 BC.	
10		NS 0174 5920	Promontory with bank	Low turf-covered bank reported at landward end of small promontory in cliff-face above raised beach (Jessica Herriot, pers comm). Feature not located on ground but map evidence suggests feature lies at/near W end of Dyke B37, first depicted on OS revised map 1896.	
11		NS 0221 5879 (area centre)	Clearance cairns, rig-and-furrow cultivation, dykes	Moss-covered cairn, 4 × 3m and up to 0.8m high, lies just N of Dyke B1 at NS 02190 58774. Formed of small to medium stones over larger angular stones at base. A second clearance cairn, 1.5m in diameter and 0.3m high, located nearby at NS 02186 58789. Adjacent is a small patch of rig-and-furrow cultivation, roughly 30 × 40m. Rigs are roughly 2m apart, centre to centre.	
12		NS 0242 5870	Enclosure (possible)	Site of small enclosure (Jessica Herriot, pers comm) located in area of rank vegetation; remains too slight to interpret.	
13		NS 0198 5863	Find spot (flint flakes)	Flint flakes reported to have been found in this area (Jessica Herriot, pers comm).	
14		NS 0194 5850 (site centre)	Quarry	Small slate quarry located on the present shore and old cliff line.	
15		NS 0195 5838	'Dysart' and cave/rock shelter	Built against the rock face in the angle of the cliff are the turf-covered footings, up to 0.6m high, of a small structure, roughly 4 × 2m internally. This end of the island is known locally as 'Dysart' (Jessica Herriot, pers comm).	
16		NS 0220 5836	Cave/rock shelter	Like Site 9, this cave or rock shelter, roughly 10m wide and 6m deep, is located in the old cliff-face above the raised beach. Trial excavation in 2000 identified primary Iron Age deposits in the cave, together with hearth debris – radiocarbon-dated to the late first millennium AD – in the upper part of the profile. Further excavation was undertaken in 2002. Excavation Results: Chapter 8.2.	

Table 2.1 Gazetteer of identified sites (Sites 1–35) *(continued)*

Site	NMRS no	NGR	Monument type	Description	References
17		NS 0252 5937	Corn-drying kiln/kiln-barn	Sub-rectangular mound, 6 × 3m and 0.6m high, located 70m N of Site 5. Mound aligned NNW–SSE and covered in brambles and bracken. Stone-lined hollow, 0.8m diameter and 0.6m deep at SE end, forms probable kiln-bowl; line of possible flue indicated by channel, 0.4m wide.	
18		NS 0200 6089	Cists	Five cists of unknown type are reported to have been discovered near the SW corner of the yard at Northpark in the early 1980s. Unearthed by the tenant, Dan Boag, and subsequently seen by Mr Middleton senior (Jessica Herriot, pers comm).	
19		NS 0231 6039	Boat nousts (possible)	Two adjacent hollows, dominated by wild iris. Each is roughly 6 × 3m, 0.8m deep and open to the shore, located just inside the N boundary of the Midpark holding. No stonework evident or traceable underfoot.	
20		NS 02502 58959	Fragmentary stone dyke (Dyke B28)	Previously recorded as site of standing stone (Jessica Herriot, pers comm), it is now clear that the large upright stone at NS 02502 58959 – in dense bracken – forms part of Dyke B28.	
21		NS 0220 5863 (approx location)	Cairn	Cairn recorded at roughly this location (Jessica Herriot, pers comm) but not located during the 2002 survey.	
22	NS05NW 7 (incorrect map sheet)	NS 01695 61172	Quarry (probably same as Blain's so-called 'Devil's cauldron')	Arc of prominent, curvilinear stony mound, up to 15m long, 5m wide and in places over 1m high, located in raised beach near NW corner of island. Remains of coursed drystone wall-face, formed of very large blocks of slate, present on N-facing side of feature; bulk of mound, however, comprises slate shillet. Although superficially structural in appearance, the mound may simply be a stone-revetted spoil heap, left over from slate quarrying. Almost certainly to be identified with Blain's so-called 'Devil's Cauldron' and probably associated with the late 18th–century development of Northpark (see Chapter 2.2.1).	
23		NS 01955 60282 (area centre)	Stone spread	Rectangular spread of small to medium stones, 20 × 4m and up to 0.6m high, located in corner of field between Dykes B16 and B23. Feature in this location is also depicted on OS second edition map of 1897 (revised 1896).	
24		NS 0218 6000 (area centre)	Clearance cairns	Three large turf-covered, oval stony mounds, typically up to 7 × 4m and up to 0.8m high on the downslope side, are located along break of slope in field N of Midpark. Small field clearance type stones visible on top of mounds which appear to have been formed over rock outcrop at base. Probably associated with early 19th–century expansion of cultivable land.	
25		NS 02370 59469	Burnt stones	Spread of small to medium burnt stones in matrix of dark soil visible over a distance of roughly 2m in both sides of recently cut drainage ditch, 1.2m wide. Deposit, up to 0.12m thick overlies thin layer of brown sandy silt and is, itself, overlain by field soil, 0.2–0.3m thick.	

Table 2.1 Gazetteer of identified sites (Sites 1–35) *(continued)*

Site	NMRS no	NGR	Monument type	Description	References
26		NS 0185 5935 (area centre)	Cultivation remains	Large area of rig-and-furrow cultivation located outwith head-dyke. Rigs, 5m apart centre to centre, are aligned roughly SW–NE.	
27		NS 0192 5908 (area centre)	Cultivation remains; clearance cairns	Large area of rig-and-furrow cultivation located outwith head-dyke. Rigs, 4m apart centre to centre, are aligned roughly SW–NE. Rigs appear to respect line of Dyke B9; a low bank (B36), perpendicular to B9, however, appears to predate the present system of rigs. Group of five stony mounds, 2–3m diameter and 0.4m high, are located near NE corner of cultivation plot at NS 0195 5917.	
28		NS 02131 59065	Clearance cairns	Turf-covered mound of small stones, roughly 4m diameter and up to 0.5m high, heaped against rock outcrop. A second, smaller cairn lies a few metres to S, adjacent to Dyke B7. Located at break of slope above and to W of peat basin near S end of island.	
29		NS 02015 58962 – NS 02005 59017	Structures/stock-pens	Robbed-out remains of two rectilinear structures, possibly stock-pens, each roughly 12 × 2m internally, located against E side of Dyke B6. Defined by a series of low, turf-covered stony banks up to 2m wide and 0.4m high. Arc of turf-covered stony bank, 10m long, 1.5m wide and 0.4m high, may represent remains of a third structure – located W of Dyke B6, adjacent to Dyke B2 at NS 02012 58959.	
30		NS 02039 58856	Clearance cairn	Moss- and bracken-covered stony mound, 6 × 2m and 0.7m high, lies in area between Dyke B2 and Dyke B6. Bisected by modern sheep-track.	
31		NS 02233 58847	Structure (possible)	Robbed-out remains of possible structure/stock-pen, roughly 5 × 5m, located against W side of Dyke B5.	
32		NS 02298 58795	Structure (possible)	Robbed-out remains of possible structure/stock-pen, roughly 5 × 5m, formed of low turf-covered stony banks, 1.5m wide and up to 0.35m high, located against N side of Dyke B1.	
33		NS 02102 58664	Cairn; 'shepherd's cairn'	Single moss- and bracken-covered, low stony mound, 2m in diameter and 0.3m high. Located on exposed ridge within clearing in woodland. Marked as a 'Shepherd's cairn' and benchmark on the 1897 OS map.	
34	NS06SW 16	NS 022 602	Find spot (stone axes)	Chipped polished porcellanite stone axe and part of another found by the Middletons at NS 022 602 and NS 022 604 respectively in summer of 1978.	Middleton *et al* 1979
35		NS 02116 60921	Boat-house	Rectangular drystone enclosure, aligned E–W and up to 15 × 6m internally. Walls, 0.9m wide, are well coursed and stand up to 0.85m high. Much of the N side of the structure – against the slope – has been robbed; wide and off-set openings, up to 5m wide, are located in the E and W end-walls. A boat-house is first depicted in this location on the OS 2nd edition map (revised 1896), indicating a construction date within the period 1863 x 1896.	

Table 2.2 Prehistoric sites on Inchmarnock

Site	NGR	Monument type
1	NS 0202 6132	Burial cairn (kerbed)
2	NS 01998 61227	Bronze Age burial cists
3	NS 0176 6078	Cup- and ring-marked stone
9	NS 0202 5834	Cave/rock shelter
13	NS 0198 5863	Find spot (flint flakes)
16	NS 0220 5836	Cave/rock shelter
18	NS 0200 6089	Cists
25	NS 02370 59469	Burnt stones
34	NS 022 602	Find spot (stone axes)

finds which are both geographically and chronologically diverse.

At the north end of the island there is a very obvious group of funerary-related monuments (Chapter 4.5 below). Sites 1 (cairn) and Site 2 (short-cists) very clearly belong with a funerary function, as would the reported discovery of further cists (Site 18) at Northpark in the 1980s, although, of course, we do not know whether these were prehistoric short-cists or later long-cists. A funerary context could also

Plate 2.5
General view of old cliff-line at south end of island, facing east, with Site 9 in foreground (with figure) and Site 16 in distance

apply to the cup-and-ring-marked stone (Site 3). Such decorated slabs are commonly incorporated into the construction of Early Bronze Age cists as side- or cap-stones.

Two of the recorded prehistoric sites relate to the discovery of stray finds (Sites 13 and 34). A possible burnt mound (Site 25) may be indicated by the presence of burnt stones, observed in the sides of a modern drainage ditch, near Southpark. Meanwhile, at the south end of the island, later prehistoric activity was identified in the primary levels of the two rock shelters (Sites 9 and 16: Plate 2.5) that were subsequently investigated as part of this project.

These, together with the small but interesting assemblages of prehistoric material recovered from the recent excavations, are discussed in detail by Stephen Carter in his tentative reconstruction of the island's prehistoric cultural landscape (Chapter 4).

Medieval/post-medieval sites (Table 2.3)

The key site in this group is, of course, the church itself (Site 4). This was the focal point of settlement on the island from the medieval period onwards. We see the improved version of this settlement structure in the Ordnance Survey maps of the 19th century; and we see an earlier 'clachan-like' version in the scatter of buildings that are depicted on the mid-18th century pre-Improvement plans of Foulis (Figure 2.6) and Leslie (Figure 2.7). In terms of actual buildings, however, we have only the structure at our Site 5 which, in its present form, is a building of 17th-century and later date, although we can be confident that the site must have occupied from the late first millennium AD onwards (Chapter 8.3). The building at Site 5 is exceptional, however, in the sense that it was abandoned and thus became available for investigation; the earlier versions of the buildings at Midpark and Southpark, on the other hand, will lie in and around and under the present-day steadings.

In addition to Sites 4 and 5, included in this group are also some of the places where the medieval or later population worked, such as the quarries (Sites 6 and 14), or where they will have come together to dry their corn (Sites 8 and 17) at harvest-time, as well as structures and features associated with the clearing of land for cultivation (Sites 11 and 28–30). Also attributable to this period will be the possible boat nausts (Site 19), where the boats will have been brought up from the beach and sheltered when not required. The rock shelter (Site 15) and the '*Dysart*'[1] place-name, meanwhile, potentially take us back to

Table 2.3 Medieval/post-medieval sites on Inchmarnock

Site	NGR	Monument type
4	NS 0237 5965	Medieval church/site of Early Christian monastery
5	NS 0252 5930	Post-medieval building
6	NS 0665 5931 (site centre)	Quarry
8	NS 0235 5916	Post-medieval kiln; medieval kiln-site
11	NS 0221 5879 (area centre)	Clearance cairns, rig-and-furrow cultivation, dykes
14	NS 0194 5850 (site centre)	Quarry
15	NS 0195 5838	'Dysart' and cave/rock shelter
17	NS 0252 5937	Corn-drying kiln/kiln-barn
19	NS 0231 6039	Boat nousts (possible)
28	NS 02131 59065	Clearance cairns
29	NS 02015 58962–NS 02005 59017	Structures/stock-pens
30	NS 02039 58856	Clearance cairn

Table 2.4 18th- and 19th-century sites on Inchmarnock

Site	NGR	Monument type
22	NS 01695 61172	Quarry (probably same as Blain's so-called 'Devil's cauldron')
23	NS 01955 60282 (area centre)	Stone spread
24	NS 0218 6000 (area centre)	Clearance cairns
26	NS 0185 5935 (area centre)	Cultivation remains
27	NS 0192 5908 (area centre)	Cultivation remains; clearance cairns
31	NS 02233 58847	Structure (possible)
32	NS 02298 58795	Structure (possible)
33	NS 02102 58664	Cairn; 'shepherd's cairn'
35	NS 02116 60921	Boat-house

the very earliest Christian times and the possible use of this and the other caves as a place of retreat by hermits in search of solitude and an ascetic way of life. And of course we know from the radiocarbon-dating evidence, recovered during the excavation (Chapters 5, 8.2 and 8.3), that at least two of the sites in this group (Sites 4 and 5) and one from the 'prehistoric group' (Site 16) also have an Early Christian, late first millennium AD chronology.

In terms of their distribution, it is very noticeable that there is a concentration of sites on the east side of the island, in and around the Midpark/Southpark area, where six of the twelve sites in the group are located (Sites 4–6, 8, 17 and 19). Of the others, there is a group of four (Sites 11 and 28–30) on the southern fringes of the old cultivable ground; and another two (Sites 14 and 15) to the south-west.

Late 18th- and 19th-century sites (Table 2.4)

The final chronological group that can be identified is simply a sub-group of the former category whose chronology can be roughly tied down to the late 18th or 19th century. In some cases, such as the stone-spread (Site 23) or the boat-house (Site 35) at the north end of the island or the shepherd's cairn (Site 33) at the south, the map evidence might even imply a tighter chronology, focused on the latter part of the 19th century. In others, such as the 'rediscovered' 'Devil's Cauldron' (Site 22), its very presence would be best explained as a development that went hand-in-hand with the late 18th-century creation of the Northpark holding and its need for stone.

2.3 MAP EVIDENCE AND LANDSCAPE RECONSTRUCTION

CHRISTOPHER LOWE

2.3.1 Introduction

The sites and monuments of prehistoric and medieval Inchmarnock belong to an earlier landscape, very different to the large, enclosed fields that we see today.

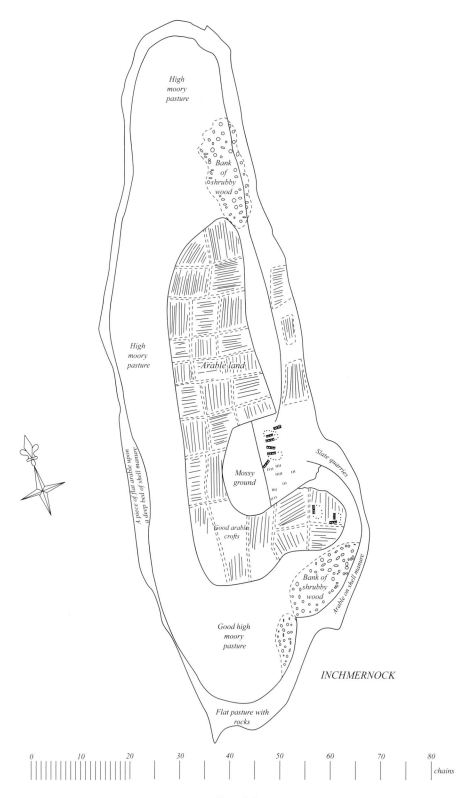

Figure 2.6
Inchmernock – a survey of the Isle of Bute by John Foulis 1758–9

A tentative reconstruction of the island's prehistoric landscape is explored by Stephen Carter in Chapter 4. But how much, if any, of the island's relatively more recent, medieval landscape survives and can it still be recognised in amongst the fields and enclosures of the modern-day, post-Improvement landscape?

The Agricultural Improvements of the late 18th and early 19th centuries wrought great changes on, and in places swept away, a managed landscape that was already centuries old. However, the extent to which the pre-Improvement landscape preserved or fossilised the fields and boundaries of medieval Inchmarnock is by no means clear. Thus, whilst it is possible to reconstruct, at least in outline, the pre-Improvement landscape, by stripping away the later accretions of the 19th and 20th centuries, it does not necessarily take us back to a landscape that would have been familiar to the island's medieval inhabitants. It does, however, represent the best chance we have of coming at least a little closer to that time so that we can begin to understand how the landscape was exploited by the island's medieval inhabitants, the nature of its resources and, importantly, the limitations that it presented.

2.3.2 Sources and method

We are particularly fortunate in that we have a very good series of maps and plans of the island. The mid-18th-century Bute Estate maps by John Foulis (Figure 2.6) and John Leslie (Figure 2.7),[2] together with the First Edition Ordnance Survey map (Figure 2.8) surveyed roughly one hundred years later, provide a series of snap-shots of the pre- and post-Improvement landscape. Additional detail is also provided by Samuel Girdwood's 1821 sketch plan of the land-divisions at Midpark (Figure 2.9). Samuel Girdwood was much employed at this time in improvements throughout the Bute Estate (Andrew McLean, pers comm). Subsequent changes can be traced in the Second Edition (revised 1896) and later Ordnance Survey maps. During the course of the sites and monuments survey, the opportunity was therefore taken to look at the actual field boundaries themselves, to see if their physical remains and the map evidence could throw any light on the chronology and development of the island's cultural landscape.

2.3.3 Results (Table 2.5; Figure 2.10)

Six different types of field boundary can be identified on the basis of their appearance and mode of construction (Figure 2.10, Types I–VI). The various boundaries are

described and their mapping evidence summarised in Table 2.5. A note of any chronological implications follows each classification and this is developed further in the discussion section below.

TYPE I: BROAD TURF-COVERED STONY BANKS
(B3–B6 AND B38)

Type I banks were only recognised at the south end of the island, principally in the woods immediately to the south of the area of bog and on the higher ground above it to the south-west. The banks are characterised as broad and stony (Plate 2.6). B3 and B5 (probably one and the same bank, but incorporated into and under the extant stone dyke, B1) are 4–5m wide and up to 1m high. B4 and B6 are less substantial. Bank 38, adjacent to the excavated late- or post-medieval building at Site 5, probably also belongs with this group.

Banks B3, B4, B5 and B38 have not been previously mapped; B6 corresponds to the line of the hill-dyke which is depicted on the 1863 Ordnance Survey map and which was subsequently replaced by the extant stone dyke (B2) in the period 1863 x 1896. B6 possibly also features on the 1758 Foulis map as the western extent of cultivated ground. The broad arc of an intermittent dyke (not traced on the ground), depicted by Leslie in the area to the west, may be associated with these boundaries.

Map evidence suggests that the Type I boundaries form part of the pre-Improvement landscape. They are not, however, necessarily contemporary elements of the same field system; a *prima facie* case might suggest that the less substantial banks B4 and B6 represent a later

Plate 2.6
Bank B3, facing south-west: broad stony bank at south end of island, cut by modern access track

21

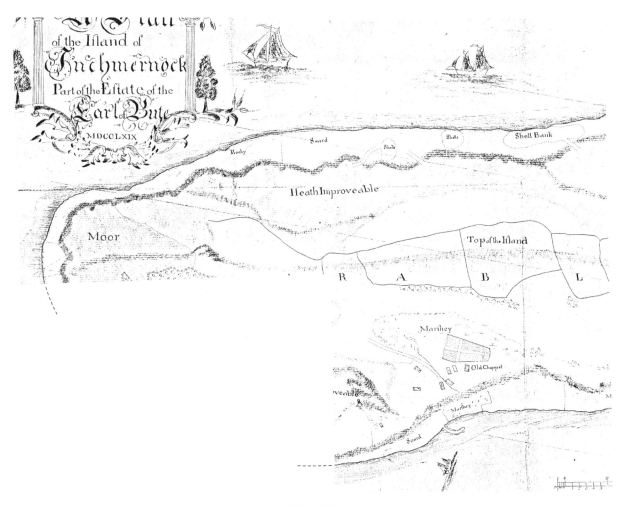

Figure 2.7
A Plan of the Island of Inchmernock by John Leslie 1769 (*see Note 2*)

division of the area possibly enclosed by banks B5, B3 and the unlocated boundary depicted on Leslie 1769. The intermittent nature of this latter boundary and the apparent absence of any enclosure to the south may suggest that this part of the field system was abandoned some time prior to 1769.

Bank B38, meanwhile, appears to define the western edge of the area of improved ground below the excavated building at Site 5. The extent and complexity of the old field boundaries in this area, however, is unknown.

TYPE II: LOW FOUNDATIONS OF DRYSTONE DYKES/ VEGETATION-COVERED (B16, B20–B24, B26–B29, B33 AND B35)

Type II boundaries are found principally in two areas of the island; along the south-east side of Southpark's

lands and, to the north, enclosing the areas of 'old arable' that were divided off in the late 18th century to form Northpark. A group of late enclosures nearby, on the west shore of Midpark, can also be similarly classified.

Traceable as low stone foundations, typically turf- or bramble-covered, Type II boundaries may subsume a variety of original construction types. They could, for example, represent drystone dykes (cf Types V and VI) that have been subsequently robbed; alternatively, stone footings to an essentially turf-built dyke, or stone footings to a post-and-wire fence.

Map evidence suggests that some elements of Type II are coincident with boundaries that were laid out in the pre-Improvement period; others belong with the late 18th and early 19th century; yet others to the late 19th century.

Table 2.5   Gazetteer of boundary-types and land divisions

	Ht	W	Description	Foulis 1758	Leslie 1769	Girdwood 1821 (Midpark only)	OS 1863	OS 1896	Comments
B1	1.1	0.5	Drystone dyke; horizontal coursing at base with vertical topping.	X	X		*	*	Course laid out 1769 × 1863 but much modified 1863 x 1896. B1, in present form, probably dates to 1863 x 1896.
B2	1.1	0.5	Drystone dyke; horizontal coursing at base with vertical topping.	part	part		part	*	S end constructed 1863 × 1896; N end coincident with course of pre-1758 boundary (probable line of old hill dyke). B2, in present form, probably dates to 1863 x 1896.
B3	1.0	4.0	Substantial turf and bracken-covered stony bank; occasional exposures of stone core; cut by modern access track; western extent obscured by rank vegetation.	X	X		X	X	Not previously mapped; probably associated with B5 to the E and incorporated into later boundary B1. Date unknown: possibly medieval.
B4	0.5	2.0	Substantial turf and bracken-covered stony bank, 10m long and aligned NS; occasional exposures of stone core; northern extent obscured by rank vegetation.	X	X		X	X	Not previously mapped; associated with B3. Date unknown: possibly medieval.
B5	0.6	5.0	Substantial turf and bracken-covered stony bank, 65m long and aligned NS; at S end turns W and underlies stone dyke B1.	X	X		X	X	Not previously mapped; probably associated with B3 to the W and incorporated into later boundary B1. Date unknown: possibly medieval.
B6	0.3	2.0–3.0	Low turf-covered stony bank, bramble- and bracken-covered; lies roughly parallel and to E of stone dyke B2.	?	?		*	*	Course laid out prior to 1863 (possibly present on Foulis & Leslie as W extent of cultivated ground); replaced by stone dyke B2 in latter half of 19th century; line visible as area of rough ground on OS survey of 1896.
B7	0.3	2.0	Low turf dyke with hawthorn hedge.	?	?		*	*	Extends from lochan in W and crosses area of boggy ground in basin to E; probably coincides in part with S boundary of enclosed ground depicted on Foulis 1758 & Leslie 1769.
B8	0.3	2.0	Low turf dyke with hawthorn hedge.	X	?		*	*	Boundary aligned EW, between cultivable land to N and basin to S; possibly depicted in part on Leslie 1769; extended E in late 18th/early 19th century.
B9	0.6	3.0	Broad low turf dyke, aligned NE–SW, perpendicular and to W of boundary B2; associated with rig-and-furrow cultivation; western extent obscured by rank vegetation.	X	X		X	X	Not previously mapped; similarity to B37 to N may suggest a similar late 19th century construction date.

Table 2.5   Gazetteer of boundary-types and land divisions (continued)

	Ht	W	Description	Foulis 1758	Leslie 1769	Girdwood 1821 (Midpark only)	OS 1863	OS 1896	Comments
B10	1.2	0.5	Drystone dyke; horizontal coursing at base with vertical topping.	part	part	★	★	★	Major shore-to-shore boundary; partially depicted on Foulis 1758 and Leslie 1769 but extended to W shore in period 1769 x 1821, probably in the 1780s as a result of the threefold division of the island. Although described as a stone dyke in 1821, B10, in its present form, probably dates to 1863 x 1896.
B11	0.3	2.0	Low turf dyke with hawthorn hedge, forming avenue up the hillside, to NW of Midpark.	?	X	★	★	★	Although possibly recognisable on Foulis 1758, its absence on Leslie 1769 suggests that the layout is not earlier than the late 18th century Improvements. First depicted (albeit as a single boundary) on Girdwood 1821.
B12	0.3	2.0	Low turf dyke with hawthorn hedge.	?	X	★	★	★	Although possibly recognisable on Foulis 1758, its absence on Leslie 1769 suggests that the layout is not earlier than the late 18th-century Improvements. First depicted on Girdwood 1821.
B13	0.3	2.0	Low turf dyke with hawthorn hedge.	?	X	★	★	★	Although possibly recognisable on Foulis 1758, its absence on Leslie 1769 suggests that the layout is not earlier than the late 18th-century Improvements. First depicted on Girdwood 1821.
B14	0.3	2.0	Low turf dyke with hawthorn hedge.	?	part	★	★	★	Probably laid out prior to 1758; prominent NS aligned boundary along upper edge of slope, extending between the shore-to-shore boundaries B10 and B15. Probably also partially depicted on Leslie 1769.
B15	1.7	0.5	Drystone dyke; horizontal coursing at base with vertical topping.	part	part	★	★	★	Major shore-to-shore boundary; partially depicted on Foulis 1758 and Leslie 1769 but extended to W shore in period 1769 x 1821, probably in the 1780s as a result of the threefold division of the island. Depicted by Girdwood 1821 in same style as B10 which was stone-built, suggesting that B15 may have been similarly constructed. B15, in present form, probably dates to 1863 x 1896.
B16	0.4	0.5	Low foundations of drystone dyke, brambled-covered. Ht 0.8m at junction with B15 but much reduced elsewhere.	X	part		part	★	Probably depicted on Leslie 1769; shown as sinuous boundary on OS 1863.
B17	1.0	0.5	Drystone dyke; horizontal coursing at base with vertical topping.	?	?	★	★	★	Coincident with course of pre-1758 boundary (probable line of old hill dyke). B17, in present form, erected after 1821 (note on Girdwood 1821), probably in period 1863 x 1896.

Table 2.5   Gazetteer of boundary-types and land divisions (continued)

	Ht	W	Description	Foulis 1758	Leslie 1769	Girdwood 1821 (Mid-park only)	OS 1863	OS 1896	Comments
B18	0.3	2.0	Turf dyke, up to 0.8m high on N, 0.3m on S.	?	part		★	★	Partially depicted on Leslie 1769 (and possibly indicated on Foulis 1758).
B19	0.8	0.5	Drystone dyke; horizontal coursing at base with vertical topping and incorporating orthostats with drilled holes on upper surface for post-and-wire fence.	?	?	★	★	★	Coincident with course of pre-1758 boundary (probable line of old hill dyke). B19, in present form, erected after 1821 (note on Girdwood 1821); probably in period 1863 x 1896.
B20	0.3	0.5	Low foundations of drystone dyke, brambled-covered.	?	?		★	★	Roughly corresponds to course of pre-1758 boundary (probable line of old hill dyke); N end laid out in period 1863 x 1896.
B21	0.4	0.5	Low foundations of drystone dyke, brambled-covered.	?			★	★	Possibly depicted on Foulis 1758 [Leslie 1769 not seen].
B22	0.4	0.9	Fragmentary drystone dyke.	?			★	★	Probable N edge (with B23) of cultivated ground depicted on Foulis 1758 [Leslie 1769 not seen]; extended to W in period 1863 x 1896.
B23	0.4	1.0	Low turf-covered footings of stone dyke	?			★	★	Possible NE edge (with B22) of cultivated ground depicted on Foulis 1758 [Leslie 1769 not seen].
B24	0.7	1.5	Low turf-covered footings of stone dyke, moss and bramble-covered, up to 0.7m high but much reduced elsewhere; stone core exposed in places but generally not traceable within extensive brambles.	X	?		★	★	Forms E side of track, to south of Southpark; area depicted as marshy on Foulis 1758; trackway [albeit on slightly different alignment] depicted on Leslie 1769. Possibly laid out in 1760s.
B25	0.3	1.0	Hawthorn hedge on low bank with drainage ditch or leat along east side leading to mill-dam at Southpark.	X			★	★	Forms W side of track, to S of Southpark; area depicted as marshy on Foulis 1758; trackway [albeit on slightly different alignment] depicted on Leslie 1769. Possibly laid out in 1760s.
B26	0.4	1.0	Low turf-covered footings of stone dyke.	X	X		X	★	Large U-shaped enclosure, evidently first depicted on OS 1897. Clearest at its junction with B24 but disappears into rank vegetation to N and E; one of the Southpark buildings and two others, to the S, are depicted in this location on Leslie 1769, suggesting perhaps a greater antiquity for the enclosure.
B27	0.5	1.4	Substantial turf-covered footings of stone dyke; stone core exposed in places; generally 0.3–0.5m high but up to 1.3m in woodland area to south. Late 19th-century modifications are constructed with horizontal coursing and vertical stones on top.	?	?		★	★	Extensive woodland enclosure; may be broadly indicated by extent of woodland shown on Foulis 1758 and Leslie 1769; constructed pre-1863, probably as part of the late 18th century Improvements; S side of enclosure modified in period 1863 x 1896.

Table 2.5 Gazetteer of boundary-types and land divisions (*continued*)

	Ht	W	Description	Foulis 1758	Leslie 1769	Girdwood 1821 (Midpark only)	OS 1863	OS 1896	Comments
B28	0.4	1.8	Turf-covered footings of stone dyke with occasional orthostats.	X			*	*	Coincident with track depicted on OS 1863 forming E side of large clearing; area shown as 'bank of shrubby wood' on Foulis 1758 [Leslie 1769 not seen]. Probably a late 18th-century clearing of former woodland.
B29	0.3	1.5	Low turf-covered footings of stone dyke with hawthorn hedge.	?	?		*	*	Probably laid out prior to 1758; prominent NS aligned boundary along upper edge of slope, delimiting E extent of old arable prior to late 18th-century Improvements.
B30	0.3	2.0	Low turf dyke with hawthorn hedge.	X	X		*	*	Extension of enclosed ground onto lower E slopes; late 18th or early 19th century.
B31	0.3	2.0	Low turf dyke with hawthorn hedge.	X	X		*	*	Extension of enclosed ground onto lower E slopes; late 18th or early 19th century.
B32	0.4	1.0	Drystone dyke, much robbed; horizontal coursing at base with vertical topping and incorporating orthostats with drilled holes on upper surface for post-and-wire fence.	X	X		*	*	Division of old arable; late 18th or early 19th century.
B33	0.7	1.5	Ruinous stone dyke, bracken- and bramble-covered.	X	X		*	*	Extension of enclosed ground onto lower W slopes; late 18th or early 19th century.
B34			Possible dyke, bracken- and bramble-covered, between old cliff-face and shore [viewed from bank, not visited].	X	X		X	*	Map evidence suggests construction in late 19th century.
B35	0.6	0.7	Stone dykes forming enclosure on raised beach.	X	X		X	*	Map evidence suggests construction in late 19th century.
B36	0.4	2.5	Low turf bank, parallel and to west of B2, joining B9 to north; appears to predate rig-and-furrow adjacent.	X	X		X	X	Not previously mapped; similarity to B37 to N may suggest a similar late 19th century construction date.
B37	0.4	2.5	Low turf bank, perpendicular and to west of B2, delimiting area of rig-and-furrow to north.	X	X		X	*	Map evidence suggests construction in late 19th century; may represent formal enclosure of ground that had been previously cleared (cf OS 1863).
B38	0.5	2.5	Turf-covered stony bank, bracken-covered; associated with excavated structure at Site 5. Extends from rock-face at S; lost in dense bracken to NE.	X	X		X	X	Not previously mapped; associated with excavated late- or post-medieval building at Site 5.

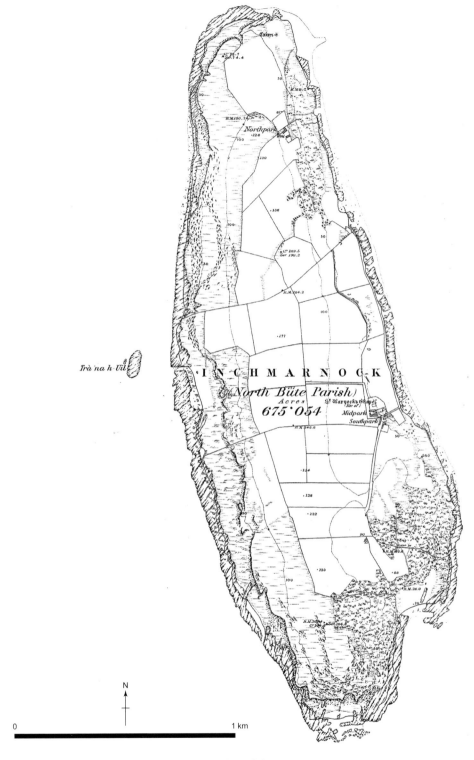

Figure 2.8
Inchmarnock in the middle of the 19th century (Ordnance Survey 1:10,560 map *Buteshire*, sheets CCII and
CCXIV, surveyed 1863)

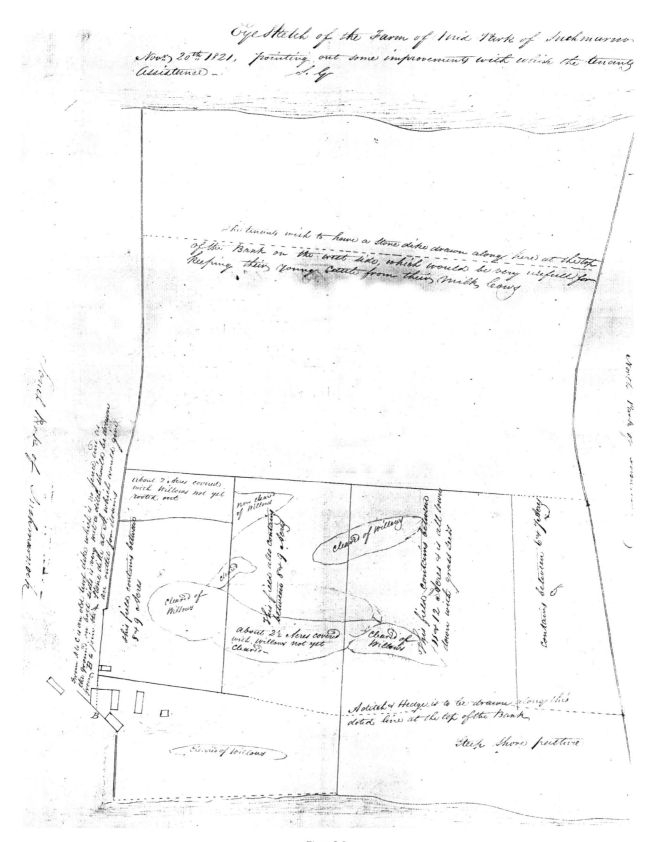

Figure 2.9
Eye Sketch of the Farm of Mid Park, Inchmarnock (20 November 1821) by Samuel Girdwood [Mount Stuart Archive]

TYPE III: HAWTHORN HEDGE IN LOW TURF DYKE
(B7, B8, B11–B14, B25, B30 AND B31)

Type III field boundaries are marked by low turf dykes, typically 0.3m high and 2m wide, along which hawthorn hedgerows have been established. With the exceptions of B25, which forms the west side of the track to the south of Southpark, and B14, which closely follows the east side of the 'old arable' along the top of the bank above Midpark, it is noticeable that the Type III boundaries generally lie east-west and occupy the lower slopes to the north and south-west of Midpark, coincident with areas of less well-drained and boggy ground.

Although a few elements of this group, such as B14, B25 and possibly B7, appear to coincide with pre-Improvement boundaries depicted on Leslie's map, it is clear that the majority (and possibly the boundary type itself) belong with the Improvement period landscape: B11, B12 and B13, for example, were established in the period 1769 x 1821; B8 was extended in the period 1769 x 1863; B30 and B31, meanwhile, were in place prior to 1863. In functional terms, the Type III boundaries represent an expansion of enclosure into the wetter and heavier soils along the eastern side of the island.

TYPE IV: LOW BROAD TURF DYKE (B9, B18, B36 AND B37)

Type IV field boundaries are marked by low, broad turf dykes, similar to Type III but unplanted. They also appear to lack the stone content that distinguishes the boundaries of Type I.

With the exception of B18, which corresponds to part of the area of 'old arable' as depicted on Leslie's map, the remaining elements of this small group are located on the south-west flank of the island. Located outwith the hill-dyke (B2), the banks are associated with areas of rig-and-furrow cultivation (Sites 26 and 27). Neither B9 nor B36 have been previously mapped; B37 is first depicted on the second edition OS map, revised in 1896. The banks may be associated with late 19th-century expansion of cultivation onto the hill-ground.

TYPE V: DRYSTONE DYKE, HORIZONTAL COURSING AT BASE WITH VERTICAL TOPPING (B1, B2, B10, B15, B17 AND PART B27)

The drystone dykes of Type V form the most substantial and most prominent elements of the current landscape. Standing up to 1.7m high, the dykes are constructed of drystone rubble, laid in courses and overlain with a capping formed of large edge-set stones placed perpendicular to the wall-line.

In terms of distribution, the Type V dykes demarcate the principal land-holdings on the island. The shore-to-shore dykes (B10 and B15) delineate the boundaries of Northpark, Midpark and Southpark; meanwhile, the south and much of the west hill-dyke are marked by dykes B1, B2 and B17. Part of dyke B27 is also constructed in this manner.

In terms of general course and alignment, it is clear that these boundaries belong with the Improvement period landscape of the late 18th century which saw the creation of the three 'park' holdings and the division of the 'old arable'. With the notable exceptions of the detailed changes that were made to Dyke B27 and the south end of Dyke B2 in the late 19th century, all were already established by the time of the first edition Ordnance Survey in 1863; indeed, the shore-to-shore boundaries were in place before Girdwood's map of 1821 (Figure 2.9). However, elements of this group can also be recognised as parts of the pre-Improvement landscape, such as the central elements of B10 and B15, as well as the north end of B2 and B17.

Although the boundaries formed by the Type V dykes are chronologically diverse, with parts dating to the late 18th century or earlier, it is clear that the dykes themselves, as structures, are somewhat later. It is clear, for example, from field evidence and comparison of the first and second edition Ordnance Survey maps, that the south end of Dyke B2 was realigned in the late 19th century; parts of Dyke B27 were similarly altered at this time. Meanwhile, there is documentary evidence that Dyke B17 and the Type VI boundary, Dyke B19, which together form the west hill-dyke of Midpark, were not constructed in stone until after 1821. A note on the Girdwood map (Figure 2.9) remarks:

> The tenants wish to have a stone dike drawn along here at the top of the Bank on the west side, which would be very usefull [sic] for keeping their young cattle from their Milk Cows.

This suggests that the earlier dykes shown in this position on Foulis and Leslie (Figures 2.7 and 2.8) were probably constructed of turf; and, perhaps significantly, that this area (formerly arable) had reverted to pasture, presumably in connection with the development of a dairy-based economy.

The Type V dyke, in summary, appears to be a diagnostic, late 19th-century type of land enclosure that was probably erected in accordance with a specification provided to its tenants by the Bute Estate.

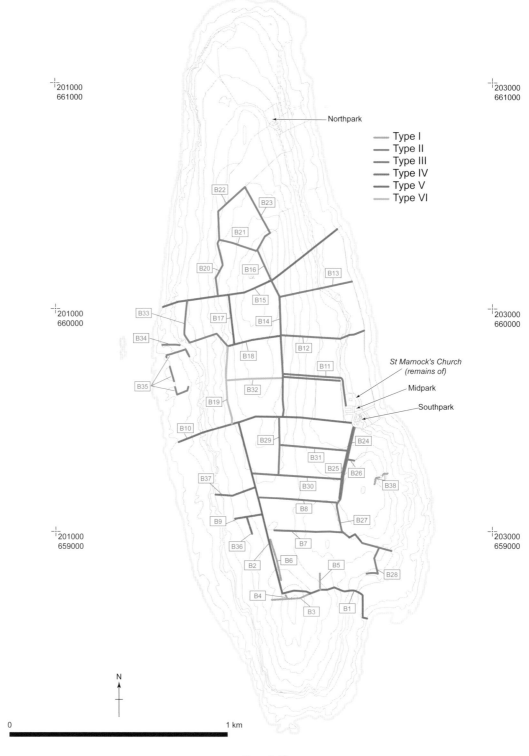

Type I
Type II
Type III
Type IV
Type V
Type VI

Figure 2.10
Mode of construction for the Midpark and Southpark field boundaries

TYPE VI: DRYSTONE DYKE, HORIZONTAL
COURSING AT BASE WITH VERTICAL TOPPING,
INCORPORATING ORTHOSTATS (B19 AND B32)

The Type VI dyke represents a variation of Type V,
similarly constructed but with the addition of earth-
fast orthostats at regular intervals along their course.
On the upper surface of the orthostats are drilled holes,
presumably for the erection of a post-and-wire fence
to contain stock.

Only two examples of this type were traced; both
are located in the area of 'old arable' above Midpark.
Dyke B19 corresponds with the line of the old hill
dyke, as depicted by Foulis (1758) and Leslie (1769);
Dyke 32 represents an Improvement period division of
the 'old arable'.

2.3.4 Interpretation

The pre-Improvement maps (Figures 2.7 and 2.8)

The key sources for recreating the pre-Improvement
landscape of Inchmarnock are the mid-18th century
surveys of the island by Foulis (1758–9) and Leslie
(1769), undertaken on behalf of the Estate as 'base-line'
surveys of its holdings and resources. It is not known,
however, why the island should have been surveyed
twice in ten years. Possibly the earlier Foulis map
simply failed to provide the Estate with the necessary
detail required for the Improvement programme of
works?

The Leslie map of 1769 is clearly the more proficient
and technically accomplished of the two maps. It
also presents considerably more detail; it shows, for
example, major vegetation changes, the topography
of the former cliff-line and what are probably rock
outcrops on the hill-side, as well as a small harbour
below Midpark.

Foulis' plan, on the other hand, has a sketch-like
quality. The extent of arable, for example, appears
to be disproportionately wide, given the evidence
of the later map; equally, the neat 'patch-work' of
small, enclosed cultivation plots seems 'formulaic',
rather than an accurate representation of the physical
landscape. Leslie's depiction of the buildings at what
were to become Midpark and Southpark, and the
settlement to the south-east (Excavation Site 5),
also appear to be more accurately located: Leslie's
buildings, for example, are drawn in plan; Foulis',
by contrast, are depicted in sketch elevation, showing
gable-ended structures with a low roof, a central
doorway and paired windows to either side. There are
also significant differences between the two plans with

regard to the disposition and number of buildings,
both at Midpark/Southpark and Site 5. The impression
gained from Foulis' map is that Inchmarnock in the
16th to mid-18th centuries was a multiple tenant farm
with perhaps seven households; five are located in what
would become Midpark/Southpark, with another two
groups to the south-east, probably our Sites 5 and 17.
Leslie's map, on the other hand, appears to show an
eighth household, between Midpark/Southpark and
those to the south-east.

Nonetheless, there is a broad agreement between
the two maps. Both, for example, show the extent
of 'mossy ground' around Midpark/Southpark, the
'banks of shrubby wood' at the south-east corner and
north end of the island, as well as the deep 'beds of
shell' along parts of the raised beach.

Leslie's map of 1769 forms the basis for identifying
any surviving elements of the pre-Improvement
landscape. Together with Girdwood's plan of 1821
and the later 19th-century Ordnance Survey maps, a
preliminary phasing of the boundaries and enclosures
that go together to make up the present-day enclosed
landscape can begin to be established (Figure 2.11).
Three broad phases can be recognised:

> pre-Improvement period
> Improvement period (*c* 1782 x 1820)
> late 19th-century modifications/extensions

The pre-Improvement period landscape

It is possible to recognise large elements of Leslie's map
in the modern-day landscape. It is clear, for example,
that the west side of the enclosed area of arable
corresponds closely to the line of Dykes B2/B6 and
B19. The 'dog-leg' between Dykes B17, B18 and B19
can also be recognised. The east side of the 'old arable'
is formed largely by Dyke B14 in Midpark, by Dyke
B29 in Southpark and probably by Dykes B16 and B23
in Northpark, the latter continuing the topographical
setting of the plots to the south.

In addition to the areas of old arable that lie along
the central crest of the island, there are hints of a large
enclosed area to the south-west of the bog or 'moss'.
A shortened form of what is probably Dyke B7 can be
seen to extend eastwards to the margins of the bog;
to the south-west is the arc of a prominent boundary
which appears to fade out in moorland. The enclosure
is possibly completed by Dyke B3 to the east and its
continuation to the north (Dyke B5) which terminates
close to the south margin of the bog. Examination of
the complete Leslie map may resolve this issue.

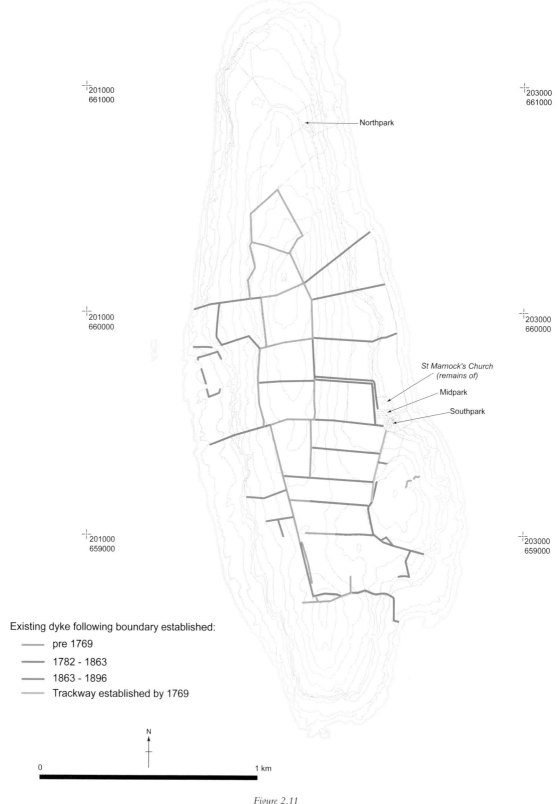

201000
661000

203000
661000

Northpark

201000
660000

203000
660000

*St Marnock's Church
(remains of)*

Midpark

Southpark

201000
659000

203000
659000

Existing dyke following boundary established:

———— pre 1769

———— 1782 - 1863

———— 1863 - 1896

———— Trackway established by 1769

N

0   1 km

Figure 2.11
The field boundaries and the expansion of the pre-Improvement field system, pre-1769 to 1896

The track-way to the south of Southpark would also appear to be a relatively early feature of the landscape, providing access to the bog for peat and rough pasture at the south end of the island.

The Phase 1 landscape is represented by a wide variety of boundary-construction types, reflecting the reuse and refurbishment of the various boundaries over time. The only original elements of this early landscape still surviving today are probably represented by the broad stony banks of boundary Type I, preserved as relict features in the woodland and rough pasture at the south end of the island.

Improvement period landscape (c 1782 x 1820)

The dominant feature of the Improvement period is the division of the 'old arable' by the construction of the shore-to-shore dykes (B10 and B15), extending to east and west elements of the earlier field system. A note on the Girdwood plan clearly establishes that Dyke B10 was stone-built; Dyke B15, by implication and drawing convention, was probably similarly constructed. The present walls, however, were probably refurbished in the latter part of the 19th century.

Contemporary with the division of the island into the three '-parks' and the division of the 'old arable' between them, is the expansion of enclosures onto the lower, east-facing slopes. Extensive drainage work, particularly of the fields to the west and south-west of Midpark/Southpark, would have gone hand-in-hand with these developments. Dykes B11–B13 and the complete line of Dyke B14 were all in place prior to 1821. Nonetheless, it is clear from the notes on the Girdwood plan that the programme of improvements was still ongoing in the 1820s. This is almost certainly the historical context for the creation of the large clearance cairns (Site 24) in the newly created field to the north of Midpark; cleared of willow scrub and drained, probably shortly before 1821, this field was sown with grass seed at the time of Girdwood's survey.

In constructional terms, the Improvement period landscape is partly represented by stone dykes of Types II and V, but overwhelmingly by the turf dyke and hedge of Type III. The use of stone appears to be confined to the outer elements of the field system; the shore-to-shore dykes B10 and B15, the hill-dyke B1 at the south end of the island and B27 which delimits the adjacent area of woodland. The Type III boundaries, by contrast, divide up the inner elements of the field system and are notably associated with the enclosure and improvement of ground on the lower, east-facing slopes.

Late 19th-century modifications and extensions

Later 19th-century improvements are characterised principally by a series of enclosures and outsets around the fringes of the enclosed landscape. The formal enclosure of the plots of rig-and-furrow cultivation at Sites 26 and 27 probably dates to this period, associated with the improvement of pasture on the old hill-ground. In constructional terms, map evidence clearly suggests that many of the stone dykes (Types V and VI) owe their present appearance to realignments and rebuildings that were undertaken at this time.

NOTES

1 The south end of the island was known to the Middletons, Inchmarnock's last tenants, as *Dysart* (Jessica Herriot, pers comm). The term is cognate with the Latin *desertum* and the Middle Irish *dísert* ('desert'), with the sense of 'hermitage' or 'retreat'. However, there is no early, or indeed pre-modern, documentation for this place-name. Although potentially of great significance, it may simply be a Victorian antiquarian invention that has been adopted in only relatively recent times to describe an archetypal landscape of eremitical cave-dwellers.

2 I am particularly grateful to Ian Fisher for providing the photocopy extracts of this map which have been reassembled here to form Figure 2.7. These were received from the late Dorothy Marshall in the 1970s; she is understood to have found the plan in the former Bute Estate office in Rothesay. The original drawing is believed to have been transferred to the Bute Estate archive in Mount Stuart when the Rothesay office was closed but it has not yet been traced (Andrew McLean, pers comm).

Chapter 3

Historical Framework

RICHARD D. ORAM AND RACHEL BUTTER

3.1 INTRODUCTION

The following narrative and discussion attempts to set the island of Inchmarnock into its general historical context and to offer an account of the main historical themes identified within the period *c* 560 to 1600. Throughout this account, the aim has been to keep Inchmarnock as a central point in a wide-ranging exploration of the outer Firth of Clyde, but the nature of the surviving documentation renders it difficult always to keep the island in view. In this sense, it is difficult to view the island other than as a piece of real estate whose fate was decided by greater and external forces. The overarching aim, however, has been to take Inchmarnock as a microcosm of wider events that moulded the development of the Clyde estuary region throughout the historic era, and illustrate a succession of key themes in Scottish history in general.

3.2 MEDIEVAL INCHMARNOCK TO *c* 1600

RICHARD D. ORAM

3.2.1 Introduction

The earlier medieval landownership of Inchmarnock is an unresolved but not irresolvable problem. Documentation specific to the island is extremely scanty, the earliest material dating from the 1390s, but material relating to its wider Clyde estuary hinterland enables an outline narrative for its earlier history to be synthesised. While it is only in the 16th century that the island emerges clearly into the records, by which date it was a component of the propertied estate of the Cistercian abbey of Saddell in Kintyre, there are a series of small clues from the 11th to 14th centuries which throw some light on what is otherwise an obscure period in the history of the outer Firth of Clyde region, and earlier fragments that may carry the story back to the 6th century. Although it constitutes our earliest piece of hard documentary evidence, the first clear reference to the island in 1391 lies at the end of a long period in which Inchmarnock lies like

an eye of calm at the heart of a hurricane of activity. By examining the events occurring all around it, it is possible to identify the stresses and influences that would have worked themselves upon the island.

Inchmarnock came into Saddell's possession shortly before January 1391 by means of an 'excambion' or exchange of property with the Cluniac abbey of Crossraguel in Carrick (MacPhail 1934, 142–4). There is, however, no corresponding record amongst the surviving fragmentary documentation for Crossraguel to indicate beyond question the route by which the island came into its hands (*Crossraguel Charters*, 1886). Together, however, the surviving evidence for both Crossraguel's and Saddell's monastic estates reveal sequences of landed endowments spanning a period from the early 13th century until the 16th century, which offer many clues as to the general pattern of power within the outer Firth of Clyde zone in the 13th and 14th centuries and point towards shifts in the political pattern of the region. They provide, moreover, a series of links through which the island can be tied into a wider context and viewed against the dynamic process of state building and rebuilding that was occurring throughout the medieval period. Inchmarnock, although almost invisible in the records, lay at the heart of this process.

3.2.2 Historical setting

In any attempt at placing Inchmarnock into its historical setting, there are major problems to be overcome. Traditional Scottish historiography is overwhelmingly centred on the processes by which the medieval kings of Scots created the kingdom that we would recognise as Scotland. This traditional approach presents the process from the perspective of a 'core' looking outwards to an increasingly peripheral zone in the Highlands and Hebrides. In short, Scottish history has been written from the perspective of the eventual winners and, more importantly, with a use of hindsight that presents their victory as inevitable. This problem is compounded by a trend within Scottish history that has treated the country almost like an hermetically sealed unit, wholly cut off from any interaction with neighbouring zones (other, of course, than its relationship with England). This is a deeply unsatisfactory method, especially for the West where close ties with Man and with Ireland remained of vital importance on political, economic and cultural levels into the Modern era. It is only through exploring those relationships that a better understanding can be gained of the processes that shaped the histories of what are now treated as peripheral areas, for, instead of marginal zones, they can be shown instead to form central links in structures radically different to those set out in the pages of most current historical textbooks. A further complication is the issue of modern perceptions of core and periphery, a product largely of the concentration of population in the lowland districts of the country and reinforced by modern patterns of communication. All roads in Scotland nowadays emanate from the central lowlands and the nature of the medieval and earlier lines of communication in the country are interpreted in the light of that fact. Road transport, too, is regarded as the primary means of communication, to the point where even the location of ferry terminals for those inconvenient sea-crossings that cannot be avoided has been determined largely by the associated land-based routes. A glance at a Caledonian McBrayne map of ferry routes underscores this point, with most of the Western Isles services cutting east-west across the natural north–south lines of communication within the islands. The same pattern holds true for the Firth of Clyde. From both a historiographical and a perceptual perspective, then, Inchmarnock has been relegated to the margins.

3.2.3 The early historic period

At Inchmarnock, the excavated remains point to the existence of a Christian centre of some importance in the early historic period. Christianity had a presence in the Clyde estuary region (Figure 2.1) by the second half of the 6th century at the latest, with the mainland powers of Dál Riata in what is now Argyll to the west and Strathclyde to the east being substantially converted by the 560s. The earliest unequivocal indication of an organised Christian presence in the Clyde islands dates from *c* 659 when the Annals of Tigernach record the death of one Daniel, described as bishop of Kingarth (Table 3.1). Lying in an elevated position at the southern end of Bute, and just hidden from Inchmarnock by the hill above Dunagoil, Kingarth has been identified as a monastic and episcopal centre which functioned from at least the early 7th century through to the 9th century. Its site was later occupied by St Blane's Church, one of the two original parish centres for Bute (Fisher 2001, 73–7; Pringle 2000; Macquarrie 2001, 111–14).

The last bishop of Kingarth to be mentioned in the annals is Iolan, who died in 688. Thereafter, only abbots and a cleric of unspecified rank are noticed (Table 3.1).

This is not absolute evidence that the early bishopric had ceased to function, but there is nothing to say that it continued to operate through the 8th century. Reference to Kingarth ends after the obituary in 790 of Abbot Noah, and it seems reasonable to infer that in view of the recording four years later of the first Viking raids on the Western Isles that the monastery was one victim of the Scandinavian onslaught (Anderson 1922, i, 255).

Table 3.1 Historical notices to the bishops, abbots and clerics of Kingarth

Name	Status	Obit.	Reference
Daniel	bishop of Kingarth	*c* 659	Anderson 1922, i, 176
Iolan	bishop of Kingarth	688	Anderson 1922, i, 198
Temnen	'a religious priest'	*c* 732	Anderson 1922, i, 228
Ronan	abbot of Kingarth	737	Anderson 1922, i, 236
Maelmanach	abbot of Kingarth	776	Anderson 1922, i, 248
Noah	abbot of Kingarth	790	Anderson 1922, i, 254

Inchmarnock's proximity to Kingarth has led to the suggestion that it was a dependency of the Bute site (Fisher 2001, 3); indeed, the relationship between these two sites is something that is explored in some detail in Chapter 9. Kingarth is historically-attested; there is, however, no early documentary evidence for the possible monastery on Inchmarnock, although in his later 14th-century *Chronica Gentis Scotorum* John of Fordun, within a description of the islands of Scotland, mentions a monastic cell there (Skene 1871, 39; Scott 1979). It has been suggested that the name *Kildauanach* (church of the monks) in the mid-17th-century atlas produced in Holland by Blaeu from notes made by the Scot Timothy Pont refers to Inchmarnock (Fisher 2001, 77), but it more probably refers to Kildavanan on the mainland of Bute, 5km north of Inchmarnock. An alternative view, however, is explored by Rachel Butter (Chapter 3.3) in her analysis of the place-name evidence.

3.2.4 Gall-Gaidhel

At the end of the 8th century a new threat appeared in the waters off western Scotland, Scandinavian raiders. By the middle of the 9th century, the major monasteries down Scotland's west coast and in the islands had been the targets of repeated attacks and even Iona had eventually been all but abandoned in favour of safer centres at Kells and Derry in Ireland. The raiders, too had begun to settle in the Hebrides, intermarrying with the indigenous Gaelic-speaking peoples and producing a distinctive hybrid culture, the Gall-Gaidhel.

That the Clyde islands suffered from Viking attack during the early part of that period and saw colonisation by Scandinavian settlers in the latter part of it is without question. In 860, Dumbarton, the fortress of the kings of Strathclyde, was captured and sacked by the Dublin Vikings (Anderson 1922, i, 302) in a campaign aimed most probably at establishing control over the strategic routeways through central Scotland that would have provided the quickest link for sea-borne Scandinavians between Dublin and York (Crawford 1987, 50–1). Soon after that, the Vikings may have gained control of the Clyde islands, opening a new phase in the history of the region which saw the Clyde estuary integrated into a sea kingdom centred on Man. Raids clearly continued into the 870s and were not only directed against the indigenous Gaelic peoples but also against other Scandinavians. *Gretti's Saga* mentions one such clash between Scandinavian raiders and settled

Scandinavians, locating the conflict in the waters off Bute in *c* 874 (Anderson 1922, i, 326).

It is likely that there was already a considerable degree of colonisation of the Clyde islands by Scandinavians and Gall-Gaidhel before the end of the 9th century, but the event that had the most profound impact on the whole of the Irish Sea and Hebridean zone was the expulsion in 902 of the Norse colony from Dublin (*AU* s.a. 901). While the largest single warband of the exiled Norse focused its attentions first of all on Strathclyde, then the heartland of the emergent kingdom of Alba in Strathearn before moving south to take control of York (Oram 2000, 2), other groups established themselves in places all around the littoral of the Irish Sea from northern Wales to the southern Hebrides.

Perhaps the most significant long term development from this period of upheaval was the emergence of a zone of Gall-Gaidhel power in the Western Isles and the south-west mainland of Scotland. Ideas as to who these people were vary, with most modern accounts rather loosely and inaccurately labelling them as hybrid Norse-Gaels with a reputation for savagery, violence and a deep-seated antipathy towards Christianity. Later medieval Irish sources present them as apostate Gaels who had abandoned their native culture and religion to embrace that of the invaders (MacQueen 1973, 26–8). The earliest reference to them, from the 12th-century material known as the *Fragmentary Annals*, which survives in a 17th-century copy, describes them as:

> A people who had renounced their baptism and they were usually called Northmen, for they had the customs of the Northmen, and had been fostered by them, and though the original Northmen were bad to churches these were worse …'
>
> *Annals of Ireland: The Three Fragments by Dubhaltach mac Firbisigh*, ed. J. O'Donovan (1860), 138–9

Modern commentators have tended to focus on the 12th-century and later identification of Gall-Gaidhel with Galloway (Oram 2000, 6–7), but there is evidence for a much wider cultural and political distribution. Versions of Irish annals produced in the 12th century, for example, describe Kingarth and Bute as being in the territory of the Gall-Gaidhel (Macquarrie 2001), while contemporary Scottish sources (using the label 'Galloway') indicate that much of the south west mainland from what is now Renfrewshire down to Galloway lay under Gall-Gaidhel lordship into the 1100s (Oram 2000, xxii–xxiii). One point that may merit further examination is the wider cult of

Ernán in the Clyde estuary area, and the possibility that its presence on the mainland in Cunningham at Kilmarnock may represent a comparatively late introduction by the Gall-Gaidhel from their island territories, as has been postulated for the cluster of dedications to Hebridean and northern Irish saints in western Galloway and Carrick (Oram 2000, 10–11).

By the middle of the 10th century, much of the island portions of Gall-Gaidhel territory, probably including the Clyde estuary islands, had been brought under the lordship of one of the greatest Scandinavian rulers of his day, Óláfr Cuarán, king of Dublin and York. His strong Isles-based links were underscored by his decision to enter monkhood and retire into Iona abbey in 980 (*Annals of Ulster* s.a. 979). Óláf's kingdom, like most of the sea-kingdoms of the west in the earlier Middle Ages, relied on his personal authority to hold it together, and after his removal other powers vied for control over portions of its former territories. Brief phases of domination by the Earls of Orkney and by Knútr, the Anglo-Danish king, followed, before after *c* 1030 a new sea-lord, Echmarcach mac Raonaill, emerged (Oram 2000, 16–18). Intermittently from 1036, Echmarcach ruled as king in both Dublin and Man, but his power base appears to have been western Galloway. His successors in Man were probably to retain domination of the Clyde estuary for the remainder of the 11th century.

The establishment of the kingdom of Man as an enduring political entity should probably be seen as the work of one man, Gofraid Crobán, a great-grandson of Óláfr Cuarán. Gofraid's power was founded on his control of the Isles. Certainly, his reign saw the fixing of Manx lordship over most of the Hebrides, and Islay, where he died, was one of his principal bases (Oram 2000, 19). It was Gofraid's naval power, which he used to project his might around the Irish Sea and which was feared and courted by Scottish and Norman rulers alike, which secured him control of western waters. Indeed, it is quite likely that he may have exercised some form of lordship over parts of the eastern side of the Clyde estuary as well as the Clyde islands (Oram 2000, 26–7).

3.2.5 *Kingdom of Man and the Isles*

At the beginning of the 12th century, then, the western seaboard of Scotland was dominated by the kingdom of Man and the Isles. It was ruled by a dynasty of mixed Norse-Gaelic ancestry based on the Isle of Man. Their kingdom, which comprised Man,

the Hebrides and, probably, the Clyde islands, had been formed in the course of the late 10th and 11th centuries, largely through the successful projection of its rulers' military and naval power. The kingdom's strength was based on sea-power and the control of the already important trade routes that ran up the western side of Britain from Biscay, Iberia and the Mediterranean to Norway and Iceland. Its strategic location, moreover, gave it a pivotal role in the political development of both Britain and Ireland, where it was a powerbroker in the struggles to achieve domination of the kings of Alba and Wessex on the British mainland, and of the kings of Connacht, Munster and Leinster in Ireland.

The kingdom's position was a weakness as much as a strength, for the weaker kings after Gofraid Crobán found themselves caught as the meat in the sandwich between aggressive and expansionist neighbours. For much of the 11th century it was Irish potentates, the Uí Néill of Ulster, the Uí Briain of Munster and Uí Conchobair of Connacht, who vied for control, but other predators waited in the wings (Oram 2000, 9–22). In 1098, the pattern of power in the region was given a violent shake by the arrival in Hebridean waters of Magnus Barelegs, king of Norway, who proceeded to impose Norwegian overlordship on what had been a region of Norse colonisation since the mid 9th century. For the next 165 years, this Norwegian link threw an unpredictable factor into an already complex political situation.

King Magnus is widely credited with establishing the territorial demarcation between the island kingdom and its mainland neighbours (Oram 2000, 42). There is only circumstantial evidence for the treaty that Magnus is said to have arranged with the Scottish king, Edgar (1097–1107), but tradition states that it assigned to Magnus all the island territories off Scotland's west coast, and all mainland territories to the Scots. There is no strong evidence for the claim that Kintyre was included in Magnus's domain, although the story of him being dragged across the Tarbet isthmus in a boat with sail set is fixed deeply in historical tradition. The clearest evidence for the nature of the division comes from the boundaries of the dioceses of Argyll and the Isles, which emerged in the course of the 12th century. These placed all of the Western Isles, including the Clyde islands but excluding those in the Firth of Lorne north of Scarba, in the diocese of the Isles, a bishopric set up by the king of Man in the 1070s to serve his entire kingdom (Oram 2000, 166–7). Around 1100, therefore, Bute,

Inchmarnock, Arran and the Cumbraes lay within the kingdom of Man and the Isles under the overlordship of the Norwegian crown.

Following the death of King Magnus in a plundering raid in Ulster in 1102–3 (Anderson 1922, ii, 127–35), a direct Norwegian presence in the Isles receded for over a century, although successive Manx kings continued to acknowledge Norwegian overlordship and seek Norwegian aid in their struggles against their enemies. For around a decade, the kingdom of Man was rent by civil war and various portions of its territories passed into the hands of other warlords. From 1112 until 1153, however, it was ruled by Óláfr Godredsson, who reimposed Manx lordship over most of the Western Isles. King Óláfr enjoyed a strong relationship with King David I of Scotland (1124–53), and during their reigns the boundaries agreed in 1098 appear to have been respected. David may have been extending his reach westwards (Oram 2000, 64), but his target was Argyll and the Gaelic powers of the western mainland, not the island territories of the Manx king. Down to Óláf's death, therefore, Inchmarnock and the other Clyde islands remained part of the Manx sea-kingdom. All that, however, changed in the turbulent decades that followed the assassination of the aged Óláfr in 1153.

3.2.6 New patterns c 1150–1263

Somairle mac Gillebrigta and the Scots

The political structures of the outer Firth of Clyde zone had begun to be redrawn in the second quarter of the 12th century as two new powers extended their spheres of influence. From the east, King David I of Scotland had consolidated his grip on what had been the heartland of the old kingdom of Strathclyde and in the 1130s and 1140s had started to stretch his controls into the district to its west, running from Renfrew south through Cunninghame and Kyle into Carrick. The second key player was Somairle mac Gillebrigta (Somerled), the ruler of Argyll, whose relationship with the kings of Scots was one of only nominal dependence. In parallel with David's consolidation of control to the east and south of the Clyde, Somairle was extending his power out of a heartland in Lorn to create a personal lordship in Argyll and Kintyre (McDonald 1997: McDonald & McLean 1992). By c 1150, therefore, the kingdom of Man and the Isles had as neighbours in the outer Clyde zone two ambitious and aggressive mainland-based powers.

The trigger for change within the region was the deaths within months of each other of both David I and Óláfr. Although Óláf's son, Godred, was soon able to call on Norwegian aid and secure his father's throne, the old king's assassination and the resulting political instability in the Isles blew apart the status quo that had prevailed for nearly half a century. Parts of Óláf's kingdom may have quickly broken away from Manx control as local lords sought to build personal empires. One such area where Manx lordship may have disintegrated was in the Firth of Clyde.

In 1154, a long-running conflict for the domination of Ireland between Toirrdelbach ua Conchobair, king of Connacht, and Muirchertach mac Lochlainn, king of Cenél nEógain, erupted into renewed violence (Oram 2000, 73). Ua Conchobair's fleet had plundered mac Lochlainn's territories in what is now County Londonderry and in response mac Lochlainn recruited a mercenary fleet from 'Galloway, Arran, Kintyre, Man and the shores of Scotland also' (Anderson 1922, ii, 227). The distinct reference to Arran as well as to Man suggests that the Clyde islands were seen as forming a separate power-bloc. The cohesion of the sea-kingdom was breaking down and external forces now sought to capitalise on those divisions.

For the Scots, the relationship with Man down to 1153 had been one of mutual benefits. A strong, stable Manx kingdom provided the Scots with security on their otherwise vulnerable western flank whilst they consolidated their domination of the mainland. After Óláf's death, however, the political instability of his kingdom was seen to pose a threat to Scottish interests, as other powers moved to fill the political vacuum. The Scots themselves, however, were in a position to capitalise on the situation, for David's political settlement of the region had provided a launchpad for more aggressive intervention in the area. The key development in this was the grant c 1147 to one of David's friends from his days at the court of King Henry I of England, Walter I fitz Alan, founder of the Stewart family fortunes in Scotland, of a lordship based on Renfrew (RRS i, Barrow 1960, no 87). A build up of Stewart power in this district continued under Malcolm IV (1153–65) and into the reign of William I (1165–1214) (RRS i, Barrow 1960, nos 184 and 310). In the 1150s and 1160s, Walter received further grants that created a substantial lordship along the southern shores of the Clyde around Renfrew, a second lordship in northern Kyle, and before his death in 1177 had begun to extend his power into Cowal on the northern side of the Firth, the Cumbraes and, possibly, Bute. With the encouragement of the crown, Scottish power was being extended to the fringes of Argyll.

Such rapid extension of Stewart influence provoked a direct confrontation with Somairle mac Gillebrigta. Somairle is a somewhat shadowy figure who, in the 1140s and 1150s, through a combination of military aggression and diplomatic marriages created a substantial sea-based kingship that controlled most of Argyll and the southern Inner Hebrides (McDonald 1997). In 1153, he revealed his hostility towards the descendents of David I in Scotland by backing a rival claim to the throne, signalling the start of what was to be a decade of alternating antagonism, conflict and unstable peace between Somairle and the Scottish crown (Oram 2000, 74). Somairle, however, was the ultimate opportunist, and in 1157 he abandoned his allies in Scotland to pursue a plan to wrest the kingship of Man from Godred Olafsson, who was his brother-in-law, for his own son, Dubgall mac Somairle, Godred's nephew (Anderson 1922, ii, 231–3: Oram 2000, 75–6). According to the *Chronicle of Man*, Dubgall was recognised as king in the islands, and, after a naval battle off Man with Godred's supporters, Somairle succeeded in forcing the Manx king to partition his kingdom and cede most of the island territories to his nephew (*Chron.Man*. s.a. 1144 [recte 1154–6]; Duncan & Brown 1957). It is most likely that the Clyde islands formed part of this settlement. By 1157–8, therefore, Somairle had gained control, through his son, of a highly strategic group of islands in a territory that the Scottish crown considered vital for its security. Given Somairle's fractious relationship with the Scots, further conflict was likely.

Somairle's settlement with Godred lasted only until 1158, when the Argyllman launched a surprise attack on Man, defeated Godred and drove him out. Godred fled first to England and then to Scotland in search of aid against Somairle, but failed to secure help in either kingdom (*Pipe Roll 4 Henry II*, 155, 168; *RRS*, i, no 131; Oram 2000, 76–7). By late 1160 or early 1161 Godred was in Norway, where he distinguished himself fighting on behalf of King Ingi (*Heimskringla*, Håkon Broad-shoulder, *c* 17). Somairle, therefore, was left to consolidate his hold over the kingdom of Man and the Isles for a period of years. He did so secure in the knowledge that the Scots were not going to interfere with his plans, for by Christmas 1159 Somairle had reached an understanding with King Malcolm IV (*RRS*, i, no 175). It was perhaps negotiations leading to this agreement that prevented

the Scots from backing Godred earlier in that year. For the Scots, perhaps, the stability that Somairle had imposed on the region was preferable to the threat to them posed by the internal problems of Godred's kingdom.

Somairle's understanding with Malcolm IV was short-lived. In 1164, he gathered a fleet and army from Ireland, Man, Argyll and the Hebrides and led it across the Clyde (*AU*, s.a. 1164). Why exactly he launched what was clearly a well-prepared attack on the Scots remains unknown, but its direction offers us some clues. According to the *Chronicle of Melrose*, the invasion force made its landfall at Renfrew (Anderson *et al* 1936, s.a. 1164). Clearly, Somairle's target was the centre of the Stewarts' lordship and it is likely that he was striking at a family whose own ambitions in the Firth of Clyde region were in direct conflict with his own (Duncan & Brown 1957). The chronology of the spread of Stewart power in the region at this time can only be sketchily reconstructed, but it was probably Walter fitz Alan's extension of his influence into Cowal, perhaps with Malcolm IV's encouragement, that provoked Somairle. The good fortune that had followed the ruler of Argyll to this point now deserted him and in what appears to have been a rather confused skirmish by the Clyde both he and one of his sons were killed. With the removal of his strong hand, the kingdom that he had built in the west disintegrated.

The Heirs of Somairle and Stewart expansion

Somairle's death brought another phase of instability and political reordering. Within months of the events at Renfrew, Godred Olafsson had returned from Norway to reclaim his kingdom, and succeeded in reimposing his power over most of the northern Hebrides and Skye as well as Man (McDonald 1997). While the Manx kings may have aspired to some limited overlordship of the other islands into the 13th century, their authority never recovered from the blow it had received at Somairle's hands. Although much of what their father had gained in the late 1150s passed quickly from their possession, Somairle's family, however, did succeed in retaining control of some of his conquests, in particular in Kintyre and the southern Hebrides including Mull, Jura and Islay. Arran and Bute, too, may have remained in their grasp, but the evidence is late and unreliable. The leadership of Somairle's kin fell to his eldest surviving son, Dubgall, who succeeded to his father's patrimony in Lorn and who also controlled the adjacent islands. Raonall, Somairle's second son, claimed the title of lord of Kintyre and king of the Isles, which appears to have involved control of Islay, Jura and, possibly, Arran. His efforts to consolidate his hold over this southern portion of Somairle's domain, however, led to decades of conflict with other, more shadowy members of his family and prolonged the instability that had begun in 1164.

The void left by Somairle was something that Walter I fitz Alan and, after his death in 1177 his son, Alan fitz Walter, were eager to fill. This was a dangerous ambition, for while the Stewarts may have enjoyed royal encouragement in the past the political climate had changed considerably after the 1170s and the expansion of Stewart influence was in itself considered as a threat to Scotland's security. The Stewarts, however, were being actively courted by other powers in the region and were forging alliances with other kindreds who had ambitions to expand their influence in the northern Irish Sea and Firth of Clyde zones, such as the rulers of Carrick. Their most significant ally, however, was Raonall mac Somairle, who controlled Islay, Kintyre, Arran and Bute, who appears to have turned to Alan fitz Walter for aid in his struggle to impose his kingship over his own kin (Murray 2005). In 1192, Raonall was defeated in battle by his brother Aongus (*Chron. Man.* s.a. 1192). Shortly afterwards, Raonall made a grant to Paisley Abbey of the annual render of one penny from every house on his lands which had a hearth (*PR*, no 130). Was this part of Raonall's moves to secure an alliance with the powerful head of the Stewart family, the patrons of Paisley? The emergence of a Stewart lordship in Bute around this time suggests that either they had exploited the conflict between Raonall and Aongus to seize control of the island or that it had been given to the Stewarts by Raonall as the price for their support in a struggle that he was clearly losing in 1192. Before 1200, then, it seems that the Stewarts had extended their western frontier to the waters between Bute and Kintyre.

Royal concern at Stewart activities can be read clearly in King William's decision to allow Roland, lord of Galloway, to inherit his brother-in-law's lordship of Cunningham in 1196, and the plantation of a royal castle at the mouth of the River Ayr in 1197 (Oram 2000, 106). The king was certainly aiming to curtail Stewart expansion and when in November 1200 Alan fitz Walter used William's absence in England to complete the marriage without royal permission of his daughter, Avelina, to Earl Donnchad of Carrick, his displeasure was made immediately obvious (*Chron. Howden*, iv, 145: Murray 2005). As part of the measures

insisted upon by King William to limit Stewart power, Alan was required to grant the church and chapel of Bute to the monks of Paisley Abbey, a move perhaps designed to neutralise the problem of Stewart control of a territory that was not only technically outwith the Scottish kingdom, but which lay under the jurisdiction of a foreign archbishop (*PR*, no 16: Murray 2005), given that the diocese of the Isles was part of the Norwegian archdiocese of Nidaros and was not considered to be part of the 'ecclesia Scoticana'. Alan fitz Walter was still in disgrace when he died in 1204 and, with his son Walter II fitz Alan, a minor, Stewart expansion in the Clyde estuary was brought to a grinding halt (Oram 2000, 133).

Meic Raonaill, meic Ruaidrí and Alexander II

The activities of Raonall mac Somairle's children were a cause of growing concern to the Scottish crown from the 1180s onwards, but events in 1209 underscored the threat that this powerful military kindred posed to the stability of the maritime west. In that year, there had been growing disturbances in the region, caused by Ruaidrí mac Raonaill and his brothers' efforts to extend their influence into Skye (*AU*, s.a. 1209). Warfare in the Isles was always the harbinger of disorder in the adjacent mainland, for the meic Uilleim family, claimants to the Scottish crown, had become adept at using the regional destabilisation caused by such events as launch-pads for successive bids to win the throne. A further complication was the arrival in 1210 of a predatory Norwegian force in the Isles (Anderson 1922, ii, 378–81). When in the same year King John of England invaded Ulster and drove out its earl, Hugh de Lacy, and sent his fleet to raid Man (Oram 2000, 115–16), the destabilising of the region was complete.

In the 1220s, it was the young Scottish king, Alexander II, who was the principal aggressor in the west. In early 1221, Alexander conducted a campaign in the Highlands from a base at Inverness against one Domnall mac Niall, a man whose name suggests a connection with the Ulster Uí Neill. This campaign was the opening round of a protracted struggle of which we possess few recorded details. Although the contemporary Melrose chronicle contains no reference to further campaigning, the late 14th-century chronicler John of Fordun notes a naval campaign against Argyll in the weeks immediately following the king's marriage at York in June 1221 (*Chron. Fordun* s.a. 1221: Duncan 1992, 528). Fordun implies that this operation ended in failure, with Alexander's fleet scattered by storms, and that the king mounted a second naval campaign in the west in 1222. These campaigns almost certainly targeted the meic Raonaill, who had provided the meic Uilleim with military aid (Oram 2000, 122). Although there is some circumstantial evidence to support these claims of major naval operations in the Clyde estuary in 1221–2 (the *Newbattle Registrum* (no 27), for example, shows Thomas of Galloway, earl of Atholl, and some of his vassals in Cunninghame, possibly in connection with the campaign), what we know of Alexander's itinerary for both years makes it difficult to provide a time frame for his personal involvement in an extended fleet-based campaign in either year.

We can only conjecture what the consequences of Alexander's campaign in the region in 1221–2 were. It appears that his principal target had been Ruaidrí mac Raonaill, who had certainly controlled Kintyre at least in the early 1200s. He seems to have been ejected from Kintyre by Alexander, who instead granted the lordship to Domnall mac Raonaill, Ruaidri's brother (McDonald 1997, 84). The king followed this up with the construction of a castle at Tarbert, controlling the important portage way across the neck of the peninsula (Dunbar & Duncan 1971). In July 1222, Alexander also erected Dumbarton into a royal burgh, and granted it trading privileges that extended to the head of Loch Long (Dennison 2005), and may also have given formal recognition to the Stewarts of their position in Cowal. In basic terms, the result of the campaign appears to have been a consolidation of Scottish authority over the territories flanking the northern and western sides of the Firth of Clyde, coupled with a consolidation of Stewart power in Bute and Cowal.

Alexander II returned his attentions to the west in the late 1220s. He clearly cherished ambitions to expand his authority into the nominally Norwegian Isles, from where the meic Uilleim had earlier drawn mercenary aid. The Scottish king also wanted to prevent the further spread of Uí Neill influence from west Ulster into the Hebrides. To help keep the Uí Neill in check, he encouraged Alan, lord of Galloway's efforts to win the kingship of Man and the Isles for his bastard son, Thomas. The king manipulated Alan's ambitions to bring the crisis to a head, but he got more of a reaction than he had bargained for. Instead of the quick victory that Alexander expected, Alan's chief opponent, Óláfr Godredsson, king of Man, escaped to Norway, won King Håkon's active support, and returned to the Isles at the head of a Norwegian fleet.

In spring 1230, Óláfr and his nephew Godred Dond sailed from Norway with a fleet commanded by another Hebridean warlord, Gilleasbuig mac Dubgaill (known to the Norwegians as Uspak Håkon), who had been given the kingship of the Isles by King Håkon of Norway. Gilleasbuig's 12 ships were joined by a further 20 from Orkney, and the initial stages of the campaign in the west passed relatively successfully with the capture of some of Gilleasbuig's rival half-brothers, who had joined Alan of Galloway's attack on Óláfr the previous year. Word of the expedition was brought to Alexander II, who immediately headed for Ayr, which was to become his headquarters during the unfolding crisis. There, he was met by several of his principal commanders, including Alan of Galloway. While Alexander gathered his forces, however, the Norwegian fleet was bearing down rapidly on the Firth of Clyde, where the Stewarts became their next target.

According to the saga accounts of the campaign, Gilleasbuig's fleet had by this stage swollen to about eighty galleys, probably carrying in excess of 3,000 men. Leaving the waters around Lorn, where the meic Dubgaill had their power-base, the ships rounded the Mull of Kintyre and entered the Firth of Clyde, probably in early June. There is no reference to any other action during this stage of the campaign than the invasion of Bute and the siege and capture of Rothesay Castle. The steady expansion of Stewart power into the outer Firth of Clyde was clearly a matter of grave concern to the leading meic Somairle kin and merited specific action. According to the most detailed saga account, probably composed soon after the events it described,

> … they sailed south round the Mull of Kintyre, and so in to Bute. The Scots were there in the castle; and a certain steward was over the Scots. [The Norwegians] attacked the castle, but the Scots defended it, and they poured out boiling pitch. The Norwegians hewed the wall with their axes, because it was soft. The torch-bearer who was called Skagi shot the steward to death. Many of the Norwegians fell before they won the castle. There they took much treasure, and one Scottish knight, who ransomed himself for three hundred marks of refined silver.
>
> *Eirspennill's Hakon Hakon's son's Saga*
> (Anderson 1922, ii, 476)

One version of the text states that the siege lasted for three days.

Their next move, however, was to withdraw in the face of the news that Alan of Galloway was moving north against them with a fleet rumoured to be two hundred strong. They fell back into Hebridean waters where, according to the saga account (Anderson 1922, ii, 476–7), Gilleasbuig, who had apparently been wounded during the three-day siege of Rothesay, died and was taken to Iona for burial. The Chronicle of Man account, on the other hand, states that Gilleasbuig was hit by a stone during the siege and died immediately (Anderson 1922, ii, 472). Following his death, command of the fleet fell to Óláfr, who now directed it towards his own purpose of regaining his kingdom in Man. In the autumn, he succeeded in capturing the island with little opposition and his Norwegian allies over-wintered in Man before heading for home in the spring (Anderson 1922, ii, 477). On their north-bound voyage, the Norwegians raided Kintyre, but were driven off with heavy losses.

The events of 1230–1 coincided with the last bid by the meic Uilleim to secure the Scottish throne. It appears that Ruaidrí mac Raonaill may have used this rising as a means of renewing his pressure on the Scottish king, and the lord of Garmoran should probably be identified with the ally of the last meic Uilleim pretender in that venture (Oram 2000, 130–2). It is unclear if he died along with the last meic Uilleim in 1230–1, but there is no other evidence for his actions after that date. By the 1240s, the meic Ruaidrí kindred, while remaining a powerful military and naval force in the west Highlands and Islands, with a lordship centred on Garmoran and the Uists, ceased to play any part in the political life of the Clyde estuary region.

The 1240s saw Alexander's authority within Scotland reach its zenith. On the mainland, only the meic Dubgaill lordship of Lorn still had an ambiguous relationship with the crown, and beyond it beckoned the Hebrides. For Alexander, the Isles constituted both unfinished business and a continuing challenge, for so long as they remained under even nominal Norwegian sovereignty they posed a potential threat to the security of his kingdom. The perennial instability of the region had long provided a breeding-ground for challengers to Alexander's segment of the royal dynasty and, although the meic Uilleim had been eliminated, the region remained a potential source of succour to disaffected elements within mainland Scotland. In 1244, Alexander offered to buy the Isles from Norway, an offer rejected out of hand by the Norwegian king, Hákon IV, who was steadily reasserting his own authority after the ending of the long civil wars that had so debilitated his kingdom. Hákon similarly dismissed subsequent offers (Anderson 1922, ii, 539–40). Suspicions that the meic Dubgaill, who were vassals of both kings, were also

involved in negotiations with Henry III, prompted Alexander to end the ambiguity for once and for all. In the summer of 1249 a royal fleet set out from the Clyde ports and cruised the waters of the Inner Hebrides. In early July, it anchored off the island of Kerrera in Oban Bay, poised to strike against the heart of meic Dubgaill power at nearby Dunstaffnage Castle (*Chron. Melrose* s.a. 1249: *Chron. Bower*, v, 191). On 8 July, at the height of his power, Alexander II died suddenly in his tent on Kerrera, struck down, it was rumoured, by the power of St Columba, protector of the Isles.

The king's death brought the campaign to an abrupt conclusion with most of its objectives unrealised. While arrangements were set in place for the transportation of Alexander's body to Melrose for burial (*Chron. Melrose* s.a. 1249), the political elite scrambled and jostled to establish their positions in control of the child Alexander III's administration. Indeed, the old king's corpse was all but abandoned as his former lieutenants raced to Scone for the inauguration of the boy king. From the first, it was clear that the political stability that Alexander had imposed would be subjected to great stress as the political community of the kingdom began to manoeuvre for power. With his heir a child of eight, it remained to be seen if the realm that Alexander II had welded together through blood and violence would remain intact through the inevitable long minority that would follow.

Alexander II's death brought to a temporary halt the Scottish advance into the west. The mainland, it is clear, was now firmly under Scottish royal authority, but the question of the status of the Isles remained unresolved. Even although Stewart control of the Clyde islands had been consolidated by 1249, technically the area remained under Norwegian sovereignty. Scottish influence over the islands was considerably strengthened in 1255 when Eoghan of Lorn was received into the Scottish king's peace and was restored to his lands (Duncan & Brown 1957, 212). The meic Dubgaill chief quickly became a pillar of the Scottish political community.

3.2.7 Scottish sovereignty achieved 1261 to 1296

The Scottish offensive in the Isles resumed in 1261 on the coming of age of Alexander III. The opening moves in the Scottish campaign were again played in the Firth of Clyde, where the Menteith branch of the Stewart family headed by Walter Stewart, earl of Menteith, younger son of Walter II fitz Alan and brother of Alexander Stewart, probably received royal encouragement to move against the powerful meic Suibne kindred, who controlled a substantial lordship in northern Kintyre and Knapdale, centred on Castle Sween on Knapdale's west coast (Munro & Munro 1986, xxv–xxvi: McDonald 1997, 240–1), Skipness Castle on Kintyre's east coast at the northern end of Kilbrannon Sound, the lands of which were 'granted' in 1262 to Walter, earl of Menteith, by Dubgall mac Suibne (OPS, ii, 29), and possibly Lochranza in Arran. The meic Suibne were a powerful military kindred, whose resources made them an unwelcome and unpredictable neighbour on the Stewart's western flank in both Bute and Cowal. Crown and Stewart interests probably coincided in respect of the fate of the meic Suibne. Whether largescale military action was involved is unknown, but the meic Suibne first of all made a series of property concessions to Menteith before being deprived of their power base. Clan tradition records how the meic Suibne subsequently pursued successful careers as mercenaries, largely in northern Ireland and the Isles. Walter Stewart, earl of Menteith, had succeeded spectacularly in creating a new Stewart controlled lordship in southern Argyll, signalling his success by confirming earlier meic Suibne gifts of the churches in his newly acquired territories to the monks of Paisley (PR, nos 124–6). The deprivation of the meic Suibne should then be seen as a final component in a sustained Scottish strategy in the Firth of Clyde which had seen either the expulsion or destruction of families whose loyalties were suspect, the forging of new political relationships with others, especially the emerging meic Dubgaill and meic Domnaill kindreds amongst the heirs of Somairle, and the intrusion of committed allies of the Scottish crown into key lands and castles throughout the region.

That control of the southern Hebrides, Argyll and the Clyde islands was now felt to be secure can be seen in the direction of the renewed onslaught. While Alexander II had directed his efforts against the south-west Highlands, Alexander III's pressure was in the north-west and the adjacent islands (Anderson 1922, ii, 605). It was this attack, amongst other issues, that prompted King Håkon IV of Norway to mount his famous expedition to the Isles, which culminated in early October 1263 in the inconclusive skirmish on the beach at Largs. The campaign drew support from Dubgall mac Ruarídh, the ruler of the outer Isles, and his brother Alan, both of whom had claims through their father to lands in Kintyre and, probably the Clyde islands (Duncan & Brown 1957, 213). Aongus Mor and Murchaid mhic Domnaill, sons of Domnall

mac Raonaill, lord of Islay, submitted to Håkon under threat of having their lands ravaged, which gave the Norwegians a powerful grip over the Argyll side of the Firth of Clyde.

By mid-August, Håkon's fleet lay in the Sound of Kerrera where it menaced the lands of Eoghan mac Dubgaill, but the lord of Lorn refused to come into the Norwegian king's peace against his other lord, Alexander II (Anderson 1922, ii, 617). From there, he sent fifty ships south to plunder in Kintyre and five ships round the Mull to raid Bute (Anderson 1922, ii, 617). A short while after, Håkon also headed south with the remainder of his ships and took up station off Gigha, where he received a deputation from 'a certain abbot of a monastery of Grey-friars', presumably the abbot of Saddell, who asked for the king's protection for himself, his community and their property (Anderson 1922, ii, 617). Håkon clearly considered himself to be gaining the upper hand through such submissions. While at Gigha, word was received that Bute had fallen to the Norwegians and that the castle at Rothesay had surrendered (Anderson 1922, ii, 620). Håkon granted the island to a certain Ruaidrí, who claimed the island as part of his birthright. The identity of this man has never been confirmed beyond doubt, but he is probably a son or grandson of the Gilleasbuig who seized Bute in 1230, or a descendant of Ruaidrí mac Raonaill, who had been ejected from Kintyre by Alexander II in the 1220s (Cowan 1990, 120–1). Quite clearly, those Hebridean kindreds who had lost out in the course of Alexander II's ruthless annexation of the western mainland were seeking restoration of their inheritance under the aegis of the Norwegian crown.

With Bute securely in Norwegian hands, the invaders carried the war into Scotland. The Norwegian garrison of Rothesay and Ruaidrí's men launched raids into the mainland, presumably attacking Stewart properties in Cowal and Ayrshire (Anderson 1922, ii, 621–2). Håkon now rounded Kintyre and brought his fleet to Arran, where it anchored in the sheltered waters between the island and Holy Island (Anderson 1922, ii, 622). Throughout September 1263, Håkon was involved in protracted negotiations with Alexander III, who had based himself at Ayr. The negotiations centred on the issue of sovereignty and possession of Arran, Bute and the Cumbraes (Anderson 1922, ii, 623). When it became clear that the Scots were spinning out the talks in anticipation of the deterioration of weather with the arrival of autumn, Håkon decided to turn up the pressure on the Stewarts and sent a detachment of his fleet up Loch

Long, across the portage point at Arrochar, and into Loch Lomond, where it proceeded to raid throughout Lennox and Menteith (Cowan 1990, 120–2). Indeed, the attack on Menteith may be linked directly to Earl Walter's role in Knapdale. Unfortunately for Håkon, at this juncture the equinoctial gales arrived and his main fleet, anchored between Great Cumbrae and the mainland, was battered by a storm out of the south. The result was the so-called battle of Largs, an inconclusive skirmish along the beach and shingle banks of the Ayrshire coast (Alexander, Neighbour & Oram 2002).

Inconclusive though the fight at Largs had been, Håkon knew that time was against him. Short of supplies, he withdrew first to Holy Island off Arran, then south round Kintyre to Gigha and Islay (Anderson 1922, ii, 634). He clearly intended to return in the spring to continue the campaign and, as he withdrew towards winter quarters he confirmed his earlier disposal of lands. Ruaidri was granted Bute and Murchaid mac Domnaill, lord of Kintyre, was also given the lordship of Arran (Anderson 1922, ii, 635). With Norwegian assistance, this reversal of Scottish fortunes may have been made more substantial, but in mid December 1263 King Håkon died in his winter quarters in Orkney and the last great Norwegian campaign into the west fizzled out. Deprived of Håkon's driving will and military resources, the Hebrideans knew that they stood no chance against the superior resources of Alexander III.

Although Håkon may have recovered physical possession of the islands during the autumn of 1263, however, the withdrawal of the Norwegian fleet after Largs handed the initiative back to the Scots. It is clear that in the following campaigning season control of the Clyde islands and Kintyre had swiftly been restored, evidently by a force commanded by the earl of Mar (ER, i, 5–6, 11). Scottish sovereignty over the Western Isles was finally secured by the 1266 treaty of Perth, which ceded lordship over the kingdom of Man and the Isles, and all its territories, from the Norwegian to the Scottish crown. The *de facto* control of the previous decades was converted into *de jure* possession.

3.2.8 A Stewart lake: Stewart lordship in Bute, Arran and Knapdale

The next three decades saw the consolidation of that possession and the steady integration of the rulers of the island districts into the ranks of the Scottish nobility. The Stewart lordships around the Clyde estuary

played a substantial part in that process. In 1293, King John Balliol and his parliament drew up a scheme for the extension of the full structures of Scottish royal government into the region in the form of three sheriffdoms centred on Skye, Lorn and Kintyre. The sheriff of Kintyre, whose territory also embraced Bute and Arran, was to be James Stewart, the dominant lord of the district (APS, i, 477b). In a century and a half, the Clyde estuary had been converted from a distinct component of the kingdom of the Isles into a Scottish fiefdom dominated by the Stewart family.

The Knapdale lordship of the Stewarts of Menteith passed to a junior branch of the family, who took the territorial surname of *de Menteith*. The Menteith lordship on the west side of the Clyde estuary continued to expand through the 13th and into the 14th centuries. Probably in 1308, Sir John Menteith, the betrayer of William Wallace in 1305, and initially an opponent of Robert Bruce, received a remission from the king and a grant of the earldom of Lennox (RRS v, Duncan 1988, no 419). His power in the Lennox area was further built up through the award to him of the sheriffdom of Dumbarton. In 1323, Sir John received the lands of Glen Breackerie in Kintyre and Ailsa Craig from the king for the service of one ship of 26 oars (RRS, v, Duncan 1988, no 239), a grant which extended Menteith power from the mouth of the firth to the head of Loch Lomond and Loch Long. In *c* 1357, Sir John Menteith II was described as lord of Arran and of Knapdale in the charter recording his gift to the monks of Kilwinning of the churches of Kilmory and Kilbride in Arran (RMS i, no 182: Cowan 1967, 96 and 107). Sir John II died without issue and his lands passed into the possession of the senior branch of the Stewart family. In 1366, Robert the Steward, the future King Robert II, held the lordships of Arran and Knapdale in addition to his hereditary lands (APS, i, 500). All of the Clyde islands and substantial areas of the north, east and west shores of the firth were under the lordship of a single man.

The stability of this zone did not rest solely on the military and naval power of the Stewarts, although that in itself was formidable. Through the late 13th century, the Stewarts had worked increasingly in alliance with the mhic Domhnaill lords of Kintyre and Islay, who were their principal neighbours to the west. The long-standing ties between the Stewarts and the mhic Domhnaill were strengthened in 1350 when John, lord of the Isles, married Margaret, daughter of Robert the Steward (Munro & Munro 1986, no B25, 286). In 1376, King Robert II granted the Stewart lands in Kintyre and half of the lordship of Knapdale conjointly to John and Margaret (*RMS* i, no 569). Through that grant, the mhic Domnaill gained possession of Castle Sween on the west of the peninsula, possibly Skipness on the east, and were able to increase their influence on the western side of the Firth of Clyde generally (Munro & Munro 1986, xxvi–xxvii). Nevertheless, the Stewarts remained active and aggressive lords of this great sub-Highland territory that centred on the Firth of Clyde, maintaining their stranglehold on the region despite their succession to the throne of Scotland. For King Robert III, who was denied any significant role in the political life of his kingdom, Kyle on the mainland and Bute formed the core of his personal power base. This continuing close identification of the Stewarts with their original lordships was underscored in 1398 when Robert III created the dignity of Duke of Rothesay for his elder son and heir, David. To Robert III, therefore, it would appear that this ancestral core was seen as the vital springboard from which his children would draw the power they needed to re-establish their grip on the throne of Scotland (Boardman 1997).

In the later 14th and 15th centuries it becomes clear that a complex land-holding pattern, in which families with bases on both sides of the Firth of Clyde played a part, had emerged under Stewart patronage. In 1430, as part of James I's attempts to curb the power of his cousin, Alexander, lord of the Isles, the crown resumed control of the castles of Sween and Skipness, placing them in the hands of Alexander Montgomery of Ardrossan and Robert Cunninghame of Kilmaurs (*RMS* ii, no 163). This arrangement started a long tradition of land-holding by both families on both sides of the region, which by the early 1500s (see below) had turned into a rivalry which spilled over into feud. The Montgomeries appear to have quickly established a close working relationship with the major Gaelic powers of the region, Alexander Montgomery in 1456 witnessing an instrument of John, lord of the Isles, on the island of Cara (Munro & Munro 1986, no 64). A less important Ayrshire laird, Adam Rede of Starquhyte or Barskimming, was in 1498 granted the castle and lands of Airds near Carradale in Kintyre, plus other properties in northern Kintyre, by King James IV, forming part of a general employment of men from the eastern side of the Clyde to control the territories of the recently forfeited mhic Domhnaill lordship of the Isles (Munro & Munro 1986, xxxviii–xxxix, nos A56 and A60). His tenure appears to have been long-term, for he was still in possession of crown lands in Kintyre in 1507 (Munro & Munro 1986, no

A56). The mhic Domhnaill themselves were part of the cross-Clyde nexus, holding land in Carrick at Greenan, just south of Ayr, which was simply treated by them as an extension of their Kintyre properties (Munro & Munro 1986, xxxvii–xxxviii). As patrons of Saddell Abbey, moreover, they enjoyed an influence that extended beyond their territorial heartlands into Arran and, of course, Inchmarnock.

What emerges from this picture of cross-Clyde contacts and exchange is the degree of cultural interaction and the essential hybridity of the culture of the Clyde islands. Bute, whilst tied politically into a 'lowland' structure of lordships, was essentially 'highland' in character. The 'Brandanes' as the men of Bute were labelled by lowland Scots on the mainland, were viewed as distinct, politically and culturally, from the inhabitants of the eastern shore of the firth. Their role as key components in the military retinues of the Stewart family gave a distinctly Gaelic or Highland character to their power. The blend of Gaelic and lowland cultures is most evident in the families who were established by the Stewarts in and around Bute and Inchmarnock. One of the best examples of this is the Leitch family, who were in possession of Kildavanan on Bute by the beginning of the 15th century. In 1429, James I confirmed one John Leitch, son of the late Gilzequhome, in possession of the property (*RMS* ii, no 123). In 1466, the property was in the hands of Gilchrist Leitch and was designated to descend to his son, David. The naming patterns of this family underscore the interchanges that were occurring in this zone of cultural interface, with the Christian names alternating between Gaelic and lowland forms. Their surname, too, is very significant, for its points towards a background as mediciners, possibly linked to the famous West Highland MacBeth or Beaton family (Black 1946, 419–20). It is possible that these men were members of a Gaelic medical dynasty in the service of the Stewart family, something which would underscore the cultural cross-over that was occurring within the wider household and retinue of the lords of Bute. A similar cultural duality can be seen in the Bannatyne family, who emerge as tenants of Inchmarnock in the 16th century but who were based on Kames in Bute by the 15th century and who probably had a much older connection with the island (*RMS* ii, no 1214). The Bute Bannatynes appear to be quite distinct from the Lanarkshire family of that name (Black 1946, 52), and their occurrence with the Gaelic patronymic of Macaomlinn suggests that this may be a native family who were embracing aspects of lowland culture (Black 1946, 453). Macaomlinn, significantly, may derive from the family of the earls of Lennox, with whom the Stewarts were allied closely from the late 12th century. This blurring between Gaelic and lowland traditions is a phenomenon recognisable all around the Firth of Clyde in the later 14th and 15th centuries, with it not always being a one-way process. In Arran, for example, a branch of the Ayrshire family of Fullarton was introduced early in the 14th century and by the 15th century had 'gone native', adopting Gaelic name forms and operating as a Gaelic kindred whilst still maintaining a separate identity as a member of the wider lowland nobility of Scotland. Study of this phenomenon is an issue that would reward further study.

3.2.9 Inchmarnock as monastic property

The records of Saddell Abbey would probably have been able to resolve many of the questions concerning Inchmarnock down to the 16th century. Unfortunately, Saddell is possibly the most poorly documented of all Scotland's medieval abbeys. Modern research has thrown some light on its general history, but there is little substantive evidence upon which to build a fluent narrative for its origins, development and ultimate demise (McKerral 1952: Brown 1969: Scott 1970). Unlike most Scottish Cistercian houses, Saddell did not belong to the network of colonies ultimately dependent on Rievaulx Abbey in Yorkshire, from which monks were sent in 1136 to found Melrose and in 1142 to found Dundrennan, the two communities from which all other Scottish Cistercian abbeys derived. This is a clear indication that it was not a foundation made by a king of Scots, as most Scottish Cistercian abbeys founded before c 1220 were established by the crown (McDonald 1995). Late 14th-century evidence reveals that it was instead a daughter of the great Irish Cistercian abbey of Mellifont near Drogheda (CPL, 195), an association that underscores how radically different the political and cultural alignments of southern Argyll and the Firth of Clyde zone were at this period. Rather than looking towards mainland Scotland to the east and the growing power of the Scottish crown, the rulers of this western district were pursuing their own independent course.

For the identity of the founder of the abbey we are again reliant on 14th-century evidence, but this states explicitly that it was Raonall mac Somairle (Reginald son of Somerled), ruler of Argyll and of most of the Inner Hebrides (Brown 1969, 131: CPL, 193). There

is, however, a persistent counter tradition that it was Raonall's father, the great Somairle mac Gillebrigta, the ancestor of the meic Dubgaill, meic Domnaill and meic Ruaidrí families, who established the community, and it is possible that he may have begun a process that was only completed in the lifetime of his son (Brown 1969, 131–2). There is no substance to the 17th-century Clan Donald tradition that Somairle was buried at Saddell. Certainly, the earliest of the charters produced by the abbey for papal confirmation in 1393 was given as a charter of Raonall (CPL, 193), and it was similarly identified in 1508, with the added rubric 'who named himself king of the Isles, lord of Argyll and of Kintyre' (RMS ii, no 3170[1]). Architecturally, what can be identified at the fragmentary ruins of the abbey points to building in the later 12th century or very early 13th (RCAHMS 1971, no 296), which would conform to the dating of its foundation to the lifetime of Raonall.

Raonall's original endowment of the abbey comprised Glen Saddell itself and property worth 12 marks at 'Baltebeam' (identified as Ballevain, on the west side of Kintyre at the northern end of Machrihanish Links NR 6525 and NR 6626). He followed this with a grant of 20 marks of land at Shiskine in the Blackwater Valley in Arran, almost directly across Kilbrannan Sound from the abbey (RMS ii, no 3170[2]). Probably before c 1220, his younger son, Ruaidrí, lord of Kintyre, added the lands of Glentorrisdale and Ugadale, immediately adjoining Saddell Glen to the north and south (RMS ii, no 3170[3]). Last in the sequence of 13th-century endowments was the gift of two pennylands in Carrick at Lesenmarg and the unidentified 'Creisbog', which were given to the abbey by Niall, earl of Carrick, and his wife, Isabella (RMS ii, no 3170[4]). The sequence of grants begins again in the 14th century with the gift by John MacDonald, lord of the Isles (d. 1386), of two marklands at the unidentified 'Lesenmarg', the first in a sequence of grants by the MacDonalds, who appear to have taken on the mantle of patron of the abbey (RMS ii, no 3170[5–7]). In addition to John's charter, there were endowments by his grandson, Alexander (d. 1449), giving two marklands at Craigvan on Gigha and the island of Davaar in Campbeltown Loch (island of St Barr at Lochkilkerran), and by John II, lord of the Isles, and his son Angus, granting Knochantebeg and Kellipul near Machrihanish. John II was forfeited by the crown in 1493. The final recorded grant was that of Barrandaimh and Blarantibert near Crinan in Knapdale, given by Duncan Campbell of Loch Awe between 1425 and 1450. It is hardly an impressive landed endowment, constituting a core of properties in southern Kintyre, mostly within a few kilometres of the abbey itself, and with outlying properties in Knapdale and Gigha to the north and west. The properties on Arran and in Carrick, however, serve to emphasise again the unity that water-borne communication gave to this region, and, although Inchmarnock is not listed amongst the monastic properties in the schedule of endowments, there is no reason to consider such a connection unlikely or impossible. In a similar vein, the priory at Whithorn in Galloway possessed properties in Kintyre. Crossraguel Abbey in Carrick held properties and rights on Arran, while its mother-house at Paisley enjoyed various possessions around the Firth of Clyde and drew income from fiscal renders throughout the southern Hebrides

Why Inchmarnock was not listed in the 1393, 1498 or 1508 schedules of Saddell's properties is unknown, for on 17 January 1391, the Avignon-based Pope Clement VII issued a commission to the Bishop of Glasgow to ratify a property exchange that had been arranged between the monks of Saddell and Crossraguel (MacPhail 1934, 142–4). This referred to the transfer from Saddell's possession of the chapel of the Holy Trinity at Kildomine (in Barr parish in southern Carrick) in exchange for the 'parish church' of Inchmarnock (MacPhail 1934, 142–4: '*parrochialem ecclesiam de Inchmernolz*'). According to the commission, the exchange had been arranged as long ago as *c* 1360. Kildomine had formed a portion of the 13th-century endowment of Saddell in Carrick given by Earl Niall, but when had Inchmarnock come into Crossraguel's hands?

The early history of Crossraguel is as obscure as that of Saddell. As early as the 1230s, Donnchad, earl of Carrick, had been making arrangements with the monks of Paisley Abbey for the foundation of a daughter-house in his earldom (*PR*, nos 382 and 383). It may have taken the threat of litigation by Donnchad's successors to force Paisley into honouring its agreement but it may only have been in the 1260s that Crossraguel was established as a fully functioning monastery (*PR*, no 380: Easson & Cowan 1976). As discussed above, Crossraguel's mother-house at Paisley possessed a clutch of important properties on the western side of the Firth of Clyde and in the Clyde islands, and had benefited greatly from its close relationship with the Stewarts. Indeed, the westward spread of its properties had moved with the steady expansion of Stewart power through the late 12th, 13th and 14th centuries. Links between the Stewarts and the earls of Carrick were

traditionally strong: in 1200 the head of the Stewart family, Alan fitz Walter, had arranged the marriage of his daughter, Avelina, to Earl Donnchad (Oram 2000, 132–3). It was possibly via this link that Inchmarnock, a property almost certainly in Stewart hands by the early 1200s, came into Crossraguel's possession. One alternative to this interpretation is that it had been given originally by the Stewarts to Paisley and had been made over to Crossraguel subsequent to that abbey's establishment in the 1260s. Indeed, the 'church and chapel' of Bute were amongst properties granted to Paisley by Alan fitz Walter before 1204 (*PR*, no 16). A second alternative which cannot be altogether dismissed, however, would place the Crossraguel connection in the 14th century. In 1368, the earldom of Carrick was granted by King David II to John Stewart, the future King Robert III (*RRS*, vi). John, earl of Carrick, became patron of Crossraguel and may have marked his connection with the abbey by an act of patronage. A grant of Inchmarnock, even if it were just of its revenues, may have been considered problematic by Crossraguel and its exchange with Saddell may have represented a simple act of rationalisation of the property portfolios of the two communities.

The physical remains of the church on Inchmarnock appear to be 12th-century in date (Fisher 2001, 77), indicating that it was probably constructed before the Stewarts gained possession of Bute in the 1190s. As we shall see, this is a point that may be reinforced now by a radiocarbon-date which provides a relatively early *terminus ante quem* date, a date before which the church (or at least the chancel) was constructed (Chapter 5.5 and Chapter 9.3). The building's style has clear affinities with the traditions of Kintyre and should probably be seen as the product of a native Gaelic patron, perhaps Raonall mac Somairle, rather than as the work of a colonising lord. While they probably did not build the church, it is likely, however, that it was the Stewarts' control of the island that led to the redevelopment of the cult of Ernán around the Firth of Clyde. The Stewarts made great use of association with the cults of native saints to tighten their influence within areas into which they were intruding their power, and it is likely that some relics of the saint, possibly removed from a shrine on Inchmarnock, were taken to Paisley. The possibility of a link between Inchmarnock, the Stewarts and Paisley is strengthened by the fact that when in August 1488 James IV erected the town of Paisley into a free burgh, one of its two annual fairs was on St Marnock's day (*RMS* ii, no 1768). There is no clear evidence for relics or even an altar of the saint in Paisley (*RMS* iv, no 2627: Malden 2000, 14), but the link does not appear to be made via any obvious alternative source, such as Kilmarnock, which was not under Stewart lordship and whose church was not appropriated to a Stewart monastery (*RRS* v, nos 67 and 422: Cowan 1967, 104). The St Marnock's Day fair and its association with Paisley suggests very strongly that the Stewarts saw the cult of this saint as an important instrument in reinforcing their identity as lords of what was essentially a Gaelic sea-kingdom.

3.2.10 Parish status

The residual traces of a wider regional cult of Ernán/ Marnock in the late Middle Ages points towards a more significant role for his church or chapel on Inchmarnock than the surviving documentation might otherwise suggest. A possible indication of the early high status of the church at Inchmarnock, perhaps reflecting its origins as a monastic centre, is its description in 1391 as 'parochial'. While this styling could simply be the result of a clerical error at the papal chancery, as the clerks were usually copying detail of that type straight from the appeals sent in by the beneficiaries, it is likely to be a correct representation of the status of the church on the island in the mid-14th century. Parish status meant that, as well as offering burial in a consecrated cemetery and sacraments such as marriage, Inchmarnock possessed the key symbol of parish status, a font for baptisms. It was the function of being a baptismal church which bestowed parish status, not size or economic base. It is interesting in itself that Saddell took control of a parish church, for the Cistercian rule prohibited the acceptance of revenues from parochial teinds and the other renders due to parish priests. Of course, by the 14th century those strictures were largely ignored, and Melrose Abbey, the chief Cistercian house in Scotland controlled 11 parish churches by the end of the 14th century: Cavers Magna, Dunscore, Ettrick, Hassendean, Hounam, Mauchline, Melrose, Ochiltree, Tarbolton, Westerkirk and Wilton (Cowan 1967). The description given in the Clement VII mandate, however, is the first and last time that it is so styled in a surviving document.

Why Inchmarnock evidently lost its parochial status and when is, and will remain, unknown. The most probable reason is that the size of the community on the island was inadequate to meet the economic level required to support a parish priest. By the later Middle Ages, it had simply become unviable as a distinct ecclesiastical entity. It is unlikely that Inchmarnock

itself was ever either sufficiently prosperous or populous to support a full parish apparatus, which would again point towards the church on the island having at some stage possessed a much wider territorial authority or some more elevated function. One conjecture is that revenue from pilgrim traffic may have boosted the teinds from the island, but that those revenues had declined as patterns of pilgrimage and popular devotion were realigned in the later medieval period. Indeed, it is possible that any relics of the saint may have been moved to Paisley by the Stewarts, with the result that pilgrims and their donations were diverted away from the island.

This distinct medieval status is one reason why the parish authorities on Bute were at something of a loss in the 17th century as to how to deal with moral discipline issues on the island and what the island's position in regard to church revenues was (*OPS*, ii). Tradition that it had been incorporated into the *parish* of Saddell is not entirely fanciful, as this may indeed have happened, with the former parish church being reduced to the status of a dependent chapel. This would have entailed the loss of its baptismal function, which would have required children born on the island to be taken to their appropriate parish church or blessed by a visiting priest. It is probable, however, that the tradition of annexation to the parish of Saddell is a garbling of the island's incorporation into the monastic estate, compounded by its later annexation to the *mensa* of the Bishop of Argyll as part of his barony of Saddell. Certainly, when Fordun was compiling his account of the islands of Scotland in the later 14th century, Inchmarnock was still included within the diocese of Sodor or the Isles, not Argyll (Fordun, *Chronica Gentis Scotorum* ii, 39). There is, indeed, no record evidence that the spiritual jurisdiction over the island ever was moved from the Isles into Argyll. The late Ian Cowan, however, suggested that on annexation to the bishopric of Argyll, Inchmarnock was probably served from the parish of Killean in Kintyre, which the bishops of Argyll had controlled since the 13th century (Cowan 1967, 85–6, 101). Killean, however, is on the west side of Kintyre and if any parish controlled by the bishop of Argyll was to have responsibility for providing spiritual services for Inchmarnock it must surely have been Saddell.

3.2.11 The suppression of Saddell

Probably in 1507, James IV wrote to the Cardinal of St Mark, explaining the situation in the diocese of Argyll

(*Letters James IV*, no 149: Hannay & MacKie 1953). It was, he said, 'very extensive and mountainous' and despite its size very poorly endowed financially. Furthermore, he stated that the bishop's problems were compounded by the difficulties of imposing ecclesiastical discipline 'upon a rude people, unsettled and not amenable to law'. The bishop himself, however, was conscientious and well qualified, and as such was deserving of better provision. To aid him in the running of his diocese, the king proposed that Saddell, which 'has within living memory seen no monastic life and has fallen to the use of laymen ... there is no hope of restoring monastic life', should be annexed to the episcopal *mensa* and that the Archbishop of Glasgow be granted a commission to investigate the situation. James added that the revenues of the house at that time amounted to only £9 sterling, and that other properties had been alienated beyond recovery.

On 1 January 1508, the king, having inspected the evidence presented to him by David Hamilton, bishop of Argyll, and on account of the pope's union of the abbacy of Saddell with the bishopric of Argyll, granted the bishop a charter under the Great Seal erecting the abbey's lands into the free barony of Saddell (*RMS* ii, no 3170). Bishop David's 'evidences' are listed as the eight charters discussed earlier dating from the early 13th to mid-15th centuries, which granted properties in Kintyre, Knapdale, Arran, Gigha and Carrick. Again, no mention was made of Inchmarnock or Bute.

Nothing more is heard until 22 April 1512, when James wrote to Pope Julius II with a further request (*Letters James IV*, no 446: Hannay & Mackie 1953). Alluding once again to the problems of the see of Argyll ('inadequately endowed, in a solitary and sterile region, among a people rude and uncultured'), he proposed that the cathedral of the see which 'has fallen into ruin and at present lies deserted' should be relocated from Lismore to Saddell. The plan proved abortive, not least because James's attention very quickly became diverted towards international diplomacy and the complex affairs that would lead him to renew the Auld Alliance between Scotland and France and invade England in the autumn of 1513. With the king's death at Flodden and the political instability in Scotland that followed, there were other priorities to be addressed.

The first clear evidence for Saddell's ownership of the island occurred on 30 April 1540 when William Cunningham, bishop of Argyll, granted the five-poundland of Inchmarnock to his brother, Hugh Cunningham, and to his heirs and assigns. The land was described as pertaining to the bishop by reason of the union of the abbey of Saddell with his see (*RMS* iv, no 2115). The property had already been set to Hugh, who was to pay £20 of ancient ferme and 20d. increase, and double feuferme on the entry of heirs. The feuing of Church property was increasingly common at this date, brought about partly by the senior clergy's need to obtain cash to pay King James V's taxation of the Church and partly by their readiness to divert lands, rights and offices into the hands of their lay kinsmen. Grants in feuferme, although retaining the fiction of the superiority remaining with the donor, were tantamount to alienation. Lands feued in this way were rarely recovered by the superior. In the case of Inchmarnock, the feuferme appears to have been converted into a grant in heritage, for on 8 January 1568 Hugh was said to possess the property heritably (*RSS*, vi, no 94). There appears to be no surviving record of its conversion from a feuferme tenure to a heritable tenure. Inchmarnock, however, was just one amongst many pieces of landed property held by Cunningham, who took his title from his principal holding at Waterston in Ayrshire, and he had no residence on the island. Indeed, the property was sub-infefted to tenants, probably continuing the arrangements that had been in place during its possession by the monks of Saddell and the bishopric of Argyll. By 1568, Hugh was evidently having difficulties with his tenants for he received letters under the privy seal granting him the escheat of the goods of the newly outlawed William Bannatyne 'in Inchmarnock', presumably his tenant. Hugh had obtained the letters following a determination by the Lords of Council concerning William's failure to vacate the five-poundland of Inchmarnock. Six years later, Hugh received a confirmation of his ownership under the Great Seal (*RMS* iv, no 2115).

3.2.12 Continuing cross-Clyde bonds: the bishops of Argyll, 1475–1580

The pattern of cross-Clyde landholding and political connections which had been established during the Stewarts' rise to regional dominance in the 13th century extended into the ecclesiastical as well as secular spheres. The clearest evidence for this is in connection with the bishopric of Argyll, which kings of Scots from James I onwards had used as an instrument for control of a region that was a source of anxiety to the crown. In 1475, the first of a succession of men of west coast background was provided to the see, setting a trend that would continue down to the Reformation. This was Robert Colquhoun, brother of Sir John Colquhoun of Luss, both of who were loyal adherents of James III (Watt 1969, 27: Macdougall 1997, 37). He was succeeded in 1497 by David Hamilton, a prominent member of a kindred that was to emerge as dominating force in the region through the course of the 16th century (Macdougall 1997, 27). A half-brother of James Hamilton, first earl of Arran, David was 'young, active in the royal interest and well connected' (Macdougall 1997, 216). The king was keen to show his commitment to this loyal servant in the West and the improvement to his financial position offered by the annexation of Saddell was an obvious means to that end. Hamilton was the intended beneficiary of the suppression of Saddell, receiving control of the monastic properties in addition to the rather slender resources of his see. His nephew, John, a bastard son of Earl James, received the commendatorship of Paisley Abbey in 1525, beginning Hamilton possession of the main religious house of the Clyde estuary that lasted until its erection into a temporal lordship for Claude Hamilton in 1587 (Watt & Shead 2001, 171). Hamiltons also controlled Kilwinning Abbey in northern Ayrshire almost without interruption from 1527 until 1571 (Watt & Shead 2001, 129–30). For much of the 16th century, then, the Hamilton family dominated the outer Firth of Clyde region, effectively replacing the MacDonalds and the Stewarts as the major kindred of the region and blocking the southward spread of Campbell power out of Argyll. Within their own backyard, however, they had rivals.

Inchmarnock, of course, was little more than an item of landed property in the dealings between these families, but title over it marked an extension of a particular kindred's power base. Thus, in 1525, a second north Ayrshire kin that was enjoying a rapid revival in its regional authority was able to project its power westwards into the Clyde islands and Argyll mainland through securing the provision of one of its own to the diocese. Robert Montgomery, a member of a family that was pushing itself into the upper circle of the aristocratic elite in the first quarter of the 16th century, and which had enjoyed strong connections with mainland Argyll since the 1430s, was provided to the see in July 1525 (Watt 1969, 27). He was succeeded in 1539 by William Cunningham (Watt 1969, 27), youngest son of William, lord Kilmaurs, Master of Glencairn and, from 1541, fourth earl of Glencairn, head of a family that was at feud with the Montgomeries intermittently through the first half of the 16th century and who eventually eclipsed them

in the 1540s and 1550s (Cameron 1998, 140–3). The Cunningham expansion into Argyll was achieved at the expense of their Montgomery rivals. William's appointment to the see in 1539 was followed by an entrenching of the family position in the western Clyde district in the early 1540s. In 1540 and 1541, the bishop's father, had been James V's naval commander in the Isles during the so-called 'Daunting', and in June 1541 he took up residence at Saddell Castle as one of the king's commissioners in the region (Cameron 1998, 247). Earl William and his son, Alexander, received possession of various properties in Kintyre and appear to have established something of a good reputation and authority in the region by late 1542, when the earl was captured in the Battle of Solway Moss (Cameron 1998, 247). Bishop William's gift of Inchmarnock to his elder brother, Hugh, which was made within a year of his appointment to the see and at the same time that their father and eldest brother were tightening the family's grasp on Kintyre, should be viewed as part of this general process of Cunningham intrusion into Argyll. It was evidently the considered view of James V that Glencairn and his family were ideally placed geographically and politically to bring stability to a region that had been experiencing protracted disturbance since his father had first intervened there in 1493.

After 1542, the Cunninghams were increasingly identified with the pro-English and Reformist party in Scotland, the earl having secured his release from captivity in England through entering an undertaking with Henry VIII's government to work for a marriage between the infant Queen Mary and Henry's son, the future Edward VI. It was probably the support of Cunningham for this position that encouraged an English sponsored raid in 1545 against Arran and Bute, centres of the Hamilton and Stewart families, who were opposed to plans for the Anglo-Scottish marriage. The strength of the Cunninghams' position in Kintyre may have been one factor that persuaded the Hamilton regime in Scotland to intrude their own supporters into this highly strategic area. Cunningham influence in Kintyre remained strong, however, even after the resignation of the see of Argyll by William Cunningham in 1553 (Watt 1969, 27). Cunningham exchanged the see with his successor, James Hamilton, for the deanery of Brechin (Watt 1969, 45). If anything, their position became even more deeply entrenched as the earl of Glencairn forged close political associations with the earl of Argyll. In the 1550s, Glencairn and Argyll emerged as two leading elements in the Reform movement in Scotland, in 1557 being principal signatories of the Bond of the Lords of the Congregation of Christ, which threw down the challenge to the pro-French regime of the Queen-Mother, Mary of Guise (Donaldson 1970, 116–17).

William Cunningham's successor as bishop was James Hamilton (Watt 1969, 27–8), whose family were the principal political opponents in the kingdom to the Campbell and Cunningham alliance. His appointment marked the intrusion of a kinsman of the earl of Arran into a region that had been dominated by the Cunninghams for two decades and marks a further shift in the political balance of power in the outer Clyde district. It would take more than the appointment of a Hamilton bishop, however, to dislodge the Cunninghams, for Bishop James's predecessor had given his kinsmen good title to the various portions of church property that they held. Alienated properties, such as Inchmarnock, were never recovered and remained in Cunningham hands until the late 16th century.

3.2.13 Back to the Stewarts

Cunningham possession of Inchmarnock ended before 1598, when control of the property passed into the hands of the Stewarts of Ardnahoe or Ardmaleish, from Bannatyne of Inchmarnock. It seems that, despite Hugh Cunningham's securing of crown charters down to 1574, that he was unable to dislodge the troublesome Bannatyne tenants from the island. At some point between 1574 and 1598, it would seem, Hugh, or more likely his heirs, disposed of the property. There was plenty of competition for control of such a valuable property and it soon attracted the attention of the Stewarts of Ardnahoe, who at that time were an important cadet line of the Stewarts of Bute. John Stewart of Ardnahoe, sheriff of Bute, evidently acquired the island as a straight purchase from the Bannatynes (who may have held it in feu from the Bishop of Argyle). Stewart was buying up properties throughout Bute and so raised the prominence of his family that he was summoned to attend Parliament at Edinburgh in 1579. His ambitions were also marked by his marriages. His first wife was Mary, daughter of John Campbell of Skipness, by whom he had a son John who succeeded him, and who may have been intended to provide Ardnahoe with a political link to the then all-powerful Campbell earls of Argyll (Reid 1864, 200–1). The Stewarts already dominated the mainland of Bute opposite Inchmarnock, where the

Bannatynes of Kames were being slowly squeezed out, and enjoyed a wide regional authority as sheriffs. Despite the marriage link with the Campbells of Skipness, the Stewarts' emergence onto the political planet was considered as something of a challenge by older established families in the region, such as the Campbells, who by the early 1500s had been given control of both Knapdale and Cowal by the crown, and who through the 16th century were extending their influence into Kintyre. The friction caused by the breakdown of the old networks of power across the Clyde sea-lanes soon spilled over into conflict, where personal family animosities rubbed shoulders with naked political ambition.

In late 1602, bad blood between John Stewart of Ardnahoe/Ardmaleish, sheriff of Bute, and the Argyll laird Dougal Campbell of Auchinbreck, spilled over into violence. Ignoring attempts by James VI to pacify the situation, in November 1602 Auchinbreck assembled a force described as 1,500-strong and armed with hagbuts and pistolets. Comprising 'sornars' (originally meaning warriors who received free board and lodgings from their lord's tenants but later tending to mean idle and masterful beggars) from various Highland and Hebridean clans, plus many of the earl of Argyll's own men, the force had gathered on the coasts opposite Bute with the intention of staging an invasion. According to Stewart's later complaint against him, Auchinbreck sent thirty of the 'maist disordourit lymmaris of his haill oist' across into Bute, where they shot many sheep and committed other 'insolenceis'. Stewart appealed to Argyll for aid, and the Earl ordered Auchenbreck to stop. Despite Argyll's orders, on 19 November 1602, Auchenbreck and four other Campbell lairds, with some 1,200 men, crossed to Bute under cover of darkness and proceeded to ravage the lands of Stewart and his tenants systematically. Their first target was the widow Marion Stewart, whose husband had died at the hands of Auchenbreck's friends. Her lands were spoiled (the ten-poundland of Wester Kames is specifically mentioned), her corn was burned, and all her plenishings and those of her tenants stolen. All told, John Stewart reckoned that 1,000 merks worth of damage had been inflicted. From Wester Kames, the raiders moved on to Ardmaleish, where they burned Stewart's corn and slaughtered his stock. They then recrossed Bute and descended on Inchmarnock, where they stole ten sheep, a fat cow and plenishings worth £20, and from Stewart's tenant there, also called John Stewart, they took plenishings valued at £30. It was a highly destructive raid and the sheriff was able to obtain a Privy Council order for the perpetrators to submit themselves for trial and for Argyll to present Auchenbreck in court. By January 1603, however, none of the defenders had appeared and the Privy Council issued a further order against Argyll and the raiders *RPC*, vi, 517–18). There is no further record of action against Auchenbreck or of how the issue was settled.

3.3 INCHMARNOCK AND KILDAVANAN: THE PLACE-NAME EVIDENCE

RACHEL BUTTER

3.3.1 Introduction

Place-names can throw light on the nature and dating of sites, on language change and the movement of peoples and cultures, and on characteristics of past landscapes. A name containing the name of a saint seems to be particularly promising. Although the notion that the saint in a place-name must have been the founder of the site has long been abandoned, it might still be thought possible to discover the identity of the saint commemorated, and so to deduce something of the place's affiliations, both cultural and geographical, and perhaps to refine our sense of the date at which a site was used and named. This is far from straightforward, however, as we will see in the case of the name Inchmarnock itself, and of Kildavanan, a name which is now applied to a place on the west coast of Bute, but which may once have referred to a site on Inchmarnock.

Even if one cannot read off a simple answer from a name there may still be something to be gained in such explorations. There is a dynamic relationship between people and names, in which names do not just reflect the situation at any given stage. They themselves give rise to stories: they influence the way people understand their cultural and physical environment, and give rise to new stories, cults and names which are created to explain the existence of the original one. Thus a mistaken understanding of the meaning of a place-name, or of the saint who is thought to be commemorated in that name, can have as powerful an effect on people's imagination as the original meaning.

3.3.2 Inchmarnock

Inchemernoc late 14th century *Chron. Fordun* 1, 43 ['Insula Inchemernok et ibi cella monachorum']

Inchemernolz 1391 MacPhail 1934, 143 [*Inchemernolz* is evidently a mistranscription of *Inchemernok*. This is a confirmation of an exchange between the abbot of Saddell Abbey, Kintyre and the abbot of Crossraguel, Ayrshire of the chapel of the Holy Trinity of *Kyldomine* and the parish church of Inchmarnock, Sodor diocese]

Inche Mernoche 1549 Dean Monro in Macleod 1934, 487. [This is the form which heads the entry; it goes on to describe 'ane little iyle callit *Inch Mernocke*'.]

Inchemerno 1573 *RMS* iv no 2115 [to William bishop of Argyll, '5 librat. terrarum de *Inchemerno* … vic *Bute*']

Marnoch 1580 Abraham Ortelius *Scotiae tabula*, NLS Marischal 2

Marnoch c 1595 Mercator *Scotia Regnum*, NLS Marischal 5

Mernoch 1654 Blaeu Pl 21 *Buthe Insula* NLS WD3B/24

Mernock I 1726 Herman Moll, *The north part of Britain called Scotland*, NLS Marischal 33

Inch Marnock 1734 John Cowley, *A New Map of North Britain*, NLS *Aq.1/1[10]*.

This name contains as its first element Scottish Gaelic *innis* 'island'. The second element is probably a personal name deriving from Gaelic *Mo Ernóc*, my Ernóc The use of *mo-* (my) or *do-* (your) followed by a personal name, often in modified form, is common in saints' names. Thus Kilmachalmaig in Bute contains a form of Colum (Columba in Latin) with the *mo-* affix, and the suffix *-óc* often found with the *mo-/do-* affixes. In the case of Marnock the name is Erne, Ernán, Ernaíne or the like, all of which probably have their origin in Old Irish *íarn* 'iron'.

A search of the Irish and Scottish calendars and martyrologies reveals many saints called Ernán, Mo Ernóc or variants, with over 20 in the *Martyrology of Tallaght* alone. It is not possible to say which of these, if any, is commemorated at Inchmarnock, despite the confident assertions of some commentators.

It is tempting to link the dedication with the St Marnock or Marnan who had a powerful cult in Scotland with a focus in the north-east. He was said, in the 16th century, to be buried at Aberchirder near Banff, where his head was used to solemnise oaths and to heal the sick. Early references to Marnocks or Marnans include a 'Sanctus Marnocus de Loychel' (Aberdeenshire) in *c* 1200 (Watson 1926, 292), a church dedication at Foulis-Easter in 1242 (Forbes 1872, 392 quoting *Regist. Priorat. S. Andree*, 348) and an annual mass *de Sancto Marnoco* in Brechin in 1348 (Forbes 1872, 392 quoting *Regist. Episcopat. Brechin*, 12). Both the *Aberdeen Breviary* and the *Martyrology of Aberdeen* give the feast day of Marnan of Aberchirder as March 1 (Forbes 1872, 113, 129).[1] Place-names and wells from Sutherland to Kincardineshire suggest the cult was widespread, though whether it was this or a different saint (or saints) of the same name being commemorated we do not know.[2] Several Scottish calendars commemorate a Marnock on 25 October, and in some he is associated in particular with Kilmarnock in Ayrshire (*Martyrology of Aberdeen*, Adam King, Dempster 1620: Forbes 1872, 135, 165, 216). This latter Marnock, who seems to have been also remembered in Paisley,[3] might be considered to have had a cult with a more westerly focus and therefore more likely to include Inchmarnock, but this is far from certain. Both cults may, of course, have their origin in a single saint.[4] Conversely the many dedications in Scotland could derive from any number of holy men called Ernán or the like, a very common name.[5]

A search in the Irish calendars for a saint who might correspond to the Marnock commemorated in Scotland on 1 March reveals in the *Martyrology of Tallaght* two potential candidates both on the previous day, 28 February: Ternóc mac Maelduibh, associated with a church in County Tyrone, and a female saint, Ernéne ingen Airchinnig. Nothing further is known about either of these two saints. There is also a possible Irish match for the Marnock remembered in Scotland on 25 October: an Ernán on 26 October who first appears in the 12th-century *Martyrology of Gorman* and who, according to the gloss is from *Michluachra icCill na saccart* (*MG*, 205). This has been identified with Kilnasaggart in County Armagh where there is a pillarstone bearing an inscription commemorating *Ternohc mac Ceran bic* (Macalister 1949, vol 2, 115). This Ternóc (another name deriving from Erne) is assigned, in genealogies compiled in the mid-12th century, to the Cruithne or Dál nAraide (*CGSH* no 101), southern neighbours of the Dál Riada in north-east Ireland. His death is recorded in the *Annals of the Four Masters* in 714 (*AFM* 714.3: *T'Ernóc mac Ciarain d'ecc*), and in the *Annals of Tigernach* (*AT*, 225 *Ternóc mac Ciarain obit*). If this obit is correct it might be thought to decrease the chance that it is this Ernán who is commemorated at Inchmarnock, as there is some evidence that Inchmarnock's Ernán was already culted by the 7th or 8th century, the date range

assigned to some writing, including the name Ernán, found three times on an inscribed slate pebble that was found during the present investigation (Forsyth & Tedeschi, Chapter 6.3.3 below).

The saint of Inchmarnock is often identified not with any of the saints above, but rather with one of the saints called Ernán who appears in Adomnán's *Vitae Columbae*, in particular Columba's uncle, who was sent to be prior of the monastery on the island of *Hinba* (*VC* i, 45) and who was among Columba's original companions in Scotland.[6] If Jura is accepted as being Hinba, as some scholars argue, then the place-name (and chapel) Cill Earnadail on its east coast might represent a dedication to this saint.[7] He is undetectable in either the genealogies of saints or in any of the martyrologies. An Ernán who does appear in the martyrologies, and who is noticed in the annals, is Ernéne mac Craséni who, according to Adomnán (and in fulfilment of a prophecy by Columba), was 'famous through all the churches of Ireland (*Scotiae*) and very highly regarded'.[8] There are two other Ernáns mentioned by Adomnán, one a monk and one a layman, and a Mernóc is named as Columba's nephew.[9] Aside from the Ernáns associated with Columba, and in view of the Stewarts' apparent devotion to St Brendan (Boardman 2008), it is interesting that a key character in the *Navigatio Brendani* is Mernóc who lives on the Delightful Isle and whose voyage with his godson Barrinthus inspires Brendan's adventures (Selmer 1959, 4–5). It is tempting to wonder if Island Davaar (*Insula de Sanctbarre* 1508 *RMS*, vol 2, no 3170) off the west coast of Kintyre is in some way connected.

Finally, it is worth considering the possibility that the *marnock* of Inchmarnock is not a personal name at all. There are several place-names in which the other element is not ecclesiastical: Ardmarnock in Cowal, Lawmarnock in Renfrewshire, Dalmarnock in Perthshire and Glasgow, and, in Ireland, Portmarnock. It is worth noting the case of the *marnock* of Sillymarnock in Old Deer parish, Aberdeenshire which seems to have come to be understood as deriving from the name of a saint (perhaps influenced by strength of cult of Marnock nearby) but whose earliest form is *merlec* 'thieves' (Taylor forthcoming).

3.3.3 Kildavanan

Douenaldo clerico de *Kildufbenin* 1269 x 1299 *PR*, no 128 [The cleric is a witness. The previous witness in the list is *Ferchar filio Nigilli de Buyt*] terr<ae> de *Kyldavanan* 1429 *RMS* ii, no 123

Kilmavanane 1467 *RMS* ii, no 917

Alex. Stewart de *Kildovanane* 1530 x 1534 *RMS* iii, no 1379

Kildavanark 1548 *RSS* iii, no 2839

40 sol. de *Kildovannane* 1588 *RMS* v, no 1541

3 mercat. de *Kildovanane* 1610 x 1615 *RMS* vi, no 1206

Kildauanach 1654 Blaeu Plate 21 *Buthe Insula* NLS WD3B/24

Kildavanna 1753 Roy 13/5

The first element is Scottish Gaelic *cill* from Latin *cella* via Old Irish *cell*.[10] In Scotland the term is applied to a range of sites from burial grounds and tiny chapels, to buildings which in the 12th century became parish churches. The second element, as in Inchmarnock, is probably a personal name with an affectionate prefix. However, there are other options.

The name is now applied to a farm on Bute, 5km north of Inchmarnock. It is of interest because it is close to Inchmarnock, and also because it seems on Blaeu's map of 1654 (drawing from data gathered by Timothy Pont probably in the late 16th century) to be referring to a place not on Bute, but on Inchmarnock. It is possible that this is simply a mistake and that the name *Kildauanach* has been misplaced. This is supported by the fact that the positioning of several names elsewhere on Blaeu's map of Bute is inaccurate, and by the fact that it would take only a small shift of the name east to land it in roughly the position of present-day Kildavanan. Another explanation is, however, worth exploring.

Elsewhere in Argyll there are examples of ecclesiastical names (or at least dedications) which migrate between the mainland and a nearby island, and this may be what we are seeing here. On the south coast of Kintyre, for instance, is Kilmanshennachan with, on the nearby Sanda island, the remains of a chapel which is said by a 19th century source to have formerly been called *Kilmashenaghan* (Howson 1842, 80), a name no longer appearing on the island. Both of these names seem to commemorate a saint called Senchán, Senach or Senán. Another example is Kilmacormack in Knapdale, a name which has been attached both to the remains on Eilean Mòr and to the church on the mainland at Keills (MacLean 1983). The name has now disappeared from both mainland

and island sites. Yet another example is Lamlash on Arran, a name commemorating one of the saints called Molaisse. The name used to be attached to the island now known as Holy Island (the name actually contains a contracted form of Gaelic *eilean* 'island') but is now attached to a settlement on Arran itself (Watson 1926, 306).

Watson considered the saint of Kildavanan to be 'probably the same as in Kilvannan in Uist' pointing out that Kilbannon near Tuam in County Galway in Ireland commemorates 'Benignus, the disciple and successor of St Patrick, Nov 9' (Watson 1926, 301). The situation is not quite as simple as Watson implies, however, as there is more than one Benignus (Benén in Irish) associated with Patrick and though the successor at Armagh is sometimes cited as the dedicatee at Kilbannon, the latter is thought by other authorities to be one of the other Benéns (Etchingham 1999, 230n, for example). It is of course possible that the cult of one original Benén has split into separate strands represented by some or all of these 'different' Benéns.

The cult of a person or persons called Benén is widespread in Ireland. It may be significant that the name, not a common one (none in *MT*, only one in *MG*, and one in *CGSH*), is almost always associated with Patrick. It is interesting, too, that a pairing of dedications near Kilbannon in County Galway (St Benén and, at the neighbouring parish of Kilconly, St Conla) may be replicated on Bute where 5km south-east of Kildavanan is Kilwhinleck.[11] This illustrates the problem with this kind of evidence: it is capable of widely varying interpretation. Kilwhinleck may possibly commemorate a Findlug or a Findláech, and Kildavanan may not contain the name Benén at all.

The earliest form of the name, *Kildufbenin*, suggests that a personal name containing Old Irish *dub*, Scottish Gaelic *dubh* 'black', might be present. There are many personal names beginning *dub-* in the Irish record, with five pages or so in the index to the secular Irish genealogies alone (*CGH*, 598–603), but Black (1946) finds very few in Scotland (names include Dougal < Dubgall 'black stranger', and Dufscolok < Dubscolóc, 'black scholar'), and there is no other example of Dub-Benén or the like in either Scotland or Ireland. The possibility that Kildavanan is not a name with the element *do-* must be taken into account, however, remembering that this would not then necessarily be a saint's name.

There is also the suggestion that the name derives from the Gaelic *manach* 'monk', in which case its meaning would be the same as Fordun's *cella monachorum* (Fisher 2001, 77). This theory falters on the difficulty of explaining the persistent *do-* or *duf-*, and the termination in *-n* in almost all of the forms. The possibility that there is a link with an 8th-century abbot of Kingarth, Mael Manach (*AU* 776.6 *Mors Mele Manach abbatis Cinn Garadh*), is similarly weakened.

Finally, since he is an authority so often quoted on the history of Bute, we must consider Hewison's suggestion that the name comes from Adomnán (Hewison 1893, i, 209). Early forms do not support this view, a view which may simply be an example of the tendency to find evidence of Iona influence everywhere, and the temptation to attribute dedications to saints whom we already know about. The saint of Kildavanan, if indeed it was a saint, may be someone with only local recognition, unrecorded in martyrologies, *vitae*, or genealogies. The same, of course, applies to Inchmarnock.

In short, we have no way of being sure of the identities of the two saints who seem to be commemorated in the names Inchmarnock and Kildavanan. Without ascertaining their identities, we cannot begin to ascertain which (if any) of the wider *paruchiae* of monasteries in the Gaelic world they might have belonged to, nor to which monasteries or churches the settlement on Inchmarnock might have been affiliated. Without this information it is difficult to glean information about the possible political implications of the cult of these two saints (as we can, for example, with St Brendan and the Stewarts). What these two saints do allow us to do is to illustrate the slippery nature of the cult of saints in the Gaelic world, and the danger of placing too much weight on any supposed identification of any saint.

NOTES

1   He has a feast on 1 or 2 March in the following calendars, though without a link to Aberchirder: Arbuthnott, Adam King, Dempster, Camerarius. In the first he is Marnoc, a bishop. In the others he is Marman, bishop and confessor. All these calendars are printed in Forbes 1872.

2   Inchmarnock parish in Aberdeenshire, two Dalmarnocks in Perthshire and one in Glasgow, Ardmarnock and Kilmarnock, both in Cowal in Argyll, Marny's well in Kincardineshire, a Killearnan in Ross-shire and one in Sutherland. Marny's well is noted by Watson 1926, 292. The others are existing place-names with the exception of one of the Dalmarnocks in Perthshire, which appears in the Dunfermline Register, 1153 x 1161, 1282, 1404 etc (Simon Taylor, pers comm).

3   A fair was established in Paisley on S. Marnoc's day in 1488 (*RMS* ii, no 1768). The day of the year is not specified but a 17th century almanac records a fair in Paisley on 26 October (Whyte Almanac, 1632, NLS F.7.6.17).

4   For arguments regarding the process by which devotion to one saint can develop into multiple cults, each later understood to commemorate a distinct saint, see work by Padraig Ó Riain especially Ó Riain 1982.

5   Three Ernán-types are listed among the martyred companions of Donan of Eigg in the *MT* (April 17), for example. The Killearnan in Kildonan parish, Sutherland might commemorate one of these. There is some evidence for dates other than 1 March and 25/26 October being observed in Scotland: Dempster has on 22 February *In Banzenoche Marnokdubi Eremitae*, Camerarius on 25 November has *Sanctus Marnochus Episcopus & Confessor*, and Arbuthnott has on 5 December *sci mernoci abb & conf* (Forbes 1872), In addition there was a November fair of St Marnoch in Kilmalcolm, Renfrewshire (Paul 1918, 168), and note that there is a Lawmarnock Farm near Kilmalcolm.

6   He appears in a list appended to one of the MSS of *VC*. Sharpe accepts this as dating to around the early 8th century (Sharpe 1995, 354).

7   *Kilharnadull* 1545 *RMS* iii, no 3085, *Kilaridil* 1654 Blaeu, *Killearn* 1695 Martin Martin in Macleod 1934, 269.

8   *VC* i, 3. *AU* 635.5: *Quies Fintain m. Telchain & Ernaini m. Creseni*. August 18 in *MT*: *Ernine mac Cresine o Raith Nui i nUíb Garrchon*.

9   *Ernéne moccu Fir Róide*, *VC* iii, 23; *Ernán mac Glasderc VC* i, 16. The son of Columba's sister is said in an appendix to the B MS of *VC* to be Mernóc mac Dícuil (Sharpe 1995, 354).

10 The early forms of the name are backed up by references to a chapel here. (Ordnance Survey first edition map 1869 and Hewison 1893, i, 209 suggest that this is the correct reading, but note that modern names containing Kil- can sometimes derive from Gaelic *cùl* 'back', *coille* 'wood' or *ceann* 'head'.)

11 Early forms include *Kilconlik* 1440 *ER* v, p 80. Conla can be equated both with Conláed and with Conláech, the form which may be present in this name.

Chapter 4

Inchmarnock in Prehistory

STEPHEN CARTER

4.1 INTRODUCTION

The Inchmarnock Project was conceived with a clear chronological focus on the early medieval period up to the recent past. The rationale behind this research design has been set out in Chapter 1.2. It is recognised, as a result of this focus, that most of the 12,000 year post-glacial history of the island has not been explored by the project. However, in preparing this volume, it was considered appropriate to include an assessment of the prehistory of Inchmarnock for two reasons.

Firstly, and more importantly, the arrival of the Irish monastic community in the 7th century AD did not involve the colonisation of a new-found-land. Inchmarnock was an island with a long cultural history when Ernán (or his followers) stepped ashore and this prehistoric context must be set out if the establishment of the monastic community is to be better understood.

Secondly, the prehistory of Inchmarnock is of interest in its own right. Given the opportunity presented by the present research programme, it is appropriate to offer an overview of our knowledge of this long period. In the future, others may wish to follow up various lines of research not explored in the present project.

The prehistoric narrative has been divided up here, for convenience, into three chronological periods. These should not be seen as distinct and meaningful stages in the development of Inchmarnock; rather they reflect the nature of the available evidence and our level of understanding of the contemporary landscape. The three periods are:

Early Holocene (10,000 to 5000 BC): A long period of natural landscape evolution from the end of the last glaciation, with no evidence for human activity in Inchmarnock.

Early prehistory (5000 to 2500 BC): The later Mesolithic and Neolithic periods when human impact in Inchmarnock is first detectable but evidence is limited to isolated artefacts.

Later prehistory (2500 BC to AD 500): The Bronze and Iron Ages with substantive evidence for settlement and funerary sites.

4.2 SOURCES OF INFORMATION FOR PREHISTORIC INCHMARNOCK

In compiling an overview of Inchmarnock in prehistory, two sources of information have been utilised.

4.2.1 Existing records of sites and artefacts

Firstly, there are the accumulated records of prehistoric sites and artefacts, the products of earlier archaeological investigations in Inchmarnock. In this respect, we are particularly indebted to Dorothy Marshall, both for her own publications (see Bibliography) and for her encouragement of the Middleton family of Midpark to report their own discoveries of prehistoric artefacts (D Middleton 1977: J Middleton 1977: Middleton *et al* 1979).

The key excavated prehistoric site from these earlier investigations is the Bronze Age cist burial from Northpark, known as 'the Queen of the Inch' because of her fine jet necklace (Marshall 1963: Scott 1963). This necklace has recently been the subject of a detailed analysis by Alison Sheridan of the National Museums Scotland as part of her wider research project on jet artefacts in Scotland. We are grateful for early sight of the results of this analysis prior to formal publication (Sheridan *et al* forthcoming).

4.2.2 New archaeological investigations

The second source of information is the limited investigation or accidental discovery of prehistoric sites and artefacts during the present project.

Evaluation and survey work was undertaken in the initial stages of the present project to clarify the nature and location of archaeological sites previously recorded on the island (*AIR* 2.2; *AIR* 3) and to explore the potential for palaeoenvironmental investigations (Tipping *et al* 2000; Tipping *et al* 2001). The following archaeological sites were investigated in May 2000 and proved to be of prehistoric date:

Site 1 Burial cairn (topographic survey and trial trench excavation)

Site 2 Bronze Age burial cists (accurate relocation)

Site 3 Cup-and-ring marked stone (trial excavation)

Site 9 Cave (trial excavation)

Site 16 Cave (trial excavation)

Further discoveries of prehistoric material were made in the course of the later stages of the project:

Site 4 St Marnock's Church: residual prehistoric lithics in later contexts (Ballin 2002)

Site 16 Cave: further excavation of Iron Age deposits below early medieval occupation (*AIR* 10)

Site 25 Burnt stones, possible prehistoric burnt mound (*AIR* 2.2)

4.3 EARLY HOLOCENE (10,000 BC TO 5000 BC): EVOLUTION OF THE NATURAL LANDSCAPE

People probably entered Scotland very soon after the loss of ice cover at the beginning of the present inter-glacial period and radiocarbon dates from archaeological sites on the west and east coasts of Scotland demonstrate that Mesolithic communities of hunter-gatherers were widespread by 7500 BC. Their mobile lifestyle continued until 4000 BC when settled agricultural communities are first recorded. Evidence for these first settlers in Scotland is slight: generally only scatters of flint tools and debris have been recorded, so an absence of direct evidence from Inchmarnock for human activity is neither surprising nor significant.

4.3.1 An Early Holocene palaeoenvironmental record for Inchmarnock

Evidence for the evolution of the natural landscape at this time in Inchmarnock does survive as a palaeoenvironmental record. A small basin on the late-glacial raised beach, 500m south of Midpark, contains sediment dating from the early Holocene period (Figure 2.2, above). This basin was evaluated by Dr Richard Tipping and co-workers from the University of Stirling to assess the potential of the deposits to yield palaeoenvironmental information (Tipping *et al* 2000; Tipping *et al* 2001).

The basin, which measures roughly 300×120m, was found to contain up to 2.65m of sediment at its deepest point. Radiocarbon dates (Table 4.1) demonstrate that the basal 1.1m of sediment is of late-glacial date (14,000 to 10,000 BC) with organic Holocene sediments starting at 1.56m below the current ground level. A sample of gyttja (organic lake mud) dated from this level returned a calibrated date of 10380–9610 BC. Roughly 1m of lake mud accumulated in the basin before emergent vegetation completely covered any open water and peat accumulation started. A second sample taken from the base of the peat returned a calibrated date of 5720–5550 BC. The surface 0.5m of sediments was not dated and appears to be disturbed.

It is clear from the upper of the two radiocarbon dates that there has been significant loss of sediments above this level and no deposits survive from the Neolithic period onwards. It is assumed that more recent peat deposits were cut away for fuel and it is known that the basin was drained (probably around AD 1800) during the improvement of Southpark. A deep drain and the remains of a thorn hedge running across the bog testify to this attempt (ultimately unsuccessful) to bring the area into productive agricultural use.

The Southpark peat basin therefore contains a truncated sediment accumulation that has the potential to provide a palaeoenvironmental record of Inchmarnock for the first 5,000 years of the Holocene. Given the medieval focus of the current project, no attempt was made to undertake detailed pollen or other analyses. However, the age and nature of the deposits have been proved and offer a resource for future

Table 4.1 Radiocarbon dates from the Southpark peat basin

Lab. Code	Depth (cm)	Sediment	${}^{14}C$ Age ($\pm 1\sigma$)	$\delta^{13}C$	Age Range cal BC ($\pm 2\sigma$)
Beta-149075	152.0–156.0	gyttja	10160 ± 60	−24.3	10380–9610
Beta-149074	46.0–49.0	peat	6810 ± 50	−29.6	5720–5550

research into landscape evolution and the impact of human activity during this early period.

4.3.2 Early Holocene landscape evolution in Inchmarnock

In the absence of local archaeological and environmental information for this period, it is necessary to fall back on our knowledge of regional landscape evolution to suggest a likely history for Inchmarnock during the early part of the Holocene (Mithen 2000; Sutherland 1997; Tipping 1994).

This period was one of considerable environmental change: rapid evolution of woodland vegetation and variations in sea level. Open grass and heathland vegetation had been replaced by birch and hazel woodland before 8500 BC which, in turn, developed into a diverse deciduous woodland by 7500 BC with oak, elm, ash, hazel and birch. This woodland would have formed a complete cover over the island, except for the relatively exposed west and south coasts where a narrow strip of land along the shore probably remained clear of trees.

The actual size of the island changed during this period. Before 7000 BC sea level was lower than at present and Inchmarnock would have been significantly larger. However, it is unlikely that it was ever low enough for Inchmarnock to have been connected to Bute. The sea level then rose until roughly 5000 BC at which point it was some 12m above its present level on Inchmarnock. The sea would have covered the raised beach platform that now rings the island and washed into the caves in the low cliffs at the back of the beach on the south and west coasts. This platform is up to 150m wide on the west coast so the island would have been somewhat reduced compared with its present-day size, but the main impact would have been on the nature of the shoreline. The majority of the shore would have been ringed with low cliffs, best developed on the exposed west and south coasts, making the island much less accessible than it is today.

Despite this, the island would have been attractive to the hunter-gatherer communities, offering plant and animal resources that could have been harvested during visits to the island by boat from Bute. Hazel nuts were collected as a staple food by Mesolithic people and there is a 19th-century record of abundant hazel nuts preserved in peat on the island (Hewison 1893, i, 132). The island may also have contained substantial numbers of seabirds, which could have been exploited for their eggs, flesh and feathers.

4.4 EARLY PREHISTORY (5000 BC TO 2500 BC): ISOLATED ARTEFACTS AND HUMAN IMPACT

After 5000 BC the sea level began to fall again, exposing the low raised beach platform and abandoning the sea cliffs with their caves. Parallels from sites elsewhere on the west coast (for example Oban, Mull and Jura) suggest that the raised beach platform and its caves offer potential for the discovery of late Mesolithic occupation sites. This potential has yet to be realised for Inchmarnock. Two caves were investigated at the south end of the island (Sites 9 and 16) but, in both cases, the primary deposits were found to be no older than the Iron Age (Table 2.2, Chapter 2.2 above). This does not rule out the presence of earlier use of the other caves on the island but further exploration of this potential lay outside the research design of the Inchmarnock project

Actual evidence for the presence of humans at this date in Inchmarnock remains extremely limited (Figure 4.1). Two small flint cores recovered from much later deposits at St Marnock's Church (Site 4) have been assigned to the late Mesolithic or early Neolithic (Ballin 2002). This age range reflects the fact that there is no clear change in flaked flint tools at this important cultural boundary. Indeed, other non-diagnostic flint flakes and tools collected in residual contexts from Sites 4, 5 and 13 could also be of late Mesolithic date.

Four fragmentary polished stone axes provide the earliest unequivocal evidence for people in Inchmarnock (Marshall 1978b, 1978c, 1980; Middleton et al 1979). They are characteristic Neolithic artefacts (4000 to 2500 BC) and symbolise one of the key innovations of the Neolithic period: the felling of trees for agriculture. We can therefore be confident that Inchmarnock was cleared, at least in part, and settled by a farming community at this time. The Neolithic farmers would have introduced the first grazing animals to the island (other than deer that swam the channel from Bute) and this would have placed pressure on woodland, also exploited for fuel wood and building timbers.

The only other diagnostic Neolithic find from the island is a detached stone slab (Site 3) at the north end of the island bearing one cup and ring and one cup mark (J Middleton 1977; Marshall 1985). This is a modest example of a style of rock art that has some of its most complex examples in Argyll, particularly from the Kilmartin area of Mid-Argyll (Stevenson 1997).

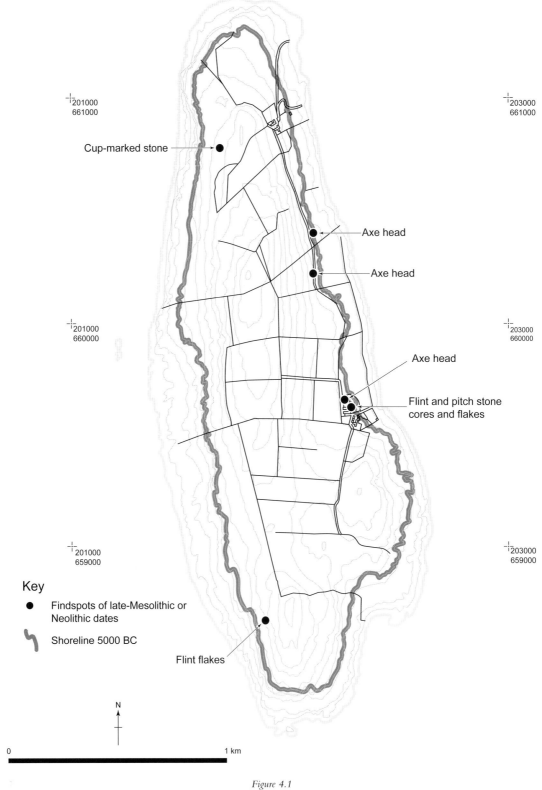

201000
661000

203000
661000

Cup-marked stone ●

Axe head

Axe head

201000
660000

203000
660000

Axe head

Flint and pitch stone
cores and flakes

201000
659000

203000
659000

Key

● Findspots of late-Mesolithic or
Neolithic dates

Shoreline 5000 BC

Flint flakes

N

0   1 km

Figure 4.1
Early prehistoric Inchmarnock, 5000–2500 BC

Whilst impossible to date directly, their frequent reuse in early Bronze Age funerary monuments is taken to indicate a Neolithic origin.

There is no direct evidence for the location of Neolithic settlements, or the extent of cultivated fields and pastures. This mirrors the situation throughout Argyll where the evidence for Neolithic settlements remains insubstantial (Marshall 1978a; Rennie 1984). The distribution of the stone axes (Site 34) on the island probably reflects the movements of the Middleton children who discovered them in the 1970s rather than the extent of cleared land. However, it is reasonable to assume that the original farmers exploited the better land and therefore would have been attracted to the central ridge of the island. This offers relatively well-drained, less-stony soils and has remained in cultivation to the present day. It is this continuity of cultivation that has erased the evidence for the prehistoric settlements in Inchmarnock.

The few stone tools that provide most of the evidence for Neolithic settlement also illustrate some of the wider contacts of the island community in the Firth of Clyde and further afield, dispelling any notion that this was an isolated or insular community. Three of the four axe heads are made from porcellanite, only quarried at Tievebulliagh on the coast of County Antrim, Ireland (Marshall 1980). Stone suitable for axes was a rare and valuable commodity in Scotland before the advent of metal and axes were traded widely from a few production centres where the stone occurred. Numerous porcellanite axe heads have been discovered around the Firth of Clyde and further into Scotland along with flint tools also traded from Antrim where flint occurs in the chalk that outcrops on the coast. The coast of Antrim is visible from as far up the Firth of Clyde as Arran and the crossing from the Mull of Kintyre is only 20km, no obstacle to Neolithic boatmen.

The fourth axe head from Inchmarnock is made from basalt and is also an import as the island is composed entirely of schist. The source of the basalt is not unique like the porcellanite and it could have been produced as close as the south end of Bute. There are also two flakes of pitchstone from Inchmarnock, one from earlier collections (Marshall 1980) and a second from the recent excavations at St Marnock's Church (Ballin 2002). Pitchstone is a glassy igneous rock that can be worked like flint and all of the Scottish examples derive from Arran where it occurs in many outcrops. It was widely traded during the Neolithic as far as the Northern Highlands.

All of these tools (porcellanite, basalt and pitchstone) would have been distributed by sea and, throughout the history of this part of Scotland, travel by sea has been the most effective means of transport. Sea travel and, in particular, links to Ireland feature prominently in the medieval history of Inchmarnock and the scraps of prehistoric evidence reported here demonstrate the antiquity and persistence of these distant connections. Inchmarnock's relative isolation at present reflects our reliance on land-based transport and is a historic aberration.

4.5 LATER PREHISTORY (2500 BC TO AD 500): DEVELOPMENT OF A CULTURAL LANDSCAPE

It must be admitted that the evidence base for the Inchmarnock narrative up to this point has been extremely small; little more than a few stray artefacts supported by a regional archaeological and palaeoenvironmental framework. In this context, the evidence available from the island for the most recent part of the prehistoric period is abundant: artefacts, structures and deposits relating to settlement and burial, all contributing to an understanding of cultural landscape. However, a note of caution should be raised as this apparent abundance is only relative. The evidence discussed below spans three millennia and most sites or artefacts are not closely dated or fully explored. The concept of a single unchanging 'later prehistoric landscape' is not something that would have been recognised by the contemporary inhabitants over this prolonged period. So, whilst making the most of the available evidence, we should not exaggerate our understanding of this long period that covers the entire Bronze Age and Iron Age.

4.5.1 The recorded later prehistoric sites

There are seven sites on the island that may be assigned to the later prehistoric period with more or less confidence and these are listed in Table 4.2. To this might also be added the lithic scatters that were recovered during the current excavation at the church (Site 4), and others (Site 13) reported by the Middletons in the south-west part of the island. If the locations of these sites and find-spots are plotted (Figure 4.2) it reveals an intriguing division between funerary and ritual monuments at the northern tip of the island and evidence for subsistence activity at the south end of the island.

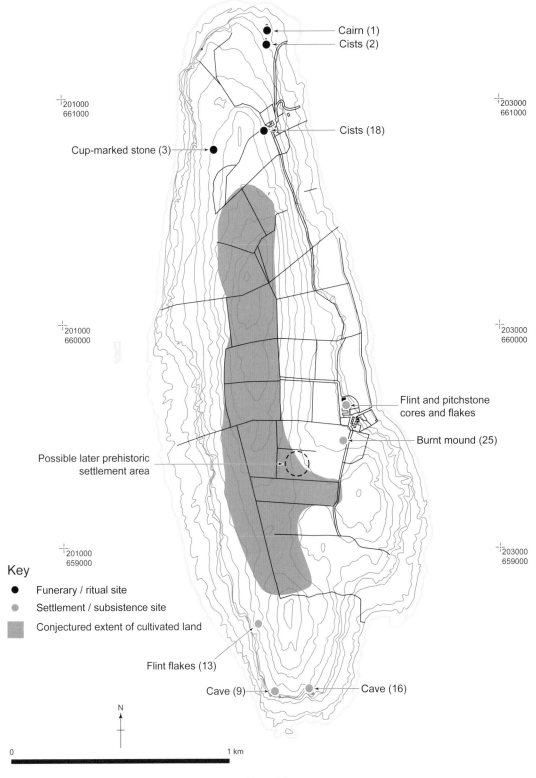

Figure 4.2
Later prehistoric Inchmarnock, 2500 BC–AD 500

Table 4.2 Later prehistoric sites on Inchmarnock

Site number	Site type	Description	References
1	Cairn	Large cairn at northern tip of island, 27.6 × 18.8 m and up to 2m high. Probable kerb identified on west side, assumed to be an Early Bronze Age funerary cairn.	Marshall 1980; *AIR* 3, 2000
2	Cists	Group of three burial cists discovered during ploughing in 1960 and excavated by Dorothy Marshall. Two were already disturbed and earth-filled, containing only a fragment of jet spacer plate. The third had its lid intact and contained a female skeleton, flint knife and an impressive jet necklace.	Marshall 1963; Scott 1963; Sheridan forthcoming
3	Cup and ring-marked stone	The stone is a detached slab, 1.5 × 1.3 m and 0.10–0.17 m thick with one cup-and-ring mark (170mm diameter) and one cup mark (120mm diameter). Discovered in 1976 and originally described as three cup-and-ring marks and two cup marks; this appears to be an error.	Middleton 1977; Marshall 1985; *AIR* 3, 2000
9	Cave	Rock shelter on south coast of island with sediments dated to 346–4 BC.	*AIR* 3, 2000
16	Cave	Rock shelter on south coast of island with sediments relating to two episodes of use dated to 355–59 BC and AD 340–540; below early medieval occupation deposits.	*AIR* 3, 2000; *AIR* 10, 2002
18	Cists (possible)	Five cists are said to have been discovered near the south-west corner of the yard at Northpark in the early 1980s. This report has not been confirmed.	*AIR* 3, 2000
25	Burnt mound (possible)	A deposit of small to medium sized burnt stones in a dark matrix, up to 0.12m thick. It is visible on both sides of a drainage ditch over a distance of 2m.	*AIR* 3, 2000

The large cairn on the northern tip of Inchmarnock (Site 1: Plate 4.1) has always been suspected to be a funerary cairn (Marshall 1978c) and the identification of a kerb during the present investigations would appear to confirm this view. While the cairn itself has not produced any dating evidence, a date within the Early Bronze Age is likely; comparable large cairns in the Kilmartin Valley are likely, from their contents, to date to between 2200 and 2000 BC (Sheridan, pers comm).

The cairn is therefore broadly contemporary with the most well-known prehistoric site on the island: the burial known as the 'Queen of the Inch' (Site 2), which is located only 70m to the south, and which forms part of a flat cist cemetery on the low gravelly ridge overlooking the cairn. This intact cist burial of a young adult female, discovered in 1960 and excavated by Dorothy Marshall (Marshall 1963), produced a flint knife and one of the finest jet spacer-plate necklaces ever found and the only one with ten strands of beads

(Plate 4.2). A reconstruction drawing of her burial is offered in Figure 4.3.

Plate 4.1
Cairn (Site 1) from Site 2, facing north, looking across to the Kyles of Bute

Plate 4.2
The spacer plate necklace of jet and jet-like materials from the grave of the
'Queen of the Inch' (Site 2). *Reproduced by courtesy of the Trustees of the
National Museums Scotland*

Recent reanalysis of this spectacular find by Alison Sheridan and Lore Troalen of National Museums Scotland (Sheridan *et al* forthcoming) has demonstrated that all the plates and many of the beads are of Whitby jet. The necklace has a complex history. Its components (some old when buried) had been assembled from five or six different necklaces, and the largest spacer plates had been rebored, and an entire string of non-jet beads added, in order to achieve the impressive ten strands at the front. The necklace has the largest number of beads found in any 'jet' spacer plate necklace and, as Alison Sheridan (forthcoming) points out, it is not impossible that its owner wished to outshine the woman who was buried at Mount Stuart on Bute, wearing a similar, newer necklace, comprising the more normal eight strands, and made almost entirely of Whitby jet.

The cist was re-excavated[1] by Alison Sheridan (together with Anne Speirs of Bute Museum and Jessica Herriot, formerly of Midpark) in 2006 to retrieve the skeletal remains that Dorothy Marshall had reburied (Sheridan 2006). These have yielded a radiocarbon date of 3635 ± 35 BP (2111–1943 cal BC at 1σ, 2133–1902 cal BC at 2σ, calibrated using OxCal v.3.10), and stable isotope analysis of bone and of tooth enamel (undertaken by Mandy Jay, Janet Montgomery and Jane Evans) have revealed that the woman was probably of local stock, and that her diet was markedly terrestrial, despite the proximity of the sea.

The 'Queen of the Inch' was one of a group of three cists excavated by Marshall, but the other two were found disturbed and earth-filled. The only find from one of these was a fragment of jet, now identified as an old, worn spacer plate which had been rebored and worn as a pendant (Sheridan, pers comm).

A second group of cists is reported to have been found a further 350m to the south at Northpark (Site 18). The discovery in the early 1980s is said to have involved five cists but there was no record made at the time and the cists do not appear to have been investigated further (*AIR* 2.1). Assuming that this record is reliable, it is of course possible that the cists were early medieval long cists and not Bronze Age short cists.

Another cist at the north end of the island may be represented by the detached slab of rock with one cup-and-ring mark and one cup mark (Plate 4.3). Investigation of this slab as part of the Inchmarnock Project confirmed that it was

Plate 4.3
Cup-marked slab (Site 3), prior to and after excavation

Figure 4.3
The 'Queen of the Inch', laid to rest; shown here lying on a bed of meadowsweet. *Reconstruction drawing by Anna Faraś-Pągowska*

simply a loose stone lying on the ground surface with no outcropping bedrock in the immediate vicinity. Its dimensions (1.5 × 1.3m and only 0.10–0.17m thick) suggest that it could have been used as a side slab or the lid for a burial cist. The association of decorated Neolithic slabs with early Bronze Age burials is strong but a search of the locality failed to locate a disturbed cist.

Evidence for prehistoric subsistence activities, as noted above, is limited to three sites at the south end of the island. The identification of a burnt mound (Site 25), just south of the Southpark steading, is based on very limited observations but seems secure. A

characteristic deposit of burnt stone in a dark matrix was recorded in a typical poorly drained location. In fact, this is one of the few locations in the island with a permanent surface water supply. The absence of any surface trace of a mound can be explained by the history of drainage and agricultural improvement in the early 19th century. Whilst it is recognised that dates as late as the medieval period have been recorded for burnt mounds in Scotland (Barber 1990), the majority of dated sites fall into the Bronze Age, including those excavated in Arran and Kintyre (Barber 1997: Siggins & Carter 1993). It is this age range that is assumed for the Inchmarnock site.

Two rock shelters (Sites 9 and 16) were investigated as part of the Inchmarnock Project. Both were located in the mid-Holocene raised beach cliff-line at the southern tip of the island and both contained sediments that yielded Iron Age radiocarbon dates (Table 4.3). Site 16, discussed further in Chapter 8.2 below, also contained deposits of early medieval date.

At Site 9, limited evaluation work revealed a simple sediment sequence with one deposit containing shell, bone and charcoal between sterile subsoil and surface sediments. Hazel nutshell from this deposit returned a calibrated date range of 346–4 BC (AA-39966).

At Site 16, extensive investigations revealed a more complex stratigraphic sequence. Sterile basal sediments were covered by a deposit with shell, bone and charcoal and an area of possible rough stone surfacing. This was dated to cal 355–59 BC (AA-39967) using hazel nutshell. It was overlain by sterile sediments and then a sequence of ash and charcoal-rich deposits, including *in-situ* hearth deposits. Most of this upper sequence of cultural deposits has proved to be of early medieval date (three radiocarbon dates, all later than AD 670). However, the basal charcoal-rich sediment (below the hearth deposits) returned a significantly earlier date: cal AD 340–540 (AA-53164). The Iron Age portion of this sequence (ie pre-AD 500) is therefore interpreted as two distinct episodes of activity in the rock shelter, separated by an interval of 400 to 800 years.

What was the nature of the Iron Age activity in either of the two rock shelters? It is clear from Christopher Tolan-Smith's recent publication of *The Caves of Mid-Argyll* (Tolan-Smith 2001) that later prehistoric use of caves or rock shelters is not unusual and he identifies both 'economic' and 'ritual' types of activity. In the case of the two Inchmarnock rock shelters the activity is clearly economic rather than ritual. There is evidence for sporadic use involving fires and the preparation or consumption of food. It is not possible to be more specific than this other than to stress the evidence that the rock shelters were not used for most of the time: use was exceptional.

4.5.2 *The later prehistoric landscape*

Whilst admitting the caveat noted at the beginning of this discussion of the later prehistoric period, the evidence summarised above provides the basis for an assessment of the island landscape in this time. The lack of peat deposits covering the later prehistoric period in the Southpark basin means that we have no knowledge of landscape-scale development of vegetation and therefore land-use at this time. Similarly, analysis of the historic landscape of Inchmarnock, undertaken as part of the present project (Chapter 2.3), has demonstrated that the modern landscape is essentially a late 18th-century creation (albeit one that incorporates and fossilises a number of pre-Improvement field boundaries).

Only one possible example of an early (pre-medieval) boundary or enclosure has been recorded during survey work in the island but the date and interpretation of this site (Site 7) remains in doubt. It comprises two linked alignments of set stones in an area 20 × 20m, located within the wood to the south of Midpark. These set stones could be the robbed remnants of a stone enclosure or boundary wall and, as they do not obviously relate to features in the post-medieval landscape, could be much older. Regardless of the actual age and nature of this obscure site, it may be concluded that there is no relict prehistoric landscape surviving in any part of the island and we are therefore largely dependent on evidence derived from the seven individual archaeological sites, discussed above.

Table 4.3   Radiocarbon dates from Iron Age deposits in rock shelters (Sites 9 and 16)

Lab Code	Material	Context	Uncalibrated	Calibrated 2-sigma
SITE 9				
AA-39966 (GU-9143)	hazel nutshell	1603	2110±35 BP	346–4 BC
SITE 16				
AA-39967 (GU-9144)	hazel nutshell	1655	2150±35 BP	355–59 BC
AA-53164 (GU-10635)	hazel nutshell	16022	1620±35 BP	AD 340–540

Given the capacity of the island in recent times to support a permanent population of several households based on subsistence farming (as demonstrated by 18th-century maps and estate rentals), there is no reason to doubt that the island supported a permanent population during later prehistory. However, our evidence is limited to sites with specific or temporary functions. The activity in the two rock shelters represents occasional use on a temporary basis, probably for a specific activity that we cannot identify. Similarly, the burnt mound is a site with a very specific (if uncertain) function dependent on a good water supply. The fact that no permanent prehistoric settlement site has been identified largely reflects the relative invisibility of such sites in the archaeological record. In this context, the absence of any record of a dun or fort in Inchmarnock is perhaps of some significance. It seems unlikely that a substantial drystone structure like a dun would have been destroyed without trace before detailed records were made of the island in the late 18th century as demand for stone would not have been high. This suggests that such a structure never existed and Iron Age settlement comprised unenclosed roundhouses built of wood, turf and stone, all readily destroyed by later agricultural activity. The so-called 'Devil's Cauldron' described by Blain, and tentatively interpreted by Marshall as a dun (NMRS site NS05NW 7), has been identified by Lowe as something quite different and significantly later (Chapter 2.2), a feature of the late 18th century Improvement period.

Despite the absence of direct evidence for later prehistoric settlement and land-use, it is possible to extrapolate backwards in time from the more recent past to reconstruct the prehistoric landscape. The starting point for this exercise is the pre-Improvement island landscape mapped in detail by Foulis (1758–9, Figure 2.6) and Leslie (1769, Figure 2.7). It is clear from both of these 18th-century maps that the arable land of Inchmarnock prior to agricultural improvement was limited to the summit of the main ridge and the spur of higher ground running off it to the east, south of Midpark. This distribution reflects the natural land capability for agriculture. The western slopes of the island are too rocky with only small pockets of suitable soils and they remain largely uncultivated to the present day. The eastern slopes were too wet prior to modern drainage and were only brought into cultivation in the 19th century. This is demonstrated by a sketch plan of Midpark, dating from 1821 (Figure 2.9). It was drawn whilst improvement was in progress and shows the uncultivated eastern slope still covered in thickets of willow trees. Examination of a drainage ditch in this area during fieldwork recorded a peat deposit still surviving below recent ploughsoil even after 180 years of drainage.

In the absence of a relict prehistoric field system, it is reasonable to conclude that the extent of cultivated land in later prehistory was similar to that mapped in the mid-18th century; in other words, that it would have exploited all of the land suitable for agriculture prior to recent mechanisation and improvement of drainage. If this assumption is correct, where was the associated settlement or settlements located? We know that it was not on the same site as the main medieval and post-medieval settlement at Midpark. Substantial archaeological excavation in the vicinity of St Marnock's Church has demonstrated the existence of a settlement here from the 6th or 7th century AD onwards but the absence of prehistoric structures or artefacts is striking. The excavations have yielded only a few, largely undiagnostic, flints dating back as far as the late-Mesolithic period. It appears therefore that the Irish monastic community settled on a greenfield site, but this site subsequently became the focus of the island's population. It may be suggested that earlier settlement was located further inland and adjacent to the cultivated fields. The area some 400m south-west of Midpark offers a well-drained and gently sloping site, close to a permanent water source.

These tentative conclusions regarding the location of settlement and cultivated land are illustrated in Figure 4.2, which offers a reconstruction of the later prehistoric landscape. No woodland is shown on this map and the status of any woodland at this time is largely a matter for speculation. It is assumed that no ancient woodland survived after several millennia of human settlement on a small island but wood was still available for fuel and buildings so some areas of trees probably remained on the island. The tree species represented by charcoal in later prehistoric and early medieval archaeological deposits are alder, birch, hazel and willow. This matches the composition of present day woodland on the island and is typical of naturally regenerating secondary woodland. Areas of woodland, mapped in the 18th century on the east side of the island, have survived up to the present day (Figure 2.3). This reflects the long-term management of trees as a resource and the protection of woodland from grazing livestock, a practice that can reasonably be extended back into prehistory. It is therefore possible that the present-day woodland has been managed and maintained since the prehistoric period.

Figure 4.2 tends to reinforce the impression gained from the distribution of known sites that there is a division between funerary and ritual sites at the northern tip of the island and settlement/ subsistence sites over the remainder. However, given our limited knowledge of the prehistoric landscape of Inchmarnock, this apparent functional division is best offered as a testable hypothesis for further research.

4.6 INCHMARNOCK AT AD 600

The preceding sections have offered an interpretation of the long prehistory of Inchmarnock from its emergence as an island after the last glaciation up to the period immediately preceding the establishment of the Irish Christian monastic community on the island in the decades after AD 600. What did this community encounter when it arrived?

The interpretation offered above for later prehistory is of a settled and cultivated island with a resident population of subsistence farmers exploiting the better quality land along the main ridge of the island. If this picture is substantially correct, Inchmarnock was no remote and deserted refuge for the incoming religious community. Rather, the new settlers were fitted into a functioning cultural landscape. In this context, the precise choice of location for the new community is potentially revealing. The monastery was fitted into a rather confined site close to the shore with the raised beach cliff to the east and a boggy terrace to the west. As noted above, this was apparently not a settlement site utilised by the indigenous population. Quite how this new settlement was incorporated into the existing cultural landscape is explored in Chapter 9.

This choice of location suggests either that the monastic community was literally obliged to settle at the margins of the existing population or that it had different priorities. It is probably significant that the monastery was located immediately above the only sandy beach and the best landing place for boats on the island. Was this community in frequent communication with distant places (other related monastic settlements perhaps) and therefore selected a site conveniently close to the landing place?

The fact that this coastal site became the principal place in the island for the next 1400 years reflects both the early influence of the monastic community and the rising importance of regular communication by sea. The establishment of this site soon after AD 600 marks a key break with the continuity of the prehistoric past and the beginnings of medieval Inchmarnock.

NOTE

1   The re-excavation of the cist and post-excavation work, along with a proposed facial reconstruction, have also been kindly funded by Lord Smith (Sheridan 2006; Sheridan *et al* forthcoming).

Chapter 5

Archaeological Survey and Excavation in and around the Church (Site 4)

CHRISTOPHER LOWE

5.1 INTRODUCTION

It was clear from the beginning of the project, given the presence and range of early sculpture that was known from the site, that excavation at the church would be the key site for understanding the medieval and later archaeology of the island, particularly with regard to issues such as settlement and land-use. In 1990 the late Dorothy Marshall (1990, 6), in what was to be her final paper concerning the archaeology of Inchmarnock, said:

> Much could be learnt of the chapel site and its surroundings from further excavation. It is hoped that this may be carried out some time and a complete report written.

This, then, was what we were about to do. Part of the brief for the job required that the fabric of the medieval church would be retained and this necessarily restricted the extent to which it would be possible to investigate deposits and features below it. Only the north-west part of the site, therefore, was fully excavated; elsewhere, the excavations have been only partial. This can have implications for understanding the nature and extent of some of the features and deposits encountered during the excavation. Nonetheless, the area around the church has revealed a long sequence of burials on the site and has confirmed the presence of an earlier structure (Structure 4, presumably a church) below the medieval building. The identification of this, in itself, was a welcome bonus, given the numbers of inter-cutting graves on the site, the fragmentary nature of the surviving stratigraphy and the extent to which earlier features had been truncated by later activity.

The area in and around the church would be the focus of our effort, involving survey and excavation in each of the five fieldwork seasons (2000–4). It was clear, however, that ours would not be the first excavation at the site. The site was partially excavated in the early 1970s by the then tenants, the Middleton family, overseen by the late Dorothy Marshall. The site, however, had also witnessed much earlier, 'intrusive works' of a different kind, the stone-robbing episodes of 1718 and 1829.

5.2 ST MARNOCK'S CHURCH IN THE 18th AND 19th CENTURIES

It is clear that the church survived as an upstanding building down to at least the 18th century. In our earliest detailed record of it we find the tenant, Alexander MacDonald, trying to explain his actions in a letter that was relayed to the Rothesay kirk sessions on 24 April 1718. He confessed that

> lately, when his House was abuilding, the masons without his Knowledge, had carried away sundry stones out of the Chappell, and put them in the walls of his House.

NAS CH2/890/2: Hewison 1893, i, 133–4

The same sources go on to record that he was 'highly displeased' with their actions and that he offered the value of the stones (10 guineas) to the kirk session 'to be by them applied to ye behoof of ye poor, as they thought meet'. There are indications, however, that there was some lapse of time between the building work and the letter of contrition. According to Blain, writing in 1818 but not published until 1880 (Ross 1880, 94–5), 'he and his family afterwards met with some adverse strokes of fortune, which he attributed to the sacrilege of his tradesmen' and this was what led to the presentation before the kirk session. After this, Blain tells us, 'fortune … ceased to frown upon him' (Ross 1880, 95). The account illustrates well the ambivalent attitude in which the site was held; it was a tempting source of stone but it still retained some of its ancient sanctity.

The extent of the stone-robbing is not known. There are indications, however, that it survived the century relatively intact. John Leslie's plan of 1769 shows the building as a simple rectangle, labelled '*Old Chappel*' (Figure 5.1b). Foulis' plan of a decade earlier, on the other hand, shows it (and the other buildings at Midpark) in sketch profile (Figure 5.1a). The domestic

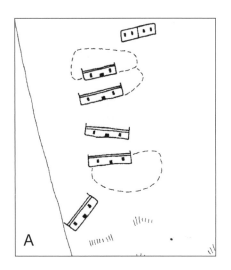

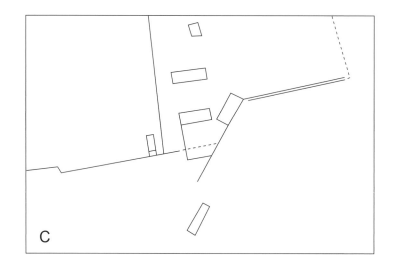

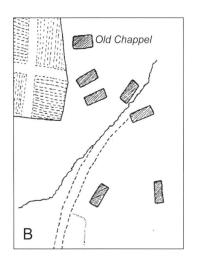

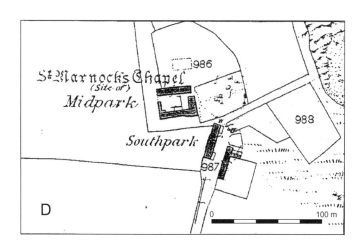

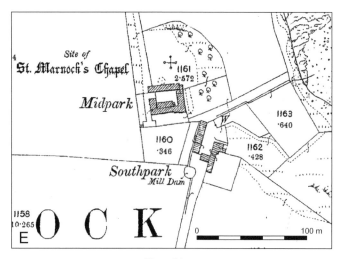

Figure 5.1
Map evidence for Midpark and St Marnock's Church, 1758–1896

buildings are depicted with high gables, a low roofline and two windows, one either side of a central doorway. Although obviously schematic, the domestic buildings are clearly differentiated from the discrete building to the north that we know from the Leslie plan and other evidence as the church. It is shown as a roofless structure, arranged in two units, representing the nave and chancel, with two windows in each. This, or something very much like it, is presumably how the church would have appeared to Thomas Pennant, one of the great travellers of the late 18th century, when he anchored his boat 'under Inchmarnoc' during his *Tour* of 1772. His account refers to 'the ruins of a chapel where (according to Fordun) had been a cell of monks' (*Pennant's Tour of Scotland, 1772*: Simmons 1998, 157).

According to Blain, writing in 1818:

> Considerable part of the walls of the chapel at Inchmarnock still remain, and there had been an extensive cemetery adjoining, from whence may be inferred that the island has been resorted to occasionally in the times of superstition as a place of more than ordinary sanctity
>
> Ross 1880, 94

However, if it owed its survival to the memory of MacDonald's misfortune and an appreciation of its ancient sanctity, things were about to change in the age of the agricultural improvements. In a Bute Estate inventory of 1821 (BE/6, p. 731), the site is described simply as 'an old wasteage', valued only for its stones. Samuel Girdwood's plan of Midpark, dated 20 November 1821, shows a small, unlabelled square feature in this location (Figure 5.1c), roughly one-third the length of the adjacent barn. The incoming tenant at this time, John Muir, is likely to be the man — as we shall see — who finally demolished the church, probably in 1829 or shortly before. The church is shown only in outline and is marked as 'site of' on the first edition Ordnance Survey map (Figure 5.1d), surveyed in 1863. On the second edition Ordnance Survey map (Figure 5.1e), revised in 1896, it is depicted simply by an antiquity symbol.

When the Ordnance Survey were recording names in Inchmarnock in 1863 (*Original Name Book [Buteshire] 5*, p. 65) they were told contradictory versions of the history of the church. The tenant of Midpark, the same John Muir who took over the lease in 1821, showed the surveyors 'a little irregular lump' that was the remains of the church and told them that it had not been seen 'in the memory of any one now living'. Subsequently the factor of the Bute Estate, also a Mr Muir, told the surveyors that the

building 'was entirely removed by the present tenant Mr Muir who is a very old man'. John Muir appears to have had good reason to forget his act of demolition if (as seems likely) the following tradition refers to him. According to Hewison, when gravestones were robbed for use as 'bissen-stones' (stalls) in an adjoining cow-house early in the 19th century, the cows became ill and died.

> The unhappy victim is said to have reverted to an old custom, once prevalent in the Highlands, for appeasing the offended deity, and offered a burnt offering of a sheep or a cow upon the fore-shore.
>
> Hewison 1893, i, 134

How do we know of this incident? To Hewison's credit (and doubtless John Muir's great embarrassment) the account was commemorated in 'a doggerel diatribe … which was sung through the Rothesay streets in 1829' (Hewison 1893, i, 134).

At the time of Hewison's visit, presumably some time prior to 1889 as he omits to mention the rune-inscribed cross (EMS.13) and the sandstone cross-shaft (EMS.10) which were discovered in that year, little of the site remained. The account does, however, contain an early notice of what is probably the lower end of EMS.9, which was found in the stack-yard wall (Chapter 6.2 below). It also gives us the intriguing reference to the unlocated 'women's burial-place':

> the only visible remains were the extra verdant turf of the cemetery, now converted into a stack-yard, and a single slab or cross-shaft carved with three small crosses on one face, and a larger cross on the reverse. A few of

Plate 5.1
Church facing east with bracken removed, revealing the site as it had been left after the excavations of 1974

the ancient cists still lie under ground unmolested. The churchyard … continued to be used within the memory of the last generation. Another graveyard known as 'The Women's Burial-place' was traceable in a field adjoining the church about thirty years ago.

Hewison 1893, i, 133

Quite what and where this separate burial-ground may have been is considered further in Chapter 9.

5.3 ARCHAEOLOGICAL SURVEY

St Marnock's Church is located in an area of level ground in the old stack-yard, immediately to the north of the steading at Midpark. No written records of the 1970s excavations survive although, as previously mentioned, Jessica Herriot (formerly Jessica Middleton) was able to bring her knowledge of the

earlier excavations and of the island in general to the project. As we have seen (Figure 5.1), the site of the church is depicted on the mid-18th-century plans of Foulis and Leslie, on Girdwood's sketch of 1821 and is precisely located in outline on the first edition Ordnance Survey map, which was surveyed in 1863. The dense cover of bracken and bramble was removed in 2000, revealing the site as it had been left in 1974 (Plate 5.1). The excavations had not been back-filled, and over and around the surviving wall-head were the remains of the old spoil-heaps. The site and its immediate environs were subsequently surveyed (Figure 5.2).

The church is located slightly east of centre of the old stack-yard. Rows of circular stack-bases, 2.6–2.8m in diameter, were evident underfoot across the west half of the yard. One or more bases were also encountered during the 1973/74 excavation (Jessica

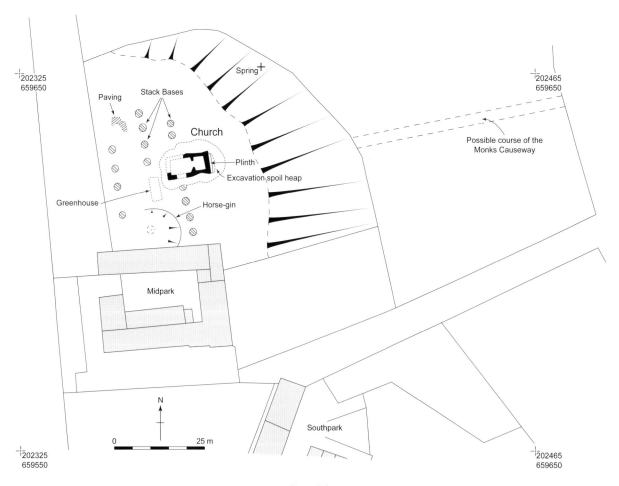

Figure 5.2
Pre-excavation plan of St Marnock's Church, the Midpark stack-yard and environs

Herriot, pers comm). Near the south-west corner of the yard, butted against the north range of the Midpark steading, are the turf-covered remains of a horse-gin. This was constructed sometime between the survey and revision dates of the First and Second Edition Ordnance Survey maps (1863 x 1896). Between the gin and the church were the brick foundations of a greenhouse. Around the church, and largely obscuring the line of the exterior wall-face, lay the spoil heap from the earlier excavation.

The church is a bicameral structure, consisting of a nave, 5.8 × 4.4m internally, and, to the east, a chancel, 3.1m long and 3.8m wide. The walls are up to 0.7m high and 1m wide; their full width, however, was only traceable at the east end of the building where an external face was visible. Traces of a plinth or platform, 0.8m wide, were also evident at this end of the building. There was no trace, however, of an entrance and none was identified during the earlier excavation.

The church is constructed of rubble masonry, roughly coursed and in places levelled up with slate pinnings, with a chamfered plinth along its south side. Where exposed on plan, the masonry appeared to have been set in clay and pointed with hard, shelly lime mortar. Occasional pieces of dressed red sandstone were evident in the building. Two sections of an ornate moulded fragment, set over a sandstone base, formed the south jamb of the chancel entrance. Another fragment, possibly a reused sill-stone, had been incorporated into the north wall of the nave.

The interior of the church had been excavated down to a series of arbitrary levels. The east and west ends of the nave, for example, had been dug to a greater depth than the central part. The floor in the chancel, meanwhile, lay roughly 0.3m above the excavated level in the north-east corner of the nave. The exposed floor in the chancel comprised several flat slabs; some may be floor-slabs, others were clearly grave-covers, at least one of which was set over a stone-edged cist. A cross-marked slab (EMS.8: Fisher 2001, 78 and Chapter 6.2.2 below) lay in the south-west corner. Next to it is a large slab, presumably an architectural fragment derived from a medieval tomb or some such similar structure, perhaps a screen; on its face has been carved a column and its foot end has been roughly shaped to form a 'tenon'. Meanwhile, in the north-west corner of the chancel is a coped stone of later-medieval type, on which faint traces of a sword can just be made out.

The church lies near the centre of a walled enclosure which is markedly curvilinear in its north and east sectors. This wall, which is recorded on the earliest

Ordnance Survey mapping of the site (surveyed 1863), delimits the lower edge of the slight spur of land on which the church and the Midpark steading stand. Although of no great antiquity itself, the wall, nonetheless, may preserve the line of a much older enclosure.

Within the enclosure, to the north-west of the church, is an area of paving, exposed during the course of the 1973/74 excavation. Meanwhile, on the lower ground, near the bottom of the slope to the north-east of the church, there is a natural spring.

To the east of the enclosure, between it and the shore, is the site of a linear stone feature which was known locally as 'the monks' causeway' (Jessica Herriot, pers comm). The causeway is reported to have been exposed and removed during ploughing of the lower field in the late 1950s. No surface remains, however, survived.

5.4 EXCAVATION METHODS AND SCHEDULE

The 2000 fieldwork season at the church not only included the survey of the building and its local setting but also a preliminary trial-trench investigation of the field to the west. The purpose of this was to assess the nature of the deposits outwith the immediate vicinity of the church. Also on the agenda, however, was the aim of seeing whether we could throw any light on the location of the 'women's burial-ground', reported by Hewison (1893, i, 133). In the event, there was no trace of a burial ground in this area. We did, however, find a previously unrecorded enclosure ditch, elements of which would be explored again in 2002 and 2003.

The excavation at the church was undertaken over four seasons, 2001 to 2004. The focus of the 2001 season was to remove the old spoilheaps from the wall-head, to open up an area around the church, roughly 17 × 13m overall, and to excavate a series of trial trenches radiating out from it. The purpose of these was to assess the nature, depth and extent of archaeological deposits at the site, to give us a better feel for the archaeology and what might be reasonably achievable within the research programme. A back-actor with a wide ditching bucket was used under archaeological supervision to remove the old spoil heaps and for the removal of turf and topsoil around the church and along the four transects. Most of the work, however, was undertaken by hand.

The first season's excavation in and around the church threw considerable light, not only on the later phases of the church itself but also on the nature of

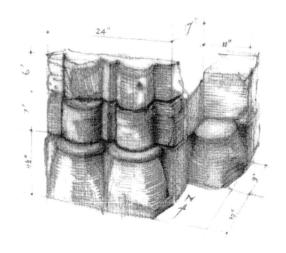

Figure 5.3
The south jamb of the chancel arch, in 1974 (RCAHMS archive drawing)

In addition to the excavations in the stack-yard, two further evaluation trenches were also excavated. One was excavated in the trackway to the north-west of the church, to investigate the site where the rune-inscribed slab (EMS.13) had been discovered in 1889; the other was opened across the site of the stone feature previously reported in the field below the church and known locally as the 'monks' causeway'.

Excavation in the north-west sector of the stack-yard was completed in 2003. In the same season, a programme of geophysical survey and trial-trenching was undertaken in the field to the west of the church. This revealed further evidence of the enclosure ditch, related to those fragments seen in 2000 (*AIR* 3) and 2002 (*AIR* 9). There would still be no trace, however, of the 'women's burial-ground'.

The last field season, in 2004, saw the team return to the church itself, with the aim of resolving questions about the development of the cemetery around it and the archaeological deposits in the immediate vicinity of the building. The present appearance of the yard was found to owe much to relatively recent changes, associated with the laying out and levelling of the stack-yard itself. This had led to truncation and disturbance of early deposits in some areas, and burial of early horizons in others.

Dense vegetation throughout the stack-yard was cleared prior to excavation. The dense root-mat, however, not only made excavation difficult; it was also clear that it had effectively destroyed the stratigraphic integrity of the uppermost deposits inside and around the church. This was exacerbated by the problem that the site had not been backfilled after the earlier excavations. This not only left the exposed archaeological deposits more vulnerable to root-damage, from the invasive bracken and bramble, but it also left the soft sandstone exposed to the elements. A considerable amount of carved detail, evident, for example, in the 1974 RCAHMS photographs and drawings of the chancel arch responds, would be lost over the next 25 years (Figure 5.3; Plate 5.2).

It was evident from the results of the 2001 evaluation that, in addition to the church itself, the area to the north-west also had the potential to contain well-preserved and significant archaeological deposits. The excavation area was therefore extended in 2002 to incorporate the area between the previously investigated northern and western trial trenches.

Plate 5.2
Detail of carved sandstone shafts forming base of chancel arch

Plate 5.3
The Phase 1 metalworking area: Structure 1 facing north-east

the nature and extent of any earlier structures that underlay it.

The results of the excavation at and around the church are set out below in Richard Conolly's account of the structural remains on the site and its stratigraphic sequence (Chapter 5.5). Detailed discussion of the artefacts from the site is presented by the various named specialists in Chapter 6. Meanwhile, the human remains from the cemetery are discussed by David Henderson in Chapter 7.

5.5 STRATIGRAPHIC SUMMARY AND SEQUENCE

RICHARD CONOLLY

5.5.1 Introduction

Prehistoric activity on the site is attested to by the presence of residual worked flint. Some of this may be associated with the later working of oil shale and related materials but some pieces, such as a Mesolithic core, are more datable. Probably also dating to the late mesolithic period, the period from about 5000 to 3500 BC, are the pieces of pitchstone and bloodstone. Torben Ballin's report on the material is summarised in Stephen Carter's analysis of 'Inchmarnock in prehistory' (Chapter 4) and can be consulted in the Project Archive.

It is possible, of course, that amongst the early historic and later features described below, particularly among the cut features (the pits and post-holes that are a feature of the north part of the excavated site) that there may be features of prehistoric date. The likelihood of this, however, is considered to be low and confidence

in this assessment receives support from the absence of any 'rogue' prehistoric radiocarbon dates from the site. The adopted phasing scheme, therefore, begins with what is interpreted as an early ecclesiastical foundation which was newly established on the site in or around the year AD 600 (Chapter 9, below).

The structural development of the site is fairly clear. However, the phasing of the graves has proved problematic. Very few graves contained datable artefacts, either in their primary context or redeposited in their fill. Radiocarbon dating was not an option for many of the graves as skeletons were frequently absent and any charcoal present was evidently residual, thus predating (potentially by several hundreds of years) the excavation and construction of the grave itself. Consequently, the dating and precise phasing of most of the graves is necessarily speculative.

5.5.2 Phase 1: the early monastery (Figure 5.4)

Phase 1 comprises a series of structures (Structures 1–3) associated with metalworking, located at the northern edge of the excavated area. Also forming part of this phase are several graves and, to the south, a

Plate 5.4
Stone-lined feature (4435), facing north-east

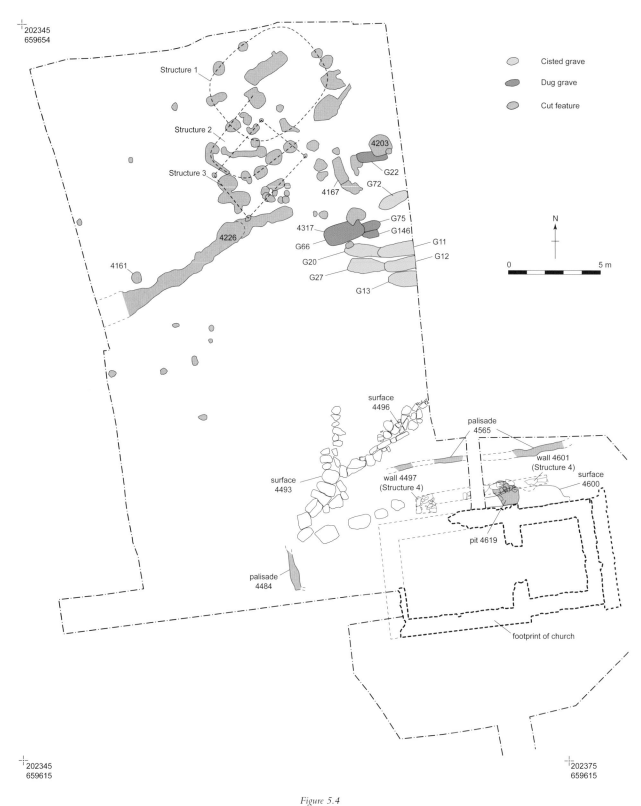

Figure 5.4
Site 4 (Phase 1) – the early monastery AD 600–1000

Figure 5.5
Detail of Structures 1–3 and associated metalworking features

fragmentary paved surface and the remains of what is probably an earlier church (Structure 4).

At the north end of the excavation area was a palimpsest of post-holes, pits and other cut features forming, what is interpreted here as, the remains of three intercutting buildings, sub-oval to sub-rectangular in shape. All three share the same north-

east to south-west alignment and are defined by possible beamslots, clusters of post-holes and features associated with metalworking.

The largest and most easily reconstructable of these buildings (Structure 1) measured roughly 6 × 5m overall with rounded corners (Figure 5.5; Plate 5.3). The west end, comprising an arc of post-holes, was relatively well-defined; the east end, however, was less clear. The bedrock is relatively close to the surface in the north-east corner of the site and the surviving features were relatively shallow as a result. Posts in this area may have been set on stone pads, leaving little trace in the subsoil.

In the centre of Structure 1 were two features, a stone-lined pit (4197) and another stone-lined feature (4435: Plate 5.4), both of which exhibited signs of intense burning. Immediately to the east of the latter lay a rectangular pit or trough (4466), possibly originally timber-lined, as the basal deposit appeared to be the result of silting up and there was no sign of the sides having been weathered. At the end of its operation it appears to have been deliberately backfilled. Although packing-stones were present in all of the post-holes, post-pipes (representing the remains of the decayed posts themselves) were generally absent, with the packing-stones appearing somewhat disturbed. This may indicate demolition and reuse of the building stance rather than its abandonment.

Partly overlying the south side of Structure 1 was a second post-built structure, Structure 2, although only the west end of what is assumed to be a sub-rectangular building is well-defined. The northernmost post-hole identified as part of this structure cuts the fill of Pit 4197, a feature associated with the earlier building, Structure 1. The post-holes tended to contain relatively dark fills with more metalworking waste and charcoal than those assigned to Structure 1, indicating that they incorporate material from earlier activity. A beam slot (4092) to the west may be associated with Structure 2.

Within Structure 2, lay Feature Group 1. This comprised a circular bowl (4193) with a flue (4073) entering from the west. The bowl appeared to have been subjected to heat and a quantity of plano-convex slag cakes and other metalworking debris were recovered from the feature (Heald & McLaren, Chapter 6.11 below). The fill of the flue has been radiocarbon dated to cal AD 780–980 (AA-53159).

Structure 3 comprises four rather slight post-holes, forming a 4 × 3m rectangle. No features are associated with it.

To the east of these buildings lie further features likely to be connected with metalworking; Pit 4167 and Pit 4202. These have been dated to cal AD 460–660 (AA-53162) and cal AD 810–1020 (SUERC-7543)

Table 5.1 Radiocarbon-dated features associated with metalworking area, arranged by date order

Code	Material	Context no	Context/comment	Uncalibrated date	Calibrated 2-sigma date
AA-53161 (GU-10632)	hazel nutshell	4160	Fill of pit 4161, metalworking area.	1450±95 BP	AD 410–780
AA-53162 (GU-10633)	alder charcoal	4168	Fill of pit 4167, metalworking area.	1480±35 BP	AD 460–660
SUERC-2631 (GU-11764)	birch charcoal	4439	Basal fill of pit 4437, metalworking area.	1415±35 BP	AD 560–680
AA-49299 (GU-10022)	alder charcoal	465	Redeposited grave fill, from G11 located N of church, adjacent to metalworking area.	1320±60 BP	AD 610–880
AA-53160 (GU-10631)	hazel nutshell	4076	Fill of NE-SW aligned gully, adjacent to metalworking area.	1310±35 BP	AD 650–780
AA-53159 (GU-10630)	hazel nutshell	4005	Fill of linear feature 4073, associated with metalworking activity.	1150±35 BP	AD 780–980
SUERC-7543 (GU-13346)	alder charcoal	4203	Secondary fill of pit 4202, associated with metalworking area.	1120±35 BP	AD 810–1020

Figure 5.6
Distribution of metalworking debris and whetstones

202345
659654

Cannel coal

Cut feature

N

0   5 m

202345
659615

202375
659615

Figure 5.7
Distribution of cannel-coal fragments

respectively. A possible tuyère plug (SF752) was recovered from Pit 4167.

In addition to these features, there were several pits and post-holes in the area to the south of Structure 2. These features cannot, however, be readily resolved into individual structures. All contained characteristically dark fills. They are presumed to relate to relatively short-lived structures built, perhaps, on an *ad hoc* basis.

Large quantities of metalworking debris, dominated by slag, were recovered from the features assigned to this phase and the surrounding area (Figure 5.6). It is difficult to relate the material to any particular process, but the general assemblage has the appearance of resulting from smelting rather than smithing (Heald & McLaren, Chapter 6.11 below). However, it does appear that some 'finishing' of products did occur on site as there was a distinct concentration of whetstones to the west of Structures 1–3. A possible stone anvil was also found and some work involving non-ferrous metals is evinced by a fragment of a crucible with traces of copper (Heald, Chapter 6.12 below).

The chronology of this activity is indicated by a series of radiocarbon-dated features (Table 5.1) which are either clearly associated with the metalworking site or, as in the case of the charcoal from the fill of Grave G11, derive from features that were sited in proximity to it. At face value, these dates span the period from the 5th to 10th century; only one (cal AD 460–660: GU-10633), however, has a weighted probability that the date lies before rather than after AD 600. None of the Phase 1 dates needs necessarily predate AD 600.

Ironworking is the most clearly attested industry on site, but industrial activity in the vicinity during this phase also included the working of oil shale and related materials (Figure 5.7). No features can be related to this activity, but it is clear that the material itself was being worked and shaped somewhere in the immediate vicinity. Dating of this activity is based on black jewellery having fallen out of favour by the medieval period (Hunter, Chapter 6.10 below).

The north-west corner of the site is intriguingly empty during this phase, and appears to have remained so through subsequent phases, up until the construction of the stack-yard in the 19th century. A rather irregularly shaped gully (4226), aligned roughly north-east/south-west and interpreted as the line of a hedge, extended part way across the site. It seems to have formed a boundary, demarcating an area of industrial activity to the north and burials to the south.

Plate 5.5
Foundation of Structure 4, facing east

A fragment of hazel nutshell from its fill has been radiocarbon dated to cal AD 650–780 (AA-53160). Given that the north-west corner remained empty until the 18th or 19th century, it is possible that this boundary persisted in one form or another until this time.

Early dates were recovered from deposits below the north side of the extant church, where the fragmentary remains of what is possibly an earlier church were found (Figure 5.8). The building (Structure 4) is marked by a fragmentary wall-foundation (4601), 0.75m thick and aligned east – west, with a return wall (4497), approximately 1m thick, at its west end (Plate 5.5). Between the early wall-foundation and the north wall of the extant church to the south, and indeed cut by the foundation trench (4697) associated with the latter building, was a silty clay floor surface (4600). The eastern extent of the surface, where any walling has been robbed or removed by later grave-digging, indicates that the building was about 7m long internally. From the surface was recovered a probable cross-incised slab (EMS.29: Fisher, Chapter 6.2 below). There was no trace of either the wall or floor surface inside the church: the area inside the nave had been subject to later disturbance, both in the construction of the surviving building itself and by later grave digging; meanwhile, the chancel was not excavated. The width of the earlier building, therefore, is unknown. Comparative data, however, would suggest that the internal foot-print of the building would probably be of the order of 7 × 3.5m; if this is the case, then the south wall of the early building would lie roughly along the centre line of the later structure (Figure 5.8).

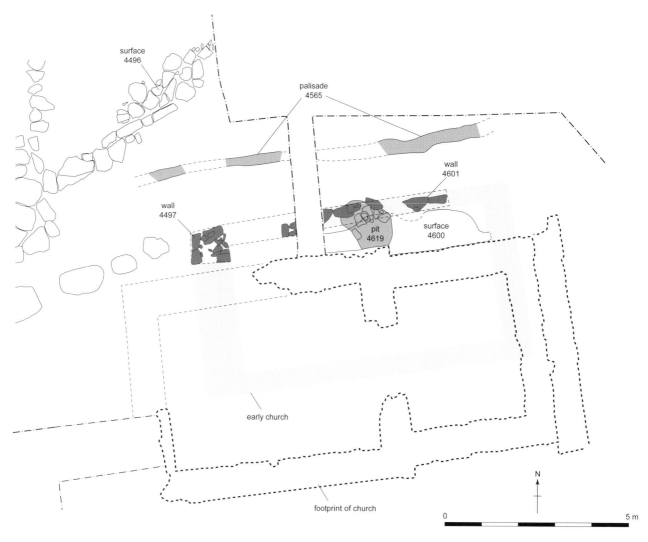

Figure 5.8
Detail of Structure 4 and associated features

Sealed below the floor surface was a stone-lined pit (4619), the fill (4617) of which contained birch charcoal which has been radiocarbon-dated to the period cal AD 650–780 (SUERC-7540). This provides a *terminus post quem* date for the construction of Structure 4, a date after which it must have been built. Material was also obtained from a charcoal lens (4675) within the floor itself. Willow charcoal from this deposit was radiocarbon-dated to cal AD 430–660 (SUERC-5466), statistically earlier than the pit sealed below the floor. Clearly, this latter material must be residual, derived from an earlier context. It does, however, indicate early activity on this part of the site, contemporary with the metalworking activity to the north.

Immediately to the north of Structure 4 and parallel with it were the fragmentary remains of a stone-lined palisade slot (4565). A possible fragment of a north/south return to this slot (4484) was excavated to the west of the existing church (Figure 5.4). The limits of a paved surface (4493) roughly coincide with the west end of the palisade. This surface comprised large flat slates and had been truncated by later graves, as had the palisade slot. Reused in Surface 4493 were a cross-marked slab (EMS.34) and an inscribed slate (SF1256, Appendix 5). Both the surface and the palisade slot had been truncated by later graves and their full extents could not be established. The surviving shape of the surface gives no indication of its function. To the north

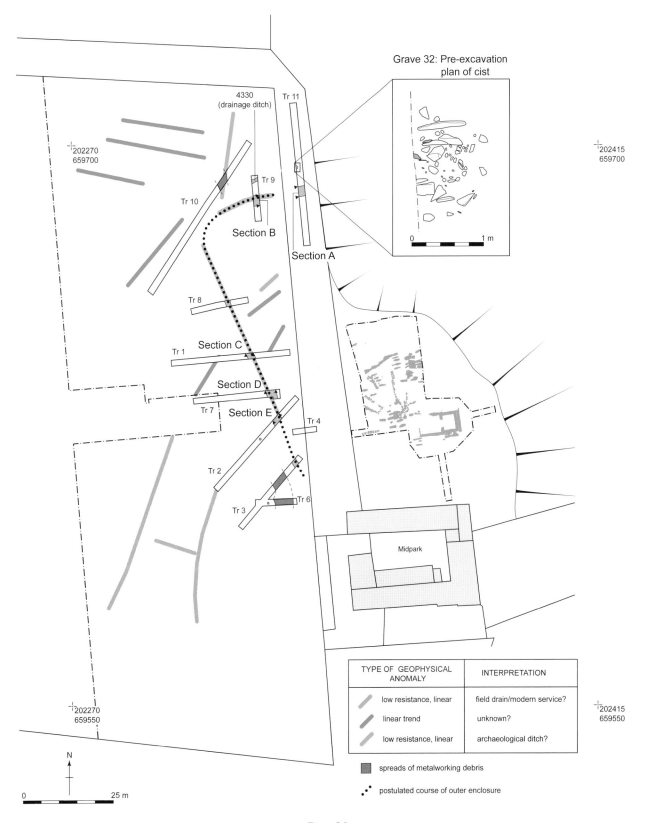

Grave 32: Pre-excavation
plan of cist

0   1 m

TYPE OF GEOPHYSICAL ANOMALY	INTERPRETATION
low resistance, linear	field drain/modern service?
linear trend	unknown?
low resistance, linear	archaeological ditch?

spreads of metalworking debris

postulated course of outer enclosure

N

0   25 m

Figure 5.9
The Phase 1 outer enclosure

of the palisade slot, and also assigned to Phase 1, was a cluster of early graves.

That there were graves on site before the construction of Structure 5, the medieval church of Phase 2, is indicated by the reuse of cross-marked slabs in the construction of later graves (G80 and G136 with EMS.17 and EMS.23 respectively) and in the fabric of the later church itself (EMS.20). The presence of cross-marked slabs in Path 431 (EMS.16) or the early stone surface (4493: EMS.34) might also lead to the same conclusion, although these are not necessarily grave-markers. However, it is difficult to disentangle these graves from those relating to the medieval church, if indeed any of the excavated examples do belong to this phase. Bone did not survive in this part of the site and, in its absence, dating of these graves is problematic, as any datable material present is clearly residual. One grave has been radiocarbon-dated. Alder charcoal from the primary fill of Grave G11, part of the grave cluster at the east side of the excavation area, yielded a date of cal AD 610–880 (AA-49299), demonstrating that it post-dates at least some of the industrial features. This is perhaps reflected by the small quantity of slag recovered from it. In the absence of other means, three potential, but not definite, indicators of phase have been identified; stratigraphic relationships, form and the presence/absence of metalworking debris in the grave-fill.

Given that the dated features and finds from the north end of the excavated area appear to belong exclusively to the period around the last quarter of the first millennium AD (and it is notable that there is virtually no later artefactual material that might indicate later activity at this end of the site), it is assumed that any graves in this area that are cut by pits or post-holes will belong to Phase 1. On this basis, the following graves have been assigned to Phase 1: G20, G22, G66, G75 and G146, and also probable grave 4317.

The second potential indicator is form. The graves fall into two groups, those with cists and those without. Most of the cisted graves are clustered to the south of the metalworking area, at the eastern edge of the excavated area. Those located elsewhere were less well constructed, and their cists appear to utilise stones disturbed in the course of their being dug, rather than being brought especially for the purpose. Many, but not all, of the graves that can definitely be assigned to Phase 2 (considered below) were shallow scoops lacking any stone-built cist. Graves with well-constructed, stone-built cists, unless demonstrably later, have therefore

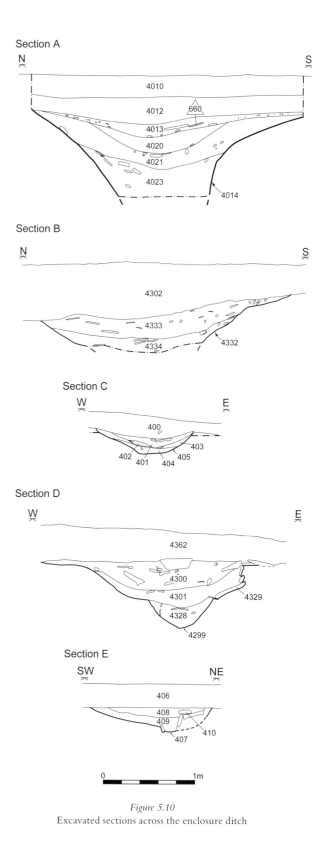

Figure 5.10
Excavated sections across the enclosure ditch

been assigned to Phase 1. This group comprises Graves G11, G12, G13, G59 (which underlies G27), G72 and G75.

The final potential indicator is the presence or absence of material associated with metalworking in the fill of graves; absence of metalworking debris could be taken as indicating that the grave predates metalworking activity on site. This would only be meaningful in the immediate vicinity of the metalworking area. Unfortunately, there is no stratigraphic sequence involving graves with and without metalworking debris.

All of the graves assigned to this phase lie in a cluster with other graves at the eastern edge of the northwest quadrant, and it is suspected that many of the other graves in the cluster also belong to Phase 1. None of these (nor indeed the graves belonging to the medieval cemetery), however, was marked by an inscribed gravestone or name-stone of the kinds known from Iona, Lindisfarne and elsewhere (Fisher 2001, 127–9, 141; Cramp 1984). As Anna Ritchie (pers comm) has commented, the apparent absence of such stones, given the evidence of the inscribed slates that this was a literate community, suggests that this was either a conscious decision or that wooden markers and name plaques were used. The latter, however, seems somewhat unlikely, given that slate was readily available on the island.

Also assigned to this phase is the enclosure ditch located in the field to the north and west of the church and also identified in Trench 11, where it crossed the track to the north of the excavated area (Figure 5.9). Here the ditch (4014) was steep-sided and rock-cut. It was 2.75m wide and, although it could not be bottomed in the narrow exploratory trench, it was excavated to a depth of 0.8m. No clear indication of the possible location of any associated bank could be discerned. Elsewhere, in the field to the west, the ditch was typically 2.1–2.7m wide, 0.34–0.75m deep, with a V-shaped profile (Figure 5.10). Stone revetting (410 and 4329 respectively) was identified on the east, inner side of the ditch sections investigated in Trenches 2 and 7. The ditch was traced in all of the exploratory trenches with the exception of Trench 10, suggesting that the north-west corner of the enclosure must lie somewhere, as indicated on Figure 5.9, in the space between Trenches 8, 9 and 10.

Miscellaneous features and deposits, probably broadly contemporary with the enclosure ditch, given the absence of demonstrably later material, were also identified in proximity to it. To the south-west of

the ditch in Trench 2 was a post-hole (418), 0.68m in diameter and 0.18m deep with a well-defined post-pipe. In Trench 6 and continuing into Trench 3, adjacent, was a thin spread of burnt material containing quantities of slag (4303) including a fragment of hearth-bottom and, nearby, a second post-hole (4304). A spread of slag (4358) was also identified in Trench 10. Whilst to the east, in Trench 11 and roughly 4m to the north of the ditch that was identified running across the modern track-way, in the area where the rune-inscribed slate cross-head (EMS.13) was found in 1889, was a stone setting formed of edge-set stones. It was roughly 1m long and at least 0.7m wide, continuing below the west side of the trench. Although not excavated, it is identified as the 'cist' (G32) that is referred to in the 1889 excavation account (Black 1890, 438). Its location, outwith the enclosure, however, is anomalous and an alternative explanation is explored elsewhere (Chapter 9.2.4 below).

No direct dating evidence could be identified for the stone-setting or 'cist'. Datable material, however, was recovered from the sediments filling the ditch. Birch and alder charcoal from the primary fill of the enclosure ditch (4301), from Trench 7, has been radiocarbon-dated to cal AD 650–810 (SUERC-7542). Material from the upper fill of the ditch, from Trench 11, where it had been deposited with a series of inscribed slates (Forsyth & Tedeschi, Chapter 6.3.2 below) and a cross-incised slab (Fisher, Chapter 6.2, below), has been radiocarbon-dated to the period cal AD 780–1000 (AA-53163). The dates effectively encompass the primary settlement phase on the site, the period of the early monastery and its schoolhouse.

Plate 5.6
Church, facing west, with end-plinth visible in foreground

Figure 5.11
Site 4 (Phase 2): the medieval church AD 1150–1550

Phase 2: the medieval church (Structure 5) and graveyard (Figure 5.11)

Phase 2 comprises Structure 5, the surviving church itself, deposits associated with its construction, and a series of radial stone paths which appear to be aligned on the west end of the building. Also assigned to this phase are those graves not already assigned to Phase 1 and those that are not demonstrably later, part of the Phase 3 or Phase 4 graveyard.

The church (Plate 5.6)

The church appears to have been terraced into the natural subsoil (4027), with a fairly shallow foundation trench with a clay 'lining'. It was constructed in local slate and finished in red sandstone (Figure 5.12), probably sourced from quarries at the south end of Bute. The walls appear to have been laid in clay, pointed with a shelly lime-mortar and externally harled, at least along the more exposed north wall-face where small patches of harling were preserved by the raised ground surface. It is assumed that the chancel and nave were built at the same time but

without excavation, and the original brief required the retention of the existing fabric of the medieval church, it was not possible to determine whether the chancel was keyed into the nave. No trace of an entrance into the building could be identified. However, it clearly did not lie in the south wall of the church and it must, therefore, have been sited towards the west end of the north wall or in the west wall, but these were areas where the masonry had been thoroughly grubbed out. Given these alternatives, the entrance is most likely to have been sited in the centre of the west gable.

Built into the south wall of the chancel was a carved cross-marked stone (EMS.20); other carved stones were found loose inside the building during the 1970s excavations (Fisher 2001; Chapter 6.2 below) and, likewise, may have been built into the structure. Indeed, the poorly preserved and worn nature of EMS.7 may suggest that it latterly formed part of a paved floor inside the medieval church.

Alder charcoal from the fill (4557) of the church foundation trench (4558) was radiocarbon-dated to cal AD 780–990 (AA-53163) but this is clearly residual

Figure 5.12
Detail plan of Structure 5, the 12th-century church

material, incorporated into its backfill. Nonetheless, it is indicative of late first millennium activity on this part of the site. A significantly more useful date was to come from the radiocarbon-dating of the articulated human remains in Grave G102, stratigraphically the earliest of the excavated graves immediately to the south of the church. The grave was located immediately next to the south wall of the chancel; its cut was seen to truncate the foundation trench of the chancel itself and the skeleton was tucked under the basal course of the wall. The skeleton was radiocarbon-dated to cal AD 1020–1210 (SUERC-7544), providing an early *terminus ante quem* date for the construction of the church or, strictly, the chancel. In other words, if we take the mid-point of the assay (AD 1020–1210), then the church was already in place when Skeleton 102 was interred in or around, say, AD 1115. This has fundamental implications for the chronology and attribution of the church (Chapter 9.3).

A mortared surface (470) covered almost half of the nave's floor. Its original extent is unknown as it had been truncated by Phase 4 graves and the excavations of the 1970s. As not all the excavated Phase 4 graves within the nave contained mortar in their backfill, it is possible that the surface had not covered the entire floor. Alternatively, the mortar may have been removed before they were dug. Sealed below the surface was a cisted burial of a child (G142). This was not fully excavated and no reliable dating material was recovered.

A stone-lined drain (4550) running southwards from the south wall of the nave appears to have been a relatively late addition to the church. The cemetery soils (deposits 448 and 4245) into which it was cut were well established by the time it was dug and the fill of the drain contained pottery dating as late as the 16th century. The drain overlay at least two graves (Graves G130 and G134), one of which contained 13th to 15th-century pottery, giving a broad *terminus post quem* date for the feature. Incorporated into the stone lining of the drain were fragments of two stone gaming boards (IS.32 and IS.33, Ritchie, Chapter 6.3.2) and part of an inscribed slate board (IS.41, Forsyth & Tedeschi, Chapter 6.3.3). A series of lightly incised lines and other marks were noted on a fourth fragment (SF1086: Appendix 5). The letter-form on IS.41 indicates that the feature must be later than the 13th or 14th century.

The cemetery

Surrounding the church was its associated cemetery. Burials were densest in the area immediately to the south of the church but grave clusters and individual graves were located elsewhere in the excavated area. A series of paved paths radiated from a point to the west of the church.

Grave G102, as remarked above, is the earliest excavated grave in a sequence of graves to the south of the church that extends up to at least the middle of the 17th century. Other Phase 2 graves in this area, the lowest levels of the cemetery here, are depicted in Figure 5.11. The digging of these frequently intercutting graves clearly caused extensive disturbance, reworking the sediments and mixing skeletal material and finds of different periods together in the cemetery soils (436, 448 and 4245), hence the mixed nature of the fill deposits in the graves. Because of this mixing it is not possible to draw a precise line between the Phase 2 graves and the Phase 3 graves to the south of the church. From the cemetery soil came fragments of pottery, mostly dated to the 14th to 16th century with an appreciable concentration in the area to the south-west of the church. It is suggested below (Franklin, Chapter 6.4) that the pottery may be associated with the post-Reformation burial of communion vessels, other liturgical practices or simply the debris from a domestic midden, although the relatively low levels of charcoal, animal bone and shell appear to be anomalous for such a deposit. Moreover, a mechanism for the incorporation of midden material into the cemetery soil is not easily envisaged. Also recovered from these deposits and the fills of graves were medieval incised slates, including IS.30 (Ritchie, Chapter 6.3.2, Figures 6.29 and 6.30), IS.54 (ibid, Figure 6.28), IS.43 (Forsyth & Tedeschi, Chapter 6.3.3, Figure 6.26) and IS.64 (Lowe, Chapter 6.3.4, Figure 6.33) and a bone and antler comb (Cat. no 56, Franklin, Chapter 6.7, Figure 6.41).

In the western half of the excavated area, there is a clear relationship between several graves (Graves G23, G24, G25, G63, G64 and G65) and Path 4025, with the graves set back from the path by a reasonably consistent distance. While to the east, a similar relationship may be observed between Graves G19, G21, G76, G77 and G79 and Path 4030. It would seem most likely that the graves were dug to respect the paths rather than the other way round. These graves therefore clearly belong to Phase 2. Meanwhile, the series of graves that were either cut through the Phase 1 paved surface (4493) or lay to the west of it are also assigned to Phase 2.

There was some variation in the form of the graves assigned to this phase. Most were shallow and unlined,

Plate 5.7
The pathways of Phase 2, facing north

but four (G10, G16, G80 and G131) had rough cists. With the exception of Grave G131, these all lay in the area to the west of the church, and the cists may simply result from their having been cut through earlier stone surfaces or paths, which furnished the stone for the cist. This certainly appears to be the case for Graves G10 and G80. A cross-marked slab (EMS 17, Fisher, Chapter 6.2.2, Figure 6.7) was reused in the rough cist of Grave G80. Grave G131 cut through a Phase 1 palisade trench (4565) which probably supplied most of the cist. This palisade trench was also truncated by Grave G136, but in this case the stone had been thrown in randomly. Amongst the stone was a cross-marked slab (EMS 23, Fisher, Chapter 6.2.2, Figure 6.11).

In some instances quartz pebbles were associated with graves. These appeared either loose in the fill of the grave (G3, G8, G9, G11, G30, G36 and G71), or pressed in between their capstones (G10, G16, G45, G68 and G69).

Five stone paths (431, 4025, 4026, 4030 and 4036) were located to the north-west and west of the church (Plate 5.7 and Plate 5.8). All appeared to be incomplete and were constructed using slabs of local slate; a simple grave marker (EMS 16, Figure 6.6) had been reused in one (Path 431). The five paths are considered to be contemporary with each other as they are near identical in form and their projected lines converge some 4.5m to the west of the church. Path 4030 was the only one to differ significantly and it is thought that this is the result of it having been relaid. While the other paths were

roughly straight and lay directly upon the subsoil, Path 4030 incorporated two slight dog-legs and, at its southern end, overlay a patchily-preserved ground surface (4280, 4281 and 4312), from which sherds of Saintonge Polychrome pottery (13th/14th century), Redware (13th–15th century) and White Gritty ware (12th–15th century) were recovered, while its northern end overlay Phase 1 structural features. The northern end of the path appeared to respect Phase 1 Gully 4226. The greater part of the path is aligned upon the point of convergence, and the quality of the stone-work changes south of the north kink, which leads to the suggestion that the path has been

Plate 5.8
View across the excavated site, facing SE, with path and graves in foreground, church in background

89

relaid, perhaps to accommodate the cluster of graves that lay at the point of convergence. Paths 431, 4025, 4026 and 4036 all stop short of these graves, whilst the kinks in Path 4030 take it neatly around them. It seems likely that all five paths originally met, but that there was a change in patterns of use, with the paths to the west falling out of use, the graves being dug and Path 4030 being rerouted in order to skirt around the area now given over to graves. Possibly the cluster of graves itself became the new focal point of the pathways?

5.5.4 *Phase 3: the post-Reformation cemetery (16th–17th century)*

Phase 3 comprises a series of graves and deposits relating to the continued use of the area around the church as a burial ground, once the church itself fell out of use following the Reformation. During this period the church appears to have fallen into disrepair, but amongst the graves is one belonging to someone who was probably a priest (SK 15), suggesting that some medieval practices persisted. Moreover, given the results from the radiocarbon dating of his bones,

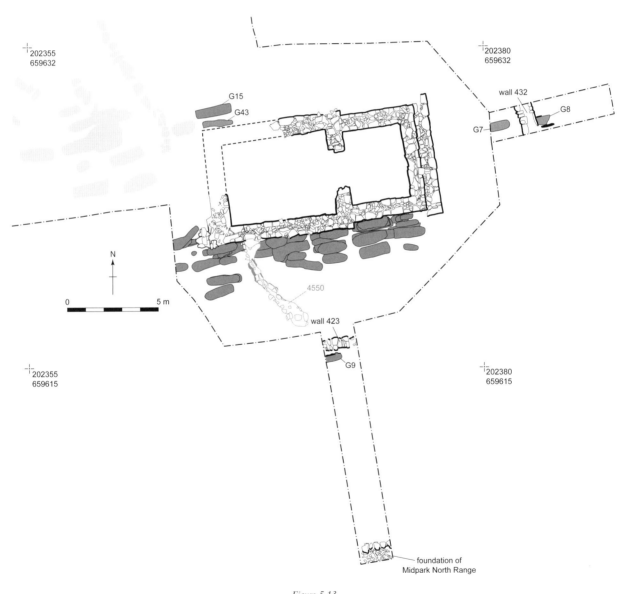

Figure 5.13
Site 4 (Phase 3): the post-Reformation cemetery (16th to 17th century)

we might speculate that he was possibly the island's last catholic priest. No excavated graves from within the church can be assigned to this phase.

As previously remarked, across much of the site it is difficult to draw a sharp distinction between the medieval graves of Phase 2 and the post-Reformation graves of Phase 3, because of the reworking of the cemetery soils and the paucity of primary dating evidence from the bones themselves. Indeed, given the presence of the probable priest burial (SK15), it may be false in some respects to draw such a distinction; the loss of the church may have had little effect upon the burial practice of the islanders.

A silty clay horizon provides the best indicator of the Phase 2/Phase 3, or the medieval/post-medieval or post-Reformation, divide. This comprises two spreads to the north and south of the church (4003 and 435 respectively) that appear to date to the end of the medieval period. Both deposits yielded sherds of White Gritty (12th–15th century), Greyware (15/16th century) and Redware pottery (13th–15th century). Deposit 4003 was cut by Grave G15, the possible priest burial (Plate 5.9). This contained the bones of a male over 55 years old who was buried with his head to the east, the reverse of usual practice, which is traditionally associated with the burials of priests (Mytum 1992, 94–5). The skeleton was radiocarbon-dated to cal AD 1440–1640 (SUERC-2630). Precisely the same calibrated date (AA-49611) was also obtained from Skeleton 7, located immediately to the west of the East Boundary wall (432).

The source of the silty clay horizon is poorly understood, although much of it is assumed to derive from the fabric of the building itself. Its basically uniform nature, however, would imply that the deposits accumulated relatively rapidly, perhaps as the result of deliberate (but partial) demolition, rather than as a gradual accumulation of outwash material as a result of neglect and decay. It seems unlikely that Alexander MacDonald or his masons (Chapter 5.2) in 1718 would have been the first to see the site as a handy quarry for stone and the presence of roofing slates and fragments of red sandstone in the grave-fills, including that of Skeleton 15, our probable priest, indicates that stone-robbing had begun by the mid-16th century (on the basis of the mid-point of the SK15 date range).

With the exception of Skeleton 15 to the north and Graves G7 and G8 to the east, the burials of Phase 3 are concentrated in the area to the south of the church (Figure 5.14), with no apparent selection in terms of

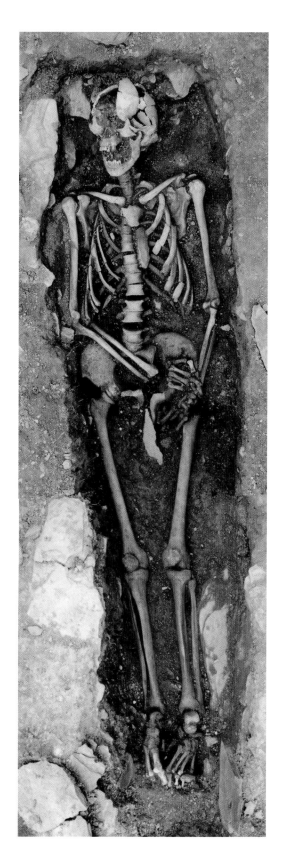

Plate 5.9
Probable priest burial (SK15), facing east

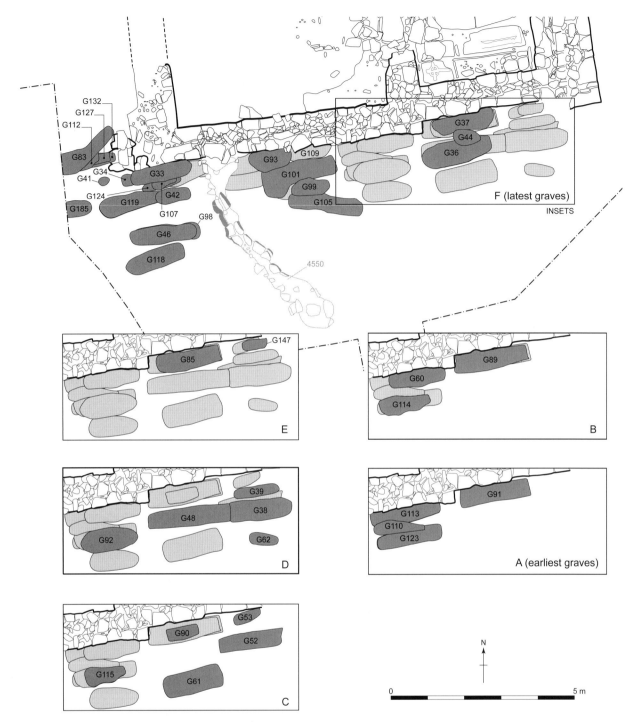

Figure 5.14
Detail of graves (Phase 3) in area south of church

age or gender. The graves here frequently cut earlier graves, with the area immediately to the south of the chancel being particularly densely populated. Coffins were generally absent, with convincing evidence, in the form of *in situ* coffin nails, occurring in just two of the Phase 3 graves (G101 and G115). It is presumed, therefore, that shrouds were used, although only two shroud pins were recovered, both from the burials of

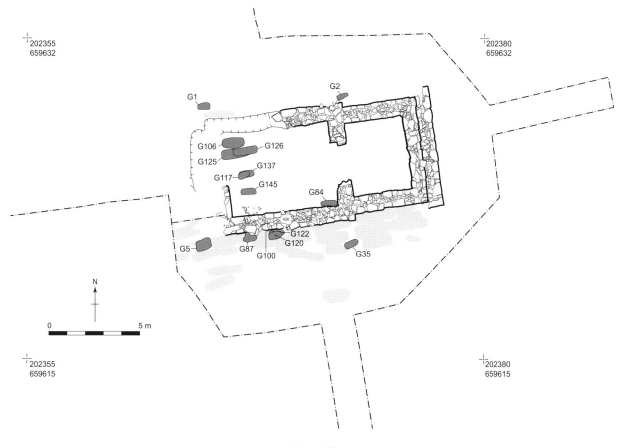

Figure 5.15
Site 4 (Phase 4): the 'children's cemetery' (late 17th to 18th century)

children aged two to three years (G40 and G99), with circumstantial evidence in three further cases; Grave G91, where remnants of cloth on the face of a buckle (SF900, Franklin, Cat. no 11, Chapter 6.5 below) suggest the presence of a shroud; Grave G96, where a perinatal infant was buried face down, presumably in error; and Grave G123, where a coin (SF1240) was recovered from the base of the grave, below the left foot of the skeleton, the preserved cloth on its underside suggesting that the burial was originally in a shroud. The coin has been identified as a Charles I second issue turner dating to 1632–9 (Holmes, in Franklin, Chapter 6.5).

The buckle (SF900, Franklin, Cat. no 11, Chapter 6.5 below) recovered in association with Skeleton 91 is the only example of an accoutrement recovered from its primary context in this phase. It was located in the pelvis of this adolescent boy, who had been killed by three blows from an edged weapon (Henderson, Chapter 7.9.4). It is possible that the unusual

circumstances of the boy's death may have led to him being buried with his clothes on. This appears to be

Plate 5.10
Excavation of graveyard to south of nave, facing south-east, with quern (SF1096), reused as grave-marker

Plate 5.11
The late enclosure wall (Phase 3) in the east transect, facing west.
The capstone of Grave G8, which extends beneath the wall, can be
seen bottom left

a departure from the norm given the lack of similar finds from other graves.

Skeleton 91 was buried on top of a second victim of violence, Skeleton 97, a middle-aged woman. There was a gap of, at the very least, ten years between the two burials, as the woman's corpse had decomposed fully by the time the later grave came to be dug. The woman had also been killed by several blows from an edged weapon (Henderson, Chapter 7.9.4). The two burials were made close to the chancel's southern wall and it is assumed that the juxtaposition is coincidental.

In situ grave markers were present in only two cases; Grave G110 where a quernstone (SF1096: Figure 6.43 –67; Plate 5.10) had been set on its side and Grave

Plate 5.12
Excavated burial of child, Grave G42, facing south

G114 where a plain slate slab (SF1169: not illustrated) had been set on edge. It may be significant that these graves lay side by side, perhaps indicating that the same person or group was associated with the two burials and, possibly, therefore that this distinctive practice may reflect a family group or burial area within the cemetery.

The assemblage of small bird bones recovered from graves of this phase is consistent with raptor activity

Plate 5.13
Grave G119 under excavation, facing east

or nesting in and around the ruins of the church and graveyard. This suggests that there was relatively little activity on the site at this time.

Phase 3 saw the construction of a wall (423/432). Recorded in the south and east transects, the wall may have been built to define the post-Reformation churchyard and mark its boundary with the farm of Midpark immediately to the south. Drystone-built and formed of angular slate blocks with occasional rounded beach cobbles, the wall was up to 0.6m wide and 0.15m high. Constructed over the medieval cemetery soil, this is a relatively late feature on the site. It overlay Grave G9 in the south transect and Grave G8 in the east transect (Plate 5.11) and is almost certainly stratigraphically later than Grave G7 as well. The pottery evidence from the relevant grave-fills would suggest that the enclosure wall was erected not earlier than the 15th or 16th century.

It is not possible to place a precise date upon the end of this phase. That the sequence of graves extends well into the 17th century, however, is amply demonstrated by a sequence of burials commencing with that of Skeleton 123 with its associated coin, dated 1632–9. A succession of three graves (G110, G114 and G115) and a charnel pit (4535) followed this. There was a gap of at least ten years between the burials of SK123 and SK110, as SK123 was fully decomposed by the time of the later burial. Similar minimum intervals preceded the burials of SK114 and SK115. This suggests that the graveyard continued to be used into the late 17th century at least.

5.5.5 Phase 4: the children's cemetery (late 17th– 18th century)

Phase 4 represents the final phase in the use of the church as an acknowledged burial place. The stratigraphically latest graves are dominated by those of young children, leading to the suggestion that the unbaptised were interred here as a matter of course well into the 18th century (Plate 5.12 and Plate 5.13). During this period the interior of the nave was intensively used for burial, with upwards of seven inhumations being made (Graves G84, G106, G117, G125, G126, G137 and G145). In addition several burials of perinatal infants were made outside the church (Graves G1, G2, G35, G87, G100, G120 and G122).

Bone preservation in these graves was generally poor, presumably as a result of the infants' fragile bones being more susceptible to destruction than those of adults. Unlike the graves of Phase 3, coffin-stains and/or fittings were present, occurring in seven of the thirteen child graves assigned to this phase (Graves G84, G87, G106, G117, G125, G126 and G137). The use of shrouds is attested to by the presence of shroud pins in two graves, G84 and G117.

Lying on the remnants of the coffin base in Grave G106, were 93 glass beads (Plate 5.14: Cat. no 53, Franklin, Chapter 6.6). These were located in the chest region (no skeletal material survived) in a random

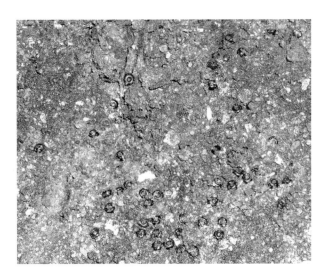

Plate 5.14
Glass beads (SF1069; cat. no 53) as found in base of Grave G106. No scale but beads are 2.5–3mm across

pattern, which probably reflects post-depositional movement as the coffin and corpse decayed.

One adult grave (SK5) may also belong to this phase. The young adult male here was buried in an unusual pose (Figure 5.16). Although interred with his head to the west and supine, in conventional fashion, his knees were drawn up to the shoulders and the left hand appeared to be clasping the back of the right thigh (Henderson, Chapter 7). Two lace tags (SF658, Franklin, Cat. nos 15 and 16, Chapter 6.5) were

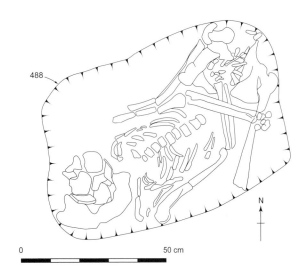

Figure 5.16
Burial SK5

located beneath him, indicating that a shroud or similar covering had been used. The unusual disposition of the body might also suggest that the corpse was bound in some way.

5.5.6 Phase 5: stone-robbing and reuse (18th–early 19th century) (not illustrated)

Phase 5 accommodates a series of features and deposits associated with the robbing of stone from the church in the 18th century, its eventual demolition in the early 19th century and its subsequent reuse.

Although roofing slates were present in deposits around the church these represented only a small percentage of those that would have been present, indicating that these were probably systematically removed, presumably by 1758–9 when Foulis depicted the church as upstanding but roofless. The north-western angle of the nave was almost completely removed during this period and the remaining walls were virtually razed to the ground.

Following this some attempt seems to have been made to build a very rough revetting wall (4247 and 4541) in those places where the nave wall had been removed, suggesting that some use was intended to be made of the hollow formed by the church. Possibly it represents an undocumented or token 'rebuilding' of the church by MacDonald or his successors following the 1718 stone-robbing episode?

Context 4541 contained a sherd of modern white earthenware dating to the late 18th or early 19th century. Throughout the west end of the hollow, formed by the nave, was an extensive dump of maerl (442), containing pottery of 14th to 17th century date. Meanwhile, a wall (4676) immediately to the west of the nave was built using rubble from the church but its function is unknown. That the site of the church was still significant to the islanders is indicated by the burial of a foetus (SK122) in the top of the revetment.

5.5.7 Phase 6: modern features (not illustrated)

Phase 6 features and deposits take in the remnants of the stack-yard and the exploratory excavations of the 1970s.

Chapter 6

The Finds from the Church and Graveyard (Site 4)

JULIE FRANKLIN, CHRISTOPHER LOWE, IAN FISHER, ANNA RITCHIE, KATHERINE FORSYTH,
CARLO TEDESCHI, FRASER HUNTER, ANDREW HEALD AND DAWN McLAREN

6.1 INTRODUCTION AND SUMMARY

JULIE FRANKLIN

The finds fall into three broad chronological groups: early historic, medieval and post-medieval. The earliest finds were predominantly found in the north-west quadrant of the site, north of the church. Many were found in later layers, but very little medieval material seems to have travelled this far and the spatial location of the finds seems a more secure guide to dating than their stratigraphic position. The movement of finds in the soil, in other words, tends to have been in the vertical, rather than the horizontal plane. Much of this disturbance has doubtless been caused by bracken roots; movement across the site, however, appears to have been minimal. In the case of some of the incised slate refits, such as IS.46 or IS.47, it is clear that these fragments remained within roughly 1 to 4m of each other. Context 4001, in particular, a spread of material across the north part of the excavated area contained many early finds, with only a small amount of modern contamination.

The later finds, found in and around the medieval church at the south end of the excavated area are related either to burials or to a midden deposit of uncertain origin which has been mixed through the graveyard soil. The extensive redeposition caused by grave cutting means that there is no useful stratigraphy within this midden to help date the finds within it, but broadly it seems to be of mixed finds spanning the 13th to 16th centuries.

The finds are grouped by material and then type of find. Information on the finds in the various catalogues include small finds (SF) number, where appropriate, context number and phase. Where finds were found in a grave fill, the grave number (G) is also given.

SUMMARY

Early historic artefacts

Most of the earliest finds were recovered from the north-west quadrant of the site, north of the church. There

is clear evidence of metalworking in this area and the iron finds such as the weapons and clench bolt (no 36) may have been produced on site. The whetstones are clearly of use in this context. Many of the finds are of stone tools of various kinds, some of uncertain function (eg no 71). Other pastimes and activities are indicated by the possible fishing weights, the quernstones, and the gaming pieces and boards. The finds suggest a settlement site specialising in metalworking. The only structural remains are pivot stones, implying the structures were built entirely of organic materials. In the vicinity was also evidently a workshop specialising in the production of oil shale artefacts (Hunter, Chapter 6.10); and, as the incised slate assemblage implies, there was also a monastic 'school-house' or equivalent somewhere nearby (Lowe, Chapter 6.3.5).

It might seem a relatively low status site, if not for the presence of a ringed pin and glass beads. The ringed pin and striped glass bead were found near graves and may be redeposited grave goods. Equally, the beads are small enough to have been chance losses, and the pin may have been discarded when broken. Though some wealth, then, was clearly attracted to the site, there is little evidence of it remaining. Glass and metalwork are, of course, recyclable, whereas this is rarely the case with stone tools. Many of them are also worn, broken or bulky, the kind of finds to be left behind when a site is abandoned.

The chronological implications of the early sculpture and the incised slate assemblage are explored in detail below (Chapters 6.2 and 6.3). These collections aside, few finds are datable by typological means. The ringed pin is of probable 10th-century date. The arrowhead is approximately contemporary. However, some finds may well be earlier, as radiocarbon dates suggest activity in this area throughout the second half of the first millennium.

Medieval artefacts

The medieval finds are limited to the area of the church itself and the graveyard to the south. Many of these finds derive from midden material mixed through the cemetery soil, but some may have originally been items buried with the dead, such as the buckle (no 10) or comb (no 56). Though some finds derived from medieval grave fills (eg the knife tip, no 32), none was convincingly *in situ*, and the assumption, therefore, is that the finds were accidentally incorporated into the fill deposits.

The derivation of this midden is unclear. It appears domestic in nature, particularly the earlier finds, with a number of cooking pots. Domestic occupation somewhere in the vicinity is therefore implied. However, in proportion to the pottery, there is relatively little animal bone, in an area where the human burials indicate that bone survives well. There is also a high proportion of jugs. Though it is hard to imagine an ecclesiastical use for cooking pots, jugs would have been of use in the church for transporting and storing water and wine. The Saintonge jugs, in particular, being unusual and attractive may have been kept specifically for the communion wine and may therefore have been of some age when eventually discarded. The large handled jars may also have had a ritual purpose.

The assemblage dates between the 13th and 16th centuries. There is very little later pottery, but for a few modern sherds clearly relating to the neighbouring 19th-century farmstead. Thus the midden roughly dates to the approximate lifespan of the church. However, even if the bulk of this material was used inside the church, pottery middens are not usually found in graveyards and the implication is that there was nearby domestic activity.

Post-medieval artefacts

The post-medieval finds are almost entirely graveyard-related. Several finds were found *in situ* in graves, either to accompany the dead, such as the coin (no 9), or shroud fastenings and coffin fittings. Graves in which objects were found tended to be the exception, rather than the rule. Though shroud pins are not unusual, found in seven burials, other finds are from burials which are unusual in some way. The only lace tags came from a burial of a man (G5) buried in an irregular position in the children's cemetery. The only two bodies which appear to have been clothed in death, were a small child (G106), who was apparently wearing bead-embroidered clothing and whose wooden coffin indicates that she was from a relatively wealthy family; and a teenage boy (G91) who died

by violence, probably at the end of a sword, whose clothing is indicated by a buckle (and might also be inferred, as Henderson points out in Chapter 7.9.4, by the anatomically-incorrect position of his severed left arm). Other finds, principally roof slates and nails, relate to the collapse of the building.

The individual finds reports are presented as follows:

early medieval sculpture
incised slate
pottery
metalwork
glass
bone and antler
stone and ceramic
building materials
oil shale and related materials
ferrous metalworking debris
crucibles and related ceramics
modern finds

Separate numbering sequences have been used for the early medieval sculpture and incised slate assemblages, prefixed with EMS- and IS- respectively. All other finds are numbered sequentially from 1 to 110 without prefix.

6.2 EARLY MEDIEVAL SCULPTURE

6.2.1 Introduction

CHRISTOPHER LOWE

Cross-marked stones and other pieces of early medieval sculpture have been discovered on the island since at least the late 19th century (Figure 6.1). The rune-inscribed cross-head (EMS.13) was the first to be found, in 1889. According to Hewison (1893, i, 223), the find-spot was on the west side of the farm-track, '50yds north of the graveyard'. It was found by the tenant, although the actual circumstances of its discovery are not known. The stone was subsequently reported by the estate factor in correspondence with the Museum of Antiquities in Edinburgh (Letter 222, in Bute Estate Archive BE/18/11; partially reproduced in Black 1890, 438).

Subsequent examination of the site not only discovered an empty stone cist but also led to the discovery of EMS.10, in 'a mound'.

> The farmer showed me the place where he found the runic stone and he opened what appeared to be a grave at the place, it was lined with thin flat stones evidently waterworn and brought from the shore, but there was

nothing inside it not even a bone – we tried another place, a mound, and found a fragment of soft sandstone, after washing which there appeared some carving, little flowers or some thing of that sort … The farmer is going to carefully remove the mound and if anything further is found he will bring it to Rothesay and I will inform you of it.

Letter 222, dated 27 February 1890,
in Bute Estate Archive BE/18/11

According to local island tradition, the site of the mound lay some 20m to 30m to the north of the EMS.13 find-spot, in the hedgerow beside the present farm-track (Jessica Herriot, pers comm). Having got his eye in, the factor then went off on something of a 'sculpture-hunt', involving some minor works in the tenant's kitchen. This presumably refers to the house at Midpark:

I saw several stones which were said to have come out of the graveyard but there was nothing on any of them. I had a bar with me and we lifted the hearthstone in the kitchen, as to which there was a tradition that it had writing on the under side but we found it was not the case.

Letter 222, dated 27 February 1890,
in Bute Estate Archive BE/18/11

In the following year, 1891, EMS.1 was found in the so-called 'Women's Burial-place', described as a short distance to the north of the stack-yard (Hewison 1893, i, 133, 222–3). Interestingly, the same source also seems to associate the discovery of EMS.1 with the presence nearby of what are described as short-cist burials. Nothing of this kind, however, was encountered during our excavation (Chapter 5.5 above); possibly, therefore, these were further examples of children's graves? The precise location and form of the 'women's burial-place' is explored in Chapter 9. Around the

same time the bottom half of EMS.9 was found in the stack-yard wall, to the north-west of the church (Fisher 2001, 79). The rest of the assemblage (EMS.2–9, 11 and 12), prior to the present study, was to turn up in the early 1970s during the Middletons' partial excavation of the church itself and detailed examination of the stack-yard wall.

In all, 34 pieces of early medieval sculpture have now been recovered from the site and its immediate environs. Ian Fisher's Gazetteer of the Inchmarnock stones from the recently-published RCAHMS monograph (Fisher 2001), with Ian Scott's fine drawings, is reproduced below (EMS.1–13), permission for which is gratefully acknowledged. This is now augmented by Ian Fisher's study of the newly-discovered fragments (EMS.14–34). This is a large assemblage of early medieval carved stone. Similarly large assemblages in the West Highlands and Islands are known from Cladh a' Bhile, Ellary in Knapdale (with 29 examples) and from Kingarth on Bute (with 24). In terms simply of numbers, only Iona (with 111) has more (Fisher 2001, 8).

The complete carved stone assemblage from Inchmarnock is illustrated in Figure 6.1 (EMS.1–13) and Figure 6.2 (EMS.14–34) and the find-spots of the various stones are shown in Figure 6.3. For the approximate locations of those recovered in the 1970s we are indebted to Jessica Herriot for her record of those finds. The new discoveries, with EMS.14 and EMS.19, extend the distribution to the south of the church; overall, however, they largely reinforce the pattern already established by the earlier finds (Table 6.1).

The largest single group (Group 1, with 14 examples) is focused on the church itself. In part this may represent burial within the building but, mostly, it probably reflects the practice of reusing the stones in

Table 6.1   Principal concentrations of early medieval carved stones, relative to the church

Group	Location	EMS nos
1	inside or immediately adjacent to church	3, 4, 7, 8, 11, 12, 15, 20, 22, 24, 29, 32, 33 and 34
2	south of church	14 and 19
3	west of church	2, 5, 9b, 16, 17, 23 and 25
4	approx 25m north-west of church	6, 9a, 18, 26, 28, 30 and 31
5	approx 50–75m north-west of church, outwith stack-yard	10, 13 and 21 (and possibly EMS.1 also)

Figure 6.1
The early medieval sculpture assemblage from Inchmarnock (down to 1973/74), after Fisher 2001 (EMS fragments 1–13)

its construction. However, at least two of this group were recovered from Phase 1 deposits: EMS.34 formed part of a stone surface below and to the north-west of the church; EMS.29 was found in the floor of what is interpreted as an earlier church on the site.

The Group 2 stones, already noted, comprise two cross-marked slabs (EMS.14 and EMS.19) that were found away from and to the south of the church, in the trial trench that was opened between it and the Midpark buildings to the south. The Group 3 stones comprise seven fragments, including those from the stack-yard wall, which were found to the west of the church. Two of these (EMS.17 and EMS.23) had been reused in the construction of cists; another (EMS.16) had been incorporated into one of the medieval paths. Meanwhile, another seven (Group 4), again including fragments from the stack-yard wall, were found in the area well to the north-west of the church. Finally, as indicated by the late 19th-century finds, it is clear that there is another focus (Group 5), outwith and to the north-west of the stack-yard, in the vicinity of what we have identified as the outer enclosure ditch (Chapter 9.2.3). And indeed, it is this group that probably gives us our best clue as to the location of the 'women's burial-place' which, as Hewison (1893, i, 133, 222–3) noted, lay a short distance to the north of the stack-yard. However, if local tradition is correct then at least one of these stones (EMS.10, as discussed above) was found well outside the enclosure, opening up the question of whether further burial areas or 'zones' remain to be discovered. That, however, would be another project.

6.2.2 Catalogue and discussion

IAN FISHER

EMS.1 (Figure 6.1/1)

Slab of blue schistose grit found in the 'Women's Burial place' in 1891 and donated to Bute Museum in 1913. It measures 0.57 × 0.17m and 50mm thick and is irregularly tapered in the lower part. It bears a Latin cross, about 0.28m high, incised with a V-section groove up to 50mm width. There is a transverse bar across the lower part of the shaft, and the top side-arms have triple-forked terminals which at the left extend on to the edge of the slab (Hewison 1893, i, 222–3; Cross 1984, M4).

EMS.2 (Figure 6.1/2)

Fragment of a rounded igneous stone, 0.21 × 0.17m and 0.32mm thick, found in the west wall of the stack-yard in 1974. It bears a sunken cross with a rounded upper terminal, incomplete at the ends of the side-arms and lacking the lower part of the shaft (Cross 1984, M15).

EMS.3 (Figure 6.1/3)

Slab of carefully smoothed schist, found in the nave of the church in 1974. Measuring 0.52 × 0.27m and 90mm thick, it has been cut down for reuse and preserves about half of a cross-of-arcs about 0.48m in original diameter. Within a 13mm groove the design is indicated by incisions which form 30mm margins enclosing the deeply-sunken and spade-ended interspaces (Marshall 1974; Cross 1984, M5).

EMS.4 (Figure 6.1/4)

Fragment of slate, 0.21 × 0.19m and only 16mm thick, found in the church in 1974. It bears the outline of a slightly-curving cross-arm or shaft, about 50mm wide within a groove 9mm wide and 6mm deep (Cross 1984, M10).

EMS.5 (Figure 6.1/5)

Slab of greenish schist, 0.65 × 0.25m and 85mm thick, found in the west wall of the stack-yard about 1970. It bears a Latin cross with a pecked and grooved outline, having a small equal-armed cross incised at the centre of the crosshead. The ends of the arms extend to the edges of the slab, and the shaft, which is also open, is prolonged by a vertical spike although this may be natural in origin (Marshall & Middleton 1972; Cross 1984, M6).

EMS.6 (Figure 6.1/6)

Slab of schist, broken at the foot, measuring 0.52 × 0.39m. It was found in the same wall as EMS.5 in 1972. It bears an incomplete cross on each face and the edges of the slab have rounded projections corresponding to their top and side-arms. That on face (*a*) has arms varying from 70mm to 90mm in width, defined by a groove about 20mm wide, and the small circular armpits are more deeply sunk. At the centre of the cross-head there is a small recessed boss. The cross on the other face (*b*) is executed in low relief and its arms are less regular in alignment and width. The armpits are plain, and there is a central recessed boss about 70mm in diameter (Marshall & Middleton 1972; Marshall 1980; Cross 1984, M7).

EMS.7 (Figure 6.1/7)

Slab of greenish schist, 0.64 × 0.55m and 65mm thick, found in the nave of the church in 1974. It

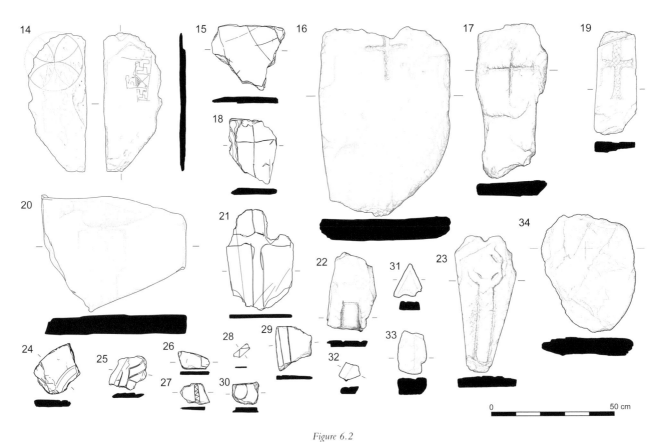

Figure 6.2
The early medieval sculpture assemblage from Inchmarnock (2001–4), (EMS fragments 14–34)

is incomplete at the foot and much worn, especially at the right, although the full width appears to be preserved. One face bears a cross-potent with a square central expansion, executed in low relief. Despite the wear it can be seen that the outline of the cross has been defined using a fine punch, and the background has been reduced with a coarser tool (Cross 1984, M11).

EMS.8 (Figure 6.1/8)

Rectangular slab of schist, lacking the foot, 0.94 × 0.64m and 90mm thick, found in the chancel of the church in 1973. It bears an outline ringed Latin cross with square sunken armpits, 0.58m across the arms and 0.33m in diameter. The arms and shaft are of varying width, and the sections within the ring are conspicuously out of alignment with those beyond it (Marshall 1973; Cross 1984, M12).

EMS.9 (Figure 6.1/9)

Two fragments of a massive cruciform stone of greenish schist. The lower and smaller piece was

found in the stack-yard wall north-west of the church about 1890 and was donated to Bute Museum in 1913. In 1987 it was reunited with the upper part, which was found in the same wall in 1974. A section about half the width of the shaft is broken away at the oblique break between the two fragments, but the surviving surfaces of the break match closely, and the correspondence of the foliations on the edge confirms beyond all doubt (*contra* Marshall 1990) that the stone is complete except for some damage at the top and the loss of one side-arm. It measures 1.54m in length, the shaft is 0.32m in maximum width, and the maximum thickness is about 80mm. The surviving side-arm projects obliquely upwards and is about 0.15m long and 0.35m high. The stone is carved on both faces, except for a slightly expanded butt about 0.22m high. One face (*a*) is filled by an irregular Latin cross defined by a groove up to 50mm wide except at the ends of the arms which continue into the broad margin. Just below the top of the lower fragment the shaft swells out to interrupt the groove, possibly indicating a lower transom or else defining a pedestal, but the detail is obscured by the break and associated flaking. On face (*b*) the lower fragment bears two saltires in false relief within a rectangular panel, separated by a transverse bar from a single saltire. Above the break two deep grooves define a central vertical bar which splits at the cross-head to run into the margins of the side-arms. The crude interlace filling the cross-head, executed with deep grooves of V-section which retain coarse punch-marks, has affinities with the 'stopped plait' found in carvings of Anglo-Scandinavian character in west Cumbria and Galloway, and at Govan (Bailey 1980, 196, 204–6; Ritchie 1994, 73, 117–20, 125). It may incorporate two birds shown beak-to-beak, but the crudity of the carving and extensive surface-flaking make interpretation difficult. The top arm, whose upper part is lost, retains a vertical central bar which may have been the shaft of a small Latin cross (Hewison, 1893, i, 223; Marshall 1990; Spiers 1996; Cross 1984, M2 and M14).

EMS.10 (Figure 6.1/10)

Cross-shaft fragment of yellow sandstone, 0.43 × 0.30m and about 65mm in incomplete thickness. It was found in 'a mound' in 1889 (Black 1890, 438) and donated to Bute Museum in 1913. Despite heavy wear the face preserves, within a 20mm edge-roll, a series of interlinked trumpet-spirals springing from flat roundels and having small lentoid projections in some of the interspaces. The technique provides the closest parallel from western Scotland for the 'chip-carved' style of spiral-work seen on the crosses at Ahenny (County Offaly) and on a fragment from Tarbat (Easter Ross), although it lacks the zoomorphic features of the former. One edge preserves a simple two-strand plait in false relief (Black 1890; Hewison 1893, i, 224; Cross 1984, M3).

EMS.11 (Figure 6.1/11)

Surface-flake of schist, 0.22 × 0.21m, found in the chancel in 1974. Although the surface is much shattered it retains a fret-pattern formed by flat-bottomed L-shaped depressions and surface incisions executed with a fine-pointed tool. This fragment presumably came from a cross or cross-slab, and similar horizontal frets are found on carvings at St Blane's and Rothesay (Cross 1984, M9).

EMS.12 (Figure 6.1/12)

Fragment of greenish schist, 0.31 × 0.15m and 60mm thick, found in the chancel in 1974. One end is broken obliquely and the other has a concave-sided taper, suggesting that it was the base-tenon of a small gravemarker, or the arm of a cross. Above the taper there is a transverse flat band linked to much-weathered edge-mouldings which enclose a saltire-in-square motif of four inward-pointing triangles (Cross 1984, M8).

EMS.13 (Figure 6.1/13)

Fragment of the head of a cruciform stone of schist, 204mm × 198mm × 25mm thick. It was found in 1889 on the west side of the farm-track, '50 yards [45m] north of the graveyard' (Hewison 1893, i, 223), and was presented to the National Museum of Antiquities of Scotland the following year (NMS reference: X.IB 93). The shaft, which is broken off obliquely, originally measured about 0.12m and the span of the cross arms was at least 0.24m, but the right is broken off and the ends of the left and top arms are incomplete. The shaft and left arm form a right angle, slightly rounded in the armpits and having a ring whose quadrants are defined by single incised arcs.

Running up the centre of the cross there is a band 45mm wide formed by two incised lines which enclose an Old Norse runic inscription, incomplete at beginning and end. Most of the letters are firmly incised, although flaked in places, and the words are divided by pairs of dots:

]krus : þine : til : kuþ*e★★[

This begins with the words 'this cross', and ends with a personal name such as Guthleifr or Guthleikr, but the preposition til ('to') is not commonly used in memorial inscriptions, and the reconstruction of the inscription is uncertain.

Further letters are faintly incised on a horizontal band, only 16mm high, across the head of the back, which is otherwise plain. This fragmentary inscription was interpreted by Liestøl as the continuation of that on the front, but this is unlikely. The only identifiable letters are krus ('cross') (Black 1890; *NMAS Cat.* 1892, 264; Hewison 1893, i, 134–5, 223–4; Allen & Anderson 1903, 412–13; Shetelig 1954, 172–3; Liestøl 1984; Cross 1984, M1; Barnes & Page 2006, 232–7 (SC10), pls 54–5).

EMS.14. SF406 (Figure 6.4)

Context 422, Phase 2

Incomplete slab of slate, 0.56m long by 0.24m in width and 30mm thick. It appears to have been originally rectangular, with a tapered foot, and about 0.26m

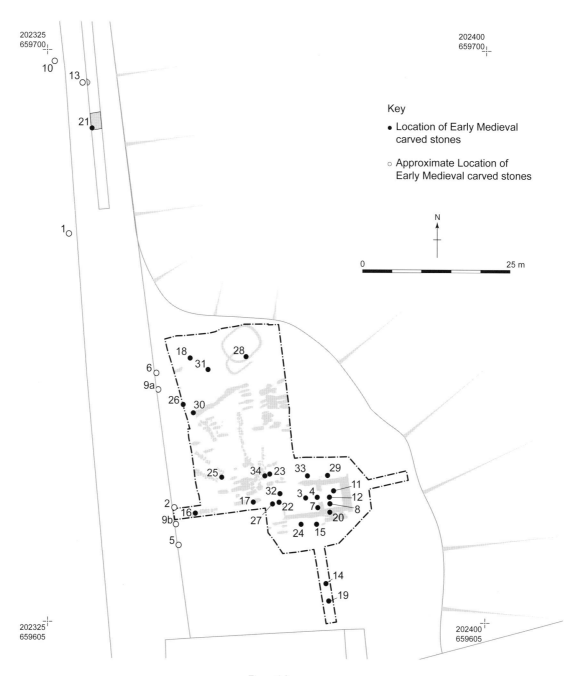

Figure 6.3
Location of early medieval sculpture finds in and around the church on Inchmarnock

wide. A straight right edge and the oblique lower part of the left edge are preserved, but the upper left edge and top have been roughly chipped away to give a D-shaped outline. Filling the top there was a thinly but firmly-incised cross-of-arcs, 0.24m in diameter. Most of the perimeters of the left and top arms have been removed in the later recutting of the slab and

the bottom arm has been lost through lamination, but enough survives to show that the opposed arcs touched at the centre. There is a minute 'pin-hole' at the centre of the cross, but the surface shows other holes formed by the weathering of mineral inclusions, and it is possible that an existing one was used in laying out the design.

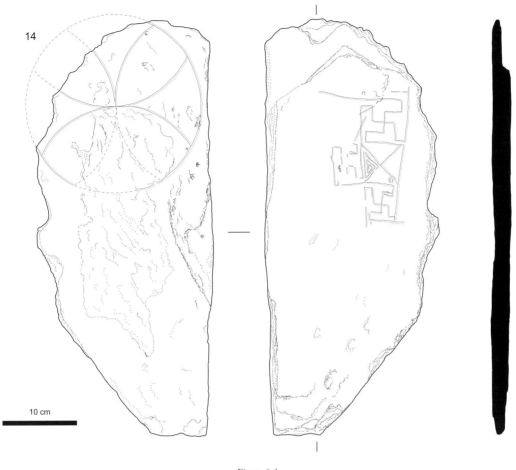

Figure 6.4
EMS.14

The back of the slab bears further lightly-incised carving, of practice-piece type and irregular execution. If it is assumed that the slab stood on its original vertical axis, the carving was towards the curved right edge. It comprises three linked almost-square panels set vertically, with remains of a fourth at mid-height to the left. The central panel is divided by a saltire cross into four triangles of which that to the left is filled with a single triangular straight-line spiral (RA 861). The panels above and below incorporate swastikas, and the left panel was probably similar.

Encircled crosses-of-arcs, and the related six-petalled 'marigold' crosses, which were regarded as equivalent, were popular in Mediterranean and Gaulish art from Late Antique times. They spread to western Britain and Ireland, where they occur in manuscript art and sculpture from at least the early 7th century (Henry 1965, pls 14, 15, 50, 58, III;

Crawford 1980, pls 19–20; Fisher 2001, fig 169*A*–*F*, *K*) and were common in southern Argyll and the Clyde area (Fisher 2001, 12, fig 37). In most examples the ends of the cross-arms or the interspaces were linked by peripheral arcs, and mouldings or recesses were used to distinguish the arms or petals from their backgrounds, as on the slab with both types of cross at Millport, Great Cumbrae (ibid., 70–1, no 5(3)). The fragmentary cross-of-arcs found on Inchmarnock in 1974 (EMS.3, above), trimmed for reuse as a building-block, was about 0.48m in original diameter and had incised margins enclosing deeply-sunk interspaces. The present example, 0.24m in diameter, is of the simplest type, related to the chi-rho cross at Whithorn, 0.27m in diameter, which is however more firmly incised, with opposed arcs not meeting at the centre, and enclosed in a double circle with a curved pedestal (ibid., fig 169*A*). The recently-

15

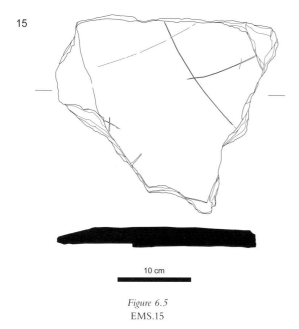

10 cm

Figure 6.5
EMS.15

identified fragment at Kilmoluag, Raasay, was 0.26m in diameter, but the arcs just failed to meet at the centre (ibid., 104, no 34(3)). However the cross-of-arcs from Papa Westray, Orkney (Kirkness 1921, 134; Fisher 2005, 161), although a little larger at 0.27m and embellished with a crosslet on the perimeter, is identical to the Inchmarnock one in proportions and fine-line execution. Dates within the 7th century seem likely for all four of these carvings.

The saltire-in-square sketched on the back of this slab is paralleled on a small tenoned slab found in the church in 1974 (EMS.12, above), which has a full set of inward-pointing triangles, but without the straight-line spiral treatment. In a technique closer to that on the back of the cross-of-arcs, a small swastika is incised on one of the motif pieces (IS.47, Chapter 6.3.4 below).

EMS.15. SF966 *(Figure 6.5)*

Context 436, Phase 3

Roughly triangular fragment of slate, 155mm × 150mm × 12mm thick. One face is smooth, although laminated at the edges, and bears two lightly-incised slightly-curving grooves which intersect near the end of the shorter one. It is possible that these were part of a cross-of-arcs, although this would have been very faintly-drawn in relation to its diameter of about 0.29m.

EMS.16. SF861 *(Figure 6.6)*

Context 431, Phase 2 (reused in path, west of church)

Slab of slate, measuring 0.75m × 0.63m and tapering in thickness from 70mm at the foot to 35mm at the top. The foot has a natural rounded taper and there is an irregular break across the top, which has removed part of the top arm of a linear cross. This is 0.15m in surviving height by about 0.16m in span, and the grooves are of U-section, about 10mm in width at base, but their surface width of up to 30mm is the result of heavy weathering.

EMS.17. SF846 *(Figure 6.7)*

Context 4476, Phase 2 (reused in Phase 2 Grave G80)

Roughly tapered slab of slate, heavily laminated in the lower part and the back. It measures 0.65 × 0.30m and 20mm in thickness at the lower end. The right edge projects in a possible cruciform outline with slightly curved armpits, in line with the cross in the upper part, but the corresponding widening at the left is damaged. The upper part is weathered with many small laminations, and bears a Latin cross, 0.24 × 0.19m, with worn bar-terminals (possibly original triangular) at the top and sides. It is defined by crudely-formed shallow grooves up to 15mm wide, with some discontinuous sharp incisions in the bottom. The lowest 35mm of the shaft is a single narrow incision, possibly representing a basal spike or pedestal, or else an initial marker-line which was not used. The cross is contained within an oval frame, and it is possible that the whole area within this was slightly sunken.

If this stone was indeed of cruciform outline, there were two parallels bearing Latin crosses at Iona (Fisher 2001, fig 56*M, N*). Two other carvings at the same site bear Latin crosses with triangular terminals at top and sides but not the foot (Fisher 2001, fig 31*EE, GG*).

EMS.18. SF455 *(Figure 6.13)*

Context 400, Phase 6

Irregular slab of slate, 130mm × 95mm × 10mm in thickness. Three straight lengths of the rounded edge of the original waterworn slab survive, showing a naturally-tapered foot. Two irregular grooves span the slab at right angles to form a simple Latin cross, whereas a meandering line which crosses the lower part of the shaft appears to be a later addition.

Since there was no provision for the slab to be fixed upright, it may have been designed to lie on or inside a grave, or to be a pilgrim's votive cross. A similar although slightly larger slab was found beside a well at

16

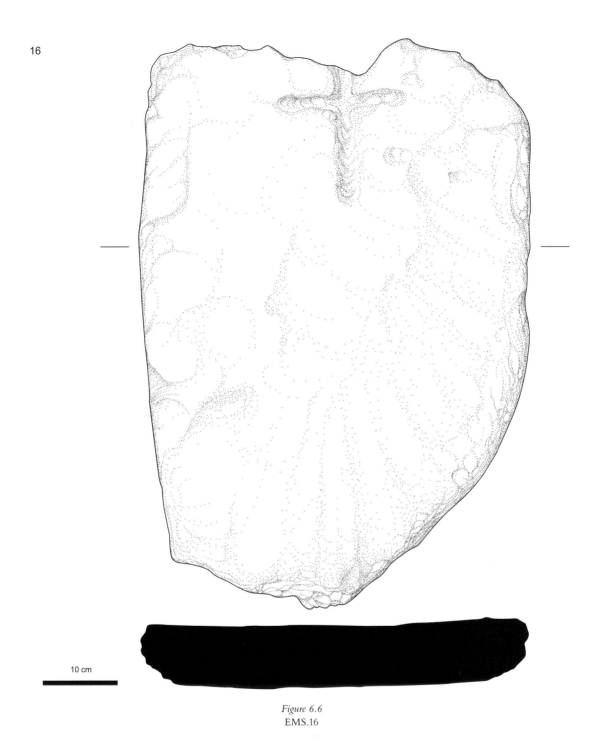

10 cm

Figure 6.6
EMS.16

Cill Ashaig, Skye (Fisher 2001, 102, no 32) and graffito linear crosses are found at several caves, including St Molaise's Cave on Holy Island, Arran (Fisher 2001, 60–5, no 1). Despite the 'primitive' character of these irregular linear crosses, some of those at the latter site are associated with a runic inscription of 1263, while two slabs with similar crosses were included in the kerb of a rich late 9th-century burial at Kiloran Bay, Colonsay (Fisher 2001, 136 (Argyll 5, no 298), fig 28 *X, EE*).

17

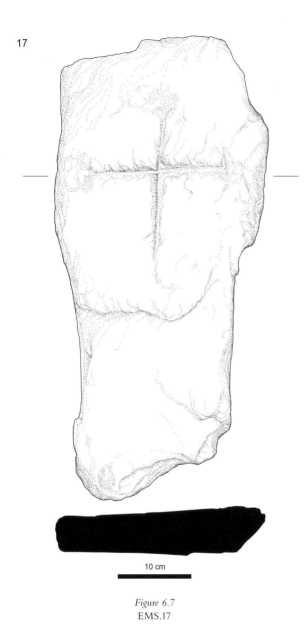

Figure 6.7
EMS.17

presumably been of Latin form but lacks the top and left terminals because of lamination. It now measures 0.24m in incomplete height while the centre of the cross-head is 0.14m above the foot, and the original span was about 0.14m. The surviving part of the top arm and most of the shaft are of fairly uniform width, about 28mm to 30mm, but the lower part of the shaft flares out to meet a concave base-line, 55mm wide. The side-arms widen from about 20mm at the cross-head, and the right arm preserves a similar flared terminal, about 45mm high. The interlace filling the base of the recess, although damaged in places, is a regular four-cord plait with pointed loops in the terminals and plain flat bands.

Sunken crosses appear to have been more common in western Scotland than in other areas, and there are examples of similar scale to this one on Iona, Rum and Tiree (Fisher 2001, 13, fig 22). The crosses are normally of very simple form and are not ornamented. Relief crosses filled with interlace are most common on Pictish cross-slabs, while western examples are found on Iona and at Kilmory Knap and Rosneath

19

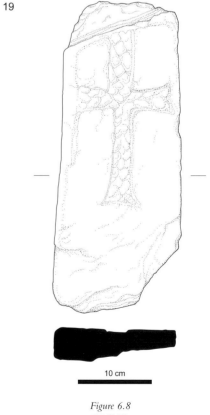

Figure 6.8
EMS.19

EMS.19. SF401 (Figure 6.8)

Context 422, Phase 2

Almost rectangular slab of slate, probably intended to stand upright. It measures 0.42m long by 0.17m in maximum width and 45mm in maximum thickness. The long edges are very regular and taper slightly towards the top, which is broken irregularly and laminated obliquely. The butt appears to have been carefully thinned below the foot of the cross, but is broken obliquely at the right. The upper part of the slab is filled with a sunken interlaced cross whose recess has steep sides, rounded at the upper surface. It has

(Fisher 2001, figs 41*D*, *F*, 44*B*). Crosses filled with interlace and plain ones on interlaced backgrounds occur on the Govan graveslabs (Cramp 1994) and both types are numerous on the Manx cross-slabs (Kermode 1907). Irish examples are not common but there is a notable one whose date remains controversial at Fahan Mura, County Donegal (Henry 1965, pls 52, 54). Many of these comparisons are probably of 10th-century date, and most of the Scottish occurrences of plain four-cord plait listed by Romilly Allen (RA503), which often comprise short space-fillers, are also late. An interesting comparison is the plait on the shaft of an incomplete cross-slab at Tullylease, County Cork, which has been described as 'deeply sunken', although it seems rather to be in false relief (Henderson & Okasha 1992, no 4, 2, 19, 21, pl VIa, b). Many of the late instances of this plait are double-beaded, but the one closest in appearance to the Inchmarnock slab, with similar tightly-meshed

plain bands although less carefully disposed at the cross-head, is on the 10th-century rune-inscribed slab from Cille Bharra (Kilbar), Barra (Fisher 2001, 107–8, figs 107*D*, 108*A*). The Inchmarnock slab lacks the tight circular armpits of this and many other 10th-century crosses, but this is also true of some of the Govan slabs. Its flared terminals are found in Irish manuscripts from the early 7th century (Henry 1965, pl 58), but also, although without the curving base-line, on an Iona slab bearing an interlaced ringed cross (Fisher 2001, fig 41*F*). This slab is again of the 10th century, which also seems the most likely period for the unique Inchmarnock carving.

EMS.20. SF711 (Figure 6.9)
Context 425, Phase 2 (recovered from masonry forming south wall of church)
Irregular slab of slate, 0.62m × 0.48m × 75mm thick. Its original slightly tapered outline is preserved at the

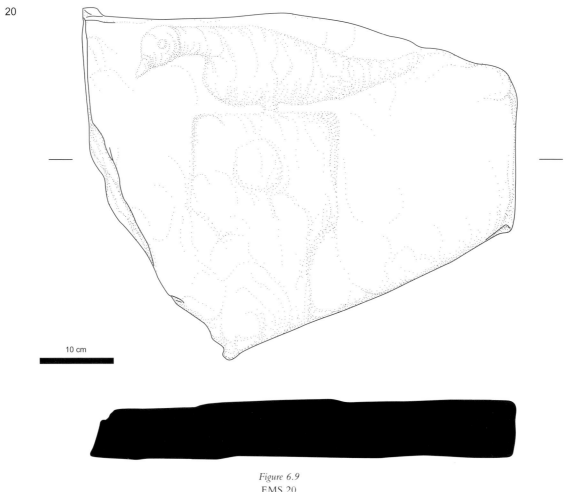

20

10 cm

Figure 6.9
EMS.20

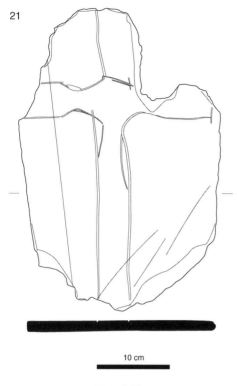

21

10 cm

Figure 6.10
EMS.21

right and upper left edges, while the top appears to retain its original alignment but has been chipped away later. The surface is heavily laminated, and many sharp curved edges make interpretation of the carving difficult. This shows in low relief a rectangular cross-arm or pedestal, at least 0.15m high at the right by 0.20m wide, on which is perched a bird, 0.38m long. It is shown with low-curved back, rounded breast and neck and head extended to the left, but the form of the beak, which appears rounded, has been damaged by flaking. The rest of the body has also been affected by laminated edges, except for a few possible tail feathers, and a single short leg is shown resting on the pedestal, but no feet.

Although lamination in the lower part of the slab interrupts the possible link with a complete cross below, iconographical comparisons suggest this as the most likely reconstruction. In insular Christian art three species of bird predominate, the eagle representing St John the Evangelist and the peacock symbolising immortality, as seen on the Kildalton Cross (Fisher 2001, 19, figs 49*B*, 138*C*). From early Christian times in Rome doves symbolised faithful Christian souls and were commonly shown on or flanking the cross, as on the cross-slab at Kilmory Oib, Knapdale (Fisher 2001, 19, figs 41*A*, 150*B*). However, a closer comparison for the position of the Inchmarnock bird is that in the top arm of the cross-slab at Brechin, probably of 9th-century date (Fisher 2001, fig 18*B*). The body has the same curved back and the head, again facing left, is similarly lowered, perhaps to respect the Virgin and Child in the cross-head below. The Brechin bird is associated with the eagle-headed symbol of St John flanking the cross, and is probably a dove representing the Holy Spirit. It would be characteristic of early medieval symbolism for this meaning as well as that of the soul to be intended at Inchmarnock.

EMS.21. SF660 (Figure 6.10)

Context 4013, Phase 1 (recovered from upper fill of enclosure ditch)

Roughly rectangular slab of slate, 0.40m × 0.28m × 18mm. The left edge, which utilised a natural line of cleavage, tapers slightly towards the foot, as does the less complete right edge. However, the foot of the slab has been broken, perhaps deliberately, to a rough curve, and the top is similarly broken. Indeed, the top right quadrant is completely lost, perhaps as a result of its possible reuse as a socket-stone (discussed below). The slab is filled with an outline Latin cross with wide rounded armpits, whose top and left terminals are lost. The lower angle of the right terminal is preserved 12mm from the right edge, and the shaft may have terminated in an open foot just above the present break-line. The original outline was very irregular, the upper part of the shaft being particularly asymmetrical, and some recutting appears to have taken place to rectify this. Crosses of the same type are found on rather larger slabs on Isle Maree and at Kildalton, Islay (Fisher 2001, fig 35*L*, *M*).

The possible reuse of the slab as a socket for an upright stone has been suggested on the basis of the rectilinear notch, about 45mm wide, which has removed the upper right-hand side of the stone (*AIR* 9, 14) and it has been likened to the fragmentary socket-stones that have been identified from Iona and elsewhere (Fisher 2001, 54–5). The shaft of the rune-inscribed cruciform stone discovered near the find-spot of this slab in 1889 (EMS.13, above) was 25mm thick and at least 120mm wide. This width would extend beyond the present broken edge of the slab, but it is not known how much of the top is lost. Nonetheless, the association is possible.

EMS.22. SF763 (Figure 6.13)

Context 447, Phase 5

Fragment of slate preserving one original long edge, 0.32m × 0.20m × 23mm thick. The lower part of the back is split off, but the detached surface-flake fits closely. Both main faces bear considerable traces of lime mortar, indicating that it was roughly trimmed for reuse in the 12th-century church. The main face shows an incomplete rectangular outline, presumably the shaft or arm of a cross, measuring 115mm to the narrow edge of the slab by 50mm in width within the outline. This is defined by a firm but irregular shallow V-section groove, 10mm to 15mm wide, and a series of small incisions at the closed end may have been intended as an 8mm margin. Two thin grooves intersecting at right angles at the lower right corner of the outline may have been setting-out marks for it.

A fragment of slate found in the church in 1974 (EMS.4, above) bears a very similar although slightly smaller ?cross-arm within a broad groove. It has not been possible to compare the two fragments geologically, but it seems likely that they belonged to the same slab.

EMS.23. SF1260 (Figure 6.11)

Context 4682, Phase 2 (reused as cover-stone of Grave G136)

Kite-shaped slab of slate, 0.69m long and 50mm thick, and tapering from a maximum width of about 0.34m to 0.13m above the curved base. It was laid face-down over an unexcavated grave, Grave G136. The long edges are well preserved, and most of the top, although the presumed central peak has been obliterated by a notch, but the upper right edge is damaged. The top left corner and foot have laminated, and much of the upper part of the surface is worn and shattered. The slab is filled by a ringed Latin cross with rounded armpits, 0.19m in diameter. The lower part of the slightly curving shaft, 0.37m in surviving length and 65mm to 80mm wide, is represented in outline but its upper part and the cross-head rise in relief up to 15mm high. Weathering has removed most traces of tooling, but there are remains of pocking in the outline of the shaft. Its foot and all three arms of the cross-head have laminated, but the spaces between the armpits and the ring-quadrants are narrow oval hollows giving proportions similar to those of a graveslab on Iona (Fisher 2001, fig 40*M*).

23

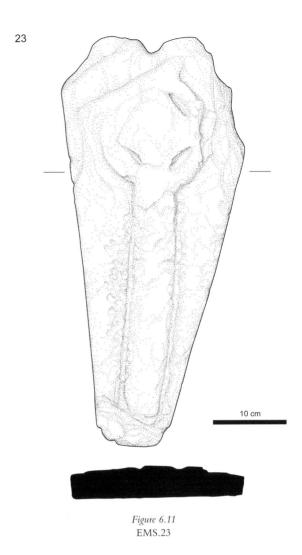

10 cm

Figure 6.11
EMS.23

EMS.24. SF420 (Figure 6.13)

Context 400, Phase 6

Fragment of slate with no preserved worked edges except for a possible outer curve, 0.20m × 0.16m × 30mm thick. On the opposite side of the surface a flat curved moulding 30mm wide is defined by a 10mm hollow, and its inner edge by a deeper recess at the broken edge of the fragment. This has probably been the ring of an outline cross with sunken armpits, of a type which is already known from Inchmarnock (EMS.8, above).

EMS.25. SF629 (Figure 6.13)

Context 4001, Phase 3

Irregular fragment of slate, smooth at the back but without any worked edges, 145mm × 130mm × 16mm.

34

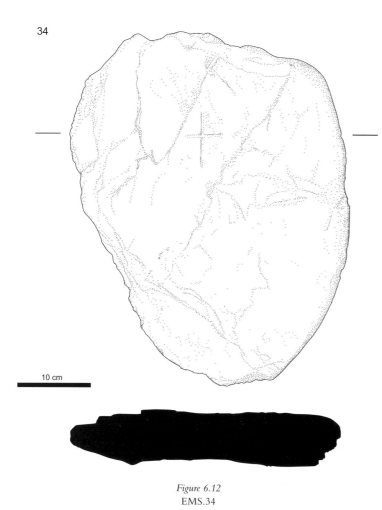

10 cm

Figure 6.12
EMS.34

The carved surface is heavily weathered and shows many mineral inclusions, and several of the edges are sheared obliquely. The principal features are a band spanning the surviving surface, and two concentric curving bands which abut it at right angles. Within the inner curve there are slight remains of a recessed surface, and it is possible that the fragment belonged to a graveslab whose cross had a double ring. There are examples of such rings on slabs from Iona and Laggan, Islay, and possibly on a lost slab from Keills, Knapdale (Fisher 2001, figs 36*M*, 37*U*, 38*C*).

EMS.26. SF564 (Figure 6.13)

Context 4001, Phase 3

Tapered fragment of slate, 135mm × 70mm × 12mm thick. The two preserved edges meet at an obtuse angle to give a shallow gabled form, and the only ornament is an incomplete outline formed by two lines which also meet at a slightly obtuse angle. They show similar irregularities to those on EMS.28, but are incised with a firmer V-shaped groove. While the shape of this outline would be more appropriate for a cross-base than a cross-arm, there is no space for a cross above it.

EMS.27. SF710 (Figure 6.13)

Context 4002, Phase 5

Fragment of slate, 125mm × 85mm × 12mm thick. An irregular but firmly-incised round-ended outline, 16mm to 21mm wide, defines a possible cross-shaft or arm filled with equally irregular zig-zag or chevron ornament. An alternative interpretation is a medieval sword-blade in a decorated scabbard, or a pommel with bindings, but the thinness of the slab suggests that it could not have been large enough to show a complete sword.

Zig-zag or chevron ornament is used in the 10th century and later, for example on the shaft and margins of a coarsely-decorated slab at Kirkclaugh, Kirkcudbright (Collingwood 1988, pl 13, no 42). It occurs on a roughly-shaped cross at Glendalough, County Wicklow (Leask 1950, 46–7, no 8) and on the edges of a small gravemarker at Auckland St Andrew, County Durham (Cramp 1984, part 2, pl 6 (19–20)). Comparable rectilinear ornament is found on graveslabs in the Dublin area, while chevrons were used on bone and antler artefacts from Scandinavian levels in the Dublin excavations (Ó hEalidhe 1973, 56, 58).

EMS.28. SF469 (Figure 6.13)

Context 4005, Phase 1 (recovered from fill of Gully 4073)

Rectangular fragment of slate, broken obliquely at both narrow ends; 74mm × 24mm × 3mm thick. The only ornament is two lightly-pecked oblique grooves which converge at slightly different angles at the edge of the stone to form a chevron. In view of the thinness of this piece, it was presumably a surface-flake of a larger stone, but it is difficult to judge its context.

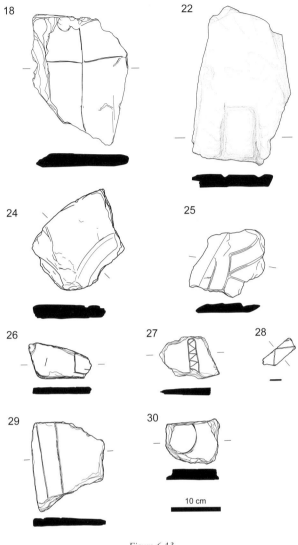

18 22

24 25

26 27 28

29 30

10 cm

Figure 6.13
Cross-incised slate fragments: EMS.18, 22, 24–30

church on the site) also indicates that this must be a relatively early piece.

EMS.30. SF719 (Figure 6.13)

Context 4059, Phase 1 (slag-rich deposit cut by Gully 4226)

Fragment of slate, 122mm × 83mm × 21mm thick, with flat top and bottom surfaces but no surviving worked edges. Firmly incised on one surface, and with a double outline in places, there is an arc of a circle, about 80mm in diameter and flattening slightly at one end. It is possible that this was a rounded armpit of an outline cross on a grave-slab rather larger than EMS.21.

EMS.31. SF518 (Figure 6.14)

Context 4001, Phase 3

Triangular fragment of buff sandstone, 0.13m high by 0.13m wide at the damaged base. The two surviving edges meet at an acute angle and have slightly faceted edge-mouldings 15mm to 20mm in width whose hollows on one face are almost worn away. Interpretation is made difficult by the incomplete state of the fragment and by its uneven thickness, which tapers from 45mm at the apex to 32mm near the base. This taper, and the acute angle, do not seem appropriate for a grave-slab or a cross-arm. The angle would be suitable for the gable of a composite stone shrine but again the overhanging taper is an objection to this. Another puzzling feature is a series of small pick- or punch-marks on the edges of the stone and cutting into the mouldings. Similar marks are found at the lower edge of the fragment, where a deep semicircular hollow and a shallower curve have been cut. It is possible that the fragment was reused to practice tooling, since the shape produced does not appear to be significant.

EMS.29. SF1205 (Figure 6.13)

Context 4600, Phase 1 (early floor surface in Structure 4)

Irregular fragment of slate, 0.18m × 0.15m × 15mm thick. Close to the least damaged edge the stone is spanned by two firm but irregular incised parallel grooves, 38mm to 40mm apart. These may have belonged to the shaft of an outline cross, or a medieval sword-blade, but against the latter it may be noted that the present thickness of the slab is too slight for it to have belonged to a large grave-slab. The archaeological context (from the floor of what is probably an earlier

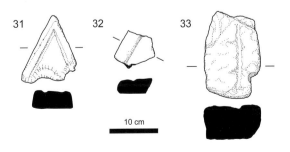

31 32 33

10 cm

Figure 6.14
Carved sandstone fragments: EMS.31–33

EMS.32. SF407 (Figure 6.14)

Context 400, Phase 6

Fragment of buff quartzitic sandstone with one straight edge, 75mm × 70mm × 27mm thick. A straight hollow defines a shallow rounded margin, 30mm wide. The area contained within the margin, and the back of the fragment, are dressed flat. Too little of this stone survives for its function to be decided, as it may have been part of a grave-slab or an architectural item. The very shallow character of the margin is not typical of the later medieval period.

EMS.33. SF806 (Figure 6.14)

Context 4003, Phase 3

Roughly rectangular fragment of buff sandstone, broken on three sides, and measuring 0.16 × 0.13m and tapering in thickness from 70mm to 50mm. A shallow V-section groove with punch-holes forms a margin up to 50mm wide at one damaged edge, and a broken area within this preserves remains of a conical drilled hole 33mm deep. Several surfaces bear chisel tooling, suggesting a probable medieval origin, but the tapering thickness is not appropriate for a grave-slab, and it may have had an architectural function.

EMS.34. SF1258 (Figure 6.12)

Context 4493, Phase 1 (from paved surface, below and north-west of church)

Rounded slab of slate, measuring 0.48 × 0.34m and roughly 50mm thick. On its upper face and located off-centre is an incised Latin cross, 85mm tall and 50mm wide.

6.3 THE INCISED SLATE ASSEMBLAGE

CHRISTOPHER LOWE

6.3.1 Introduction

In all, over a hundred pieces of incised slate were found in and around the church during the course of the excavation. The material ranges from well-executed pieces containing fragments of text, others with sketches of animals, boats and buildings or geometric motifs, to yet others with less involved markings. Some of these designs also appear on several of the gaming boards (Ritchie, below).

With the exception of those pieces which are just gaming boards (eg IS.33) or which only contain text (eg IS.37), most of this assemblage can be classified

as examples of 'motif-pieces'. Previously known in the archaeological literature as 'trial-pieces', these are small, portable scraps of (mostly) bone or stone laminae, especially slate, upon which patterns or designs have been carved or incised. The classic work on the subject is contained in the writings of Uaininn O'Meadhra, particularly the two volumes that make up her work on the Irish material, *Motif-pieces from Ireland* (O'Meadhra 1979 and 1987a). Examples on wood or leather are also known but these materials of course require particular ground conditions in which to survive and these were not present on Inchmarnock. As we will see (Chapter 6.7), bone artefacts from the site are few and far between; indeed bone, generally, is poorly preserved in all but the latest phases of the site's use (Chapter 7). In the Inchmarnock assemblage, therefore, we are concerned solely with examples of incised slate fragments and pebbles.

O'Meadhra (1987a, 170; 1987b, 159) has categorised the Irish material on the basis of a functional classification:

1 leisure activity
2 learning attempts
  a) apprentices' exercises
  b) artisans' trial working drawings
3 *modelli* and *exempla* (including model books and display pieces)
4 formers or dies for casting moulds, impressing foils or leather decoration
5 talismans

At least three of these functional areas (1, 2a and 2b) will be seen among the Inchmarnock incised slate assemblage and, as Forsyth and Tedeschi (below) suggest, the special resonance of the saint's name *Ernán* on IS.35 may also be an indication of a fourth, the 'talisman' function. There is no indication of *modelli* and *exempla*, in the sense used by O'Meadhra (1987a, 110) to include 'model books' or 'display pieces'; nor in their use as souvenirs, a functional area which O'Meadhra (1987a, 161) had previously identified. Meanwhile, the stones are too lightly incised to be relevant to the question of their potential use as formers or dies.

Material and manufacture

The slate (technically a schist, derived from the Dalradian schist formation) forms the bedrock of the island and there is no reason to think that any of the inscribed material is other than local. There are abandoned slate quarries, for example, some 400m to

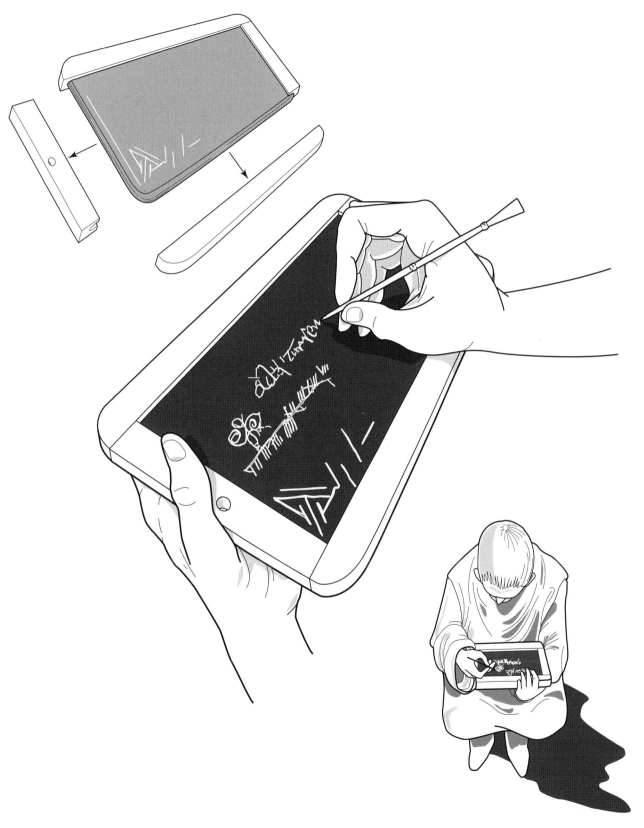

Figure 6.15
Reconstruction of a framed slate board by Craig Williams (based on IS.58)

the south-east of the church and another at the north-west end of the island (Site 6 and Site 22 respectively, Chapter 2.2 above). Meanwhile, rounded, flat slate cobbles and pebbles, which were also used to inscribe the full repertoire of motifs and other graffiti at the site, could have been picked up from the beach below the church.

In terms of form, the assemblage includes fragments that have clearly been dressed and smoothed, as well as other more work-a-day pieces that have been inscribed on pieces of quarried or roughly shaped blocks of slate. Beach pebbles and other water-worn blocks of slate, for example, were also used.

In terms of function, it is clear that a number of the fragments derive from *bona fide* slate-boards, that is to say flat pieces of slate, typically 4–9mm thick which have been trimmed around the edges and bevelled, presumably so as to fit inside a grooved wooden frame. Some are smoothed on both faces, others only on one. The most complete example (IS.58), with surviving bevelled and trimmed edges on three sides of the slab, suggests that the boards, together with their wooden frame, would have measured something in the order of 240 × 120mm (roughly 10″ × 5″) when complete (Figure 6.15). The majority of the other pieces appear to have been impromptu 'note-pads'. A good example is IS.55, a poor quality piece of slate, heavily veined with quartz, but which, nonetheless, was chipped to the round to form a small 'slate-pad' which sits comfortably in the palm of the hand. Indeed, there are several examples of similarly-sized fragments.

Among the incised slate assemblage are also several gaming boards, discussed by Anna Ritchie (below). Some of these were incised upon dressed slate-boards which display graffiti and other marks; other gaming boards were simply marked out on flat beach cobbles and whatever other pieces of slate came to hand.

Derived in the main from pieces of slate that would have been carried in the hand or laid upon one's lap, it is not surprising that most of the incised fragments are small, with sides less than 150mm long. However, among the larger pieces of incised slate are reused pieces of early sculpture and what are probably grave fittings (in the sense of the stone linings of cists), as well as at least one example of what appears to be a piece of stone 'furniture' (IS.76), a table- or work-top that has been covered in graffiti and various laying-out marks. Among the larger pieces of incised slate are also two probable grave-markers, one (IS.77) associated with the medieval cemetery of Phase 2; the other (IS.78), a reused roof-slate, that appears to have been used as

an informal grave-marker in the post-Reformation graveyard of Phase 3.

Classification

The classification of the incised slate assemblage has been based primarily on *content*, that is to say on the basis of the principal form of the incised designs or marks themselves. In the case of the gaming boards, this is also of course related to the question of function but the 'content' approach has the merit of bringing to the fore-front any similarities or differences that may be present in the assemblage. The assemblage, together with numbers of examples, is considered under the following headings:

> Gaming boards (35 examples)
> Inscriptions/letter-forms (including ogham) (14)
> Sketches/figurative scenes (11)
> Curvilinear and rectilinear motifs (14)
> Miscellaneous/other (51)
> Informal grave-markers (2)

Clearly, there are examples that cross these categories (gaming boards with motifs or sketches, figurative scenes with motifs or other, less involved markings and so on) and these counts include those cases where an individual piece may appear under more than one classification. In such cases, the stone has been classified in what is perceived as its 'dominant type'. It is then cross-referred to in any subsidiary group to which it also belongs.

Detailed discussion precedes the catalogues for the gaming boards (Ritchie, below) and those pieces of inscribed slate containing texts or letter-forms (Forsyth & Tedeschi, below). This is then followed by the catalogue for the remaining motif-pieces and an overall discussion of the assemblage.

6.3.2 *Gaming Boards*

ANNA RITCHIE

Introduction

Evidence of board games is perhaps unexpected on an ecclesiastical site, but there can be no doubt that playing such games was part of everyday life on Inchmarnock. Among the incised slate assemblage there are eight complete gaming boards, two almost complete boards, and parts of 25 others, a grand total of 35 boards. In addition there are small fragments with incised grid-lines that may be parts of gaming boards, and one unfinished board. This rich haul is but a sample of the total that is likely once to have existed, but there is an important factor that puts their role into a realistic perspective: these boards are ephemeral, in the sense that they took just a few moments to create and were discarded after a game or two. The gaming pieces may have been more lasting, simply for the convenience of having a set to hand, despite the fact that only one certain piece has survived.

Manufacture

Most of the surviving boards and fragments of boards were incised on slabs of local slate, as ideal a medium for this purpose as for graffiti. The depth and width of the incised line varies from very fine and shallow to relatively wide and deeply cut, and it is clear that several types of tool were involved. The fine lines could easily be cut with the tip of an ordinary domestic knife, and freshly cut they would be easier to see than they are now. The wider and more heavily scored lines required a more substantial tool, perhaps a large awl or the corner of an axe, and there are traces of overcutting on IS.1. The wide and shallow lines again required a substantial tool such as an axe or a chisel. The grids were drawn freehand, some more accurately than others. It seems likely that there were stacks of slate on site, ready for use in lining graves or replacing roof tiles, and some slabs were used more than once, both for gaming boards and for graffiti. In some cases where there is superimposition of grids or very fine incision, some form of 'whiting' may have been used (Lowe, Chapter 9.2.5).

A carefully drawn and deeply incised grid such as that on IS.1 is likely to have had longer usage than the hastily scratched grids, but none of the Inchmarnock boards would have been in circulation as long as the few surviving examples from elsewhere of carved wooden gaming boards. Most of these have peg-holes at the points or intersections of the grid, which made them particularly suited to play on board ship, because the gaming pieces would not shift with the motion of the sea, and long idle hours at sea made board games a welcome diversion. Three such pegged boards have been found in Ireland: Ballinderry (Hencken 1937, 175–90), Knockanboy (Simpson 1972) and Waterford (Hurley *et al* 1997), and the wooden board from York, though pegless, had a raised border, which would similarly have helped to prevent pieces falling off the board (Morris 2000, 2350–1, no 9032, fig 1158). There is likely to have been a similar raised border to the board found in the Gokstad ship-burial, Norway (Heyerdahl-Larsen 1980).

Dating and context

The gaming boards were mostly residual finds from silt and rubble deposits and from the fills of graves of the 16th century (G33, G46, G113 and G124), but two *merels* boards had been reused to line a drain (IS.32 and IS.33) contemporary with the use of the church in the 12th century or later, and two *hnefatafl* boards came from possible Phase 1 graves (G11: IS.1, G72: IS.8). One fragment of a *hnefatafl* board, IS.7, came from a well-stratified Phase 1 context and can be assigned to the last quarter of the first millennium AD. None is therefore closely datable, but in broad terms they are likely to belong to the period from the 9th to the 14th centuries. This time-span is entirely compatible with the range of games represented by the surviving boards and with the associated graffiti.

Games

Certainly three and possibly four known board games are represented: *hnefatafl, alquerque, merels* and possibly chess. Apart from chess, all these games were played on the points or intersections of the grid rather than in the cells, although *hnefatafl* could also be played from the cells. *Merels* is classed by Parlett (1999, 11–12, 121) as a space game, because the aim is to form lines or mills of three playing pieces, whereas *hnefatafl* is a chase game and *alquerque* a war game of capture.

HNEFATAFL (Figure 6.16)

Hnefatafl is one of a series of Norse board games that Bell (1979, 41) defines as games in which 'sides of unequal strength, and with different powers of movement or mode of capture, struggle to achieve different objectives'. One player has a king, set in the centre of the board, and a number of defenders around him, and the other player has twice as many attackers as the king has defenders. The aim of the defenders is to get the king safely to the edge of the board, while that of the attackers is to capture the king by surrounding him. All the Inchmarnock *hnefatafl* boards have 7 by 7 points or intersections, and thus there are likely to have been eight defenders and 16 attackers. This is the common form of *hnefatafl* board found in Scotland and Ireland. Sometimes the central point is marked by a circle, which can be seen on IS.1 and IS.6, and the latter also has circles denoting the positions of four defenders around the king, and circles marking three of the corners of the grid. The fourth corner, at bottom right, appears to have 'fallen' off the edge of the slate, and its marker circle has been placed

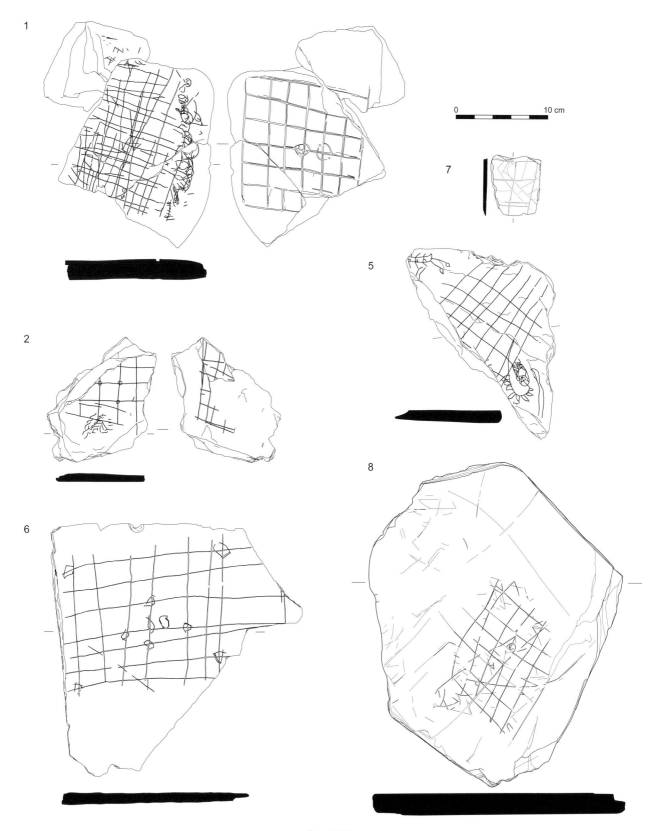

Figure 6.16
Selected gaming boards: *hnefatafl* boards (IS.1, 2, 5–8)

one cell up (Figure 6.16). Despite its informality, IS.6 echoes the beautifully crafted wooden board from Ballinderry in Ireland on which the central point is marked by a circle and each of the four corners by an arc (Hencken 1937, 175–90; it may be noted that Riddler (2007, 256) has cast some doubt on the purpose of the Ballinderry board, but it has sufficient parallels among stone boards to make it acceptable). Stone boards with just the central point circled include three from Buckquoy, Orkney (Ritchie 1977, figs 9 and 10, nos 90–2), one of which, no 92, was recognised by Sterckx (1973a, figs 1 and 2) below a later palimpsest. A board from Dun Chonallaich, Argyll, has the positions of four, possibly five, defenders marked by small pits and is comparable to IS.6 (Ritchie 1987, 62–3), and in both cases the defender positions presumably reflect an essential opening lay-out at the start of the game. The fragmentary board, IS.2, has three points marked by circles. A board from Howe, Orkney, has no fewer than 11 points marked, not including the central point (Ballin Smith 1994, illus 108, SF700), which suggests that it was in use for playing another Norse *tafl* game known as *hala-tafl*, the Fox game. This is mentioned in *Grettis Saga* in the 14th century (Parlett 1999, 187–9) and was doubtless played in earlier times.

Hnefatafl could also be played on the cells of boards with an uneven number of cells. It seems likely that a broken stone board from Whithorn in Wigtownshire originally had seven by seven cells and was played on the cells, for there are crosses and single diagonals in five cells (Hill 1997, illus 10.112). Parlett (1999, fig 12.21) has reconstructed a fragmentary stone board from Jarlshof in Shetland as a nine-celled grid on which five central cells are cross-marked, but the grid is only 130mm across with cells 10–16mm square, and one of the cross-marked cells appears to be at the edge of the grid (Hamilton 1956, pl xxxi.1). Too small for play, and with an even smaller celled grid on the other side, this is more likely to be some sort of trial piece.

It is possible that the larger-celled plain grids were used for chess as well as for the earlier game of *hnefatafl*, for chess was introduced into western Europe in the 10th century and was well established in Scotland by the 12th, as witnessed by the merchant's hoard of playing pieces known as the Lewis Chessmen (Stratford 1997). The cells on the boards in this group from Inchmarnock are 35–80mm in size.

The assemblage includes three complete *hnefatafl* boards (IS.1, IS.6 and IS.8), two almost complete boards (IS.5 and IS.9) and seven fragmentary boards (IS.2, IS.3, IS.4, IS.7, IS.10 (two boards) and IS.11),

together with five fragments of large-celled boards (IS.12, IS.13, IS.14, IS.15 and IS.16).

ALQUERQUE (Figure 6.17)

Alquerque is a war game between two players, which is played on a grid of cells with diagonal lines (a reticular grid). The term was used in the 13th century in Spain to describe a game that was ancestral to modern draughts, involving capture of the opponent's men by jumping over them (Bell 1979, 48; Parlett 1999, 121–3, 243–4). The board on IS.30 is the classic *alquerque* grid with 25 points, on which to start the game each player would place 12 playing pieces to fill all but the central point. Inchmarnock has yielded one complete (IS.30) and 10 fragmentary *alquerque* boards (IS.22, IS.23, IS.24 (two boards), IS.25, IS.26, IS.27, IS.28 (two boards) and IS.29). Two small fragments were found in excavations at Castle Sween, Argyll (Ewart & Triscott 1996, illus 15.51, illus 16.52), which came from a 16th- or 17th-century context but may have been residual from an earlier period from the 13th century onwards.

The related game of draughts, played on a chequered board, is thought to have been invented in southern France around AD 1100 (Bell 1979, 71).

MERELS (NINE MEN'S MORRIS) (Figure 6.17)

The ancient game of *merels*, or *merelles*, was introduced into England by the Normans in the 11th century (Parlett 1999, 109), but it had reached Scandinavia by the start of the 10th century and could have been introduced into northern and western Scotland by Norwegian settlers earlier than into England. In England it became known as morris: Three Men's Morris, Six Men's Morris and Nine Men's Morris, according to the size of the board and the number of playing pieces. Until the Inchmarnock boards were found, the earliest Scottish *merels* boards were those from 13th-century Dryburgh Abbey and Arbroath Abbey (Robertson 1966). The aim of the game is to place playing pieces on the board to form lines of three, at which stage an opponent's piece may be removed.

Inchmarnock can boast four complete Nine Men's Morris boards (IS.30 (two boards), IS.32 and IS.33), and three possible fragmentary boards (IS.30 (two boards) and IS.31). None displays consistent diagonal lines linking the corners of the squares, a feature that appears in England by AD 1400, though there is a diagonal line at one corner of the 'Layer' 3 board on IS.30.

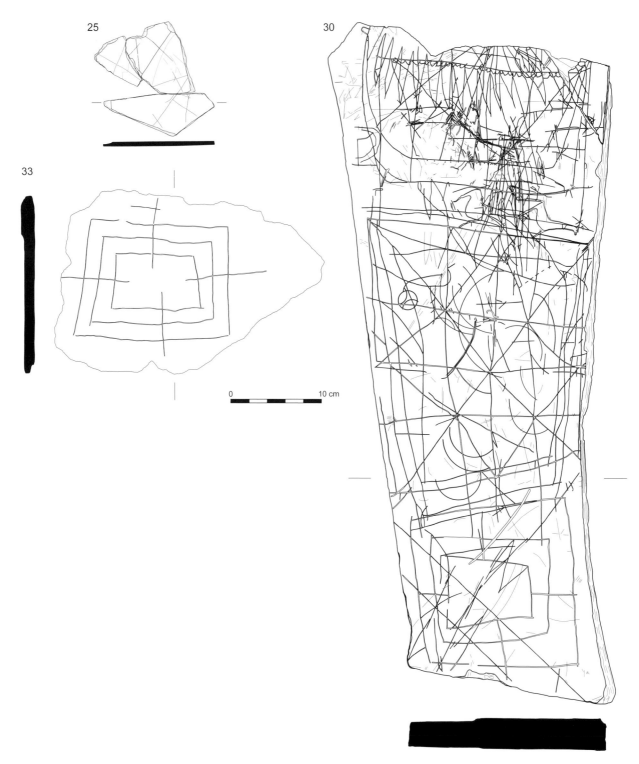

Figure 6.17
Selected gaming boards: *alquerque* and *merels* boards (IS.25, 30 and 33)

Double-sided boards and two-game boards

Two slates have a playable plain grid on both sides (IS.2 and IS.10), and others have unplayable 'doodle' grids on the reverse (eg IS.1 and IS.2). IS.28 has part of a reticular grid on each side. IS.30 is unique in the assemblage in having both *merels* and *alquerque* on the same face, and it is clear from the chronological analysis of the carving on this stone that the two games were broadly contemporary. The gaming-board aspects of this slab are summarised here in Figure 6.18. Detailed discussion of the phasing of the various incised marks on the stone (ie the 'Layers' referred to below) is explored in connection with its figural scenes in Chapter 6.3.4 below. There are traces of a regular *merels* board, perhaps recut (to account for the doubling of the medial lines), on the wider end of the stone in 'Layer' 1, which was augmented in 'Layer' 2 by an *alquerque* board, and in 'Layer' 3 another *merels* board was cut at the narrow end of the slab. There need have been no significant lapse of time between the three phases of carving, all of which largely respect one another, but in 'Layer' 5 the *alquerque* board was replaced by an unplayable 'doodle' version of a *merels* board. Here the points are too close together to allow play, despite an unnecessarily large central area.

The double-sided board from the Gokstad ship-burial has a finely decorated *merels* board on one side and a 13 by 13 celled board on the other, which is assumed to be for *hnefatafl* (Heyerdahl-Larsen 1978, 39; Parlett 1999, 200). Some cells are decorated, however, and their location on the board does not tally with a central position for the king-piece. Bell (1979, 94) is also cautious about identifying the board as *hnefatafl*. Another double-sided wooden board with *merels* and *hnefatafl* has been reported from an excavation at Toftanes, Leirvík, in the Faroes (Hansen 1988, fig 11; Hansen 1991), but it has yet to be confirmed by full publication.

Playing pieces

For comfortable play, a gaming piece should be significantly smaller than the width of an individual cell on the grid, whether the game is played on the cells or on the points. A circular slate disc (no 72: Franklin, Chapter 6.8 below), is a likely candidate for a playing piece, with a diameter of 25mm that would be suitable for play on a grid with cells no smaller than 30mm across. Its edges are carefully chipped and it was probably part of a relatively formal set of playing pieces. A small square piece carefully made from a sherd of greyware (no 80: Franklin, Chapter

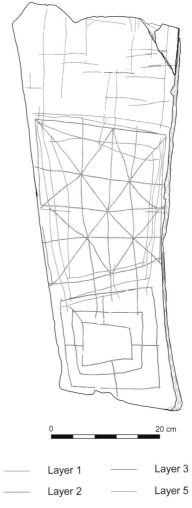

0   20 cm

——— Layer 1   ——— Layer 3
——— Layer 2   ——— Layer 5

Figure 6.18
Gaming boards on IS.30 and their phasing

6.8 below) seems best interpreted as a playing piece, and seven rectangular or sub-triangular pieces of stone (nos 73–9: Franklin, Chapter 6.8 below) could have been used as playing pieces.

The informality of the Inchmarnock boards suggests that most of the playing pieces may have been small pebbles or shells or other small natural items. Two colours or two shapes were required for most games, one for each player, and *hnefatafl* also called for a distinctive 'king' piece, and for these reasons it is likely that habitual players might retain sets of pieces however humble a material was used. Truncated antler tips were used at Whithorn (Hill 1997, 487), Dun Cuier in Barra (Young 1956, 320), Broch of Burrian (MacGregor 1974, 88) and Brough of Birsay in Orkney

(Curle 1982, illus 38.251), and deposits of 15 and seven small flattish quartz pebbles were found in House 1 at Jarlshof (Curle 1935, 304–5). Stone counters are a common find. One from Castle Sween in Argyll, from the same context as the fragments of *alquerque* board, has a rough decorative graffito on either side (Ewart & Triscott 1996, illus 16.50).

Ox phalanges have been used in the past as playing pieces, as David Clarke suggested for the two decorated phalanges from the Broch of Burrian in Orkney (MacGregor 1974, 88). Their use would require boards with large cells, perhaps 50–60mm across, and some of the large-celled boards from Inchmarnock would be suitable. In addition to the chessmen in the Lewis hoard, there were 14 plain discs of walrus ivory, 55–56mm in diameter (Stratford 1997, 10, 54), which may have been destined for *hnefatafl* or *alquerque* play.

More formal and carefully crafted playing pieces also exist, and there is evidence of painting in order to distinguish the pieces of one player from those of the other. At Upper Scalloway in Shetland, conical playing pieces made of some kind of silicate were used in the second half of the first millennium AD, some painted with a manganese-rich coating (Wilson & Watson 1998, 174–5). In Viking-Age York, playing pieces were made of trimmed pottery sherds, antler, stone and chalk, and some of the chalk pieces were painted red (Mainman & Rogers 2000, 2566). A complete set of playing pieces for *hnefatafl* was found in a 10th-century grave at Baldursheimur in Iceland, consisting of a carved king and 24 men, ie eight defenders and 16 attackers (Eldjárn 1956, 159–61; the board was presumably made of wood and did not survive). Pegged wooden boards could be smaller than unpegged boards, because the playing pieces could be literally narrow pegs, hence the 'travel' board from Waterford with a grid that is only 95mm across (Hurley *et al* 1997, fig 16:14.1).

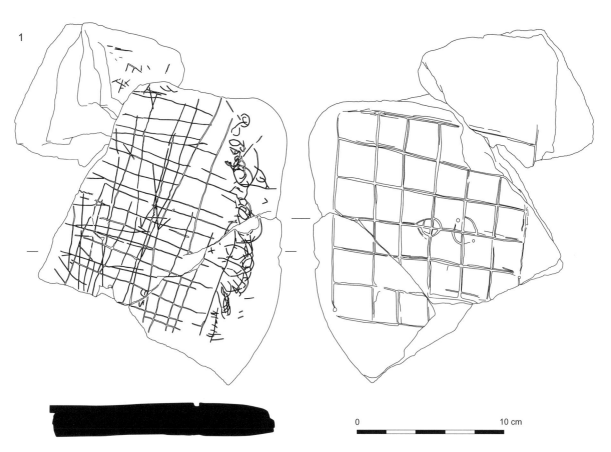

Figure 6.19
Gaming board IS.1: obverse and reverse faces

Conclusions

Board games in early medieval times were popular across the social spectrum and, to judge by the Inchmarnock evidence, were not confined to the secular world. Slate was an ideal medium for the creation of gaming boards, and its local abundance on the island encouraged the use of relatively ephemeral boards. Inchmarnock is unique among Scottish sites of the period in yielding so many boards and such a variety of known games.

Despite the fact that most extant *hnefatafl* boards point to a Norse context from the 9th or 10th century onwards, the Inchmarnock boards need not be assigned necessarily to a similarly Norse cultural context. It is clear from early Welsh literature that a form of *hnefatafl* was played in Wales from the 10th century under the name *tawlbwrdd* (Parlett 1999, 202–3), and the existence of an earlier board game known as *gwyddbwyll* indicates

the possibility of a common stratum of board games of *tafl* type in western Britain. An early medieval Irish legal text known as *Mellbretha* (Sport-Judgements) includes liabilities for injuries to children at play, and three board games are mentioned specifically as being excluded from liability: *brandub, fidchell* and *buanfach* (Ó Cróinín 1995, 132–3). *Brandubh*, or Black Raven, is also mentioned in early Irish literature and may have been a form of *tafl* (Parlett 1999, 200–4; Sterckx 1973b).

Familiarity with *alquerque* and *merels* may have spread north and west through Britain as it did through northern Europe, but it is equally possible that *merels* at least was introduced into Scotland by Norse settlers. Their occurrence on informal boards at Inchmarnock suggests that knowledge of these games was more common in Scotland than the very few previous discoveries had indicated.

Plate 6.1
Gaming board IS.1, with stone counter (cat. no 72)

123

Catalogue

The boards are mostly incised on local slate. The playing area of complete boards is given as two measurements across the centre of the board. The boards are described under the relevant games, hence IS.30 appears twice, under *Alquerque* and *Merels*, and IS.12 appears both under *Large-celled boards* and under *Alquerque*.

Hnefatafl boards

IS.1. SF402/625/430 (Figure 6.16; Figure 6.19; Plate 6.1)

Contexts 437 and 4001 (both Phase 3) and 459 (Phase 1: fill of grave G11)

Three conjoining fragments of a flat beach pebble incised on both faces.

Face 1: very heavily incised and regular complete grid of 6 by 6 cells, 49 points, 138mm × 130mm overall. Heavy scoring involved multiple strokes which occasionally missed the main groove. There is clear evidence that deep incision led to surface flaking. 28 complete cells, *c* 22mm square, seven incomplete cells (one cell missing). Central point marked by a circle, and one adjacent point marked by a less heavily incised circle (perhaps mistaken initially for the centre).

Face 2: at least two highly irregular sets of lines at right angles. Attempts to separate out primary and secondary grids failed to produce any playable board. Curvilinear graffiti and ogham inscription (Forsyth & Tedeschi, below). There are a few small natural pits on both faces.

A gaming piece (no 72) was recovered from the same context as fragment SF430.

Together the three fragments represent a slab *c* 235mm L, 193mm W, 20mm Th

IS.2. SF403 (Figure 6.16)

Context 437, Phase 3

Fragmentary board

Face 1: part of edge of very finely incised grid overlain by graffito. Five complete cells, *c* 20mm square, and nine incomplete cells. Three points marked by small circles, one at a distance of one cell and two at a distance of two cells from the edge of the board.

Face 2: corner of very finely incised and very irregular grid, six complete cells 14mm × 16mm to 15mm × 6mm.

156mm L, 95mm W, 8mm Th

IS.3. SF424/425

Context 400, Phase 6

Two fragments with part of a finely-cut grid with a cell 20mm × 48mm, possibly unfinished. Secondary line leads off one short end of cell. Remains of peg-hole for later use as a roof-tile.

97mm L, 67mm W, 5mm Th

IS.4. SF503

Context 4001, Phase 3

Fragment with part of a lightly incised and worn grid with three complete cells, *c* 24mm × 30mm.

123mm L, 95mm W, 12mm Th

IS.5. SF533 (Figure 6.16)

Context 4001, Phase 3

Face 1: finely incised grid of seven by >five cells, *c* 103mm × >76mm, originally probably seven by seven cells. 26 complete cells *c* 22mm × 11mm, plus six incomplete cells. Partially overlain by motif at bottom right corner; sketch of boat-like vessel present at top left corner of slate. The boat graffiti from the site are examined in detail by Atkinson in Appendix 3.

Face 2: very lightly incised parallel lines, >19mm apart, of unfinished grid.

240mm L, 130mm W, 10mm Th

IS.6. SF632 (Figure 6.16)

Context 4001, Phase 3

Complete grid of six by six cells, 49 points, *c* 158mm × 131mm, irregularly incised. Cells vary in size between 16mm × 9mm and 41mm × 32mm. Roughly drawn circles mark the central point, four points surrounding the central point, three corner points, one perimeter point one cell away from the fourth corner, and one of the four central cells.

160mm L, 140mm W, 20mm Th

IS.7. SF676 (Figure 6.16)

Context 4066, Phase 1; reused as packing-stone in post-hole.

Corner of carefully drawn grid superimposed on earlier motif. Three complete cells, *c* 24mm × 22mm, and four incomplete cells.

60mm L, 50mm W, 3mm Th

IS.8. SF826 (Figure 6.16)

Context 4345, Phase 1; reused in lining of early grave G72

Very irregular and lightly incised complete grid of six by six cells, max 120mm × 100mm, cells from 12mm × 10mm.

345mm L, 265mm W, 20mm Th

IS.9. SF849

Context 4004, Phase 5; reused in modern fence-post setting

Two conjoining fragments of ?grave-slab. Edge of board with lightly incised grid of cells c 30mm × 27mm.

295mm L, 215mm W, 18mm Th

IS.10. SF879

Context 4245, Phase 4

Side 1: interior fragment of regular well-incised grid, three complete cells from 21mm × 15mm to 22mm × 18mm. Partially overlain by wavy line.

Side 2: edge fragment of very lightly incised regular grid, six complete cells c 11mm × 15mm.

70mm L, 54mm W, 2mm Th

IS.11. SF888

Context 436, Phase 3

Fragment

Face 1: part of edge of very lightly incised grid of one complete cell, 28mm × 25mm, and nine incomplete cells.

Face 2: single incised line 30mm long on heavily flaked surface.

112mm L, 60mm W, 7mm Th

Large-celled boards (chess?)

IS.12. SF481

Context 400, Phase 6

Heavily worn fragment bearing broad and shallow incised lines.

Face 1: possible corner of grid with one complete cell 38mm × 42mm.

Face 2: possible corner of *alquerque* board (see below, IS.22) reticular grid with one/two incomplete cells, 76mm × ?60mm.

200mm L, 126mm W, 12mm Th

IS.13. SF549

Context 4008, Phase 3

Heavily worn fragment probably of one edge of an incised grid, possibly one corner, with two complete cells 30mm × 30mm and 30mm × 39mm.

140mm L, 95mm W, 16mm Th

IS.14. unstratified

Corner of unfinished grid of very broad and shallow incised lines, two complete cells 59mm × 41mm.

307mm L, 196mm W, 12mm Th

IS.15. SF912

Context 436, Phase 3

Part of grid of incised lines overlain by myriad of linear scratches, two complete cells, 59mm × 66mm.

215mm L, 189mm W, 14mm Th

IS.16. SF1144

Context 436, Phase 3

Face 1: corner fragment of grid with sides of 140mm and 307mm. Three complete cells of c 58mm × 80mm, and parts of six adjacent cells. Broad and shallow incised lines.

Face 2: lightly incised lines, unlikely to have part of gaming board.

750mm L, 440mm W, 30mm Th

Fragments of possible large-celled boards

IS.17. SF426

Context 400, Phase 6

Fragment with single broad and shallowly cut line, 63mm long. Faint traces of another line at a right angle, in which case cell was >61mm across.

88mm L, 54mm W, 11mm Th

IS.18. SF761

Context 4251, Phase 3

Fragment with single incised line >30mm long. The type of stone and the character of the incision suggest that this fragment may have been part of the same slab as IS.19 and IS.26 (though not the same grid as the latter).

73mm L, 44mm W, 5mm Th

IS.19. SF869

Context 4251, Phase 3

Fragment with two lines at right angle, could be part of the edge of a grid with cells >32mm across. Again, the type of stone and the character of the incision suggest that this fragment may have been part of the same slab as IS.18 and IS.26 (though not the same grid as the latter).

85mm L, 45mm W, 5mm Th

IS.20. SF1158

Context 4611, Phase 3; fill of grave G113

Fragment with two very heavily scored lines at a right angle, line 22mm broad. If these represent part of a grid, the cells were >32mm across.

57mm L, 45mm W, 7mm Th

IS.21. SF1242

Context 435, Phase 3

Fragment with two heavily scored lines at a right angle. If these represent cells, cell-size was >63mm across.

77mm L, 50mm W, 6mm Th

Alquerque boards

IS.22. SF481

Context 400, Phase 6

Heavily worn fragment bearing broad and shallow incised lines.

Face 1: possible corner of plain grid (see above, IS.12).

Face 2: possible corner of reticular grid with one or two incomplete cells, 76mm × ?60mm.

200mm L, 126mm W, 12mm Th

IS.23. SF650

Context 4001, Phase 3

Fragment of edge of grid, one complete cell 25mm × 22mm, and five incomplete cells.

55mm L, 52mm W, 4mm Th

IS.24. SF726

Context 4233, Phase 3; fill of grave G33

Small part of two superimposed grids, one lightly incised and the other more heavily incised. Of the latter, parts of three cells survive; slab appears to have

fractured along an incised line, in which case the cell was *c* 60mm × 48mm.

93mm L, 81mm W, 4mm Th

IS.25. SF749/756/1228 (Figure 6.17)

SF749 and 756 from context 4233, fill of grave G33, and SF1228 from context 4646, fill of grave G124; all Phase 3

Three fragments including one edge of a carefully incised grid, incomplete cells *c* 54mm × 41mm. Traces of two earlier and lighter lines.

c 120mm × 120mm, 3mm Th

IS.26. SF762

Context 4251, Phase 3

Fragment with part of a reticular cell that was probably *c* 65mm across.

54mm L, 50mm W, 5mm Th

IS.27. SF790

Context 4278, Phase 3; fill of grave G46

Face 1: part of edge of grid, two complete cells *c* 40mm × 35mm, and three incomplete cells.

Face 2: lightly incised line forming 90 degree-angle.

127mm L, 78mm W, 8mm Th

IS.28. SF812

Context 436, Phase 3

Face 1: part, possibly of the edge, of an extremely finely and carelessly incised grid. Six complete cells, one of which is 66mm × 39mm.

Face 2: four incomplete cells on the edge of a grid, cells *c* 38mm across.

217mm L, 115mm W, 9mm Th

IS.29. SF813

Context 436, Phase 3

Part of a very carelessly drawn grid, with cells from 34mm to 57mm across.

107mm L, 81mm W, 3mm Th

IS.30. SF1087 (Figure 6.17 and Figure 6.30)

Context 4245, Phase 3; possible stone lining or cover from robbed cist grave

Side A: in the centre of the slab in 'Layer' 2 there is a reticular *alquerque* board, *c* 285mm × 210mm.

The diagonal lines are carefully incised to pass through the corners of 16 squares, creating 25 points for play.

730mm L, 240mm W, 20mm Th

Merels/Nine Men's Morris boards

IS.30. SF1087 (Figure 6.17 and Figure 6.30)

Context 4245, Phase 3; possible stone lining or cover from robbed cist grave

Side A of this intensively used slab bears three and possibly four *merels* boards.

At the wider end of the slab in 'Layer' 1 are faint traces of a regular Nine Men's Morris board, *c* 230mm across, possibly recut to account for the doubling of the medial lines.

At the narrow end end of the slab in 'Layer' 3 is an irregular triple board for Nine Men's Morris, *c* 170mm × 150mm with 22 points. Despite its irregularity, the medial lines are carefully incised from the inner square outwards. Requires small playing pieces no more than 20mm in diameter.

Plate 6.2
Merels board (IS.33)

In the centre of the slab in 'Layer' 5, and superimposed on the *alquerque* board of 'Layer' 2, there is a recognisable but unplayable Nine Men's Morris board, *c* 190mm × 300mm.

730mm L, 240mm W, 30mm Th

IS.31. SF913

Context 436, Phase 3

Corner fragment of a possible *merels* board, incised with two right-angle corners 32–44mm apart, and one median line at a distance of 108mm from the outer corner angle. The surface of the slate is very worn and thus the incised lines appear very light.

300mm L, 270mm W, 35mm Th

IS.32. SF1082

Context 4594, Phase 2; lining of drain

Lightly incised irregular board, *c* 256mm × 220mm, complete but damaged by wear and flaking.

380mm L, 380mm W, 40mm Th

IS.33. SF1083 (Figure 6.17; Plate 6.2)

Context 4594, Phase 2; lining of drain

Confidently cut complete board, *c* 158mm × 123mm, no attempt to stop medial lines at inner square. Minimum distance between points 24mm.

290mm L, 190mm W, 11mm Th

Possible gaming board trial piece

IS.34. SF965

Context 435, Phase 3

Face 1: possible trial piece for reticular board with four cells *c* 64mm × 58mm.

Face 2: grid of diamond-shaped cells *c* 35mm × 20mm.

245mm L, 125mm W, 13mm Th

Gaming pieces

Two definite playing pieces, one a circular slate disc (no 72: Plate 6.1), the other formed on a reused pot sherd (no 80), were also recovered, as indeed were several possible gaming pieces (nos 73–9). None, however, was incised and these are therefore treated in

Franklin's discussion of the general finds from the site (Chapter 6.8).

6.3.3 Text-inscribed slates

KATHERINE FORSYTH AND CARLO TEDESCHI

Introduction

Amongst the many incised stones from Inchmarnock are fourteen carved with what are certainly letters. There is also a handful of others, such as IS.57, IS.74 and IS.75, not discussed here, which may have letter-like markings, although it is difficult to be sure.

The fourteen inscribed stones fall into two distinct groups which on palaeographical grounds can be assigned to the pre-1000 and the post-1200 periods respectively. The larger, early group consists of eight stones which are most likely to date from the 7th century to the 9th. The smaller, later group comprises six stones with gothic lettering which are likely to date to the 13th or 14th century, if not later. These late stones exhibit isolated letters only. The earlier group is more varied. It includes inscriptions in both the roman and ogham alphabets, including an alphabetic sequence in each script. There are three earlier stones with isolated roman letters, two or more with isolated words or Gaelic names, and a single stone with a three-word phrase in Latin.

The incised slates from Inchmarnock are mostly fragments of natural, water-worn pebbles, presumably picked up on the shores of the island itself. These slates vary in size but most sit comfortably in the palm of the hand. Three (IS.35, IS.37 and IS.38) have sub-circular indentations in their perimeter. These are not the remains of perforations, as can be seen on IS.35 where such a 'perforation' would be far too close to the natural edge of the slate, but rather remnants of the cone-shaped voids that result when the slate is hit sharply on the reverse. There is thus no reason to think of these slates as former roof-tiles. They seem too small for much practical use, unless as pot lids, and it seems more than probable that their primary function was simply as 'note-pads'. Other inscribed slates from Inchmarnock, such as IS.36, IS.54 or IS.58, interpreted as properly dressed slate 'boards', are larger and more carefully prepared (for example, Figure 6.15).

Vellum was an expensive writing medium, reserved only for formal work. Ephemera could be committed to wax-tablets, prepared bark, or, as here, a suitably soft and smooth stone, slate being ideal. In an area with appropriate geology, beach pebbles thus constituted a handy, cheap surface on which to practice letters, work out designs, or while away some time in doodling. By their very nature, such inscriptions were only lightly incised. Although doubtless clear enough when freshly scratched, the lines have faded over time. Although the more substantial carvings are readily intelligible, the slightest (with lines little more than a hair's breadth in width) are extremely faint. The difficulty in making them out is compounded by the minute scale of some of the carving and by the fact that much of it is overlain with unrelated lines. Certainly, the Inchmarnock slates present a challenge to the epigrapher! A general discussion of techniques and methods used in the study of graffiti are set out elsewhere (Tedeschi 2000a).

Readings

There are fourteen stones from Inchmarnock which are certainly inscribed with letters. Of these, eleven have letters of the roman alphabet, two have ogham, and one has both roman and ogham scripts (Table 6.2). A full discussion and explanation of the conventions used are set out in the Catalogue below.

As is clear from Table 6.2, the texts are all very short and simple. Nonetheless they encompass a range of material and provide a surprising quantity of information about the milieu in which they were produced. The inscribed 'texts' at Inchmarnock may be categorised as follows:

ISOLATED LETTERS

Several stones exhibit casually inscribed isolated letters which have no obvious meaning and are perhaps simply practice letters or doodles. Some of these are so casual as to be somewhat doubtful, although there is sometimes a fine line between actual letters and the letter-like curves and strokes of a literate person's scribbling. Such carvings are less likely to be poor attempts at writing, than the careless doodling of someone who knew how to write. The isolated gothic letters are more carefully executed and one (IS.42) is internally decorated. They appear to be practice display letters (decorated initials).

SEQUENCES OF LETTERS IN ALPHABETIC ORDER

There are two examples of short sequences of practice letters in alphabetic order in roman script (IS.38 and IS.46) and an example of an incomplete ogham alphabet (IS.36).

Table 6.2 The inscribed texts from Inchmarnock (ogham in bold)

Ref no	Phase(s)	Face/line	Reading
IS.1	1 and 3	A:	**[BOHBADA]** ?
IS.35	1	A i:	ERNAN
		ii:	ERN
		iii:	DDERNAN
		B:	CASA
IS.36	1	A: (i)	ADEPTUSSC̄MPREMIUM
		(ii)	A<D>[E]PTUS SC̄M PR[E]MIUM
		B:	**BLFSNHDTC[Q]**—
IS.37	1	(i)	—DARI[.]—
		(ii)	—[.]TTAGAN
		(iii)	BE[R or N]IT
IS.38	1	A:	MNOP[–]—	LE
		B:	—][R]OU[—	AB
				CD
				EF
IS.39	1/2	A:	[*B*]
		B:	S
IS.40	4	A:	A
IS.41	2	A:	A
IS.42	3	A:	A[D] (or , possibly, A[B])
IS.43	3	A:	M̄
		B:	M
IS.44	3	A:	M [*O*]
IS.45	3	A:	R
IS.46	3	A:	[D] ?
		B:	AAB[—
IS.76	2	A:	**IA[G]GH[—]S[—][B]** or **[H][—]C[—]BGGAI**

INDIVIDUAL WORDS

Complete but isolated words are found in roman letters on two stones (IS.35 and IS.37) and in ogham on two stones (IS.1 and IS.76). The ogham examples are not fully legible but their length and context suggests they may be personal names, presumably scribal signatures. The roman alphabet words include three Gaelic personal names, one of which is incomplete, a single Gaelic verbal form, and a Latin noun. It is not clear whether the isolated words on each of the roman-inscribed stones are meant to be taken together. This is perhaps likely on IS.37 which has two names and a plural verb on the same face (although the verb is much fainter and on a slightly different axis to the names). It is more doubtful on IS.35 which has Latin *casa* and *Ernán | Ernán| Ern* on opposite faces.

SENTENCE

There is a single unambiguous example of a sentence or phrase (IS.36), consisting of three Latin words. It is repeated in a second line. The text *adeptus s(an)c(tu)m premium* means 'having reached the holy reward' and is a quotation from a late 7th-century abecedarian[1] hymn composed at the monastery of Bangor, County Down, in honour of its founder, St Comgall.

Language

Two languages are used: Latin (*casa, adeptus sanctum praemium*) and Gaelic (the personal names *Ernán, Dar-Í, —ttagan*; and the verb *benit/berit*). Of course, Latin is to be expected at a monastery but the evidence for Gaelic ('Old Irish') and the lack of evidence for British provides important evidence of the linguistic and cultural affiliations of Inchmarnock in this early period. The two ogham texts (as opposed to the alphabet) are not sufficiently legible to determine the language used, but the use of the script itself constitutes further evidence of a Gaelic cultural milieu.

Function

As regards function, several of the Inchmarnock inscriptions appear to be no more than doodles, and their carving may be classed as 'leisure activity'. A clear example of this is the ogham text, perhaps a signature, lightly incised on the edge of a gaming board (IS.1). Others, however, appear to be exercises and this group provide important evidence of educational instruction at the site.

The copying exercise on IS.36 is evidence of instruction in basic literacy; it exhibits evidence of difficulty in physically controlling the writing instrument. The short sequences of letters in alphabetic order on IS.38 also appear to be the work of a beginner. Other exercises may reflect more advanced work, for instance IS.46 with its mixture of capital and lower case letters, and IS.35 in which the one scribe may be trying out different grades of script. There are two instances of simple decorated capitals (IS.42 and IS.43), which may be exercises in an educational sense, or working sketches by an adept. Either way they imply training in the methods of book production, not just basic instruction in the cursive scripts used for everyday purposes such as for notes or personal correspondence. The use of drawing compasses evident on IS.76 may also point in this direction.

Ogham

Three stones carry ogham inscriptions. Two of these bear only ogham: short, probably single-word texts (ie names?) on the margins of stones covered with other carvings. One of these is a gaming board (IS.1), the other has been identified as a possible table-top (IS.76). Both inscriptions have the air of casual doodles carved on a stone while it was in use for some other purpose. They are casually carved, as befits their informal context. The third example, the incomplete alphabet (IS.36), is more carefully executed and appears on the reverse of a stone used for copying a Latin phrase.

The extant ogham corpus is overwhelmingly dominated by monumental epigraphy, both in Ireland and in Britain. Literary references to the non-lapidary use of ogham are supported by a very small number of everyday objects inscribed with ogham. If not casual finds, these have, until now, all been from secular sites. This is the first find of non-monumental ogham from an ecclesiastical site. Not only have finds of ogham ephemera been extremely rare, due largely to the vagaries of preservation, but in most cases the dating evidence is weak. The Inchmarnock discoveries are thus particularly welcome. The character of the Inchmarnock ogham inscriptions sits well with the evidence of ogham marginalia in 9th-century Irish manuscripts preserved in Continental monastic libraries (McManus 1991, 132–3). From these it is clear that Gaelic-speaking scribes were familiar with the ogham alphabet and used it in an informal, sometimes jocular way, for brief marginal glosses and comments. While it should not surprise us that the Gaelic clerics of Inchmarnock would be aware of ogham, slate IS.36 seems to imply that the script was being actively taught in the monastery's school.

The three ogham-inscribed slates from Inchmarnock are part of a small, though diverse, concentration of ogham inscriptions in the region. There are pillars of early type on Gigha (RCAHMS 1971, 96–7, no 244 fig 107 pl 16; Forsyth 1996, 288–98) and at Poltalloch, Mid Argyll (RCAHMS 1988, 204, no 350, 80–3, no 104, 4; Forsyth 1996, 443–55). Ogham is incised on bedrock at the summit of Dunadd, also Mid Argyll (RCAHMS 1988, 157–9, no 248; Forsyth 1996, 227–42), and on a puzzling block of stone from Lochgoilhead which also bears an alphabetic inscription in roman letters (as far as N) (RCAHMS 1992, 194, no 87 (1) figs a-b; Forsyth 1996, 374–84). All of these sites are only a short sea journey away from Inchmarnock (in the case of Gigha via the portage at Tarbet).

The form of ogham script exhibited at Inchmarnock is basically simple and devoid of the baroque 'supplementary' letters which are such a prominent feature of the later Scottish oghams to the east. The stem-line is drawn-in and the vowels are formed from strokes rather than notches. Interestingly, the B- and H-consonants slope, a feature common in Scottish ogham but not in Irish ogham. Such simple forms of script are difficult to date and continued in use as late as the 12th century, however, the Inchmarnock oghams would be most readily placed in the 7th- to 9th-century bracket indicated by the palaeography of the other inscribed slates.

Scripts (roman alphabet)

Given the brevity of the texts on the Inchmarnock slates, the site's corpus of inscriptions displays a remarkably wide range of letter forms, ranging from the cursive to the formal, indeed to decorated capitals. Three slates, IS.46 (aAb), IS.37 (Dar-Í) and IS.38 (alphabetic sequences), are written in forms of basically the same hand, a rounded Insular minuscule with, throughout, a half-uncial a. It is hard to date short fragments of simple and informal lettering such as these, shorn of the kind of embellishments which are more readily diagnostic. Script of this kind continued in use after the 9th century, but the general roundness of the script and the use of a half-uncial a perhaps sits more happily before c 800 than much after. A date in the 8th century is thus likely, though not certain. A different, more cursive, hand appears on IS.36 (adeptus). It is derived from New Roman cursive but clearly exhibits typical Insular

elements, like the oc-shaped A, the P descending under the writing line, and the R characterised by a very long and curved tail. An 8th- (or possibly 9th-) century date is likely. Slate IS.35 (Ernán) exhibits more than one form of script. In two cases, (i) and (iii) which may be the work of a single hand, the writing is basically derived from the capital model, with elements borrowed from minuscule − N in (iii) − or uncial − E in (i). This script bears comparison with the writing of post-Roman British epigraphy. In particular, the shape of R in (i) is noteworthy as it is found in post-Roman inscriptions of the late 6th and 7th century, but also in display script of very early Insular manuscripts (Tedeschi 2005). This R sits very well with the ligatured AN, with the uncial E and the reversed N. All these elements together suggest an early date, perhaps in the 7th century. On the reverse of IS.35 the Latin casa incorporates a mix of capital letters (C, A − in one case without horizontal stroke) and minuscule (S), in a manner which, again, is very typical of post-Roman epigraphic writing.

Six slates from Inchmarnock are incised with lettering in a very different style to the above, that of the gothic script which is found in both manuscripts and epigraphy of the period after 1200. These are IS.40–45. The lettering on IS.40 and IS.41 is so similar as to imply they are by the same hand. In all six examples the letters are rendered in outline, thus suggesting the thickness of the broad, oblique pen on vellum. The MS and AS have the characteristically fractured shafts of gothic letters, and the zig-zag decoration and spiral terminals found on IS.42 and IS.43 are also typically gothic features. The hey-day of gothic script was the 13th and 14th centuries, but it continued in use, especially as a decorative display script, into the 16th century (Bischoff 1990, 127–36). Certainly, this group of six stones is considerably later than the rest of the corpus.

Comparanda

An impressive corpus of inscribed slates is known from Visigothic Spain (Velasquez Soriano 1988) but the function of these Spanish examples is profoundly different from the kind of thing found at Inchmarnock: they were used to write private documents and their texts are much more complex than the ones studied in this paper. A closer comparison, albeit much later, is a large slate from Tuscany on which the soldiers of a besieged garrison wrote their names and made drawings in the mid-14th century (Bianchi 2003).

Apart from these, however, inscribed slates are rare in Continental Europe, perhaps because alternative media such as ostraca (pot-sherds/tiles) and plastered walls were more readily available. Nor, indeed, are inscribed slates particularly common in the British Isles. It is striking therefore that there is another collection of inscribed slates from only a few miles away, at St Blane's Monastery, Kingarth, on the mainland of Bute (Anderson 1900). There is indeed a remarkable similarity between the Inchmarnock and the Kingarth slates (actually slate and shale), both in a general sense and more specifically in the shared use of similar letter-forms (see discussion of IS.37), and at both sites there are interlace and other patterns beyond mere lettering. The link is hardly surprising if, as seems likely, there was a close connection between the two monasteries, yet it is remarkable that more than a dozen inscribed slates should survive from Bute when they are otherwise so rare. There are motif pieces from elsewhere in Dál Ríata (Dunadd, and Dervaig, Mull, see Laing 1996) but the only other inscribed stone is the *inomine* pebble from Dunadd (Okasha 1985). The Kingarth stones are little studied. They have been dated 9th to 12th century (Laing 1996, 134), but on rather slight grounds. The Dunadd pebble is earlier. Inscribed slates of a later medieval date are found further up the Clyde estuary at the royal castle of Dundonald (Ewart & Pringle 2006) and there is an important collection of inscribed slates of probably 15th-century date recently recovered from the Great Drain of Paisley Abbey (Malden 2000). The concentration of inscribed slates along the Firth of Clyde over many centuries is perhaps, at root, simply a reflection of the highly suitable local geology.

Inscribed slates have been viewed as a sub-set of the wider corpus of so-called 'Insular motif pieces' (formerly termed 'trial pieces') on stone, bone, and other organic materials, studied in some detail by O'Meadhra (1979; 1987a). Several hundred such motif pieces are extant, the overwhelming majority from Ireland or areas of Irish influence (O'Meadhra 1987a, 172). Only a small minority of these are carved with lettering, most have geometric patterns (eg interlace) or figurative art (for examples of the latter outwith Ireland see Laing 1996). O'Meadhra is adamant that Insular motif pieces are of pre-*c* 1200 date, yet clearly inscribed slates continue until the later Middle Ages, so perhaps the latter are best considered a related and overlapping category, rather than a simple sub-set (*pace* Laing 1996).

In terms of O'Meadhra's (1987b, 159) classification (Chapter 6.3.1 above), the Inchmarnock inscriptions can be assigned to at least three of her categories, namely: (1) leisure activities (IS.37 and IS.46); (2a) apprentices' exercises (IS.36 and IS.38); and (2b) artisan's working drawing (IS.42 and IS.43). The special resonance of the saint's name *Ernán* on IS.35 may also be an indication of the talismanic function (5).

Significance

Although only three of the Inchmarnock slates bear 'texts' which can be read, and these are all short, the collection is nevertheless of considerable significance. On a basic level, they swell the numbers of an under-studied category of material, namely inscribed slates. From a palaeographic point-of-view, they provide rare examples of informal script, not the writing of masters that is found in manuscripts and on formal public inscriptions, but the everyday hand of learners (presumably children).

The Inchmarnock slates provide evidence of literacy at an apparently minor ecclesiastical site, in the context of there being very little concrete evidence for literacy anywhere in Scotland in this period (Forsyth 1998). More specifically they furnish evidence of instruction in literacy, the teaching of basic skills in forming letters, writing Latin, and copying of text. They demonstrate knowledge of ogham in an ecclesiastical context, side-by-side with the roman alphabet, and hint it may even have formed part of the monastic curriculum at Inchmarnock.

The different forms of roman script used on Inchmarnock indicate that the slates cover a wide chronological range. The earliest (IS.35) could be as early as the 7th century; others are more likely to date to the 8th or 9th centuries. The *adeptus* fragment (IS.36) can be no earlier than the late 7th century, the date of the text that it quotes; in fact, the form of the script used suggests a mid-8th century date. The latest are the group of six stones with gothic letters which are no earlier than the 13th or 14th century. This palaeographical dating is useful in corroborating the dates for activity at the site obtained by other means.

In the context of the history of the site, the reference to Ernán, provides very important early evidence for the presence of his cult. Knowledge of and interest in the cult of Comgall of Bangor is indicated by the quotation from a hymn in his honour. If the Dar-Í referred to is the saint of that name the slates provide rare evidence of her cult. If a different person, then they raise the tantalising possibility of female involvement in literacy.

The slates also throw light on the Brittonic/Gaelic linguistic interface on Bute by providing evidence for the Gaelic language there in, perhaps, the 8th century.

The strong similarities evident between the Inchmarnock slates and those from Kingarth underlines the close connection between these two ecclesiastical sites.

CATALOGUE

Conventions

The following epigraphic conventions are employed, namely:

—	text incomplete
[A]	letter damaged or of unusual form
[*A*]	identification of letter not certain
[.]	one letter missing, or in doubt
[−]	an unknown number of letters missing, or in doubt
		a break in the carving due either to intervening decoration, or a fracture
<A>	letter omitted in error and inserted by carver
(A)	letter expressed by abbreviation

Inscriptions in roman script, of whatever kind, are transliterated using small capitals. Inscriptions in ogham script are transliterated using the standard key (McManus 1991) using emboldened small capitals. In the case of stones inscribed on more than one face, the labels Face A and Face B are arbitrarily assigned.

Early group (pre-AD 1000)

IS.35 SF630 (Ernán) (Figure 6.20)
Context 4013, Phase 1 (upper fill of enclosure ditch)

Description

A fragment of water-worn slate incised on both sides with a profusion of lines of various depths and widths. The carving is very similar on both sides, in terms of both repertoire and technique, and is probably the work of the same person. Much of it appears random, but recognisable features include:

pairs of long parallel lines intersecting to form loose grids or lattices
pentangles and sub-pentangular figures (ie stars)
zig-zags/triangles
Latin letters

Lettering appears on both faces. That on Face A consists of the same word repeated (or partially repeated) three times, once at the top of the slab (i), once near the middle of the left edge (ii), and once at the bottom (iii). The lettering on Face B consists of a single word.

Reading

A i: ERNAN
ii: ERN
iii: DDERNAN

B: CASA

Discussion

On face A we have the Irish male personal name *Ernán* twice (i, iii). On the second occasion it is preceded by two letters *dd* which may be considered practice letters unrelated to the name. A third time (ii), only the first three letters *Ern* have been attempted. The lettering of (i) and (ii) is of a similar size, with that of (iii) being rather larger. Each version employs a different form of script, but this need not imply they are the work of different hands. On the contrary, individual scribes would have had at their disposal a range of scripts and letter-forms of differing grades of formality, and it could be that on this slate we have a single scribe (or trainee scribe) trying out different forms using a familiar word.

Note the following features of the script of (i): the E is uncial; capital R is characterised by the position of the third stroke, which is upright. This kind of R is very typical of 7th-century British epigraphy (Tedeschi 2005, 55) and can be found in early Insular manuscripts. The first N is reversed and capital, A is conjoined to the final N which is also capital. Again, there are very close similarities in post-Roman British epigraphy.

Note the following features of the script of (iii): preceding the first letter of *Ernán* are two minuscule DS. The loop of each is formed by a curved line, closed on top by a straight stroke, a shape found in post-Roman inscriptions (Tedeschi 2005, 49). The E is capital; the loop of the R is missing, but it exhibits a long, horizontal final stroke, another shape common in post-Roman inscriptions (Tedeschi 2005, 55), as well as in early display scripts of Insular manuscripts. The first N is minuscule and the A and final N are capital.

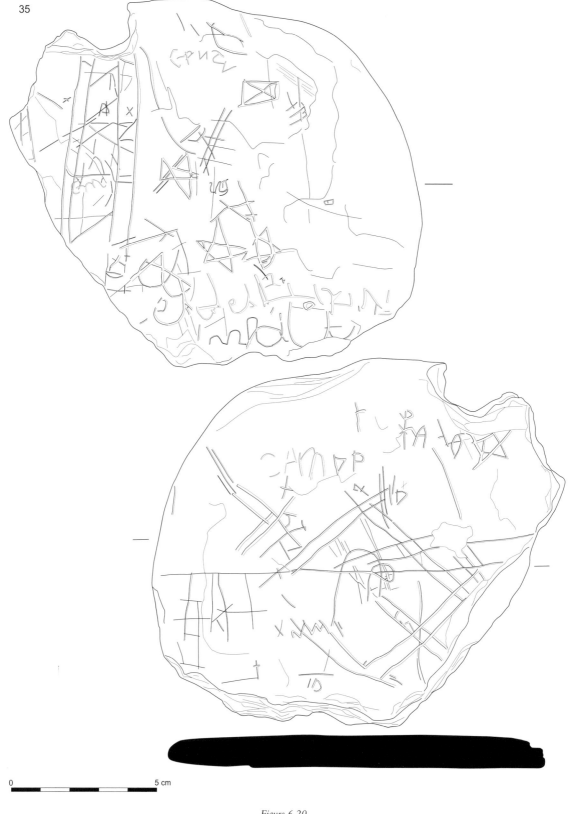

Figure 6.20
IS.35 SF630 (Ernán)

In contrast to the predominantly capital forms used in (i) and (iii), the *Ern* of (ii) represents an attempt at cursive writing. Worthy of note is the manner in which the R is ligatured to the central stroke of the E, which is close to the model of New Cursive script. On Face B, the letters are CASA, all of which are capital, except for the S, which is minuscule. The final A has no central stroke.

Several palaeographic features, then, find close parallels in 6th- to 7th-century British epigraphy including a number of specific letter forms (capital R with upright stroke, capital R with long, horizontal final stroke, minuscule D with a flat-topped bowl) and more general features such as the use of reversed and conjoined letters, and the combination of minuscule and capital forms. The writing on this slate, therefore, is likely to date to a very early phase, probably 7th century.

Interpretation

Ernán is an Old Irish male personal name, apparently derived for *iarn* 'iron' with the common diminutive ending *–án* (Thurneysen 1946, 175, §274b). The name takes on a particular significance at Inchmarnock, of course, because the island derives its name from that of a saint Ernán, in a typical hypocoristic or 'pet' form: *Mo-Ernóc*, 'my little Ernán' (Butter, Chapter 3.3 above). The latter form involves the possessive *mo* and an alternative diminutive ending *–óc*, which is in origin a British hypocoristic suffix but which was used to form hypocoristic names of Irish saints from the 6th century onwards (Thurneysen 1946, 173–4 §271). That such endings were, to some extent, interchangeable is indicated by the example of St Ernéne mac Craséni, who appears in Adomnán's *Life of* Columba (*VC* i, 3) as *Erneneus* (a Latinization of Irish Ernéne which uses a third alternative diminutive *–éne*, Thurneysen 1946, 175, §274b) and is listed as Mo-Ernóc mac Cruisíne among a list of homophonous Irish saints (Ó Riain 1985 §707.766).

The name, while not common, is certainly far from rare: no less than four different Ernáns appear in Adomnán's *Life of Columba*, for instance. Nonetheless, it would be somewhat of a coincidence for this name to appear on Ernán's island simply by chance. Nor can it be readily argued that an inhabitant would be likely to take or be given the saint's name as a mark of devotion. In the early medieval Gaelic world, saints names were not adopted or given to children in their 'raw' form, as happened in later periods (and happens today). Instead saints' names were compounded with

words such as *Máel-* 'devotee', or *Gille-* 'servant', to form names such as Máel-Coluim, or Máel-Phadraig, or Gille-Bhride, indicating devotion to Columba, Patrick and Bridget respectively. That the name appears as *Ernan* may be taken as a reference to the saint himself.

It could be that someone practising letters might consider it particularly propitious to try them out on the name of the island's patron. The dedication to Mo-Ernóc is no guarantee that Ernán ever set foot on the island. It is now accepted that a church's dedication may be due to no more than its possession of relics of the saint in question, and certainly need not imply that it was his or her personal foundation, or even existed during his or her lifetime. Nonetheless, Ernán *may* have been personally active on the island, and it is always possible that the scribe of IS.35 was writing his own name!

Whether the name is a scribal signature or a pious copying exercise, the appearance of the name *Ernán* is highly significant. The slate's palaeography indicates a date as early as the 7th century and this is consistent with the linguistic evidence. The spelling *Ernán* could be as early as the 7th century, but is unlikely to be earlier. The ending *–án* derives from older *-agnos*, (the weakening and loss of the fricative causing compensatory lengthening of the vowel) and Insular inscriptions of the 6th century still spell this with G, eg ERCAGNI > Erccán (CIIC 376) (Sims-Williams 2003, 315–16, 336). This slate therefore provides the earliest extant evidence for the presence of the cult of Ernán on the island. Furthermore, its apparently 7th-century date may assist in choosing among the plethora of possible Ernáns listed in the sources (Butter, Chapter 3.3 above).

Also of interest is the word *casa* on face B. In Classical Latin *casa* refers to a humble, or even temporary, dwelling. The Oxford Latin Dictionary defines it as 'a small, humble dwelling, cottage, hut, hovel' (Glare 1982, 280). A more precise definition of what the word meant in the early Middle Ages is provided by the early 7th-century writer Isidore of Seville, who defines it as 'a small rural inhabitation woven together with posts, twigs, and reeds' (Lindsay 1911). It is striking, therefore, that *casa* appears in the early 8th century as the name of the major British monastery of Whithorn: *Candida Casa*. This is how the site is referred to by Bede in his *Historia Ecclesiastica* (Book 3 ch 4), by the anonymous author of the late 8th-century anonymous poem *Miracula Nynie Episcopi* (Strecker 1923, 948), and by the 12th-century Aelred of Rievaulx in his *Vita Sancti Niniani* (Forbes 1874). Fraser (2002, 48–55) has shown that these three derive most of their information from the same ultimate source, a lost Latin account of the life and miracles of St Ninian, the composition of which he has been able to date to the period *c* 720 × 30. Later 8th- and 9th-century Anglo-Latin writers, including Aldhelm, also use *casa* when referring to ecclesiastical and monastic buildings of a substantial

nature (*Dictionary of Medieval Latin from British Sources, s.v. 1 casa 1b*).

Previous authors have noted that Bede's phrasing is somewhat odd. What he says is that the place was '*vulgo vocatur Ad Candidam Casam*' (*Historia Ecclesiastica* III.4). Presumably he is translating a native British name into Latin for his non-British-speaking audience, perhaps something like the Welsh *ti uuin*, 'white house' (modern *Tywyn*), the name of several early ecclesiastical sites in

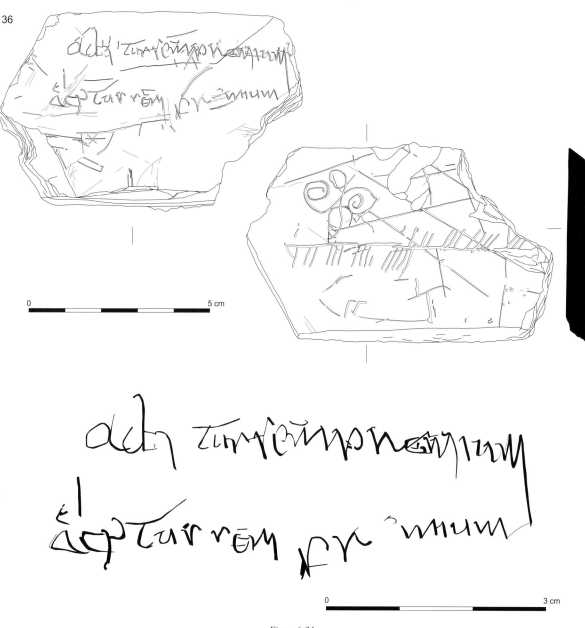

0   5 cm

0   3 cm

Figure 6.21
IS.36 SF717 (adeptus sanctum premium)

Plate 6.3
The adeptus fragment (IS.36)

Wales. The cognate term is found in the names of a number of Irish monasteries, for instance *Tech Moling* 'house of Moling'. The latter cannot, however, be considered a specifically ecclesiastical term as it is widespread in secular place-names too (Hogan 1910, 622–7).

It is interesting that the word *casa* should be found written on a slate at a monastery, given that it was the term used to name one, albeit very famous, monastery. If one were to take the two sides together, *casa Ernan* might be an acceptable translation of *Tech Ernáin* (or *Ti Ernan*), at least in a general sense. Yet, if it were really intended as a single phrase, it should be *casa Ernani*, and on balance the two words are best considered separately, especially as *casa* need not have any ecclesiastical connotations at all.

IS.36 SF717 (adeptus sanctum premium) (Figure 6.21; Figure 6.25; Plate 6.3)

Context 4059, Phase 1

Description

A small piece of slate (max 120 × 70mm.) of approximately rectangular shape. The upper break is rather straight and neat, as if obtained by trimming down the edge. On Face A there are two lines of Latin writing accompanied by other minor scratches which can probably be considered accidental. The same text is repeated on two different lines, albeit with different orthographic errors each time (as discussed below). On Face B are the first ten letters of the ogham alphabet, and a, possibly cruciform, curvilinear design involving two intersecting lines which terminate in spirals.

Reading

A(i)   ADEPTUS S(AN)C(TU)M PR[E]MIUM
 (ii)   A<D>[E]PTUS S(AN)C(TU)M PR[E]MIUM

B   BLFSNHDTC[Q]—

Letter-forms

The writing can be described as Insular minuscule. The A has the typical Insular 'oc' shape, derived from New Roman cursive. The C is formed by two strokes, a first down stroke, followed by a second upward stroke. The D is minuscule, with open bowl, while the vertical stroke (in the first D) is bent to the left. This form has a close parallel in the Insular cursive minuscule, where the vertical stroke would show a closed bowl at the top. Here the hardness of the slate surface did not allow the writer to accomplish a complete bowl, but the curve derives from the movement of a hand which was used to realising the D without lifting the writing instrument. The E has a minuscule form, with the last stroke ligatured to the following P in *adeptus* and probably to M in *premium*. The M at the end of the word is characterised by a long final stroke, descending under the line (particularly long in the last M of the first line). This kind of final M can be found in many examples

137

of Insular cursive minuscule, ie in the Leningrad Bede (St Petersburg, Public Library, Q.v.I.18), dated AD 746 (Brown 1993, 216). The P is minuscule, with open bowl. The descending stroke of P and the ascending stroke of the bowl divide to form a sort of v-shape; this form too can be easily compared to examples of cursive Insular. The R is minuscule, with the second stroke characteristically pointed and drawn out to the writing line, with a double curve. The first stroke of the R and S sits on the line. The T is minuscule, with an oblique down stroke and a long horizontal bar. The word *sanctum* is abbreviated SCM, with a horizontal *titulus* (suspension mark).

Discussion

The text was written by someone who, notwithstanding the difficulty of controlling the writing tool, due to the hardness and the small size of the surface, was able to respect the Insular cursive minuscule model coherently. This script was already in use at the end of the 8th century, as attested by the Book of Armagh (Dublin, Trinity College, 52), dated to *c* AD807, but examples dating from the 8th century provide the closest parallels. Indeed, on the basis of the close similarities with contemporary book hands, like the Leningrad Bede, a mid-8th century date can be proposed.

The physical difficulty in mastering the writing action becomes obvious if one observes the general inaccuracy of the writing and in particular how the scribe loses control over the ascending stroke of P (ii). This, and the copying of the sentence on a second line, seems to indicate that we are dealing with a writing exercise. Especially as the D was originally omitted in error from the second line and had to be inserted interlineally.

As to the meaning of the text, the words are Latin:

adeptus: past participle of *adipiscor* 'reach', 'obtain', 'obtained'
sanctum: accusative singular of *sanctus*, 'saintly', 'holy'
praemium (n): accusative singular, 'reward'

The phrase *adeptus sanctum praemium* means 'having reached the holy reward'. David Howlett, Director, Dictionary of Medieval Latin from British Sources, University of Oxford (pers comm) has identified the phrase as a line of octosyllabic Hiberno-Latin verse, a quotation from the hymn *Audite pantes ta erga*. This hymn occurs, uniquely, in the Antiphonary of Bangor, a late 7th-century liturgical commonplace book written at Bangor, County Down (Kenney 1929,

707–12), and preserved at Bobbio (Milan, Biblioteca Ambrosiana, C 5 inf., fols 15v-17v; Warren 1893, I.14; Warren 1893, II.16–19). Formal similarities between it and the final hymn in the manuscript, *Amavit Christus Comgillium*, suggested to Curran (1984) that both were written by the same author. The latter, in honour of the first fifteen abbots of Bangor, was evidently composed during the abbacy of Cronán (680 x 691) and therefore provides an approximate date for the hymn quoted here. *Audite pantes ta erga* is a hymn in honour of Comgall (died *c* 602), the founding abbot of the great monastery at Bangor, although it provides no biographical or historical information, beyond naming him. Rather, it consists of 'numerous expressions of praise for the saint's virtue, his learning, apostolic zeal and eternal reward, with constant repetition of the same stereotyped forms' (Curran 1984, 81), albeit expressed with considerable ingenuity as regards rhyme and metre.

The hymn consists of 196 octosyllabic lines, each ending in a proparoxytone, ie the accent is on the third last syllable (Curran 1984, 81). The composition begins with an eight-line introductory stanza *Recordemur justitiae nostri patroni fulgidae*, then continues for 23 verses, each of eight lines, interspersed with a four-line refrain. Each successive verse begins with the next letter of the Latin alphabet, and some verses contain multiple lines beginning with this same letter. The line quoted at Inchmarnock occurs at fol 16v, line 12, in the verse beginning 'M':

Magnum apprendit bradium	He got the great victory
Aeterna vita condignum,	truly proper to eternal life,
Adeptus sanctum proemium,	**having reached the holy reward,**
Post laborem firmissimum,	after most steadfast labour
Cujus perfectum meritum	the perfect merit on which
Vocamus in auxilium,	we call for help,
Ut mereamur omnium	so that we can deserve of all
Vitiorum excidium.	vices the destruction.

It appears that the line was written and copied on the stone simply as writing practice; but why that particular line? On a mundane level, it contains a fair variety of letter forms: A, C, D, E, I, M, N, O, P, R, S, T, U. Its theme of steadfast labour leading to heavenly reward is certainly not inappropriate to those toiling in the monastic classroom. The fact that the hymn is in honour of Comgall inevitably raises the question of a possible connection between Inchmarnock and the saint's foundation of Bangor. It seems likely that Inchmarnock was a dependency of Kingarth, and thus looked to Bláán as patron. Early 16th-century materials relating to St Bláán present him as having been a pupil of Comgall of Bangor and Cainnech of Aghaboe (Fraser 2005, 114–15; Macquarrie 2001). Pupilage is a standard hagiographic device for asserting claims of institutional subordination between the monasteries of the saints involved, but these uncorroborated claims concerning Bláán are so late that no reliance can be placed on them as having any bearing on the early medieval situation. While an institutional connection with Bangor remains a possibility, and certainly one worth exploring, it would be wrong to place too much stress on it. No monastery had a monopoly on 'their' saint and a particular saint might be honoured by anyone who thought his or her support worth having. Indeed there is liturgical evidence that Bláán himself was culted on Iona by the middle of the 8th century (Fraser 2005, 113). Thus a hymn to Comgall could be sung both within and outside the Bangor *familia*.

Although the lack of dedications to Comgall suggests that he was not widely culted in Scotland, he and his foundation would certainly have been known to Gaels in the Firth of Clyde, only about 120km away across the North Channel. He is twice mentioned in Adomnán's *Life of Columba* where he is presented as a close friend of Columba, travelling to visit him in Scotland (*VC* i, 49; iii, 17, see also reference to Comgall's monks at iii, 13). Bangor was one of the principal Irish monasteries, a renowned centre of learning, where the great Columbanus of Bobbio had studied under Comgall himself. Is it too fanciful to imagine that a more humble scholar, such as the master of the monastic school on Inchmarnock, might also have studied there? Finally, it may be worth noting that in the 7th and 8th century Bute lay within the territory of Cenél Comgaill (Dumville 2002, 201–3, §50). Indeed Fraser (2005, 112) has suggested that the dynasty's principal ecclesiastical loyalty was to Kingarth, as that of their Cenél nGabráin cousins was to Iona. Although it is simply a coincidence that the ancestor figure of this segment of the Corcu Réti shared the name of the saint, it might constitute another reason why the conversation in the schoolroom on Inchmarnock might turn to Comgalls. In the immediate context of the writing exercise, the hymn's subject matter may, however, have been of less relevance than its abecedarian nature. On the other face of the slate is an ogham alphabet (see below). If the day's lesson related to alphabets then discussion may have called to mind a well-known alphabetical hymn.

In conclusion, the Inchmarnock graffito provides direct evidence of the educational process taking place in an 8th-century Gaelic monastery. It is the writing exercise of a monk or a novice, who made use of a phrase extracted from a well-known text, perhaps included in the liturgy of his own monastery, to practise letters. Similar cases of casual writings, as writing exercises, can be easily found on the margins or blank folios of contemporary Continental manuscripts. This inscription is a unique witness to the fact that the hymn *Audite pantes ta erga*, probably composed in Bangor in the 680s or thereabouts, had a circulation beyond the monastery itself within a generation or two. Whatever its significance as evidence of a formal institutional link between Inchmarnock and Bangor, in more general terms it demonstrates unequivocally Inchmarnock's cultural and intellectual ties with the Church in north-eastern Ireland.

Ogham inscription

The ogham inscription on Face B is incomplete. The extant portion consists of the first ten letters of the ogham alphabet on a stem-line which runs horizontally across the middle of the slab.

B L F S N H D T C [Q] —

The beginning of the stem is clear, about 10mm in from the left edge, but the end of the stem is lost beyond the fractured edge of the top right corner. Although the loss of this corner is thus subsequent to the carving of the ogham, it does not impinge on the space occupied on the reverse by the Latin inscription. Therefore it cannot be used to establish the order in which the two sides were carved. The incised line on both sides is of similar character and it is possible all was carved by the same hand. While it is perhaps easier to imagine the two sides date to about the same time (ie in the 8th century), there is nothing to preclude the ogham having been added at a latter date. Its script provides no datable stylistic features.

To complete the basic, twenty-letter ogham alphabet would have required a slate twice as long (and for the ogham to pre-date the latin inscription). It may be, however, that the extant letters are complete. Although there are a number of examples of ogham alphabets in Irish manuscripts, there is only one other epigraphic example. This is on a small slab (0.33 × 0.33m) found built into the church at Maughold, Isle of Man (Kermode

1907, 214, pl lxiv). Like the Inchmarnock example the Maughold ogham alphabet runs horizontally across the face to a fractured right edge, with the tenth letter damaged and the stem beyond it lost. The ogham accompanies two lines of 12th-century runes: the runic alphabet (futhark) and a Norse text which reads 'Juan the priest carved these runes'. The extant portion

of ogham is aligned with the beginning and end of these two lines of runes which may indicate that it is complete as it stands.

The skill in writing ogham is to control the individual strokes to make them neatly parallel, and to ensure that they begin an equal distance from the stem and do not overshoot it. By and large the carver

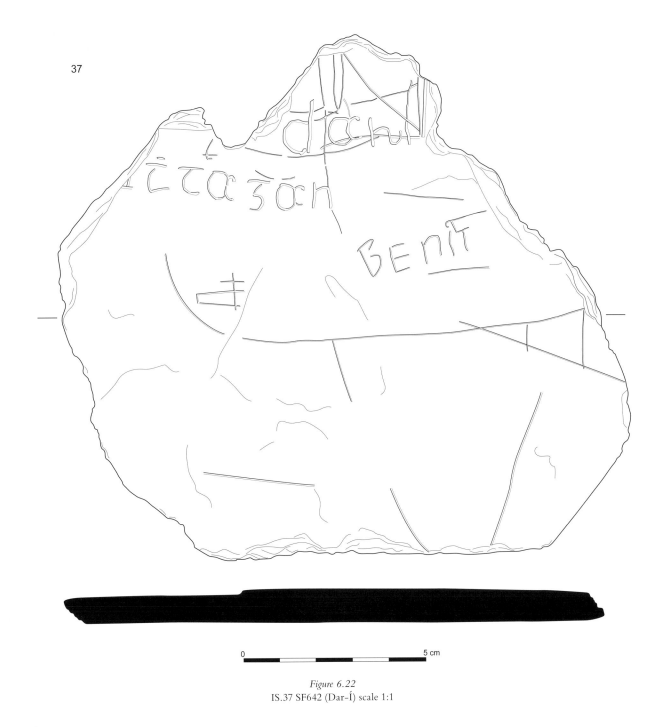

37

0   5 cm

Figure 6.22
IS.37 SF642 (Dar-Í) scale 1:1

has managed this well, although the final stroke of the fourth character (S) appears not to reach the stem. Another possible indication of inexperience is the fact that the fifth and sixth letters overlap (NH). Perhaps the H was at first omitted, then inserted (cf the D added above the line on A(ii)), or perhaps the carver got half way before realising there was insufficient space to complete the next five letters before the break and came up with the novel, and not entirely satisfactory solution, of overlapping these two letters. Nonetheless, this is a neatly carved ogham, with individual letters well spaced and clearly legible. It has been executed with more care than either of the other two Inchmarnock oghams. This is consistent with its being an exercise, and could itself be taken as a sign of inexperience.

The only palaeographical feature to note is that letters of the H-group (short consonant strokes above the stem) exhibit a consistent forward slope, ie their distal tips (furthest from the stem) are further 'forward' (to the right) of their proximal tips (where they touch the stem line). Letters of the B-group (short consonant strokes below the stem) slope on this same axis, ie their distal tips are further 'back' (to the left) of their proximal tips. A B-stroke and an H-stroke would meet to form a single oblique stroke '/', (indeed the fourth stroke of the fifth letter and the single stroke of the sixth letter do precisely this). This contrasts with the later Scottish examples which are consistent in having the two groups slope, but on different axes, such that strokes of the two would meet to form an arrow head '>'. The sloping of consonant strokes is rarer in Ireland, in both epigraphic and manuscript ogham. The Inchmarnock ogham contrasts with the Maughold alphabet which consists of strokes which are strictly perpendicular to the stem. The two differ in two further respects: the Maughold ogham begins with the non-phonetic '>' or 'feather-mark', sometimes used in late manuscript oghams to indicate the beginning of the text; and the letters at Maughold are much more widely spaced. Both of these features reflect the late date of the Maughold example.

IS.37 SF642 (Dar-Í) (Figure 6.22)
Context 4013, Phase 1 (upper fill of enclosure ditch)

Description

The slate is incised on one face only with two lines of clearly carved lettering, and a third line of less distinct, though still legible, letters. There are also several long, straight lines, apparently random and rather faint, which are, in fact, little more than scratches.

The two upper lines of lettering are neatly and carefully carved in the same manner (what might be termed the same 'hand'). They are parallel to one another and evidently go together. This lettering evidently predates the breaking of the slate as the long vertical stroke at the end of the first line disappears at the fracture, and at the very beginning of the second line the slight remains of a letter can be detected emerging from the broken edge. The third line of text is different in character, so faint as to be almost invisible, and not on the same alignment as the other two lines. It is possibly a later addition.

Reading

(i)   —DARI[.]—
(ii)   —[.]TTAGAN
(iii)   BE[R or N]IT

The final stroke in the upper line (i) is carved in the same manner as the preceding letters although it does not come down to their notional base-line. If it is an I it is about three-times the height of the i which precedes it. The upper part of the stroke is lost beyond the fracture but it would be hard to interpret it as any other letter (eg P, B, T) because of the absence of any adjoining strokes or remains of strokes in the extant area above or to the right of the vertical. The D at the beginning of this line is a little larger than any other of the letters, possibly because it marks the beginning of a new word (ie personal-name, see below). If so, then the greater size of this final stroke (I?) could be explained by its being the beginning of a new word or name. Given the informal nature of this carving, however, we cannot be certain that it is indeed (part of) a letter.

Interpretation

Whether or not the final stroke is indeed a letter, the first four characters (DARI) could be complete as they stand. They suggest the Gaelic female personal name *Dar-Í*, 'daughter of *Eo*' (*Eo* is attested as a male personal name in its own right. It is identical to the tree name 'yew', cf ogham IVO-, Gaulish *Ivorix*. The male equivalent of *Dar-Í* is also attested: *Nath-Í*, see *DIL* col. 121 s. *Dathí*). A handful of historically attested women bear this name, the most famous being the author of the lost canon law-text *Cáin Daríi* ('the law of Dar-Í') which appears to have dealt with cattle-stealing, and other legal matters relating to cows. The text also goes by the name *Cáin Bóshlechtae* 'the law of cow sections' (Kelly 1997, 167, 504) and under this name is mentioned as being promulgated in Munster in 810: *Boslechta la Mumain la Dare ocus la Adhuar mac Nechin*, 'cow-sections in Munster by Dar-Í and Adhuar mac Echin' (Annals of Innisfallen 122, s.a. 810, see Ó Riain 1990; Kelly 1988, 275). It is referred to three times in the Annals of Ulster as Lex Dari(i), 'the law of Dar-Í', where it is recorded that it was promulgated in Connacht in 812 and again in 826 (AU 812.13, 826.10). The supreme importance of cattle to the Irish economy in this period is reflected in the fact that an Old Irish gloss on Colmán's Hymn (Stokes & Strachan 1903, ii 306 n.5) lists the Law of Dar-Í ('not to steal cows') as one of the four principle laws of Ireland, along with the law of Patrick ('not to kill clerics'), the Law of Adomnán ('not to kill women') and the Law of Sunday ('not to travel [on a Sunday]') (Kelly 1988, 276).

The second line is evidently the end of a Gaelic male personal-name with a diminutive ending. It could be a name ending -*tag* with the typical male -*án* diminutive suffix, although what such a name could be is unclear. Alternatively, it could be a name ending in -*t* with a form of the longer -*ocán*/-*ucán* diminutive suffix. This is a development of the −*óc* suffix (discussed above in relation to SF 630), which is in origin a Brittonic hypocoristic suffix, cf MidW. -*awc*). On both these suffixes see Thurneysen 1946, 173 §271. There would be a problem with this latter interpretation, however, in explaining in an Old Irish context the spelling *g* = /c/ alongside the double *t*. The similarity to Modern Gaelic *taghan*, 'pine marten', is coincidental.

The third line constitutes a separate text. The first letter appears to be a very faint B, upright, with curved and open bowl. Next to it is an uncial E, and following that N or more probably R. The sequence is complete and intact. Whether read as *berit* or *benit* the sequence would make sense as an old Irish word. The former is the third person plural present indicative form of the verb *beirid* (Thurneysen 1946, 353, 349), which has a wide range of meanings, including 'carries', 'brings forth', 'gets', and 'takes'. Interestingly, in the light of the reference to the female jurist Dar-Í, it is the verb used in a legal context to mean 'judges, passes judgement' (*DIL* s. *beirid*). If the form is *benit*, it could be the equivalent form of the verb *benaid*. The basic meaning of this word is 'beat, strike, cut' but it is attested meaning specifically 'incise', with reference to ogham (*DIL* s. *benaid*). Thus the third word could

relate to the two persons named, stating, among a range of possible meanings, either 'they judge' or 'they incise'.

Letter-forms

From the palaeographical point of view, the writing is a typical Insular minuscule. The A shows the typical *oc* shape; D has a large loop with short vertical stroke, characterised by a triangle-shaped top; G has a half-uncial shape; minuscule R with long curved final stroke; minuscule T. The B of the third line is minuscule. The three texts are written in the same neat form of Insular minuscule (note the form of R, T, G, and N) with a half-uncial 'oc'–A throughout. The hand is upright, rounded and even. Serifs are missing, except for the one found in the upper end of the D stroke. Insular minuscule continued in use in the Gaelic-speaking world into the medieval period (and beyond) becoming increasingly 'square' and angular but the rounded character of this script and the use of a half-uncial form probably implies a relatively early date, perhaps 8th century. The script on this slab is similar in certain respects to that found on the slabs from Kingarth (eg half-uncial 'oc'–A, open rounded B) yet is not identical (eg the Kingarth minuscule R does not come down to the line as here). John Higgitt has commented that the Kingarth lettering 'lacked the angularity and serifs of the 9th century and later' although he cautioned 'I do not mean necessarily to argue for an early date' (*apud* Laing 1996, 133).

Discussion

This is one of the few Inchmarnock slates to bear an intelligible 'text': a Gaelic word and two Gaelic personal names, one female and one male, the former complete and recognisable, the latter incomplete and unidentifiable. The two names could have been written by the same hand but need not have been. There is too little overlap in the letters of the extant sections to judge. Is one or other a scribal signature? Is the other, then, the name of a companion? In this case the third word 'they inscribe' (reading *berit*) could refer to their act(s) of carving. If so this could constitute unprecedented epigraphic evidence for female literacy in the British Isles in this period (for a possible parallel, see the 8th/10th-century graffito signature of a Welsh pilgrim woman called *Guil*, found near Perugia, in Italy: Tedeschi 2000b). If the names are not signatures then why would they be written on a slate by a third

Figure 6.23
IS.38 SF663 and SF666 (alphabet stone) scale 1:1

party, presumably a male cleric? The Dar-Í named may have been an otherwise unrecorded woman of this name (at a time when so few women are mentioned in the historical record). However, if the third word does read *benit* and the sense 'they judge' is accepted, then it seems more likely that this is a reference to the saint. A parallel is provided, of course, by the carving of (St) Ernán's name on IS.35. There is very little evidence at all for a cult of Dar-Í, and none, it seems, in Scotland until now.

IS.38 SF663 + SF666 (alphabet stone) (Figure 6.23)

Context 4059, Phase 1

Description

Two small matching fragments of a single slate (max 66 × 55 × 4mm), treated here as a single item. The lower edge may be a natural break, the other edges appear to have been trimmed down: the sub-circular remains of two percussion cones are visible in the bottom right corner. Very lightly incised on both faces.

Face A: Two horizontal, parallel strokes across the width of the stone. Above this a line of lettering (*c* 6mm tall):

(SF663)   (SF666)

MNOP[–]— | LE

The *mnop* is clear. What follows in the second fragment are the letters L and uncial E.

Face B (shown inverted in Figure 6.23): Very similar in character to the carving on the other side: a layer of apparently random straight strokes of various lengths; on the left, an equal-armed outline cross with expanded bar terminals (the right terminal, unfinished); straddling the fracture, what may be an encircled, equal-armed cross with the left arm terminating in a disc and the bottom left-hand quadrant of the circle doubled; on the right a free-hand circle containing the letters A and B; under this are four more letters of the alphabetic sequence in two lines: C D E F, these last two conjoined. Below the left-hand cross are the remains of lettering: R (?), O, U.

(SF666)   (SF663)

—][R]OU[— | AB
             | CD
             | EF

Letter-forms

All the letter forms belong to the Insular minuscule style. They are in keeping with those on IS.37 (Dar-Í), but they are much less regular in size and shape. The A

has a typical '*oc*' shape, with open loop; B is capital; D is characterised by a very large and open loop; E is uncial, as is the M; the N is minuscule.

Discussion

The texts on the two faces of IS.38 are very similar, and appear to be practice sequences of letters of the alphabet, in alphabetical order. The traces of letters under the cross on Face B are read as R O U and it is tempting to see these in relation to the drawing above as [c]*rou*[x] 'cross'. Classical Latin *crux* appears on two Breton inscriptions as *crox*, a spelling which reflects Vulgar Latin change of /u/ > /o/ (Sims-Williams 2003, 102), and once with the spelling *croux* on the possibly 9th-century *croux Prostlon* at Locoal-Mendon, Morbihan, Brittany (Davies *et al* 2000, 225).

It is conceivable that the writing on both faces was carved by the same hand. Some of the other strokes on Face B appear to be random doodles, but it is possible that the pairs of straight horizontal strokes on this face (corresponding to the letters ROU) and on Face A (corresponding to the letters MNOP) were intended as rule-lines to guide the pupil. If so, the slate provides evidence, not only for the use of literacy at this site, but evidence that literacy was taught there.

IS.39 SF728 (B/S) (Figure 6.24)

Context 4009, Phase 1/2

Face A: Amongst the various lines are a series of multiple super-imposed strokes which could be a letter. If the small horizontal bar on top is disregarded

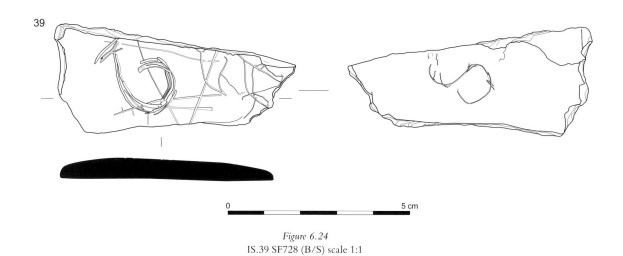

Figure 6.24
IS.39 SF728 (B/S) scale 1:1

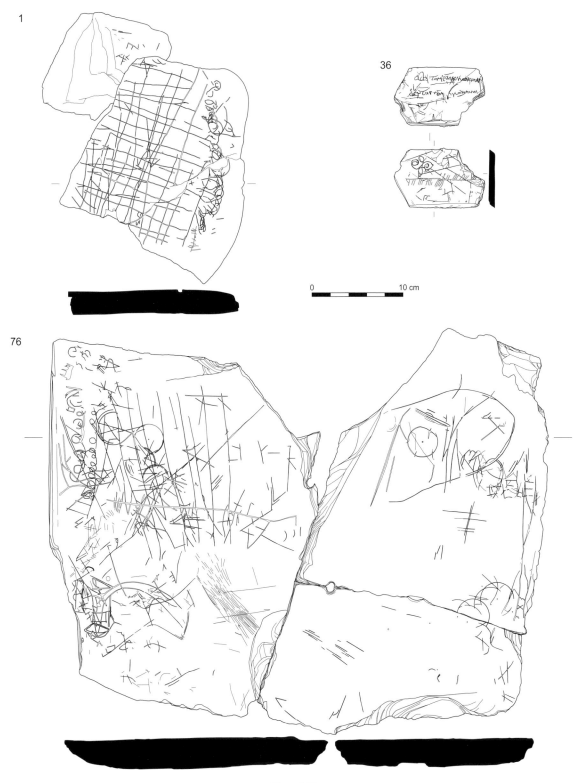

Figure 6.25
Ogham inscriptions (IS.1, IS.36 and IS.76)

it could be a typical Insular minuscule в, if not, then it could be read as minuscule т, although the lower curve would appear somewhat over-developed in that case.

Face B: An s of the typical Insular decorative form, as can be found in early Insular inscriptions (Tedeschi 2005, 56) and manuscripts (Higgitt 1994, fig 2, S1).

Other text-inscribed stones in the early group (catalogued elsewhere)

IS.1. SF402/625/430 (Gaming-board, with ogham) (Figure 6.25)

Contexts 437 and 4001 (both Phase 3) and 459 (Phase 1: fill of Grave G11)

Ogham inscription

There is a tiny ogham inscription, in total length not much more than about 20mm, lightly incised on the margin of the stone. It is very indistinct and difficult to make out, but sufficient remains visible to be confident that it genuinely is ogham, rather than, say, a score-tally relating to the game, or some haphazard combination of random strokes. It is tucked into a corner between the edge of the ruled grid and the end of the mass of curving lines, which it avoids, and presumably it post-dates both. It consists of about seven characters.

Ogham inscriptions read from left-to-right, but as the orientation of the slab at the time of carving is not known it is unclear which end is the beginning. Because of the nature of ogham script, which depends on the position of strokes relative to a stem-line, inversion affects not only the sequence of letters, but, in many cases, the actual identity of individual letters. For instance, characters aligned to a particular side of the stem would represent different letters depending on which way round the object is held: ie a five stroke letter is either ('Q') or ('N'), and a one-stroke letter, either ('B') or ('H').

Another difficulty is that the ogham has been casually rather than carefully carved. The key features which distinguish different letters, spacing, relative length and slope, are less than rigorously indicated (not surprisingly, perhaps, on this minute scale). Obviously, it is difficult to control a tool to incise tiny strokes on uneven slate and it is perhaps inevitable that certain strokes will over- or under-shoot the mark slightly. With ogham, however, this can cause particular problems. Ogham strokes should lie either to one side or the other of the stem (short-stroke consonants) or

sit on it balanced on their mid-point (vowels and long-stroke consonants). How, then, to interpret strokes which cross the stem, but only a little bit. Are they short-stroke consonants which have over-shot the stem, vowels which have gone too far beyond the stem, or long-stroke consonants which have not gone far enough?

Although the ogham on this slate now looks rather scrappy it must be borne in mind that it would not have been carved with posterity in mind. Like so many other carvings on the corpus of slates from Inchmarnock it is an occasional doodle, done for personal enjoyment. Our problems with its legibility are due to lack of care in execution rather than ignorance on the part of the carver, compounded, of course, by the fact that it is now considerably more faint than it would have been when freshly scratched.

The inscription is complete as it stands. The 'tail' of the stem-line is visible beyond the first and last letters. Notwithstanding the uncertainties of the reading (see below), the spacing of letters appears somewhat erratic, with the first half rather generously spaced yet the final letters cramped. If this is an indication that space was running out, it is our only clue that the direction of reading is from the fractured edge towards the grid. If this were the case, the reading would be as follows:

1 A single long stroke below the stem, slightly sloping, with distal end (ie the end furthest from stem) forward of the point at which it joins the stem-line: (в)

2, 3 A single stroke across the stem followed by a second, slightly shorter. If these are a pair they could be two vowel strokes (o), yet they seem rather widely spaced and may have been intended as two separate strokes. If the difference in length is significant, they could be a consonant followed by a vowel stroke (MA), if not, then two vowels (AA). There is a small curving nick before stroke 2, but it is very faint. The spacing would be oddly close if this were an independent letter stroke (H), unless it formed a pair with stroke 2 (D) (in which case it would be necessary to assume that 2 was a short-consonant stroke which had overshot the stem). According to this scenario, the inscription would open with a nicely spaced BDA.

4 A single short stroke above the stem (H). There is an insubstantial hint of a continuation below the stem, sloping backwards, but I think this may be disregarded.

5   A single short stroke below the stem (B). There is a little oblique nick between this stroke and the following bit of stem. Again, I think it unlikely to be part of a letter. Perhaps the carving tool slipped. Certainly there is a larger than expected gap before the next stroke. It may have contained up to two or three light strokes which are now completely invisible.

6   A long stroke which crosses the stem perpendicularly. The difficulty is in judging whether this cross-stroke is a vowel (A) or a consonant (M). It extends further above the stem than below, but in overall length is shorter than stroke 2. As it stands between what appear to be consonants, perhaps a vocalic interpretation is to be preferred.

7   Two short strokes above the stem, close together. These are closer at their distal tips than where they meet the stem, but this is probably not significant and they should be read as a pair (D).

8   The final stroke is a long oblique one across the stem. It is similar in length to stroke 6, but more emphatically sloping. This is perhaps to differentiate the two and indicate that this is a long-stroke consonant (M) rather than another vowel (A).

On this basis, a possible reading (with alternatives within brackets, separated by '/') is as follows:

B(AA/O/MA)HBAD(M/A)

There is nothing in the shape of the individual letters which precludes a reading in the opposite direction (ie turning the inscription 180°). In this case, the equivalent reading would be:

MLAHB(O/AA/AM)H

or

ALAHB(O/AA/AM)H

A final remaining difficulty, is the value to be assigned to the character ⊥ ('H') (Forsyth 1996, xxxix; Sims-Williams 1993, 162–70). The original sound value of this character is not known as it does not appear in Irish ogham inscriptions of the pre-7th century (see McManus 1991, 37). In Irish manuscripts of the 9th century and later, when ogham was used as a cypher for contemporary manuscript spelling, the symbol was equated with *h* and used with C and T as equivalents of the manuscript digraphs *ch*/χ/ and *th*/θ/. It is, however, never used in this way in Scottish inscriptions. Instead it tends to occur between a vowel and T or R, eg

EHT, AHT, AHR. This suggests the value was a spirant, perhaps perpetuating an older convention *h* = /χ/ seen, for example, on a roman alphabet inscription from Wales (CIIC 349, 401) BROHO- for /broχo-/. The Inchmarnock example, however, does not follow this pattern as it stands between a vowel and B (and, alternatively, also as a final letter following a vowel).

Leaving the transliteration of H ambiguous, the reading BOHBADA although pronounceable does not yield any obvious sense. From the context a name or nickname might be expected, or some word relating to the game, but nothing obviously suggests itself. As mentioned above, however, the spacing of the letters is sufficiently erratic and the carving in general so small and indistinct, that it remains possible that there were additional strokes in some of the intervals which are now completely invisible. Regardless of the interpretation, however, the carving on this slate provides important evidence of ogham literacy at the site, not just in a school-room context (see above, IS.36), but in 'recreational' use.

IS.76 SF1263 (stone 'table-top', with ogham) (Figure 6.25)

Context 4679, Phase 2 (fill of Grave G141)

Ogham inscription

The ogham inscription is one of numerous separate carvings on this palimpsest of a stone. It is written on an irregular stem-line running horizontally across, or up, the middle of the largest piece of the slab. It is cross-cut by the sequence of long parallel lines running vertically but it is difficult to tell which came first. The stem-line is mostly clear, as are the first four or five letters and the final letter. The intermediate area, by contrast, is worn and the reading in this area is very doubtful.

The stem starts *c* 60mm from the left edge of the slab, which is original. There is a gap of about 10mm before the first letter, a five-stroke vowel (I). There is a further gap of about 10mm before the next letter, a single vowel stroke (A). The next stroke crosses the stem after an interval of about 12mm. It appears to be the first of a pair of long oblique strokes, although it seems to be angled at its mid-point (>), whereas its partner is straight. The two are about 3mm apart at the stem, yet about 6mm apart at their distal tips (G?). After a gap of 8mm there is a second pair of two long oblique strokes, but these are parallel to one another and 3mm apart (G). The next letter consists of a single stroke above the stem sloping backwards. It touches the stem 16mm from the point where the preceding stroke

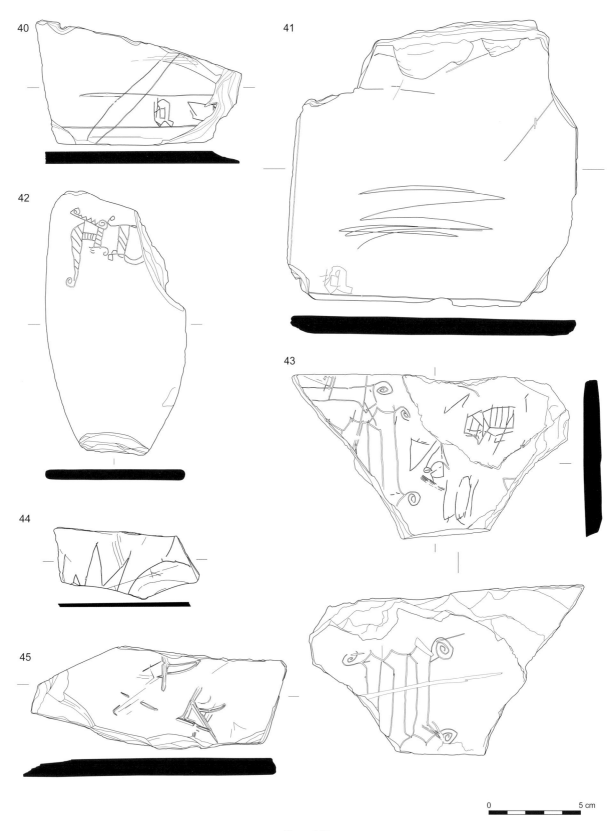

Figure 6.26
Later medieval letter-forms from Inchmarnock (IS.40–5)

crosses the stem, but they are closer at their distal tips because the two slope in opposite directions, towards one another. From this point on the lettering becomes very indistinct. There follows a section of about 78mm which may contain a second H and then, perhaps, some vowel strokes. Then comes a group of four strokes below the stem (s). The stem may continue beyond this, but the surface of the stone is too abraded to tell. There is what appears to be a final stroke below the stem about 85mm from the fractured edge (B?).

This gives a reading:

IA[G]GH[—]S[—][B]

If read from the opposite end, this would yield:

[H][—]C[—]BGGAI

Neither of these makes particular sense, but there remains little of the text to go on.

The portions of this ogham which can be made out are easier to read than IS.1 because this one is carved on a larger scale, the letters are widely spaced, and there is a clear distinction between long and short strokes, indeed its long consonant strokes are very long. The script of the two, however, is basically similar, with strokes rather than notches for vowels, and with H-strokes which slope backwards, both features typical of the Scottish ogham corpus. Angled strokes are found on Scottish oghams, but only for vowels, and it is odd that only one of the pair should be angled. It may be a slip. Like the ogham on IS.1, this text is an informal doodle.

IS.46. SF404 + SF587 (armoured warriors and boat) (Figure 6.27)

Contexts 437 and 4001, both Phase 3

Description

Face A lower portion (SF404 Face A): At the lower edge of the slab, on the right-hand side, a curved line emerges from the lower fracture. It is joined to a long straight stroke which ends in a short, right-angled stroke with a triangular terminal. This could be the remains of an upright letter D with a 'cap' and wedge-shaped serif. There are traces of what may be cross-hatched decoration under the curved line, ie within the bowl of the putative D. The identification of this carving as a letter is far from certain, however, due to its incomplete preservation.

Face B lower portion (SF404 Face B): Towards the right hand edge, aligned vertically down the stone

(ie perpendicular to the drawing on the other face), are incised three letters. Firstly, there is a half-uncial 'oc'-A, nicely rounded, which is identical in form to the As on IS.37 (Dar-Í). Next is a highly baroque-looking capital A, of a form that is reminiscent both of forms of epigraphic script, as seen in the As on the Catamanus stone, Anglesey, Wales (CIIC 970), which dates from the first quarter of the 7th century, as well as some examples of display script (see Tedeschi 2005, 47). It is joined to what follows, clearly a minuscule B with open, rounded bowl and a forked serif on the upright. The latter is formed from a single stroke which sweeps down and round to form an open bowl (ie it is not a two-stroke 'vertical-plus-bowl').

Face B upper portion (SF587 Face B): There are a variety of incised lines on the upper portion of this face but none appear to be letter-forms.

Reading

Face A: [D] ?
Face B: AAB[—

Discussion

The letters on Face B appear to be a single group of practice letters in alphabetic sequence. That they lie on a different axis from the sketch on the obverse suggests the two sets of carvings are unrelated. Given the potential for reuse of slates, they may or may not be closely contemporary. With only three identifiable letters there is little to provide dating criteria, although the rounded character of the letters is compatible with an earlier, rather than later date, ie probably pre-9th century, as is the unusual form of the capital A (if the Catamanus parallel is valid). The forked serif appears to be an Irish/Gaelic feature.

Late group: post-AD 1200

IS.40 SF890 (a) (Figure 6.26)

Context 4537, Phase 4 (fill of Grave G93)

A minuscule A is visible in the lower right angle. The double-lined strokes are constructed around a central rectangle in a manner which recalls the typical gothic writing technique (in which curves are fractured into several pen strokes). This character is almost identical to the A on IS.41 and is possibly by the same hand. This is one of six stones bearing gothic script, and is likely to date to the 13th or 14th century, if not later (see Introduction).

lower tip. The original edges are water-worn, implying this is a beach-slate. Neatly and clearly incised on one face only, with two decorated capital letters. The slate sits comfortably in the palm of the hand and would have made an ideal 'note-pad' for trying out a simple illumination of this kind which could be employed to mark chapter- or section-headings.

Reading

A[D]   (or, possibly,   A[B])

Letter-forms

This pair of gothic capitals, both decorated in the same simple style, appear to be practice letters. The A has thick, vertical sides (with the first descending low below the line and terminating in a spiral) and a horizontal bar, all internally decorated with oblique parallel strokes (cf N-like character on IS.74). This H-shaped box is

0   5 cm

Plate 6.4
The Gothic 'AD' slate (IS.42)

IS.41 SF1084 (a) (Figure 6.26)

Context 4594, Phase 2 (lining of drain 4550)

An A is visible in the lower left angle of the slate. It is practically identical to the letter described in IS.40 and may be ascribed to the same hand. This is one of six stones bearing gothic script, and is likely to date to the 13th or 13th century, if not later (see Introduction).

IS.42 SF649 (AD) (Figure 6.26; Plate 6.4)

Context 4001, Phase 3

Description

A flat, wedge-shaped slate (max 137 × 76 × 4mm), intact except for the loss of the top right corner and

0   5 cm

Plate 6.5
The Gothic 'M' slate (IS.43)

topped with a sloping 'cap' which consists of a single line terminating in spirals and surmounted by a zig-zag line. The D (or B) also has a thick vertical which is internally decorated with three parallel oblique strokes. The full-height bowl of the D/B sweeps round to the right, there is no internal decoration on the extant portion. Most of the bowl has disappeared beyond the fracture. There are two faint, in-turning strokes which emerge to the left of the fracture, almost as if part of the lower bowl of a B. Any trace of the mirroring stroke of an upper bowl would have been lost beyond the fracture, but certainly the visible strokes stop well short of the vertical. At the top and bottom of the vertical are serifs formed from straight horizontal strokes to the left, to which have been added a spiral (upper) and an indistinct s-curve (lower).

Discussion

This is one of six slates from Inchmarnock which are carved with gothic capitals of a kind typical in both manuscripts and epigraphy of the period after 1200. They are likely to date to the 13th or 14th century, if not later (see Introduction).

IS.43 SF795 (M) (Figure 6.26; Plate 6.5)

Context 436, Phase 3

In addition to some very light doodled strokes, each face of this fragment is neatly incised with an identical gothic capital M. The three minims of each letter are rendered in outline with no internal decoration. Each minim is fractured in the characteristically gothic manner, in imitation of the short oblique extensions to the shafts of the book-hand. The upper and lower corners of the Ms terminate in spirals. On face A there is an additional horizontal stroke, of similar form, above and separate from the M. This may be intended as a suspension mark. This is one of six stones bearing gothic script, and is likely to date to the 13th or 14th century, if not later (see Introduction).

    Face A: [M̄]
    Face B: M

IS.44 SF741 (MO) (Figure 6.26)

Context 4233, Phase 3 (fill of Grave G33)

A capital M, very lightly scratched, followed by what may be the upper curve of an O.

This is one of six stones bearing Gothic script, and is likely to date to the 13th or 14th century, if not later (see Introduction).

IS.45 SF796 (R) (Figure 6.26)

Context 436, Phase 3

A series of partially preserved, deep intentional cuts, some of which may be letters, others only 'letter-like'. The clearest is a large capital R on the right hand-side which has a large bowl and a horizontal bar at the base of the vertical stroke. This peculiar form is likely to be even later than the series of Gothic letters, indeed perhaps as late as the 16th century.

6.3.4 *Non–text-inscribed slates*

CHRISTOPHER LOWE

Catalogue

6.3.41 Figurative scenes and other sketches

In all, there are 11 stones containing what can be described as figurative scenes and other sketch-forms. A possible twelfth piece, depicting what may be a frontal view of a human figure (IS.69), is too faint to be certain and it has therefore been classified elsewhere (*Miscellaneous & other incised slate fragments*, below).

The subjects of the carvings include human figures, sketches of animals (both 'domestic' and what is clearly a hunting scene), as well as boats, weapons and an exceptionally fine drawing of what is almost certainly a church (IS.54). Another outstanding piece in the assemblage is IS.46 which not only depicts a group of armoured warriors and their boat but also another figure who appears to carry before him a house-shaped reliquary shrine. If correctly identified, this would be our earliest representation of this class of artefact.

IS.46. SF404 + SF587 (Figure 6.27; Plate 6.6)

Contexts 437 and 4001, both Phase 3

Description

Flat, oval slate beach pebble formed of two conjoining fragments recovered in 2001 and 2002, roughly 4m apart. The piece is essentially intact except for the loss of its upper right-hand margin and its lower edge, and measures 180 × 120 × 12mm in its present state. It was, perhaps, originally up to 30mm bigger (say, 180 × 150mm) but in any event it is clear that the slab would have been easily portable and could have been held comfortably in one hand.

Inscribed on the principal face are four human figures (Figures A–D), in profile facing to the right, a boat, a possible letter-form with a terminal serif and a number of miscellaneous other marks. On the reverse, and laid out on a different alignment to the obverse, are a series of letter-forms, a cruciform-pattern formed of four ringed shafts and further miscellaneous marks. Palaeographic aspects of the stone are considered above (Forsyth & Tedeschi, Chapter 6.3.3).

Obverse

FIGURE A: complete figure in profile but with face turned to viewer and stooped, roughly 65mm tall. The face is rounded and the eyes and mouth are formed by small cut ovals. There is a rectangular motif on the forehead and, above the figure's left ear, traces of what may be a cap or similar head-covering. Unlike the other figures on the stone, Figure A does not appear to be dressed in a mail shirt, wearing instead what appears to be a plain skirt or tunic tied at the waist, marked by a simple incised line. Below this there is a prominent hatched band. Across the lower part of the tunic there is a loose curvilinear motif, possibly a chain, which continues to the right to join with a small box-like feature (see below). The legs are cross-hatched, possibly representing cloth leg-bindings, whilst a single incised line immediately to the left of the figure may represent the outline of a cloak or cape. The right arm (or possibly both arms) sweep forward towards Figure B; around and hanging from the wrist(s) there is a small box-like feature. The 'box' is roughly 6 × 6mm, tapering slightly to the top. It is bisected by a horizontal line and, in the centre of the upper panel, there is a prominent point or 'dot'. A possible rope or chain-like device appears to link the figure's hands to the prominent figure, Figure B, to the right.

FIGURE B: complete figure, 100mm tall, with long swept-back, shoulder-length hair, a moustache and whiskers on his chin. Below a prominent forehead there is a triangular-shaped eye-brow over a small wedge-shaped eye. To the left is the ear, defined by a small spiral, whilst to the right is a stubby nose or snout. The neck and body of the figure are covered in a long coat of mail, extending perhaps to the mid-thigh or knee and represented by a series of small circles and scales. The outline of what may be part of the figure's right arm, bent at the elbow, and his hand can also be identified. The leg on the left side of the figure is cross-hatched; the other is partly hatched and partly filled with small circles. This may be a device to represent mail or, possibly, to suggest depth (Tobias Capwell, pers comm). A cross-hatched belt or strap hangs between the legs (cf Figure D).

FIGURE C: extant from his feet to just below the shoulders. The figure, like his companion to the left, is dressed in a long coat of mail that extends roughly to the mid-thigh. The mail links or scale in the upper part of the body are aligned horizontally ('c-shaped') whilst those below are arranged vertically ('u-shaped'), suggesting perhaps that the upper part of the body is leaning forwards. The legs appear to have cloth leg-bindings and at the broken edge of the stone there are traces of an extended arm holding what is possibly the shaft of a spear – or perhaps a bow, given the figure's stance and the attendant implications for the alignment of the mail.

FIGURE D: a fragmentary figure, located at the broken edge of the stone. The left leg is marked by a very thin and carefully incised cross-hatched leg, plus shoe; only part of the figure's right leg can be discerned. Meanwhile, at the top of the legs, there is the very bottom of what is probably a mail shirt; a plain rectangle, similar to the feature seen on Figure B, hangs between the legs.

BOAT: below Figures C and D is a sketch of an oared vessel. It is depicted in profile with an almost vertical stern to the left and, to the right, a sweeping bow. Extending from the stern and lying behind the vessel are what appear to be a pair of steering oars and, at the stern-post itself, there are three or four upright strokes. These may represent mountings for figure-heads or banners or, alternatively, the housing for the mast when un-stepped or not in use (D Atkinson, pers comm). At the bow are two further projections, possibly part of the stem structure or its decoration, whilst towards the centre of the vessel there is what appears to be a square sail or covered space marked by diagonal hatching.

Eleven oars are indicated along the lower or starboard edge of the vessel and a possible twelfth oar, in fact a pair, comprising a nearer, larger example to starboard and a smaller example to port, is shown at the bow in a raised position, possibly depicting the oars in the process of being shipped or deployed. The upper parts of the oars are depicted by a series of simple incised lines; however, the lower parts of the oars and the oar blades are depicted in outline and are deflected towards the stern, a device that was presumably intended to convey the idea of the vessel's movement through the water.

OTHER MARKS: (1) to the left of Figure A there is a small incised cross and triangle motif, 5mm high and

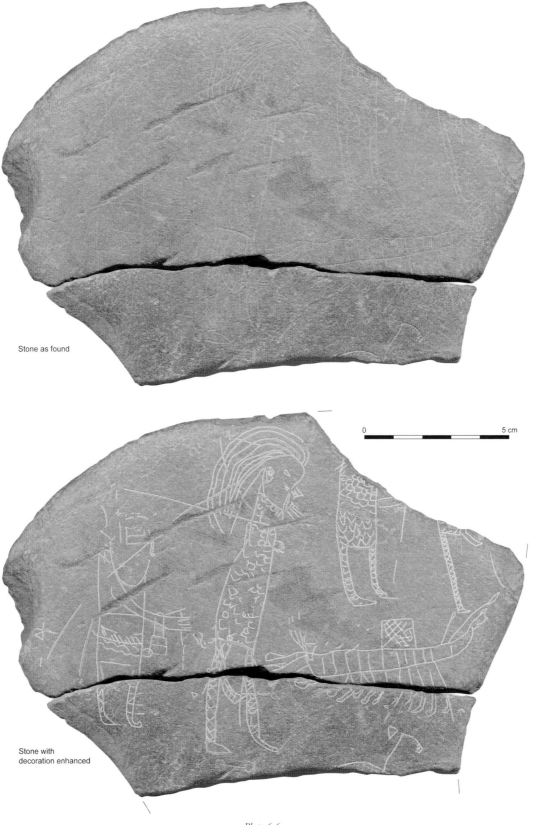

0   5 cm

Stone as found

Stone with
decoration enhanced

Plate 6.6
The 'armoured warriors' slab (IS.46)

up to 8mm wide. (2) across Figures A and B is an incised 'crossing-out' mark. One stroke extends from near the bottom left-hand edge of the stone and crosses the face of Figure A before terminating in the 'hair' of Figure B. A second, shorter stroke extends from just above Figure A and crosses into the 'neck' of Figure B. At roughly the same point is a third short stroke which extends upwards, terminating just above and to the left of Figure B and next to what appears to be a small incised cross. It is clear, however, that this is an incidental scratch mark rather than a deliberate construction. (3) below Figure B are faint traces of two small circles joined by a straight line. (4) below the boat there is a prominent right-angled line with a serif, which joins with the arc of a circle where the stone is broken. It may represent the remains of an upright letter 'd' with a cap and wedge-shaped serif. The bowl is lightly hatched (Forsyth & Tedeschi, above). (5) the latest marks on the stone comprise a series of probable plough-marks, aligned bottom-left to top-right and cutting across Figures A and B. The marks are up to 40mm long, 3mm wide and 1mm deep. Interestingly, all are located on the upper part of the stone, perhaps indicating that the slab was already broken when it acquired this latest group of marks.

Reverse

Located across the bottom right-hand edge of the stone, and on a different alignment to the scene on the obverse, are a series of letters, *aAb* (Forsyth & Tedeschi, above). At the top left edge of the stone there is a cruciform design formed of four ring-headed shafts, not dissimilar to ringed-pins, laid head-to-head. The three complete shafts are 23–26mm long and up to 2mm wide; the ring-heads up to 8mm across. Between the letter-group and the cruciform design are two pairs of incised lines, up to 2mm apart and 25mm long, as well as a series of curvilinear and other marks.

Dating

The principal dating evidence for the stone comes from the letter-forms, essentially a rounded Insular minuscule with a half-uncial 'oc' –*a*. Although it is difficult to date short fragments of simple, informal lettering, the roundness of the script and the use of the half-uncial 'oc' –*a* form is suggestive of a date prior to *c* AD 800 rather than much after (Forsyth & Tedeschi, above). This is reinforced, in a general way, by the spread of radiocarbon dates from the site and might also be indicated by the ringed-pin or

cruciform motif on the reverse of the stone (Fanning 1983, 325).

Details of the costume and armour could also be accommodated within a similar chronology. On the basis of the mail coats alone, for example, the slab could conceivably date from any time between the 8th and the 14th centuries (Tobias Capwell, pers comm). A much later date within this range, however, may be indicated by some of the specific detail of the armour. A 13th-century date, for example, would be indicated if the cross-hatching and groups of circles on the legs of Figures B–D are taken to represent mail leg armour or *chausses*. Mail *chausses* were known as early as the 11th century and some of the earliest representations occur in the Bayeux Tapestry. In Scotland and Scandinavia, however, mail *chausses* do not seem to have come into general circulation until the 13th century (Tobias Capwell, pers comm).

It is not possible to reconcile these conflicting chronologies without making a special pleading for or against the dating of script-forms or types of armour, or abandoning the idea that the carvings on the two sides of the stone are broadly contemporary and were made by the same person using, in all likelihood, the same tool. To get beyond this impasse we have to consider some other aspects of the stone.

Interpretation

One of the keys to understanding the scene is the distinction that the carver makes between the mail-suited and presumably armed figures (Figures B–D) to the right and the armour-less, unarmed figure (Figure A) to the left. These differences are emphasised by the erect, 'head-up' and dominant stance of the former, and the slightness, stooped and 'head-down' form of the latter. The group to the right are clearly identifiable as warriors and the event being depicted looks very much like slave-raiding or a hostage-taking, but what particular type of non-combatant is intended by the figure to the left? The slightness of Figure A may suggest a youth or possibly an ecclesiastical figure. Central to this interpretation is the identification of the box- or 'hand-bag-'like feature that is suspended from the figure's wrists.

The feature could represent a padlock or shackle, although there seems to be little to prevent the figure from slipping his hands out of the device. Significantly, perhaps, the object appears to be attached to Figure A himself, by means of a chain at its bottom left-hand corner, rather than to the character to the right, which might be expected if the box-like feature were

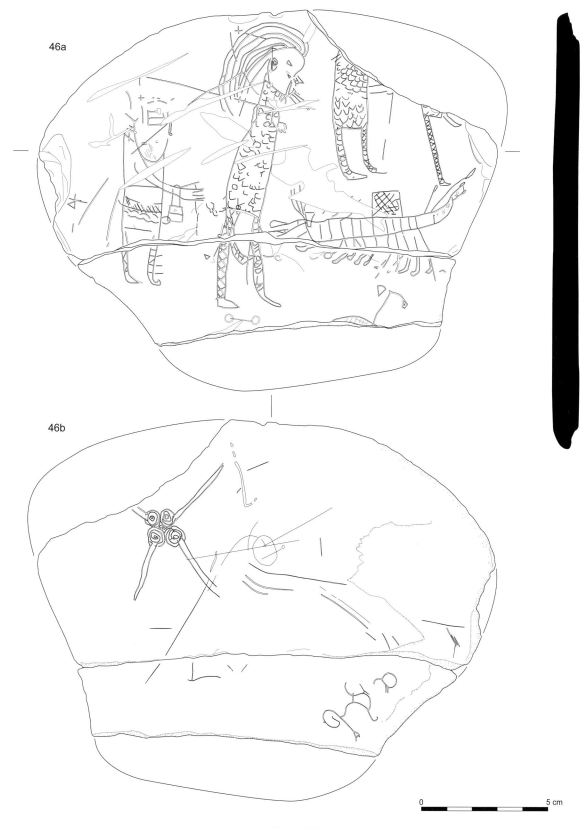

46a

46b

Figure 6.27
IS.46 SF404 and SF587 (armoured warriors and boat)

a restraining device. It may be the case that Figure B is leading Figure A by a rope that is slung over his right-shoulder (hence the bent arm and the small raised hand or fist) or that Figure A is attached by a rope or chain that extends from the bottom of Figure B's mail-shirt. Neither, unfortunately, is entirely clear. What is clear, however, is that the 'hand-bag' belongs with Figure A and there is the implication, in its physical attachment, that it was an item of some importance. Furthermore, the fact that the person who incised these lines has even bothered to include it in the scene might suggest that the object 'defines' its carrier in the same way that the spear or bow, together with the mail-shirts, define the other members in the story.

Alternative interpretations of the 'hand-bag' place it firmly in an ecclesiastical context. It could, for example, represent a book-satchel. A leather example, previously thought to be a leather jerkin, has recently been recognised among the finds from Loch Glashan crannog (Crone & Campbell 2005, 81–5). Meanwhile, pictorial representations are known from Papil and Bressay in Shetland (eg Wainwright 1962, Plates XII and XIII), as well as from elsewhere (Meehan 2005). It is clear, however, from these examples that the satchels were carried over the shoulder and were significantly larger than the Inchmarnock 'hand-bag'.

Its size and the fact that it is shown suspended from the figure's wrists might suggest that the feature is a bell. Examples of small Celtic bells and bell-shrines are, of course, well-known (Bourke 1980; Bourke 1983). An alternative interpretation, given its slightly tapered form, and the one favoured here is that it represents a contemporary depiction of a house-shaped shrine or reliquary. Many examples of these objects are known from Ireland and the Continent, as well as from Scotland and they are one of the defining artefacts of the Gaelic ecclesiastical cultural milieu. They take the form of small models of hip-roofed buildings with prominent gable finials and applied metal decoration, occasionally with inlaid precious stones and enamel. As has long been noted, these house-shaped shrines bear a strong resemblance to the depiction of the Temple of Jerusalem in the 8th-century Book of Kells (f.202V), to the finials of 9th- and 10th-century sculptured Irish high crosses and to some surviving Irish stone oratories (Ryan 1989, 129). The Inchmarnock example lacks any obvious finials. The slight taper on the upper panel, however, may reflect a hip-roofed structure whilst the central point on the same field may represent an applied decoration or mount.

Slave-raiding or relic procession?

A *prima facie* case can be made that the figurative scene represents slave-raiding or hostage-taking and the capture of an ecclesiastical figure by a group of armed and sea-going warriors. In light of the historical evidence and the many references in the Irish annals and other records, there is a natural tendency to assume that the image is that of a Viking raiding party (Lowe 2007). However, as Katherine Forsyth has suggested, we should not rule out the possibility that the image is describing something quite different; with the armed warriors as protectors, not pirates, and with the whole scene describing the departure on circuit of the ecclesiastical figure and the reliquary. As she has suggested, this would have been a major event in the life of an island monastery like Inchmarnock (Katherine Forsyth, pers comm).

Certainly, there is little evidence for Figure A having been bound in any way and, as noted above, the evidence for a rope slung over the right-shoulder of Figure B, or for a rope or chain extending from the bottom of Figure B's mail-shirt is poorly defined. Furthermore, given the attention to detail that is present elsewhere on the slab, it could be argued that we might have reasonably expected to see Figure A bound in neck-chains or leg-irons or some such similar device. The way in which the reliquary is held might also suggest procession rather than 'imprisonment'.

Against the idea of the 'ecclesiastical relic circuit', however, we would have to offer two, not-unrelated observations. One concerns the stooped posture of Figure A, his relative size and the subservient position that he adopts in relation to Figure B. The second concerns the central role that is accorded to Figure B and the way in which he – and not Figure A, despite his reliquary – dominates the scene as the largest character and focal point of the image. One might wonder, for example, why the ecclesiastical figure was not given this position and size on the stone.

The scene may represent a contemporary display of a contemporary event or one that is historical. In either event, however, it is likely that the 'display-forms' (the nature of the dress and the type of boat adopted) are local, based on types that would have been familiar to the scene's creator.

The purpose of the stone is less clear but its very form, as a simple water-worn pebble that was picked up off the beach, suggests that it was a piece of ephemera. Given the evidence elsewhere on the site for training and instruction, it may have been used as a teaching aid for story-telling.

Figure 6.28
Figurative scenes and other sketches (IS.47–54)

IS.47. SF635 + SF747 (Figure 6.28)

Contexts 4001 (Phase 3) and 4510 (Phase 2)

Description

Sub-rectangular fragment of a dark grey dressed slate board formed of two conjoining pieces, recovered in 2002 and 2003. The fragments were found roughly 1.2m apart The larger fragment (SF747), from Phase 2 deposits, was found some 80mm below the level of the piece (SF635) found in 2002. The left-hand edge of the slab has been trimmed square and both faces are smooth, with some evidence of surface-flaking. Overall, it measures 150 × 95mm and is 7mm thick.

HUMAN FIGURE: incised outline of a fragmentary human figure, 47mm tall, located at the broken edge of the stone. Like those on IS.46, the figure is in profile facing to the right and is extant from the feet to possibly just below the shoulders, although there is no trace of either arm on the surviving fragment. The legs are flexed and the upper part of the body appears to be leaning forwards.

MOTIF: below the figure there is a series of less deeply incised lines which terminate in a square frame with sides 17mm long, inside of which is an incised swastika, its upper arm set to the left. At the corner of the frame are indications of an incised 'loop' or 'handle'.

MOTIF: below the swastika is a sub-triangular motif up to 14mm across and resembling a shell or spiral, infilled with a series of perpendicular cut lines.

OTHER MARKS: incised underneath the sub-triangular motif and continuing to the edge of the stone is a pair of parallel lines, 3mm apart.

Comparanda

Larger versions of the swastika motif, up to 50mm across (with two complete and one partially preserved

Plate 6.7
Slate-board fragment with incised sketch of horses (IS.48)

example, all of them with their upper arm facing to the right) are present on the reverse of the large cross-of-arcs incised slab (SF406: EMS.14). A closer parallel is offered by a fragment of incised slate that was recovered from the Cathedral Hill excavations in Armagh in 1968. It depicts three swastika motifs, the upper arms on two of them left-facing, with each set within a square field or frame, the largest with sides roughly 8mm long (O'Meadhra 1979, 29, plates 1 and 2, Cat 7A). The line-and-bar motif on IS.55 may represent a poorly conceived or executed version of the symbol.

There are no immediate parallels for the sub-triangular motif. It may, however, represent a crude representation or a poorly executed version of a triquetra knot (cf example incised on a piece of slate from Beal Boru ringfort, Ballyvally, County Clare: O'Meadhra 1979, 34, plates 3 and 4, Cat. 15B7).

IS.48. SF718 (Figure 6.28; Plate 6.7)
Context 4059, Phase 1

Description
Sub-rectangular fragment of a dark grey dressed slate board, 94 × 75mm and 6mm thick, with a surviving edge along the top of the stone and incised figures on both faces. Only the upper surface, however, is smooth. The piece was recovered from a ground surface which was cut by features that are associated with the structures of Phase 1.

Obverse
QUADRUPEDS AND HUMAN FIGURE: incised outline sketches of five quadrupeds, almost certainly to be identified as horses by their pricked ears, long tails and manes. Set in profile and facing to the right, each is roughly 25mm across and 15mm high. The legs of the animals terminate in small circles, representing hooves, and the creatures are shown in a grazing position, with the end of their angular snouts on a level with their hooves. A rectangular feature on the snout of the creature at the upper right-hand edge of the stone may represent its mouth or part of its harness or bit. Astride the horse at the bottom-left of the group is a crude stick-man figure, in profile facing right. Its foot, leg and torso is marked by a single incised line; a single arm, reaching forward to the base of the horse's neck, is similarly depicted. The head, meanwhile, is sub-triangular with a single round eye; on the back of the head is a crude hairstyle, marked by a series of scratched lines.

Reverse
QUADRUPEDS: incised outline of another horse-like creature together with, below it, a single incised wavy line, marking the beginnings of another. Both sketch-forms are set at right-angles to the figures on the obverse.

Discussion
The horse-forms and the simple stick-man display a certain naivety and crudity, and the whole piece has about it a certain child-like quality. Indeed, the piece may be the work of a child or a young adult whose writing or drawing skills were not fully developed.

The purpose of the sketch is not clear. It may simply be a 'doodle' or an observational sketch of a group of grazing horses. Alternatively, the sketches may represent trial pieces for the construction and treatment of a stylised letter M and the repetitive nature of the image, on both sides of the stone, possibly reinforces this. In either event, the addition of the elemental stick-man is a humorous personal touch, akin to the drolleries that are present in some of the early Insular illuminated manuscripts (Rynne 1994), that would not have been out of place in a monastic schoolhouse or scriptorium.

A similar form, albeit larger and possibly set out over a grid, is displayed on IS.49.

IS.49. SF595 (Figure 6.28)
Context 4001, Phase 3

Description
Sub-triangular fragment of grey slate, 75 × 70mm and 5mm thick, broken on all edges, the surface of its incised face heavily spalled. The fragment was recovered from a Phase 3 deposit, some 2.5m to the south of IS.48 with which it shares a possibly similar sketch-form.

POSSIBLE ANIMAL FORM: incised outline of possible creature marked by an elongated snout similar to that displayed on IS.48. The design is set over a lightly incised rectilinear lattice formed of cells with sides roughly 10mm long.

Discussion
Only one end of the creature, if correctly identified, survives, the other end lost through spalling of the flaky surface. The sketch, when complete and if similarly proportioned, would have been roughly twice as large as those on IS.48. The underlying lattice

possibly represents a scaling device for the resizing of such sketch-forms.

IS.50. SF722 (Figure 6.28)
Context 461, Phase 1

Description
Fragment of flat sub-oval slate beach pebble, 65 × 58mm and 2–5mm thick, with part surviving original edge. The fragment was recovered from a Phase 1 ground surface which was subsequently cut by Grave G11, part of the Grave Complex in the north part of the excavated area.

Obverse
POSSIBLE BOAT FORM: series of lightly incised lines forming in outline the bow or stern section of a possible double-ended, clinker-built vessel. Possible oars with circular oar blades extend diagonally across the vessel from the left-hand margin of the stone and a triangular flag or banner appears to extend from the tip of the stem or sternpost.

Reverse
Miscellaneous incised lines; no coherent form.

Discussion
The boat graffiti from the site are discussed by Atkinson in Appendix 3.

IS.51. SF744 (Figure 6.28)
Context 4510, Phase 2

Description
Largely intact oval slate beach pebble, 110 × 80mm and 7mm thick. The fragment was recovered from the fill of Linear Feature 4469, possibly a drain.

BOAT AND OARSMEN: palimpsest of lightly incised lines representing stylised depiction of a small vessel and four or five oarsmen. The orientation of the oarsmen suggests that the bow is to the left and the stern to the right. The bow is particularly stylised, comprising a backward sweeping prow with a scroll or swan-neck terminal.

Discussion
The boat graffiti from the site are discussed by Atkinson in Appendix 3.

IS.52. SF588 (Figure 6.28)
Context 4001, Phase 3

Description
Sub-rectangular fragment of smooth grey slate, 90 × 50mm and 7mm thick, recovered from area adjacent to Linear Feature 4226. The straight edge to the stone is a natural break, coincident with a quartz vein.

WEAPON: distinct lentoid-shaped motif, 10mm long, with attached line representing shaft of probable spear.

OTHER MARKS: across the opposite end of the stone is a pair of parallel lines, 4mm apart and hatched. Overlying this is what appears to be a crossing-out mark; along the left-hand edge of the piece are faint traces of one or more incised circles, 4mm in diameter.

IS.53. SF824 (Figure 6.28)
Context 4312, Phase 2

Description
Two conjoining fragments forming near complete lozenge-shaped slate lamina, 198 × 94mm and 7mm thick, recovered from the medieval ground surface near the north-west corner of the church.

WEAPON: the principal face of the stone is covered with a palimpsest of lightly scratched lines, depicting what is possibly a sword-handle, with a rectangular grip, guard and pommel.

IS.54. SF1094 (Figure 6.28; Plate 6.8)
Context 4605, Phase 3

Description
Sub-rectangular fragment of grey slate, 80 × 55mm and 4m thick, smooth on both faces and probably originally part of a formal slate-board. No original edges, however, survive. The fragment was recovered from the fill of a post-medieval grave (Grave G110), part of the late children's cemetery, located up against the south exterior wall-face of the church. Coin-evidence (SF1240) from a stratigraphically-related earlier grave (Grave G123; context 4643) indicates that Grave G110 was inserted some time after 1632–9.

BUILDING: part of an aisled basilican-type building, almost certainly a church, is depicted in sketch-profile in lightly incised freehand lines. Two complete and two incomplete round-headed arches are shown, formed by columns with ornate capitals. Behind the right-hand column is a finely-drawn face, in profile facing left; behind the column to the left there are

Plate 6.8
Slate-board fragment with incised sketch of aisled basilican-style church (IS.54)

indistinct traces of one or two further figures. Above the main arcade is a line of pointed-arched openings, corresponding to an upper gallery. Above this is a tiled roof, marked by cross-hatching. Two lines, possibly representing the beginnings of towers, extend above the roof-line. On the reverse, there is a palimpsest of miscellaneous incised lines.

Discussion

Dating of the piece is problematical and the circumstances of its discovery, from redeposited material comprising the fill of a post-medieval grave, are not helpful. The form of the sketch bears a superficial similarity with the way in which canon tables are depicted in illuminated manuscripts of the 8th century and later, such as those, for example, in the *Lindisfarne Gospels* (f.14v: *c* 700), the *Canterbury Codex Aureus* (f.6v: *c* 750) or the *Book of Kells* (f.4r: *c* 800). It may belong, therefore, with the way in which buildings were depicted in Late Antiquity.

In terms, however, of the structural detail of the building, particularly with reference to the way in which it is depicted as a sectional profile, it more

closely resembles the way in which buildings are portrayed in the early 10th-century *Athelstan Psalter* in, for example, the miniature of the Christ-in-majesty scene.

A similar drawing style is also present in the early 11th-century *Echternach Codex Aureus* in, for example, the 'Presentation' or 'Temptation of Christ' scenes, as well as elsewhere in the manuscript. Like the Inchmarnock fragment, the human figures in the scene are shown in a large format that is not in scale with the adjacent buildings. A similar approach to the depiction of buildings is also evident in the late 11th-century Bayeux Tapestry, in for example the depiction of Harold's Church at Bosham.

On balance, therefore, a 10th- or 11th-century date may be indicated for the Inchmarnock fragment. It presumably represents a sketch-form of a building that the artist had seen or had had described to him; in either event, there is no suggestion, of course, that such a building was ever constructed on Inchmarnock itself.

Other examples of incised stones with figurative scenes and other sketches (catalogued elsewhere)

IS.5. SF533 (Figure 6.16)

Context 4001, Phase 3

Description

Sub-triangular fragment of large flat slate, 240 × 130mm and 10mm thick, with traces of its original edge surviving in places along two sides. Gaming board (Ritchie, Chapter 6.3.2) with sketch of boat at top left corner and curvilinear motif at bottom right.

BOAT: incised outline of one end of an oared vessel, 25mm long, with two steering oars extending from the stern to the right. The boat graffiti from the site are considered in detail by Atkinson in Appendix 3.

IS.30. SF1087 (Figure 6.29 and Figure 6.30)

Context 4245, Phase 3

Description

Large trapezoidal fragment of mid-grey slate, 730 × 240mm and 30mm thick, recovered from the disturbed cemetery soil (Phase 3) immediately outside the south wall of the church. The slab is incised with several gaming boards, including examples of merels and alquerque (Ritchie, Chapter 6.3.2), as

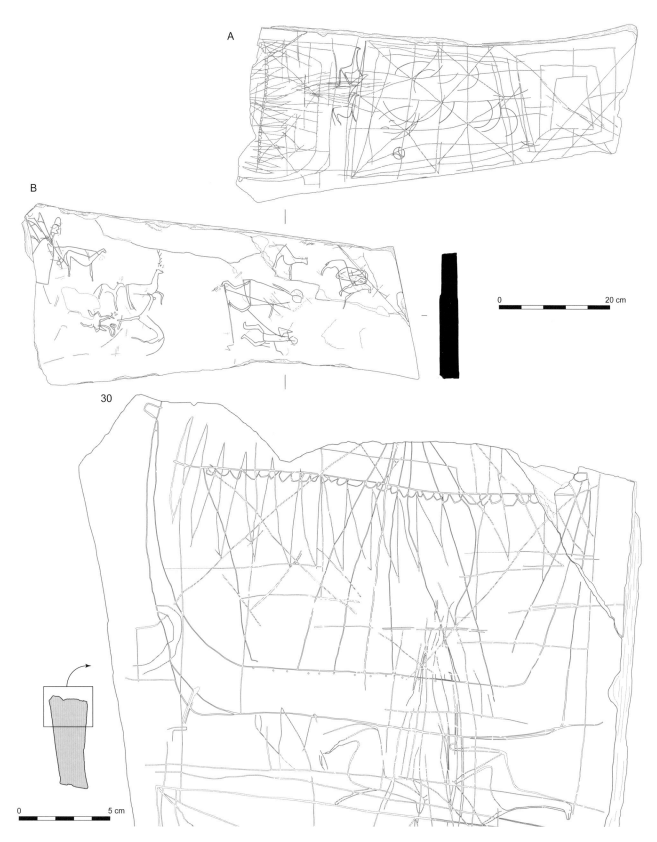

Figure 6.29
The hunting scene and other graffiti on IS.30

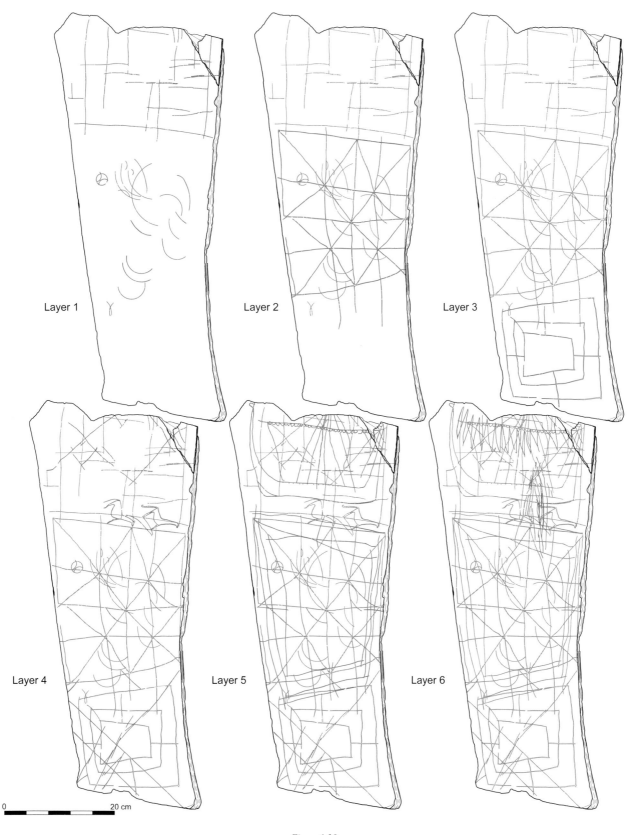

Layer 1

Layer 2

Layer 3

Layer 4

Layer 5

Layer 6

0   20 cm

Figure 6.30
Phasing scheme for IS.30

well as multiple incised motifs including a Highland galley, animals, human figures and compass-drawn circles.

BOAT: located at top of slab on Side A is the incised outline, in profile, of a double-ended vessel, 245mm long, with a high stem and sternpost, identifiable as a typical West Highland galley. Twelve oar ports, mast, yard with furled sail, rigging, and decorative adornments on ends of stem and sternposts are also evident. The boat graffiti from the site are examined in detail by Atkinson in Appendix 3.

HUNTING SCENE: located at the upper end of Side B but perpendicular to the galley on the other side is a hunting scene. At the broken left-hand edge of the slab is a deeply incised, 'bottle-' or 'bell-shaped' figure with a long neck, in profile facing to the right. Over his left shoulder is a long-handled implement, possibly an axe; to right a line, marking a leash, extends to the neck of a small quadruped, probably a dog. The dog is also deeply-incised, with a long neck, prominent belly and a lightly-incised tail with a curly tip. Set below and to the right of the leashed dog is a lightly-incised stag, in profile, facing to the right. The antlers (35mm long) are depicted by a curving line from which emerge five tines. The rear legs of the animal are straight; its front legs are raised as if jumping.

Faint traces of a second dog, up to 50mm long and 50mm tall, in profile facing to the right, can be identified immediately behind the stag, biting its rear. The surface is badly flaked but the legs and neck survive. Meanwhile, a third dog is located underneath the stag, seemingly biting the underside of the animal. An amorphous shape to the left of the two dogs may represent the stag's entrails.

QUADRUPEDS, HORSE AND RIDER: located across the lower end of Side B, beyond a natural split in the rock where the surface has sheared off, is a probable dog and (to the right of that) a horse and rider. There is no indication that they formed part of the hunting scene at the opposite end of the slab.

The dog-like animal, 50mm tall with a rounded belly, a long tail and short ears, stands on the natural fault-line in the rock. To the right and at an angle is an incised image of a figure on horseback, 70mm tall. The rider has a trapezoidal body, a triangular head and sits noticeably forward on the horse, at the base of the animal's neck.

Meanwhile, on Side A there are two further long-necked quadrupeds. They lie just below the galley and

are perpendicular to it. Like the animals on Side B, they probably depict hunting dogs.

HUMAN FIGURES: across the centre of Side B and at right-angles to the adjacent hunting scene are the faint traces of two human figures, up to 105mm tall. The left-hand figure appears to be in profile, facing to the right; the other is possibly a frontal view of a jumping figure.

COMPASS-DRAWN CIRCLES: located across the central part of Side A is a large number of compass-drawn circles, centre-points and arcs of circles. There is one very distinct complete compass-drawn circle (27mm diameter), together with intersecting arcs of the same diameter, just below the primary merels board at the top of the slab.

Discussion

IS.30 is one of the largest worked stones from the site; it is certainly the most extensively decorated. Indeed, it brings together onto one stone many of the motifs and incised designs that are evident elsewhere in the assemblage. Analysis under a microscope of the various incised lines on Side A has enabled a rough phasing or sequence to the palimpsest to be constructed (Figure 6.30); the phases are described here as 'Layers', to avoid confusion with the overall site-phasing.

The time-interval between these layers is difficult to gauge. Whilst the compass-drawn circles could represent an early or primary use of the stone, the time-interval between the later motifs (particularly the gaming-boards) is likely, however, to be counted in hours or days rather than months or years. In other words, the various designs, with the possible exception of the compass-drawn circles, are likely to be closely contemporary.

The earliest features on the slab ('Layer' 1) appear to be the compass-drawn circles and/or the uppermost merels board, followed by an alquerque board and another one for merels ('Layers' 2 and 3). In 'Layer' 4 a series of diagonal lines, in part continuing the axes of the earlier alquerque board, and two small quadrupeds (similar to the hunting dogs on Side B) were carved into the surface. This was followed, in 'Layer' 5, by what looks like a very crude (and unplayable – Ritchie, Chapter 6.3.2) merels board, together with a simple but competent sketch of a Highland galley. A series of scoring out marks comprise 'Layer' 6.

The boat graffito, although not closely datable, indicates a date in the later medieval period. Very similar vessels are depicted on a series of late gravestones, typical of the monumental sculpture of Argyll and the west Highlands and dating to the period 14th to 16th century (Steer & Bannerman 1977). Interestingly, among this same group are several examples on which hunting scenes are also featured, including examples from Kintyre (Keils, Kilmory, Kilchenzie and Saddell) and Iona. The example on the shaft of the MacMillan Cross, at Kilmory in Knapdale shows a hunter and two dogs chasing a stag (Wilson 1857).

Hunting scenes of dogs and stags, typically known as the 'hart-and-hound' motif, is a long-lived and popular Christian motif symbolising the conversion of sinners or the soul in pursuit of Christ and salvation. The theme appears on Mediterranean mosaics as early as the 5th century and, in England, it has been identified as a feature of Viking-period and later workmanship (Alcock 1998, 521; Alcock 2003, xxvi, 307; Bailey 1980, 174). The earliest datable example of the hart-and-hound motif from the west Highlands and Islands is probably the decorated slab from Kildonnan on Eigg, dating to the 9th century (Fisher 2001, 93–4). Examples are also preserved among the graffiti on the walls of the King's Cave on Arran (Fisher 2001, 69). Significantly, the same motif (similarly incised on a piece of slate) is also found at St Blane's Church at Kingarth, Bute (Anderson 1900, figs 14–16). Its appearance, in sketch-form, in an informal setting on a slab from Inchmarnock, some 500 or 600 years later, confirms the long-lived popularity of the motif; meanwhile, its association with the boat graffito suggests that the two sides of the slab may have been carved in imitation of the local monumental sculpture.

The function of the slab itself is unclear. On the basis of its location, shape and the circumstances of its discovery, it was assumed to have originally formed part of a stone-lined cist that had subsequently been reused as the 'compendium games-board' and as a surface for other graffiti. The identification of IS.76 as a possible stone 'table-top', however, suggests that IS.30 itself may also have originally been part of the furniture or fittings of a building on the site. If so, the fact that it has been worked on both sides would imply that the slab must have been easily movable. In any event, the absence of mortar clearly indicates that the slab was not used in the construction of the church.

6.3.42 Curvilinear and rectilinear motifs

There are six stones with curvilinear motifs. These include examples of simple interlace and cable patterns, as well as various types of spiral motif. The example on one of the gaming boards (IS.2) is particularly important as it appears to have been cut by two different hands, one more confident than the other. It is identified as an exemplum-and-copy teaching piece. Significantly, the incised lines of the cable motif overlie and thus post-date the grid of the gaming board, providing an insight into what we might recognise as a leisure activity, although it is not possible to say, of course, whether these were pursued inside or outwith the monastic school-room.

There are eight stones with rectilinear motifs. These include examples of fret or step patterns, as well as triangle, rectangle, square, diamond and chevron motifs.

The earliest *in situ* pieces in the group are IS.57, which looks like a practice piece for the laying out of a filled border, and IS.36, the 'adeptus' fragment with its ogham inscription (Forsyth & Tedeschi, above) and the conjoined S-spiral and C-spiral motifs. Both fragments were recovered from Phase 1 features and deposits in the northern part of the excavated area.

Curvilinear motifs

IS.55. SF417 (Figure 6.31)
Context 400, Phase 6

Description

Oval, quartz-veined slate pebble, 120 × 85mm and 11mm thick, roughly worked to the round by chipping of its edges. Topsoil find. The reverse face of the stone is extensively flaked. On the better-preserved face are faint traces of five lightly incised spiral motifs set within a rectangular frame. Along the top edge of the frame there is a pelta motif, executed in a similar style to the adjacent spirals. Near the right-hand side of the frame, there is a more deeply cut line-and-bar motif, 5 × 5mm, possibly intended as a swastika. On the reverse are faint traces of a knotwork motif, formed of interlace bands, 2mm wide, part-removed by surface-flaking of the stone.

IS.56. SF589 (Figure 6.31)
Context 4001, Phase 3

Description

Sub-triangular spalled fragment of slate, 65 × 37mm and 4mm thick, with iron-staining on its upper surface. Towards one edge of the stone there is a small spiral

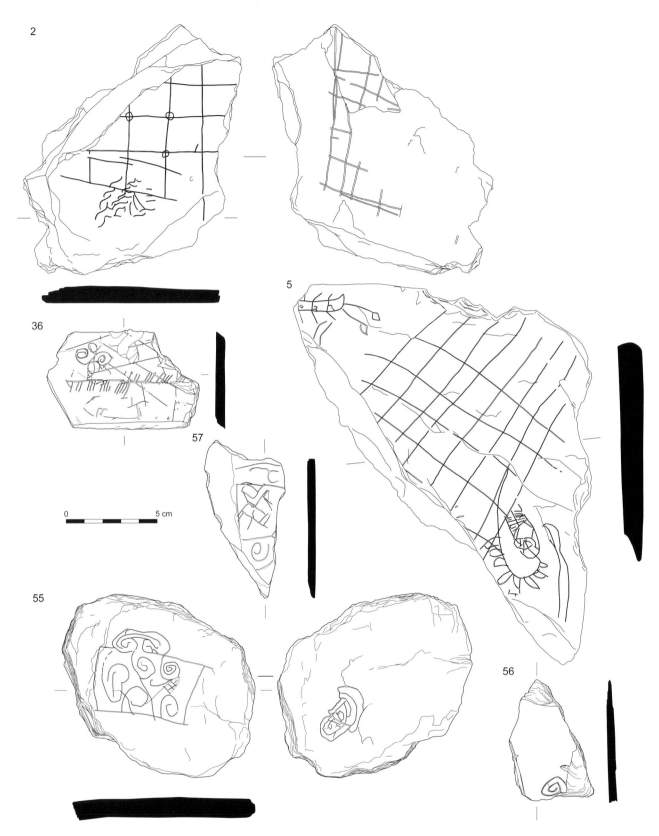

2

5

36

57

55

56

0   5 cm

Figure 6.31
Curvilinear motifs (IS.2, 5, 36 and 55–7)

motif, 14 × 10mm. The same motif also appears in the lower frame of IS.57 and as a flourish to the letter-forms on IS.43.

IS.57. SF679 (Figure 6.31)
Context 4076, Phase 1

Description

Sub-triangular fragment of slate, 70 × 45mm and 4mm thick, broken on all sides. The upper face is a dull light grey; the reverse darker and shinier. Three very obvious parallel quartz veins, together with a fourth at the top edge of the stone, are evident on both faces, although more prominent on the reverse. The fragment was recovered from the fill of the Phase 1 linear feature (4226) that marks the boundary between the early cemetery and the workshop area to the north.

Set within a rectangular frame, 29 × 20mm, is a simple interlace motif. In the lower frame, although only its upper part survives, there is a C-spiral motif, similar to those on IS.56 and IS.43, whilst across the upper edge of the stone is the Insular minuscule letter-form T. The same letter-form is also seen on the 'adeptus' (IS.36) and 'Dar-Í' (IS.37) fragments.

Other examples of incised stones with curvilinear motifs (catalogued elsewhere)

IS.2. SF403 (Figure 6.31)
Context 437, Phase 3

Description

Across the bottom edge and post-dating the carving of the gaming board (Ritchie, above) on Face A are a series of wavy lines. The left-hand group of five incised marks, set out in a shallow reverse-S form, create an outline cable motif. The incised lines have been cut with a controlled hand and are roughly equidistant and parallel to each other. This is in contrast to the group to the right which appears to be a less-confidently executed copy. Like the repeated text on IS.36, this fragment would appear to represent a teaching piece in the manner of exemplum-and-copy.

IS.5. SF533 (Figure 6.31)
Context 4001, Phase 3

Description

Gaming board (Ritchie, above) with sketch of boat at top left corner and curvilinear motif at bottom

right. The curvilinear motif comprises an oval with eight attached loops around its perimeter and a series of hatched fields along its open side. The motif (which possibly represents petals around the head of a flower, although precise parallels have not been identified) overlies and thus post-dates the gaming board.

IS.36 SF717 (Figure 6.31)
Context 4059, Phase 1

Description

Like IS.48 with its sketch-form 'horses' and IS.72 with its hatched rectangles, the 'adeptus' fragment was recovered from a ground surface which was cut by features that are associated with the structures of Phase 1. Next to the ogham inscription is a conjoined S-spiral and C-spiral motif, forming a curvilinear cross 9mm across.

Rectilinear motifs

IS.58. SF476 (Figure 6.32)
Context 400, Phase 6

Description

Near-complete rectangular slate-board, 213 × 105mm and 9mm thick, bevelled along its longer sides and trimmed square on its surviving end. Topsoil find. There is an incised margin at left and the outline of a triangular or diagonal fret pattern along its bottom left-hand edge.

IS.59. SF1127 (Figure 6.32)
Context 436, Phase 3

Description

Sub-rectangular fragment of grey slate, 105 × 85mm and 8mm thick, recut in antiquity. One edge, coincident with a 10mm diameter hole that has been drilled from both sides, is rough; the remaining three are smooth and abraded. Parallel to the longer edge of the fragment and continuing the full width of the stone in its present state (although the surface has spalled at one end) is an 11–15mm wide step-motif or key-pattern. A second narrower step-motif (7mm wide) lies roughly parallel to the recut edge and abuts the wider fret-pattern.

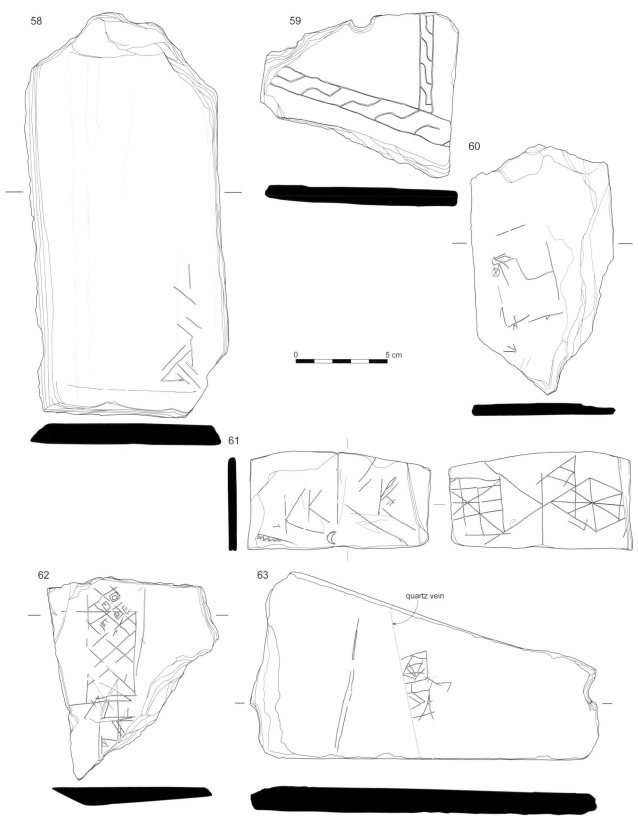

Figure 6.32
Rectilinear motifs (IS.58–63)

IS.60. SF550 (Figure 6.32)
Context 4001, Phase 3

Description
Sub-rectangular fragment of grey slate, 135 × 77mm and 5mm thick. The upper face is quartz veined with extensive surface flaking. Preserved on the surface are the faint remains of a rectangular frame, 50 × 30mm, inside of which is a single step or key-pattern. To one side there is a slightly more deeply cut diamond motif and a series of miscellaneous other marks.

IS.61. SF776 (Figure 6.32)
Context 4243, Phase 4

Description
Flat, sub-rectangular beach pebble, 98 × 52mm and 4mm thick, broken at both ends. Recovered from fill of Grave G43, located immediately to the north-west of the church. On the upper face is a series of incised rectilinear and triangular lattices or grids; on the reverse are several chevron or diagonal frets, along with a quarter-moon motif.

IS.62. SF580 (Figure 6.32)
Context 4001, Phase 3

Description
Flat, sub-rectangular fragment of grey slate, 120 × 90mm and 8mm thick, with an orange-brown deposit on its upper surface, the remains of a clay render which was used to 'reset' the slate and so allow further incised marks to be cut (Chapter 9.2.5). The long edge of the stone (possibly an original edge) is bevelled; the others, however, are all broken.

Incised on the face of the stone is a rectilinear frame, diagonally hatched. Several of the cells are filled with a rectangular straight-line spiral motif. Traces of a second rectilinear lattice, this time divided into squares, lie below at the broken edge of the stone.

IS.63. SF468 (Figure 6.32)
Context 400, Phase 6

Description
Flat, trapezoidal beach pebble, 190 × 98mm and 10mm thick. Topsoil find. Set against the line of a quartz vein are two rectilinear frames with sides 12–15mm long. The frames are filled with concentric rectangles and miscellaneous diagonal lines. Two close-set and roughly parallel incised lines lie adjacent.

Other examples of incised stones with rectilinear motifs (catalogued elsewhere)

IS.35. SF630 (Figure 6.20)
Context 4013, Phase 1

Description
Flat oval beach pebble, 148 × 116mm and 11mm thick, recovered from upper fill of enclosure ditch along with the Dar-Í stone (IS.37) and an incised outline cross (EMS.21: Fisher, Chapter 6.2.2 above). In addition to the various inscriptions to *Ernán* and the Latin word *Casa*, both sides of the stone are covered in various rectilinear motifs and symbols, including pentangles, triangles, saltire-in-rectangle and several examples of parallel incised lines forming larger squares and rectangles.

EMS.14. SF406 (Figure 6.4)
Context 422, Phase 2

Description
Sub-rectangular slate slab, 560 × 240mm and 30mm thick, with incised cross-of-arcs on front (Fisher, Chapter 6.2.2). On the reverse is a series of lightly-incised lines forming three roughly square panels, one on top of the other, and a mid-panel to one side. In the latter and in the top and bottom panels adjacent is a swastika; in the central panel there is a saltire cross, one quarter of which is filled with a single triangular straight-line spiral.

6.3.43 Miscellaneous and other incised slate fragments

The 'miscellaneous and other' category accommodates the rest of the incised slate assemblage and, perhaps not unnaturally, its members make up the largest group. There are, altogether, some 51 pieces of which 13 are illustrated and described in some detail as examples of the type. The rest, essentially pieces with less involved markings, are listed in Appendix 5

One of the pieces (IS.64), almost certainly, and another two (IS.65 and IS.66) possibly, may be associated with the writing of music. Another piece (IS.69) contains a palimpsest of incised marks, including what looks like a frontal view of a human figure. However, it is, perhaps, too faint to be sure –

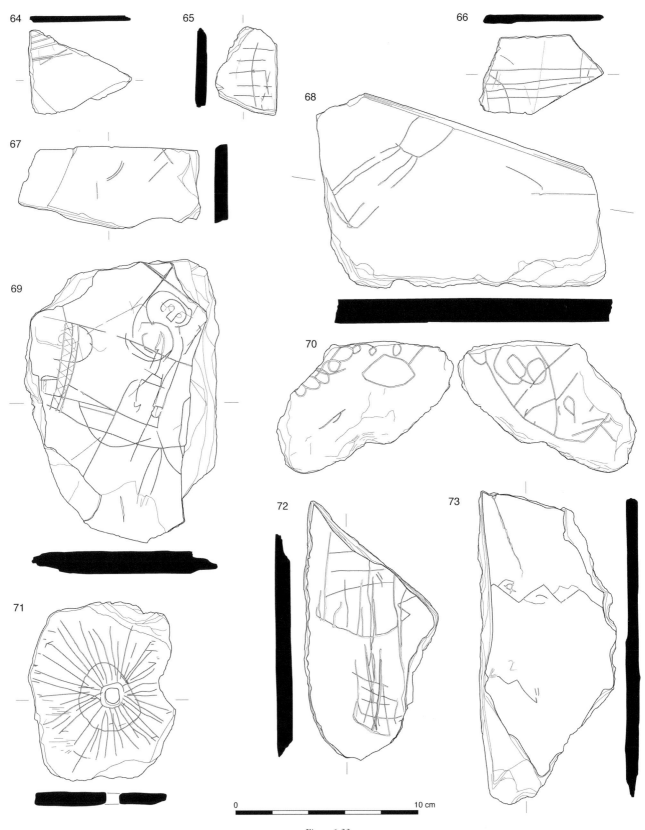

Figure 6.33
Miscellaneous and other incised motifs (IS.64–73)

hence its inclusion here rather than among the sketch-forms above.

Others in the group could be classified as 'doodles' or 'miscellanea', though that is not to say that they are necessarily less significant than those fragments with recognisable letter-forms, sketches or well-known geometrical or other motifs. The creation of 'doodles', for example, would have been very much concerned with learning how to control the stylus, as a prerequisite for learning how to create the various letter-forms and, ultimately, how to read and write. Interestingly, one of the pieces in the group (the graffiti-covered surface of IS.76) would appear to have been part of the furniture from some building on the site, possibly a workshop.

IS.64. SF1257 (Figure 6.33)
Context 448, Phase 2

Description

Triangular fragment of dark grey slate, 55 × 45mm and 3mm thick, broken on all three sides and recovered from the Phase 2 cemetery soil west of the church. Across the fragment are three deeply incised and parallel, ruled lines, 1mm wide and 4mm apart; a fourth line, not quite parallel and seemingly cut with a narrower point, lies below the group.

The original size of the stone and any pattern that the incised lines may have formed is not clear. They are too close together to be guidelines for the practice of letters and they may, therefore, simply represent part of a larger rectilinear design. The stone, however, recalls a similar piece of incised slate that was recovered from the monastic latrines at Battle Abbey in Sussex (Hare *et al* 1985); on it were incised a series of staves, each of five lines, for musical notation. A similar function may be proposed for this piece from Inchmarnock (cf IS.65 and IS.66).

IS.65. SF720 (Figure 6.33)
Context 4432, Phase 2

Description

Subtriangular fragment of smooth grey slate, 47 × 34mm and 5mm thick, with one surviving edge to right. It was recovered from the Phase 2 cemetery soil in the area to the north-west of the church, just to the south of the earlier workshops.

On the face and perpendicular to the surviving edge are five lightly incised parallel lines, 5–7mm apart. One or two transverse lines appear to be later additions to the stone. Like IS.64, although less precisely cut, the piece may represent a fragment of a music stave.

IS.66. SF757 (Figure 6.33)
Context 4233, Phase 3, fill of grave G33

Description

Sub-rectangular fragment of light grey slate, 65 × 40mm and 4mm thick, with major spalling on reverse. The fragment was recovered from the fill of Grave G33, at the south-west corner of the church. On the upper face are four lightly scratched and roughly parallel lines, 3–7mm apart, set perpendicular to two further lines 20mm apart. Across the corner of the fragment is an arc. Like IS.64 or IS.65, although less precisely cut and less carefully laid out than either, the piece may represent a fragment of a music stave.

IS.67. SF774 (Figure 6.33)
Context 4255, Phase 3, fill of grave G36

Description

Sub-rectangular fragment of mottled reddish grey slate, 98 × 43mm and 7mm thick with an original edge along top but broken elsewhere. The upper face of the stone is extremely smooth and polished, the reverse rough and flaked. The fragment was recovered next to the skull of the skeleton in Grave G36, immediately south of the church.

On the smooth face are several incised lines, not dissimilar to those seen elsewhere in the assemblage. They form no coherent pattern, although the pair of incised parallel curving lines, executed in freehand rather than compass-drawn, clearly indicate the handiwork of a competent scribe.

The possible significance of the stone lies less in its incised work than in the nature of the stone itself. This type of mottled red slate is unique among the assemblage and, given its polished surface, the possibility arises that the piece may have been incorporated into the furniture or fittings of the church.

IS.68 SF612 (Figure 6.33)
Context 4001, Phase 3

Description

Trapezoidal fragment of grey slate, 150 × 100m and 13mm thick. On the upper face and continuing to the broken edge of the stone is an incised oval, roughly 20mm across. Below the oval and appended to it are two thin incised rectangles, the ends of which are joined

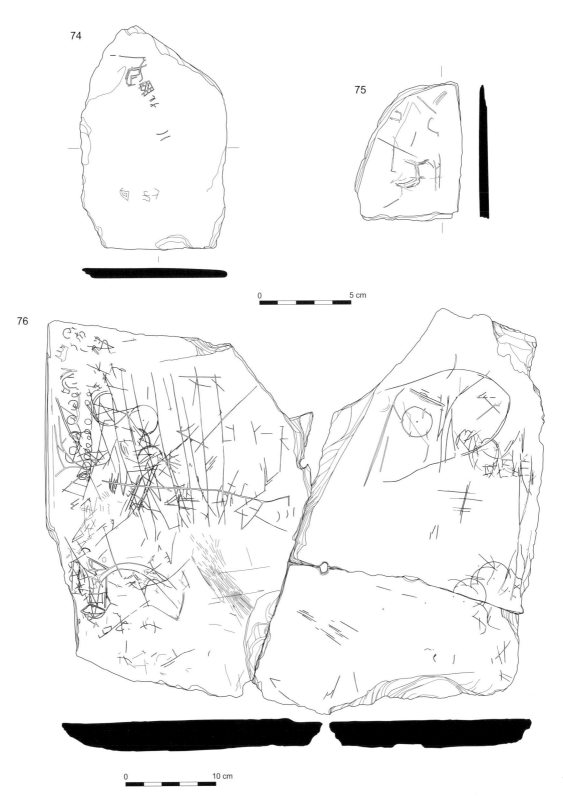

Figure 6.34
Miscellaneous and other incised motifs (IS.74–6)

by a further pair of lines. The whole may represent the lower torso and legs of a child's drawing of a human figure or elements of an abstract design or 'doodle'.

IS.69 SF708 (Figure 6.33)
Context 4221, Phase 1

Description

Sub-oval fragment of grey slate, 150 × 100m and 10mm thick, roughly chipped around the edges to sit comfortably in the palm. The upper face is smooth, the reverse rough and uneven. It was recovered from a spread of small stones forming a possible surface adjacent to the workshops in the north part of the excavated area.

On the upper face there is a palimpsest of miscellaneous incised marks and patterns. Across the very upper edge of the piece there is a deeply scored cut mark and traces of another, shorter cut at right-angles to it (where the stone has fractured). The remainder of the marks, however, are considerably fainter.

There are indications of a rectilinear lattice and, near the left-hand side, two hatched rectangular bands, 46mm long and 7mm wide overall. Meanwhile, near the upper right-hand side of the stone are faint traces of what looks like a frontal view of a face with a long central nose and two eyes. It is reminiscent, in a simplistic way, of the figures that were carved on the late 7th-century coffin of St Cuthbert, now preserved at Durham (Battiscombe 1956). Immediately below the 'face' is a crude spiral motif, whilst to the right are indications of the figure's left shoulder and arm.

IS.70 SF405 (Figure 6.33)
Context 437, Phase 3

Description

Irregular oval fragment of grey slate, 105 × 60mm and 4mm thick. Given the rounded profile evident in its surviving edges, the piece is probably a modified beach pebble which, when complete, would have sat comfortably in the palm of the hand. A repertoire of incised 'loops' and other curvilinear marks are present on both sides of the fragment. Although not recognisable as writing as such, it is likely that such 'doodles' were practised to familiarise the pupil with the practice of writing and to gain confidence in the use and control of the stylus.

IS.71 SF532 (Figure 6.33)
Context 4001, Phase 3

Description

Sub-rectangular, perforated dark grey slate, 97 × 85mm and 5mm thick, with minor flaking to one side but otherwise essentially intact. Given the rounded profile of its surviving edges the piece is probably a modified beach pebble. Like others of its kind and size, it would have sat comfortably in the palm of the hand.

On the upper face is a simple 'sunburst' motif, formed of a series of rays emanating from a circle that has been incised around the central perforation. A second complete circle lies a little way out.

On the reverse there is simply an incised line around the perforation, together with a more deeply scored line that extends to the edge of the stone.

IS.72 SF693 (Figure 6.33)
Context 4059, Phase 1

Description

Flat, oval grey slate beach pebble, 140 × 70mm and 6mm thick, broken at its upper end and originally probably some 20mm longer, essentially another palm-sized piece. Miscellaneous incised marks or 'doodles' are present on both sides of the stone. Those on the upper face form a series of rectilinear lattices; those on the back form no coherent pattern.

IS.73 SF952 (Figure 6.33)
Context 4541, Phase 5

Description

Irregular fragment of light grey slate, 167 × 72mm and 7mm thick, broken on all edges and with surface-flaking on both sides. It was recovered from the backfill of the late robber-trench, associated with the demolition and stone-robbing of the church.

Across one face is a very pronounced incised zig-zag motif, 60mm long and 8mm high. In the angles of the motif are a series of further incised marks or 'doodles'. Below it is another fragmentary zig-zag motif and, next to it (and upside down in this view), a possible Insular minuscule letter-form τ.

IS.74 SF453 (Figure 6.34)
Context 400, Phase 6

Description

Trapezoidal fragment of water-worn slate, 117 × 81mm and 3mm thick, with fractured edge. Irregular row of short, predominantly upright strokes, aligned almost vertically on the slab. Possibly practice strokes for components of letters or merely doodles. Lines appear random except for one group which appears to constitute a capital N with the uprights internally embellished with parallel oblique strokes, similar to that seen in IS.42.

IS.75 SF804 (Figure 6.34)
Context 4003, Phase 3

Description

Sub-rectangular fragment of probable slate-board, 73 × 55m and 5mm thick, smooth on both faces. Series of short, roughly parallel lines, 2–6mm apart, appear to form faint outline of an 'n-shaped' figure, up to 15mm high and 24mm wide, including the 'flourish' on its left-hand side. Miscellaneous, lightly incised marks are also present on the reverse.

IS.76 SF1263 (Figure 6.34)
Context 4679, Phase 2

Description

Large sub-rectangular block of slate, 530 × 455mm and 28mm thick, formed of three conjoining fragments. The slab appears to have been reused as a cover-stone for Grave G141, located immediately north of the church. Two drilled holes, 8mm in diameter and roughly 110mm apart, are located near the centre of the slab. Its upper surface is generally smooth but the stone is crossed by three quartz veins which form low ridges, like 'ripples', on the surface; the reverse side is flaked. A straight edge survives along part of the left-hand side of the slab; the others, however, are all broken.

On the upper surface of the slab is a palimpsest of incised lines and other marks. These include examples of several compass-drawn arcs and complete circles, together with their centre-points. At the left-hand edge of the stone are a series of 'loops' or scribbles, similar to those on IS.70. These too probably represent practice writing or exercises in the control and use of the stylus whilst across the centre of the same fragment

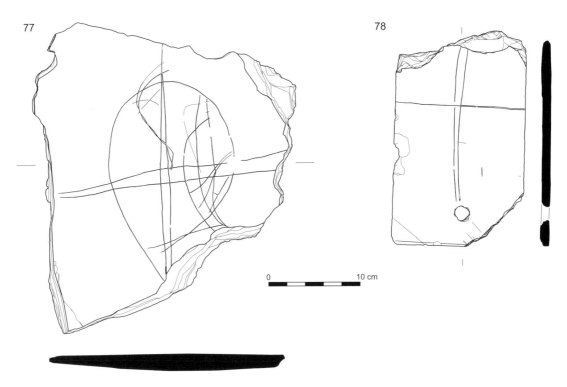

Figure 6.35
Informal cross-incised slabs (IS.77 and 78)

174

there is an ogham inscription (Forsyth & Tedeschi, above).

Discussion

The size of the slab and its rough-and-ready nature set it apart from virtually all of the other incised stones in the assemblage and only IS.30, with its multiple gaming boards, ship graffiti and the hunting scene on the reverse possibly comes close. The present stone, however, was incised on only the one face, leading to the suggestion that it was probably originally part of the furniture and fittings of a building on the site. It is interpreted as a work-top and the most likely context for such a piece would be a school-house, a stone equivalent, in other words, of the graffiti-covered school desk-lid.

The purpose of the two drilled holes is not clear. If associated with its use as a writing surface, they may have held wooden pegs and lines for the laying out of patterns on, for example, an adjacent slate-board (or sheet of vellum?). Alternatively, of course, the holes may be associated with some later use of the slab.

6.3.44 Informal cross-incised slates

Among the miscellaneous incised slate fragments from the site are two cross-incised slabs that would seem to have been intended as informal grave-markers. One (IS.77) was recovered from the upper surface of Grave G63; the other (IS.78), clearly a reused roof-slate, was recovered from the late rubble surface to the south-west of the church.

IS.77 SF853 (Figure 6.35)

Context 4502 (fill of Grave G63), Phase 2

Description

Large rectangular block of slate, 335 × 285mm and 8–14mm thick. On one face is a lightly scratched oval (200 × 140mm) with a crudely incised outline cross at centre whose arms extend beyond the 'ring'. Further lightly scratched curvilinear marks are evident to one side.

IS.78 SF765 (Figure 6.35)

Context 436, Phase 3

Description

Rectangular roof-slate, 228 × 142mm and 6mm thick, dressed on both faces and pierced at one end by a drilled hole. On one face there is a simple incised cross with arms 165mm and 142mm long.

6.4 POTTERY

JULIE FRANKLIN

Grass-tempered wares

There are three sherds from hand-made pots of a grass-tempered fabric. This is dark grey with buff surfaces, a sandy texture and clear voids visible on the surface and in the thickness of the wall where grass or similar vegetable temper has burnt out during firing. Two of the sherds are sooted on the exterior surface, suggesting they have been used for cooking, though equally this could have occurred during the firing process. In terms of form, the vessels seem to be rounded, globular forms. There are two base sherds, one sagging, the other flatter with a slight thickening along the edge of the basal angle.

There is a long tradition of hand-made grass-tempered wares in the Highlands and Islands, surviving from prehistory and continuing, in remote places, as late as the 19th century. There are records of this 'craggan ware' tradition surviving, with very little change, even into the 19th century in the Hebrides and Western Isles (Holleyman 1947; Quail 1979). It is therefore worthless as a chronologically diagnostic fabric. Sherds have been found from the Hebrides to Caithness and the Northern Isles dating from the late Iron Age to the 19th century (eg Dalland & MacSween 1999; Ross 1994; Carter *et al* 1995, 469–70; Gaimster 1995, 136; Turner & Dunbar 1970, 182).

The Inchmarnock sherds are all from late contexts, but were found in the north-west quadrant, quite separate from the medieval pottery around the church. Associated finds and radiocarbon dates in this area imply a date in the second half of the first millennium AD. There is no evidence of this 'craggan' tradition surviving into the medieval period in the Firth of Clyde. Wheel-thrown pottery is clearly being imported from the mainland from at least the 13th century onwards, and there are no grass-tempered sherds from the medieval midden.

Early cooking pots (Figure 6.36–1)

This is a group of 71 sherds from approximately 18 vessels. The sherds are thin walled (3–5mm thick) of a relatively fine soft fired fabric, with a sandy texture,

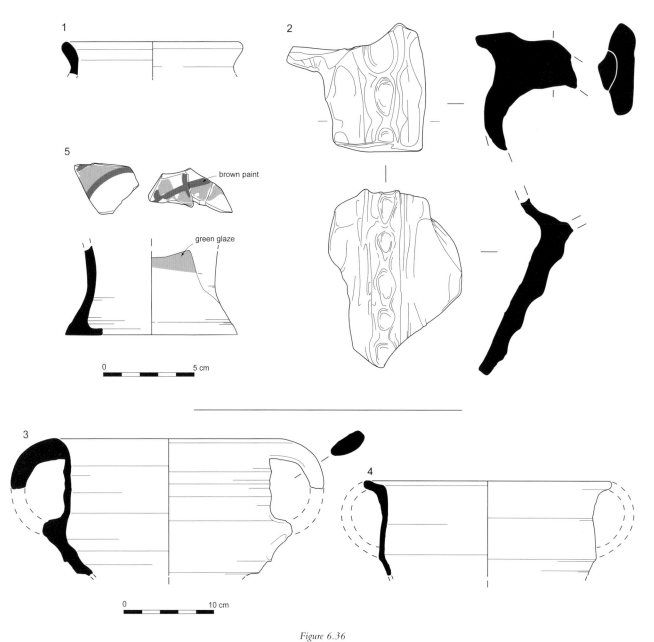

Figure 6.36
Pottery from the excavation of the church and graveyard (nos 1-5): 1. Early cooking pot rim; 2. Greyware jug handle with applied thumbed strip; 3. White gritty jar; 4. White gritty jar; 5. Saintonge polychrome jug base

containing fine grits of quartz and occasionally other minerals. Typically it is buff in colour, varying to greyish, pinkish or orange-buff. At least one sherd is treated with a white slip, while some others have a red external skin or patches of thin glaze.

The small size of the sherds hinders form identification but all the sherds appear to be from small

globular jars, sooted from use as cooking pots. Rims are all simple everted types and several sherds show pronounced wheel rilling.

The most likely source for these vessels is Ayrshire. They are similar, both in fabric and form to a type found in Ayr (Franklin & Hall, forthcoming). There they were identified as a locally made type of cooking

Table 6.3   Quantification of medieval and later pottery

Fabric/Phase	Phase 2	Phase 3	Phase 4	Phase 5	Total
Early Cooking Pots	47 (30%)	23 (16%)	1		71 (19%)
White Gritty	55 (35%)	56 (40%)	6		124 (33%)
Greywares	34 (22%)	53 (38%)	4	15	125 (33%)
Saintonge Green Glaze		5 (4%)			5 (1%)
Saintonge Polychrome	13 (8%)	2 (1%)			15 (4%)
Modern	8 (5%)	1? (1%)		2	35 (9%)
Total	157	140	11	17	375

pot. They probably date to around the 13th and 14th centuries.

Greywares (Figure 6.36–2)

The greywares form a heterogeneous group. Sherds are typically reduced to grey, with an external olive glaze. All are apparently from jugs. However, the shade of grey varies from light to dark, the coarseness of the fabric, from gritty to sandy. The variation probably reflects different dating and provenance, however, the small size of the assemblage and mixed nature of the stratigraphy, mean this is impossible to quantify. A general date for this group of 13th to 16th century would fit all the evidence.

All the sherds represent strap handled jugs. Decoration includes a fragment of a face mask motif, a small circular impressed grid motif, a Yorkshire style thumbed base, grooved strap handles, and a handle with a central thumbed strip which continues down onto the body of the vessel.

White Gritty Wares (Figures 6.35–3 and 4)

Though more often thought of as a south-east Scottish fabric, there is some evidence that White Gritty wares were produced in the West, though a source has yet to be identified. They make up a significant proportion, for example, of the medieval pottery found in Ayr (Franklin & Hall, forthcoming). There is some evidence from Ayr that whiteware production

continued later than in the east and survived into the 16th century or possibly even later.

There is considerable variation in the fabric, from white to pale buff, grey or pink. Often the external surface has a pink or orange skin. It is coarser and thicker walled than the fabric of the Early Cooking Pots.

Most of the sherds appear to be from plain jugs, however, the two most complete vessels are large two handled bowls or jars. Similar jars are well known in 16th-century deposits elsewhere, generally interpreted as cooking or chamber pots. However, the diameter of these seems too large for either and there is no evidence of heat damage. Both have a slight bevel inside the rim, possibly to hold a lid in place. It is easy to imagine many domestic or industrial uses for such bowls. However, in view of the ecclesiastical context, there is the possibility that they were used as receptacles for holy water. A similar bowl was found under the floor of Innerpeffray church in Perthshire, interred intact on top of a 16th-century infant burial (Robertson 1974). This was linked to French funerary customs, the vessels holding holy water during the ceremony, and then buried with the body. Two bowls were found at Cadzow Castle near Hamilton, close to the site of the castle chapel (Franklin forthcoming), while an odd handled bowl is among the Glenluce Abbey assemblage (Cruden 1951, fig 10). The forms and fabrics of these bowls vary, according to the contemporary local pottery industry, but all are of similar proportions. Though both of the Inchmarnock vessels are fragmentary and clearly redeposited, they are much less so than the rest of the assemblage, suggesting they are more closely related than other vessels to the use of the church or graveyard.

Saintonge Wares (Figure 6.36–5)

The imported vessels were all from the Saintonge area of south-west France. There are a handful of body sherds from a Saintonge whiteware jug, glazed with the typical mottled green glaze. These were found in the graveyard to the south of the church mixed with the rubble and in the fill of G101.

There was also a small collection of Saintonge polychrome sherds, possibly all from the same jug. These were distinctive jugs, decorated with heraldic, bird or vine leaf designs outlined in brown and coloured in green and occasionally yellow (Brown 2002, 26). Most of these were found to the west of the church on a possible Phase 2 ground surface. There is very little evidence for the exact design of the polychrome jug, but there is certainly a green band running around the lower part of the jug (see Figure 6.36–5) and a suggestion of a vertical outlined green band running up the pot (cf Platt & Coleman-Smith 1975 fig 185:1023; fig 186:1025). Another sherd shows a curving band of outlined green, suggesting a vine leaf design (cf Brown 2002, fig 22:213). Polychrome jugs are found in contexts dating between about 1250 and 1350 (Haggarty & Will 1996, 653; Platt & Coleman-Smith 1975, 138–46; Watkins 1987, 129–33), while the green glazed versions may have had a longer life span and are generally more common finds.

Despite being well made and attractive, Saintonge jugs were probably of no great monetary value. They rarely travel inland from the coast or major ports and were probably only a sideline for merchants involved in the more lucrative Gascon wine trade out of Bordeaux, Rochefort and La Rochelle (Brown 2002, 26; Courtney 1997, 102). They are found in North Sea ports, particularly Hull (Watkins 1987, 129–33), but they have a wider distribution in the West and in Ireland (eg Gahan & Walsh 1997, 111–12), possibly due to the relative scarcity of locally made pottery in those areas. Medieval Saintonge wares are more common on the west coast than the east. They have been found in the nearby ports of Dumbarton (Hall 2004, 339; Franklin 2004, 355) and Ayr (Franklin & Hall, forthcoming), where they make up the largest group of medieval imports. Polychrome sherds have been found at Carrick Castle on Loch Goil, at the north end of the

Firth of Clyde (Franklin 1998, 960), and are common on Islay (George Haggarty, pers comm).

6.5 METALWORK

JULIE FRANKLIN

6.5.1 Copper alloy

Ringed pin (Figure 6.37–6)

Ringed pins are predominantly a Hiberno-Norse type of dress fastening, best known in Ireland, where most were probably made. They are widely distributed along Norse trade routes, including the Western seaboard of Scotland (Fanning 1983: Fraser Hunter, pers comm).

Polyhedral headed pins are the most common type found in Scotland, mainly in the Western Isles and Orkney, though others have been found as nearby as Whithorn (Nicholson 1997, 369), Lochlee Crannog in Ayrshire, and an unprovenanced pin possibly from Lanarkshire (Fanning 1983). The earliest form of this type of pin has a plain ring, and is mainly found in Scotland in 10th-century contexts. A later development has a closer fitting kidney shaped ring, dated in Ireland to the 11th and 12th centuries. Though the ring is missing from the Inchmarnock example, most Scottish examples are plain ringed, with kidney ringed pins concentrated in the Western Isles, and it is therefore most likely to belong to the earlier group.

The Inchmarnock pin is from the north end of the site, close to, though not directly associated with a medieval grave (G19). No skeletal material survives in this grave. The pin may have been associated with an earlier grave or may simply have been discarded because it was broken. The break in the shaft, could well be the result of bending the pin, commonly done to prevent the fabric slipping during use, but often weakening the metal at this point.

6. Polyhedral headed ringed pin. Ring missing and shaft broken off approximately half-way down. Head decorated on all facets with simple borders, quartered lozenges and dots. Three grooves around top of pin shaft. Length 63+, max head width 8mm. SF576, Context 4001, Phase 3.

Coins (not illustrated)

N M McQ HOLMES

Edwardian pennies were the main currency in Scotland during the 14th century. There was another coin, from

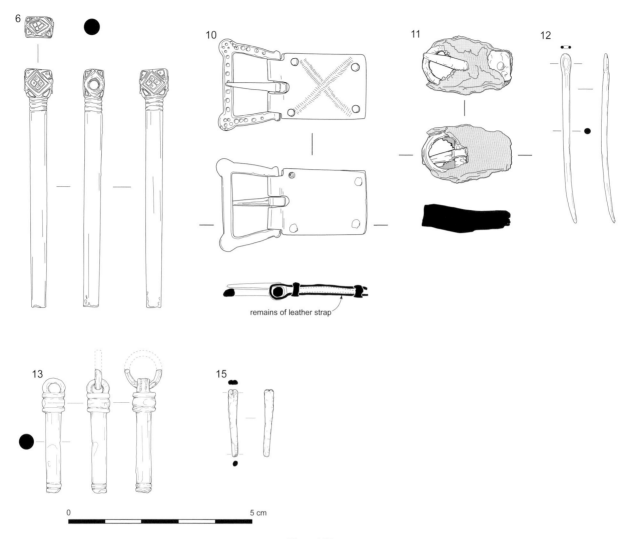

Figure 6.37
Copper-alloy artefacts from the excavation of the church and graveyard (nos 6, 10–13, 15); 6. Polyhedral ringed pin (SF575); 10. Trapezoidal buckle (SF1071); 11. D-shaped buckle (SF900); 12. Needle (SF1029); 13. Balance arm (SF915); 15. Lace tag (SF658)

the topsoil, of possible medieval date, but this was too worn and corroded to identify.

7.   Edward II, 1d, Durham, class 11a^2–11b1 (1310–14). SF709, Context 400, Topsoil

Of the post-medieval coins, one was found inside the nave of the church; the other in a grave to the south of the nave. This latter was found under the left heel of an adult, with cloth impressions on the underside indicating it was placed within the shroud. This helps to date the burial, though the coin could have been in circulation for some decades.

8.   Charles I, turner, second issue, twopence, 1632–39, good condition. SF1111, Context 491, Phase 4

9.   Charles I, turner, second issue, twopence, 1632–9, worn, corroded. SF1240, Context 4643, G123, Phase 3

Buckles (Figure 6.37–10 and 11)

Buckle (no 10) is well made and in very good condition. Whitehead dates this type as 1250–1400 (Whitehead 1996, 30). This is a particularly fine example, decorated

179

on the frame and the plate and must have been an item of personal dress. The unusual saltire pattern on the plate would seem to be symbolic of Scotland. Found loose in the graveyard soil, this may have been disturbed from an earlier burial, or be part of the midden.

10. Buckle. Trapezoidal buckle with ornate front end and folded sheet plate. Frame decorated with impressed dots. Cast pin with transverse ridge. Plate decorated with hatched saltire, held by four rivets, one in each corner. Remains of leather strap retained between plate. Length 41, max width 24, width of plate 17mm. SF1071, Context 4245, Phase 3

Buckle (no 11) appears to be *in situ*. It was found inside the pelvis of one of the post-reformation burials, an older juvenile, 12–15 years old, who met a violent end. It is possibly the remains of a belt worn around the waist of the deceased, though is very small for a belt buckle. The cloth preserved on top of the buckle is probably remains of the shroud cloth, while cloth impressions on the underside are probably from clothing. Both are of a fine fabric of plain weave, probably linen.

11. Buckle. Small D-shaped buckle. Frame made in two pieces, with a bent strip forming the frame and a separate bar riveted between each end. Small pin made from bent strip. Folded sheet plate, fixed with at least one rivet. Remains of strap retained inside plate. Mineralised textile preserved on top and part of underside, obscuring some detail. Length 24mm, width 12mm, width of plate 8mm. SF900, Context 4534, G91, Phase 3

Other finds (Figure 6.37–12 and 13)
The needle was found in a drain deposit at the south end of the site, with several other medieval finds.

12. Needle. Solid needle with eye pierced through flattened end. Slightly bent at tip, probably accidental. Length 45mm, width 2mm. SF1029, Context 4574, Phase 3

Small balance scales of the type represented by no 13 were used for weighing precious substances such as metals and spices. Both portable folding types and fixed arms balances are known from contexts as early as Saxon England (Oakley & Webster 1979, 258) and are well known in the Viking, medieval and later worlds. The complete arm would have been pivoted

from a stirrup in the middle, with loop terminals at both ends, from which pans were suspended by chains. However, there was no sign of any other pieces of this balance in the surrounding area.

A folding balance with similar terminals was found in an Anglo-Scandinavian context in York (Mainman & Rogers 2000, 2559, fig 1258:10405). Another from Colchester was found in a medieval pit but is thought to be possibly residual Roman (Crummy 1988, 67, fig 66:2989). Medieval examples tend to have simpler terminals (eg Ford 1987, ill. 63:54; Ford 1996, illus 17:5; Margeson 1993, fig 155:1572–3). The Inchmarnock example was found in the fill of a post-medieval grave, that of an adult female, *c* 35–45 years old, south of the chancel. It was found towards the head end of the grave, though there was no definite association with the burial. The grave was badly intercut and it may have been part of the midden, incorporated in the graveyard soil. A medieval or post-medieval date is therefore more likely. However, the medieval midden is fairly low key and domestic in nature and a balance scale seems to fit better with the higher status evidence and industrial activity, predating the church, in the north-west quadrant. None of this earlier material has demonstrably travelled to the south end of the site, but it is not impossible that it might have. The dating for this object must therefore remain uncertain, but it does add a further dimension to the site, of trade in expensive goods.

13. Balance arm. Moulded terminal with grooved decoration. Two grooves incised further down shaft, at which point shaft broken. Found with part of small wire ring, *c* 10mm diam, threaded through hole. Possibly some silver content. Length 30mm+, max head width 6mm. SF915, Context 4547, G97, Phase 3.

Wire pins and lace tags (Figure 6.37–15)
Both wire pins and laces were used in everyday dress but equally both were used to secure shrouds and are common finds in late medieval and post-medieval graveyards.

There were only three lace tags. These were of typically simple construction, made from rolled sheet, with edges abutting or slightly overlapping. One was found with other material in a drain fill, close to the burials at the south end of the trench, the other two were found as a pair under the skeleton in G5. The only burial with associated lace tags, it was unique in

Table 6.4 Wire shroud pins (not illustrated)

No	SF	Context	Phase	Grave	Skeleton	Location	Length	Tinned
17	820	4263	3	40	Infant	?	23	
18	778	4270	3	44	Perinatal	Across pelvis	8+	
19	779	4270	3	44	Perinatal	Between knees	26	X
20	874	4516	4	84	Child	Under right skull	19	X
21	926	4551	4	99	Child	On ribs	16+	
22		4554	4	100	Perinatal	?	11+	
23	1164	4624	4	117	Infant	Around left shoulder	–	
24	1165	4624	4	117	Infant	On skull	17+	
25	1166	4624	4	117	Infant	Around right shoulder	24	X
26	1183	4624	4	117	Infant	At feet	24+	
27	1196	4635	4	137	No skeleton	?	–	

other ways. It was of a young man, buried lying on his back, but with his knees drawn up to his chest. It implies he was laced up inside a tight shroud, or possibly a sack. This may have been to fit him into an awkward space in the graveyard, or possibly he was already partially decomposed at the time, such as a drowning victim. He dates to Phase 4, when the area had become a children's cemetery, and it may be that there was something unusual about his death or life, or something uncertain about his faith, that is reflected in his atypical burial.

14. Lace tag. In three pieces, edges abutting. Length *c* 21mm. Context 4574, Phase 2 (not illustrated)

15. Lace tag. Complete, edges abutting, tapering towards free end. Length 18mm. SF658, Context 487, G5, Phase 4

16. Lace tag. Broken at one end, edges overlapping. Length 13mm+. SF658, Context 487, G5, Phase 4 (not illustrated)

Shroud pins are more numerous. All have small heads made of coiled wire, stamped into a spherical shape, typical of the early post-medieval period. No 17 was found with associated fibres, presumably the remains of the shroud. All are associated with child, infant or perinatal burials, dating to Phases 3 and 4, from either inside, or to the south of, the church. The number of pins used varied as did their locations relative to the skeleton. There is also one possible iron shroud pin (Franklin, Iron Finds, below). The burial with the most shroud pins, G117 (Table 6.4), was also the only one to have evidence for a wooden coffin.

6.5.2 Iron

Weapons (Figure 6.38–28 and 29)

The arrowhead was found in the fill of a grave to the north of the church. Other finds from the fill, iron slag, a broken knife tip (SF699) and another unidentifiable iron object, suggest these might all represent debris from the ironworking in the area redeposited in the grave backfill. However, the arrowhead, unlike the knife, is complete, and though very corroded, otherwise in good condition, and the wood preserved on the tang indicates at least part of the shaft was attached when it was deposited. It is tempting to suggest the arrowhead might have

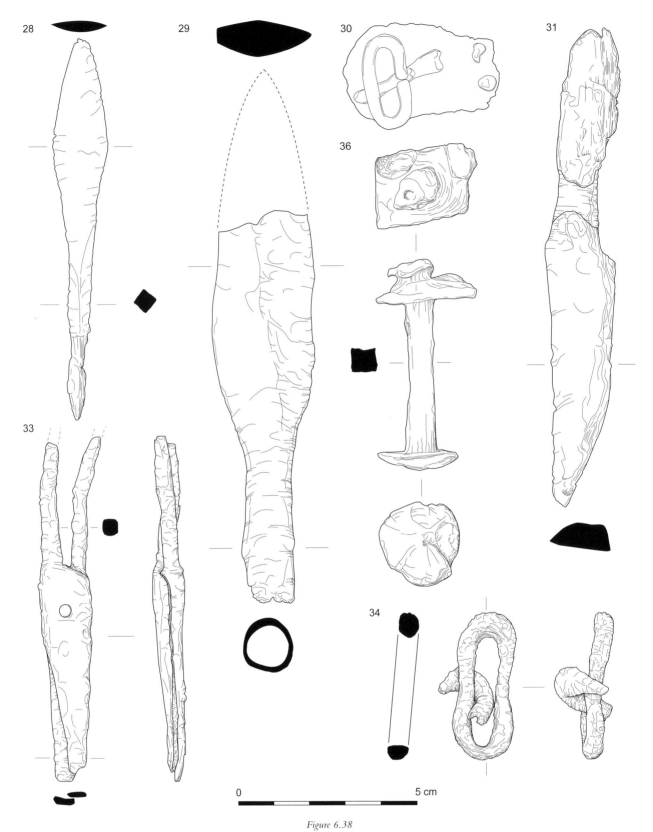

Figure 6.38
Iron artefacts from the excavation of the church and graveyard (nos 28–31, 33, 34, 36): 28, Arrow-head (SF702); 29. Spear-head (SF844);
30. Oval-framed buckle (SF611); 31. Knife (Context 4135); 33. Scissors (SF1252); 34. Chain (SF531); 36. Clench bolt (SF664)

been the cause of death, though no skeletal material survived in the grave and there were no traces of any of the victim's bone or clothing preserved on the blade. It is also possible that it is the remains of a bow and arrow placed in the grave of an archer.

Medieval arrowheads are generally socketed rather than tanged, providing a stronger join with the shaft. In his typology, Jessop (1996) dates this type of leaf-shaped tanged form to between the 9th and the 11th century, based largely on a series of arrowheads from York (Ottaway 1992, 710–14).

The dating of the spearhead is more difficult. The blade, though incomplete, appears to have been quite long, in keeping with Norse and early medieval types (Ward-Perkins 1940, 74). Again, the spearhead may be a product of the on-site metalworkers, though this, again has clearly been hafted.

28. Arrowhead. Narrow pointed leaf shaped blade with lentoid sectioned blade and square sectioned tang. Mineralised remains of wooden shaft adhering to end of tang. Length 103, width 15mm. SF702, Context 4111, G30, Phase 2

29. Spearhead. Leaf shaped blade, of lozenge shaped section with blunt edges. Post-depositional break in blade. Socketed tang with remains of wooden shaft surviving inside. Length 106mm+, width 29mm. SF844, Context 4009, Phase 1/2

Dress accessories (Figure 6.38–30)

30. Buckle. Small oval framed buckle, with pin and sheet buckle plate, fastened by two rivets. Length 37mm, width 26mm, plate width 18mm. SF611, Context 4001, Phase 3. (Drawn from X-ray).

The buckle is rather plain, but its small size suggests a human dress accessory rather than horse gear. It was found in the topsoil in the middle of the north-west quadrant, and thus is possibly of early historic date. It may have derived from one of the graves to the east.

Tools/Fittings (Figure 6.38–31, 33 and 34)

The knife, no 31, is an unusual shape. It appears to be complete, though the concavity of the blade could be due to wear or corrosion. It may have been designed for a specialist purpose. It was found in an early feature, possibly a post-hole.

31. Knife. Slightly concave blade with back curving down towards point. Mineralised remains of

antler, possibly bone handle. Context 4135, Phase 1

The knife fragment, no 32, is more typically shaped. It was found in the backfill of a medieval grave, though is not necessarily related to the body.

32. Knife. Tip of knife blade, triangular section, blade and back gently curving towards pointed tip. Length 42mm, width 12mm. SF699, Context 4111, G30, Phase 2 (not illustrated)

Scissors are known from Dark Age and medieval sites, but they did not come into everyday domestic use until the 16th century. Contemporary illustrations show shears were routinely used in the home while medieval scissors are generally associated with trades such as tailoring (Ward-Perkins 1940, 150). Finds of scissors are generally post-medieval. These were found in very poor condition, directly to the west of the church on an old, post-medieval ground surface.

Chains had many uses, for suspending or securing items, or for tethering animals. This is a relatively delicate example for an iron chain. It was found on the north-east side of the excavated area, in a post-medieval layer containing many apparently first millennium finds. Further fragments of this chain were found, totalling six links, though all from surface contexts.

The pin was found with the body of an old woman, buried to the south of the chancel. It was found around the area of her hands, which were folded over her pelvis. It may have been a shroud pin. No other iron shroud pins were found, but many may have corroded away to nothing. Another iron object was found under her hands, a U-shaped object, though unfortunately this was too corroded to identify. It may have been a broken buckle, though equally it may have been a redeposited staple. The fact the pin was found around the woman's hands makes it tempting to suggest she was buried with a needle, possibly the tool of her trade.

33. Scissors. Blades and arms of pair of scissors. Rivet at top of blades clearly visible in X-ray. Missing loops and tip of blades. Length 93mm. SF1252, Context 4662, Phase 3

34. Chain. One and a half waisted oval links. Length of link 40mm, width 16mm. SF531, Context 4001, Phase 3

35. Shroud pin/needle. Very fine pointed iron object, with round section. Broken at wide end, with no evidence of eye or head. Length 38mm, width

Table 6.5 Clench bolts (not illustrated except no 36)

No	SF/<>	Context	Phase	Context type	Rove Shape	Rove Size	Wood Thickness
36	664	4001	3	Deposit	Lozenge/ Rectangular	22–24	41
37	–	422	2	Sandy layer	Lozenge	*c* 25–30	24
38	975	4579	3	Fill of grave G105, S of chancel, male 15–23	Square/ Lozenge	26–27	19
39	1046a	4574	2	Fill of drain 4550	Square	24–26	18
40	934	436	3	Rubble to SW of church	Lozenge	*c* 25	33–36
41	1113	436	3	Rubble to SW of church	?	?	19–24
42	732	4003	3	Deposit	Square	30	22
43	733	4245	3	Deposit against S wall of church	Square	21	22
44	1136	4245	3	Deposit against S wall of church	Square	22–3	20
45	1246	4245	3	Deposit against S wall of church	Round?	25	25
46	766	4255	3	Fill of grave G36, S of church, female 25–35	Square	25–29	17
47	875	4524	4	Fill of grave G87, S of chancel, infant 0–2	Concave Square	30–32	13
48	–	4002	5	Levelling deposit	Rectangular	20–30	*c* 24
49	–	400	–	Topsoil	Lozenge/ Square	25-27	17+

1.8mm. SF878, Context 4507, G60, Phase 3 (not illustrated)

Clench bolts (Figure 6.38–36)

There were 14 clench bolts. These were large iron rivets, formed from a nail and a square or lozenge shaped holed plate, used to join thicknesses of wood together. They are often associated with boat building, riveting together the planks of clinker built boats and ships, in both the Viking and medieval periods. However, they were also used by joiners to fix planks together, such as in the construction of doors. It seems unlikely that the church site would have been used for boat building and repair, as near to the sea as it is, it sits on a raised beach, a considerable slope upwards from the present beach. Nails and roves may have been made at the metalworking site in Phase 1, but as all the bolts here have already been clenched, they have clearly been used for whatever purpose they were intended. None shows any traces of attached wood, though as most are intact, it seems unlikely they were wrenched out of place. Possibly the wood to which they were attached was used as firewood. All the nails used were of the same type, with flat round heads, about 20mm wide.

Most were clustered in the graveyard to the south and west of the church, in contexts dating from Phase 2 and later. They are probably part of the medieval midden found in this area. Three were found in post-medieval grave fills (G36, G87 and G105), suggesting they may have been used in coffin construction. These were also the shortest, joining wood of 13–19mm total thickness, and one of the roves appeared to be decoratively shaped, a square with concave sides, all of which, again suggests a different usage. However, very few of the burials (including these three) bore any trace of wooden coffins.

Only one was found in the north-west quadrant (no 36), from a post-medieval layer which contained much early material. It is by far the longest, clenching wood some 41mm thick. It may, conceivably therefore, be from boat-building or repair.

Coffin nails and fittings

There was very little evidence for wooden coffins. Only five burials (G106, G115, G117, G125 and G126) contained convincing coffin remains, all from post-medieval children's graves. All but one of these (G115) were from inside the nave, though the survival of metalwork in deposits outside the church suggests this is not simply a matter of differential corrosion.

The remains generally are no more than some nails, coated with mineralised wood, found in a coffin shape around the body. There were not enough remains to glean anything about coffin construction techniques. The nails, where enough remained to tell, were all small woodworking type nails, with flat round heads about 15mm in diameter. The number of nails varied in approximate proportion to the size of the grave. The most nails found were 18 in a child's grave 1.3m long.

In three examples (G106, G117 and G126), corner brackets were also visible in the ground, though these disintegrated upon excavation. They appeared to be simple angled straps, joining the corners. There was no evidence for handles, linings, or any other kind of coffin fitting. The infant buried in G117 was the only burial with evidence for both shroud and coffin.

Other structural ironwork

Nails were the most common iron find. Not including *in situ* coffin nails, there were 388 in total. Some are probably redeposited coffin nails, but the evidence for wooden coffins is so slim that it seems unlikely to account for all of them.

It seems more likely that most of the nails were related to the structure of the church itself, either for large structural timbers, internal fixtures and fittings, or for fixing roof slates. Only 11 nails were found in Phase 1 contexts predating the church. All appeared to be unused and they are possibly the products of on-site iron working. In Phase 2, there were 85, and in Phase 3, 230, 60% of the total. This implies that the nails were mainly deposited as the church fell out of use. Fittings and roof slates may have been stripped out of the church, or allowed to slowly decay, probably a combination of both.

Other structural fittings included a staple and a possible hinge strap.

6.6 GLASS

JULIE FRANKLIN

Beads (Figure 6.39–50, 51, 52 and 53)

The three large beads were all found in the north-west quadrant, and all probably predate the church. Beads

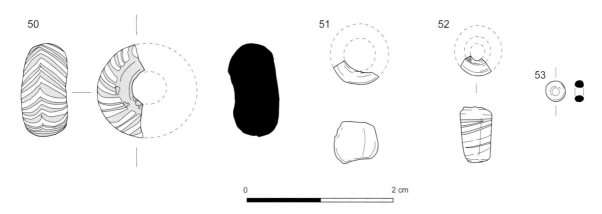

Figure 6.39
Glass beads from the excavation of the church and graveyard (nos 50–3); 50. Blue glass bead (Context 4124); 51. Blue glass bead (SF608); 52. Green glass bead (SF514); 53. Orange/'black' glass bead (SF1069)

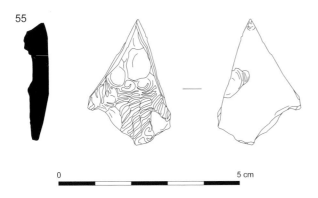

Figure 6.40
Vessel glass from the excavation of the church and graveyard (no 55)

of these types are known in Britain from the Iron Age and Roman periods onwards (Guido 1999). The shapes of the beads are described according to Guido (1999, 13).

50. Bead. Thick annular bead of translucent blue glass with opaque white stripes dragged around circumference to form chevrons. The stripes end before the central perforation, an area which would have been hidden if the bead was strung. Length 6mm, diam 12mm, hole diam 6mm. Cleaning over Phase 1 Graves G20 and G11.

51. Bead. Fragment of globular bead of translucent blue glass. Length 5mm, diam *c* 6mm, hole diam *c* 4mm. SF608, Context 4001, Phase 3

52. Bead. Fragment of barrel-shaped bead of opaque green glass with paler green streaks. Length 7mm, diam *c* 6mm, hole diam *c* 2mm. SF514, Context 4001, Phase 3

The small orange glass beads (no 53) were found together within a grave in the north-west corner of the nave. No bone survived in the grave, but at 90 × 30cm, it could have held only a small child or toddler. There was evidence for a well-constructed wooden coffin with iron fittings. The beads were scattered around the chest area. There is no observable pattern, but there would have been considerable movement in this area after burial, as the body and then bones decomposed. The orange colour is possibly meant to imitate amber. A similar group of small beads of probable 16th-century date found at Stoneypath Tower in East Lothian were interpreted as part of a piece of dress fabric that had rotted *in situ* (Franklin 2001). The beads may have been threaded onto a necklace, or embroidered onto the bodice of a dress, of a relatively well-to-do little girl. Glass beads were a popular way to embellish fabric, as a cheaper alternative to jewels or pearls. An identical bead was recovered from the floor of the turf-built structure

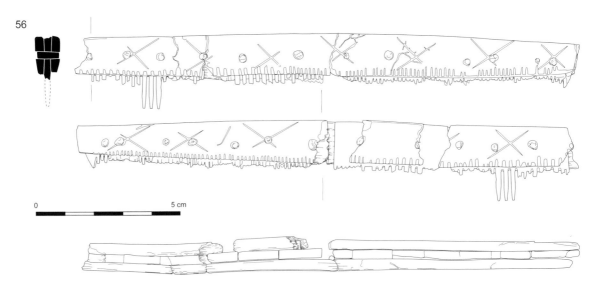

Figure 6.41
Bone and antler comb (no 56)

57

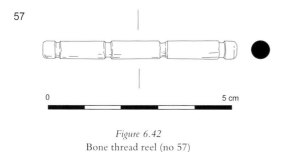

0   5 cm

Figure 6.42
Bone thread reel (no 57)

at Site 5, dating to the final phase of its occupation in the early 18th century (Chapter 8.3). It is very tempting to speculate that that building may have been the child's home. The turquoise bead (no 54) is of identical form and may have had a similar function. Unfortunately, however, it was unstratified.

53. Beads. 93 small globular beads (Plate 5.14). Colour appears opaque black, but translucent orange colour observable when held to the light. Length 1–1.5mm, diam 2.5–3mm. SF1069, Context 4588/4589, G106, Phase 4.

54. Bead. Small globular bead of opaque turquoise glass. Length 1mm, diam 2mm. Unstratified, from north transect (not illustrated).

Vessel Glass (Figure 6.40–55)

The sherd of glass is one of the more enigmatic of the Inchmarnock finds. The glass in distinctly curved, implying it is from a vessel, but the decoration is on the concave side. It is in extremely good condition, was found to the north-west of the church, in a deposit of uncertain date, containing finds, most of which appear to be early, such as the spearhead, oil shale fragments and a stone gaming piece. Decoration of this type is not unheard of in first millennium contexts (eg Peers & Radford 1943, 73).

55. Decorative ?vessel glass. Small sherd of clear yellowish glass decorated with rods of similar clear glass with opaque pale yellow stripe, twisted and applied in a pattern on concave side of sherd. Length 33mm. SF703, Context 4009, Phase 1/2.

There were a handful of other small fragments of clear glass from both Phase 1 and Phase 2 contexts. Two Phase 2 pieces are very thin walled and may represent

medieval glass vessels, though with no evidence of form, they could equally be later intrusive sherds.

6.7 BONE AND ANTLER

JULIE FRANKLIN

Comb (Figure 6.41)

The comb was found in three pieces in the fill of a post-medieval grave of a 12–15-year-old child (G109), immediately to the south of the church. However, the comb is clearly earlier than this. It may have been displaced from an earlier grave and redeposited here or may have been part of the medieval midden. One part of it (SF1073), for example, came from the fill of an adjacent, earlier grave (G106). In some respects it is rather crudely made, with poorly executed decoration and uneven riveting, but in others, such as the faceting of the teeth it is very fine.

It is of a type dated by MacGregor to between the 10th and 13th centuries, but more commonly found in Scandinavia (MacGregor 1985, 90, fig 50k). The closely spaced copper alloy (rather than iron) rivets indicate this is a late example. Narrow, nearly straight backed, simply decorated combs such as this are known from 13th-century contexts in Scandinavia (eg Long 1975, 27, fig 9e–f). A similarly decorated, though better executed comb was found in medieval deposits in the Earl's Palace, Kirkwall and dated stylistically to the late 12th to 14th century (Cox *et al* 1998, 572–5, illus 5–6), and examples are also known from Shetland (*PSAS* 1936, 22; Hamilton 1956, pl XXXII). A plainer example with iron rivets was found in Aberdeen, in a late 12th- or early 13th-century context (MacGregor 1982, 182, ill.105:30). The two gauges of teeth are an unusual feature, more often found on double-sided combs. The comb was probably made in or around the 13th century, dating to the early years of the church. It also indicates continuing contact with Scandinavia.

56. Bone and antler comb. Composite single sided comb, with antler side plates and bone tooth plates. Narrow, near straight backed side plates with rectangular profile, decorated with roughly executed incised crosses on both sides. Coarse teeth at one end (5 per cm), fine teeth at other (8 per cm). Cracked and broken off at one end, side plate complete at other, but break in tooth plate suggests this originally extended beyond the side plate. Teeth made up of at least nine

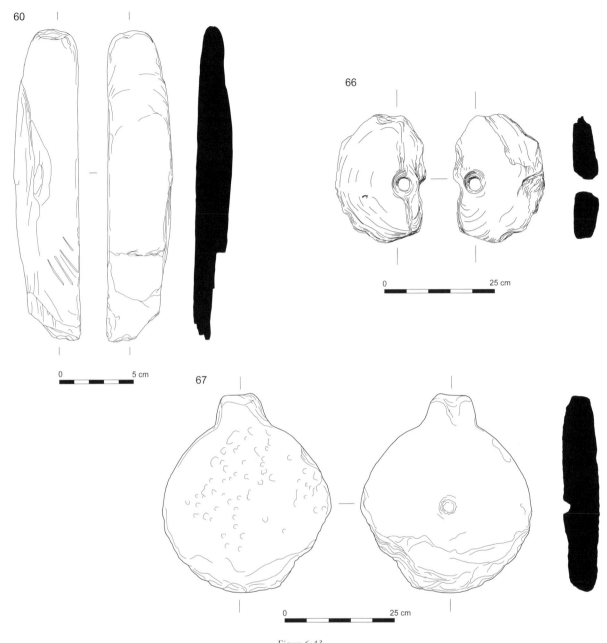

Figure 6.43
Whetstones and quernstones from the excavation of the church and graveyard (nos 60, 66, 67)

individual plates of varying lengths, though damage means this is possibly an over estimate. Three complete teeth remaining, facetted at end to hone into points. Little wear visible on teeth. Fixed with 13 remaining unevenly spaced copper alloy rivets. Length 177mm (estimated complete 200mm), height 24mm, thickness 10mm. SF1073/1091/1093, Contexts 4589 and 4599, G106 and G109, Phases 3 & 4

Other finds (Figure 6.42)

Find no 57 was found in rubble to the west of the church. It may have originally have derived from a grave or the medieval midden. Thread reels were probably more often made of wood, such as a medieval example found in London (Egan 1998, 270).

57. Bone thread reel? Turned, four grooves. Length 53mm, width 5mm. SF807, Context 436, Phase 3

6.8 STONE AND CERAMIC OBJECTS

JULIE FRANKLIN (WITH GEOLOGICAL IDENTIFICATIONS
AND COMMENTS BY DIANNE DIXON)

There are two main types of stone utilised for the manufacture of stone tools: sandstone and schist. The various types of sandstone are probably from southern Bute, though could have originated in Ayrshire. The smaller sandstone objects could have been made from erratic beach pebbles. The Dalradian schist forms the local bedrock on Inchmarnock.

Whetstones (Figure 6.43–60)

All the whetstones were found at the north-west quadrant, all but one from the north-west corner. The associated iron slag from this area suggests it was used for production or repair of iron tools and weapons. Though all are from late contexts, their location implies they are part of the pre-church industrial activity in this area. There is well established evidence for trade in Norwegian schist whetstones during the Norse and medieval periods, from a quarry in the Eidsborg area of southern Norway (eg Gaunt 2000; Moore & Oakley 1979). However, there is no reason to suspect that the Inchmarnock stones were imported when there was a ready and extremely local supply. Though all perfectly functional, none of the whetstones is particularly well finished, and it seems most likely that they were made on the island, probably using beach pebbles from near the site, as need arose.

No 59 has a series of incised lines towards broken end, probably from sharpening of small points, eg pins or needles. Three other slabs of stone (SF547, Context 4001; SF452, Context 400; SF806, Context 4003) have deep grooves worn into the surface possibly wear sustained during the sharpening the tips of pointed tools or weapons.

58. Whetstone. Dalradian schist. Large stone, ovoid section, tapering towards one end. Traces of wear on both faces of wider end. Broken both ends. Length 173mm, width 48mm, thickness 29mm. SF414, Topsoil. (not illustrated)

59. Whetstone. Dalradian schist. Large stone, ovoid section, tapering towards one end. Little trace of wear. Badly chipped and scratched. Length 195mm, width 47mm, thickness 29mm. SF 473, Topsoil. (not illustrated)

60. Whetstone. Dalradian schist. Large stone, sub-rectangular section, traces of wear on both faces.

Chipped at one end, broken off at other. A series of incised lines towards broken end. Length 210, width 43mm, thickness 25mm. SF492, Context 4001, Phase 3.

61. Whetstone. Dalradian schist. Small stone, rounded section. Little trace of wear. Length 120mm, width 28mm, thickness 23mm. SF538, Context 4001, Phase 3. (not illustrated)

62. Whetstone. Devonian/Carboniferous reddish fine grained sandstone. Rectangular section, broken at one end, other end well squared. Length 60mm, width 26mm, thickness 17mm. SF526, Context 4001, Phase 3. (not illustrated)

63. Whetstone. Devonian/Carboniferous red fine grained sandstone. Rectangular section, broken at one end, other end cut diagonally. Length 75mm, width 21mm, thickness 15mm. SF556, Context 4001, Phase 3. (not illustrated)

64. Whetstone fragment. Devonian/Carboniferous grey fine grained sandstone or siltstone. Long thin sliver of stone, worn concave on one face, rounded at one end, broken at other. SF543, Context 4001, Phase 3. (not illustrated)

Quernstones (Figure 6.43–66 and 67)

The local schist used for no 66 is very soft and flaky and seems unsuited to its purpose. It may have broken during manufacture and been abandoned. No 67 also appears to be unfinished. It was reused as a grave marker for a Phase 3 child's grave south of the church. No 65 was found in the north part of the trench and probably belongs to the early historic period of activity, the date of the other two is more speculative. However, the greater degree of industrial and domestic activity on site in the early historic period suggests they are most likely to belong to this time, but they may in fact be medieval.

65. Quernstone. Devonian/Carboniferous red sand-stone. Segment of quernstone with well rounded smooth outer edge. Damaged on one face and towards centre with no remains of central hole. Diam 360mm, thickness 37mm. SF528, Context 4001, Phase 3 (not illustrated)

66. Quernstone. Dalradian schist. Large plano-convex semi-circular slab of stone, with rough faces and roughly rounded edge. Large hole through thickest part of stone towards centre of circle, hole drilled from both sides. Either extensively

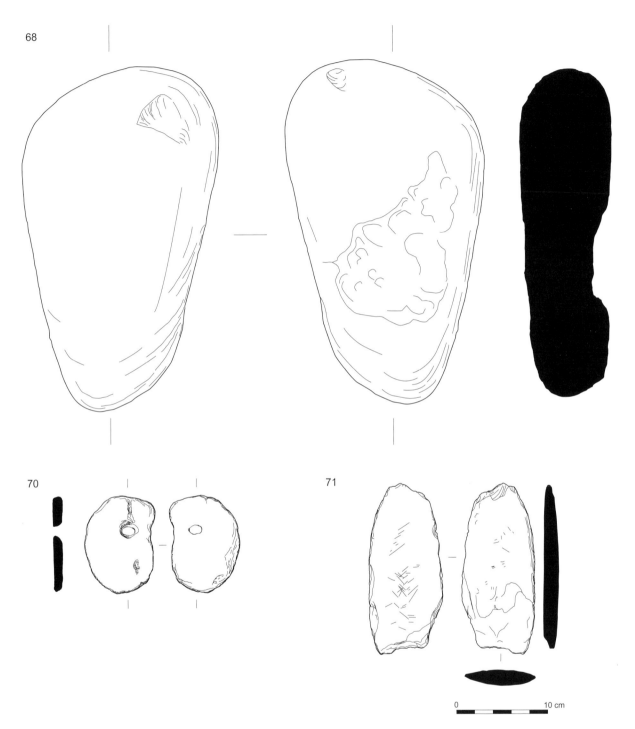

Figure 6.44
Other stone implements from the excavation of the church and graveyard (nos 68, 70, 71)

damaged or broken during manufacture and unfinished. Max diam 340mm, max thickness 52mm, hole. Unstratified.

67. Quernstone rough out. Buff sandstone. Large circular slab of sandstone with lobe on edge. Top face uneven with roughly pecked 30mm wide depression in centre and traces of a spout cut into lobe. Rough peck marks on underside and around edge. Diam 375mm, thickness 70mm. SF1096, Context 4605, G110, Phase 3

Other tools (Figure 6.44–68, 70 and 71)

The igneous stone used for no 68 is extremely weathered, and thus may well be a glacial erratic. Though dolerite dykes are found in Southern Bute, it is more likely to have been found on the beaches of Inchmarnock, possibly transported from further north.

There are two slate weights, nos 69–70, both waterworn, suggesting they are worked beach stones. Both were found in early grave fills, in the cluster of graves on the east side of the north-west quadrant. They may have been loom weights, though there is no other evidence of textile manufacture in this area. It is more likely that they were used as fishing weights or net sinkers and it is possible they were deliberately deposited as grave goods.

No 71 is similar in shape and size to a number of shale tools found at Kebister, Shetland (Clarke 1999, 157, illus 146–7), where it was suggested they were hafted either as ards or hoes. However, the fine polish on the surface of this object suggests a finer use, such as a weaving sword or linen smoother.

68. Tool. Igneous stone, probably dolerite. Large rounded stone with one flatter face. Large rounded roughly pecked hollow on this face, apparently from being used as some kind of mortar or anvil. Underside also has possible wear traces and surface crazing, possibly from heating? Possibly a rough-out for a pivot stone? Length 370mm, width 200mm, thickness 90mm. SF692, Context 4101, Phase 1

69. Weight? Slate. Irregular sub-ovoid piece of slate, with drilled hole towards one end, at which point slate has broken. Smoothed and waterworn edges. 135 × 110 × 21mm, weight 441g. SF413, Context 463, G12, Phase 1 (not illustrated)

70. Weight? Slate. Irregular sub-ovoid piece of slate, with roughly drilled hole towards one

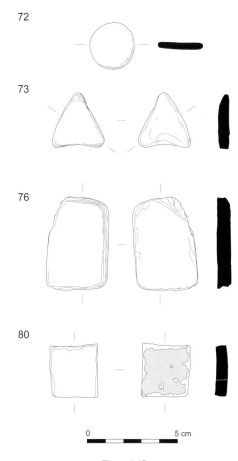

Figure 6.45
Stone and ceramic gaming pieces from the excavation of the church and graveyard (nos 72, 73, 76, 80)

end, smoothed and waterworn edges. Grey slate has white mineral vein running down centre. 110 × 80 × 11mm, weight 163g . SF687, Context 4087, G26, Phase 2

71. Tool. Slate. Large ovoid slate with polished rounded lozenge shaped section. Chipped at both ends. Length 184mm, width 80mm, thickness 16mm. SF493, Context 4001, Phase 3

Stone and ceramic gaming pieces (Figure 6.45–72, –73, –76 and –80)

The gaming pieces, like the gaming boards are all roughly made using materials ready to hand. Most are of slate, one of other locally available stone, and one is made from a sherd of greyware pottery. In view of the number of gaming boards, it seems likely that many gaming pieces have gone unrecognised, among the

191

profusion of slate fragments found on site. These nine pieces have been identified as gaming counters, as their regular shape and polished edges seem unlikely to be natural.

The best made is no 72, found in close association with gaming board SF430 (part of IS.1: Plate 6.1), and recovered from the upper fill of a Phase 1 grave (G11). Other pieces are triangular, rectangular or square, of various sizes, to fit the various sized boards found. Pieces of similar shape and size tend to be found together, probably part of the same set. The different shapes may have helped to distinguish between opponents men, as there was little material available to make pieces of different colours. There was a game that specifically used triangular pieces, rithmomachy was an arithmetical war game played on a double chess board, using round, square and triangular pieces, each numbered and coloured white on one side, black on the other (Murray 1951, 84). According to Eales (2007, 166), the game first appears in the 11th century and has been been characterised as a teaching aid for the new skills of calculation (Evans 1979). The stone pieces were all from contexts to the north of the church, suggesting an early date.

72. Gaming piece. Dalradian schist. Circular. Diam 25mm, thickness 3mm. SF432, Context 459, G11, Phase 1 (Plate 6.1).

73. Gaming piece. Slate. Triangular, rounded edges. 27 × 30mm, thickness 6mm. SF680, Context 4009, Phase 1/2.

74. Gaming piece. Slate. Sub-triangular. 33 × 41mm, thickness 5mm. SF862, Context 4087, G26, Phase 2 (not illustrated)

75. Gaming piece. Slate. Sub-triangular. 37 × 49mm, thickness 9mm. SF862, Context 4087, G26, Phase 2 (not illustrated)

76. Gaming piece. Slate. Rectangular, well polished faces and edges, chipped corner. 49 × 33mm, thickness 9mm. SF489, Context 4001, Phase 3

77. Gaming piece. Slate. Sub rectangular, rounded edges, made from reused roof slate, retaining peg hole. 47 × 36mm, thickness 7mm. SF497, Context 4001, Phase 3 (not illustrated)

78. Gaming piece. Slate. Small roughly formed rectangular piece, rounded edges. 18 × 14mm, thickness 6mm. U/S, associated with no 79 (not illustrated)

79. Gaming piece. Schist. Small roughly formed rectangular piece, sharp edges. 18 × 13mm, thickness 7mm. U/S, associated with no 78 (not illustrated)

The ceramic counter is the only inherently datable piece and must post-date the 13th century. It was found in rubble to the south-west of the church.

80. Ceramic gaming piece. Square, chipped edges, made from reused gritty, olive glazed greyware pot-sherd. 29 × 26mm, thickness 6mm. SF1163, Context 436, Phase 3

Stone discs (not illustrated)

Three slate discs are too large for gaming counters and have been interpreted as pot lids for small or narrow necked vessels. They may be medieval or earlier.

81. Smooth slate disc. Diam 74–69mm, thickness 8mm. SF427, Context 400.

82. Rough slate disc, smooth edges, chipped. Diam 68–65mm, thickness 9mm. SF427, Context 400.

83. Rough slate disc, smooth edges. Diam 86–82mm, max thickness 16mm. SF427, Context 400.

6.9 BUILDING MATERIALS

JULIE FRANKLIN

Pivot stones (not illustrated)

Very few objects from the early period related to building. There were a few fragments of burnt daub, which are more likely to relate to metalworking furnaces, rather than wattle and daub structures. There were however, five pivot stones. One of these (no 85) was from the area south of the church and may in fact be related to medieval or later structures. Two (nos 86 and 87) were from the north end, associated with many redeposited early finds. One (no 88) was found reused in a wall predating the church, on its north side. This was not removed and measurements are therefore approximate. None was found *in situ*, or appeared to be associated with any specific structure. They all appear to have been made from any piece of stone to hand. Many appear to be beach stones.

83. Pivot stone. Slate. Rough slab with irregular edges. Rough circular shallow depression in approximate centre of flattest face, more worn on one side than other. 201 × 153mm, 35mm thick,

hole 42mm wide, 10mm deep. SF418, Context 400, Topsoil

84. Pivot stone. Buff sandstone. Rough lump, broken off on one side, originally sub-triangular. Hole in top face worn deep and very smooth with steep sides and rounded bottom. 160 × 120mm, 96mm thick, hole 46mm wide, 30mm deep. SF422, Context 400, Topsoil

85. Pivot stone. Slate. Sub-square slab with worn edges. Shallow round depressions in centre of both faces. 174 × 145mm, 33mm thick, holes 30mm wide, 7mm deep and *c* 25mm wide, 4mm deep. SF793, Context 4003, Phase 3

86. Pivot stone. Grey schist. Ovoid rounded slab, shallow depression in approx centre of flattest face. 197 × 170mm, 45mm thick, hole 45mm wide, 12mm deep. SF502, Context 4001, Phase 3

87. Pivot stone. Grey schist. Irregular unworked slab, small shallow depression towards centre of one face. 260 × 160mm, 43mm thick, hole *c* 25mm wide, 9mm deep. SF605, Context 4001, Phase 3

88. Pivot stone. Shale or schist. Large sub-rectangular roughly squared block with round depression. 350 × 260mm, hole 50mm wide. Context 4497, Phase 1

Window glass

There was very little evidence of window glass from the site. A few crystallised fragments were found in a grave (G44) to the south of the chancel. Soil conditions, however, were clearly not conducive to glass preservation and it is therefore impossible to say to what extent the church may have been glazed.

Roof slates

Slate is readily available on Inchmarnock. The site was littered with pieces of slate, some entirely natural, some incised (Chapter 6.3, above), some fashioned into roof slates. It seems likely that the roof of the medieval church was slated. There are no examples of tiles. The use of organic roofing materials such as shingles or some kind of thatch is entirely possible, particularly in its early years, but it seems likely that towards the end of its life at least, the church was slated.

The only complete slate (Context 455, Phase 3) measured 270 × 135mm, with a variable thickness up to 22mm. It had a nail still in place, with a domed

square or lozenge shaped head inside a 15mm wide nail hole. There are some slates which appear to be wider than this. There are only two pieces of holed slate from Phase 1, both are small and abraded and may have been used as weights. Most of the slates are from Phase 2 and especially Phase 3. There are very few large pieces, suggesting that most of the usable slate was stripped from the roof and reused elsewhere on the island.

6.10 THE OIL SHALE ARTEFACTS AND RELATED MATERIAL

FRASER HUNTER (WITH A CONTRIBUTION BY J M JONES)

Introduction

The Inchmarnock church excavations produced a small but informative range of debris from the manufacture of items of black jewellery, primarily bangles of oil shale and related material. The 19 items cover most stages of the production process, although no finished ornaments are present. Unusually, two different production techniques were used, suggesting either different phases of activity or craft-workers trained in different traditions.

The individual items are listed below in the catalogue. The craft process is then discussed and the material considered in its wider context. The following abbreviations are used: *L*ength, *W*idth, *T*hickness, *D*iameter, *int*ernal, *ext*ernal, *max*imum, *min*imum. Where no abbreviations are given, measurements are in the order L × W × T. With bangles, W is the radial width of the original circular form and T the thickness of this circle. All dimensions are in millimetres.

Catalogue

Prepared roughouts (Figure 6.46)

89. Rounded block, abandoned due to excessive flaking during edge shaping. Edges generally bifacial, either flaked or knife-trimmed (?after flaking). One natural face, the other with some flaking. The natural face has remains of an incised line marking the outer edge, two grooves from an incipient perforation, and an unexplained short radial groove from a notch on the edge. It is notable (and unusual) that considerable effort was expended on shaping the edges before perforation was begun. 90 × 76 × 10mm; max ext D 90 SF462. Context 4001, Phase 3.

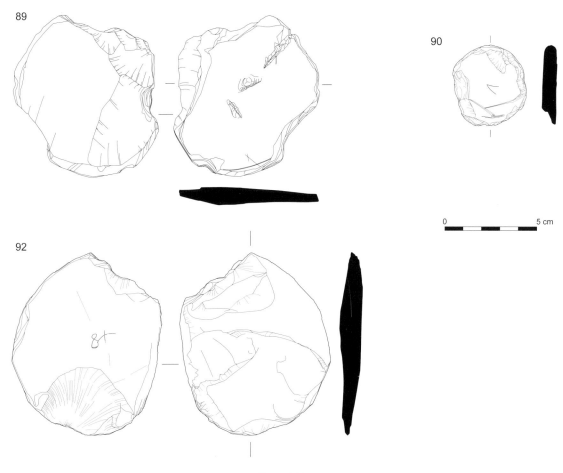

Figure 6.46
Cannel coal jewellery: prepared roughouts (nos 89, 90, 92)

90. Unfinished disc, probably a waste core removed from a bangle which was then itself used as a smaller roughout. One (natural) face has a central marking-out dot; the other is gouged and flaked flat, with a central mark and a couple of grooves crudely locating the perforation. The edge shows varied treatment; in places it has been snapped, in others knife-trimmed, while on one face a circular groove was cut to smooth the edge. This postdates removal of the core, and confirms it was being prepared for further use. D 39–44, T 7.5mm. SF484. Context 4001, Phase 3.

91. Rounded block, broken at one edge. Natural surfaces and one naturally square edge, the others shaped by gouging. Its size suggests it was for a small item such as a ring-pendant.

76.5 × 61 × 11.5mm, max ext D 60mm. SF542 (not illustrated). Context 4001, Phase 3.

92. Rounded block, the edges natural in places, elsewhere both unifacially and bifacially flaked, gouged and perhaps knife-cut. Faces partly flaked, one with a near-central incised figure-of-eight marking the centre of the intended perforation. Perhaps abandoned because flaking left it over-thin in places. D 97 × min 81.5, T 13.5. SF592. Context 4001, Phase 3.

93. Prepared roughout, broken prior to perforation. Part-rounded block with two naturally-square parallel edges, the others bifacially flaked to shape. One face has been partly flaked, the other apparently split. Two lines on this face (a fine straight one and a deeper curved one)

194

may mark the very beginning of perforation attempts, prior to the piece breaking. 117 × 66 × 18mm. SF615 (not illustrated). Context 4001, Phase 3.

94. Chunk, perhaps from a broken squared block. One face natural, one flaked; one, perhaps two prepared edges, others apparently broken. Probably a broken corner, although it could be a very small roughout. 37 × 29 × 9mm. SF673 (not illustrated). Context 4001, Phase 3.

95. Fragment of broken prepared block. Thick, with natural edges; a band of markedly inorganic stone within it probably caused it to fracture. Surfaces partly trimmed with long-bladed knife (cut-marks *c* 70mm L). 100 × 53 × 34mm. SF745 (not illustrated). Context 4510, Phase 2.

Perforated roughouts, finishing in progress (Figure 6.47)

96. Intact perforated roughout with perforation in process of expansion; probably abandoned because the material was not working well. Edges unifacially flaked then knife- and gouge-trimmed; all surfaces extensively flaked and gouged. Biconical perforation, formed by near-vertical pecking and ?gouging, with deep radial knife-cut grooves to expand it. There is a distinctive 'signature' pattern on the gouge marks, a phenomenon noted in toolmarks on wood (eg Sands 1997); it was not noted on other pieces. D 97 × 88mm, T 17.5mm; perforation 17 × 12.5mm. SF456. Context 4000, Phase 5.

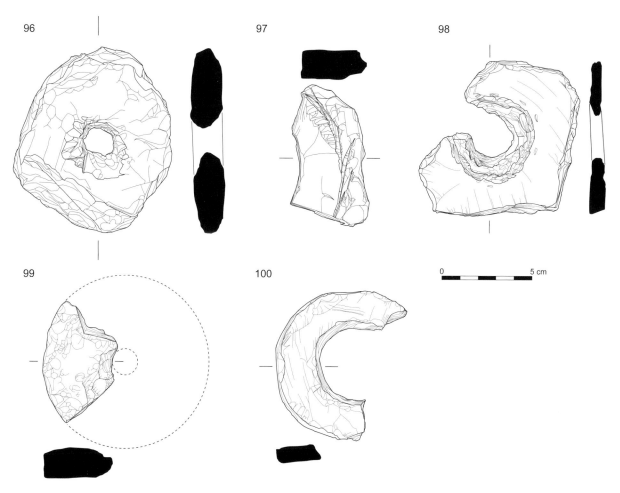

Figure 6.47
Cannel coal jewellery: perforated roughouts, finishing in progress (nos 96–100)

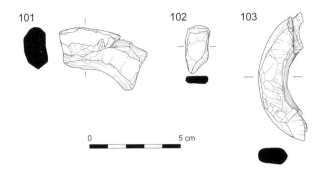

Figure 6.48
Cannel coal jewellery: near-complete items (nos 101–3)

97. Faces flaked, outer edge bifacially flaked and in process of being shaped by chopping from either side with a heavy knife, creating deep cut facets of L 20–30mm. The inner edge is a very smooth flake, unusual as a working trace and more likely from accidental flaking than deliberate shaping. 93 × 47 × 18.5mm, intended W *c* 27mm. SF458. Context 400, Phase 6.

98. Squared roughout with disc removed from centre. The two intact edges were shaped by cutting straight grooves on either side and snapping. One surface natural, other split and flaked. The perforation was created by removal of a central disc *c* 30mm D by bifacial chiselling or gouging around the margins (using a tool *c* 4mm W). An outer gouged line in areas marks initial unsuccessful attempts to remove the disc. One surface bears random knife cuts. It is unusual to leave the block so square at such a late stage, suggesting this perforation technique was recognised as hazardous. 115 × 115 × 11mm. SF621. Context 4009, Phase 1/2.

99. Broken perforated roughout with limited finishing. Flat faces, one gouged to shape, the other with some abrasion; the edge also shows abrasion to round off the gouged facets from shaping. Biconical perforation with marks from a fine gouge (2.5–3mm wide). 65 × 39.5 × T 17mm; ext D *c* 95mm. SF633. Context 4009, Phase 1/2.

100. Roughout with expanded perforation. Unusually thin, its non-biconical perforation suggesting this was a thicker roughout which was split horizontally to make a thin bangle. Edge carinated in places, with extensive gouging and areas of abrasion; the perforation was expanded by cutting and abrasion. One face split, the other natural with some flaking. D ext 93, int 45, T 9. SF645. Context 4001, Phase 3.

Near-complete items (Figure 6.48)

101. Two joining fragments of an unfinished bangle. Faces trimmed and flaked, with some natural surface remaining; outer edge with extensive knife-trimming facets; angular perforation with pronounced knife facets. Ext D 95–100, int D 50–55mm; *c* 20% survives. 49 × 21 × 12.5mm. SF541, Context 4001, Phase 3 and SF715, Context 4059, Phase 1.

102. Flat, thin bangle roughout with natural surface; biconical perforation with knife-cut facets, outer edge facetted. 25.5 × 13 × 5mm. SF590. Context 4001, Phase 3.

103. Unfinished bangle, near its final shape although still uneven. Flat D-section, the surfaces and inner face with fine knife-trimmed facets (typically 1.5mm W), and some abrasion on the exterior. The latter appears to predate the trimming, implying it was from earlier stages in the shaping. Ext D 70–75, 42% surviving. L 67.5, W 15–17.5, H 9–12mm. SF661. Context 4001, Phase 3.

Working debris (Figure 6.49)

104. Edge-trimming flake, removing a knife- or gouge-trimmed corner; ?natural faces. 24 × 14 × 10.5 mm. SF558. Context 4001, Phase 3.

105. Either a large thinning flake or an accidentally spalled surface from a prepared roughout. Sub-oval disc, with one natural face apart from

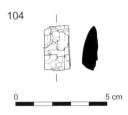

Figure 6.49
Cannel coal jewellery: working debris (no 104)

Table 6.6 Phasing of the Inchmarnock oil shale

Phase	Context	No of finds
1	4059	1
1/2	4009	2
2	4510	2
3	4001	13
5	4000	1
recent	400	1

limited edge-flaking, the other flaked. Naturally rounded, with some cutting and flaking of the edges in places. 94.5 × 79 × T 7.5mm. SF561 (not illustrated). Context 4001, Phase 3.

106. Edge-trimming flake, removing the corner of a squared block. Two edges flaked, then snapped. One, perhaps both sides flaked. 44 × 24 × 7mm. SF742 (not illustrated). Context 4510, Phase 2.

Other

107. Unidentified fragment, either a thin block or a flake. All edges broken; flake scars on faces. 70 × 60 × 7mm. SF.638 (not illustrated). Context 4001, Phase 3.

Discussion

The working of black organic-rich stones into jewellery was a long-lived tradition in Scotland, but bangle production was largely a phenomenon of the later prehistoric and early historic periods. Their popularity continued in Norse areas (eg Grieg 1940, 24, 70, 87; Hamilton 1956, 114, 121), but there is no evidence of production in the medieval period. Only one of the Inchmarnock finds (part of no 101) comes from a stratified early historic context (4059), although fragments of the same bangle were also found in 4001 (Table 6.6). Two fragments were recovered from a Phase 1/2 horizon; the remainder are residual in later contexts, but there is no doubt they are connected to the pre-medieval use of the site. However, they cannot be more closely dated typologically. The degree of post-depositional disturbance is seen by the existence of joining fragments spread between Phase 1 and Phase

3 contexts. Two stray finds of manufacturing debris are also known from the island (Marshall 1980, 16), but the recorded provenance is too unclear to know if they are connected to the current finds.

The craft process

What is preserved are traces of the process of jewellery manufacture. No finished products were found, but the debris indicates the main product was bangles, some of which (eg nos 100 and 102) were quite fine. The size of roughouts 90 and 91 shows that smaller items, probably rings or ring-pendants, were also produced.

Two different production methods for bangles are represented. The normal sequence of manufacture was as follows. Blocks of raw material were gathered and roughly worked to a square or sub-circular shape by trimming the edges and thinning one or both faces. This allowed the craftworker to assess the working properties of the block. Natural edges were utilised where possible, but various shaping techniques were used: snapping, unifacial and bifacial flaking, knife-trimming and gouging. A number of pieces bear incised guidelines, with central points to guide the initial perforation (nos 89, 90 and 92) or circles to mark the intended edges (no 89). A small central hole was made by bifacial pecking and gouging, and then expanded by knife and gouge. Normally the shaping of the outer edge was delayed until the initial perforation was completed, as this was one of the riskiest parts of the operation, although the edge of block 89 was rounded and well-finished before perforation had even begun. Final shaping involved fine knife-trimming of the roughout to shape, and abrading and polishing it to its final form and finish. No 103 is important as it shows abrasion preceding knife-trimming, suggesting cycles of increasingly fine abrasion and trimming to get the piece to its desired form. This general sequence is well-attested elsewhere (Callander 1916, 235; Hunter 1998; Hunter forthcoming).

A second technique is also represented at the site, where a solid disc was removed from the centre of the roughout to make the perforation. This is represented by no 98 (where some trial and error can be noted) and by disc 90, a waste disc which was being reused to make a smaller item. There is a stray find, poorly located, of another disc from the island (Marshall 1980, 16, fig 2, 2). This technique is attested elsewhere, although less widely than the perforation method (Callander 1916, 236–7). With the exception of Carn Liath in Sutherland there is a marked concentration in west and south-west Scotland, suggesting it was a regional tradition. Similar finds are known from early historic sites in northern

Table 6.7   Raw material identification

Group	Finds	Identity	Petrological sample and results
A	95, 97, 100, 101, 103, 104 and 106	Canneloid shale	100: canneloid shale, very fine-grained, rich in small plant fragments
B	89–94 and 98	Oil shale	91: shale, rich in algae – Torbanite or Boghead coal 98: amorphinite-rich shale, rich in algal fragments
C	102, 105 and 107	Oil shale	107: shale, rich in amorphinite and algae
D	99	Lignite	Coal containing algal fragments
E	96	Oil shale	Shale, amorphinite-rich with inertinite fragments and algae

Ireland (eg Armagh: Crothers 1999, 63, fig 13), raising the possibility that the tradition may have been shared between these areas, but further research is required on the Irish material to clarify this.

Inchmarnock is so far unique in having these two different processes represented on the one site, although both were known in the area. The relationship between them is unclear: this may represent different phases of working (which is impossible to prove on the available evidence), or craftworkers trained in different traditions. It does not seem to be a response to different raw materials. There is no sign of the unusual technique represented at nearby St Blane's, Bute, where a partial core was removed and the remaining thin layer of material then perforated and cut away (Callander 1916, 236).

The small amount of working debris (the flakes and chunks carved off the main block in the process of shaping it) is surprising. This may be an issue of recovery: such material is often not recognised by excavators. However, this lack was noted at the assessment stage and sample residues were checked for debris, to no avail. It is likely that, since most of the finds are from secondary contexts, the smaller debris had been broken up and dispersed, and the centre of production lay outwith the excavation area.

The raw material (with J M Jones)

To identify the raw materials used, the pieces were inspected visually for key characteristics (such as conchoidal fracture and evidence of laminar structure) and analysed by surface X-ray fluorescence (XRF; for methodology, see Davis 1993; Hunter *et al* 1993). This technique provides broad groupings of the material (Table 6.7). Five groups were defined in the Inchmarnock assemblage. Representative samples were then studied by J M Jones for petrological characterisation (Allason-Jones & Jones 2001).

Amorphinite is amorphous organic material, rich in hydrogen and the source of oil. The algae are all *Botryococcus*, which is a freshwater algae. This strongly suggests that these are carboniferous 'oil shales' from the Midland Valley. When they are very rich in algae they are termed Torbanites or Bog Heads after Torban Hill and Bog Head near Bathgate. All the samples, except possibly the Group A canneloid shales, probably come from the Midland Valley sources.

Visually there are two clear outliers, confirmed by XRF: no 99 (lignite) and no 96 (an oil shale with poor working properties). Fragments 101 and 104 are a distinctive highly organic material; they were not studied petrologically, and may be cannel coal or a high-quality compact lignite, as the visible pore structure may suggest. Otherwise clear groups were not distinguished in the analytical data, suggesting use of a related group of sources with similar inorganic inclusions. Many of the pieces had noticeable levels of barium, which is unusual but has been noted previously in Clyde coast finds (Hunter 1998, 48).

The Midland Valley Carboniferous deposits occur extensively, but the source of the raw materials is likely to have been the eastern shore of the Clyde. The raw material occurs abundantly in Ayrshire and neighbouring areas (Gibson 1922); a thin seam of Coal Measure deposits is known across Bute, north Arran and south Kintyre (MacDonald 1982, 184; Gibson 1922, 30; Gunn *et al* 1903, 37, 48–9, 54, 146; Mann 1915), but it is unclear if this is usable. The Bute raw material

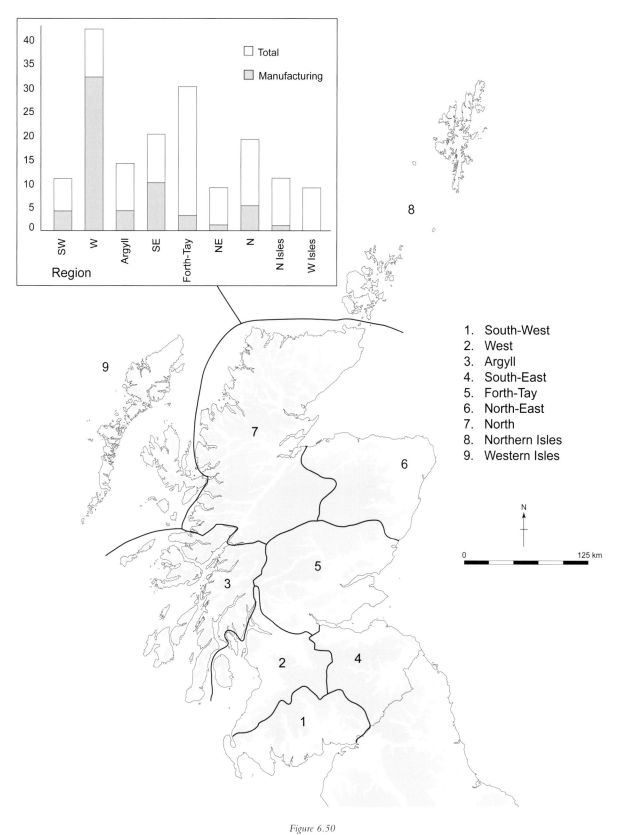

Figure 6.50
Regional variety in the occurrence of cannel coal and related materials on settlement sites in Scotland, *c* 1000 BC–AD 1000. The proportion of sites with evidence for manufacturing is indicated.

Table 6.8 Scottish sites with evidence for jewellery of oil shale and related material, most likely of early historic date. (The Cumbrae find is included as sculpture indicates the presence of an early church (Waddell 1932, 411–12; Curle 1962, 223–5). The Lasswade fragment is unworn and thus need not be residual, as the excavator implies; it may be a token thrown into the burial.)

Site	Island/county	Site type	Production evidence	Finished products	Reference/notes
RELIGIOUS SITES					
Inchmarnock	Bute	Church	X		This volume
St Blane's	Bute	Church	X	X	Anderson 1900
St Ninian's Chapel	Bute	Church		X	Aitken 1955, 70
Great Cumbrae Churchyard	Bute	Church?	X		*PSAS* 27 (1892–3), 244; NMS FN 80
Holy Island	Arran	Church?	X		Balfour 1909, 151 (possible early chapel under medieval tower)
Govan Old	Renfrew	Church	X		Unpublished
Barhobble	Wigtown	Church	X	X	Hunter 1995
Whithorn	Wigtown	Church	X	X	Hunter & Nicholson 1997
St Andrew's	Fife	Church		X	Hay Fleming 1909, 412 (from a burial)
Isle of May	Fife	Church		X	Peter Yeoman, pers comm
Tarbat	E Ross	Church		X	Unpublished
OTHER SITE TYPES					
Little Dunagoil	Bute	Settlement	X	X	Marshall 1964, 18, 20, 22, 39–45
Auldhill	Ayr	Fort	X	X	Hunter 1998
Buiston	Ayr	Crannog	X	X	Crone 2000, 142, 148
Lochspouts	Ayr	Crannog	X	X	Munro 1882, 13; 1884, 15–16
Dunadd	Argyll	Fort	X	X	Lane & Campbell 2000, 192–5
Kildalloig	Argyll	Dun		X	RCAHMS 1971, 87–8
Kildonan	Argyll	Dun		X	Fairhurst 1939, 215
Ugadale Point	Argyll	Fort		X	Fairhurst 1956, 19
Parkburn, Lasswade	Midlothian	Cemetery		X	Henshall 1956, 264–5
Jonathan's Cave	Fife	Cave		X	MacKie 1986

Table 6.9 Composition of the Inchmarnock finds compared to other early historic assemblages with ten or more finds of oil shale and related materials. (The Auldhill assemblage is a mixture of Iron Age and early historic date; Little Dunagoil is excluded because the material has not yet been studied by the writer.)

Type	Inchmarnock	St Blane's	Govan	Auldhill	Buiston	Dunadd	Whithorn
Gathered blocks	–	2	–	–	–	1	–
Prepared roughouts	7	6	7	2	2	3	–
Part-perforated roughouts	–	2	–	3	–	1	–
Perforated roughouts	8	10	3	2	3	5	8
Finished items	–	3	–	5	5	18	12
Working debris	3	10	11	9	–	–	1
Unidentified	1	2	–	–	–	–	–
Total (objects + debris/unidentified)	15 + 4	23 + 12	10 + 11	12 + 9	10 + 0	28 + 0	20 + 1

samples seen by the writer are unworkable, and it is unclear if the Arran deposits (which are immediately adjacent to Inchmarnock) included suitable material. Similar transport of raw materials is attested at Dunadd (Lane & Campbell 2000, 192–5).

Comparisons (Figure 6.50)

The presence of manufacturing debris at Inchmarnock is not surprising. Both this area and this type of site regularly produce such evidence. However, the comparanda have not been synthesised, and it is worth considering in more detail how Inchmarnock fits into its regional and cultural context.

There is evidence for the production of oil shale or cannel coal bangles in the Firth of Clyde area on the vast majority of excavated sites in the later prehistoric and early historic periods. Figure 6.50 provides a regional summary of the evidence for the manufacture and use of oil shale and related items in Scotland in the period *c* 1000 BC–AD 1000. It is clear that there was considerable regional variety both in availability of such jewellery and in its production. Unsurprisingly it was most common in areas near major coal seams such as Ayrshire, Fife and the Lothians. However, there are also hints of differences in production systems: in western Scotland most sites have working debris while in the Forth–Tay area only a minority do, suggesting more centralised control over production. Manufacturing evidence is

all but unknown in the north-east and the Atlantic island archipelagos, and finds generally are rarer there.

This general picture undoubtedly conceals chronological and sub-regional variety. For the early historic period, Table 6.8 lists all the Scottish evidence known to the writer; Table 6.9, meanwhile, looks at the composition of those early historic assemblages with ten or more finds and the relative proportions of finished objects to working debris.

It can be seen that manufacture was common at many religious sites in western Scotland, one of a range of craft processes carried out under the wing of the church. Yet church sites were only one centre among many: a range of other site types was producing similar jewellery. Unlike the production of non-ferrous metalwork, where centralised control has been suggested (Campbell 1996, 84–6), the manufacture of black jewellery was widely dispersed. However, there are indications of regional variety: in Argyll, so far only Dunadd has produced manufacturing evidence, and thus may have been a central site for this as with other craft processes.

Table 6.9 compares the major early historic assemblages known from the area. Differing excavation scales and styles will cause some variation, but the broad patterns are likely to be robust; with Dunadd, for instance, the more recent excavations have a similar picture to the early ones. There appear to be

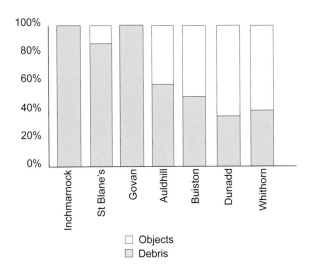

Figure 6.51
Proportions of finished objects and manufacturing debris in early historic assemblages with ten or more finds (working debris excluded).

two different patterns, summarised in Figure 6.51: sites where debris far outweighs products; and those where products equal or exceed the debris. The three 'producer' sites in the former category are all churches around the Clyde estuary. It seems the jewellery saw only limited use at these religious sites, suggesting that, despite manufacturing evidence being commonplace in the area, there was some localised exchange system for the products.

The Inchmarnock assemblage is a valuable addition to our knowledge of oil shale and cannel coal working in the early historic period. It is the first site to have produced evidence of both major production methods, which raises questions of the relation between them that require further work. The debris provides a vivid insight into this craft process, and also feeds into wider questions on the nature of craft production and exchange in the region and beyond.

6.11 FERROUS METALWORKING DEBRIS

ANDREW HEALD AND DAWN McLAREN

Introduction

A total of 32.3kg of material was visually examined, which allows it to be broadly categorised using the criteria of morphology, density, colour and vesicularity. In general, assemblages of slag can be divided into two broad categories. The first group includes the diagnostic material which can be attributed to metalworking. In the case of ironworking a range of slag morphologies are produced. Only a few, for example tapped slag and hammerscale, are truly diagnostic (of smelting and smithing respectively). The second category includes the non-diagnostic slags, which could have been generated by a number of different processes but show no diagnostic characteristic that can identify the process. Within this group there is often a significant amount of material which is unclassifiable, making the allocation of individual pieces (particularly small samples) to specific types and processes difficult (Crew & Rehren 2002, 84). That said, in many cases these undiagnostic residues, such as hearth or furnace lining, may be ascribed to a particular process through archaeological association.

The slag has been described using common terminology (eg McDonnell 1994; Spearman 1997; Starley 2000). A full catalogue of the material is given in the archive report. Further scientific analyses would be necessary to classify the material more conclusively. This was only undertaken on a few samples by Lore Troalen and Jim Tate in NMS Conservation and Analytical Research Department [noted in the catalogue].

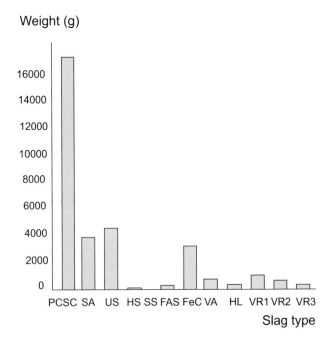

Figure 6.52
Total quantities of ferrous slag and other residues (weight g)

Classification

There are five diagnostic ferrous slags and residues present:

1. *Plano-convex slag cakes (PCSC)*: a plano-convex accumulation of slag formed in a pit, which can come in a range of sizes. It is difficult to be sure whether these were produced during smelting or smithing although their dimensions and weight compare closer to slag cakes associated with smelting on other Iron Age sites (eg McDonnell 1994, 230; McDonnell 2000, 219). That said scientific analysis illustrates that their compositions vary (eg some have a high manganese content, others do not) suggesting that different cakes may be related to different parts of the ironworking process.

2. *Slag Amalgams (SA)*: randomly shaped pieces of slag including plano-convex slag cakes and hearth lining which have fused together to form larger masses.

3. *Unclassified slag (US)*: randomly shaped pieces of iron silicate slag generated by the smelting or smithing process.

4. *Hammerscale (HS)*: small flakes of iron produced by the impact of hammers on hot iron during either the refining of iron blooms or the working of wrought iron. When found in sufficient quantities this is usually indicative of *in situ* metalworking.

5. *Slag spheres (SS)*: spheres ejected as spherical globules of molten slag during ironworking. When found in sufficient quantities this is usually indicative of *in situ* metalworking.

In addition, there are other non-diagnostic slags and residues:

1. *Hearth or Furnace Lining (HL/FL)*: The clay lining of an industrial hearth, furnace or kiln that has a vitrified or slag-attacked face. It is not always possible to distinguish between furnace and hearth lining. Often the material shows a compositional gradient from unmodified fired clay on one surface to an irregular cindery material on the other (Starley 2000, 339).

2. *Fuel ash slag (FAS)* and *vitrified amalgams (VA)*: slag formed when material such as sand, earth, clay, stones or ceramics are subjected to high temperatures, for example in a hearth. During heating these materials react, melt or fuse with alkali in ash, producing glassy (vitreous) and porous materials. These slags can be formed during any high temperature pyrotechnic process and are not necessarily indicative of deliberate industrial activity.

3. *Vitrified residues*: due to the sampling strategy employed on the site a fair quantity of small vitrified residues (*c* 1mm–10mm) were recovered. Again, these are mixtures of various types of material, fused together through heat. Three different types were recovered: those that were comprised mainly of sand, clay, stone and other material and were magnetic (VR1), those that shared similar constituents but were not-magnetic (VR2) and finally fused masses of soil (VR3). Although it is impossible to relate these small pieces to any specific process it is likely that VR1 was related to ferrous-metalworking.

4. *Fe conglomerate*: Random pieces of compact conglomerate with a significant Fe chemical component.

Table 6.10 Total quantities of ferrous slag and other residues (weight g)

Short description	Abbreviation	Weight (g)
DIAGNOSTIC SLAGS		
Plano-convex slag cakes	PCSC	17,293
Slag amalgams	SA	3,830
Unclassified slag (Fe?)	US	4,509
Hammerscale	HS	39
Slag spheres	SS	12
UNDIAGNOSTIC SLAGS		
Hearth lining	HL	401
Fuel Ash slag	FAS	272
Vitrified amalgams	VA	709
Vitrified residue 1	VR1	1,038
Vitrified residue 2	VR2	636
Vitrified residue 3	VR3	364
Fe conglomerate	FeC	3,223

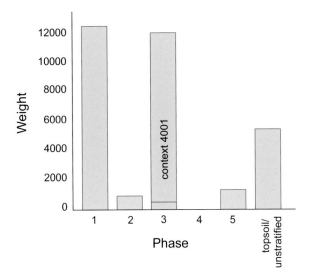

Figure 6.53
Distribution of slag by phase and weight

The total quantity of debris recovered is shown in Table 6.10 and Figure 6.52.

Visual analysis suggest that the assemblage is composed predominately of plano-convex slag cakes, both by weight and by number of specimens. There are 31 PCSCs and another 25 possible fragments. The slag amalgams should also be viewed in this class; all are composed of plano-convex cakes, with additional slags. There are, therefore, almost 60 plano-convex slag cakes from Inchmarnock. Together with the unclassified slag, which is likely to be derived from ironworking, the slag assemblage represents one of the largest ironworking assemblages from early historic Scotland. Differentiating between smithing and smelting slags visually is difficult. As noted, the weight and size of the cakes make many examples closer to smelting than smithing slags (see McDonnell 1994, 230; McDonnell 2000). That there was little diagnostic iron smithing micro-slags (hammerscale and slag spheres) from Inchmarnock may, therefore, be instructive.

Site distributing and phasing

Contextual and distributional analysis, set out in detail in the archive, shows that slag was found throughout much of the excavated area. Furthermore, it was recovered from a range of features including soil layers, levelling layers, gullies, pits, post holes and the like. Many of the contexts are clearly redeposited.

In order to tease out further patterns in the material it is pertinent to analyse the distribution and phasing of the material more closely (Figure 6.53). Three patterns emerge. First, almost 20% of the material, classified as topsoil or unstratified finds, cannot be assigned to a phase. Second, the largest proportion of slag comes from Phase 1. Finally, a large proportion of the assemblage derives from context 4001, a Phase 3 deposit comprising a thick, homogenised layer directly below topsoil, and prevalent across the whole of the site.

Context 4001 is particularly important. It was dominated by bracken roots which mixed a great deal of material (eg prehistoric flint, medieval pottery and small 20th-century items, such as cartridge cases) from the underlying contexts. While this renders all of the finds – including the slag – unstratified, it is of particular note that when the slag from this context is plotted spatially across the site almost all of the finds derive from an area of the site which saw metalworking in Phase 1. It is arguable, therefore, that some of the slag from 4001 is derived from earlier Phase 1 metalworking contexts. That no micro-slags (eg hammerscale, slag spheres or vitrified resiudes) were recovered from 4001 suggest that this is probable. It is suggested here, therefore, that the overwhelming majority of slag from Inchmarnock (*c* 75–68%) derives from a specific area: the northern part of the site, which was associated with metalworking, predominantly during Phase 1.

Although slag from Phase 1 was scattered across much of the excavated area the majority comes from the northern end. Excavation here indicated the presence of a possible 'craft zone' associated with the early historic monastic settlement. Excavation identified a series of early ironworking features and a series of intercutting buildings defined by possible beamslots and clusters of postholes. The area primarily in and around Structure 1 is of note. At least 10 features have notable distributions of slag (Table 6.11). Of these, four are particularly important.

Feature Group 1 (4228; 4193; 4195/4073; 4192; 4005; 4072)

Feature 4228 comprised 4193 (a 'bowl') and 4195/4073 (a possible 'flue'). These features were filled by 4192 (the 'bowl') and 4005, 4072 (the 'flue'). All of the fills produced varying types and quantities of ironworking debris. Context 4005 had the largest range and quantity including plano-convex slag cakes, hearth lining, and unclassified ironworking slags. A small quantity of

Table 6.11 Features probably associated with ironworking (weight g)

Feature	C14	PCSC	PCSC?	US	HS	SS	VR1	VR2	FeC	VC/ HL	FAS	VA	Total
4228 4073 4195 4193 4072 4005 4192	AD 780–980	2503	1023	914	36		453	526		83			5538
4136 4135		705	209	170	1	1				132			1218
4226 4077 4079 4086 4076 4078 4085	AD 650–780	673	263	177.9	1		12.8	0.1				130	1257.8
4160 4161	AD 410–780	298		266	1	1	355.7			7	28		956.7
4083 4074 4075			97		1		3.8						101.8
4308 4307				50	1								51
4146 4143 4145					1		32.1						33.1
4154 4153						1	20.1						21.1
4197 4198							2.2						2.2
4202 4220 4203								0.3	990				990.3

hammerscale was also recovered. Radiocarbon dates indicate that this activity took place around cal AD 780–980.

Feature Group 2 (4136; 4135)

Beside the above feature was an irregular scoop (4136), filled by 4135. Again, plano-convex slag cakes,

unclassified ironworking slags and minute quantities of micro-ironworking slags were recovered.

Feature Group 3 (4226; 4077; 4079; 4086; 4076; 4078; 4085)

A shallow gully (4226, comprised of 4077, 4079, 4086) was located to the south of the above features.

Three fills from this feature (4076, 4078 and 4085) produced evidence of ironworking including plano-convex slag cakes, unclassified ironworking slags and magnetic material that may be associated with ironworking. Radiocarbon dates indicate that this gully was filled around cal AD 650–780.

Feature Group 4 (4160; 4161)

Beside Feature Group 3 was a pit (4161), filled by 4160. A plano-convex slag cake, unclassified ironworking slags and small amounts of micro-ironworking slags were also recovered. Radiocarbon dates indicate that this feature was filled between cal AD 410–780.

In summary, four groups of features produced a suite and quantities of slag suggestive of *in situ* ironworking. It is also noteworthy that other features excavated in the area (the majority listed in Table 6.11) also produced varying amounts of slag. Although few are diagnostic of ironworking, merely some unknown pyrotechnic process, it is likely that much of the slag was associated with this industrial activity. Ironworking requires a suite of features and areas to undertake the work; we should not expect diagnostic slags from all of them. The radiocarbon dates indicate that the area saw more than one episode of metalworking activity.

Wider discussion

Monastic sites are well known for being foci for crafts, including metalworking (Price 1982, 52–6; Barber 1981, 366; Alcock 2003, 334), and specific areas appear to have been set aside for such crafts. In this light the evidence from Inchmarnock fits well with the slag evidence from other monastic sites across Scotland, for example Iona (Barber 1981, 349), Tarbat (Carver 2004) and Whithorn (eg Hill 1997, 27, 67, 129, fig 3.1). The stratified Inchmarnock ironworking debris from a series of features and associated radiocarbon dates provides a further opportunity to study where smiths worked and the suite of accoutrements they used. The distribution of whetstones, concentrated in the area to the west of Structures 1–3 (Conolly, Chapter 5.5; Franklin, Chapter 6.8), clearly complements that of the ironworking debris. A possible anvil stone was recovered from the same area (Franklin, Chapter 6.8).

Assessing the role of the smith in the social and economic life of Inchmarnock is more difficult. In his review of Irish ironworking Scott (n.d., 101) highlights the different type of smiths we should

expect on monastic settlements. On the one hand Scott views most of the industrial activity as the equivalent of that on 'lower-tier secular sites' where the making or repair of a knife or an axe for use in the work of the community would be a part of its self-sufficient internal economy. On the other hand, he admits that we must be conscious of the possible presence of master smiths working in some monastic communities.

In order to understand the role of the monastic smith it is necessary to take a broader look into the organisation of ironworking in the early historic period. This is far from easy, hindered by the lack of systematic analysis of ironworking both in the immediate area and beyond. There have been few useful discussions of ferrous metalworking in Iron Age Scotland (although see McDonnell 1994; McDonnell 1998 for an initial model of iron-working in Orkney and Shetland) and recent discussions of the practice in western Scotland in the first millennium AD have been superficial (eg Photos-Jones 2005). This is undoubtedly due to the difficulty in finding comparable sites and contemporaneous production (see also Alcock 2003, 93). Many slag assemblages were excavated decades ago and slag finds were often not retained. Even when slag was kept it is difficult to ascertain what process it is related to.

Despite this predicament it is pertinent to raise some issues that should be addressed in the future. If we are to understand the meaning of slag on archaeological sites we need to relate the material to other objects on the site and assess assemblages in the surrounding area.

It is clear that other sites in and around the area of Inchmarnock have produced slag. Although identifying and dating the material is often difficult – many come from either sites where there is no context or that saw millennia of use, such as caves (eg Columba's Cave, Tolan-Smith 2001, 51) – a number have evidence of ironworking during the early historic period. These include: Auldhill, Portencross (Cullen 1998, 59–60); Kildonan Bay (Fairhurst 1939, 212); Loch Glashan (Photos-Jones 2005); Dunadd (McDonnell 2000); Iona (Barber 1981, 349) and Bruach an Druimein (RCAHMS 1988, 204).

This shows that ironworking took place on a range of sites including nuclear forts, duns, monastic sites, crannogs and open settlements. In other words, almost every site type in the area has produced evidence for ironworking. This is hardly surprising. Most iron objects were largely functional and everyday, such as knives, agricultural tools and structural fittings (see Alcock 2003, 95–101 for a useful summary). In other words, the occurrence of slag on many archaeological sites may represent everyday repair or manufacture of prosaic, functional objects (see also Mytum 1992, 211). That said, this does not mean that we should assume that the practice was common place everywhere. There are many areas for fruitful research.

A starting position should be analysis of the iron objects from sites which have also produced slag; it is not the slag that will indicate what was made, nor the status of the smith, but the surviving objects. For example, we should expect that the ironworker on a monastic settlement would be required to make a range of objects, from nails for buildings to tools for sculpture, and bells for religious purposes. Do any of these survive and what do they infer about the scale and status of the craft?

From here we should broaden analysis to the slag and iron objects from a range of contemporary sites. For example, are there sites which have produced no evidence for ironworking debris, but where iron was in use? Was there ironworking, but little or no consumption? Did ironworking and use go on together? Quantity and survival should always be considered; some sites may produce slag but not of the type or quantity to suggest that a full-time specialist existed on them. Are there differences between sites?

These are questions which were first raised over 30 years ago (reviewed in Rahtz 1973) but still remain unanswered. Previous studies have shown that the presence and absence of object types and crafts may give insights into questions of status, hierarchies and inter-site relationships. This has largely been confined to the exotic end of the spectrum: imported pottery, fine metalworking and jewellery (eg Dark 1994: Campbell 1991: Campbell 2007). It is clear that sites such as Dunadd stood apart from other settlements in the area, with their inhabitants able to acquire, use and distribute exotica (Alcock & Alcock 1987; Alcock 1988; Campbell 1996: Campbell 1999). These studies into local and regional politics are now being augmented by analysis of the more prosaic material. For example, analysis of the Argyll data set has suggested that there may well be differences in the range of iron objects used on different sites (Hunter & Heald forthcoming). It is time that the slag was brought into the discussion.

What the Inchmarnock smiths produced, for whom, and what status this conferred is difficult at present to answer. However we should be content with the recovery of one of the few *in situ* metalworking areas in early historic Scotland.

6.12 CRUCIBLES AND OTHER VITRIFIED CERAMICS

ANDREW HEALD

Two crucible fragments were recovered; reconstruction of their original shape is not possible. They were analysed non-destructively by energy dispersive X-ray fluorescence (EDXRF) by Jim Tate and Lore Troalen of the NMS Conservation and Analytical Research Department to give broad characterisation of the alloys melted.

108. Body fragment of crucible. Broken on all sides and lacking diagnostic features (rim, base etc). Heavily vitrified on the outside. 47mm × 32mm × 9mm. SF606, Context 4001, Phase 3. XRF analysis reveals traces of copper.

109. Rim, corner and body fragment of crucible. The outside is fractured and the inside coloured grey due to heating. Although the original shape is difficult to reconstruct the surviving fragment suggests that the vessel would have been fairly substantial, and probably triangular in shape. Although XRF analysis did not reveal any metallic traces the object does have the characteristics of a crucible. 58mm × 52mm × 12mm. SF714, Context 4001, Phase 3.

Crucible fragment 109 was recovered from the heavily turbated deposit (4001), over the site of a pit (4154), part of the metalworking area; fragment 108 was found in the same mixed deposit, some 9m to the south. Although the context of the material does not aid discussion of on-site metalworking the crucibles are a welcome addition to the ever-expanding corpus of non-ferrous metalworking from Iron Age Scotland.

Evidence for the practice has been found on a range of sites in and around Inchmarnock. Assemblages from forts, such as Dunadd (Christison & Anderson 1905, 311–4; Craw 1930, 120–3; Lane & Campbell 2000, 106–49) and Dunollie (Alcock & Alcock 1987, 140–1), and the monastic sites of St Blane's (Anderson 1900, 311, 6; Laing, Laing & Longley 1998, 559–61, illus. 6), Iona (McCormick 1992; Graham-Campbell 1981; Barber 1981, 349–50, fig 42, nos 303/1; 304/1) and Whithorn (Hill & Nicholson 1997) are best documented. Indeed, these sites, particularly forts, have been the focus for past discussions of metalworking during the period. Structural characteristics, together with artefactual analysis and literary sources demonstrate that these sites stood apart from other settlements, with their inhabitants controlling access to exotic goods and maintaining their royal power through redistribution. It seems that, at least on some sites, the production of precious objects was under the direct control of aristocrats at the top of the social hierarchy. This has led to a common social interpretation, that the control of jewellery manufacture was the '... prerogative of the elite' (eg Crone 2000, 9) and '... a means of obtaining and maintaining hierarchical status' (Nieke & Duncan 1988, 16).

It is well known that these sites were important power centres in the early historic period and their importance for understanding the organisation of metalworking cannot be denied. However sites of a different nature have also produced evidence for non-ferrous metalworking, such as Loch Glashan crannog (Campbell 2005), Ardifuar dun (Christison & Anderson 1905, 267–9), St Columba's Cave (Tolan-Smith 2001, 49–51, fig 24) and the open settlement of Bruach an Druimein (Hunter & Heald forthcoming). This association is mirrored in other areas of Scotland. There is, therefore, emerging evidence that during the early historic period a wider range of sites than hitherto appreciated were domains for metalworking activity. Many are of a different nature than traditional foci, being undefended, isolated sites and not of apparent high status. Further, the smiths working on many of these apparently everyday sites were using precious metals (Heald 2005). This accumulating evidence shows that the production of non-ferrous objects was *not* confined to high-status settlement sites. Whether this reflects itinerant smiths producing material for distribution to other areas or a more egalitarian distribution of wealth in this region is a question for further research. At the very least it forces us to appreciate that there were regional differences in the control of the production of fine metalwork (see also Campbell & Heald 2007).

Other vitrified ceramic

A cylindrical fired object, broken at both ends was recovered from Inchmarnock. Although not directly related to any metalworking feature the object could be a tuyère plug. It was recovered from a Phase 1 pit (4167) at the north end of the excavated area, part of a series of features associated with metalworking activity. Alder charcoal from the pit has been radiocarbon-dated to cal AD 460–660 (AA-53162).

110. A cylindrical object, broken at both ends, with signs of being fired. 39mm × 39mm × 32mm. SF752, Context 4168, Phase 1. XRF analysis revealed no metal traces.

6.13 MODERN FINDS

JULIE FRANKLIN

Only ten clay pipe fragments were recovered during the excavation. Two of these were of 17th-century date, including an unmarked bowl fragment, probably dropped by grave-diggers or visitors. The rest were of 19th-century date. Two marked stems were from Glasgow makers John Warnock who was active in the 1870s and, probably, Alexander Coghill who was trading in the period 1826–1904.

There were two pieces from modern bottles, including the base from a wine bottle, of probable 19th-century date. There are four buttons, a four-holed example of bone or horn, and three flat disc types with integral loops of copper alloy. These were common types of the 18th and 19th centuries. Modern iron finds include a pitchfork blade, some pieces from very large horseshoes, some large ring fittings and a heavy duty chain. All of these later finds relate to the use of the area as a stack-yard and horse gin in the late 19th and 20th centuries.

NOTE

1 abecedarian: structured alphabetically, with each successive verse beginning with the next letter of the Latin alphabet.

Chapter 7

The Human Remains from the Church and Graveyard (Site 4)

DAVID HENDERSON

7.1 INTRODUCTION

The remains of a minimum of 43 adults (on the basis of number of right femurs recovered) and 43 infants (left humerus) were excavated from the burial ground. Sixty-three graves contained *in situ* inhumations, and a further 19 contexts (mostly soil layers in the areas surrounding the graves) also contained some human bone. Each grave was given a Grave Number (eg G7), any *in situ* remains within a grave were allocated that same figure as a Skeleton Number (SK7). Many graves to the north of the church no longer contained any surviving human remains, hence the gaps in the sequence of SK numbers. Many of the graves had been dug through one, or more, earlier graves so that the material used to backfill them contained disarticulated remains. As is normal in medieval and post-medieval graveyards, disturbed bones were not systematically replaced in the backfill; however, in several cases bones could be matched and rearticulated with partially disturbed skeletons lower in the stratigraphic sequence. Four nearly complete skeletons were reconstructed, with a high degree of confidence, solely from bones in the backfill of later graves. The graves of three of these individuals had been completely removed by later activity, while the fourth, SK36B, from G36, probably represents the disturbed remains of the individual SK48, who survived only as an *in situ* left hand. SK33x and SK33y were skeletons recovered mostly from the fill of G33; SK36A was also reconstructed from material in the fill of G36. All material was analysed to determine age at death, sex, stature and health.

Most of the inhumations excavated followed the normal Christian pattern of lying supine, head to the west with the arms by the side or crossed over the body. In four cases, however, as discussed below, this pattern was not followed.

7.2 METHODOLOGY

Some methods of estimating age at death in adults are now thought to be less accurate than was previously supposed (Molleson 1995: Mays 1998, 49–66). Tooth-wear analysis (as outlined by Brothwell 1981, 72) was used to determine the age classes of the adult skeletons. Other methods were used to estimate a more exact skeletal age. These were examination of the pubic symphyses (Brooks & Suchey 1990) the auricular surface of the ilium (Lovejoy *et al* 1985), and the sternal end of the fourth rib (Iscan *et al* 1984 and 1985). The age of the infants was estimated from tooth eruption and development, or from the state of development of the skeleton (Scheuer & Black 2000).

Sex was assessed by examining the form of the skull and the pelvis (W E A 1980), with more emphasis being given to pelvic form. Stature was reconstructed using the standard regression formulae from longbone lengths of Trotter and Gleser (in Bass 1987). Skeletal measurements were taken as per Cross & Bruce (1989) and indices were calculated using the formulae in Bass (1987). Non-metric traits were recorded from those in Brothwell (1981, 93–100). All bones were examined for pathological lesions and, where possible, these were classified according to cause.

7.3 PRESERVATION

Bone preservation on the site was generally very good, where bone survived at all. However, more than approximately 2m away from the walls of the church, to the north and west, no bone was recovered (except from Grave G66, where a few fragments of bone were recorded). It appears that this is due to the acidic nature of the groundwater, away from the protection afforded by the alkaline mortar of the church leaching into the ground immediately surrounding the building itself. An exception to this was the young adult male SK129, where preservation was very poor, but in this case a later drain may have provided the source of acidic water.

Many skeletons were largely intact, although the weight of overlying material had often caused the skulls and other bones to fragment somewhat. However, the standard of preservation and of excavation was generally excellent, so that in 15 of the 23 skeletons

Table 7.1 Demography: age, sex and stature distributions of the assemblage

SK #	Phase	Sex	Age class	Ht (m)	Pathology	Arthritis (counted only in cases of eburnation)	EH (enamel hypoplasia)	cribra orbitalia	Notes
2	4		PE						
5	4	M	SA	1.70			none	Y	Buried with knees by ears, complete to knees.
15	3	M	OA	1.75	Left 5th rib fracture. Scoliosis to right at T3. Hallux valgus bilaterally.	Left fingers, lumbar spine.	1.5, 2, 2.5, 3.5, 4	N	Buried with head to the east. Complete.
33	3	F	OA	1.56	Crush injury to tip of Left 3rd finger. Groove worn in left lower I1.	Left fingers.	none	Y	Almost complete.
33x	2?	M	MA	1.62	Os acromiale ensethopathy at head of Left tibia.	Shoulders.	2	Y	Skull, limbs and pelvis, not *in situ*, backfill GR33.
33y	2?	F	MA	1.57	Gout, Osteoporosis with vertebral collapse, lumbarised 1st sacral vertebra.	Neck, lower back.	none	N	Skull, limbs and pelvis, not *in situ*, backfill GR33.
34	3		FO						Skull and neck only.
35	4		PE						Complete.
36	3	F	SA	1.54	5th toe DIP fused.		2,3,4,8, 10,12	N	Complete.
37	3	F	OA	1.59	Osteoporosis. Rickets. Left ankle sprained.	Left fingers.	none	N	Almost complete but very fragmented.
38	3	F	OA	1.66	Cracked Left ribs, scoliosis, Right 5th toe DIP fused. Possible blow to mouth.		none	N	Skull to waist. Some elements in Grave 40 backfill.
39	3		YJ				2,3	Y	Complete.
40	3		CH				none	Y	Complete.
41	3		FO						Skull to waist present.
42	3		CH				none	Y	Complete.
43	4		CH				9 months, 1.5 years	N	Almost complete, right forearm missing.
44	3		PE						Almost complete.
46	3	M	OA	1.72	11th rib and 3 vertebrae fractured. Ulnar fracture (Colle's) Clay-shoveller's fracture. Osteomyelitis right tibia.	Spine, left fibula proximal, right acromion.	none	Y	Complete.
48 (36B?)	3	??F	??OA	1.57	Fracture, left fibula.				Left hand only *in situ*. Possibly SK36(B) (F OA).

Table 7.1 Demography: age, sex and stature distributions of the assemblage (continued)

SK #	Phase	Sex	Age class	Ht (m)	Pathology	Arthritis (counted only in cases of eburnation)	EH (enamel hypo-plasia)	cribra orbitalia	Notes
52	3	F	SA	1.66	5th toe fused.		none	N	Skull and left side in situ. Other elements in 4259/4263.
53	3		YJ		Scurvy.		3	N	Skull, right humerus, chest to mid-thorax only.
60	3	F	OA	1.68	Osteoporosis. Rheumatoid arthritis.	See pathology notes.	none	Y	Complete.
83	3	M	MA	1.63	Osgood-Schlatter's disease. Right thumb crushed. Lesions on frontal and R scapula.	Right acromion, spine.	1.5, 3, 3.5, 4, 5	N	Complete.
84	4		PE						Poorly preserved. Skull and major limb bone fragments
85	3	F	YA	1.56	Obstetric casualty. Left calcaneus fracture.		3.5, 5	N	Complete, with perinatal SK88 in utero
87	4		IN						Almost complete.
88	3		PE						Almost complete, in utero SK85.
89	3	M	SA	1.62	5th toe DIP fused. Rectus capitis lateralis tendon ossified.		1.5	Y	Feet, legs and hands in situ. Most of rest in Grave 90 backfill.
90	3		IN		Severe porosity of parietals.			Y	Almost complete.
91	3	M	OJ		Perimortem blade trauma; sword cuts. Non-ossifying fibromae on both femurs.		1.5, 4	Y	Almost complete.
93	4		CH				none	Y	Complete.
94	5		FO						Skull fragments, right arm, lower legs only.
96	3		PE						Almost complete, buried prone.
97	3	F	MA	1.61	Perimortem blade trauma.	Right wrist.	none	N	Left side of thorax and feet in situ, rest in Grave 91 backfill.
98	3	M	YA	1.73	Left MT I sesamoid fractured.	4th lumbar disc.	none	N	Feet only in situ, rest in Grave 46 backfill.
99	4		CH				none	N	Complete, buried prone.
100	4		PE						Complete.
101	3	M	OA	1.70	R MT I fracture, benign osteoma on frontal bone.	Right 4th MTP joint.	none	N	Complete.

Table 7.1 Demography: age, sex and stature distributions of the assemblage (*continued*)

SK #	Phase	Sex	Age class	Ht (m)	Pathology	Arthritis (counted only in cases of eburnation)	EH (enamel hypoplasia)	cribra orbitalia	Notes
102	2		CH		Right ribs 5 and 6 fused together at the head (probably congenital).		none	N	Complete.
103	3		PE						Skull, spine, thorax, right arm, shins and feet.
105	3	M	SA	1.72	5th toe DIP fused.		none	Y	Complete, skull recovered from Grave 103 backfill.
107	3		FO						Complete.
109	3		YJ				2	N	Complete, very fragmented.
110	3		YJ		Caries cavities on deciduous molars.		1.5, 2, 3	Y	Left arm and leg missing.
112	3	M	MA	1.61	5th toe DIP fused.				Legs and feet only.
113	3	M	MA	1.68	Right 13th rib present.		2	Y	Complete.
114	3		CH		Scurvy.		none	Scurvy	Skull, chest and upper arms *in situ*, most of rest in Grave115.
115	3		CH				none	Y	Complete.
116	3	M	MA	1.83	5th toe DIP fused.	Left shoulder and lumbar spine.	none	N	Right arm, spine, left shin and feet *in situ*. Rest in Graves 105, 101.
117	4		PE						Almost complete.
118	3	M	MA	1.62	Kidney stone.	Feet and hands.	none		Skull to waist very fragmentary, almost complete.
119	3	M	SA	1.80	5th toe DIP fused. Pelvic/colonic infection, possibly actinomycosis. mandible fractured.		none	Y	Complete.
120	4		IN						Complete to waist-level.
122	4		PE						Skull, left ribs, left femur and left ilium only.
123	3	M	MA	1.70	Feet, left tibia and fibula healed fractures. Right iliosacral joint fused.	Right 4th toe.	none	Y	Feet only *in situ*, rest in Grave 114 and 115 backfill.
124	3		YJ				5		Almost complete.
127	3	?	AD	1.64	Right patella and left tibia fractures.	Right 1st TMT joint.			Legs, feet and right fingers only.
128	3		PE						Complete.

Table 7.1 Demography: age, sex and stature distributions of the assemblage (*continued*)

SK #	Phase	Sex	Age class	Ht (m)	Pathology	Arthritis (counted only in cases of eburnation)	EH (enamel) hypoplasia)	cribra orbitalia	Notes
129	2	M	YA		Childhood middle ear infection.		3,4,5		Badly preserved fragments.
132	3	M	MA	1.70	Right tibia osteomyelitis, 5th toe DIP fused.				Pelvis, legs and feet only.
		Male Av	1.70						
		Female Av	1.60						

Age class: FO = pre-birth; PE = birth ± 2 months; IN = 2–24 months; CH = 2–6 years; OJ = 12–18 years; SA = 18–25 years; YA = 25–35 years; MA = 35–45 years; OA = over 45 years

with feet *in situ* the very smallest bones of the tips of the little toes were recovered.

7.4 BURIAL PRACTICE

Most of the burials, where evidence survives, show the normal Christian layout of being buried supine, with head to the west, legs straight and arms either by the sides or crossed over the lower abdomen. Exceptions to this were

> SK15 buried with the head to the east. Traditionally, skeletons buried in this reverse orientation are interpreted as being Catholic priests, the rationale being that on Judgement Day the priest rises from the grave in a position to begin preaching to the congregation. While the radiocarbon dating of this skeleton may place the burial post-Reformation (cal AD 1440–1640: SUERC-2630 (GU-11763)), it is possible that a priest may have been interred in the vicinity of an important, abandoned religious site. The location of this burial to the north of the church is also unusual, in that few burials were discovered here, and this may also reflect a different status for this individual.

> SK5 was buried in a remarkable position (Figure 5.16). The knees of this 18–20-year-old male were drawn up to the shoulders, and the left hand of the skeleton was clutching the back of the right thigh in order to maintain the position. It is very difficult to explain why this bizarre posture was chosen for this individual, one of the later burials on the site, but it may simply reflect a lack of room in the graveyard at the time. Certainly, to the east of the burial there was a large, flat stone slab, so that digging a full-sized grave would have been difficult. It has been speculated that the individual may have been of low status to the community on Inchmarnock (for example a washed-up drowning victim) and so there was less pressure to give him a more dignified position.

> SK96 and SK99 (a perinatal baby and a three-year-old child, respectively) were both buried prone. As both were most likely buried in shrouds, it may be that this was simply a mistake, as it will not have been obvious which was the front and back of the little bundle to be buried.

7.5 DEMOGRAPHY

The age, sex and stature distributions of the assemblage are set out in Table 7.1

As shown in Table 7.1, the *in situ* material consists of a total of:

> 33 immature individuals (it is not possible reliably to separate males from females by visual inspection of children's remains, although one individual, SK91, adolescent, was definitely male). The youngest recorded

was SK107, a foetus of about seven month's gestation. Altogether, thirteen skeletons were from perinatal deaths, *ie* stillbirths, or those dying under two months of age.

16 adult males (four 18–25 year olds, two 25–35 , seven 35–45 and three over 45 years)

Nine adult females (two 18–25 years, one 25–35, one 35–45, five over 45 years, counting SK36B as the rest of the skeleton represented by *in situ* hand, SK48).

One adult (SK127) was recovered only from the thighs down and was not assigned to a sex.

The left ilia (hipbones) from the non-articulated material were examined, as these bones can provide good indications of the sex and age of adults. Ignoring two bones which may have derived from *in situ* skeletons which were missing left ilia, a further seven males (two 25–35 and five aged 35–45 years) and three females (one 18–25, one 35–45 and one over 45 years) were identified.

A more accurate breakdown of the age profile of the assemblage was constructed, using the stage of tooth-development of the immature remains and the changes to the auricular surface of the ilium of the adult remains (Lovejoy *et al* 1985). All the skeletal material (ie including the disturbed, non-articulated bones) was included in this analysis, so that numbers of individuals are higher than in the discussion above, as set out in Table 7.2, below.

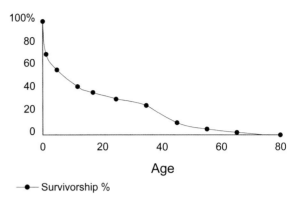

Figure 7.1
Percentage survivorship by age group

Figure 7.1 shows this data converted into a survivorship graph. Here, the percentage of individuals surviving through each age category is plotted (with an arbitrary maximum age of 80 years), the steeper the curve indicating the greater death-rate at that age category.

While the graph ignores the fact that the burials took place over perhaps 500 years or so, and the later burials are almost exclusively of new-born infants, the general shape of the curve is likely to be a fair representation of the death-rates of the population at any one time. High infant mortality is typical of societies before the advent of modern medicine, but once an individual reached teenage years, there was a good chance of surviving to around 40 years of age.

7.6 LOWER LIMB SHAPE

Flattening of the femur and tibia (platymeria and platycnemia) are commonly reported findings from among pre-industrial populations. In both cases it is suggested (Brothwell 1981, 89) that the flattened shape of the bone is a biomechanical response to the stress produced on the leg by a more robust lifestyle (eg long-distance walking on rough ground). All female femurs recovered from the *in situ* material were flattened from front to back (eight left, six right), as were 25 of 31 male femurs (12/15 left, 13/16 right). Rates of platycnemia were much lower, as is commonly recorded (eg Roberts 2001); only one male tibia was flattened (of 14 left and 14 right) and two left and one right female tibiae (of seven left and eight right), although the tibiae of SK33, an old aged female, were particularly flattened. This finding ties in with the high proportion of fractures found in the lower legs

Table 7.2   Numbers of individuals in each age band

Age at death	Number
0–1 year	27
1–5	13
6–12	12
13–17	1
18–25	5
26–35	11
36–45	14
46–55	4
56–65	3
>65	3

and feet (see below) which indicate a lifestyle which placed great stress on the legs. In modern Scotland, these rates of flattening and injury are likely to be found only in highly specialised occupations, such as professional footballers.

7.7 METRICAL DATA

Nine male and eight female crania were measured to give craniometric indices, indicating the shape of the skulls in various dimensions. Five of eight male skulls, but only two of eight female skulls, were 'long-headed' (dolichocranic). Females showed a tendency towards high skulls relative to length (6 of 8). Both men and women had narrow noses. The estimated living stature of individuals was calculated, giving a male average of 1.70m (about 5' 7") and female average of 1.60m (5' 3"). The range of male heights was 1.61m to 1.80m (5' 3½" to 5' 11") and that of females 1.54m to 1.68m (5' ½" to 5' 6").

The estimated stature of both the male and the females falls into the range found in many medieval Scottish sites eg Aberdeen and Linlithgow (Cross & Bruce 1989, 126) and St Giles, Edinburgh (male range 1.55–1.80m (n = 38) female range 1.49–1.67m (n = 25) (Henderson 2006), indicating that the population represented by the assemblage was not markedly undernourished compared to contemporary people. The comparison to modern people is highlighted by the rate of growth of the children (Figure 7.2). Here, the lengths of the femurs and humeri of children of known age (from tooth development) are plotted against modern children's femur and humerus lengths (Scheuer & Black 2000, Tables 9.6 and 11.6, adapted from Maresh 1970).

It can be seen that the differences between modern foetuses and new-born babies and those from Inchmarnock are small initially. Babies in the womb will grow to near normal size even if their mothers are on the point of starvation. By a year or 18 months of age, however, the slower growth of the less well-nourished Inchmarnock children becomes apparent and is marked by the later childhood years. A ten-year-old child from the assemblage would have been about the size of a modern seven-year-old. A full list of measurements is available in the archive.

7.8 NON-METRIC VARIATION

Small variations in the form of the skeleton, traits that are either present or absent, come under the designation

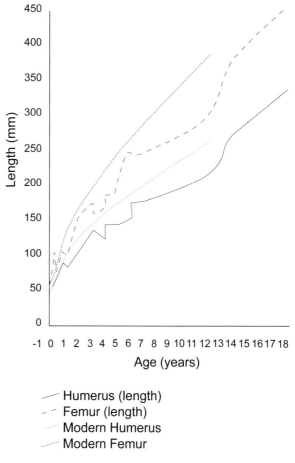

Figure 7.2
Humerus and femur length plotted against age

non-metric variation. These are usually of no clinical significance, but may be significant as indicators of changing populations and relatedness, although environmental conditions can have a large effect on the expression of these traits (Mays 1998, Chapter 5). Four individuals (out of 39 for which the trait could be recorded, including non-articulated bones) were metopic, that is the frontal bone of the skull remained in two halves beyond infancy. This is a fairly low incidence in a Scottish population. Frequencies of metopism at various Scottish sites range between 3% and 64% (Roberts 2001), although the lower frequencies do tend to be found at sites in the west.

Other common cranial traits were the presence of parietal foramena (23 of 38 individuals, small holes in the top of the skull for blood vessels to pass through) and the presence of Wormian bones in the lambdoid suture (30 of 39, 'islands' of bone created by the meandering path of the juncture between the bones at the back of the skull). Of the latter, three individuals had a particularly florid expression of this trait, which has been linked to poor nutrition in childhood (Bouquet-Appel 1984).

On the post-cranial skeleton, 26 of 34 left tibiae had lateral squatting facets, small extensions of the distal joint surface which are thought to be caused by habitually adopting a squatting position when sitting.

Rare skeletal anomalies included a left *Os acromiale* in SK33x (the right was normal). This variation is where the acromial process of the scapula remains a separate bone beyond puberty, and may be linked to repetitious strain on the shoulder. The archers aboard the *Mary Rose* had a high incidence of *Os acromiale* (Stirland 2000). In the child SK102, the heads of the right ribs 5 and 6 were fused together, in a manner which appeared to be developmental rather than as a result of trauma. This is likely to have been asymptomatic (Scheuer & Black 2000, 237).

7.9 PATHOLOGY

Detailed technical lists of pathological, dental and osteoarthritic lesions, as well as periosteal lesions of the tibia, are set out in the Project Archive.

7.9.1 Arthritic lesions

As would be expected with nine individuals in the Older Adult (OA) category, degenerative changes to joint surfaces were commonly recorded, six of these individuals having severe osteoarthritis in at least one joint. Three Middle Adult (MA) individuals also exhibited the most severe category of joint degeneration, Sager's Grade III (Brothwell 1981,150), where cartilage has been completely lost in some areas, causing bone to grind directly on bone. Five of the severe cases were in the fingers or wrist, four were in the feet, five in the spine (usually the lower back region) and three were at the shoulder.

The OA female, SK60, showed the lesions of rheumatoid arthritis, with a classical distribution of affected joints at the atlas and axis, mandibular condyle, shoulders, elbows, wrists, left hip and knee. The fingers of the hands were beginning to show the 'claw deformity' typical of the disease. This disease, of poorly understood origin, has been present in Britain at least since Roman times (Roberts & Cox 2003, 150), but was apparently very rare until the 18th century, and not clinically described until 1800.

7.9.2 Deficiency diseases

Cribra orbitalia was observed in 22 of 59 right orbits examined. This condition, of porosity in the roofs of the eye-sockets, is a consequence of certain iron-deficiency anaemias, caused, for example, by a heavy load of gut parasites or a gastric infection interfering with uptake of iron from the diet. At over 37%, this represents a very high prevalence compared to many graveyard assemblages (Roberts & Cox 2003, Tables 5.4 and 6.6, average prevalence 9 to 10%). It is not clear what the reason for this might be, even without counting the under-18-year-olds with the condition, 10 of 33 right eye-sockets showed the symptom, indicating that the high rate is not a result of unusually high numbers of 'sickly' children being recovered.

Two children (SK53 and SK114, approximately six and five years old, respectively) showed lesions associated with scurvy, Vitamin C deficiency. These included 'woven' new bone growth in the roofs of the eye-sockets and around the attachments of the muscles used in chewing. This is caused by a loosening of the membrane surrounding the bone due to the inability of the body to build connective tissue properly. The teeth may also become loose in the gums, some signs of which were recorded in SK53. Scurvy also affects the efficiency of the immune system, and so will have been a contributory factor to the death of these children. Even small amounts of leafy vegetables in

Table 7.3 Percentage of dentitions showing enamel hypoplasia, by age

Age at death	Immature	18–35	35–45	over 45
Total dentitions examined	14	10	6	7
% of dentitions with enamel hypoplasia	50	40	33	14

the diet (kale, for example) can prevent scurvy, so it is perhaps surprising that it should occur in a farming community. It may be that it set in towards the end of winter, before the first leafy crops were available, so that the diet consisted largely of stored grain.

One OA female, SK37, showed evidence of child-hood rickets with bowed femurs and tibiae. It is unusual, again, to find many cases of rickets before its great increase among the urban poor in the 19th century.

Three females (SK37, SK60 and SK33(y) a complete skeleton from the backfill of Grave 33) showed signs of osteoporosis, with the cancellous ('spongy') bone inside the vertebral bodies and at the ends of longbones being very thin and eroded. This is a common finding in women of post-menopausal age.

7.9.3 Childhood morbidity

Some evidence of childhood ill-health may be preserved in the adult skeleton in the form of furrows in the enamel of the teeth (hypoplastic lines) whose position reflects the state of development of the permanent tooth when an episode of illness or nutritional stress occurred. The occurrences are listed in Table 7.1 and summarised in Table 7.3 above.

The older adults may have lost some evidence of early episodes of stress due to the greater attrition of their teeth, but it is a common finding, as here, that more frequent lines of enamel hypoplasia are found in the dentition of those individuals who died at younger ages. It has been suggested (eg Stroud & Kemp 1993,

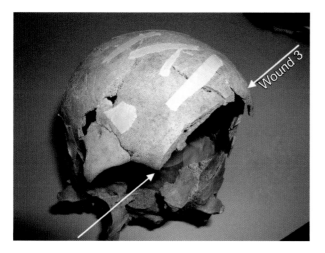

Plate 7.1
Blade injuries on Skeleton SK91 (Wound 3)

204) that children experiencing greater bodily stress may be more likely to die in young adulthood.

It is probable that the lines which were formed at 18 months to two years of age were caused by the nutritional stress which can occur during the switch to solid foods at weaning, while the lines at five to six years of age may reflect the occurrence of 'childhood infectious diseases' passed on from child to child as individuals become more independent of their mothers and begin to interact more with their con-temporaries.

7.9.4 Blade injuries

Two individuals displayed marks of violent assault with an edged weapon, in both cases almost certainly a broadsword of some type. SK91 was a boy of 14 or 15 years, buried adjacent the south wall of the church, just at the junction of the nave and the chancel. SK97 was a middle-aged woman buried in exactly the same spot, but, at a minimum, ten years earlier (possibly considerably longer). The later Grave 91 had disturbed Grave 97, only the left shoulder, spine and feet of SK97 remaining *in situ*, the rest of the skeleton being recovered from the back-fill of Grave 91.

The boy, SK91, had sustained three massive blows with a very sharp weapon, two of which would have been fatal on their own. Wound 1 was an extremely powerful chop, delivered horizontally from behind and to the left of the boy, completely severing the left arm halfway down the humerus, continuing through the left scapula, the third thoracic vertebra and stopping on the anterior (ie the inside) surface of the right scapula. Essentially, the body was very nearly completely chopped in twain.

Reconstructing the position of the body when the blow was struck indicates that the left arm was being held almost straight out from the body, while the right was raised up beside the head. It seems probable that the youth was lying on his right side, with his head on his right arm, perhaps having been incapacitated by a previous wound and facing away from his assailant, who brought the blade straight down through the boy's upper arm and chest. This wound would have cut three main arteries coming off the aorta as well as severing the spinal chord and death would have been near instantaneous.

Wound 2 on SK91 was another horizontal blow, parallel to Wound 1 and also delivered from behind, cutting through the left hip bone and cutting the body of the fifth lumbar vertebra. Although potentially not

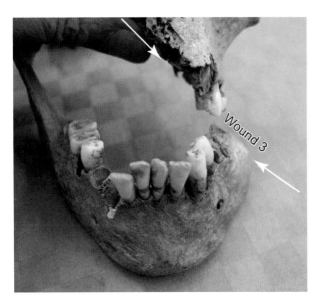

Plate 7.2
Blade injuries on Skeleton SK97 (Wound 3)

fatal in itself, this blow would have completely disabled the left leg.

Wound 3 was a blow to the skull, again delivered from the left and behind, slicing the skull open from the right eyebrow to just above the left ear canal, penetrating deep into the brain (Plate 7.1). This blow would also have been almost instantly fatal.

It seems probable that Wound 3 was the first blow struck, with the following two chops delivered to the dying youth while he lay on the ground, This 'overkill' is suggestive of an attack during battle, where the priority would be to make absolutely certain that a downed opponent would never get up to retaliate. Without an exact date for the skeleton, it is idle to speculate on which conflict the lad was involved in when he met his end, there is no shortage of possible candidates in 17th- and 18th-century Scotland. It is interesting that this individual is one of only two burials where there is evidence of clothing (buckle SF900: Franklin, Chapter 6.5 above, Figure 6.37–11), further suggested by the fact that his severed left arm had been replaced in a 'natural' (though actually anatomically impossible) position, probably while concealed in the arm of a shirt or jacket. The head was also tilted to the left in the grave, possibly to conceal the massive wound on that side.

In the case of SK97, five edged-weapon blows were recorded, all on the skull. Wound 1 was to the root of the right zygomatic arch, from the front and slicing off the temporal part of the zygomatic arch (ie cutting the cheek to just in front of the right ear). Wound 2 was also vertical from the front, striking the outer corner of the left eye and slicing through the cheekbone.

Wound 3 was a thrust from the front, a diagonal blow passing through the bottom of the right eye-socket, through the nose and mouth and cutting through the lower jaw just in front of the left wisdom tooth (Plate 7.2). The position of the wound in the lower jaw indicates that the mouth was slightly open at the time the blow was delivered. The blade used appears to have had a fuller (gutter) at the edge. Wound 4 was from behind, slicing off a part of the outer surface of the skull between the back of the skull and the left ear. Wound 5 appears to have been another thrust through the mouth severing the spinal chord and cutting the left occipital condyle. The angle of this blow is perpendicular to that of Wound 3. Wound 5 would have been instantly fatal, while Wound 3 would almost certainly have been so, the other three wounds would possibly have been survivable on their own.

A small area on the back of the right ulna and radius, just above the wrist, may also be a blade injury, possibly a defensive wound, but equally may be a spade-mark occurring when Grave G91 was dug through burial G97. The blows to the skull, on the other hand, were very clearly inflicted on the woman whilst she was still alive. The sharpness of the instrument used suggests an edged weapon, the breakage pattern on the bone is consistent with that observed on fresh, rather than dry, skeletonised, bone (Lyman 1994) and the direction and nature of Wound 4 show that it was delivered from directly behind the skull and met with some resistance, impossible if the woman was lying on her back in the grave. Again it is impossible to reconstruct the events which led up to such a sustained and deadly attack on a middle-aged woman.

7.9.5 Other trauma

A few healed fractures were recorded, mostly in the foot or lower leg. Several skeletons also show evidence of trauma to the ligaments and tendons of the lower leg (where a sprain of the ankle causes slight bleeding where the ligament attaches to the bone, and the blood subsequently ossifies). Six individuals had suffered fractures of the shin or of the feet. This represents 16% (6/38) of the adult population on the site where these areas were preserved, a high incidence of such trauma

(Roberts & Cox 2003, 239). Of note was SK98, a young adult male, who had sustained a fracture of a sesamoid bone of the left first metatarsal. Sesamoids are small bones, shaped like a split pea (the name is from the sesame seed) which occur in tendons in areas of high wear (the kneecap is actually a large sesamoid bone), in this case at the ball of the left foot. Fractures of this type are most frequently seen in young track athletes and army recruits and are caused by excessive impact of the foot with the ground, as in 'square bashing'. The fracture causes disabling pain on walking, especially at the end of each step. In another male, SK123, the sacrum was fused to the ilium (on the right side only) probably due to having a fractured left tibia and fibula which had healed slightly out of alignment, producing a halting gait which would have stressed the sacro–iliac joint.

An unusual finding was that nine of the adults (of 15 individuals for which the observation could be made) had the last joint of one or both of their little toes fused. It is unclear if this was the result of repeated trauma to the toes, or was an inherited trait. If the latter case it suggests a close relationship between the individuals buried on Inchmarnock over a considerable span of time.

Two skeletons had experienced crushing injuries to the fingers. All these injuries would be expected in a population engaged in walking over rough ground and manual labour, such as farming.

Two individuals had collapsed vertebrae; in SK33(y), a middle-aged female, this was due to osteoporosis, while in SK46, an older male, it may have been caused by a fall. The collapsed second lumbar vertebra was so severe that the first lumbar actually sits 'inside' the body of the second, producing a spine angled sharply forward at the waist. This individual also had 'clay-shoveller's' fractures of the seventh cervical and first thoracic vertebrae. In this condition, the tips of the vertebral spines are pulled off by the force applied by the trapezius muscles; anyone who has attempted to shovel sticky clay will appreciate the amount of force generated. Further fractures were on the right eleventh rib, and of the right ulna, the latter a 'Colle's fracture' near the wrist, typically sustained when falling forward onto an outstretched hand.

SK15 and SK38 had both suffered fractured ribs. Skeleton 38 had lost her lower front teeth and right canine, and the right third premolar was broken off to a stump before death. SK119 had an old, healed fracture of the right mandibular joint. These may have occurred because of blows to the mouth, although it is

Plate 7.3
Excavation record photograph of the young woman (SK85) who was found with the skeleton of a full-term baby (SK88) within her pelvis

impossible to say if it happened because of interpersonal violence or an accident.

The young adult female, SK85, was found with the skeleton of a full-term baby (SK88) within her pelvis (Plate 7.3). It appears that the baby's head had not fully engaged ready for birth, possibly because the mother was a very slight young woman of only 1.52m to 1.58m in height (5' to 5' 2").

Middle adult male, SK83, had Osgood-Schlatter's disease of the right tibia, where the tubercle (the lump just below the kneecap) has become detached from the rest of the bone, usually due to (often quite slight) trauma in childhood or early adolescence.

7.9.6 *Infectious diseases*

Several individuals showed signs of infection of one sort or another. Very few infectious diseases leave traces on the skeleton, but it is almost certain that most of the individuals in the assemblage would have died because of some type of infection. All rib surfaces were examined for signs of pulmonary tuberculosis lesions, but none was observed.

Direct infections of the bone (osteomyelitis) were seen in three cases; the right tibiae of SK46 and SK136, and in an unarticulated left radius from [433]. Before the advent of antibiotics these infections could easily have been a cause of death.

Infection of tissues overlying a bone can affect the membrane surrounding the bone (periosteum) causing a rough deposit of new bone growth to be laid down on the normally smooth outer cortex. This phenomenon is regularly observed on the tibia, in pre-modern skeletal material, as the shin is one area where the bone directly underlies the skin and is often subject to slight trauma. Periostitis, as it is known, was seen on 12 of 43 left and 10 of 39 right adult tibiae in the assemblage. Again this rate is higher than in many archaeological populations where rates at about 10% (eg Whithorn: Cardy 1997, 538) are common, reflecting the general high levels of trauma to the legs of the population on Inchmarnock.

Three individuals (SK46 and SK101, both older adult males, and SK118, middle adult male) had maxillary sinusitis (of 33 observable sinuses). Here periostitis occurs in the maxillary sinuses (to either side of the nose) probably as a result of recurring irritation which has been linked to poor air quality and to dental abscesses (Roberts & Cox 2003, 173). All the cases above were linked to dental abscess.

SK119, a sub-adult male, had a small patch of periostitis on the visceral surface of the sacrum, indicating an infection in the overlying tissues within the pelvis, probably in the colon. This may have been actinomycosis (Aufderheide & Rodriguez-Martin 1998) which can lead to septicaemia if untreated.

The left temporal bone of SK129 (a ?young adult, ?male) showed evidence of a severe middle ear infection (otitis media), with a fistula connecting the middle ear canal to the mastoid sinuses, surrounded by unresolved periostitis, indicating that the infection was active at the time of death. It is possible that the infection was the cause of death due to secondary septicaemia or meningitis, and would certainly have caused excruciating ear-ache. The 'sacs' of the mastoid sinuses were small, suggesting that an initial infection had occurred in childhood (Aufderheide & Rodriguez-Martin 1998, 234); if the childhood infection had caused a perforation of the eardrum, this would have left a route through which reinfection could easily occur.

7.9.7 Neoplasms

Benign or 'button' osteomas (harmless, round growths of bone, usually found on the skull) were observed on three specimens, all frontal bones (a minimum of 29 adult frontals were observed). One was the skull of SK101, an older adult male, the other two coming from the non-articulated material.

A further non-malignant tumour was observed on the femurs of SK91, the boy with the blade trauma. These lesions were diagnosed as benign fibroblastic tumours (also called non-ossifying fibromas), which are usually asymptomatic, relatively common in teenagers and which usually resolve with time (Aufderheide & Rodriguez-Martin 1998, 383). The lesions were on the posterior side of the femurs, on the supracondylar lines. They presented as sharp-edged irregular lobate fossae, that on the left almost completely invested in normal cortical bone.

SK83, a middle adult male, had two round excavated lesions, one at the point between the eyebrows (glabella) and one on the underside of the right scapular spine. Both were apparently lytic lesions with some evidence of sclerotic healing. It is not clear what caused these, but one possibility is that it was breakaway fragments of a malignant tumour (metasteses) from elsewhere in the body.

7.9.8 Other pathology

The female, middle adult skeleton recovered from Grave 33 backfill (catalogued here as SK33(y)) had sharp-edged excavated lesions around the heads of the first metatarsal and the fourth proximal phalanx of the right foot, indicative of gout. This condition is caused by the presence of excess uric acid in the blood, due to failure of the kidneys to excrete it properly, often as a consequence of excessive alcohol consumption, damage caused by lead poisoning or by high blood pressure and a range of other factors. The uric acid

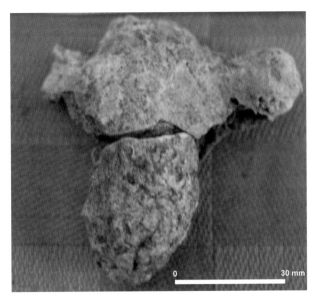

Plate 7.4
Renal calculus (kidney-stone) from Skeleton SK118

Table 7.4 Number of dentitions showing pathology, by age category

Age	Immature	SA/YA	MA	OA
dentitions	17	10	7	7
abscess	0	0	5	6
caries/tooth-loss	2	2	4	7

is deposited out of the blood into the joint spaces (especially of the feet, ankles and knees) as crystals which erode the surrounding bone. Sufferers describe the pain as exquisite.

A remarkable find was recovered from the grave of SK118, a middle adult male, in the form of what appears to be a large renal calculus or kidney-stone (Plate 7.4). The excavation photograph shows it overlying the right ninth or tenth rib, approximately the correct position for the kidney, and the shape and structure correspond very closely to what would be expected of a renal calculus. It is a rough-surfaced mineral accretion (ie with a lamellar structure) with a central void, somewhat pear-shaped, 32mm long with two lobes off the sides of the thicker end, giving a total width of around 30mm. This shape and size would be a good fit for the lumen of the kidney, with the two lobes fitting the calyces of the lumen. Kidney stones accrete around foreign matter in the kidney (often pus from an infection) and continue to grow, eventually blocking the ureter and causing pain, inflammation and kidney damage. Death from kidney failure or infection is not uncommon.

7.9.9 Dentition

The *in situ* skeletons from the site provided 41 dentitions, excluding infants with no erupted teeth. Of these, 15 individuals had suffered from caries cavities or had lost teeth, and 11 had abscesses in the jaw. The incidence and severity of these lesions increased with age, as might be expected. Teeth are the only parts of the skeleton which do not heal if injured, so that damage tends to be cumulative over time (see above for discussion of enamel hypoplasia). Table 7.4 above lists the numbers of dentitions in the *in situ* sample in each age category with the number suffering abscesses and caries and/or *ante-mortem* tooth-loss (excluding the natural loss of 'milk-teeth' during maturation)

The severity of the lesions also increased with time; in the sub-adult/younger adult category, eight teeth were carious in the two affected dentitions, while in the older adult category, 87 teeth were carious or had been lost *ante-mortem* out of the seven affected individuals. The low rates of caries in the children is in marked contrast to the modern situation; only four teeth (all upper molars) were carious of the 176 milk-teeth available for study (ie those which had erupted but were not lost *post-mortem*. This is a consequence of the small amount of refined food available in the diet, especially sugar. In general, caries rates are quite low compared to today, both for this reason and because of the very coarse nature of the diet, often containing particles of grit from the grind-stones or mill wheels used to process grain. Because of this there was a high rate of attrition of the teeth; often a colony of bacteria starting a cavity would be abraded away before they could cause much damage.

A few dental anomalies were also noted in the assemblage. Three individuals had retained some of their milk-teeth beyond the age at which they would be expected to have been replaced by the adult teeth. In SK89 (male, SA) an upper right canine had been retained, and in SK98 (male, YA) the lower right second molar was retained. In the case of SK91, the adolescent who suffered the sword attack, all his upper milk-molars and both lower second milk-molars had been retained, with the adult premolars which should replace them not having formed in the jaws. A line of enamel hypoplasia was recorded on the upper incisors, corresponding to a disruption to the development of the teeth at about 18 months of age. It may be that this problem with the system completely prevented the 'buds' of the premolars from forming at about this time.

The old woman SK33, had a groove worn in her lower left first incisor, in the gap between her two front teeth. This may have been caused by pulling some sort of fibre through the gap, possibly related to some handicraft.

Chapter 8

Archaeological Excavation (Minor Sites)

KIRSTY DINGWALL, ELIZABETH JONES AND CHRISTOPHER LOWE
(WITH CONTRIBUTIONS FROM JULIE FRANKLIN, TIMOTHY HOLDEN
AND BRUCE WALKER)

8.1 INTRODUCTION

CHRISTOPHER LOWE

Intrusive evaluation was undertaken at a number of sites during preliminary investigations in May 2000 (*AIR* 3). This work succeeded in clarifying the nature and date of, for example, the previously unrecorded rock shelters (Sites 9 and 16), as well as accurately locating others, such as the cup-and-ring-marked stone (Site 3), for the very first time. Other, previously poorly-located sites were also accurately located during the course of the survey programme (Chapter 2.2).

The cairn and the cup-marked stone (Sites 1 and 3) and the significance of the Iron Age dates that were recovered from primary levels in both of the rock shelters investigated (Sites 9 and 16) have been discussed above (Carter, Chapter 4).

Excavation at the medieval church and burial ground (Site 4) had been identified at the outset of this enquiry. It was also clear that the excavation programme would include Site 5 (the building on the hillside to the south of Southpark) given the map evidence and the results of the Middletons' earlier excavations there (Table 2.1, Chapter 2.2 above). It would be important not only to try and clarify the chronology and structural development of the existing building but also to determine whether earlier remains were preserved within or under it.

In addition, then, to the planned excavations at the church and on the hillside below Southpark (Sites 4 and 5), the May 2000 programme of fieldwork also identified which other sites might warrant further, more detailed investigation. Once we had the radiocarbon dates to hand – and these are discussed below – it was clear that the medieval corn-drying area (Site 8) and one of the rock shelters (Site 16) would also repay further investigation.

8.2 SITE 16: THE ROCK SHELTER

8.2.1 Introduction

Site 16 is a small cave or rock shelter, roughly 10m wide at the mouth, 2m wide at the rear and 6m deep, located in the cliff-face above the old raised beach at the south end of the island (Figure 8.1; Plate 8.1). This part of the island was known to the Middletons, the island's last tenants, as *Dysart* (Jessica Herriot, pers comm; Chapter 2.2 above), cognate with the Latin *desertum* and the Middle Irish *dísert* ('desert'), with the sense of 'hermitage' or 'retreat'. The antiquity of its usage, locally, however, is by no means clear. There is no early documentation for the name on Inchmarnock and it could, for example, be a Victorian or later antiquarian invention.

The site was partially excavated in 2002, following the earlier investigation in 2000 which had established that it contained evidence of both Iron Age and early medieval activity. Primary deposits in the cave had been radiocarbon-dated to the period cal 355–59 BC (AA-39967). Meanwhile, a sample of carbonised oats from its upper levels had been radiocarbon-dated to the period cal AD 679–888 (AA-39968). The purpose

Plate 8.1
View of rock shelter (Site 16), facing north

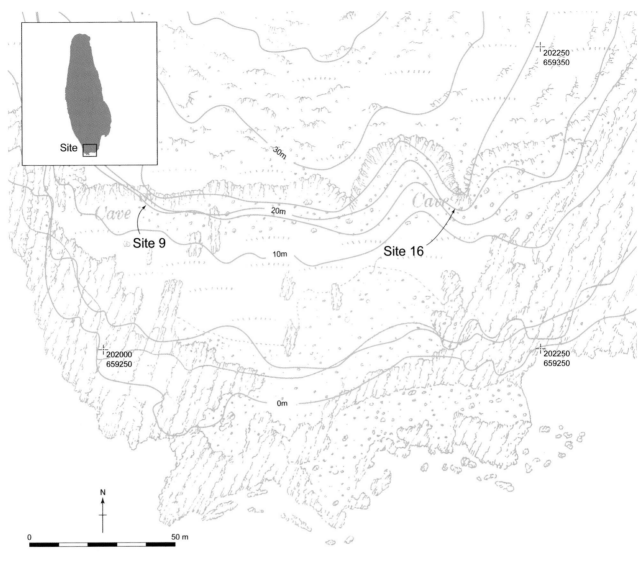

Figure 8.1
Rock shelter (Site 16) in its local context

of the 2002 excavation, therefore, was to clarify the nature and chronology of the activity in the rock shelter, and to consider how it related to other, contemporary settlements on the island.

An area roughly 6.50 × 5.50m was opened across the south-east side of the cave (Plate 8.2); only a metre wide sondage along the north-west side of the area, however, was taken down to the natural bedrock (Figure 8.2). Deposits were up to 0.6m deep and extensive rabbit burrowing was identified throughout the rock shelter, particularly in the drier areas towards the rear of the cave.

8.2.2 Stratigraphic summary

ELIZABETH JONES AND KIRSTY DINGWALL

Five principal phases of activity were identified. These comprise: (1) Iron Age occupation deposits and a possible surface; (2) a period of abandonment; (3) a series of hearths and occupation deposits covering a wide range of dates during the early medieval period; (4) medieval occupation deposits; and (5) 19th-century and later activity. Overall, the sequence indicates that the rock shelter has been used periodically over the last two thousand years, although as Stephen Carter

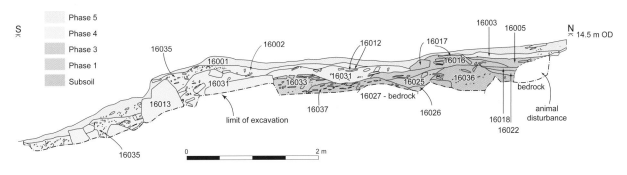

Figure 8.2
Excavation section through rock shelter (Site 16)

has noted above (Chapter 4), its use was exceptional, attracting only occasional, temporary or perhaps seasonal use. Given its size, however, this is not surprising.

Phase 1 (Figure 8.3)

Phase 1 was represented by two sandy silt layers containing animal bone, shell, charcoal and other evidence of domestic activity, and a possible surface. Layer [1655/16026] extended across the main covered part of the cave, while [16025] above was confined to the rear part of the shelter. This contained smaller amounts of domestic waste. At the front of the cave was an area of round cobbles [16033], associated with a deposit of broken and angular stones [16032].

Dating for this phase is provided by hazel nutshells from layer [1655/16026], which have been dated to

cal 355–59 BC (AA-39967). In addition, fragments of metal finds were recovered from [16025] and [16033], although these are identified below (Franklin, below) as almost certainly intrusive, presumably the result of rabbit burrowing. The presence of burnt material within the deposits indicates that there is likely to have been a hearth during this phase although no direct evidence for one was seen.

Phase 2

The primary Iron Age activity in the cave was followed by a long period of abandonment in which sterile layers [16023 and 16024] of light sand and sandy

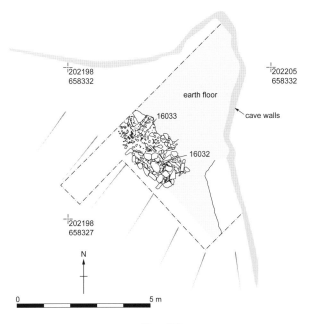

Figure 8.3
Primary deposits in the rock shelter (Site 16, Phase 1)

Plate 8.2
Close view of the interior of the rock shelter (Site 16) during excavation

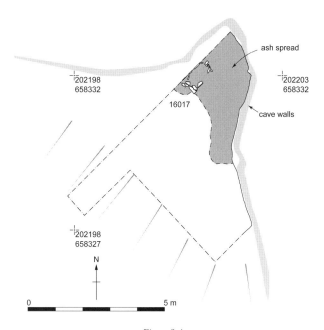

Figure 8.4
Early hearth and burnt deposits in the rock shelter (Site 16, Phase 3)

content and associated with a series of fires or hearths within the rock shelter. Most of the ash and charcoal concentrations and lenses are interpreted as raked-out and redeposited hearth material. Radiocarbon-dating of hazel nutshells from the basal element of the group [16022] indicates that the shelter was used sometime in the period cal AD 340–540 (AA-53164).

The only stone-built hearth surround (16017), together with an *in situ* deposit of ash and charcoal (1651) was preserved in the upper part of the Phase 3 deposits. Carbonised oats from this layer have been radiocarbon-dated to the period cal AD 679–888 (AA-39968). Very similar dates were obtained from fragments of hazel charcoal from layers 16007 and 16016, forming the upper levels of the Phase 3 deposits (Table 8.1).

No clearly defined abandonment horizon could be identified in the Phase 3 deposits. Charcoal and evidence of burning events, for example, were present throughout, albeit in varying concentrations. In addition to charcoal, the Phase 3 deposits also contained marine shell, fragments of animal bone (including burnt pig bones), occasional fish bone, charred cereal grains (hulled barley, oat and rye) and weed seeds. A number of samples produced burnt animal droppings, reflecting the use of animal dung as fuel. There is no indication, however, that the cave was resorted to throughout the period indicated by the upper and lower Phase 3 dates, and the low levels of charcoal and other cultural material in the intervening layers are probably due to rabbit disturbance.

Phase 4

The cave continued to be used as a temporary shelter in the medieval period. Sherds of medieval pottery dating from the 13th to 15th centuries were recovered

silt accumulated in the cave. Neither of these deposits, unfortunately, extended into the excavated section (Figure 8.2). Samples from these deposits contained occasional bones of small mammals such as water vole, field vole, wood mouse, common shrew and at least one pygmy shrew (David Henderson, pers comm). All, however, are most likely to have been deposited by raptors (*AIR* 10, 15–17).

Phase 3 (Figure 8.4)

Phase 3 deposits comprise a series of sandy silt layers, differentiated only by their ash and charcoal

Table 8.1 Radiocarbon dates from Site 16

Laboratory code	Material	Context no	Phase	Radiocarbon date BP	Calibrated 2-sigma radiocarbon date
AA-39967 (GU-9144)	hazel nutshell	1655	1	2150±35 BP	355–59 BC
AA-53164 (GU-10635)	hazel nutshell	16022	3	1620±35 BP	AD 340–540
AA-53165 (GU-10636)	hazel charcoal	16007	3	1260±35 BP	AD 670–880
AA-39968 (GU-9166)	oats	1651	3	1245±35 BP	AD 679–888
AA-53166 (GU-10637)	hazel charcoal	16016	3	1195±40 BP	AD 690–970

from the upper deposits in the cave, as well as some later (probably intrusive) material (Franklin, below). The collection of iron finds from deposit 16015 possibly indicates the use of the cave for storage by fishermen.

Phase 5

The topsoil deposits in the cave contained fragments of a porcelain teacup and a blue transfer-printed white earthenware saucer, dating to the late 19th – or early – 20th century, the remnants perhaps of a Victorian or later picnic in the cave.

8.2.3 The artefacts from Site 16

JULIE FRANKLIN

Introduction

There are very few datable finds from the site. Some finds are clearly modern, and there is one example of a medieval pot, but others are less distinctive. Combined with a stratigraphy much disturbed by animal activity, this makes dating most of the finds largely a matter of guesswork.

Pottery

The only finds datable to the medieval period are nine sherds of White Gritty pottery, from one small buff coloured cooking pot (Figure 8.5). These were produced on the mainland, and are common finds, for example in the medieval burgh of Ayr (Franklin & Hall, forthcoming). Medieval activity on the site would therefore seem to be short-lived or occasional. Possibly it was used as a temporary shelter by passing fishermen, as it appears to have been in later times.

1. White gritty cooking pot rim. Buff fabric, slightly sooted exterior. SF1601, Context 16002, Phase 4

Figure 8.5
White gritty cooking pot rim, Site 16 (SF1601, Context 16002, Phase 4)

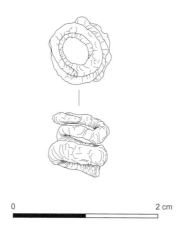

Figure 8.6
Copper alloy spiral, Site 16 (SF1618, Context 16025, Phase 1)

Metalwork

The wire spiral (Figure 8.6) and a small iron nail or hook were both from Phase 1 (Iron Age) deposits, the basal element of which has been radiocarbon-dated to cal 355–59 BC (AA-39967). These, however, would be extremely unusual finds for this period and it is likely that both are intrusive. Other metal finds include a lead tube and a copper alloy wire pin, both from Phase 3 (early medieval) deposits, though again, both are probably intrusive post-medieval finds. Other fragments of nail are from a medieval context, but again, this contained some modern contamination and again, they may be later.

2. Copper alloy object. Tight spiral of copper alloy wire, pointed at one end. Forms total of 2½ turns of wire, possibly two individual rings/spirals. Diam 8, length 8mm. SF1618, Context 16025, Phase 1

Stone

WITH GEOLOGICAL IDENTIFICATIONS AND COMMENTS BY DIANNE DIXON

The hammerstone is from a context from which hazel charcoal provided a date of cal AD 670–880 (AA-53165). There is no reason to suspect this stone is not contemporary with this. Dolerite is found on the southern tip of Bute, but the weathering on this stone suggests it may be a glacial erratic, transported by ice from further north.

3. Rubber/hammer. Dolerite. Rounded pebble with one side flattened into a concave face. Traces

of pitting at both ends suggest both ends used for hammering. Length 100mm, width 50mm, thickness 23mm. SF1611, Context 16007, Phase 3 (not illustrated).

Oil shale

An undiagnostic fragment of oil shale was recovered during the course of samples processing. It might be working debris but could equally be an accidental spall; such a small quantity of material is insignificant (Fraser Hunter, pers comm).

4. Oil shale fragment, broken in two (11.5 × 9.5 × 1.5mm; 6.5 × 6 × 1mm). Context 16022, Phase 3 (not illustrated).

Modern finds

A handful of pot sherds were from two vessels, a moulded fluted porcelain teacup and a blue transfer printed white earthenware saucer. There were also two clay pipes, with large bowls and narrow bore stem. Both were unmarked but are clearly late 19th or early-20th century in form. Also recovered were two fragments of thin vessel glass, one clear and polygonal, one rounded and blue. All of this implies the site was resorted to as a picnic spot in the 19th century or later.

Four copper alloy wire pins with cast conical heads are also of post-medieval date. Their presence on site is harder to explain, but possibly they were used to secure items of clothing by visitors to the site, or they may indicate sewing activity during picnicking.

Other finds indicate the cave was used for more practical uses. A riveted iron strap may be from a chest. A small copper alloy nail is probably from a boat. There is also a very large iron nail and staple and a short length of lead tubing. It has been suggested that the cave was used for storage by local fishermen in recent times and these finds may well relate to that.

8.2.4 *Discussion*

ELIZABETH JONES

There are many caves and rock shelters throughout Scotland with evidence of human use or occupation. This is attested to either through excavation or local lore and place-name evidence. A number of caves are found in relict cliff lines at the head of the Main Rock Platform, and at the time of the Main Post-glacial Transgression (*c* 6500 BP) were washed by the sea. The cave at Site 16 falls into this category.

The high sea levels during the fifth millennium BC would have made occupation of caves difficult at this time, and any deposits unlikely to survive. Archaeological excavation of caves demonstrates this, in that the oldest deposits are Mesolithic. Numerous caves and rock shelters have been identified at the back of the recent transgression beaches on the west coast of Scotland (Coles 1983, 21). The best known are the caves at Oban, which demonstrate human activity ranging from the Mesolithic through to the 17th century AD. In some caves initial activity begins in the Neolithic or Bronze Age and there are also many sites with evidence of funerary activity (Tolan-Smith 2001, 10).

Many caves and rock shelters do not appear to have been used until relatively late in prehistory. The earliest deposits from the Inchmarnock rock shelter, directly above the shattered bedrock, date to the Iron Age. This early horizon was not fully excavated, although the presence of charcoal indicates the use of fires in the area. Above this deposit in the front of the cave a layer of stones and beach pebbles was used to form a rough surface, perhaps to level out the floor of the cave. Small fragments of red deer bone may indicate that they were being hunted during the Iron Age (David Henderson, pers comm).

Tolan-Smith (2001, 10) has divided cave use into two categories: economic and ritual. Economic sites commonly comprise middens and some are described as having been modified with walling and entrances. Ritual sites contain funerary elements, incised crosses and burials. Incised crosses and both Christian and Pictish symbols are common on the walls of caves associated with particular saints or used as hermitages. Scoor Cave and The Nun's Cave on Mull both contain incised crosses on the cave walls. This is thought to reflect occupation in the Early Christian period, from the 6th to 9th centuries (RCAHMS 1980, no 325). St Ninian's cave at Glasserton is traditionally associated with St Ninian and the church at Whithorn. The retreat associated with a monastery is common in the Celtic church (Radford 1957). As well as incised crosses on the walls, traces of fires were also uncovered at all levels, indicating the temporary use of the cave in later periods (Radford 1957).

The cave at Site 16 is almost certainly associated with the early monastic site at Midpark (Chapter 9, below). The place name '*Dysart*', indicating a hermitage and relating to Site 15 in particular (Chapter 2.2) and this end of the island in general, also suggests

Figure 8.7
The view from the rock shelter, looking SSE to Arran and Holy Island. *Reconstruction drawing by Craig Williams*

a link with early monasticism. No incised crosses or Christian graffiti were found at either of the rock shelters (Sites 9 and 16), such as might be expected in the case of a hermitage or retreat. However this is almost certainly due to the nature of the geology, consisting of schist and slate with quartzite lenses, with few smooth surfaces. The location of the cave might suggest a spiritual focus as it looks southwards towards Holy Island, traditionally associated with St Molaise and this is the view that we have chosen for our reconstruction drawing (Figure 8.7). St Molaise's cave is a rock shelter situated on the southwest coast of the island and contains a revetment wall as well as many crosses and other inscriptions. It is thought to have originated as a hermitage and later become a focus of pilgrimage (Fisher 2001, 67).

The two caves at the southern end of Inchmarnock fall into the category of rock shelters. These are described as natural overhangs with a greater width than depth (Tolan-Smith 2001, 13). Excavations at the Ellary rock shelter revealed relatively small-scale activity, with the use of a hearth and the preparation of shellfish (Tolan-Smith 2001, 144–8). This can be compared in size with the cave at Site 16, too small to be used on anything but an occasional basis, but offering an open aspect and a degree of shelter in the landscape. The absence of structures, which would have provided a greater degree of shelter, also suggests the lack of longer occupation.

Other excavations of rock shelters in Argyll (Coles 1983, 18–20) commonly reveal middens or occupation deposits consisting of charcoal lenses

Plate 8.3
The building at Site 5, prior to excavation, with the bracken and undergrowth removed, facing east, downslope

The presence of charred cereal grains in hearth deposits indicates that small scale corn drying or cereal processing was being carried out on the site. The presence of burnt sheep/goat droppings suggest that animal dung was being used as fuel (Mhairi Hastie, pers comm). The evidence for high levels of animal dung in the caves suggests that sheep or goats were using the cave for shelter, or were sheltered there by shepherds.

8.3 SITE 5: MEDIEVAL AND LATER SETTLEMENT ON THE HILLSIDE

8.3.1 Introduction

The low, stone footings of a turf-built structure (Site 5: Plate 8.3) are located on the east-facing slope above the nearby slate quarry (Site 6: Chapter 2.2). The interior of the building had been partially excavated by the Middletons in the 1970s, the site of their investigation marked by a slight hollow towards its north-west end. That work had revealed a central hearth, sherds of late medieval pottery and two coins, reportedly dating to the 15th and the late 17th century (D Middleton 1977; Marshall 1980; Jessica Herriot, pers comm). The location of the building coincides with the smaller of the two settlements mapped by Foulis in 1758–9 and Leslie in 1769 (Chapter 2.3) and the nature of the previously reported finds suggested that the site may well have an earlier, medieval origin. The remains of an old enclosure dyke abut either end of the building and some 70m to the north are the turf-covered foundations of a previously unrecorded kiln-barn (Site 17: Chapter 2.2).

with animal bone and marine shell. This is consistent with the finds from Site 16. This material is typical of domestic waste and marine shells are commonly used as a food source on coastal sites. The relatively small amount of fish bone may have been brought to the cave by gulls.

The presence of hearths at the site probably implies overnight stays (Tolan-Smith 2001, 169). The intensity of use of the site can be related to the presence of other materials and features such as hearths and pits. The small amount of mammal bone recovered also suggests the site was not intensively occupied. The burnt pig bones from the basal layers associated with Phase 3 are probably the remains of a meal.

Table 8.2 Radiocarbon dates from Site 5

Laboratory code	Material	Context no	Phase	Radiocarbon date BP	Calibrated 2-sigma radiocarbon date
AA-49300 (GU-10024)	hazel charcoal	5030	1	1185±55 BP	AD 690–980
AA-49305 (GU-10029)	oats	5047	2	320±45 BP	AD 1460–1660
AA-49303 (GU-10027)	barley	5052	3	450±45 BP	AD 1400–1630
AA-49304 (GU-10028)	barley	5064	3	275±45 BP	AD 1480–1680
AA-49302 (GU-10026)	oats	5029	4	305±60 BP	AD 1440–1680
AA-49301 (GU-10025)	marine shell	5013	5	495±45 BP	AD 1721–

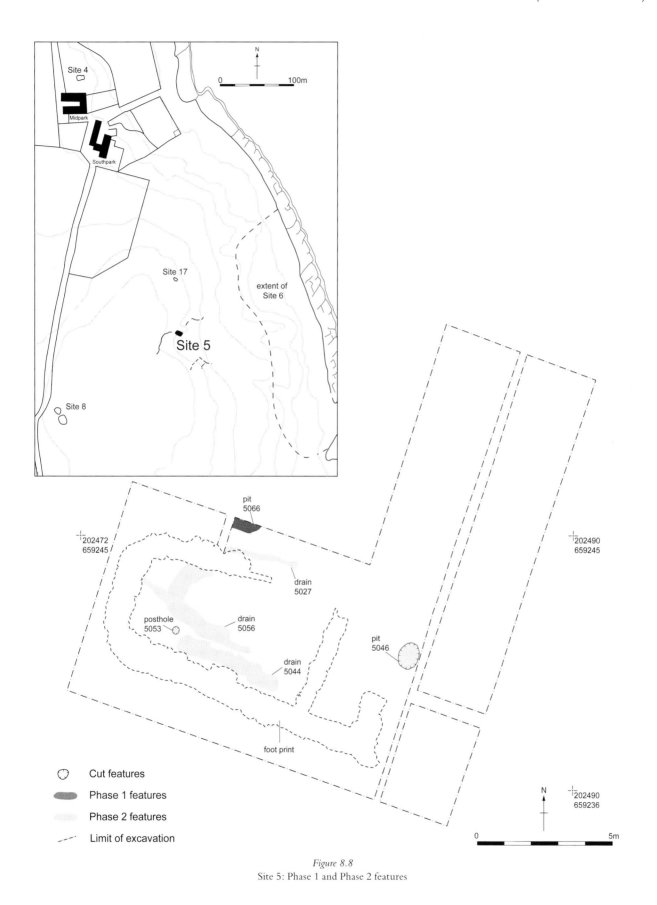

Figure 8.8
Site 5: Phase 1 and Phase 2 features

Partial excavation of the building, which was left *in situ*, was to succeed in clarifying the chronology of the upstanding remains on the site. The evidence of the finds (Franklin, below) and the radiocarbon dates (Table 8.2) concur to suggest that the Phase 3 building was probably constructed around 1600; the shortened building of Phase 5 probably dates to about a hundred years later and the site was abandoned by about the middle of the 18th century. It is clear, however, that the surviving structure here is only the latest in a potentially long line of buildings on the site. Medieval pottery, incorporated into the fill material of the surviving wall-base, indicates earlier activity on the site; meanwhile, the late first millennium radiocarbon date from a pit indicates an earlier presence still, contemporary with the monastic settlement at Midpark.

8.3.2 Stratigraphic summary

KIRSTY DINGWALL

Six principal phases of activity have been identified. The earliest features on the site, relating to Phases 1 and 2, are extremely fragmentary and could only be glimpsed below the walls of the surviving building which was left in place. Major construction activity on the site is marked by the Phase 3 building and the refurbished, shortened version that was rebuilt in Phase 5. Phase 4 deposits are associated with this reconstruction work; Phase 6 deposits relate to its final abandonment and subsequent collapse.

Phase 1 (Figure 8.8)

Phase 1 is represented by a large pit (5066), at least 0.85m across and 0.30m deep, cut into the bedrock. It

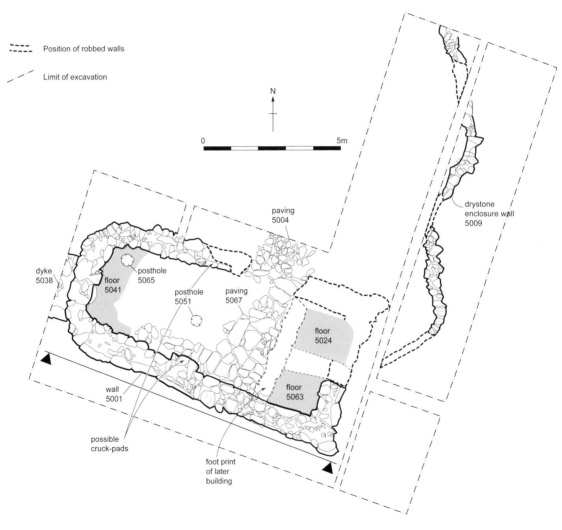

Figure 8.9
Site 5: the 17th-century building (Phase 3)

NW   SE

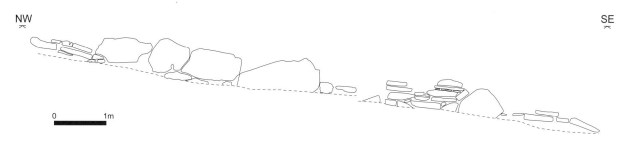

0   1m

Figure 8.10
Site 5: elevation of south long wall of building

lay immediately to the north of the later building and extended outwith the excavated area. Its fill (5030) was rich in charcoal and hazel charcoal from it has been radiocarbon-dated to the late first millennium AD (Table 8.2). No other finds were recovered from the pit.

Phase 2 (Figure 8.8)

Phase 2 comprised a series of truncated cut features that were preserved below the floor levels and walls of the later building. It is not clear how these features relate to the Phase 1 pit, to each other, or indeed if they all date to the same period of construction. The features comprise five drains or parts of drain [5027, 5044, 5056, 5060 and 5062], along with two discrete postholes or pits [5046 and 5053]. Fill deposits (5047), containing carbonised oats, from a pit (5046) below the east end of the building have been radiocarbon-dated to cal AD 1460–1660 (AA-49305) and this may indicate a late medieval date for the phase group as a whole. The drains, however, have not been dated and they could, of course, be considerably earlier.

Phase 3 (Figure 8.9)

Phase 3 is represented by the stone-built sub-rectangular structure formed by wall [5001] and its associated floor surfaces and occupation deposits. The building was 11.5m long and 5.2m wide externally and was rounded at its western end. There are indications that the building was originally divided into two rooms, along the line of the later wall [5002] which forms the east gable of the Phase 5 building. In its present form, however, this wall (unexcavated) overlies the stone floor, abuts the south long wall and is clearly a later addition to the building.

The north-east corner of the building was thoroughly robbed and only fugitive traces could be identified during the excavation. Elsewhere, however, the extant wall-base was well-preserved, with edge-set stones forming the outer face in places (Figure 8.10). Indeed, as Bruce Walker makes clear in his discussion of the techniques that were used in the construction of the building, the surviving stone wall-base is essentially preserved to its original height, on which would have stood a turf-built structure (Walker, below).

On the north and south long walls were two possible cruck pads, the southern one jutting out into the building, the northern one opposite marked by two rectangular stones. Postholes [5051 and 5065] inside the building have also been recognised as part of the cruck coupled structure (Walker, below).

Inside the building were a series of floor surfaces, although no trace of the previously reported hearth (from the Middletons' excavations in the 1970s) could be identified. The remains of an earth floor [5041] extended across the west end of the building; it was flecked with charcoal and ash and from it was recovered sherds of pottery and a spindle whorl. The remains of an earth floor [5024 and 5063] were also traced at the east end of the building.

Between the floor deposits at either end of the building was an area of paving and flagstones [5042 and 5067] and, as noted above, it is likely that the line of the later wall [5002, Phase 5] preserves an earlier division of the building. This is the structure that is explored in Bruce Walker's architectural analysis of the building (Walker, below). Meanwhile, to the north was a further area of paving [5004], albeit one formed of smaller stones, marking the location of the original entrance into the building. The building as a whole is interepreted as a probable cottar's house, with the west room used as a dwelling, the east end (4 × 1.5m) as a store-room or possibly for small livestock.

To the north-east were the remains of a drystone enclosure wall [5009], traceable to the east and west of the building as a low turf-covered stony dyke [5038].

233

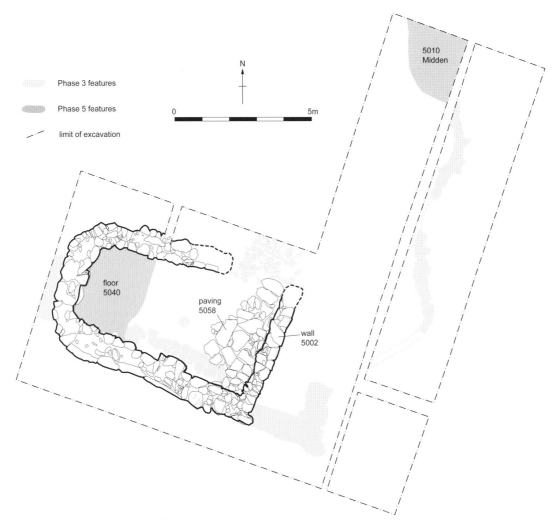

Phase 3 features

Phase 5 features

limit of excavation

N

0   5m

5010
Midden

floor
5040

paving
5058

wall
5002

Figure 8.11
Site 5: the 18th-century building (Phase 5)

Plate 8.4
The stone-foundations of the building at Site 5 in its shortened form
(Phase 5, *c* 1700), facing west, upslope

It was crudely constructed of large blocks of slate and quartz.

Radiocarbon dates from pits associated with the roofing of the Phase 3 building indicate that it was constructed in the 16th or 17th centuries (Table 8.2); pottery fragments found in association with floor surface [5041] have been dated to the period 14th to 18th centuries. A date of around 1600 may be indicated for its construction.

Phase 4

A period of abandonment is suggested by the accumulation of various rubble and silt deposits within and around the building. These were subsequently overlain by elements of the later Phase 5 structure.

Phase 5 (Figure 8.11; Plate 8.4)

Phase 5 comprises the repair and partial rebuild of the original Phase 3 structure. By this stage the east end of the earlier building had collapsed. A new wall [5002] was constructed to the west of the original gable, reducing the overall length of the building to 8.5m. The construction of this wall-base will almost certainly account for the thorough robbing of the north-east corner of the earlier structure and, as remarked above, the new east gable almost certainly coincides with the turf-couple of the Phase 3 building (Walker, below).

The remains of a clay earth floor [5040], associated with sherds of 17th- and 18th-century pottery and a small glass bead, were identified at the west end of the building; meanwhile, the earlier stone surface to the east was reused in the later building.

To the north-east of the building and dumped against the enclosure wall was an extensive midden [5010] containing a large amount of marine shell, pottery and animal bone. Pottery from the midden was of 14th- to 18th-century date; meanwhile, an 18th-century or later date (calibrated and corrected for the marine reservoir effect) was obtained from the shell midden itself.

The dating evidence associated with Phase 5 deposits suggests the building was probably modified in the early 18th century, possibly around 1700 and, like the earlier structure, it is interepreted as a probable cottar's dwelling.

Phase 6

The abandonment of the building is marked by a series of rubble and earth layers throughout the building,

in effect the collapse matrix of a turf-built structure. The absence of small finds dating to after the mid-18th century, discussed by Julie Franklin (below), suggests that it was around this time that the building finally fell into disuse.

8.3.3 The artefacts from Site 5

JULIE FRANKLIN

Introduction

The Site 5 assemblage was small and mostly post-medieval in date. The house on the site was built in around 1600 and inhabited until the mid-18th century and this is consistent with the finds. There is some evidence for late medieval activity predating the structure, with late 15th-century radiocarbon dates, but few finds date to this period.

Pottery (Table 8.3)

MEDIEVAL WARES

There were a handful of fragments of medieval gritty grey and redwares, of the type produced on the adjacent mainland. Unfortunately all were residual in later features, though they do show medieval activity in the area.

POST-MEDIEVAL REDUCED WARES

This was the most common type of pottery from the site. The fabric was generally smooth to the touch, occasionally sandy. There are few indicators of vessel form, but most of the sherds would seem to represent strap handled, olive green glazed jugs, the most common form produced at the time. This is a widespread type, known to have been produced at Throsk, near Stirling,

Table 8.3   Quantification and distribution by phase of pottery from Site 5

Fabric	Phase 3	Phase 4	Phase 5	Phase 6	Unphased	Total
Medieval Wares	8			1		9
Post-Medieval Reduced	1	3	9	27	29	69
White Salt Glazed Stoneware			3	3	10	16
Modern Red Earthenware				3	6	9
Other					2	2
Total	9	3	12	34	47	105

in the 17th and early 18th centuries (Caldwell & Dean 1992), but a source in west Scotland is also likely, as it is indicative of early post-medieval contexts in Ayr (Franklin & Hall, forthcoming). The sherds are mostly of 17th-century date, though some of the sandier sherds could be a little earlier.

OTHER POST-MEDIEVAL WARES

There is a small collection of white salt glazed stoneware, representing plates and at least one small bowl. These were produced from the 1720s in Staffordshire, and later at a number of other centres including places in Scotland. Cheaper than porcelain, it became a popular tableware with the middle classes until it was superseded by creamware in the 1770s (Draper 2001, 36–9; Jennings 1981, 222). The absence of creamware in this assemblage is extremely useful in terms of dating. It was extremely popular and widespread in the later 18th century and its absence suggests the site was abandoned around the middle of the 18th century.

Other sherds include some coarse brown glazed earthenwares, a piece of undecorated Delft ware and a fragment of fine whiteware, hand painted in blue, and possibly of Chinese origin.

Coins (not illustrated)

WITH IDENTIFICATIONS AND COMMENTS BY
NICHOLAS McQ HOLMES

Elizabethan coins are common enough finds in Scotland. They were particularly imported during the Civil War when silver was in short supply.

1a. Elizabeth I silver shilling, third issue (1583–1603). SF501, Context 5008, Phase 6

Two further coins, recovered from the site during the excavation in the 1970s, were also re-examined by Holmes in October 2001. These had previously been published as '15th century' and 'Charles II' (D Middleton 1977). This new work has confirmed the latter attribution. The other coin, however, dates to the late 13th century.

1b. Alexander III silver penny, second coinage (1280–c 1286)

1c. Charles II Irish halfpenny (1680–1684)

Iron

The blade is the most intriguing object, particularly as it was found in a drain below the floor of the house, probably dating to the late medieval period. It may be part of a dagger or sword blade, but unfortunately it is in very poor condition and is too fragmentary to be identified.

2. Blade? Fragments of a double-edged blade, with one flat side and ridge running down other, making broad triangular section, tapers towards a point. Max width 30mm, length 95mm+. Context 5043, Phase 2 (not illustrated)

The horseshoe probably relates to the last period of the house's occupation. There are also a handful of nails, generally from late contexts, and are probably related to the structure of the house or its fittings. An iron cannonball (not seen) is also reported to have been found during the course of the 1970s investigation (Jessica Herriot, pers comm).

3. Horseshoe. Slightly narrowing at toe, pointed calkin. Length, 136mm, width 133mm. Context 5000, Topsoil (not illustrated)

Glass

GLASS BEAD

The bead is of the same type as, though very slightly bigger than, the beads from the grave of one of the child-burials at the church (Franklin, Chapter 6.6 above, Figure 6.39–53). It is probably also a dress accessory of similar post-medieval date.

Bead. Small annular bead. Appears opaque black, original colour unclear. Diam 3mm, length 2mm. SF507, Context 5040, Phase 5 (not illustrated)

WINE BOTTLES AND GLASSES

A number of green wine bottle sherds were found from deposits of Phase 5 onwards, though the majority were found in Phase 6 abandonment deposits and in the topsoil. These are all late 18th or early 19th century in date and are probably contemporary with the 18th-century pottery from the site. There is the possibility that after that building was abandoned it was used by locals for drinking and other nefarious activities, but as the bottles are generally associated with the 18th-century pottery, they are probably all part of the 18th-century reoccupation of the house. Also contemporary are fragments from two fine glass vessels, a stem from a wine glass, and sherds from the bowl of another.

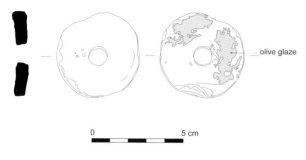

Figure 8.12
Spindle whorl formed on reused pottery sherd, Site 5 (SF503, Context 5041, Phase 3)

Ceramic object

The spindle whorl (Figure 8.12) is fashioned from a pot sherd of probable 17th-century date, and is probably therefore contemporary with the initial occupation of the house. It was found in a floor layer at the west end of the building. Spindle whorls tend to be made from any material to hand, which not infrequently includes pot sherds. Whorls vary considerably in weight and the Inchmarnock example is towards the lighter end of the scale. Lighter whorls were probably for use with lighter yarns or threads. A study of 35 whorls from Northampton found a preference for weights of 10–16g (Oakley & Hall 1979), with a more scattered group of heavier whorls, possibly used for plying two or more yarns.

Most women and girls spent a good proportion of their time spinning and consequently spindle whorls are widespread on medieval sites. Though the spinning wheel was introduced to Europe during the Middle Ages, it seems to have been slow to spread, particularly to poorer households and more remote areas. In urban contexts, post-medieval whorls are rare compared to earlier contexts. However, in the Northern Isles, there are many recorded examples made of pot sherds as late as 18th century in date, with a preference towards more exotic and attractive sherds (Melton 1999). Hand spinning in outlying areas, probably continued right up until the industrial revolution when cheaper machine-spun cotton and wool became widely available in the late 18th and 19th centuries.

5. Spindle whorl (Figure 8.12). Fashioned from a jug sherd, of post-medieval reduced fabric, soft fired smooth micaceous greyware with external olive glaze. Edges smoothed and a little abraded.

Diam 46mm, thickness 6mm, hole diam 10mm, weight 14g. SF503, Context 5041, Phase 3

Stone

WITH GEOLOGICAL IDENTIFICATIONS AND COMMENTS BY DIANNE DIXON

Both objects are made from locally available Inchmarnock stone. They were found built into walls, the quern from the wall of the house, the pivot stone from the yard wall. The quern may have been reused as a pivot stone.

6. Quernstone. Dalradian schist. Broken and unfinished quern. Flat top face with central circular depression. Edges mostly broken, underside very uneven. Possibly used as pivot stone. Diam 450mm, max thickness 80mm, hole 30mm wide, 37mm deep. SF506, Context 5001, Phase 3 (not illustrated)

7. Pivot stone. Slate. Large irregular block of slate with flat top face and large round depression. 270 × 230mm, max 140mm thick, hole 50mm wide, 30mm deep. SF512, Context 5032, Phase 3 (not illustrated)

A handful of worked roof slates from the topsoil were also recovered, although it is clear from the analysis of the building reconstruction (Walker, below) that it never had a slate roof. Two fragments of red sandstone from a Phase 6 deposit may be the remains of a flagstone floor.

Two flint flakes and a large piece of nodule were found in post-medieval contexts and were possibly used as strike-a-lights.

Discussion

MEDIEVAL FINDS

The medieval finds from the site clearly indicate earlier activity in or around the extant building but it is difficult to say what the nature of that activity may have been. The new coin evidence for the Alexander III piece and the radiocarbon dates for the truncated Phase 1 and Phase 2 features beneath the standing building, however, provide a tantalising glimpse of earlier activity on the site.

POST-MEDIEVAL FINDS

The bulk of the assemblage dates from the late 16th or 17th century to around the middle of the 18th century, the period during which the building was occupied.

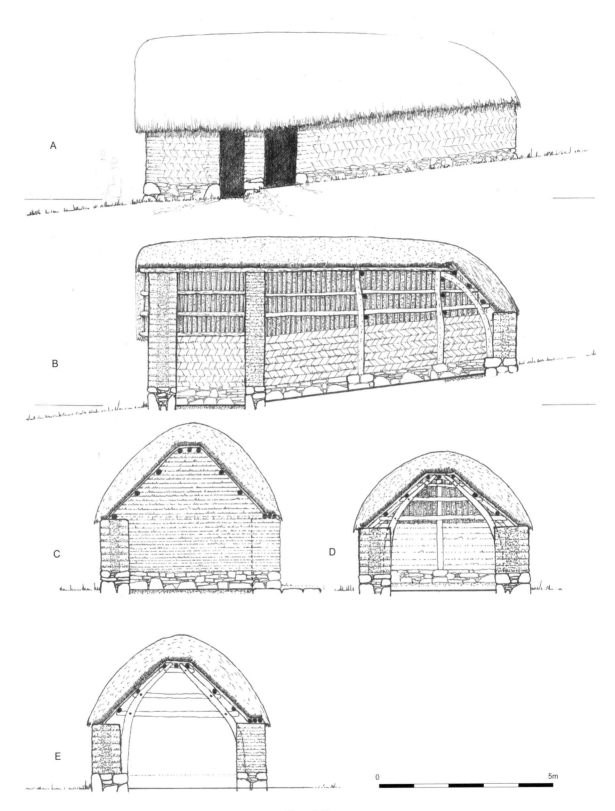

Figure 8.13
External elevation, and lateral and transverse sections across the Phase 3 building reconstruction: (a) north elevation; (b) longitudinal section; (c) transverse section of east room looking west; (d) transverse section at west end of building; (e) transverse section showing mid-cruck in west room of building

Clay tobacco pipes, usually ubiquitous on sites of this date, are notable by their absence. Presumably none of the residents was a smoker. The fragment of a possible dagger or sword blade provides a little colour, particularly so given some of the evidence from the graveyard for blade injuries (Henderson, Chapter 7.9.4), but it would be unwise to infer too much from a small fragment of iron from a drain, unless of course it was deliberately concealed there. Unfortunately, excavation was not able to clarify this and, given the size of the surviving fragment, it could have been washed through the drain at any time prior to its silting up.

The white tablewares suggest a degree of affluence involved with the later reoccupation and partial rebuilding of the house in the early 18th century. The assemblage seems almost too cosmopolitan and middle class for the tiny cottage. Possibly the reoccupation was temporary and related to incoming slate quarry workers. The co-occurrence of the same type of glass bead in a late floor deposit inside the Site 5 building and in one of the graves (G106) associated with the late children's cemetery at Site 4, however, hints at a long forgotten tragedy. The untimely death of the family's baby daughter might well explain why the reoccupation of the house was so short-lived.

8.3.4 Building reconstruction

BRUCE WALKER

The western end of the primary building (the structure of Phase 3) appears to have been a cruck-coupled structure where the crucks are set at a slight angle to

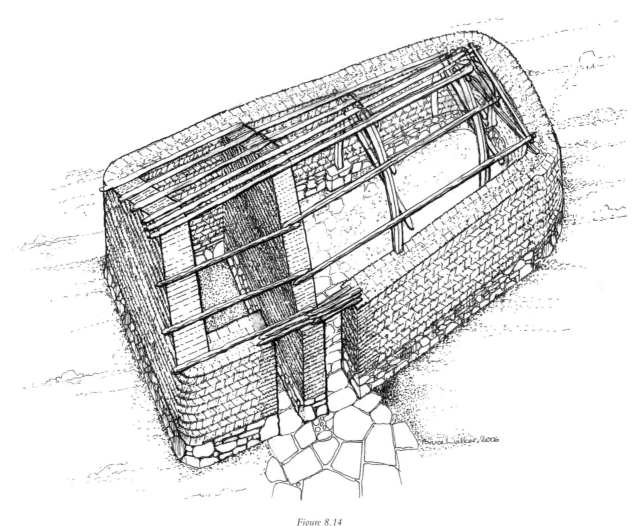

Figure 8.14
Site 5: axonometric reconstruction of the Phase 3 building at Site 5

Figure 8.15
Reconstruction of the turf-built and thatched structure as it would have appeared in the 17th century, viewed from the NE

the ridge tree forming what has been described as a parallelogram plan (Walker 2004). At the west end there is an end cruck whilst the east end has been reconstructed with what is known as an 'earth-' or 'turf-couple' and a turf gable. The couples in turn support a triple 'roof tree' or 'first', and two purlins or 'pans' supporting cabers forming the roof pitches to the north and south (Figures 8.13 and 8.14). These would probably support an undercloak of turf covered with a thatch (Walker *et al* 1996). Remains of earthen floors survive at both ends of the building.

The external face of the base-course is constructed using a mix of large quartz boulders set on edge, occasional flagstones also set on edge and drystone rubble. The inner face consists of crudely coursed masonry packed with rubble and earth mortar. The base-course walls survive to a maximum height of 0.7m and have a maximum width of 1.5m. This is consistent with a base-course for a turf wall since there was no indication of large scale masonry tumble and

the wall widths are more akin to 'fale' walls than to masonry. The outer walls have been taken as 'fale' reinforced with 'divet' at the eastern corners where a reasonably sharp arris was required. The 'turf couple' wall has been taken as 'divet' owing to its slimmer section. The possible cruck pads identified during the excavation fit with a purlin span of 2.5m, which is not uncommon in this area.

The 'turf couple' sat at an angle to the roof tree and was adapted for the angle of the cruck couples. This slight angling of the couples gives a structural advantage to the builders when erecting the structure since it reduces the tendency for the structure to rack, that is to collapse lengthwise. The extent of this advantage has still to be agreed between carpenters and engineers but even the simplest of experiments show that structures constructed on a parallelogram plan and spanned by purlins parallel to the lateral walls are much easier to erect and are more stable. End crucks of the type utilised are common in south-western Scotland

and can still be viewed at the farming museum at Auchindrain, Argyll.

The triple roof tree is again common in south-western Scotland: a number of vernacular structures on Jura, Argyll still utilise this feature and photographic evidence shows it was widespread in the south-west Scottish Borders area. The structure over the purlins is more problematical. Old descriptions tend to refer to wattle or more correctly to 'rice' (ON-*hris*: brushwood) but virtually all the surviving roofs in Scotland have cabers; thin branches or thick brushwood. The thatch is likely to have been local to the area or even to an individual farm but is likely to be loosely placed vegetation over an undercloak of turf and roped and weighted in the local fashion (Figure 8.15).

8.4 SITE 8: MEDIEVAL AND LATER CORN-DRYING KILNS

8.4.1 Introduction (Figure 8.16)

Site 8 is located roughly 450m south of Midpark on a shelf of relatively high ground that overlooks the old areas of arable to the west and north-west (Plate 8.5). Attention was initially drawn to the remains of a drystone built kiln, with a bowl 2.5m in internal diameter. Probably dating to the post-medieval period, it was partially excavated in the 1970s by the Middletons (Jessica Herriot, pers comm). Immediately to the south of the upstanding kiln is a low, oval mound, roughly 13 × 10.5m (Figure 8.16). Initially identified as a possible house-platform, an exploratory trench across the site in the May 2000 evaluation identified the fragmentary remains of a robbed corn-drying kiln (Kiln 1), radiocarbon-dated to the 13th century (Table 8.4). Excavation in 2003 was to identify the fragmentary remains of at least two further corn-drying kilns.

Plate 8.5
Site 8 and its setting: the corn-drying site – marked by the excavation team in the centre of the frame – occupies a shelf between the peat basin in the foreground and the tree-covered hillside above

Three principal structural phases were identified:

- Phase 1: possible structure/oval turf-built enclosure?
- Phase 2: Kiln 1
- Phase 3: Kilns 2 and 3

8.4.2 Corn-drying kilns on Inchmarnock (Figure 8.17)

TIMOTHY HOLDEN AND ELIZABETH JONES

The earliest structure on the site comprised an arc of edge-set stones (8028), possibly part of a turf-built enclosure. This primary Phase 1 structure was then cut by three features, interpreted as corn-drying kilns of medieval date (Plate 8.6).

Table 8.4   Radiocarbon dates from Site 8

Laboratory code	Material	Context no	Phase	Radiocarbon date BP	Calibrated 2-sigma radiocarbon date
SUERC-2633 (GU-11765)	oats	8005	2	880 ± 35 BP	AD 1030–1250
SUERC-2634 (GU-11766)	oats	8019	2	945 ± 45 BP	AD 1000–1210
AA-39965 (GU-9142)	barley	811	2	740 ± 35 BP	AD 1222–1298
SUERC-2635 (GU-11767)	oats	8037	3	745 ± 35 BP	AD 1215–1300

Plate 8.6
Site 8: view of excavated site showing arc of stones/turf-bank (8028) to left and excavated Kilns 1 and 2 to right. Facing SW

The earliest of these, the Phase 2 structure (Kiln 1), is represented by a short length of edge set flags aligned east – west, at the end of what could be the edge of a stone-lined flue running to the north. The evidence is scant and if this really is a kiln then the assumption is that the valuable flat stones forming the bowl and much of the flue were robbed and used during the construction of a second, and much better preserved kiln to the west, the Phase 3 structure (Kiln 2).

Kiln 2 (Plate 8.7) is represented by a series of edge-set flags forming a bowl approximately 1.0–1.8m in diameter and with a flue, approximately 3m long, open to the north and terminating in a fire pit some 0.2m below the level of the flue. Also attributed to Phase 3 was a third kiln (Kiln 3), similar in form and scale to Kiln 2, and located 5m to the south-east. This was only superficially exposed on plan and it remains unexcavated. A fragment of a steatite bowl and a single sherd of medieval pottery, both recovered from overlying deposits, were the only artefacts from the site.

Although Kiln 1 is very poorly preserved and Kiln 3 has only been seen in plan it is not unreasonable to suggest that all three structures are drying kilns of the distinctive 'key hole' type. Medieval kilns of this type are known on Bute, at Glenvoidean and near St Blane's (Marshall & Taylor 1979; Milligan 1963). The evidence on Inchmarnock is supported by large quantities of charred cereal grain that was recovered from the area around Kiln 1 but whether the charred grain came from the final destructive event in Kiln 1 or from the repeated raking out of charred debris from

minor accidents in Kiln 2 is difficult to determine. The composition of the charred remains does not help in this matter because in all samples barley and oat grain formed the main elements, an indication, if one was needed, that these two crops played an important role throughout the period.

In some traditional communities the kiln was an integral part of the barn (Emery 1996) but on earlier sites isolated kilns are the norm. The kilns at Inchmarnock fall into the second category which are often dug into natural banks or slopes to reduce the need for a built superstructure. They comprise a bowl and a fire stoking area connected by a flue, the length of which can vary considerably. The bowl of the kiln is often lined with stone, as in the Inchmarnock examples here, but clay or wattle and daub were also used depending on the friability of the subsoil. Over the bowl a platform of poles, commonly covered with straw or cloth, would support the drying grain (Fenton 1978, 377). There was often evidence for a timber superstructure over kilns. In 19th-century Ireland temporary and fixed roof structures were known (Gailey 1970, 66). This may have been to help with loading or to provide protection from the weather.

The earliest known corn-drying kilns in Scotland date from the 8th or 9th centuries and are generally associated with either monastic settlements or high status sites where grain would need to be stored and large numbers of people provided for. Elsewhere, it is assumed, the unthreshed cereals would typically remain in stacks over the winter only to be processed piece-meal, as and when required. Only where larger,

Plate 8.7
View along Kiln 2, facing north-west

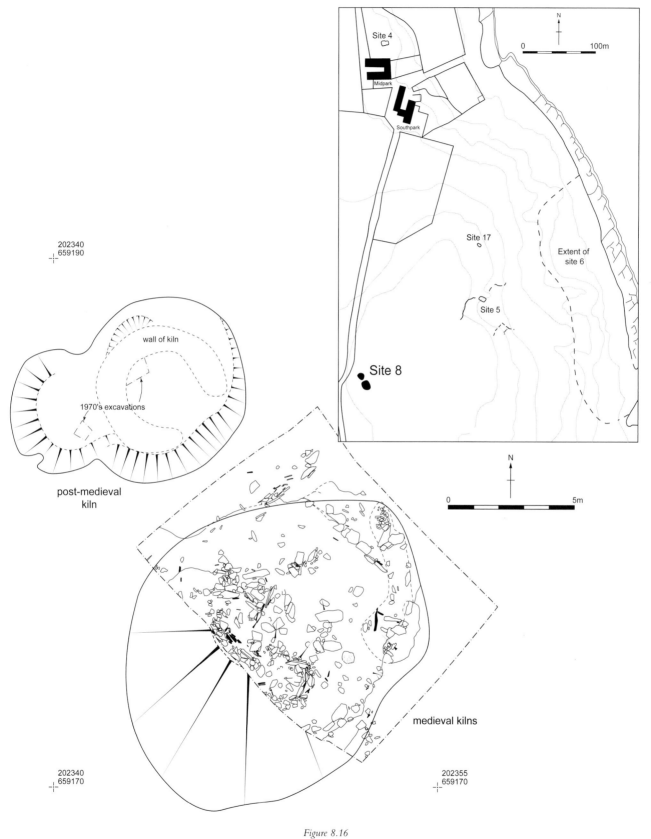

202340
659190

wall of kiln

1970's excavations

post-medieval
kiln

Site 4

Midpark

Southpark

Site 17

Site 5

Extent of
site 6

Site 8

0   100m

N

0   5m

N

medieval kilns

202340
659170

202355
659170

Figure 8.16
Site 8: location plan and principal features of the medieval and later corn-drying area

8002

8001

202350
659183

8003

Possible turf-built
enclosure 8028

8003

8043

202355
659177

Kiln 1

8044

Kiln 3

8035

8032

8003

steatite bowl

8003

[8045]

[8045]

8046

[8047]

8048

Kiln 2

8049

8052

202355
659177

Charcoal

Edge set stones

Line of earlier building

Area of individual kilns

N

0   5m

Figure 8.17
Site 8: identified features, Kilns 1–3

more organised communities existed, or where grain was required for trade or tribute were bulk processing facilities required. By the 13th century, however, smaller kilns associated with farms or small townships begin to appear and these were routinely located away from the main settlement due to the risk of fire (Evans 1957).

The charred debris from Kiln 1 has been dated to the 13th century and, like several other excavated kilns of similar date on Bute, it was probably linked to a small farm or settlement. At Glenvoidean, the chambered cairn had been partly excavated to accommodate the kiln. Stones around the rim of the bowl had been roughly arranged to form a semi-circular platform (Marshall & Taylor 1979). Three sherds of green-glazed pottery were found among these stones and similar sherds found elsewhere on the island have been dated to the 12th or 13th centuries, suggesting the kiln belongs to this period. The bowl was shaped like an upturned truncated cone, measuring 1.5m at the rim, 0.90m at the base and was 0.76m deep. Slabs set on end, supported by earth, formed the sides of the bowl. The flue was lined with flattish stones, sloping downhill from the bowl. The bowl is very shallow and the upper edge of the flue is almost level with the rim of the bowl (Marshall & Taylor 1979). It is described as a simple structure compared to other kilns on Bute, but is seen as unusual, locally, in having a bowl composed entirely of upstanding slabs.

The kiln at Ardmaleish consisted of a keyhole-shaped chamber, several courses high, with a retaining wall packed with stones to form a mound (Milligan 1963). The kiln was within a small barn, although it was not clear whether this was built at the same time as the original kiln. The kiln at St Blane's most resembles Kiln 2 at Site 8. The flue was almost 3m long and was level with the bowl as at Glenvoidean and Site 8. Traces of a low semi-circular wall supporting stones and tightly packed soil kept the walls of the kiln in place. Pottery from the 12th or 13th centuries was found associated with this revetting material. It is suggested that the structure may have been one of the outbuildings associated with the settlement at St Blane's (Milligan 1963). The construction and form of this kiln are again very similar to that of Kiln 2 and they are likely to be of a similar date. This suggests that the 13th-century Kiln 1 is unlikely to be significantly earlier than Kiln 2.

Function

The most common reasons for drying grain were:

- to parch hulled grains, primarily black oats and barley, in order to make the enclosing hulls and awns brittle and easier to remove
- to harden the grain in advance of grinding
- to stop germination in a spoiling crop or during malting
- to kill pests in advance of storage/transport

Burnt grain is not a necessary consequence of the drying process, because the fire pit and the drying floor would generally be separated by the flue in order to prevent the kiln catching fire. The length of the flue is very much dependent on the nature of the fuel used. Fuels such as cereal straw or furze (gorse), can produce sparks and long flues, often with stone cross baffles, are often used to prevent the sparks reaching the drying floor. At the other extreme short to non-existent flues would be indicative of a slow burning peat fire (Scott 1951). In the Inchmarnock kilns the flues are in the order of up to 3m long and this, combined with the presence of quantities of wood charcoal, indicated the use of wood as a fuel.

The kilns in context

The discovery of these three kiln-like structures close to the upstanding remains of a known post-medieval kiln suggests a long duration of similar activity on the site. It is possible that more than one was active at any time but it is perhaps more likely that these four kilns represent a series of replacements of structures that have burned down or collapsed through prolonged use. Evidence from other sites, most notably at Hoddom, Dumfriesshire (Holden 2006) and Chapeltown, Angus (Pollock 1985), show very clearly that corn dryers frequently burnt down and regularly required rebuilding over, or close to, the original location.

Medieval kilns are commonly found in close association with medieval and later settlement sites although often on the periphery because they represent a fire risk to the rest of the settlement. One interpretation of Site 8 is that it represents an outlying element of the medieval and later settlement at Site 5 (Chapter 8.3, above); that site, however, appears to have its own, much nearer corn-drying kiln and barn, at Site 17 on the hillside a little to the north (Chapter 2.2; Figure 2.5). The distance between Site 5 and Site 8 is, however, in the order of 300m, rather more than might be expected in a nucleated settlement. Perhaps a more likely interpretation is, therefore, that the kilns at Site 8 represent communal agricultural facilities on the periphery of an as yet unidentified settlement on the gently sloping and currently overgrown ground to the east.

8.4.3 The artefacts from Site 8

JULIE FRANKLIN

Introduction

Only two finds were recovered from the corn-drying site: a sherd of steatite and a fragment of pottery.

Steatite

The earliest find is a large rim sherd from a steatite bowl (Figure 8.18) from a demolition or abandonment deposit. The bowl is oval-shaped with the remains of an iron suspension loop. Steatite, also known as soapstone, was widely exploited in Norway and Shetland and traded all over the Norse world. It is soft and easy to shape and, as it expands very little during heating, can be used for cooking wares without fear of cracking. Vessels were shaped at the quarry face, before being split off and hollowed out (Sharman 1999, 169), thus this bowl is likely to have been made at source rather than made on Inchmarnock from imported raw materials.

The best known and most widely exploited sources of steatite are in Norway and Shetland and thus the distribution of steatite artefacts in Britain is very much centred on the Northern Isles. However, there are nearer sources, most relevantly in the Firth of Clyde, at Toward Point on Cowal peninsula, south of Dunoon, on the other side of Bute (Ritchie 1984, 64). This has been mined on a very small scale in recent times, but has never been examined from an archaeological stand point. Ritchie cites (but does not reference) a soapstone bowl found in Dunoon as possible circumstantial evidence for its use.

There is a scattering of other steatite finds in south-west Scotland. A ladle was found in Kintyre (*PSAS* 1970, 296, no 14), while a spindle whorl was found in a Norse grave of 9th- or 10th-century date on Islay (Gordon 1990, 158, illus 4g) and a mould for making beads was found in post-medieval rubble at Dunstaffnage Castle, near Oban (Caldwell 1996, 587, illus 21:47). These are generally small objects, and in the absence of scientific analysis, the most likely source for the Inchmarnock bowl still remains the well-established steatite industry of Shetland.

Typologically, oval vessels are dated between the 9th and 11th centuries and sub-rectangular vessels are even later (Sharman 1999, 173; Forster 2004).

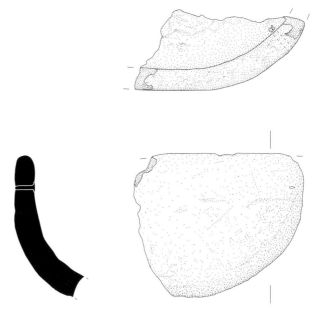

Figure 8.18
Fragment of a steatite bowl, Site 8 (SF8001, Context 8003)

This appears to be a Shetland innovation, probably due to the coarser stone, less suited than Norwegian stone for round vessels (Forster 2004, 5). Examples of iron-filled holes in vessels are widespread and are interpreted either as repairs or handles (Sharman 1999, 173). An illustration of a more complete example of such a handle from York has recently been published (Mainman & Rogers 2000, fig 1240 and 1242).

The fact that this is the only piece of steatite found on any of the Inchmarnock sites, despite large assemblages of contemporary material from the excavation at and around the medieval church (Site 4: Chapter 6), suggests there was no regular trade in steatite this far south.

1. Bowl (Figure 8.18). Oval or sub-rectangular shaped bowl with rounded profile. Roughly shaped, though few chisel marks visible, interior surface smoother, probably due to wear. Traces of sooting on exterior. Small pierced hole through wall 15mm below rim, filled with iron. Wall thickness 12–16mm. SF8001, Context 8003.

Pottery

The pot-sherd was a base fragment from a white gritty cooking pot found in the topsoil. Sooting on the exterior show it was used for heating. This type of pottery was produced on mainland Scotland. Many sherds, for example, were found during excavations in the medieval burgh of Ayr (Franklin & Hall, forthcoming). It is most likely to date to the 13th or 14th century. This is in keeping with the 13th-century radiocarbon date for the site.

Discussion

Both finds are from vessels used for heating and may therefore be related to the use of the site for corn-drying. Equally they could have been used for preparing food for people working at the site. Radiocarbon dates show activity at the site from the 11th to the 13th centuries. The steatite bowl fits best into the earlier part of this range, while the pottery belongs to the later part. However, the bowl may in fact be a little later, contemporary with the pottery. Its rarity and usefulness also mean it could have been of some age when it was deposited.

Chapter 9

Early Historic and later Inchmarnock

CHRISTOPHER LOWE

9.1 INTRODUCTION

This final chapter takes up the narrative where we left it in Chapter 4, with Ernán and his followers landing on the island in or around AD 600 and establishing what we will be identifying as an early monastic settlement. Whether an actual *Ernán* made the land-fall, climbed up the old raised beach and laid the first stone is, of course, hardly susceptible to proof. Ernán, however, is a convenient short-hand by which to refer to the holy man who founded the settlement and whose name is attached to the island and, of course, whose name is commemorated in the dedication of the later church itself. And as we have seen, among the inscribed stones from the site, carved in what has been described as an early hand of possibly 7th-century type (Forsyth & Tedeschi, Chapter 6.3.3 above), is a piece on which the name <Ernán> has been inscribed no less than three times. Finally, when we add in the evidence of the radiocarbon dates, the corpus of carved stones and the chronological implications that arise from the incised slate assemblage we may wonder what room there is to doubt that an Irishman called Ernán founded a monastery here some 1,400 years ago.

We do not and cannot know what circumstances lay behind the establishment of Ernán's new foundation. The island, however, would not have been an empty place, ripe for the picking by any 'saint' who happened to be passing by. The settlement must have been at the 'invitation' of a secular authority and there are many recorded examples of such secular donations. Bede, for example, writing in the early 8th century but referring back to the events of the 630s, records how the Northumbrian king, Oswald, gave Aidan the island of Lindisfarne as his monastic and episcopal seat (*HE* iii, 3). He also relates the account of how Columba received Iona from Bruide, king of the Picts (*HE* iii, 4), although of course in Irish tradition, the island is said to have been given to Columba by his kinsman, the overking of the Dál Riata, Conall son of Comgall. The Irish tradition is recorded retrospectively in the *Annals of Ulster* under the year 573. It was not, however, recorded in Adomnán's *Life of Columba*, a work that

was completed in the 690s and Anderson (1991, xxxi) suggests that the entry in the *Annals* was not made much before 750. The point, however, is that cultivable land in the Firth of Clyde at this time would have belonged to one of the main secular kin-groups. According to the *Senchus Fer nAlban*, the 'History of the Men of Scotland', a 10th-century compilation incorporating earlier material from the mid-7th century (Bannerman 1974, 27; Sharpe 2000), Inchmarnock will have lain within the region of the *Cenél nGabráin* kin-group, the second branch of the Dál Riata whose lands extended from Kintyre to Cowal, together with the islands in between (Figure 9.1).

Stephen Carter's analysis (Chapter 4) of the island's palaeotopography and its soils, in conjunction with the observation (Chapter 5.5) that only low levels of prehistoric activity could be identified on the excavated site, come together to suggest that the 'Midpark' site that Ernán acquired was not a prime piece of real estate. On the contrary, it appears to have been, quite literally, a rather 'marginal' place; and relatively isolated too as a small plot of dry (or drier) land, surrounded on all sides by poorly drained ground that was, until very recently, persistently wet. This would be the practical context for the enclosure ditch to the west and the stone causeway to the east of the settlement.

Such a marginal location could be likened to the setting of an 'island-within-an-island', giving rise perhaps to ideas of ascetic withdrawal, isolation and extreme eremitical practices. Such views, however, would be wrong. We will see eremitical behaviour, associated with the cave and rock shelter sites at the south end of the island. The 'marginality' of the Midpark site, however, is relative to the settlement structure of what had gone before, rather than what was still to come.

Ernán's foundation at 'Midpark' would become the new central-place on the island and this part of the island would remain the principal focus of settlement down to the present day. Then, in the medieval period, we see the site attracting further investment, in the form of a fine Romanesque church which was erected

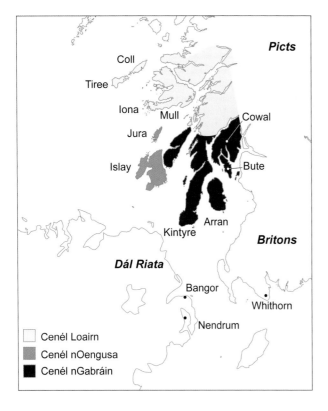

Figure 9.1
The kindreds of early Dál Riata

Legend:
- Cenél Loairn
- Cenél nOengusa
- Cenél nGabráin

track-way to the north-west of the site would appear to be associated with some form of an enclosure. A possible reconstruction of the size, shape and extent of this enclosure is explored below. It would be useful, however, to first consider the role that the enclosure played in the life of the settlement and to set out some comparative data.

9.2.2 The enclosure of early ecclesiastical sites

Early monastic sites, both large and small, were normally enclosed. The boundary of the enclosure, the *vallum monasterii*, not only served to define the physical extent of the site but also, as Thomas (1971, 29) has pointed out, formed 'a spiritual and legal ... boundary between the monastic establishment and the world outside it'. In the Rule of Columbanus, for example, penances were due if a monk went 'outside the wall (*extra vallum*), that is, outside the bounds of a monastery without asking' (Bieler 1963, 106–7). The Rule of Ailbe, meanwhile, insisted 'that he may not leave his enclosure' (Walker 1970, 154–5: O'Neill 1907, 105). Internal subdivisions of the enclosure, which served to control and allow access to different parts of the monastery, are also referred to in contemporary documents.

The *vallum monasterii* is referred to in a host of early saints' *Lives*, penitentials and other early ecclesiastical documents. The *Betha Mochuda* (Plummer 1922, I, 299, ii, 290), for example, describes the construction of the rampart at Lismore. The Irish law tract, *Coibnius uisci tairidne* ('the kinship of conducted water': Binchy 1955), meanwhile, refers to ditches around churches. In a Northumbrian context, there are Bede's references to the hermitage that Cuthbert established on Inner

inside the old monastic enclosure. Such largesse was not easily come by. It suggests that there was something special about the place, about Ernán's foundation and the reputation that he or it had in the wider world of Scottish Dál Riata, the Irish settlement of Argyll. The archaeological evidence provides some clues as to what this may have been but before we do this we need to consider what Ernán's settlement would have looked like.

9.2 'CASA ERNANI', 'TECH ERNÁIN': THE EARLY MONASTERY AND ITS LANDSCAPE

9.2.1 Introduction

The archaeological evidence from the excavation has been very much focused on the remains in and around the later, medieval church. Exploratory work was undertaken outside the stack-yard (Chapter 5), to try and clarify the extent of the site and whether it was enclosed and the fragmentary evidence that was discovered in the field to the west and in the

Table 9.1 Selected curvilinear-enclosed ecclesiastical sites from western Scotland

	Area
Iona	8ha
St Blane's, Kingarth, Bute	2ha
Ardnadam, Cowal	0.3ha
Cladh a Bhearnaig, Kerrera	0.3ha
Nave Island, Islay	0.2ha
St Patrick's Chapel, Ceann a'Mhara, Tiree	0.14ha
Sgor nam Ban-naomha, Canna	0.13ha

Farne and its construction inside a circular stone and earth rampart and ditch (*VCB*, 17); similarly (*vallo circumdata*), the retreat that Bede tells us John of Beverley established near Hexham (*HE* v, 2). Others may have been specified, not because of the personalities involved, but perhaps because of the unusualness of the materials used in their construction. According to Rudolf's *Life of St Lioba*, the double-monastery at Wimborne was enclosed by high and stout walls (Whitelock 1955, 715). Wilfrid's foundation at Oundle, meanwhile, was enclosed by 'a great hedge of thorn' (*sepes magna spinea*: *VW 67*, Colgrave 1927, 145–7), although possibly this was established on or over an earlier rampart.

Early monastic enclosures can take a variety of shapes, sizes and forms. Curvilinear enclosures are particularly well-represented in the archaeological record. In

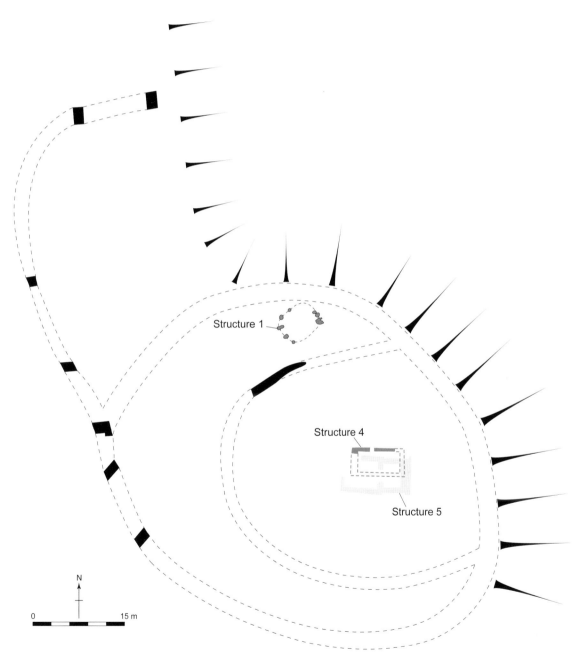

Structure 1

Structure 4

Structure 5

N

0   15 m

Figure 9.2
Reconstruction of the monastic (Phase 1) enclosures at Inchmarnock

Ireland, for example, large numbers of curvilinear-enclosed ecclesiastical sites have been recognised from cartographic and aerial survey, most notably associated with the work of Leo Swan (1983). He has noted a hierarchy of sites, ranging from very small enclosed sites, in the order of 25m to 50m across (area <0.2ha), a group of larger enclosures, 90m to 120m in diameter (area roughly 0.5–1ha) and yet others, 140m to 400m across (area, roughly 1.5–12ha) (Swan 1983, 274). A similar range in scale is also evident among broadly contemporary sites known from Scotland (Table 9.1).

However, before we can say how Inchmarnock compares, we need to define the size and extent of its enclosure. We also need to clarify its shape.

9.2.3 The Inchmarnock enclosure (Figure 9.2)

It seems clear that there are probably two, quite discrete elements to the line and extent of the enclosure at Inchmarnock. One is defined by the ditch fragments that were identified during trial-trenching in 2000 and 2002, along with the geophysical survey undertaken in the latter year; the other is defined topographically by the small promonotory, formed by the old cliff-line (now an eroded bank) above the raised beach, on which the site is located.

If this interpretation is correct, then the north-west and west sides of the enclosure would have been marked by a rampart (since removed by cultivation) and an external ditch. In addition to any 'legal' or 'spiritual' requirement that the enclosure may have had, a ditch in such a location would have had the added, practical bonus of draining away water from the boggy ground adjacent and the hillside above. Given the topography of the site, it seems likely that the south and south-west sides of the enclosure would have been similarly delimited. The projected line of the rampart and ditch

would have lain under the north range of the later steading.

We cannot be certain how the eastern side of the site was defined, whether by a turf bank or a stone wall. Nor do we know its precise line, whether it followed the course of the modern enclosure around the base of the small promonotory on which the site lies or whether it was sited higher up at the break of slope. A bank in the latter position, however, is assumed for the purpose of this reconstruction. If this is the case, then the natural spring that was traced during survey will have lain outwith the enclosure. The resultant shape thus comprises an oval-shaped enclosure, roughly 70 × 55m, with its longer axis aligned north-west to south-east, together with, at its north-west end, what looks like an annexe. The annexe is sub-rectangular in shape, roughly 40 × 25m and with its longer axis aligned roughly north to south (Figure 9.2). The possible relationship of this annexe, both in terms of its function and its chronology, is explored below in the context of how the space inside the enclosure may have been used (Chapter 9.2.4). However, in terms of 'site-scale' (Table 9.1: Figure 9.3), it is clear that the enclosed space at Inchmarnock (reconstructed as 0.3ha or 0.4ha with the northern annexe) is considerably smaller than anything we see at Iona or even Kingarth, yet equally larger than the type of hermitage site that we see at Sgòr nam Ban-naomha on Canna.

Two radiocarbon-dates were recovered from the enclosure ditch; one from the upper fill of the fragment identified in the evaluation trench that was located in the track-way to the north-west of the excavated area; the other from a lower fill of the ditch that was traced in Trench 7, in the field to the west of the site (Table 9.2).

Neither, of course, provides a construction date for the feature and ditches are such dynamic archaeological

Table 9.2 Radiocarbon dates from the enclosure ditch at Inchmarnock

Code	Material	Context no	Context/comment	Uncalibrated date	Calibrated 2-sigma date
SUERC-7542 (GU-13345)	birch/alder charcoal	4301	Lower fill of ditch, revetted on east side with large stones	1285 ± 35 BP	AD 650–810
AA-53163 (GU-10634)	hazel nutshell	4020	Upper fill of ditch; provides *terminus post quem* date for deposition of inscribed slates SF630 and SF642 and cross-marked slab SF660	1130 ± 35 BP	AD 780–1000

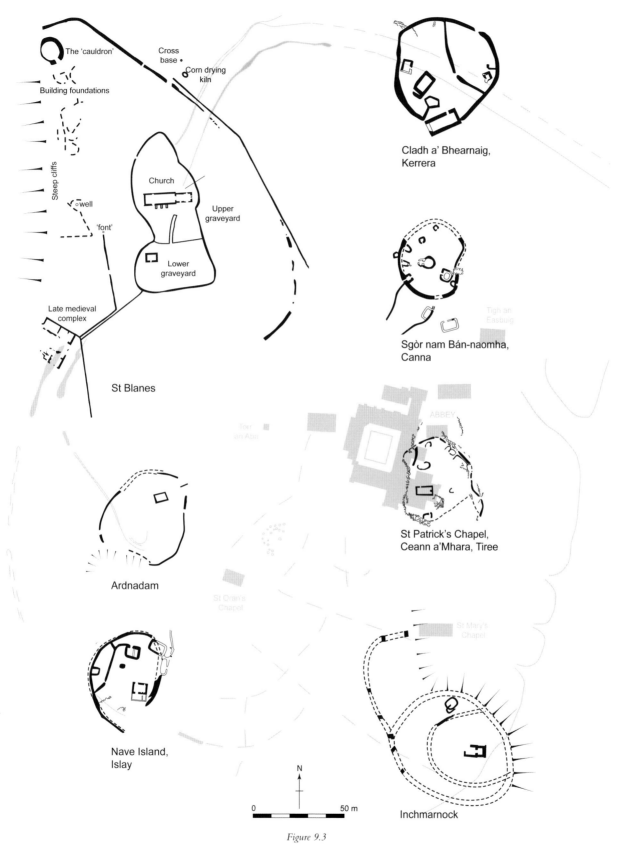

Figure 9.3
Early Historic monastic enclosures: selected comparanda (with Iona shown in the background at the same scale)

253

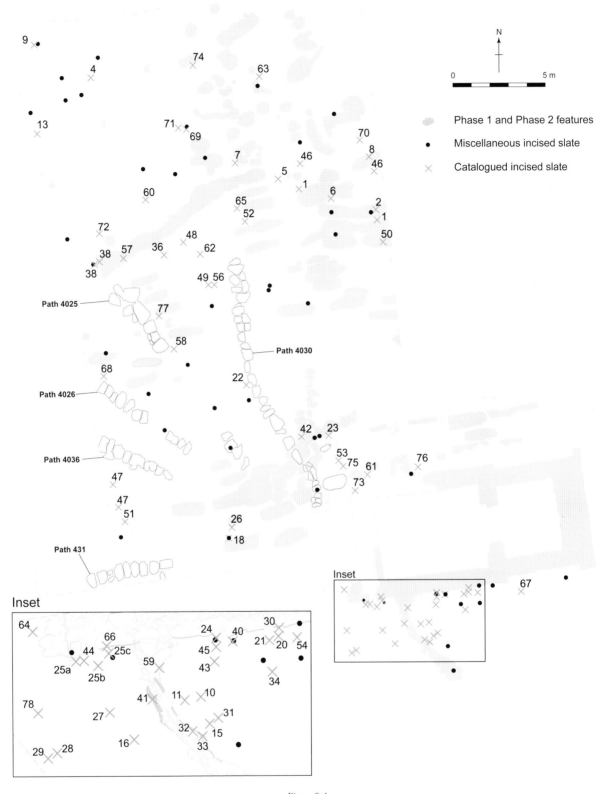

Figure 9.4
Distribution of incised slate

environments that primary dating evidence (unless structural) will rarely be preserved since deposits will be removed by water-action, as well as by the actions of those whose job it will have been to maintain the ditch in a working order. Clearly, such features would rapidly silt up without regular maintenance. Nonetheless, the earlier date would not contradict the idea, that we see, for example, in the dating of some of the text-inscribed slates, that the enclosure was a primary feature on the site, constructed perhaps in the early 7th century, in or around the year AD 600.

9.2.4 The use of space

The site of the medieval church and indeed Structure 4, the fragmentary building that was identified below and to one side of it, are located east of centre of the oval enclosure. In very general terms and using very round numbers, the dating evidence suggests that Structure 4 could have been built as early as around 800, given the cal AD 650–780 date (SUERC-7540) for the pit sealed below its floor. A much later date, say around 900, however, may be indicated by analogy with the documentary evidence from Ireland for the construction of churches in stone (Hare & Hamlin 1986, 131). The present church, meanwhile, was probably constructed closer to the year 1100 than 1200 given that it must predate the insertion of Grave G102 which is dated to cal AD 1020–1210 (SUERC-7544). It is not unreasonable to assume that Ernán's Church, presumably a post- and turf-built structure, would have occupied roughly the same location.

Around the church, the ecclesiastical focus of the site, lay the cemetery. There was possibly an early cluster of graves in the area to the north of the church, as indicated by the phasing plan (Figure 5.4), but the distribution of the cross-marked and related stones from the site (Figure 6.3) indicates that the primary cemetery almost certainly extended to the south and west of the church as well. There is, however, a very clearly defined northern limit to the cemetery, marked by a shallow gully aligned north–east to south–west. Extrapolation and projection of this line around the inside of the enclosure suggests an inner area roughly 45m across, centred on the church, and an outer zone up to 20m wide (Figure 9.2).

In this outer zone was sited a series of workshops associated with metalworking (Heald & McLaren, Chapter 6.11) and there are indications that the working of oil shale and related materials, for the fashioning of bangles, was also being undertaken close to but outwith the excavated area, perhaps in that part of the site immediately to the north-west. Interestingly, as Fraser Hunter (Chapter 6.10) has pointed out, the manufacture of black jewellery is a well-recognised phenomenon at several religious sites in western Scotland and was presumably one of a range of craft processes carried out under the auspices of the church. We might characterise, therefore, the north and north-west areas of this outer zone as a workshop area. However, for the rest of the outer zone, we can only speculate as to how these areas may have been used and what buildings may have existed there.

Around the south side of the enclosure, coincident with and under the footings of the Midpark farmstead, is probably where the members of the monastic community will have lived, probably in small individual post-built huts or drystone cells. A barn, byre and possibly a corn-drying kiln will have been located nearby. To the east, perhaps outwith the enclosure, on the bank next to the causeway, may have been a rudimentary guest-house. But what lay to the west of the cemetery, in the area between the identified craft area to the north and the presumed accommodation zone to the south? Here we can possibly infer quite a lot.

Fragments of incised slate were recovered throughout the excavated area (Figure 9.4). It is clear, however, that the demonstrably early pieces, that is to say those text-inscribed fragments that have been assigned to Forsyth and Tedeschi's pre-800 group, tend to lie in the area to the north and west of the church. The suggestion, therefore, is that somewhere in the vicinity, outwith the excavated area, is where the monastic school-house was located, between the industrial zone to the north and the living quarters to the south. Interestingly, this was also the location of Building 22, the monastic school-house at Nendrum (Lawlor 1925, 143–149, Plate 1). It too lay directly to the west of the church, outwith the inner cashel wall (Figure 9.5). And precisely the same thing is also evident in St Molaise's foundation on Inishmurray, off the coast of Sligo, where a circular stone clochán known as the 'school-house', lies to the west of the principal church, beyond the cashel wall in an outer enclosed area (Figure 9.5). Interestingly, the inner enclosed area around the church on Inishmurray is traditionally known as the men's burial-ground (Wakeman 1893, 50; O'Sullivan & Carragain 2007). The significance of the Inchmarnock school-house and the incised slate assemblage is considered further below (Chapter 9.2.5).

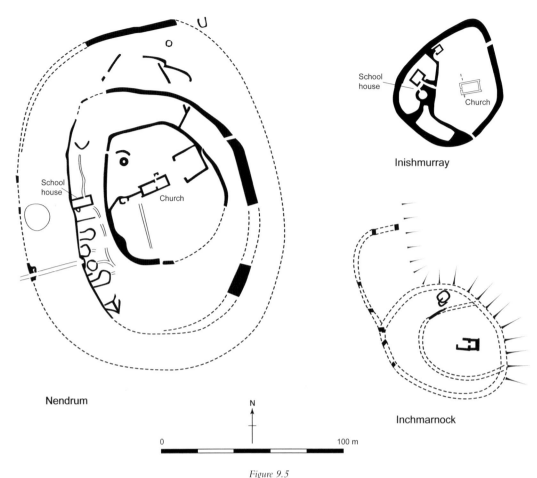

School
house
Church

Inishmurray

School
house
Church

Nendrum

N

0   100 m

Inchmarnock

Figure 9.5
Nendrum, Inishmurray and Inchmarnock: comparative plans

Our reconstruction of Ernán's monastery (Figure 9.6), and clearly some elements of this are more speculative than others, suggests that the site comprised five or possibly six quite distinct elements: (1) a spiritual space at its centre, represented by the church and cemetery; (2) a living space, to the south; (3) a working space to the north; and (4) a learning space to the west. A fifth zone may be indicated by an 'access space' to the east, represented by the causeway which led up from the beach. In this area, as suggested above, may have been sited a 'guest-house' or cell for visitors to the island. But what was the purpose of our sixth zone, the 'northern annexe'? How does it fit into these ideas of zoning and is it contemporary with our oval-enclosed site?

There are no easy answers to any of these questions. The suspicion, however, based simply on its alignment and position in the landscape, is that it is probably a secondary feature that has been appended to the earlier enclosure. For example, there is a noticeable 'dog-leg' in the line of the enclosure ditch at the east end of Trench 7, between it and Trenches 1 and 2 to the north and south. Meanwhile, radiocarbon-dating of hazel nutshells from its upper fill (cal AD 780–1000: AA-53163) indicates that the ditch probably went out of use some time after AD 1000. The presence of metalworking debris in its lower fill and fragments of inscribed slate in its upper fill (including pieces that were probably well over 200 years old at the time of their deposition) suggests that the site witnessed a major phase of reorganisation at or around the turn of the millennium.

Dumped in the upper fill of the ditch was also the cross-marked slab (EMS.21). Evidence of recutting on the stone suggests that it may have been reused as part of a composite cross-base for a freestanding

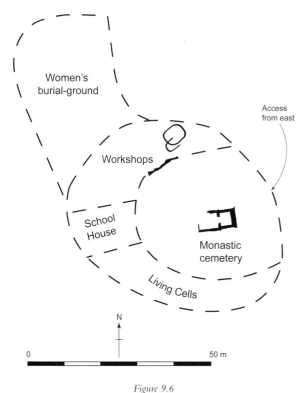

Figure 9.6
The use of space: an interpretative plan

cross-shaft, of the type known, for example, from Iona (Fisher 2001, Figure 29). The unexcavated 'cist' (G32) that was identified in the side of the evaluation trench, some 4m to the north of the enclosure ditch (Chapter 5.5), may in fact be the below-ground element of just such a cross-base. And, in terms of size, it is not impossible that the probable cross-base (EMS.21) was associated with the rune-inscribed cross-shaft (EMS.13) that was found in the vicinity in 1889 (although if it was, then the dating of the upper ditch deposits (cal AD 780–1000: AA-53163) might imply that it only stood for a generation or two before it was cast aside). Possibly, then, EMS.13 replaced an earlier shaft in the same position? In any event, such a monument at this location would have marked the line of the boundary ditch and, possibly, the site of an entrance into the ecclesiastical enclosure itself.

But what was the northern annexe used for? Here, we are necessarily on even thinner ice and the small areas examined in the various trial trenches provide no clues as to its function. Past discoveries and local tradition, however, may give us the answer. It can only be a suggestion but possibly this corresponds to the site of the 'Women's Burial-place' that Hewison

recorded in the 1890s, noting that it 'was traceable in a field adjoining the church about thirty years ago' (Hewison 1893, i, 133). The use of separate burial-grounds for women (and other groups) is a well-known phenomenon of the early church in Ireland (Hamlin & Foley 1983) and the practice is also known in Scotland (O'Sullivan 1994, 359–360). Examples have been recorded from Iona, Taransay and, in a local context, from St Blane's, at Kingarth on Bute. However, if the Inchmarnock burial-ground has been correctly identified then this probably gives us our best-dated example known to date: it would suggest a chronology that lies between the 7th and the 11th century, albeit most likely towards the latter part of this range.

9.2.5 The Inchmarnock school-house

Introduction

The identification of a probable school-house on the site, although we only see it through the debitage of its day-to-day activity, is one of the most significant findings of the project. The incised slate assemblage is the largest collection of such material from Scotland, known to date. Similar finds are known from a number of Early Christian and Viking sites (O'Meadhra 1979: 1987a), including locally the early monastic site of St Blane's at Kingarth on Bute (Laing 1996; Laing *et al* 1998; Anderson 1900) and the nearby, broadly contemporary settlement at Little Dunagoil (Marshall 1964). Examples on the whole, however, although relatively common in Ireland are rare in Britain (Laing *et al* 1998, 559). As potential 'pattern books', these scraps of slate are important not only for the archaeology of the island itself but also potentially for broader art-historical studies of the Early Christian period.

O'Meadhra's work suggests that motif-pieces are essentially an Insular Celtic, possibly even Irish, phenomenon (O'Meadhra 1987a, 78–83; 1987b, 159). As for the corpus of Scottish motif-pieces (that is to say material that is found on sites in what is now Scotland), it is clear that there are two very specific distributions. There is the larger, Scottish Dalriada group that is closely related and essentially forms an extension to the material from Ireland; and there is a second, much smaller, group from Orkney and Shetland although its cultural origins, whether Pictish or Norse, and its relationship, if any, to the Irish and Dalriadic material are difficult to discern (O'Meadhra 1993, 435).

257

In terms both of geography and 'content', it is clear that the Inchmarnock material belongs with the Scottish Dalriada group and that it is closely related to the material from Ireland. The early monastic site of Nendrum, on Mahee Island off the western shore of Strangford Lough, provides a very useful context for what we see at Inchmarnock in the latter part of the first millennium. Excavations at Nendrum produced a large assemblage of motif-pieces, as well as several iron styli which were used to inscribe the fragments. The building in which the pieces were found was interpreted as a monastic 'school' (Lawlor 1925, 144–8) and these have been dated by O'Meadhra (1987a, 72) on stylistic and palaeographical grounds to the period 7th to 9th centuries. A similar chronology, although possibly continuing down to the 10th or early 11th century if the dating of pieces like the sketch of the church arcades (IS.54) is correct, may apply to the Inchmarnock assemblage. It is clear, however, given the presence of the later gothic script that we see on a handful of pieces from the site (Forsyth & Tedeschi, Chapter 6.3.3 above), that there is also a later medieval literate presence on the island. Among the island's later medieval inhabitants, there was also, of course, someone who was familiar with the layout, design and composition methods of the so-called 'West Highland school of sculpture', given the presence of the slab (IS.30) with the sketch of the Highland galley and hunting scene (Chapter 6.3.4).

One of the key themes that runs through the various pieces that make up this assemblage is that of learning and instruction (O'Meadhra's Class 2a and Class 2b functions). Indeed, as she has noted, the association seems mainly to be with training activity, and only rarely are motif pieces found in association with workshops or manufacturing: 'In most cases, motif-pieces seem to be unique evidence for design as an activity separate from manufacture' (O'Meadhra 1987a, 169).

The juxtaposition of school-house and workshops, then, that we see at Inchmarnock is potentially very significant indeed, and it is these activities that are given pride of place, therefore, in our reconstruction drawing of *Casa Ernani* and its stone-built church (Figure 9.7). Unfortunately, however, no evidence of a direct linkage between design and manufacture was forthcoming although this is likely to have more to do with the type of workshop activity identified. General ironworking and shale bangle production, for example, are unlikely to have presented much of a 'design' opportunity, unlike (say) fine metalworking or stone sculpture which the community may have been actively engaged in elsewhere on the site.

Meanwhile, among the doodles and other graffiti in the assemblage we can also see elements of O'Meadhra's Class 1 function, reflecting 'leisure' activity of one kind or another; and in the *Ernán* stone we can see what is probably a talismanic function (O'Meadhra's Class 5 function). These themes are explored below but we also need to address the question of how old were the scholars whose handiwork this is. Before we can do this, however, we need to consider a very basic question concerning the manufacture of the boards and whether their surfaces were prepared in any particular way and how these stone fragments might relate to the waxed tablets that are referred to in early saints' Lives and other literature.

Tabulae: waxed tablets and stone slates

There is a large number of references to the use of tablets (Latin: *tabulae*) in early Irish and other sources. The 6th-century Rule of St Benedict, for example, required every monk to have a wax tablet and stylus, the metal or bone implement that was used to write on the tablet, as part of their essential everyday equipment (Peers & Radford 1943, 64). There are references in the early Irish Lives of Saints (Plummer 1910, I, cxv, note 11) to the use of waxed tablets for the practice of letters; and Adomnán tells us that Columba's prophecy to Colcu, Cellach's son, was written down *in tabula* (*VC* i, 35).

But it was not just words that were set out on these tablets and a key work is Adomnán's account of *De locis sanctis*, describing the holy places of Palestine. The work was based on the account of Arculf, a Frankish bishop, who visited Adomnán on Iona some time before 686 or 688 when Adomnán presented his copy of *De locis sanctis* to King Aldfrith of Northumbria; significantly, 'he wrote down first on wax tablets, then transferred it to parchment' (*primo in tabulis describenti ... quae nunc in membranis brevi textu scribuntur*: De locis sanctis [Bk.I, preface], Meehan 1958, 36). Of particular interest, however, is the fact that, when asked to describe the appearance of the Church of the Holy Sepulchre in Jerusalem and its surrounding chapels, Arculf took the stylus and drew a rough sketch in the wax (*sanctus Arculfus in paginola figuravit cerata*: De locis sanctis I.2,15: Meehan 1958, 46).

In addition to references regarding their use, there are also descriptions in the Irish material of what these wax boards actually looked like, as well as what are probably depictions of the same in

Figure 9.7
'Casa Ernani' in the 9th century: a group of young scholars practise their letters under the watchful eye of the school-master; a cut-away provides a view into the adjacent workshop. *Reconstruction painting by David Simon*

contemporary illuminated manuscripts. The *Hisperica Famina*, a 7th-century Irish colloquy, for example, describes a wax tablet in a carved oak frame which has been 'fashioned with various painted designs and has decorated borders'; it goes on to tell us, in the grandiose language typical of the document, that 'the embellished tablet ... is carried in the right hand of the scholars and contains the mysteries of rhetoric in waxen spheres' (Herren 1974, 106). Meanwhile, in the Book of Kells, dating to around 800, on folio 8r there is a figure of a sitting man holding what may be an open book or a pair of wax tablets set within a wooden frame (Meehan 1994, 13 and 43).

Moreover, actual examples of waxed wooden tablets have survived. Six small boards of yew wood, known as the Springmount Tablets, were recovered from Springmount Bog in County Antrim, where they had been preserved in the anaerobic conditions

of the peat (Armstrong & Macalister 1920). The boards are 210 × 77mm (8¼" × 3") and along one edge are two holes for gathering the boards together into a 'book'. The two outer boards are recessed only on their inner faces, whilst the four inner boards are recessed on both sides. The resultant hollows have been filled with a layer of beeswax and preserved in the surface of the wax are verses from the Psalms. Although traditionally dated to the 7th century, there are palaeographical arguments that might suggest a 5th- or more likely a 6th-century date for the tablets (O'Meadhra 1987a, 105; Ó Cróinín 1995, 182; Charles-Edwards 2002).

Wax tablets, then, feature prominently in the documentary record, they appear to have a place in the visual representations of the time and they also occasionally make an appearance in the archaeological record. Slate-boards and slate pebbles, on the other hand, seem to occupy an almost inverse universe, rarely referred to in the documentary and manuscript record but dominant, because of the survivability of stone, in the archaeological record of, at least, some sites. Interestingly, the size and proportion of the most complete slate-board (IS.58) from Inchmarnock, with extant dimensions of 213 × 105mm (reconstructed as 240 × 120mm with its wooden frame: Figure 6.15), is of a similar order to the boards that make up the Springmount Tablets (210 × 77mm).

A rare record of slates being used is preserved in an Old Irish account concerning Cenn Fáelad's convalescence in 636 at the monastery of Tuaim Drecain (Tomregan, County Cavan) (quoted in O'Meadhra 1987a, 105–106). It tells us that:

> everything that he would hear of the recitations of the three schools every day, he would have it by heart every night. And he filled a pattern of poetry to these matters and wrote them on slates and tablets and set them in a vellum book.

Like the *De locis sanctis* account, noted above, where Adomnán describes writing things down *in tabulae* before transcribing them to vellum, the Cenn Fáelad account also emphasizes the fact that wax tablets and slates were simply a means to an end, not an end in themselves. Clearly, in these two particular cases, the tablets or slates were intended only as temporary media prior to transcribing the works onto vellum; in the Inchmarnock material and elsewhere, therefore, what we are seeing is essentially a collection of ephemera. As temporary pieces of 'work-in-progress', however, they can acquire a tremendous significance, out of all proportion to the actual incised design or motif itself because it is here that we see the individual scholar and the individual novice coming to grips with his letters, learning how to set out motifs and fill borders with interlace and other designs, and possibly – among some of the later fragments (Chapter 9.3.4 below) – how to set out pieces of music. Without this basic, lower level of instruction and training there would have been, for example, no Book of Kells or any of the other great illuminated manuscripts of early insular Christianity.

Palimpsests and their implications

The slate on Inchmarnock varies in colour from light- to dark-grey but its surface, when freshly scratched, leaves a very clear, white incised mark. It is this appearance that we have tried to recreate in the 'white-line' method that has been used to illustrate some of the finer pieces from the excavation (Middleton, Appendix 4).

Experimentation indicates that the 'whiteness' of the line and its visibility is long-lasting. It dulls over time but, if left untouched (and, importantly, so long as it is kept out of the soil), it is clear that any marks will remain perfectly legible for many years. Meanwhile, although the marks can be temporarily 'erased' by wetting and a new mark made in its place, once the stone has dried out then the earlier mark reappears to obscure any later design. This strongly suggests, therefore, that those pieces on which palimpsests of marks have been preserved must have been coated with clay or 'whiting'. Indeed, some such process is described in a late 12th-century account, *De Utensilibus* by Alexander Neckam, an English goldsmith who was teaching in Paris in the period *c* 1180–1200:

> And let his untaught apprentice have a waxed tablet or one anointed with whiting or rubbed over with clay so that he may portray and draw little flowers thereon in various manners.
>
> *Habeat autem discipulus eius rudis tabellam ceratam vel aeromate unctam, vel argilla oblita, ad flosculos protrahendos variis modis, ne in offensione proceda.*
>
> Quoted in O'Meadhra 1987a, 107

In all, leaving to one side the large and the heavily graffitoed 'furniture-like' pieces of incised slate (the possible grave-cover or side-slab, IS.30 and the 'table-top', IS.76) which are hardly relevant to a discussion of manual slate-boards, there are only ten fragments in the assemblage where it is possible to identify at least an element of superimposition of design and marks (Table 9.3).

In two cases (IS.2 and IS.5), the extent of the superimposition is literally marginal and both the earlier grids for the games and the later motifs remain perfectly legible and the gaming board entirely playable. The other gaming board in this group (IS.7), the grid of which overlay an earlier design, would have also remained easily playable. The marks on IS.53, on the other hand, may simply be a 'scribble' or a crossing-through of an earlier sketch. Meanwhile, given the likely talisman function of the *Ernán* stone (IS.35), it is debatable whether any of the incised marks were ever intended to be seen or read by another party; in other words that what mattered was the act itself of actually carving the words and other motifs on the stone rather

Table 9.3 Slate-boards and related hand-sized fragments with superimposed designs

Cat. no	Nature and extent of palimpsest
Cat. no 2	probable slate-board with grid of gaming board and overlying cable motif across edge of grid.
Cat. no 5	irregular large fragment of slate with gaming board and overlying curvilinear motif across edge of grid.
Cat. no 7	possible slate-board with gaming board grid overlying earlier set of lines forming possible 'F-' or 'E-shaped' design with bulbous terminal to central bar.
Cat. no 35	slate beach pebble with various inscriptions – Ernan and Casa – plus miscellaneous motifs and other marks, palimpsested on both faces: probable talisman object.
Cat. no 36	slate-board with accipitur text on Face A; light palimpsest of ogham inscription, lattice and scroll-motif on Face B.
Cat. no 38	slate-board with letter-sequence on Face A; heavy palimpsest of further letter-sequences, doodles and sketches of encircled, equal-armed crosses on Face B.
Cat. no 43	slate-board with manuscript tradition capital M on both faces; light palimpsest of miscellaneous marks on both faces.
Cat. no 53	irregular slate fragment with sword-like motif and miscellaneous other marks forming palimpsest on Face A.
Cat. no 62	probable slate-board with light palimpsest of rectilinear grids.
Cat. no 69	irregular slate fragment with palimpsest of grids, hatching and possible human figure.

than their external display. In none of these cases is there any reason to suppose that a clay coating would have been present to facilitate the creation of the palimpsest.

In the remaining five examples, however, it would not be unreasonable to suppose that some form of 'whiting' would have been required to facilitate the legibility of the characters and other marks inscribed. This is particularly so in the case of the heavy palimpsest that we see on IS.38. None, however, is now present and it is assumed that its coating has been lost. There is, however, the remains of a 'clay wash' on IS.62 and the remains of what may be a very fragmentary coating on IS.43. Microscopic examination has identified the residue as a fine silty clay sediment which, in places, has become impregnated with iron oxide (Dr Stephen Lancaster, pers comm). This is a natural process which will have hardened the silty clay sediment and possibly helped cement it to the stone. This would suggest that a clay whiting may have been used on Inchmarnock, at least for the more formal slate-boards that were used in the monastic school-house; whether it survives, however, is very much down to serendipity and the precise conditions of its burial environment.

The incised slate assemblage as evidence of instruction and training

The Inchmarnock slates containing script and letters clearly indicate the presence of a literate, Gaelic-speaking community on the island in the early medieval period. Significantly, as Forsyth and Tedeschi (above, Chapter 6.3.3) have noted, this group of slates also provides an insight into how instruction and training in literacy was delivered.

The impression that we get from the surviving documentary record is very much focused on the notion of master and pupil. In Chapter 5 of the early medieval Life of St Daig, for example, we are told that on the island of *Daiminis* (Devenish) on Lough Erne in County Fermanagh, there was 'a little monastery called a school' (*monasteriolum quod schola dicitur*) in which Daig taught the elements of lettering and the art of manuscript decoration (Heist 1965, 390). And this individual relationship of master and pupil, as represented in the cases of exemplum and copy, is one that we also seem to see in parts of the archaeological record.

We get to see, for example, the pupil practising his 'abc' and not only in Latin but also, significantly, in ogham as well; elsewhere, we get to see him practising the basic skills required in forming letters. There are also some intensely private moments, in the writing exercise (*adeptus sanctum praemium*) where we see the novice as he struggles to get to grips not only with his Latin but also with his writing implement.

The age of the novices, whose handiwork we mostly see, is difficult to gauge. According to Adomnán, Columba's training for religion began in boy-hood; he was the foster-child or pupil of a priest called Cruithnechán (*VC* iii, 2). Meanwhile, we know that Bede was only seven years of age when he was taken into the care of Benedict Biscop at the Anglo-Saxon monastery at Wearmouth in 680 (Colgrave & Mynors 1979, xx). It is assumed that such an age would not be out of place for the Inchmarnock scholars; indeed, Abigail Burnyeat's (pers comm) work in looking at children's cognitive development would suggest that the pictorial finds from the site are very much indicative of the work of children of this age.

Part of what we may be seeing at Inchmarnock, therefore, may reflect the practice of fostering. This is a well-known feature of early Irish secular society, particularly among the aristocracy who would typically foster out their children from the age of seven until 17 for boys and 14 for girls (MacNiocaill 1972, 59: Mytum 1992, 102–65). This practice, which helped develop ties and alliances between and outwith the various kin-groups, was quickly seized upon by the early Irish church. It recognised that it would not only provide income but was also a very effective way of spreading its influence, particularly through education and the use of writing. The fosterage of young children has been suggested as a likely explanation for the presence of the children's remains in the early monastic cemetery on Illaunloughan Island, County Kerry (White-Marshall & Walsh 2005, 84–5) and the same mechanism almost certainly also applies to Inchmarnock. One of the disappointments here, of course, is that bone does not survive among the earliest graves from the site; however, among the Phase 1 graves (Figure 5.4), particularly the shorter ones (for example, G72, G75 or G146), are probably those of some of these early scholars whose handiwork we otherwise have in an abundance. The discovery of a simple gravestone with the inscription *Fínán puer* ('the student Fínán'), from Peakaun in County Tipperary (Manning 1991), traditionally identified as a 7th-century foundation associated with St Beccan, also reflects the presence of children or young adults at these early monastic schools.

Examples of instruction and training are also evident among the non-text-inscribed slates from the site. The idea of exemplum and copy is very evident in the cable motif that has been carved over and across one edge of a previously incised gaming board (IS.2: Figure 6.16). The curve and sweep of the example to the left is controlled and regular; the marks to the right, however, show what is clearly meant to be a copy of the more accomplished hand. The poor quality of the pupil's copy suggests, perhaps, that the trainee should have spent more time in practising control of his writing implement, less in the pursuit of games!

Other aspects of the monastic curriculum clearly involved the use of pairs of compasses. For example, among the assemblage of early medieval sculpture (including the pre-2000 discoveries) there are no less than three pieces featuring the 'cross-of-arcs' motif (EMS.3, EMS.14 and EMS.15). But we also see compass-work among the heavily-graffitoed 'table-top' (IS.76) with its arcs, circles and centre-points and the same are also found in the primary layer of the palimpsest on the later medieval, possible 'mock' or imitation grave-slab with its Highland galley and hunting scene (IS.30).

There is also evidence, seen in IS.57 (Figure 6.31) with its framed panels of interlace and spiral motifs, for practising the types of design that were used to fill the borders or decorated capitals that we see in the illuminated manuscripts. There is also possibly some evidence for the use of grids, although whether as a design tool or as a scaling or resizing device is not clear. Lightly incised grids, for example, are present on IS.49 (Figure 6.28), with its possible quadruped, and IS.69 (Figure 6.33) which possibly depicts a frontal view of the upper torso and face of a human figure.

The training and instruction that the pupils underwent was not, however, entirely formal in the sense of learning script or instruction in the use of pair of compass and grids. The simple sketches and doodles that we see among the material, and these could easily be classified as examples of O'Meadhra's leisure-pieces, would have also had a place in the curriculum as examples, respectively, of a narrative tradition and as practice pieces to gain experience and confidence in controlling and using the stylus.

The sketch of the armed warriors, the boat and the figure with the 'handbag' (IS.46: Figure 6.27), for example, could have been used for story-telling. What that story may have been we can only guess. It could, for example, represent an anachronistic and corrupted version of Patrick's enslavement; or alternatively, a narrative local to the island or to Bute, including as Katherine Forsyth has suggested (pers comm) a relic procession, with the warriors as guardians and protectors instead of pirates. Meanwhile, the 'loops' or 'scribbles' that we see on IS.70 (Figure 6.33) and on the *Ernán* stone (IS.35: Figure 6.20) could simply represent practice strokes in the use of the stylus. They look, respectively, very much like two ends of a spectrum; one, the work of a novice, unfamiliar with writing and unused to controlling the stylus; the other the work of a significantly more mature hand.

Maturity of writing and control of the stylus will have come with practice, with the copying out of set pieces of text, such as the *adeptus* fragment (IS.36: Figure 6.21), or designs like the cable motif on IS.2 (Figure 6.16). It would also come about through the copying of shapes and this may be the context for the multiple quadrupeds that we see on IS.48 (Figure 6.28). The piece, however, would acquire an added significance if it represents an experiment in the stylisation of the capital letter-form M; and the addition of the 'stick-man' gives a humorous and personal flavour to the piece, not dissimilar to the 'drolleries' or humorous sketches that the medieval manuscript illuminators would sometimes incorporate into their work (Rynne 1994).

9.2.6 The status of Ernán's monastery

In terms simply of its size, we have already seen that the early monastery on Inchmarnock lies towards the 'small' end of the scale (Chapter 9.2.2 above). Provided with an enclosed area of, at most, 0.4ha, the site is dwarfed by its near-neighbour, St Blane's (2 ha). Differences on this scale, between what must be broadly contemporary foundations, presumably reflects a local hierarchy. But what can the island's school-house tell us of the relative status of Ernán's foundation?

If our conclusions concerning the age of the island's pupils are correct, then all the indications are that the Inchmarnock school-house was functioning very much as a primary or elementary school. This was a place where young children, perhaps as young as seven, were taught the basics of design and writing prior to their transfer to other, larger, better-resourced, higher-status establishments. Young children, for example, are notable by their absence from Columba's Iona (Anderson 1991, li). And there are hints of this educational hierarchy, the ecclesiastical equivalent of the secular Late Roman system of elementary school and *grammaticus*, in the documentary sources. Adomnán's *Life of Columba*, for example, tells us that Columba's early schooling was with his foster-father, the priest Cruithnechán (*VC* iii, 2). Later, when he

was a young deacon, he was taught by an aged cleric called Gemmán (*VC* ii, 25), and by 'the holy bishop Findbarr' (*VC* i, 1; ii, 1), also described as 'the venerable bishop Finnio, his master' (*VC* iii, 4) who instructed him in holy scripture, although it is not clear whether this refers to Finnian of Moville in County Down or the founder of Clonard in County Meath (Anderson 1991, xxix). Similarly, we are told that Columbanus was first taught by Mo-Sinu maccu Min at the island hermitage of *Crannach Dúin Lethglaise* (Wood Island, near Downpatrick, County Down) prior to going on to Comgall's monastery at Bangor (*Life of Columbanus*, Chapter 9: Krusch 1905). Meanwhile, Comgall himself received his early instruction from a cleric who lived *in quadam villa in rure* ('a rural hamlet'?) (Plummer 1910, ii, 3: *Vita Comgalli*, Chapter 3) and we have already had cause (Chapter 9.2.5 above) to refer to St Daig's teaching in his school at Devenish on Lough Erne.

Ó Cróinín (1995, 180) stresses the importance of the relationship between an individual master and his pupil but there is another point that also emerges. And that is the undoubted association of at least some small island monasteries with the provision of what looks like an elementary schooling. The prime archaeological example, of course, is Mochaoi's foundation of Nendrum on Mahee Island in Strangford Lough (Lawlor 1925). But it is clear from the documentary sources that a secondary level of education was also available in what we might recognize as larger, regional centres. Possibly, then, Ernán's school on Inchmarnock was the local equivalent of Daig's foundation on Devenish or Mo-Sinu maccu Min's on Wood Island? If so, then it invites the suggestion that Ernán's foundation on Inchmarnock may have been in the same relationship to Blááan's monastery on Bute as Wood Island was to Comgall's house at Bangor.

Columbanus's writings, as Ó Cróinín (1995, 178) has pointed out, show us the work of the trained scholar, the finished product of the Irish schools in general and Bangor in particular. In the monastic library of somewhere like Bangor, the trained scholar would have had access to a wide range of sources, patristic commentaries as well as collections of canon law, ecclesiastical history and church synodal decrees. By contrast, other than the Bible, it is difficult to envisage what teaching materials or books would have been available to a master at one of these elementary schools. However, thanks to David Howlett's identification of the *adeptus* fragment (IS.36: Figure 6.21) as a quotation from the hymn *Audite pantes ta erga*, it is clear that the monastery is likely to have had a copy of the Antiphonary of Bangor, a late 7th-century liturgical commonplace book. Whether this implies a formal or institutional link between the two monasteries, however, is not clear. It may, as Forsyth and Tedeschi (Chapter 6.3.2 above) have suggested, simply mean that the master of the monastic school, like Columbanus before him, had been trained at Bangor. In more general terms, however, as they also note, it clearly demonstrates Inchmarnock's cultural and intellectual ties with the Church in north-eastern Ireland in the 7th and 8th centuries.

9.2.7 Ernán's monastery at the end of the first millennium AD

It is difficult to trace the transition from the small monastic settlement that Ernán established in the 7th century to the construction of the medieval church in the twelfth. The sanctity of the site and any traditions that may have been preserved concerning, perhaps, its fame as a place of learning, however, would have been key factors in this development.

Doubtless the site will have developed and changed over these several centuries and (if our identification of the 'Women's burial-ground' is correct) we have already seen, for example, that the primary enclosed area was extended in the latter part of the first millennium. We do not know who the women were who were buried here. There is no indication that there was a house of female religious on the island and it might be expected that the presence of a nunnery or a double-house would almost certainly leave some record in local tradition or dedication evidence. However, as Hamlin and Foley (1983, 44) have pointed out, clerics in the early church could often be married. The monastic tenants, meanwhile, would have certainly been married and clearly there must have been women and children in and around all but the most isolated monasteries. Burial in the 'women's burial-ground' would have also been a useful source of income to the church and it is not difficult to envisage how burial in proximity to such an early foundation would have been much sought after, not only on Inchmarnock but also possibly from Bute as well.

The monastery would have been a self-contained and self-suffcient community. Without tracing its accommodation areas, it is difficult to establish its size. Columba, for example, founded his original community on Iona with twelve disciples and the apostolic number may not be wide of the mark for Inchmarnock. Most of their time will have been spent in the company of

the community, in prayer, in work and, clearly, some or perhaps one will have been involved in teaching. A more austere, eremitical life of meditation and fasting, however, could also be followed and this is almost certainly the context for the temporary activity that we see in the rock shelters at the south end of the island (Jones & Dingwall, Chapter 8.2). This is also, of course, the context for the *Dysart* place-name that has been locally recorded for this part of the island (Chapter 2.2) and, as was remarked in Chapter 1.1, it neatly presages John Foulis' comment in 1759 that the island would make an appropriate setting 'for one in Love with a Hermetical Life'.

The monastic life on Inchmarnock, therefore, could offer both a communal experience, for those in the monastery at 'Midpark', as well as the opportunity for a more eremitical way of life for those who wished to reaffirm their faith through isolation. It brings to mind Adomnán's account of Virgno, an Irish monk who spent his latter years in the monastery on *Hinba*, an unidentified island (possibly Jura or Colonsay/Oronsay: Macquarrie 1997, 91–102). However, in his last years there, he is said to have left the monastery in order to lead the life of a hermit 'in the place of the anchorites, in *Muirbolc már*' (*VC* iii, 23), the 'great sea bay'. This dual focus of monastery and hermitage is also evident on Iona where the site of *Cladh an Dìsirt* (the 'burial-ground of the hermitage': RCAHMS 1982, 242–3, no 7) is located some 400m north-east of the abbey. Meanwhile, Ian Fisher (1996: 1997, 191) has identified a similar relationship on the island of Canna, with the site of the medieval church at A'Chill as a possible early monastic centre and the outlying *Sgòr nam Ban-naomha* ('the cliff of the holy women': Dunbar & Fisher 1973) as an eremitical retreat.

The daily life of the community revolved around the church and its ecclesiastical and spiritual offices. On a lighter, more personal note, however, it is clear that the playing of board games (and, indeed, a wide variety of games) was extremely popular here. Ours is the largest collection of gaming boards known from any single site in medieval Britain (Ritchie, Chapter 6.3.2). Despite initial impressions to the contrary, such items would not have been out of place on an ecclesiastical site because board games were an aristocratic pastime and many of the monks would have come from relatively good families; the unusual number of boards at Inchmarnock might also be a by-product of the school-house. As Eales (2007, 164) has pointed out, the earliest documentary evidence for chess comes from monastic contexts, and Anna

Ritchie (pers comm) has suggested that the same is probably also true for merels and alquerque.

In addition to the religious community, there would have also been a contemporary secular population of monastic tenants (known in Irish sources as the *manaig*) who would have farmed the land, either with or on behalf of the religious community. Their fields, to all intents and purposes, would have been those that we see in the pre-Improvement plans of the mid-18th century, which are, of course, in turn, not dissimilar to the extent of the cultivated landscape that Stephen Carter has suggested for the later prehistoric period (Chapter 4). And, as we have seen (Figure 2.11), it is possible to still see, in broad outline at least, some elements of these early fields in the present-day landscape.

We have very little idea where the *manaig* would have lived but one possible site is the artificial building platform at our Site 5. Fragments of hazel charcoal from a large pit below the later house were radiocarbon-dated to the period cal AD 690–980 (AA-49300). Such a setting would not be inappropriate for a contemporary secular population. Here they would be far enough removed from the monastery so as not to interfere with the internal workings of the monastic day but near enough to provide service when required.

If this model is correct, and certainly something like it is required to explain the dating evidence for the late first millennium activity that we see at Site 5 and in the excavated rock shelter (Site 16), then it would suggest that Ernán's foundation had a profound and long-lasting effect upon the island's landscape and settlement structure, well beyond the confines of the Midpark site itself.

9.3 INCHMARNOCK IN THE MEDIEVAL PERIOD

9.3.1 Introduction

The construction of a fine Romanesque church on the site sometime in the 12th century marks a significant departure from what had gone before. This may be the context for the final infilling of the enclosure ditch to the north-west of the site. It is not clear, however, if this was undertaken as part and parcel of the continuing development of the ecclesiastical settlement here or whether this followed a period of abandonment. In any event, the indications are that the ecclesiastical site in this later period simply consisted of the church and its cemetery.

There is no clear indication of a resident ecclesiastical community on the site at this time, although possibly a small community may have been retained. As we will see, our view on this much depends upon how we interpret a series of enigmatic pathways that were constructed across the old monastic enclosure. Certainly, there was a literate presence on the island in the later medieval period, as the evidence of the inscribed slates clearly indicates, but it is by no means clear that there was still a functioning school-house here. It seems unlikely. Nor is there any indication of workshops or industrial activity such as we see for the earlier period and, crucially (with the exception of Skeleton 102) nor are there any relevant radiocarbon-dates for this period. So, just as the absence of stray prehistoric dates from the many deposits and features examined led us to conclude that this was a *de novo* foundation in the early historic period (Chapter 5.5 above), so too the absence of any stray medieval dates leads us to conclude that activity on the site in the medieval period was significantly different from what had gone before. In other words, either the activities and structures that we see in Phase 1 were completely relocated in Phase 2 or, as seems more likely, there was a fundamental shift in the core function of the ecclesiastical site, from monastic settlement to parochial church and graveyard.

The overriding context for the island and its archaeology in the medieval period is almost certainly closely associated with the notion of pilgrimage and 'access' to the sanctity with which the island had been imbued as a result of Ernán's earlier foundation. To understand how and when this happened, we need to consider the dating of the extant church and who its builder may have been. We also need to consider the implications that arise from the very form of the building itself.

9.3.2 The church

Small bicameral churches with distinct square-ended chancels, such as we see on Inchmarnock, are a relatively rare and distinctive group among surviving church-plans from the north and west of Scotland (Table 9.4). There are several examples from Orkney and Shetland and a much smaller group from Lewis and the Uists. In terms of distribution, the emphasis is clearly northern and, culturally, Norse, representing the medieval, Christian descendants of the earlier Viking settlers (Cant 1984; Morris 1990; Morris 2004).

In the immediate context of medieval church-types in Argyll, however, the bicameral plan with an

Table 9.4   Medieval bicameral churches in western and northern Scotland (after Fleming & Woolf 1992, Appendix 1, with additions)

Site	Internal dimensions (m)		Internal area (m²)		Total area (m²)
	Nave	Chancel	Nave	Chancel	
FIRTH OF CLYDE					
St Blane's Church, Kingarth, Bute	15.6 × 5.1	4.1 × 3.9	79.5	16.0	95.5
St Marnock's Church, Inchmarnock	5.8 × 4.4	3.1 × 3.8	25.5	11.8	37.3
WESTERN ISLES					
Cille Donnain, South Uist	8.5 × 4.4	3.1 × 2.3	37.4	7.1	44.5
Teampull Eoin, Bragor, Lewis	6.1 × 3.4	2.8 × 2.1	20.7	5.9	26.6
Teampull Pheadair, Shader, Lewis	5.6 × 3.4	2.7 × 2.4	19.0	6.5	25.5
Teampull Mhuir, Vallay, North Uist	?? × ??	3.0 × 3.0	–	–	–
ORKNEY & CAITHNESS					
St Magnus Kirk, Egilsay, Orkney	9.1 × 4.7	4.6 × 2.9	42.8	13.3	56.1
Brough of Birsay, Orkney	8.9 × 4.9	3.3 × 3.1	43.6	10.8	54.4
Peterkirk, Evie, Orkney	6.4 × 5.0	3.7 × 4.0	32.0	14.8	46.8
Tammaskirk, Rendall, Orkney	7.1 × 4.3	4.4 × 3.0	30.5	13.2	43.7
St Magnus Church, Birsay, Orkney	6.0 × 5.0	4.0 × 2.9	30.0	11.6	41.6
Grimbister, Firth, Orkney	6.6 × 3.8	3.0 × 4.0	25.1	12.0	37.1
Eynhallow, Orkney	6.3 × 3.5	3.8 × 2.7	22.0	10.3	32.3
Bridekirk, Sandwick, Orkney	6.0 × 3.5	3.5 × 3.1	21.0	10.9	31.9
Kirkness, Sandwick, Orkney	6.8 × 3.3	2.8 × 2.9	22.4	8.1	30.5
Crosskirk, Westray, Orkney	5.7 × 4.2	2.8 × 2.1	23.9	5.9	29.8
St Mary's Chapel, Lybster, Caithness	5.5 × 3.3	3.5 × 3.3	18.1	11.5	29.6
Linton Chapel, Shapinsay, Orkney	5.8 × 4.1	2.4 × 2.3	23.8	5.5	29.3
St Mary's Chapel, Wyre, Orkney	5.9 × 4.0	2.4 × 2.2	23.6	5.3	28.9
St Nicholas Chapel, Papa Stronsay, Orkney	5.3 × 3.9	2.7 × 2.5	20.7	6.8	27.5
SHETLAND					
St Olaf's Church, Unst, Shetland	8.0 × 4.4	4.0 × 3.0	35.2	12.0	47.2
St John's Church, Unst, Shetland	8.1 × 4.1	4.9 × 2.7	33.2	13.2	46.4
St Ninian's Isle Chapel, Dunrossness, Shetland	6.5 × 4.9	4.0 × 3.2	31.9	12.8	44.7
Kirk of Ness, Yell, Shetland	6.3 × 4.5	4.1 × 3.5	28.3	14.3	42.6
Noss Chapel, Bressay, Shetland	5.5 × 4.0	3.6 × 3.1	22.0	11.2	33.2
Kirkaby, Unst, Shetland	4.2 × 3.7	2.9 × 2.1	15.5	6.1	21.6
Colvidale, Unst, Shetland	3.7 × 3.4	2.4 × 2.3	12.6	5.5	18.1

architecturally distinguished chancel is extremely rare. As is clear from the RCAHMS inventories for Argyll (RCAHMS 1971; 1975; 1980; 1984; 1992), surviving medieval churches here are unanimously single-cell, oblong buildings. And such information as we have for the medieval chapels of Bute itself (Marshall 1992, 41; Aitken 1955; CANMORE database) indicates a similar pattern. The Bute chapels, like their better-preserved cousins on Islay (RCAHMS 1984: Swift 1984), are not only single-cell structures but they are also relatively small. The chapel at Kilmichael has internal dimensions of roughly 5.7 × 3.8m; the excavated chapel on St Ninian's Point, directly opposite and visible from Midpark, is 6.3 × 4m internally.

The presence of a nave-and-chancel church on Inchmarnock, and another, much larger example at St Blane's, just across the water, looks, therefore, decidedly anomalous. Where and when was the inspiration for this church-plan coming from?

The existing building on Inchmarnock is a typical Romanesque nave and chancel church of 12th-century type. This chronology depends in part upon the dating of architectural features at the site, specifically the attached shafts which form the base of the chancel arch (Figure 5.3 above; Fisher 2001, 77), and partly by analogy with the better-preserved and similar, but substantially larger, building at St Blane's (Cruden 1986, 2; Laing *et al* 1998, 551). But quite when in the century does it date to? Dorothy Marshall (1992, 39), for example, assigned the Inchmarnock building to around the middle of the century; meanwhile, John Dunbar (1981, 39–40), in his discussion of the chronology of St Blane's Church, has suggested a late 12th-century date, associating its construction with the establishment of the Stewart family on Bute. The 1190s looks like the period in which the Stewarts finally gained possession of Bute and there is good documentary evidence, in the grant to Paisley Abbey, that St Blane's was built before Alan fitz Walter's death in 1204 (Oram, Chapter 3.2 above). Could this Stewart connection also provide a likely context for the construction of our church? Richard Oram (Chapter 3.2), for example, has pointed out how the cults of native saints and their foundations were exploited by the Stewarts as a means of expanding their influence throughout their newly acquired lands.

This would be a useful context for the building of the medieval church at Midpark. There is a major objection, however, in that the radiocarbon-dating evidence (cal AD 1020–1210: SUERC-7544) from one of the graves suggests an earlier, rather than a later, chronology,

with a construction date closer to the year 1100 than 1200 (Chapter 5.5 above). It is impossible to refine any further quite where within the century, whether first, second or third quarter, we place the construction event, but the implication is that St Marnock's Church is probably earlier than St Blane's by a generation or two. But under whose auspices was it built?

Down until 1153, Inchmarnock and the islands of the Clyde will almost certainly have lain within the kingdom of Man and the Isles, under the control of Óláfr Godredsson (Oram, Chapter 3.2 above). After this date we would need to look to the family of Somerled, either Somairle mac Gillebrigta himself or, after 1164, his son, Raonall mac Somairle. Indeed, the association of Raonall, in 14th-century records, with the foundation of Saddell Abbey, and the association of Saddell with Inchmarnock (Oram, Chapter 3.2) might pinpoint it precisely. This would suggest, then, that St Marnock's Church should be seen as the product of a native Gaelic patron, rather than (by analogy with St Blane's) as the work of the incoming Stewart lordship. If this is the case, then the inspiration for the church-plan will have come, not from Norse areas to the north and west, nor from Norman Scotland to the east but from Ireland where the nave-and-chancel church is a familiar feature of the Romanesque architecture of that country (Leask 1955), the Type 4 building in Harbison's (1982) classification of early Irish stone churches.

But why was such a sophisticated building built here on Inchmarnock? The presence of such a relatively prestigious building suggests that this was more than a parish church serving the needs of a small local population. And the likely context that emerges for its foundation is as a reliquary church associated with the cult of Ernán. As a local place of pilgrimage, this would not only generate income, it would also reinforce the influence of its patrons. In the 12th century, this may have been the family of Somerled; however, after 1190 or so this would have been the Stewarts. And it is this idea of pilgrimage that possibly provides an explanation, as ritual, processional footpaths, for the multiple pathways that are such a feature of the site in Phase 2.

9.3.3 The cemetery

The almost complete absence of bone from all but the latest graves on the site – those associated with the post-Reformation burial ground of Phase 3 or the children's cemetery of Phase 4 – means that it is impossible to discuss in any detail the demographic structure of the cemetery or how it developed over time. There are, however, two features which are worth drawing some attention to: the association of several graves with white quartz pebbles, and the multiple stone paths which converge on or adjacent to the west entrance to the church. For the former we can say something about comparanda with other sites; for the latter, however, as we will see, we appear to be very much on our own.

Quartz pebble graves

There are 10 graves or similar features associated with white quartz pebbles, that is to say that the pebbles are present in sufficient numbers as to suggest their deliberate inclusion. One (Grave G11) has been tentatively assigned to Phase 1; another ('Grave' G32, interpreted as the below-ground element of a possible cross-base, beside the entrance into the monastic enclosure: Chapter 9.2.4 above) has also been assigned to Phase 1, although its fill could, of course, be later. The remaining eight examples (Graves G4, G8, G9, G10, G16, G30, G68 and G71) all belong with the medieval cemetery of Phase 2. It appears, then,to be a feature of the Phase 2 cemetery, although it is present in less than 20% of the group. Most of the Phase 2 burials are not associated with quartz pebbles and the phenomenon is noticeably absent from the post-Reformation burials of Phase 3 and later.

The association of white quartz pebbles and early ecclesiastical sites, particularly with graves, is a well-known phenomenon. Evidence from the Isle of Man, for example, suggests that the deposition of quartz pebbles in graves is a relatively long-lived phenomenon (Lowe 1987, i, 361–5). The special graves or possible Early Christian *leachta* at Ronaldsway, for example, were full of quartz pebbles and were also associated with an external quartz pebble surface (Neely 1940; Cubbon 1935; Lowe 1987, i, 165–8). Evidence from Ireland, however, has suggested that the deposition of white pebbles in graves may represent a later medieval custom. Just under 7,000 white quartz pebbles were recovered by Michael O'Kelly during his excavation of the early monastic site at Church Island, County Kerry. Significantly, however, the excavator noted that none was found with the early burials, 'nor with any burial which was demonstrably earlier than the period of the post-monastic shelter builders' (O'Kelly 1958, 93). At Reask, too, also in County Kerry, it is noticeable that deposits of quartz pebbles were only found in relatively late contexts, associated with the *ceallúnach* graves, for which a post-12th-century date has been suggested

(Fanning 1981, 74). Brannon's excavations at St John's Point Church in County Down also suggest that the deposition of quartz pebbles in graves is a relatively late tradition (Brannon 1980, 59). The recovery of White Gritty Ware, a pottery fabric of 13th to 15th century date, from Inchmarnock Grave G9, reinforces the essentially post-12th century and later medieval date that appears to be indicated by the evidence from Ireland.

The stone paths

On any archaeological site, pathways provide potentially important evidence for how the various buildings or features were accessed or approached and what this might have meant for the settlement's human population. The complex of pathways that were identified across the north-west part of the excavated area is no exception. This, however, is a unique feature, without close parallel in Insular archaeology. The stone paths form a series of radii, converging on a point a few metres to the west of the medieval church, opposite the projected site of its entrance. The area, unfortunately, has been completely dug over by later graves and it is not possible, therefore, to identify what the focal point of the paths may have been.

There is no evidence to suggest that the paths are anything other than contemporary with one another and it is difficult to avoid the conclusion that the path-complex may be a 'ritual' structure, comprising a series of processional routes which are focused on the entrance to the building itself or some feature immediately adjacent.

Our interpretation of them as possibly processional routes brings to mind the practice recorded in Ireland of *an turas*, literally the journey but with the sense of the pilgrimage round. The antiquity of *an turas* is by no means clear. On the basis, however, of the monuments themselves, particularly the dating of the various cross-types, as well as documentary evidence, Herity (1995, 91–143) has suggested that the tradition goes back to the earliest centuries of Christianity.

Some of the recorded routes cover a relatively large landscape; that at Glencolumbkille in County Donegal, for example, is about 5km long and takes 3 to 4 hours to complete (Herity 1995, 92). The *turas* on Caher Island, by comparison, is a less onerous affair, occupying a compact area close to the hermitage with a circuit of about 250m (Herity 1995, 107). On Inchmarnock, we lack the various stations that are marked elsewhere by decorated cross-slabs, holy wells or drystone altars or *leachta*. But what we may have, with the paved pathways, are the beginning and end of a *turas*, possibly one that moved between a central point of the cemetery, such as a founder saint's tomb (or the church itself), and a peripheral area. It may be relevant, for example, that the traditional *turas* at Caher Island, Rathlin O'Birne and Inismurray began and ended at the tomb shrine of the founder saint (Herity 1995, 120).

The idea of pilgrimage, then, is the key feature for our understanding of the site in the medieval period. It provides the necessary context for the foundation of the church in the first place; it also leads us on to suppose that an ecclesiastical presence would have been required to service a growing pilgrimage traffic. Quite what this ecclesiastical presence would have looked like, and whether it comprised a small community or a single priest in residence, is impossible to say. That there was a permanent ecclesiastical presence of some kind in the later Middle Ages, however, may be implied by two things: firstly, by the late medieval assemblage of incised slate, considered next, and, secondly, and perhaps more tellingly, on the basis of the later settlement morphology.

It has been argued above (Chapter 9.2.4) that the south side of the old monastic enclosure of Phase 1 may be characterised as a habitation zone. Although not excavated or 'excavatable' because of standing buildings, it is clear that other activities were archaeologically identifiable to the north and west, whilst the eastern side of the enclosure would have been topographically unsuitable. The monastic living cells, therefore, are most likely to have been located on the south side of the enclosure. In functional terms, this is certainly what we see in the post-medieval period with the creation of the Midpark farmhouse and steading. Economy of interpretation, then, might suggest that this is also the likely location of the medieval priest's or priests' house. Possibly, this is what becomes the 'big house' or residence of *Kildavanach* that we see on Blaeu's map in the mid-17th century, itself, of course, almost certainly derived from an earlier, lost late 16th-century manuscript map by Timothy Pont (Stone 1989). This, then, would have been the house that would have been familiar to the island's last Catholic priest whose remains we presumably see in Grave G15, given their reversed orientation and the late medieval radiocarbon date (cal AD 1440–1640: SUERC-2630).

9.3.4 The late incised slate assemblage

Among the incised slate assemblage are examples that clearly belong with the later medieval ecclesiastical site. The most graphic of these is the 'mock' or imitation grave-slab (IS.30: Figure 6.29) with its Highland galley and hunting scene on one side and its compendium of gaming boards on the other (Ritchie, Chapter 6.3.2 & Lowe, Chapter 6.3.41 above). There are also, however, a small group of late inscriptions and another, smaller, group that may be associated with the writing of music.

The small assemblage of Late Gothic inscriptions (Figure 6.26) indicates the presence of a literate community or person on the site in the later medieval period. The assemblage comprises six pieces: two (IS.40 and IS.41) with a minuscule gothic 'a', possibly by the same hand; two decorated capitals (IS.42 and IS.43), with AD (or AB) and M; one (IS.44) with the letters MO lightly scratched; and a sixth (IS.45) with a capital R form. Fragments IS.40–IS.44 are thought to date to the 13th or 14th century, possibly later; fragment IS.45 could be as late as the 16th century (Forsyth & Tedeschi, Chapter 6.3.3 above). With the exception of fragment IS.41, which formed part of the lining of a medieval drain, all the rest were recovered from deposits and features associated with the post-Reformation and later cemetery of Phases 3 and 4 (Table 6.2). The provenances of all these pieces, therefore, would not contradict the idea that all of them date to the later medieval period.

The presence of this late group of inscribed pieces opens up the possibility, of course, that elements of the wider incised slate assemblage that has been considered above in connection with the school-house of Phase 1, may, rather, belong with this later activity. And for some individual items this may well indeed be the case. Certainly, as previously noted, much of that assemblage is poorly stratified. Nonetheless, there are pieces that are clearly associated with Phase 1 features, and which belong epigraphically with an early, pre-1000, chronology. And as we have seen, the site also has a very convincing run of radiocarbon dates for the late first millennium, and a virtual absence of such for the early second.

It is clear, then, that there is a literate presence at both Ernán's monastery of the late first millennium, and at what we are calling our reliquary church or pilgrimage centre in the later medieval period. The question we have to ask ourselves is whether a fully functioning school-house sits more comfortably with the former or the latter and our conclusion is that the balance of the evidence weighs more heavily in favour of Ernán and his immediate descendants. However, having said all that, we still have to account for these later literary fragments and their context, and it is to the local secular population that we should perhaps look.

It must be assumed that throughout the medieval period there was a resident farming population on Inchmarnock, living alongside the priest or the small religious community that maintained the church and serviced pilgrims to the site. Possibly it is among the children of this group, then, that we should be looking for our later students. Alternatively, of course, the inscribed slates of this later period, particularly the finely carved display capitals (IS.42 and IS.43), could simply represent the practice workings of the priest himself; possibly there was no training or formal instruction being undertaken on the island in this later period. It certainly seems unlikely that there was a formal school-house along the lines that we have suggested for Ernán's monastery of Phase 1 and there is no archaeological or documentary evidence to suggest that the medieval occupation of the site in our Phase 2 was monastic. Despite all this, there was perhaps one other subject on the 'syllabus', not previously recognised among the incised stone assemblage and this is, perhaps, the study of music.

The evidence comes in the form of three incised slate fragments (IS.64, IS.65 and IS.66: Chapter 6.3.43 above). On the best preserved piece (IS.64: Figure 6.33) are three deeply incised and parallel, ruled lines, 1mm wide and 4mm apart, together with a fourth which is not quite parallel with the rest and appears to have been cut with a narrower point. Because of the way in which the fragment has broken, it is not known if additional lines were originally present. It bears a strong resemblance to the incised slate fragment that was recovered from the monastic latrines at Battle Abbey in Sussex (Hare et al 1985) which depicts three complete five-line staves, together with part of a fourth group.

The Sussex fragment dates to the late medieval period, following the introduction of the five-line stave during the course of the 14th century. This, in turn, replaced the earlier four-line stave that had been developed by Guido d'Arezzo, an Italian Benedictine monk, in the early 11th century (Parrish 1957: Gallo 1977). It is not clear to which tradition the Inchmarnock fragment belongs. In either event, however, the accepted chronologies of stave-notation would imply, if it is indeed an example of musical notation, that it forms part of the site's later medieval assemblage, along with the gothic script and the 'mock' piece of 'West Highland' sculpture. And it is, perhaps, this last piece,

together with the historical evidence for the link with Saddell Abbey (Oram, Chapter 3.2 above), that really underlines the island's ecclesiastical connections in the later medieval period.

The Inchmarnock 'galley' stone, in terms of its composition and layout, takes its inspiration from the West Highland 'school' of monumental sculpture (Steer & Bannerman 1977). Close parallels survive in Kintyre, in general, and at Saddell, in particular. It was presumably, then, to Saddell that Inchmarnock looked in the latter Middle Ages for priests to tend and support its church. It was, after all, but a short sea journey away, just over 20 miles distant by boat, across to Skipness and down Kilbrannan Sound.

9.3.5 Medieval Inchmarnock beyond the church

Our understanding of medieval Inchmarnock is largely governed by the archaeology of the church and its graveyard. As we have seen (Chapter 2.3), however, fragments of the medieval landscape, in the form of its fields and enclosures, as we see them on the pre-Improvement maps of Foulis and Leslie (Figure 2.6 & Figure 2.7), can still be recognised on the ground today. Fragments of the island's medieval settlement structure, again as first depicted on the 18th-century estate maps, have also been recognised archaeologically. At our Site 5, for example, it seems likely that the surviving post-medieval building has replaced an earlier medieval structure on the site, given the presence of medieval pottery and other occupation debris (Chapter 8.3). But new, previously unrecorded elements of the island's medieval landscape have also been recognised here for the first time. From Site 8, there are the fragmentary remains of several corn-drying kilns and a handful of radiocarbon dates spanning the period 11th to 13th century (Chapter 8.4). The concentration of drying kilns in the same place leads us to conclude that this was either a central point for grain-drying or that there may be an unlocated medieval settlement somewhere in the vicinity. In any event, the presence of a later, post-medieval drying kiln on the site, adjacent to the robbed out remains of our excavated examples, would suggest that the same area was used for crop-drying over a considerable period of time. These buildings and other structures presumably represent the work of the island's monastic tenants, the descendents of the manaig. These are the people whose graves (although largely empty) we see in the medieval graveyard. It is their descendents, in turn, who we meet in the post-medieval cemetery of Phases 3 and 4.

9.4 FROM THE REFORMATION TO THE IMPROVEMENT PERIOD (1560–1850)

9.4.1 Introduction

There are three key elements to this final chapter of the island's story. On the one hand, there is the development of the modern-day landscape and how it relates to earlier settlement and land-use. Our reconstruction of this process has been set out elsewhere (Chapter 2.3 above). There is also the story of the church's abandonment and the documented accounts of its robbing and final demolition in the 1820s that was explored in Chapter 5.2. The remaining story, then, concerns the graveyard and its post-medieval inhabitants. Analysis of the human remains and their pathology, as well as data on the demographic structure of the population, are presented in David Henderson's detailed study in Chapter 7. This is where we see the very personal stories of, for example, the murdered woman in Grave G97; the extreme blade trauma on the young boy in Grave G91; the young woman in Grave G85 who died during child-birth, or (in Grave G106) the glass beads from the dress that was once worn by the young girl who probably lived in the house at our Site 5. In terms of human pathology, Henderson has also drawn attention to the fact that several of the adult skeletons have fused joints in one or both little toes and has suggested that this may be an inherited trait over several generations. But we also see a large number of perinatal and infant burials at the site and this deserves some further discussion. What remains, then, to be considered is whether we can identify how long the graveyard continued in use and whether its use changed over this period.

9.4.2 The post-Medieval graveyard

Quite what effect the Reformation may have had on the inhabitants of Inchmarnock is difficult to gauge; nor can we say with any confidence whether the church itself continued to be used much past the middle of the 16th century. Indeed, all the indications are that the church was probably an early casualty of stone-robbers; certainly we have very good reason to believe that Alexander MacDonald and his masons in 1718 were by no means the first stone-robbers on the scene. For example, roof slates and fragments of red sandstone – the detritus left behind after walls have been robbed of their good or dressed stone – were recovered from the backfill of our 'priest burial' (SK15). The radiocarbon date (cal AD 1440–1640: SUERC-2630) from this skeleton does not necessarily give us a mid-16th century or Reformation date for the burial (although, clearly, it would not be not incompatible with such a chronology) but it does seem awfully suspicious if we look at what was happening to the island in terms of who owned it at the time. Some of the physical changes to the site, represented archaeologically by the construction of a wall around the church, also probably belong to this later period.

In terms of the historical evidence and issues related to land-holding, the story of Inchmarnock at this time is very much focused on the issue of the alienation of church land and its transfer to secular hands. We know that this process of alienation, that started in 1540 when the island was granted to Hugh Cunningham by his brother, the Bishop of Argyll, was completed some time before 1568 when we see that the original grant of feuferme tenure had become one of heritable tenure (Oram, Chapter 3.2 above). In terms of the site's archaeology, this may also be the time when the late enclosure wall was built, fragments of which were identified in the trial-trenches to the south and east of the church. As we have seen (Conolly, Chapter 5.5) it was built on top of the medieval cemetery soil and stratigraphically overlay a number of medieval graves. The presence of Greyware pottery sherds, a late medieval fabric, below the wall clearly indicates that this enclosure (in effect the post-medieval graveyard) cannot be earlier than the 15th or 16th century. The context for this enclosure of the cemetery and fixing the line of its boundary with the farmstead immediately adjacent is most likely to be found in the refurbishment or development of the buildings that would become Midpark. This is also, of course, the likely destination of the dressed and other stone that was robbed from the ruins of the church.

The island's last priest may have been laid to rest in, say, the third quarter of the 16th century and its medieval church partially demolished. It is clear, however, that the graveyard continued to be used long after the church had gone out of use. The men, women and children and the age structure that we see in the Phase 3 assemblage (Henderson, Chapter 7 above; Table 7.1) is typical of a rural, pre-industrial population. The sequence of graves overlying Grave G123 with its associated coin, dated 1632–9, suggests that the graveyard must have continued in use down to at least the late 17th or early 18th century. Throughout this period, all the indications are that the site was being used as an ordinary cemetery for the island's inhabitants, in effect as the parochial graveyard. By

1718, however, the date of the MacDonald stone-robbing case, it is clear that the islanders were recognising the ecclesiastical jurisdiction of Rothesay. A date in or around the year 1700, therefore, might be suggested for the abandonment of the graveyard as an official burial ground.

Among the Phase 3 graveyard population are a number of foetal or perinatal graves. This becomes the dominant feature of the stratigraphically latest graves (Phase 4) from the site, representing the final phase in the use of the graveyard as an acknowledged, but presumably unofficial, burial place. With the exception of SK5, the 'crouched' burial of the young man who was squeezed into his grave beside the south-west corner of the church, the Phase 4 burials are characterised as those of perinatal deaths, infants and young children. On the basis of his treatment, we have suggested that SK5 may have been a shipwreck victim, or at any rate someone who was outwith the local community. Clearly, the 'regular', adult population was being buried elsewhere at this time, presumably in the parish church at Rothesay.

In terms of dating, the children's cemetery must belong to the late 17th and 18th centuries. Certainly, some of these graves will post-date MacDonald's stone-robbing exploits in 1718; others could be as late as, say, 1800, if we take Hewison's report that the cemetery was used 'within the memory of the last generation' (Hewison 1893, i, 133) at face value, although whether they would have been remembering its conventional use as a parish graveyard, or its 'irregular' use as an unofficial burial-ground is not clear. The preponderance of children's graves in the final phase of the cemetery suggests that these are clandestine, unofficial burials of the rural poor, including (for the perinatal and infant deaths at least) those who were illegitimate or unbaptised.

The practice of separate burial for different groups, such as suicides, shipwrecked sailors and children, particularly the illegitimate and the unbaptised, is a well-recognised phenomenon in Ireland (Hamlin & Foley 1983). Large numbers of children's and other separate burial grounds have been identified in County Donegal (Lacy 1983, 309–17). Near Carrickmore in County Tyrone, there is Relignaman (Old Irish *Relig na mbhan*, the women's graveyard). Nearby are two further cemeteries; *Relig-na-paiside*, 'children's cemetery', and another called *Relig-na-fir-gunta*, 'cemetery of the slain', or 'wounded men' (Hamlin & Foley 1983, 43). Documented examples in Scotland, however, are few and far between, although such examples as we

have, such as the women's burial grounds previously discussed (Chapter 9.2.4), seem to be associated with the western side of the country and areas of Irish settlement or cultural influence. The burial ground at Ardmenish on Jura, known as *An Caibeal* ('the burial place'), for example, is said to have been used for the burial of illegitimate children (RCAHMS 1984, no 316, 157); similarly, according to local tradition, one of the two enclosures at Cladh Mhic Iain, also on Jura, was 'used for the burial of sailors and stillborn infants' (RCAHMS 1984, no 344, 167). In Cowal, in Betty Rennie's excavation at Ardnadam, the absence of bone and the small size of the graves have been interpreted as relating to the later use of the site as a children's burial ground (Rennie 1999, 41). Meanwhile, Peter Hill's excavations at Whithorn identified an area of the medieval cemetery, to the east of the Northumbrian church and burial chapel, which appears to have been given over to children and infants (Hill 1997, 170–2; Cardy 1997, 557–9).

9.5 ENDWORD

Every archaeological project throws some light onto the past, onto events, people and places long forgotten. There is also, of course, an element of luck and serendipity. If we had focused on, say, the area to the south-west of the church (rather than that to the north-west), then we would have probably ended up with a very different story. With only the lower fragment of the 'warrior stone' (IS.46) we would have certainly been pondering the significance or otherwise of what we can now recognise as oar-blades being pulled through the water; in our original interpretation these were mooted as the legs of people or animals. Moreover, if our interpretation of the incised slate distribution is anything like correct, then we would have ended up with only a handful of pieces; we could have easily lost any substantive evidence for our school-house, and for the iron- and shale-working activity. It would have been a different site, a different archaeology with different insights. But we also, of course, largely make our own luck, guided by models, experience and hunches. So, what have been the key learnings from this work?

The key thing must be the inscribed slate assemblage, not only for what it can tell us about the chronology of the inscriptions themselves but also the cultural connections of Ernán's foundation; clearly, Inchmarnock looked to the Gaelic west rather than the Brittonic east, with its seat at Dumbarton. The school-house also gives us a clear focus for the function and status of the monastic settlement and its role as a place of primary schooling. We are reminded, of course, that this was a place where the very basics of literacy, of practising alphabets and controlling the stylus, were taught. It is a sobering thought that without these basic training establishments (and how many others must have existed?) that there would have been no Book of Kells or any other of the other great illuminated manuscripts of early Insular Christianity.

Was Ernán's foundation a 'feeder' monastery for the larger house at St Blane's? How many other sites of similar status might there have been within the kin-group of the Cenel nGabrain, whose lands took in Jura, Kintyre, Cowal, Arran and Bute? And if St Blane's was the principal ecclesiastical centre of the Cenel nGabrain, what was its relationship to Iona, the major monastery of the Cenel Loairn?

Further questions, then, might lead us to ask whence Ernán's foundation on Inchmarnock or Bláán's monastery on Bute might have been founded? Indeed, if we had to narrow down any particular place in the north of Ireland, as the 'mother church' for either Inchmarnock or Kingarth, we could do worse than suggest Comgall's house at Bangor. Clearly, the *adeptus* fragment (IS.36) shows us that the Bangor hymn, composed in honour of its founder, St Comgall who died in AD 602, was familiar to someone on Inchmarnock in or around AD 750. Documented, 16th-century links between Bláán and Comgall (and, by implication, between Kingarth and Bangor), however, are too late for us to place any reliance on them as evidence for the period of the late 6th and 7th centuries. Bangor and nearby Nendrum, however, look very much like a pair of functionally-related sites, not dissimilar to, respectively, the pairing of Kingarth and Inchmarnock.

The connection with Ireland is one that can be observed in the archaeological record from the earliest times down to the recent past. Clearly, the proximity of the coast of Antrim and Down to Argyll has had an impact on the archaeology of Inchmarnock from early prehistory onwards, indeed down to relatively recent times when communications would have been by sea rather than over-land. The porcellanite axe-heads, for example, come from Tievebulliagh on the coast of County Antrim. The north of Ireland, albeit mediated through the Norman settlement of that country, would also seem to have been the likely source for the island's Romanesque church. And later still, the use of old abandoned graveyards as the burial grounds of children and other social groups is a familiar feature of the Irish countryside. Indeed, we might wonder whether the old graveyard at Midpark might have been considered a particularly suitable place for the burial of children (albeit illegitimate and unbaptised) on account of the island's earlier association with children. Was there, perhaps, a folk memory of the old monastic schoolhouse and the island as a place where children were fostered?

The final point worth stressing is, perhaps, the timelessness of the place and the way in which the island's past is never far away. The ability to trace the pre-Improvement field pattern is a case in point. Similarly, it is clear that settlement and other sites, once established, have a tendency to remain in use, with earlier structures being robbed and reused. This was the story at Sites 5 and 8 and was also, of course, a feature of the monastic settlement itself. And we have suggested a mechanism here whereby today's farmhouse and an earlier priest's house on the site may have preserved the former habitation zone of the old monastery. Natural features, if useful, such as the caves and rock shelters, can similarly be resorted to over many centuries. Indeed, as Stephen Carter pointed out in the preliminary study for this project (*AIR* 1, 15), this bringing together of the past and the present, the old and the new, is neatly summed up in the story of John Muir and the stone-robbing episode of 1829. The irony will not have crossed his mind when he decided to employ the pre-Christian practice of animal sacrifice to atone for the desecration of a medieval church that he had just demolished in the cause of improvement. For us, however, it illustrates perfectly (together with a ritual twist) the classic sequence of robbing and reuse that is such a recurring feature of the island's archaeology.

Appendices

APPENDIX 1: THE RADIOCARBON DATES

Code	Material	Phase (site specific)	Context no	Context/comment	Uncalibrated date	Calibrated 2-sigma date
SITE 4						
AA-49299 (GU-10022)	alder charcoal	1	465	redeposited grave fill, from G11 located N of church	1320±60 BP	AD 610–880
AA-49611 (GU-10023)	human bone	3	Sk 7	articulated human remains from G7, located immediately W of East Boundary Wall (432). White Gritty ware present in grave fill.	365±40 BP	AD 1440–1640
AA-53159 (GU-10630)	hazel nutshell	1	4005	fill of linear feature 4073, associated with metal-working activity	1150±35 BP	AD 780–980
AA-53160 (GU-10631)	hazel nutshell	1	4076	fill of NE-SW aligned gully, adjacent to metal-working area	1310±35 BP	AD 650–780
AA-53161 (GU-10632)	hazel nutshell	1	4160	fill of pit 4161	1450±95 BP	AD 410–780
AA-53162 (GU-10633)	alder charcoal	1	4168	fill of pit 4167	1480±35 BP	AD 460–660
AA-53163 (GU-10634)	hazel nutshell	1	4020	upper fill of enclosure ditch	1130±35 BP	AD 780–1000
SUERC-2630 (GU-11763)	human bone	3	Sk15	articulated human remains from G15, located immediately next to N wall of church. Laid head to east, feet to west: possible priest burial.	375±35 BP	AD 1440–1640
SUERC-2631 (GU-11764)	birch charcoal	1	4439	basal fill of pit 4437	1415±35 BP	AD 560–680
SUERC-5466 (GU-12740)	willow charcoal	1	4675	charcoal lens within floor surface 4600 of pre-church structure, Structure 4.	1485±35 BP	AD 430–660
SUERC-7540 (GU-13343)	birch charcoal	1	4617	fill of pit 4619, sealed below floor surface 4600	1305±35 BP	AD 650–780
SUERC-7541 (GU-13344)	cf alder charcoal	2	4557	fill of church foundation trench 4558	1135±35 BP	AD 780–990
SUERC-7542 (GU-13345)	birch/alder charcoal	1	4301	primary fill of enclosure ditch	1285±35 BP	AD 650–810
SUERC-7543 (GU-13346)	alder charcoal	1	4203	secondary fill of pit 4202, associated with metal-working area	1120±35 BP	AD 810–1020
SUERC-7544 (GU-13347)	human bone	2	Sk102	articulated human remains from G102, located immediately next to S wall of church. Cuts foundation trench of chancel (TAQ for construction of chancel)	920±35 BP	AD 1020–1210

Code	Material	Phase (site specific)	Context no	Context/comment	Uncalibrated date	Calibrated 2-sigma date
SITE 5 AA-49300 (GU-10024)	hazel charcoal	1	5030	fill of pit 5066, located N of later building	1185 ± 55 BP	AD 690–980
AA-49301 (GU-10025)	marine shell	5	5013	shell midden dump against enclosure wall, 5014	495 ± 45 BP	AD 1721–
AA-49302 (GU-10026)	oats	4	5029	collapsed wall-core	305 ± 60 BP	AD 1440–1680
AA-49303 (GU-10027)	barley	3	5052	fill of post-hole 5051, associated with cruck-support	450 ± 45 BP	AD 1400–1630
AA-49304 (GU-10028)	barley	3	5064	fill of post-hole 5065, associated with cruck-support	275 ± 45 BP	AD 1480–1680
AA-49305 (GU-10029)	oats	2	5047	fill of pit 5046 below E end of building	320 ± 45 BP	AD 1460–1660
SITE 8 AA-39965 (GU-9142)	barley	2	811	burnt deposit at base of flue associated with Kiln 1	740 ± 35 BP	AD 1222–1298
SUERC-2633 (GU-11765)	oats	2	8005	burnt deposit at base of flue associated with Kiln 1	880 ± 35 BP	AD 1030–1250
SUERC-2634 (GU-11766)	oats	2	8019	burnt spread, possibly rake-out, associated with Kiln 1	945 ± 45 BP	AD 1000–1210
SUERC-2635 (GU-11767)	oats	3	8037	burnt deposit at base of fire-pit associated with Kiln 2	745 ± 35 BP	AD 1215–1300
SITE 9 AA-39966 (GU-9143)	hazel nutshell	–	1603	primary deposits in cave	2110 ± 35 BP	346–4 BC
SITE 16 AA-39967 (GU-9144)	hazel nutshell	1	1655	primary deposits in cave	2150 ± 35 BP	355–59 BC
AA-39968 (GU-9166)	oats	3	1651	burnt spread (rake-out) associated with stone-built hearth (16017)	1245 ± 35 BP	AD 679–888
AA-53164 (GU-10635)	hazel nutshell	3	16022	charcoal lens at base of Phase 3 deposits	1620 ± 35 BP	AD 340–540
AA-53165 (GU-10636)	hazel charcoal	3	16007	charcoal lens in upper level of Phase 3 deposits	1260 ± 35 BP	AD 670–880
AA-53166 (GU-10637)	hazel charcoal	3	16016	charcoal lens in upper level of Phase 3 deposits	1195 ± 40 BP	AD 690–970

APPENDIX 2:
THE FAUNAL REMAINS FROM SITE 4

DAVID HENDERSON

A total of 674 specimens of animal and bird bone was recovered from the excavation of the medieval church and its immediate environs, of which 345 (51%) could be identified to species. As with the human remains, all the material was recovered from the area immediately adjacent to the remains of the church, where the leaching of lime from the mortar protected the bone from the effects of the acidic ground water. As a consequence, almost all the faunal remains derive from backfills of intercutting graves and are almost certainly residual. In view of this, and of the small amount of bone present, this report is simply confined to a list of species present.

Over 80% of the identified animal bone is of domestic sheep and cattle (143 and 134 fragments, respectively) with all parts of the carcass represented. Pig was also recorded (23 fragments) as were two cat bones and the lower jaw of a small dog. Dog-gnawing marks were also evident on many sheep and cattle bones. The only specimen of horse was a single, shed milk tooth. Two bones of red deer, and one of fallow deer were recovered, as was an antler tine from a red deer. The antler was abraded, but showed no signs of having been used for craftwork. Both deer species are capable of swimming the short distance to Inchmarnock from mainland Bute. Other minor species recorded were frogs (six bones) and field vole. One cod vertebra was also recovered.

Of the bird bones, 12 were identified as being from chickens and (probably domestic) geese. Many of the other bones were from small songbirds and probably represent the remains of the meals of birds of prey. If this is the case, it might indicate that the burials close to the church had taken place during a period when the building was little used, or abandoned.

APPENDIX 3:
THE INCHMARNOCK BOAT AND
SHIP GRAFFITI

DANIEL ATKINSON

Introduction

The remarkable discovery of boat and ship 'graffiti' amongst the assemblage of inscribed stones discovered during the excavation at and around the medieval church are of particular interest and significance.

The information gained from the inscriptions gives a flavour of the social, political and economic atmosphere of an island community inextricably linked to a predominantly maritime cultural landscape such as that of the West Highlands and Argyll. The inscriptions also offer interesting artistic and stylistic attributes in addition to contributing to our understanding of developments in boat and ship technology from the latter half of the first millennium AD.

The study aims to describe the details illustrated in the inscriptions, using characteristics such as *size/scale*, *form*, *construction*, *propulsion*, *crew* and *function*, and to assess the nature of the stones and associated graffiti. The analysis of these characteristics could then help inform the possible type, function and date of the vessels and their historical context.

The stones (Figure A3.1)

A total of five stone fragments revealed depictions of vessels, and survive either in full or in part. The stones vary in size and type and all highlight simple doodles or graffiti. The various craft depicted reveal evidence for both small oared vessels and larger ships furnished with both oars and sail.

IS.5

Fragment of slate with a fairly crude sketch depicting what appears to be the profile of the stern half of an oared vessel, indicated by two steering oars extending from the stern to the right, complete with the oval or trapezoidal oar blades and a sweeping stern and pointed terminus of a sternpost. The sketch also appears to show oars extending across the vessel on the opposite or port side. The continuation of the oars across the vessel suggests that the sketch may be a crude depiction of a vessel in plan as well as in profile. Alternatively, the vertical lines could represent the benches for oarsmen. The three roughly circular marks to the right of the vertical lines across the hull could be interpreted as oar ports. The fragmentary survival and the simplistic nature of the sketch make the identification of the form and construction of the vessel particularly difficult. It is likely that the vessel is double-ended, although the size of the vessel and the number of crew is difficult to gauge as the sketch is incomplete. The lack of detail in the depiction of the hull also means that the mode of construction of the vessel, whether plank-built or skin, cannot be identified. Artistic attributes of the inscription include the possible representation of waves or oar splashes noted below the starboard or lower oars.

Figure A3.1
The boat graffiti

IS.30

Slate slab, covered on both sides with an array of graffiti. Among the palimpsest of incised marks, is the outline of a large masted vessel.

Although the style of the incised sketch is fairly simple, it is possible to clearly identify a double-ended vessel in full profile with a high stem and sternpost. This very distinctive form clearly identifies the vessel as a West Highland and Argyll galley. At the peak of the stem and sternpost are what appear to be roughly rectangular objects, both pointing to the left, possibly indicating decorative adornments such as banners, or some form of burgee or wind indicator. Although there is no indication of a central rudder, it is suggested that the stern is to the right and the bow is to the left. This is based on the steep, almost vertical nature of the sternpost, and the slightly more curved and sweeping stem post, inherent in the depictions of galleys elsewhere. Towards the upper edge of the hull profile are 12 small indentations. These are certainly oar ports, suggesting the galley had a total of 24 oars. On the whole, the details of the hull are relatively slight. There is no indication of the type of construction, which will certainly have been of wood, and also no smaller details such as fastenings, fittings, steering gear and crew.

The vessel is illustrated with a crude mast, yard, sail and rigging. The mast is indicated as a single line with two shrouds on either side and a possible backstay. The yard that is shown squared fore and aft has a furled sail attached and possibly two braces extending down to the deck from each end. To the right of the lines depicting the mast, shrouds and backstay is a curved line. This extends downwards from what would have been the top of the mast, crosses the backstay and ends just above the gunwale. This may well be another decorative feature such as a banner or pennant.

IS.46

Beach pebble with a crudely incised sketch of a complete vessel, showing the stern to the left and the bow to the right. The orientation of the vessel is supported by the presence of what appear to be two steering oars extending from the stern, similar to those seen on IS.5 noted above. The vessel is depicted in profile with an almost vertical stern and a sweeping bow. At the terminus of the stern it is possible to identify three or four vertical, forked projections that appear to be akin to prongs or spikes. It is uncertain as to the interpretation of these projections, although it could be suggested that they are mountings for figureheads

or banners, or alternatively, the housing for a mast when un-stepped and not in use (Steer & Bannerman 1977, 182). Two projections are also visible at the bow. These bear particular similarities to the depiction of the oars, although it appears that they form part of the prow or stem structure and therefore represent possible decoration.

In addition to the steering oars, the vessel also highlights a further 11 oars along the lower or starboard edge of the vessel, and a possible twelfth (port and starboard) at the bow, extending upwards, possibly depicting the oars in the process of being shipped or deployed. Like IS.5, the lower oars extend vertically across the vessel, where three further oars can also be seen extending above the vessel towards the stern. Of interest, particularly in terms of artistic and stylistic attributes, is the depiction of the end of the oars and oar blades below the vessel. Both the lower oars and blades are deflected towards the stern, suggesting the depiction of the refraction of the oars as seen when immersed in the water. The lower oars and blades are also drawn in a double line, possibly depicting the magnification of the oars and blades. The propulsion of the vessel is further intimated with the presence of what appears to be a square sail with diagonal hatching, although it is also possible that this feature may represent some kind of deck structure.

IS.50

Very crude and roughly drawn, but appears to depict the bow or stern section of a possible double-ended vessel. Of particular interest is the added detail of the hull that shows what appear to be three planks curving round into the terminus of the stem or sternpost. Further details include possible oars with circular oar blades extending diagonally across the vessel from the left hand margin of the stone; and a triangular flag or banner at the tip of the stem or sternpost.

IS.51

A very stylised but crude depiction of a small craft. The image shows a vessel in profile, although unlike the other examples, the waterline is included. At least four or possibly five oarsmen are illustrated, where the body, head, arm and oar are formed using a single stroke of the stylus. The top of the oar blade and the oar splash are also evident at the end of each oar. The orientation of the oarsmen suggests that the bow is to the left and the stern to the right. The bow is particularly stylised, illustrating a backward sweeping prow with a scroll or swan-neck terminus. There also appears to be what looks like a gunwale extending from the prow aft, which steps down onto the main gunwale from fore to aft. A crude bow wave can also be identified. The stern is sweeping and curves upwards and forwards to a point with a possible steering oar or side rudder and wake also depicted. Unfortunately, the vessel is incomplete where part of the lower edge of the stone cuts into the lower part of the design towards the stern. From the scale of the oarsmen and the absence of a sail, there seems no doubt that the vessel depicted is a small rowing craft. The form of the craft is also of interest, especially the bow detail with the ornate scroll or swan-neck, but it is possible that the vessel is double-ended. Immediately to the right of the vessel is the possible depiction of the upper body and head of a further figure. It is not possible to ascertain whether the figure is related to the vessel.

Discussion

The geographical position of the Western Isles and Argyll highlight an area of the British Isles that has witnessed an admixture of cultures from early times. By the early Middle Ages the area was populated by indigenous Pictish tribes and growing numbers of Dalriadic Scots from Northern Ireland. From the late 8th century AD, the Viking raids led to increasing numbers of Scandinavian settlers. What is significant is that all these cultures were predominantly maritime with their own influences and traditions in boat and ship technology. Early sources bear testament to the intrinsic maritime organisation of Dalriadic society in the *Senchus Fer n'Alban (History of the Men of Scotland)*, compiled in the mid-7th century AD. In this case each community of twenty 'Houses' was to provide and man two seven-benched vessels, as part of 'Ship Service'. This type of service also formed an integral part of the Scandinavian naval levy system or *Leidangr*, and later feudal systems of the Lords of the Isles in the later medieval period (Laing & Laing 1993, 14; Crawford 1987, 86; McWhannell 2002, 15).

After the Dalriadic settlement of Argyll, the indigenous and predominantly Gaelic population shared an increasing cultural identity with Ireland. Irish boat and shipbuilding traditions relied on both wood and skin hides with which to construct their vessels. Early medieval sources such as Adomnán's *Life of Columba* (Anderson 1991) indicate the use of both wooden and skin-covered vessels. These vessels were used for inland and coastal travel in addition to more extensive open-water voyages, such as those across the Irish Sea to the

Western Highlands and Argyll. Furthermore, mention is also given to the forms of propulsion of the vessels and the use of both oar and sail.

The Scandinavian or Viking shipbuilding tradition produced double-ended wooden vessels constructed with overlapping clinker planks or strakes. The distinctive vessels with their long sleek hulls and upturned sweeping prow and stern gave rise to the Viking *Langskip* or longship, used predominantly for raiding expeditions, and the larger, broader cargo vessels known as *knarrs*. The design of these vessels combined with both oar and sail meant that they were well suited to voyages in open sea and along coasts and inland waterways. In this way, like the Dalriadic Scots before them, the Scandinavian settlers also began to influence the traditions of the indigenous population.

The Highland and Argyll Galley is a derivative of the earlier Scandinavian Viking type, used in large numbers by the Lords of the Isles and other Chiefs throughout the Middle Ages. The larger galleys with the smaller *lymphads* and *birlinns* continued in use into the 17th century, thus preserving the building traditions of the Viking era (Rodger 1998, 67).

The Inchmarnock vessels

The analysis of the Inchmarnock boat and ship graffiti has enabled the identification of possible vessel types through a number of attributes and characteristics such as the form, type of construction, scale of craft, method of propulsion, method of steering and the crew. The only vessel-type to be positively identified is the West Highland and Argyll Galley that is depicted on IS.30.

The boat and ship graffiti fall into two quite distinct groups:

Group 1 comprising IS.5 and IS.46 forms a distinct assemblage based on stylistic attributes, and belongs to a period prior to the 12th century, probably the last quarter of the first millennium AD.

Group 2 comprising IS.30, IS.50 and possibly IS.51 represent later vessel-types, datable to the period between the 12th and 17th centuries.

GROUP 1

The interpretation of the Group 1 sketch-forms, comprising IS.5 and IS.46, brings to light a number of interesting possibilities. Their similarity of style suggests that they are perhaps contemporary. These similarities include the basic form of the vessels, the two steering oars and oar blades, and the continuation of the oars or benches across the vessel, shown as vertical lines. Unfortunately, the fragmentary remains of the vessel depicted on IS.5 offer little in terms of definite interpretation. The complete vessel illustrated on IS.46, however, presents interesting and perhaps significant implications.

The crude depiction on IS.46 makes interpretation of the form of the vessel problematic although it appears to be long (given the number of oars) and possibly double ended. The method of construction is also particularly difficult to identify. The lack of detail in the sketch has resulted in the absence of features such as the planking or strakes indicative of a wooden vessel. Furthermore, it is equally difficult to identify features that suggest the vessel is constructed with hides or skin, more in keeping with Irish vessel types such as the curragh.

The difficulty in identifying the method of construction of the vessel suggests that it cannot be ruled out that vessels made of skin were being used in the Western Highlands and Argyll in the last quarter of the first millennium AD. Early references certainly give an indication of the use of skin vessels or *currachs*, as do surviving place names in the Western Highlands such as Port na Churraigh and An Curach on Iona (Rixson 1998, 4). However, the skin boats, surviving to this day in the form of the curragh, bear few similarities to the vessel depicted on IS.46. Comparative evidence from Ireland such as the carving on the Kilnaruane Cross-shaft in County Cork support this observation (Wooding 2001). While the vessel is powered with oars, the depiction of a single side rudder is in contradiction with features such as the double steering oars noted on the Inchmarnock vessels.

This question is perhaps significant, as neither the southern Irish nor Scandinavian evidence indicates conclusive use of the long steering oar, or indeed two in tandem. The only evidence that might indicate the use of two steering oars is the Broichter boat model discovered in a gold hoard from County Derry in Ireland. This boat dates to the 1st century BC and shows quite clearly a single (surviving) steering oar with a second hole at the stern for a possible further oar (McGrail 1998, 244). The discovery of the boat model in Northern Ireland perhaps intimates an affinity with Dalriadan boat types, inherited from their ancestors and later amalgamated into the traditions that spread to the west coast of Scotland around the 7th century AD. What may be visible here is a variation in the boat building traditions of Ireland, and in particular variants in the methods of steering. Evidence of 'ship service' in the *Senchus Fer n'Alban* and reference to the

furnishing of vessels with benches perhaps highlights the depiction of benches noted as vertical lines across the Inchmarnock vessel. The presence of 12 benches, and thus 24 oars, intimates a size of vessel not dissimilar to that suggested in the Iona Chronicle. This document dating to AD 737 mentions a professional crew of 22 (Laing 1993, 64).

Unfortunately, the dearth of archaeological evidence for any vessel other than the logboat from this period means that we have to rely on two Pictish carvings for comparative analysis, both of which are located on the east coast of Scotland.

The first is the small craft depicted on the Cossans or St Orland's Stone in Angus (Graham-Campbell & Batey 1998, figure 1.2). The vessel appears on the lower panel above two beasts. It depicts five longhaired figures behind what has been described as a possible sail or a sixth person, facing forwards. The orientation of the figures places the bow to the right and the stern to the left. This is also supported by the position of a steering oar extending from the stern. This stone has been dated to the 9th century AD (Gilbert 1995, 89; Mack 1997, 63).

The second carving is the graffiti discovered at Jonathan's Cave, East Wemyss, Fife. This vessel is mastless and double-ended, showing a total of five oars. The only figure represented is the helmsman to the left, therefore suggesting the orientation of the vessel. The carving has not been securely dated but the presence of other Pictish symbols in the cave and the abundance of Pictish archaeology in the area suggests a late first millennium AD date (Johnstone 1980, 152). What is interesting are the similarities of the long steering oar shown in these examples with those depicted on IS.46. Furthermore, the depiction of a possible sail on the Cossans Stone supports the use of sails on Pictish vessels.

It could also be argued that the vessel depicted on IS.46 shows few similarities with the Scandinavian Viking type vessel. This is particularly the case when compared with incised sketches of Viking vessels from elsewhere. The incised motif from Jarlshof in Shetland (conveniently in Crawford 1987, Figure 4A) shows a similar lack of detail as the Inchmarnock inscription, while depicting a completely different vessel form, with a high prow and stern The depiction of oars (indicating the size of the vessel), and the possible square sail with diagonal hatching offers the only similarities with many depictions of Viking vessels, such as those found on the picture stones at Gotland in Sweden (Greenhill 1995, 208–9), and the archaeological remains of

Viking period vessels discovered in Scandinavia. One such vessel is the Oseberg ship, discovered near Tonsberg in Norway, constructed sometime around AD 820. She revealed a total of 15 oars (ports) on each side, only three more than the Inchmarnock vessel. Furthermore, the length of the vessel at 65m perhaps gives an indication as to the possible size of the Inchmarnock vessel, consistent with vessels used in the region for coastal raiding and trade.

It is suggested therefore that the Inchmarnock vessel may be representative of a native, pre-Scandinavian type (indicated by the two steering oars), or a hybrid, incorporating pre-existing boatbuilding traditions of the Gaelic, Pictish and Dalriadic peoples and later Scandinavian Viking influences in boat and ship construction in the Western Isles and Argyll from the late 8th and early 9th century AD. The sketch may represent the only known depiction of a vessel that illustrates ship and boat types pre-dating the Scandinavian migrations or a period of transition between the two.

GROUP 2

The Group 2 vessels, comprising IS.30, IS.50 and possibly IS.51, provide further interesting implications with regards to possible interpretations of the graffiti. Stone IS.30 provides the clearest evidence for the positive identification of the vessel type and therefore the period to which it belongs.

IS.30

The positive identification of the vessel as a Highland Galley is interesting, although hardly surprising given the geographical context of its find-spot. Unfortunately, the limited archaeological evidence for this type of vessel has resulted in the reliance upon artistic evidence from which to draw comparisons and develop our understanding. The only archaeological evidence comprises the remains of two stem-posts discovered on Eigg (Crawford 1987, Figure 3; Graham-Campbell & Batey 1998, 84). One of these has recently been radiocarbon-dated to cal AD 870–1150 (1060 ± 50 BP at 2 sigma, Beta-114594: Alison Sheridan, pers comm).

The most obvious feature confirming the identification is the profile, common to most if not all depictions of Highland Galleys. Further features from the incised design offer distinct similarities such as the oarports, mast, sails, rigging and decorative adornments. There is, however, a relative lack of detail by comparison with more formal examples. The depiction of a Highland Galley on the early 16th-century MacLeod wall-tomb in St Clement's Church at Rodel, on Harris (Rixson

1998, Plate 12) offers a particularly fine example of a galley, although examples of surviving graffiti discovered at Kilchattan on Luing (Rixson 1998, Plate 2) and Creagan on Loch Creran are not as impressive or convincing as the Inchmarnock Galley.

The majority of the evidence survives in the form of stone carvings associated with funerary monuments. Over 80 representations of Highland Galleys have been noted on grave slabs and cross-slabs discovered throughout the Western Isles and Argyll (Ritchie & Harman 1996, 103–4). These offer interesting comparisons with the depiction of the vessel that we see on IS.30. Previous work by Steer and Bannerman (1977) established four main schools of carvings associated with the late medieval monumental sculpture of the Western Highlands and Argyll. The Iona workshop is purported to be the earliest, followed by schools from Kintyre, Loch Awe and Loch Sween. The stylistic traits of the individual schools are also partly translated into the features shown in the galleys, such as orientation, degrees of decorative adornment, set of the sails and characteristics of the rigging.

The stylistic traits of the Inchmarnock Galley, in particular the use of the furled sail, are also found among the galleys that have assigned to the Iona and Kintyre Schools (Ritchie & Harman 1996, 104). The close proximity of the monastic site at Saddell would almost certainly suggest that IS.30 reflects the stylistic influence of the Kintyre School. Also there were, of course, proprietorial links between Saddell and Inchmarnock from at least the late 14th century (Chapter 3.2).

IS.50

The depiction of planking suggests that the vessel is constructed of wood, possibly similar to the Viking-type vessels and the Highland Galley. The fragmentary remains are similar to the incised drawing of a boat on the Hedin cross-slab, from Maughold, Isle of Man (Rixson 1998, Plate 1).

IS.51

The lack of detail in the sketch makes it difficult to identify the type of construction of the vessel. The form of the vessel may suggest a craft constructed of wood, although this is uncertain.

Conclusion

The discovery of boat and ship graffiti among the assemblage of incised stone on Inchmarnock represents, perhaps, the most significant corpus of this material relating to the depiction of vessel types and technology found to date in Scotland. This is accentuated by the fact that we have a group of graffiti that spans almost a millennium, from the 8th to the 17nth century. The study of the graffiti adds to the only other known graffiti from this period, discovered at Kilchattan on Luing and Creagan on Loch Creran.

The implications for the craft depicted in the Group 1 inscriptions are particularly significant. They may well be the only known depictions of vessel types indicative of those possibly used by the Gaelic, Pictish and Dalriadic maritime communities in the Western Isles and Argyll before the increasing dominance of the Scandinavian Viking influences in boat and ship construction from the early 9th century. It is interesting that a tangible link may now survive between the indigenous and Irish maritime cultures of the west with the Scandinavian maritime culture of the east.

The vessels depicted in the Group 2 inscriptions are also significant. The graffiti of the Highland Galley certainly represents the most comprehensive and recognisable depiction of a Galley to date. The smaller craft evident in IS.51 is also interesting, perhaps offering a rare depiction of an inshore rowing craft dating to the medieval or early modern period.

APPENDIX 4:
ILLUSTRATING THE INCISED STONES

MIKE MIDDLETON

The incised stone from Inchmarnock was one of the more unusual collections of material to come through Headland's drawing office. It posed a number of very specific illustrative problems and it required a variety of illustrative styles to do it justice. The main aims have been to illustrate all the incised slate to publication standard and in a style that allows comparison with similar published material.

Two principal challenges have been faced in illustrating the incised slate; (1) the issue of visibility, given the frequent faintness of the incised lines; and (2) the difficulty that arises from those examples where a palimpsest of designs has been preserved and where it is difficult to isolate which incised marks belong with which 'level'. Various techniques have been used during the illustrative process to resolve these issues.

The problem of visibility has been tackled using a range of different techniques. Talc has been used to highlight the faintly incised lines against the body of the stone; stones have been scanned at a high resolution, allowing the images to be enlarged; colour filters have been applied to the scans that 'flatten' the background colour, making the incised work easier to see. However, by far the most useful technique has been the use of a hand lens and raking light (Plate A4.1).

Transcribing and unpicking the palimpsests mainly combined the use of scanned images rectified to wax rubbings (where the stones were robust enough to allow this), prepared using brass rubbing wax and lining paper (Figure A4.1). Where the stones were too fragile, a pencil drawing was prepared, to which the images were then rectified. Fine detail was then added using a hand lens and raking light. Only one phasing was attempted. This was done using IS.30 where different phases of incised line could be seen to have been scratched through earlier incised marks. These

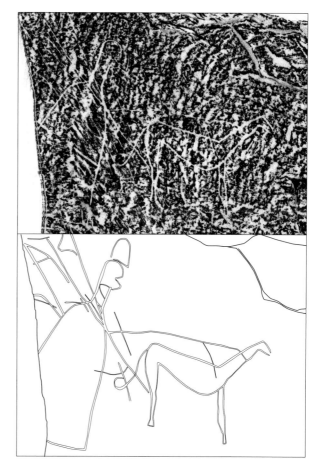

Figure A4.1
Wax rubbing, showing part of the hunting scene on reverse of IS.30
(cf Figure 6.29B)

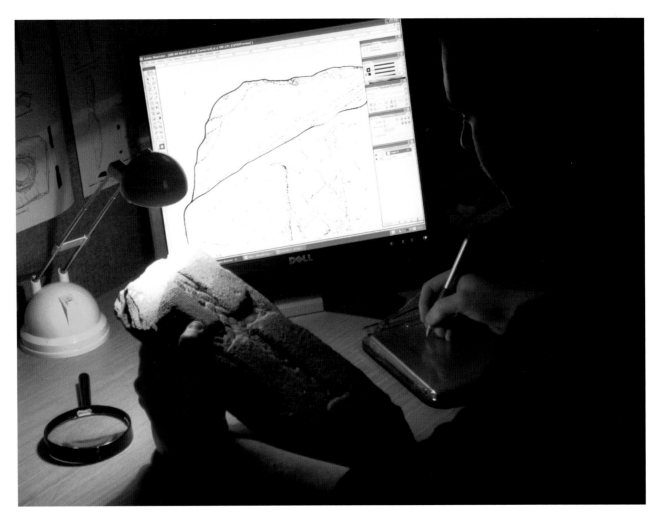

Plate A4.1
Using a hand-lens and raking light to show up the detail on the carved and incised stones

points of intersection were double-checked under a microscope to confirm their authenticity.

Three presentation styles were chosen to best reproduce the stones for publication.

The first, a traditional stipple technique using a top left light source, was used for the large sculptural stones (eg EMS.19: Figure 6.8). This style was chosen to allow the stone to be more easily compared with similar material from the region, as illustrated in Ian Fisher's recent monograph on the early medieval carved stones of the West Highlands and Islands (Fisher 2001). The pre-1974 assemblage of stones from the island, as well as those from the current research programme, are illustrated in Figures 6.1 and 6.2.

The second technique used was a simple, very clean, line technique that aimed to maximise the legibility

of complex designs and palimpsests (eg IS.30, Figures 6.17 and 6.30). The technique focused on the incised lines themselves and uses the minimum number of lines to represent the stone and its texture.

The final technique aimed to provide a technically accurate, photo-realistic representation of some of the stones, enhanced where the incised marks were too faint to see. The aim was to give the viewer a feel for not only the designs but also the colour and texture of the stone. There was also an intention to try and recreate a sense of how some of the more coherent designs may have looked when first created (eg IS.46, Figure 6.27 and Plate 6.6). It was clear from early in the project that freshly etched lines produced very clear white lines against the naturally dark background colour of the local slate. The technique involved preparing very high quality scans of the stones; these were then rectified to produce metrically accurate images and, where enhancement was required, the 'line technique' was used to depict the incised marks. To give an impression of freshness to the design, the lines were rendered white and applied to the scanned image as a transparent overlay.

Due to the importance and scale of the corpus our overriding intention has been to produce a consistent archive of illustrations that could be easily compared with published material and that would aid interpretation of the incised slate assemblage, both in this volume and for the future.

APPENDIX 5: MISCELLANEOUS AND OTHER INCISED SLATE FRAGMENTS (NOT ILLUSTRATED)

CHRISTOPHER LOWE

SF no	Context	Phase	L	W	Th	Shape/condition	Face #1	Face #2
412	422	2	135	125	6	Fragment flat, grey slate.	Two deep scored lines, up to 2mm wide.	[Blank]
416	454	2				Slate fragment.	Five parallel lines, lightly scratched.	[Blank]
423	400	6	85	58	5	Flat, grey slate fragment.	Two incised lines, forming crude crossing out mark.	[Blank]
457	400	6	145	98	12	Irregular fragment of slate.	Two incised lines forming a right angle; a third line set parallel.	[Blank]
479	400	6	85	47	7	Sub-rectangular fragment of dark grey slate with possibly one surviving square-trimmed edge.	Two short parallel incised lines, set perpendicular to incised line.	[Blank]
491	4001	3	60	40	3	Small thin fragment of slate.	Line of lightly incised arc roughly hatched.	[Blank]
517	4001	3	90	55	5	Small sub-rectangular fragment of slate; one possible bevelled edge, other broken.	Series of incised lines.	[Blank]
536	4001	3	120	110	13	Sub-rectangular fragment forming corner of possible slate-board; one edge trimmed square; the other, longer, edge is bevelled.	Miscellaneous faintly-incised diagonal lines.	[Blank]
540	4001	3	300	105	17	Large fragment of slate, broken on all sides; cones of percussion evident.	Numerous linear marks, some scored, others lightly scratched; faint traces of possible lattice.	[Blank]
552	4001	3	60	5	3	Small fragment of spalled slate.	Palimpsest of lightly incised lines.	[Blank]
573	4001	3	170	130	15	Sub-rectangular fragment with bevelled edge, possibly forming part of dressed slate-board.	Series of incised lines forming small rectilinear lattice; one of the lines is hook-ended; near centre of face is an elongated figure-of-eight form.	Small lobate 'fish-like' motif, roughly 21 × 11mm; surface-flaking on face.
604	4001	3	102	80	7	Flat, sub-rectangular beach pebble, broken on two edges.	Two roughly parallel lines, 10-16mm apart, lightly incised.	[Blank]
623	4003	3	82	33	3	Small fragment of spalled slate.	Lightly incised zig-zag design.	[Blank]
634	4001	3	159	109	9	Sub-rectangular fragment of possible slate-board with bevelled edge.	Miscellaneous lightly scratched lines; faint traces of possible rectilinear grid.	[Blank]

SF no	Context	Phase	L	W	Th	Shape/ ondition	Face #1	Face #2
640 641	4001	3	160	85	10	Sub-rectangular fragment of slate; no original edges evident.	Incised arc at edge of stone, adjacent to which are several lightly scratched lines.	[Blank]
667	4001	3	172	95	13	Sub-rectangular fragment forming edge of dressed slate-board; edge is bevelled.	Incised line set perpendicular to bevelled edge of stone; traces of diagonal line adjacent, plus other lighter scratches.	[Blank]
716	4112	2	115	100	9	Sub-rectangular fragment, flaking along two sides.	Very faint scratches forming an outline rectilinear shapef roughly 70mm long and 18mm wide.	[Blank]
750	4233	3	117	95	4	Sub-rectangular fragment, light grey slate, with possibly one surviving original edge; dressed on upper surface, rough face on reverse.	Two parallel incised lines (14mm apart), 105mm long, lightly hatched; at edge of stone are two pairs of incised lines, set perpendicular to each other.	[Blank]
760	4233	3	74	29	2	Sub-triangular spalled fragment, light grey slate.	Fine incised line with three strokes meeting it at 45 degrees and lentoid terminal, finely incised on upstroke but with wider incision on downstroke.	[Blank]
770	4251	3	70	62	6	Sub-triangular fragment, dressed on both surfaces; slight flaking on obverse.	Miscellaneous incised and scratched lines.	Palimpsest of lightly incised lines.
784	4272	2	80	35	7	Sub-rectangular fragment of flakey slate, not dressed.	Two lightly scratched lines set perpendicular to one another; traces of arc at break of stone.	[Blank]
785	4274	2	115	100	11	Sub-rectangular light grey slate with single bevelled edge; flaking on reverse.	Miscellaneous incised lines, set diagonal to surving edge of stone.	[Blank]
815	4263	3	58	44	5	Sub-triangular dark grey fragment, with smooth upper face; slight spalling.	Miscellaneous incised lines, including arc across corner.	[Blank]
850	4004	5	340	160	20	Large sub-rectangular slate block.	Lightly incised lines at one end of slab and arc of deeper cut line across corner.	[Blank]
860	4165	2	290	260	30	Large sub-rectangular slate block, naturally-tapered.	Two slightly curving grooves, 90mm and 70mm long, roughly perpendicular but not touching.	[Blank]
864	4230	3	79	46	5	Fragment of grey slate.	Miscellaneous incised lines at edge of stone.	[Blank]
865	4231	3	106	103	6	Flat grey slate, with squared end.	Miscellaneous incised lines.	[Blank]
880	4245	3	85	52	6	Irregular fragment of slate beach pebble.	Four lightly incised parallel lines roughly 9 mm apart. These are aligned with veins of quartz in stone. The space between these veins appears hatched.	[Blank]
891	4247	5	250	105	10	Sub-rectangular fragment light grey slate. One original edge part survives.	Palimpsest of finely incised lines forming a series of rectilinear and diagonal grids.	Palimpsest of finely incised lines.

SF no	Context	Phase	L	W	Th	Shape/condition	Face #1	Face #2
1063	4574	2	190	100	5	Sub-triangular fragment light grey slate. Recut as roof-tile?	Two parallel lines (22 mm apart) partly cross-hatched and miscellaneous light scratches.	[Blank]
1086	4594	2	250	150	24	Irregular trapezoidal fragment of dark grey slate, with possibly two original edges. Similar stone-type to Cat. no 30 (SF1087).	Lightly incised line 35mm long, crossed by line (8mm long) at upper end; miscellaneous lightly incised lines also present.	[Blank]
1119	436	3	1150	400	20	Trapezoidal slab of dark grey slate, with rounded ends, broken in two. Original edges survive but approx 20% of right hand side missing, broken in antiquity.	Lightly incised freehand circle Ø 270mm located roughly in middle of slab. Miscellaneous incised lines and scratches.	Two roughly drawn concentric 'squares' 205 × 200 and 140 × 110 mm. Traces of palimpsest of rectilinear grids (cell size approximately 20 × 20mm) near base of slab; miscellaneous lines and scratches.
1128	4611	3	52	45	3	Sub-rectangular fragment light grey slate. One original edge complete, two part survive.	incised irregular oval (16mm across) at broken edge of slate.	Miscellaneous light scratches.
1174	4611	3	110	73	10	Sub-rectangular fragment mid grey slate. Surface intact on one side, 50% flaked away on reverse.	Rectilinear frame formed by parallel incised lines (possibly cross-hatched), with sides at least 65mm and 45mm long, overlain by broad scored line, 4mm wide and 78mm long.	Three lightly incised parallel lines, 3mm apart; miscellaneous other lines.
1177	4623	3	63	46	8	Sub-rectangular fragment mid grey slate.	Single incised line, roughly 40mm long and 0.5mm wide.	[Blank]
1251	4656	3	195	140	19	Sub-rectangular fragment dark grey slate, broken in two, bevelled on one edge.	Traces of two ribbon-type motifs (11mm wide), lightly incised.	[Blank]
1256	4493	1	580	400	30	Irregular mid-grey slate with rough-dressed edges. Two irregular holes. (55 × 50mm and 80 × 65mm) and possibly a third broken away at edge.	Deeply incised rectangle 115 × 80mm, divided longitudinally. with four squares (38 × 38mm) along one side and three rectangles (45 × 40mm) along other.	Miscellaneous incised lines.
1265	4537	4	180	90	20	Beach pebble, edges slightly battered.	Crudely incised triangle motif, 80 × 80mm overall.	[Blank]

287

Bibliography

ARCHAEOLOGY OF INCHMARNOCK REPORT SERIES (*AIR*): UNPUBLISHED INTERIM CLIENT REPORTS

1 Carter, S 1999 *An Introduction to the Archaeology & History of Inchmarnock* (July 1999)

2 Halliday, S 2000 *Gazetteer of Archaeological Sites* (February 2000)

2.1 Halliday, S & Lowe, C E 2000 *Gazetteer of Archaeological Sites* (Revised: May 2000)

2.2 Lowe, C 2002 *Gazetteer of Archaeological Sites and preliminary analysis of the evolution of the islands field boundaries* (August 2002)

3 Halliday, S & Lowe, C E 2000 *Results of the May 2000 Survey & Evaluation* (June 2000)

4 Lowe, C E 2000 *Summary & Interpretative Overview of the May 2000 fieldwork* (June 2000)

5 Holden, T Lowe, C E & Halliday, S 2000 *Survey of the farm steadings at Northpark, Midpark and Southpark, Inchmarnock* (October 2000)

6.1 Lowe, C E 2001 *Medieval and later Inchmarnock: a framework for a multi-disciplinary Project Design* (May 2001)

7 Halliday, S & Lowe, C E 2001 *Site 5: Results of an Archaeological Excavation on a Post-Medieval Building* (September 2001)

8 Lowe, C E 2001 *Excavation (2001) at St Marnock's Chapel, Inchmarnock: Interim Report* (March 2002)

9 Conolly, R J & Lowe, C E *Excavation (2002) at St Marnock's Chapel, Inchmarnock: Interim Report* (October 2002)

10 Jones, E 2002 *Excavation at Cave Site 16, Inchmarnock: Interim Report* (September 2002)

11 Conolly, RJ *Excavation (2003) at St Marnock's Chapel, Inchmarnock: Interim Report* (November 2003)

12 Jones, E 2003 *Excavation at Corn-drying Kiln Site 8, Inchmarnock: Interim Report* (August 2003)

13 Conolly, R 2004 *Excavation (2004) at St Marnock's Chapel, Inchmarnock: Interim Report* (December 2004)

ABBREVIATIONS

AFM — Annals of the Four Masters (Ó Corrráin & Cournane)

APS — Acts of the Parliaments of Scotland (Thomson & Innes 1814–75)

AT — *Annals of Tigernach* (Stokes 1896)

AU — Annals of Ulster (Mac Airt & Mac Niocaill 1983)

CGH — *Corpus Genealogiarum Hiberniae* (O'Brien 1976)

CGSH — *Corpus Genealogiarum Sanctorum Hiberniae* (Ó Riain 1985)

Chron. Fordun — John of Fordun, *Chronica Gentis Scotorum* (Skene 1871)

CIIC — *Corpus Inscriptionum Insularum Celticarum*, 2 vols, Dublin. (Macalister 1945; Macalister 1949)

DIL — *Dictionary of the Irish Language, Compact Edition*, Royal Irish Academy, Dublin, 1983.

ER — *Exchequer Rolls* (Stuart *et al* 1878–1908)

HE — Bede's *Historia Ecclesiastica gentis Anglorum* (Colgrave & Mynors 1969)

MG — *The Martyrology of Gorman* (Stokes 1895)

MT — *The Martyrology of Tallaght* (Best & Lawlor 1931)

NAS — National Archives of Scotland

NLS — National Library of Scotland

NMRS — National Monuments Record of Scotland.

OPS — *Origines Parochiales Scotiae* (Bannatyne Club, 1851–5).

OS — Ordnance Survey

PR — *Paisley Registrum* (Innes 1832)

RA — RA (Romilly Allen) motif-number in Allen & Anderson 1903.

RCAHMS — Royal Commission on the Ancient and Historical Monuments of Scotland.

RMS   *Registrum Magni Sigilli Regum Scotorum* (Thomson *et al* 1882–1914)

RPC   Register of the Privy Council

RRS   *Regesta Regum Scotorum* (Barrow 1960: Barrow 1971: Duncan 1988: Webster 1976)

RSS   *Registrum Secreti Sigilli Regum Scotorum* (Livingstone *et al* 1908)

VC   *Vita Columbae*: Life of St Columba– Anderson 1991 (Latin & translation); Sharpe 1995 (translation)

VW   *Vita Wilfridi*: Life of St Wilfrid (Colgrave 1927)

BIBLIOGRAPHY

Primary documents (unpublished)

Mount Stuart Archives   BE/2/1, rental ledger, 1746.
BE/3, rental ledgers, 1879–1944.
BE/6
BE/18

NAS   CH2/890/2, Rothesay Kirk Session minutes, 1685–1764.

Maps (by date order)

1654   Blaeu, J *The Ile of Boot*

1734   Cowley, J *Map of such part of his grace the Duke of Argyle's Heritable Dukedom*

1747–55   Roy, W *Military Survey of Scotland* (sheet 13/5)

1758/59   Foulis, J *A Survey of the Isle of Bute (The Patrimonial Estate of the Earl of Bute)* [bound volume of plans, original in Bute Estate Archive, copy held by Scottish Record Office RHP 14107, pp 79 & 80]

1769   Leslie, J '*A Plan of the Island of Inchmernock; Part of the Estate of the Earl of Bute*' [Photocopy extract received from Ian Fisher]

1801   Langlands, G *This map of Argyllshire . . .*

1821   Girdwood, S *Eye sketch of the Farm of Mid Park of Inchmarnock, Novr 20th 1821, pointing out some improvements with which the tenants want assistance.* (Bute Estate Archive: *Plans of Farms, Enclosures etc on the Estate of Bute. Collected and bound in 1825.* Plan no 45)

1824   Thomson, J *Southern part of Argyllshire*

1869   Ordnance Survey *Buteshire 1:10560 scale map*, sheets CCIII & CCXIV (surveyed 1863)

1869   Ordnance Survey *Buteshire 1:2500 scale map*, sheets CCIII.15, 16 & CCXIV.3, 4, 7, 8 (surveyed 1863)

1897   Ordnance Survey *Buteshire 1:10560 scale map*, sheets CCIII & CCXIV (revised 1896)

1897   Ordnance Survey *Buteshire 1:2500 scale map*, sheets CCIII.15, 16 & CCXIV.3, 4, 7, 8 (revised 1896)

1919   Ordnance Survey *Buteshire 1:2500 scale map*, sheets CCIII.15, 16 & CCXIV.3, 4, 7, 8 (revised 1915)

2000   *British Geological Survey 1:50,000 scale map.* Scotland sheet 29W, Kilfinan (Solid and Drift edition)

Other sources

Aitken, W G 1955 'Excavation of a chapel at St Ninian's Point, Isle of Bute', *Transactions of the Buteshire Natural History Society* 14, 62–76.

Alcock, L 1988 'The activities of potentates in Celtic Britain, AD 500–800: a positivist approach', *in* Driscoll, S T & Nieke, M R (eds), *Power and Politics in Early Medieval Britain and Ireland*, 22–39. Edinburgh.

Alcock, L 1998 'Insular depictions of animals and people', *Proc Soc Antiq Scot* 128 (1998), 515–36.

Alcock, L 2003 *Kings and warriors, craftsmen and priests in Northern Britain AD 550–850.* Edinburgh: (=Soc Antiq Scot Monog Ser, 24).

Alcock, L & Alcock, E A 1987 'Reconnaissance excavations on Early Historic fortifications and other royal sites in Scotland, 1974–84: 2 Excavations at Dunollie Castle, Oban, Argyll, 1978', *Proc Soc Antiq Scot*, 117 (1987), 73–101 and 119–47.

Alexander, D, Neighbour, T & Oram, R D 2002, 'Glorious Victory? The Battle of Largs, 2 October 1263', *History Scotland*, 2:2 (2002), 17–22.

Allason-Jones, L and Jones, J M 2001, 'Identification of "jet" artifacts by reflected light microscopy', *European J Archaeol* 4:2, 233–51

Allen, J R & Anderson, J 1903 *The Early Christian Monuments of Scotland.* Edinburgh 1903 (reprint 1993, Balgavies).

Anderson, A O 1922 (ed), *Early Sources of Scottish History AD 500–1286*, 2 vols. Edinburgh.

Anderson, A O *et al* 1936 (eds) *The Chronicle of Melrose* (facsimile edition). London.

Anderson, J 1900 'Description of a collection of objects found in excavations at St Blane's Church, Bute, exhibited by the Marquis of Bute', *Proc Soc Antiq Scot* 34 (1899–1900), 307–25.

Anderson, M O 1991 *Adomnan's Life of Columba* Clarendon Press Oxford.

Armstrong, E R C & Macalister, R A S 1920 'Wooden book with leaves indented and waxed found near Springmount Bog, Co. Antrim' *J Royal Soc Antiq Ireland* 1 (1920), 160–6.

Aufderheide, A C & Rodriguez-Martin, C 1998 *The Cambridge Encyclopedia of Human Palaeopathology*. Cambridge University Press.

Bailey, R N 1980 *Viking Age Sculpture in Northern England*. Collins Archaeology Series, Glasgow.

Balfour, J A 1909 'The ecclesiastical remains on the Holy Island, Arran', *Proc Soc Antiq Scot* 43 (1908–9), 147–58.

Ballin Smith, B (ed) 1994 *Howe: Four Millennia of Orkney Prehistory*. Society of Antiquaries of Scotland, Edinburgh.

Ballin, T B 2002 *St Marnock's Chapel, Inchmarnock, Argyll and Bute. The lithic assemblage*. Unpublished report to Headland Archaeology Ltd.

Bannerman, J 1974 *Studies in the History of Dalriada*. Edinburgh 1974.

Barber, J W 1981 'Excavations at Iona, 1979', *Proc Soc Antiq Scot* 111, 1981, 282–380.

Barber, J 1990 'Scottish Burnt Mounds: variations on a theme', in Buckley, V (ed) *Burnt Offerings. International Contributions to Burnt mound Archaeology*. Dublin: Wordwell, 98–104.

Barber, J 1997 *The Archaeological Investigation of a Prehistoric Landscape: Excavations on Arran 1978–81*. Edinburgh: Scottish Trust for Archaeological Research.

Barnes, M P & Page, R I 2006 *The Scandinavian Runic Inscriptions of Britain*. Runrön 19, Uppsala, Sweden.

Barrow, G W S 1960 (ed) *Regesta Regum Scotorum*, i, *The Acts of Malcolm IV*. Edinburgh.

Barrow, G W S 1971 (ed) *Regesta Regum Scotorum*, ii, *The Acts of William I*. Edinburgh.

Bass W M 1987 *Human Osteology: A Laboratory and Field Manual*. 3rd edn. Missouri Archaeological Society.

Battiscombe, C F (ed) 1956 *The relics of St Cuthbert*. Oxford.

Bell, R C 1979 *Board and Table Games from many civilizations*, vol 1. New York: Dover Publications.

Best, R I & Lawlor, H J (eds) 1931 *The Martyrology of Tallaght*. Henry Bradshaw Society, London.

Bianchi, G 2003, 'I graffiti della lastra di ardesia', in *Campiglia. Un castello e il suo territorio*, II, *Indagine archeologica*, (ed.) G Bianchi (Biblioteca del Dipartimento di Archeologia e storia delle arti – Sezione Archeologica, Università di Siena, 8), Firenze, 464–77.

Bischoff, Bernhard 1990 *Latin Palaeography. Antiquity and the Middle-ages*, transl. Dáibhí Ó Cróinín and David Gantz, Cambridge.

Black, G F 1890 'Notice of a fragment of a rune-inscribed cross-slab, found on Inchmarnock, Buteshire', *Proc Soc Antiq Scot* 24 (1889–90), 438–43.

Black, G F 1946 *The Surnames of Scotland*. New York (reprinted Edinburgh, 1993).

Boardman, S 1997 *The Early Stewart Kings: Robert II and Robert III*. East Linton.

Boardman, S 2008 'The Gaelic world and the early Stewart Court', in D. Broun & M. MacGregor (eds), *Miorun Mor nan Gall, The Great Ill-Will of the Lowlander: Lowland Perceptions of the Scottish Highlands*. Glasgow.

Bourke, C 1980 'Early Irish hand-bells', *J. Royal Soc Antiq Ireland* 110 (1980), 52–66.

Bourke, C 1983 'The hand-bells of the early Scottish church', *Proc Soc Antiq Scot* 113 (1983), 464–8.

Brooks S and Suchey J M 1990 'Skeletal age determination based on the os pubis: a comparison of the Acsadi-Nemeskeri and Suchey-Brooks methods', *Human Evolution* Vol 5, no 3: 227–38.

Brothwell D R 1981 *Digging Up Bones*. British Museum (Natural History) and Oxford University Press.

Brown, A L 1969 'The Cistercian Abbey of Saddell, Kintyre', *Innes Review*, xx pt. 2 (1969), 130–7.

Brown, D H 2002 *Pottery in Medieval Southampton c 1066–1510*, Southampton Archaeol Monogr 8, CBA Research Rep 133.

Brown, Julian 1993 *A Palaeographer's View. The Selected Writings of Julian Brown*, eds J Bately, M P Brown and J Roberts. London: Harvey Miller Publishers.

Brown, M M 1997 'The Norse in Argyll', in Ritchie 1997, 205–35.

Caldwell, D 1996 'Other Small Finds', in Lewis, J 'Dunstaffnage Castle, Argyll & Bute: excavations in the north tower and east range, 1987–94, *Proc Soc Antiq Scot* 126, (1996), 579–87.

Caldwell, D H & Dean, V E 1992 'The pottery industry at Throsk, Stirlingshire, in the 17th and early 18th century', *Post Medieval Archaeology* 26, 1–46.

Callander, J G 1916 'Notice of a jet necklace found in a cist in a Bronze Age cemetery, discovered on Burgie Lodge Farm, Morayshire, with notes on Scottish prehistoric jet ornaments', *Proc Soc Antiq Scot* 50 (1915–16), 201–40.

Cameron, J 1998 *James V*. East Linton.

Campbell, E 1991 *Imported goods in the early medieval Celtic West: with special reference to Dinas Powys*. Unpubl PhD thesis, Univ Wales, Cardiff.

Campbell, E W 1996 'Trade in the Dark-Age west: a peripheral activity?', in B E Crawford (ed) *Scotland in Dark Age Britain*, 79–91. St Andrews: St John's House Papers No 6.

Campbell, E 1999 *Saints and Sea-Kings*. Edinburgh.

Campbell, E 2005 'Industrial ceramics', in Crone, A & Campbell, E *A Crannog of the 1st Millennium AD. Excavations by Jack Scott at Loch Glashan, Argyll, 1960*, 63–4. Edinburgh (= Soc Antiq Scot Monograph).

Campbell, E 2007 *Continental and Mediterranean imports to Atlantic Britain and Ireland, AD 400–800*. CBA Research Report 157.

Campbell, E & Heald, A 2007 'A "Pictish" brooch mould from North Uist: Implications for the organisation of non-ferrous metalworking in the later 1st millennium AD', *Med Arch* 51 (2007), 172–8.

Cant, R G 1984 'Settlement, society and church organisation in the Northern Isles', *in* Fenton, A & Palsson, H (eds) *The Northern and Western Isles in the Viking World*. Edinburgh, 1984, 169–79.

Cardy, A 1997 'The Human Bones', *in* Hill 1997, 519–62.

Carter, S P, McCullagh, R P J & MacSween, A 1995 'The Iron Age in Shetland: excavations at five sites threatened by coastal erosion', *Proc Soc Antiq Scot* 125, 429–82.

Carver, M 2004 'An Iona of the East: The Early-medieval Monastery at Portmahomack, Tarbat Ness', *Med Arch*, XLVIII (2004), 1–30.

Charles-Edwards, G 2002 'The Springmount Bog Tablets: their implications for insular epigraphy and palaeography', *Studia Celtica* 36 (2002), 27–45.

Charters of the Abbey of Crossraguel. Archaeological and Historical Collections Relating to Ayrshire and Galloway, 1886.

Christison, D & Anderson, J 1905 'Report on the Society's excavations of forts on the Poltalloch Estate, Argyll, in 1904–5', *Proc Soc Antiq Scot*, 39 (1904–5), 259–322.

Chronica Regum Manniae et Insularum. The Chronicle of Man and the Isles. A Facsimile of the Manuscript Codex Julius A. VIII in the British Museum. (Douglas, 1924).

Clarke, A 1999 'The Coarse Stone Tools', *in* Owen & Lowe 1999, 151–64.

Coles, J M 1983 'Excavations at Kilmefort Cave, Argyll', *Proc Soc Antiq Soc* 113 (1983), 11–21.

Colgrave, B (ed) 1927 *Vita Wilfridi* (The Life of Bishop Wilfrid by Eddius Stephanus). Oxford Medieval Texts.

Colgrave, B & Mynors, R A B (eds and transl) 1979 *Bede's Ecclesiastical History of the English People*. Oxford Medieval Texts.

Collingwood, W G 1988 *The Early Crosses of Galloway*, revised reprint. Dumfries and Whithorn.

Courtney, P 1997 'Ceramics and the history of consumption: pitfalls and prospects', *Medieval Ceramics 21*, 95–108.

Cowan, E J 1990 'Norwegian Sunset – Scottish Dawn: Hakon IV and Alexander III', *in* Reid N (ed) *Scotland in the Reign of Alexander III*, 103–31. Edinburgh.

Cowan, I B 1967 *The Parishes of Medieval Scotland*. Scottish Record Society.

Cox, E McB, Owen, O, Pringle, D 1998 'The discovery of medieval deposits beneath the Earl's Palace, Kirkwall, Orkney', *Proc Soc Antiq Scot* 128, 567–80.

Cramp, R 1984 *County Durham and Northumberland*, Oxford (Brit Acad Corpus of Anglo-Saxon Stone Sculpture, 1).

Cramp, R 1994 'The Govan recumbent cross-slabs', *in* Ritchie, A (ed), *Govan and its Early Medieval Sculpture*, 55–61, Stroud.

Craw, J H 1930 'Excavations at Dunadd and at other Sites on the Poltalloch Estates, Argyll', *Proc Soc Antiq Scot*, 64 (1929–30), 111–146.

Crawford, B E 1987 *Scandinavian Scotland*. Leicester.

Crawford, H S 1980 *Irish Carved Ornament from Monuments of the Christian Period*, revised edition, Dublin and Cork.

Crew, P & Rehren, T 2002 'High temperature workshop residues from Tara: iron, bronze and glass', *in* Roche, H (ed), 'Excavations at Ráith na Ríg, Tara, County Meath, 1997', *Discovery Programme Reports 6*. Royal Irish Academy.

Crone, A 2000 *The History of a Scottish Lowland Crannog: Excavations at Buiston, Ayrshire 1989–90*. Edinburgh (= STAR Monograph 4).

Crone, A & Campbell, E 2005 *A Crannog of the First Millennium AD: Excavations by Jack Scott at Loch Glashan, Argyll, 1960* (= Soc Antiq Scot Monograph).

Cross, J F & Bruce, M F 1989 'The Skeletal Remains', *in* J A Stones (ed) *Three Scottish Carmelite Friaries: Excavations at Aberdeen, Linlithgow and Perth 1980–1986* (= Soc Antiq Scot Monograph).

Cross, M A 1984 *Sculptured stones in the County of Bute*. Glasgow University MA dissertation; copy in NMRS.

Crothers, N 1999 'Excavations in Upper English Street, Armagh', *Ulster J Archaeol* 58, 55–80.

Cruden, S 1951 'Glenluce Abbey: Finds Recovered During Excavations', *Trans Dumf & Gall Natur Hist & Antiq Soc, 3rd Ser (1950–51), Vol.XXIX*, 177–94.

Cruden, S 1986 *Scottish Medieval Churches*. Edinburgh: John Donald.

Crummy, N 1988 *The post-Roman small finds from excavations in Colchester 1971–85* (Colchester Archaeological Report 5). Colchester.

Cubbon, W 1935 'Excavations at Ronaldsway, 1935' *Proc Isle of Man Nat Hist & Antiq Soc* IV,2 (1935), 151–60.

Cullen, I 1998 'Metalworking debris', *in* Caldwell, D, Ewart, E & Triscott, J, 'Auldhill, Portencross', *Arch J*, 155 (1998), 22–81.

Curle, A O 1935 'An account of the excavation of a dwelling of the Viking period at "Jarlshof", Sumburgh, Shetland', *Proc Soc Antiq Scot* 69 (1934–35), 265–324.

Curle, C L 1962 'Some little known early Christian monuments in the west of Scotland', *Proc Soc Antiq Scot* 95 (1961–2), 223–6.

Curle, C L 1982 *Pictish and Norse Finds from the Brough of Birsay, 1934–74* (=Soc Antiq Scot monograph). Edinburgh.

Curran, Michael 1984 *The Antiphonary of Bangor and the Early Irish Monastic Liturgy*. Dublin: Irish Academic Press.

Dalland, M & MacSween, A 1999 'The Coarse Pottery', *in* Owen & Lowe 1999, 178–200.

Dark, K R 1994 *Discovery by Design. The identification of secular elite settlements in western Britain AD 400–700*. Oxford (=Brit Archaeol Rep Brit Ser, 237).

Davis, M 1993 'The identification of various jet and jet-like materials used in the Early Bronze Age in Scotland', *The Conservator* 17, 11–18.

Davies, W et al 2000 *The Inscriptions of Early Medieval Brittany. Les Inscriptions de la Bretagne du Haut Moyen Age*. Andover and Aberystwyth, Celtic Studies Publications.

Dempster, T *c* 1620 *Menologium Scotorum.*

Dennison, E P 2005 'Burghs and Burgesses: a time of consolidation?', in Oram R D (ed) 2005b, 253–83.

Dictionary of Medieval Latin from British sources. British Academy, London, 1975–.

Donaldson, G (ed) 1970 *Scottish Historical Documents.* Edinburgh.

Draper, J 2001 *Post-Medieval Pottery 1650–1800.* Buckinghamshire.

Dumville, D N 2002 (ed.) 'Ireland and North Britain in the earlier Middle-ages: contexts for *Míniugud Senchasa Fher nAlban*', in *Rannsachadh na Gàidhlig 2000*, eds C Ó Baoill and N R McGuire, Aberdeen, 185–211.

Dunbar, J G 1981 'The Medieval Architecture of the Scottish Highlands', *in* L MacLean (ed), *The Middle-ages in the Highlands*, Inverness, 1981, 38–70.

Dunbar, J G & Duncan, A A M 1971 'Tarbert Castle: a contribution to the history of Argyll', *SHR*, l (1971).

Dunbar, J G & Fisher, I 1973 'Sgòr nam Ban-naomha (Cliff of the Holy Women), Isle of Canna', *Scottish Archaeological Forum* 5 (1973), 71–5.

Duncan, A A M 1988 (ed) *Regesta Regum Scotorum*, v, *The Acts of Robert I.* Edinburgh.

Duncan, A A M 1992 *Scotland: the making of the kingdom.* The Edinburgh History of Scotland, Volume 1. Mercat Press 1992.

Duncan, A A M & Brown, A L 1957 'Argyll and the Isles in the Earlier Middle-ages', *Proc Soc Antiq Scot*, xc (1956–7), 192–220.

Eales, R 2007 'Changing cultures: the reception of chess into Western Europe in the Middle-ages', in Finkel, I L (ed) *Ancient Board Games in Perspective*, 162–8. London: The British Museum Press.

Easson, D E & Cowan, I B 1976 *Medieval Religious Houses. Scotland.* London.

Egan, G 1998 *Medieval Finds from Excavations in London, 6: The Medieval Household, Daily Living c 1150–c 1450.* London.

Eldjárn, K 1956 *Kuml og Haugfé úr Heidnum sid á Íslandi.* Reykjavik: Bókaútgáfan Nordri.

Emery, N 1996 *Archaeological Excavations of Hirta 1986–1990: The Archaeology and Ethnology of St Kilda No 1.* Edinburgh: HMSO.

Etchingham, C 1999 *Church Organisation in Ireland* AD *650 to 1000.* Maynooth.

Evans, E 1957 *Irish Folk Ways.* London: Routledge & Kegan Paul.

Evans, G R 1979 'Schools and scholars: the study of the abacus in English schools *c* 980–*c* 1150', *English Historical Review* 94, 71–89.

Ewart, G & Pringle, D 2006 *'There was a Castle in the West'. Dundonald Castle Excavations 1986–1993, Scottish Archaeological Journal* 26.

Ewart, G & Triscott, J 1996 'Archaeological excavations at Castle Sween, Knapdale, Argyll & Bute, 1989–90', *Proc Soc Antiq Scot*, 126 (1996), 517–57.

Fairhurst, H 1939 'The galleried dùn at Kildonan Bay, Kintyre', *Proc Soc Antiq Scot* 73 (1938–39), 185–228.

Fairhurst, H 1956 'The stack fort on Ugadale Point, Kintyre', *Proc Soc Antiq Scot* 88 (1954–6), 15–21.

Fanning, T 1981 'Excavation of an Early Christian Cemetery and Settlement at Reask, County Kerry' *Proc Royal Irish Academy* 81C (1981), 67–172.

Fanning, T 1983 'Some Aspects of the Bronze Ringed Pin in Scotland', in O'Connor, A & Clarke, D V (eds) *From the Stone Age to the Forty-Five: studies presented to R B K Stevenson.* Edinburgh, 324–2.

Fenton, A 1978 *The Northern Isles.* Edinburgh: John Donald.

Fisher, I 1996 'The archaeology of the Early Christian Church in the west of Scotland', *in* J Blair & C Pyrah (eds) 1996 *Church Archaeology: research directions for the future.* CBA Research Report 104, 37–42.

Fisher, I 1997 'Early Christian Archaeology in Argyll', *in* Ritchie, G 1997, 181–204.

Fisher, I 2001 *Early Medieval Sculpture in the West Highlands and Islands*, RCAHMS and Soc Antiq Scot Monograph Series 1.

Fisher, I 2005 'Cross-currents in North Atlantic Sculpture' in Mortensen, A & Arge, S V (eds), *Viking and Norse in the North Atlantic: Select Papers from the Proceedings of the Fourteenth Viking Congress, Tórshavn, 19–30 July 2001*, 160–6, Tórshavn.

Fleming, A & Woolf, A 1992 '*Cille Donnain*: a late Norse church in South Uist', *Proc Soc Antiq Scot* 122 (1992), 329–50.

Forbes, A P 1872 *Kalendars of Scottish Saints.* Edinburgh.

Forbes, A P (1874) (ed) *Lives of SS Ninian and Kentigern* (Historians of Scotland, v).

Ford, B 1987 'Copper Alloy Objects', *in* Holdsworth, P (ed) *Excavations in the Medieval Burgh of Perth 1979–1981* (Soc Antiq Scot monogr 5), 121–30.

Ford, B 1996 'The Small Finds', *in* Ewart, G 'Inchaffray Abbey, Perth & Kinross: excavations and research, 1987', *Proc Soc Antiq Scot* 126, 498–505.

Forster, A 2004 'Steatite Vessels in the Norse North Atlantic 800–1400' (Finds Research Group AD 700–1700: Datasheet 34).

Forsyth, K 1996 *The Ogham Inscriptions of Scotland: An Edited Corpus*, PhD Dissertation, Harvard University (Ann Arbor: UMI).

Forsyth, K 1998 'Literacy in Pictland', in H Pryce (ed) *Literacy in Early Medieval Celtic Societies.* Cambridge.

Franklin, J 1998 'The Finds' in Ewart, G & Baker, F 'Carrick Castle: symbol & source of Campbell power in southern Argyll from the 14th to the 17th century', *Proc Soc Antiq Scot* 128, 955–84.

Franklin, J 2001 'The Finds from Stoneypath Castle, East Lothian'. Unpublished Headland report to client.

Franklin, J 2004 'Pottery from 75 College Street and 101-103 High Street', in Coleman, R J 2004, 'Three excavations in medieval Dumbarton: 94-102 and 101–3 High Street and 75 College Street', *Proc Soc Antiq Scot* 125 (2004), 325–370 at pp. 352–9.

Franklin, J forthcoming 'The Finds from Cadzow Castle, Hamilton'.

Franklin, J & Hall, D forthcoming *Pottery from MSC excavations in Ayr*.

Fraser, J E 2002 'Northumbrian Whithorn and the Making of St. Ninian', *Innes Review* 53 (2002), 40–59.

Fraser, J E 2005 'Strangers on the Clyde: Cenél Comgaill, Clyde Rock and the bishops of Kingarth', *Innes Review* 56.2 (2005), 102–20.

Gahan, A & Walsh, C 1997 'Medieval Pottery', in Walsh C *Archaeological Excavations at Patrick, Nicholas & Wine Tavern Streets, Dublin*, Dublin, 109–23.

Gailey, A 1970 'Irish corn-drying kilns', *Ulster Folklife* 15/16, 52–71.

Gaimster, D R M 1995 'The Pottery', in Morris, C D, Batey C E & Rackham, D J *Freswick Links, Caithness: excavation and survey of a Norse settlement*, (Highland Archaeology mongr no. 1), Inverness, 136–48.

Gallo, F A 1977 *Music of the Middle Ages*. Cambridge University Press, 1977.

Gaunt, G D 2000 geological comment on 'Hones', in Mainman & Rogers, 2484–5.

Gibson, W 1922 *Cannel coals, lignite and mineral oil in Scotland* (Memoirs of the Geological Survey of Scotland, Special Reports on the Mineral Resources of Great Britain XXIV).

Gilbert, I 1995 *The Symbolism of the Pictish Stones in Scotland*. Speedwell Books.

Glare, P G W (1982), (ed.) *Oxford Latin Dictionary*. Oxford.

Gordon, K 1990 'A Norse Viking-age grave from Cruach Mhor, Islay', *Proc Soc Antiq Scot* 120, 151–60.

Graham-Campbell, J 1981 'The Bell and the Mould', *in* Reece, R 1981 *Excavations in Iona 1964 to 1974*, 23–5. London (= Inst Archaeol Univ London Occas Pap, 5).

Graham-Campbell, J & Batey, C E 1998 *Vikings in Scotland: an archaeological survey*. Edinburgh University Press.

Greenhill B 1995 *The Archaeology of Boats and Ships*. Conway Maritime Press

Grieg, S 1940 *Viking Antiquities in Scotland*, Oslo: Aschehoug (= *Viking Antiquities in Great Britain and Ireland* Part II).

Guido, M 1999 *The Glass Beads of Anglo-Saxon England*. Society of Antiquaries, London.

Gunn, W, Geikie, A, Peach, B N & Harker, A 1903 *The Geology of North Arran, South Bute and the Cumbraes, with parts of Ayrshire and Kintyre* (Memoirs of the Geological Survey). Glasgow: HMSO.

Haggarty, G & Will, R 1996 'Medieval Pottery' in Lewis, J H 'Excavations at St Andrews, Castlecliffe 1988–90', *Proc Soc Antiq Scot* 126, 648–69.

Hall, D 2004 'Pottery from 94 – 102 High Street', in Coleman, R J 2004, 'Three excavations in medieval Dumbarton: 94–102 and 101–3 High Street and 75 College Street', *Proc Soc Antiq Scot* 125 (2004), 325–70 at pp. 337–43

Hamilton, J R C 1956 *Excavations at Jarlshof, Shetland* (Ministry of Works Archaeol Reports No. 1). Edinburgh.

Hamlin, A & Foley, C 1983 'A women's graveyard at Carrickmore, County Tyrone, and the separate burial of women', *Ulster J Archaeol* 46 (1983), 41–6.

Hannay, R K & Mackie, T L 1953 (eds) *The Letters of James IV 1505–13*. Scottish History Society, 1953.

Hansen, S S 1988 'The Norse landnam in the Faroe Islands in the light of the recent excavations at Toftanes, Leirvik', *Northern Studies* 25, 58–84.

Hansen, S S 1991 'Toftanes: a Faeroese Viking Age farmstead from the 9th – 10th centuries AD', *Acta Archaeologia* 62, 44–53.

Harbison, P 1982 'Early Irish Churches' in *Die Iren und Europa im früheren Mittelalter*, (ed) H. Löwe, 618–29. Stuttgart 1982.

Harding, D W 1997 'Forts, Duns, Brochs and Crannogs: Iron Age Settlements in Argyll' *in* Ritchie, G 1997, 118–40.

Hare, J N *et al* 1985 *Battle Abbey: the Eastern Range and the Excavations of 1978–80*, HBMC England, Archaeological Report no. 2.

Hare, M & Hamlin, A 1986 'The study of early church architecture in Ireland: an Anglo-Saxon viewpoint' in *The Anglo-Saxon Church*, ed L A S Butler & R K Morris. CBA Research Report No. 60. 1986, 131–45.

Haswell-Smith, H 2004 *The Scottish Islands*. Edinburgh: Canongate.

Hay Fleming, D 1909 'Notice of a sculptured cross-shaft and sculptured slabs recovered from the base of St Andrews Cathedral by direction of Mr Oldrieve of HM Office of Works, with notes of other sculptured slabs from St Andrews', *Proc Soc Antiq Scot* 43 (1908–9), 385–414.

Heald, A 2005 *Non-ferrous metalworking in Iron Age Scotland, c.700 BC to AD 800*. Unpubl PhD thesis, Univ Edinburgh.

Heist, W W (ed) 1965 *Vitae sanctorum Hiberniae ex codice olim Salmanticensi nunc Bruxellensi* (Subsidia Hagiographica, xxviii). Brussels 1965.

Hencken, H O'N 1937 'Ballinderry Crannog No 1', *Proc Roy Irish Acad*, xliii (1935–7).

Henderson, D 2006 'The Human Bones' in Collard, M, Lawson, J A & Holmes, N *Archaeological excavations in St Giles' Cathedral, Edinburgh, 1981–93*. Scottish Archaeological Internet Report 22, 2006, 27–41.

Henderson, I & Okasha, E 1992 'The Early Christian Inscribed and Carved Stones of Tullylease, County Cork', *Cambridge Med Celt Stud* 24, 1–36.

Henry, F 1965 *Irish Art in the Early Christian Period (to 800 A.D.)*. London.

Henshall, A S 1956 'A long cist cemetery at Parkburn sand pit, Lasswade, Midlothian', *Proc Soc Antiq Scot* 89 (1955-6), 252–83.

Herity, M 1995 *Studies in the Layout, Buildings and Art in Stone of Early Irish Monasteries*. London: The Pindar Press, 1995.

Herren, M 1974 & 1987 *The Hisperica Famina* (2 volumes), Pontifical Institute of Mediaeval Studies, Studies and Texts, volumes xxxi & lxxxv. Toronto.

Hewison, J K 1893 *The Isle of Bute in the Olden Time*. Edinburgh and London: Blackwood & Sons.

Heyerdahl-Larsen, B 1980 'The Gokstad chieftain's gaming board', in Thoresen, P & Wexelsen, E (eds) *Gokstadfunnet et*

100-års minne, Sandefjordmuseene Årbok 1979–80, 38–40 & 106–7.

Hill, P & Nicholson, A 1997 'Moulds, crucibles and related metalworking debris', *in* Hill 1997, 400–4.

Hill, P 1997 *Whithorn and St Ninian: the excavation of a monastic town 1984–91*. Stroud: Sutton Publishing Ltd.

Hogan, E 1910 *Onomasticon Goidelicum Locorum et Tribuum Hibberniae et Scotiae*. Dublin.

Holden, T G 2006 'Corn-drying Kilns at Hoddom' *in* Lowe, C E 2006, 100–13.

Holleyman, G A 1947 'Tiree Craggans' *Antiquity 21*, 205–11.

Howson, J 1842 'On the Ecclesiastical Antiquities of Argyllshire' *in Transactions of the Cambridge Camden Society* 1842. Cambridge.

Hunter, F 1995 'Report on the analysis of a finger-ring and disc of jet-like material from Barhobble, Wigtownshire', in W F Cormack, 'Barhobble, Mochrum: Excavation of a forgotten church site in Galloway', *Trans Dumfriesshire & Galloway Nat Hist & Antiq Soc 70*, 5–106 (102–3).

Hunter, F 1998 'Cannel coal' *in* D H Caldwell, G Ewart & J Triscott, 'Auldhill, Portencross', *Archaeol J 155*, 22–81 (42–53).

Hunter, F forthcoming 'Cannel coal and oil shale working at Braehead', *in* C Ellis, 'Excavations at Braehead'.

Hunter, F & Heald, A forthcoming 'Metal artefacts', *in* Abernethy, D & Campbell, E 'Bruach an Druimein'.

Hunter, F & Heald, A forthcoming 'Crucibles', *in* Abernethy, D & Campbell, E 'Bruach an Druimein'.

Hunter, F & Nicholson, A 1997 'The jet, shale and cannel coal', *in* Hill 1997, 441–3.

Hunter, F J, McDonnell, J G, Pollard, A M, Morris, C R & Rowlands, C C 1993 'The scientific identification of archaeological jet-like artefacts', *Archaeometry 35*, 69–89.

Hurley, M F, Scully, O M B, Cleary, R M & McCutcheon, S W J 1997 *Late Viking Age and Medieval Waterford: Excavations 1986–1992*. Waterford: Waterford Corporation.

Innes, C (ed) 1832 *Registrum Monasterii de Passeley*. Glasgow (Maitland Club).

Iscan M Y, S R Loth & R K Wright 1984 Age estimation from the ribs by phase analysis: White males. *Journal of Forensic Sciences* 29: 1094–104.

Iscan M Y, S R Loth & R K Wright 1985 'Age estimation from the ribs by phase analysis: White females'. *Journal of Forensic Sciences* 30: 853–63.

Jennings, S 1981 *Eighteen centuries of pottery from Norwich* (East Anglian Archaeology Report No. 13), Norwich.

Jessop, O 1996 'A New Artefact Typology for the Study of Medieval Arrowheads', *Med Arch 40*, 192–205.

Johnstone, P 1980 *Seacraft in Prehistory*. London.

Kelly, F 1988 *A Guide to Early Irish Law* (Early Irish Law series, iii), Dublin.

Kelly, F 1997 *Early Irish Farming*, (Early Irish Law series, iv). Dublin.

Kenney, J F 1929 *Sources for the Early History of Ireland. Ecclesiastical.* New York.

Kermode, P M C 1907 *Manx Crosses*, London, Bemrose (reprinted with additional material 1994, Balgavies, Forfar, Pinkfoot Press).

Kirkness, W 1921 'Notes on the discovery of a coped monument and an incised cross-slab at the graveyard, St Boniface Church, Papa Westray, Orkney', *Proc Soc Antiq Scot* 55 (1920–1), 131–4.

Krusch, B (ed) 1905 *Life of Columbanus by Ionas*. Hannover 1905.

Lacy, B 1983 *Archaeological Survey of County Donegal*. Lifford, 1983.

Laing, L 1996 'Alternative Celtic Art – Early Medieval Non-Pictish Sketches on Stone in Britain', *Studia Celtica* 30 (1996), 127–46.

Laing, L 1998 'The early medieval sculptures from St Blane's, Kingarth, Bute' *Pictish Arts Soc J.* 12 (1998), 19–23.

Laing, L & Laing, J 1993 *The Picts and the Scots*. Alan Sutton Publishing.

Laing, L, Laing, J & Longley, D 1998 'The Early Christian and later medieval ecclesiastical site at St Blane's, Kingarth, Bute', *Proc Soc Antiq Scot* 128 (1998), 551–65.

Lane, A & Campbell, E 2000 *Dunadd, an early Dalriadic capital*, Oxford.

Lawlor, H C 1925 *The Monastery of Saint Mochaoi of Nendrum*. Belfast Natural History & Philosophical Society (Belfast 1925).

Leask, H G 1950 *Glendalough, Co. Wicklow, National Monuments, Official Historical and Descriptive Guide*. Dublin.

Leask, H G 1955 *Irish churches and monastic buildings I: the first phases and the Romanesque*. Dundalk 1955.

Liestøl, A 1984 'Runes' *in* Fenton, A & Palsson, H (eds) 1984 *The Northern and Western Isles in the Viking World: Survival, Continuity and Change*. Edinburgh: John Donald Publishers, 1984, 224–38.

Lindsay, W M 1911 (ed.) *Isidori Hispalensis episcopi Etymologiarum sive originum libri XX*, Oxford.

Livingstone, M *et al* (eds) 1908 *Registrum Secreti Sigilli Regum Scotorum* (Register of the Privy Seal). Edinburgh.

Long, C D 1975 'Excavations in the medieval city of Trondheim, Norway', *Med Arch 19*, 1–32.

Lovejoy C O, R S Meindl, T R Pryzbeck and R P Mensforth 1985 'Chronological metamorphosis of the auricular surface of the ilium: a new method for determination of adult skeletal age at death'. *Am. J. Phys. Anthrop.* 68: 15–28.

Lowe, C E 1987 *Early Ecclesiastical Sites in the Northern Isles and Isle of Man: an archaeological field survey*. 2 vols. Unpublished PhD thesis, Department of Archaeology, University of Durham.

Lowe, C E 2004 'Literacy and learning in the late first millennium AD: recent discoveries from Inchmarnock' *History Scotland* vol. 4, no. 1, January/February 2004, 4–6.

Lowe, C E 2007 'Image and imagination: the Inchmarnock "hostage stone" *in* B Ballin-Smith, S Taylor & G Williams (eds) *West over Sea: studies in Scandinavian sea-borne expansion and settlement before 1300.* Festschrift in honour of Dr Barbara E Crawford. Brill, Leiden, 2007, 53–67.

Lyman R L 1994 *Vertebrate Taphonomy.* Cambridge.

MacAirt, S & Mac Niocaill, G (ed & transl) 1983 *The Annals of Ulster (to AD 1131).* Dublin 1983.

Macalister, R 1945 & 1949 *Corpus Inscriptionum Insularum Celticarum* (2 volumes). Dublin.

McCormick, F 1992 'Early Christian metalworking on Iona: excavations under the "infirmary" in 1990', *Proc Soc Antiq Scot* 122 (1992), 207–15.

MacDonald, J G 1982 'Petrology' in E J Peltenburg, 'Excavations at Balloch Hill, Argyll', *Proc Soc Antiq Scot* 112, 142–214 (183–6).

McDonald, R A 1995 'Scoto-Norse kings and the reformed religious orders: patterns of monastic patronage in twelfth-century Galloway and Argyll', *Albion*, xxvii (1995).

McDonald, R A 1997 *The Kingdom of the Isles: Scotland's Western Seaboard c.1100-c.1336.* East Linton.

McDonald, R A and McLean, S A 1992 'Somerled of Argyll: a new look at old problems', *SHR*, lxxi (1992).

McDonnell, G 1994 'Slag report', *in* Ballin Smith, B (ed), *Howe: Four Millennia of Orkney Prehistory. Excavations 1978–82*, 228–34. Edinburgh (= Soc Antiq Scot Monograph Series, 9).

McDonnell, G 1998 'Irons in the fire - evidence of ironworking on broch sites', *in* Nicholson, R A & Dockrill, S J (eds), *Old Scatness Broch, Shetland: Retrospect and Prospect.* University of Bradford (= North Atlantic Biocultural Organisation Monogr 2 & Bradford Archaeol Sciences Res 5).

McDonnell, G 2000 'Ironworking and other residues', *in* Lane & Campbell, *Dunadd: an early Dalriadic capital*, 218–20. Oxford.

Macdougall, N 1997 *James IV.* East Linton.

McGrail, S 1998 *Ancient Boats in North-west Europe: The archaeology of water transport to AD 1500.* London.

MacGregor, A 1974 'The Broch of Burrian, North Ronaldsay, Orkney', *Proc Soc Antiq Scot* 105 (1972–74), 63–118.

MacGregor, A 1982 'Bone, Antler and Ivory Objects', in Murray, J C (ed) *Excavations in the Medieval Burgh of Aberdeen 1973–81* (Soc Antiq Scot monograph series, 2). Edinburgh, 180–84.

MacGregor, A 1985 *Bone Antler Ivory & Horn: the technology of skeletal materials since the Roman period.* London.

McKerral, A 1952 'A Chronology of the Abbey and Castle of Saddell, Kintyre', *Proc Soc Antiq Scot*, lxxxvi (1951–2), 115–21.

MacKie, E W 1986 'Iron Age and Early Historic occupation of Jonathan's Cave, East Wemyss', *Glasgow Archaeol J* 13, 74–85.

MacLean, D 1983 'Knapdale Dedications to a Leinster Saint: Sculpture, Hagiography and Oral Tradition' in *Scottish Historical Review* 27, 49–65.

Macleod, D 1934 (ed), *A Description of the Western Islands of Scotland and A Voyage to St Kilda*, both by Martin Martin and *A Description of the Western Isles of Scotland* by Sir Donald Monro. Edinburgh. (First published in 1698 and 1774 respectively, and together in 1934, and here quoted from reprint of 1934 edition, Edinburgh 1994.)

McManus, D 1991 *A Guide to Ogam.* (Maynooth Monographs 4), Maynooth.

MacNiocaill, G 1972 *Ireland before the Vikings.* Dublin.

Macphail, J R N (ed) 1934 *Highland Papers.* Volume IV. Edinburgh: Scottish History Society.

Macquarrie, A 1997 *The Saints of Scotland: essays in Scottish Church History AD 450–1093.* Edinburgh: John Donald Publishers Ltd, 1997.

Macquarrie, A 2001 'The Office for St Blane (10 August) in the Aberdeen Breviary', *Innes Review*, 52:2 (2001), 111–35.

MacQueen, J 1973 'The Gaelic speakers of Galloway and Carrick', *Scottish Studies*, xvii (1973), 17–33.

McWhannell, D C 2002 'The Galleys of Argyll' in *The Mariner's Mirror* Vol. 88 no. 1 (February 2002), 14–32.

Mack, A 1997 *Field Guide to the Pictish symbol stones.* Pinkfoot Press.

Mainman, A J & Rogers, N S H 2000 *Craft, Industry and Everyday Life: Finds from Anglo-Scandinavian York* (York Archaeological Trust: The Archaeology of York vol. 17/14), CBA.

Malden, J 2000 'The Abbey and Monastery of Paisley' in J Malden (ed) 2000 *The Monastery and Abbey of Paisley*, 5–22. Renfrewshire Local History Forum.

Mann, L McL 1915 'Report on the relics discovered during excavations in 1913 at cave at Dunagoil, Bute, and in 1914 at the fort at Dunagoil, Bute', *Transactions of the Buteshire Natural History Society* 8 (1914–15), 61–86.

Manning, C 1991 'Toureen Peakaun: three new inscribed slabs', *Tipperary History Journal* (1991), 208–14.

Marshall, D N 1963 'The Queen of the Inch' *Transactions of the Buteshire Natural History Society*, 15, 5–14.

Marshall, D N 1964 'Excavations at Little Dunagoil, Bute' *Transactions of the Buteshire Natural History Society* 16 (1964), 3–69.

Marshall, D N 1973 'Inchmarnock: chapel', *Discovery and Excavation in Scotland 1973*, 21.

Marshall, D N 1974 'Inchmarnock, chapel', *Discovery and Excavation in Scotland 1974*, 28.

Marshall, D N 1978a 'Excavations at Auchategan, Glendaruel, Argyll', *Proc Soc Antiq Scot* 109, 36–74.

Marshall, D N 1978b 'Inchmarnock: axe', *Discovery and Excavation in Scotland 1978*, 24.

Marshall, D N 1978c 'Two Neolithic axeheads from Inchmarnock off Bute', *Proc Soc Antiq Scot* 109, (1978), 355.

Marshall, D N 1980 'Recent finds on Inchmarnock', *Transactions of the Buteshire Natural History Society* 21 (1980), 15–18.

Marshall, D N 1985 'The enigmatic cup mark carvings on Bute', *Transactions of the Buteshire Natural History Society* 22 (1985), 7–19.

Marshall, D N 1987 'Inchmarnock chapel site (N Bute Parish): stone carved with crosses', *Discovery and Excavation in Scotland 1987*, 42.

Marshall, D N 1990 'Carved stone cross from Inchmarnock', *Transactions of the Buteshire Natural History Society* 23 (1990), 5–7.

Marshall D N 1992 *History of Bute.* Rothesay.

Marshall, D N & Middleton, D 1981 'Mid Park Farm, Inchmarnock (N Bute Parish), carved stone', *Discovery and Excavation in Scotland 1981*, 32.

Marshall, D N & Middleton, R 1972 'Inchmarnock', *Discovery and Excavation in Scotland 1972*, 16.

Marshall, D N & Taylor, I D 1979 'The excavation of the chambered cairn at Glenvoidean, Isle of Bute', *Proc Soc Antiq Scot* 108 (1979), 1–39.

Mays S 1998 *The Archaeology of Human Bones*. Routledge.

Meehan, B 1994 *The Book of Kells: an illustrated introduction to the manuscript in Trinity College Dublin*. Thames & Hudson.

Meehan, B 2005 'Book satchels in medieval Scotland and Ireland' in Crone & Campbell 2005, 85–92.

Meehan, D (ed) 1958 *Admanan's 'De locis sanctis' (Scriptores Latini Hiberniae*, iii). Dublin.

Melton, N 1999 'Post-medieval spindle whorls in the Northern Isles: examples made with reworked potsherds', *Proc Soc Antiq Scot* 129, 841–6.

Middleton, D 1977 'Inchmarnock, small finds', *Discovery and Excavation in Scotland 1977*, 41.

Middleton, J 1977 'Inchmarnock, Mid Park - cup marks', *Discovery and Excavation in Scotland 1977*, 10.

Middleton, D, Middleton, R & Middleton, K 1979 'Inchmarnock (N Bute Parish), axe, flints, sherds etc', *Discovery and Excavation in Scotland 1979*, 35.

Milligan, I D 1963 'Corn kilns in Bute', *Trans Buteshire Nat Hist Soc* 15, 53–9.

Mithen, S 2000 *Hunter-gatherer landscape archaeology: The Southern Hebrides Mesolithic Project 1988*-98. Cambridge: McDonald Institute for Archaeological Research.

Molleson T 1995 'Rates of Ageing in the Eighteenth Century' in Saunders S R and Herring A (eds) *Grave Reflections: Portraying the Past through Cemetery Studies*. Canadian Scholars' Press Inc.

Moore, D T & Oakley, G E 1979 'The Hones' in Williams J H 'St Peter's St, Northampton: excavations 1973–1976' (= Northampton Development Corporation archaeological monogr no. 2), Northampton, 280–3.

Morris, C A 2000 *Wood and Woodworking in Anglo-Scandinavian and Medieval York. The Archaeology of York. The Small Finds 17/13. Craft, Industry and Everyday Life*. York.

Morris, C D 1990 *Church and Monastery in the Far North: an archaeological evaluation*. Jarrow Lecture 1989. Jarrow.

Morris, C D 2004 'From Birsay to Brattahli??: recent perspectives on Norse Christianity in Orkney, Shetland and the North Atlantic region', *in* Adams, J & Holman, K H (eds) *Scandinavians and Europe 800–1350. Contact, Conflict and Co-existence: Medieval Texts and Cultures of Northern Europe*. Turnhout, Brepols, 2004, 177–95.

Munro, J & Munro R W 1986 (eds) *Acts of the Lords of the Isles 1336–1493*. Scottish History Society, 1986.

Munro, R 1882 'Ayrshire crannogs (second notice)', *Archaeological Historical Collections Ayr Wigton* 3, 1–51.

Munro, R 1884 'Ayrshire crannogs (third notice). Additional discoveries on the crannog in Lochspouts', *Archaeological Historical Collections Ayr Wigton* 4, 9–16.

Murray, H J R 1951 *A History of Board-Games Other Than Chess*. Oxford: Clarendon Press.

Murray, N 2005 'Swerving from the Path of Justice: Alexander II's relations with Argyll and the Western Isles, 1214–49', *in* Oram (ed) 2005b, 285–305

Mytum, H 1992 *The Origins of Early Christian Ireland*. London.

Neely, J H 1940 'Excavations at Ronaldsway, Isle of Man' *Antiq J* XX (1940), 72–86.

Nicholson, A 1997 'The Copper Alloy' *in* Hill 1997, 360–89.

Nieke, M R & Duncan, H B 1988 'Dalriada: the establishment and maintenance of an Early Historic Kingdom in Northern Britain', *in* Driscoll, S T & Nieke, M R (eds), *Power and Politics in Early Medieval Britain & Ireland*, 6–21. Edinburgh.

O'Brien, M (ed) 1976 *Corpus Genealogiarum Hiberniae*. Dublin.

Ó Corráin, D & Cournane, M (eds) *The Annals of the Four Masters*. www.ucc.ie/celt.

Ó Cróinín, D 1995 *Early Medieval Ireland 400–1200*. Longman History of Ireland

O'Donovan, J 1860 (ed) *Annals of Ireland. The Three Fragments by Dubhaltach mac Firbisigh*. Dublin 1860.

Ó hEalidhe, P 1973 'Early Christian Graveslabs in the Dublin Region', *Journ Roy Soc Antiq Ireland* 103, 51–64.

O'Kelly, M 1958 'Church Island, near Valencia, County Kerry' *Proc Royal Irish Academy* 59C (1957–58), 57–136.

O'Meadhra, U 1979 *Early Christian, Viking and Romanesque Art. Motif-pieces from Ireland 1: an illustrated and descriptive catalogue of the so-called artists' 'trial-pieces' from c.5th–12th centuries AD, found in Ireland c.1830–1973*. Theses and Papers in North-European Archaeology 7. Stockholm, Sweden.

O'Meadhra, U 1987a *Early Christian, Viking and Romanesque Art. Motif-pieces from Ireland 2: Discussion*. Theses and Papers in North-European Archaeology 17. Stockholm, Sweden.

O'Meadhra, U 1987b 'Irish, Insular, Saxon and Scandinavian elements in the motif-pieces from Ireland', in Ryan. M (ed) *Ireland and Insular Art AD 500–1200*. Royal Irish Academy, Dublin, 1987, 159–65.

O'Meadhra, U 1993 'Viking-Age sketches and motif-pieces from the Northern earldoms', *in* Batey, C E, Jesch, J & Morris, C D (eds) *The Viking Age in Caithness, Orkney and the North Atlantic. Proceedings of the Eleventh Viking Congress*. Edinburgh University Press, 1993, 423–40.

O'Neill, J 1907 'The rule of Ailbe of Emly', *Eriu* 3 (1907).

Ó Riain, P 1982 'Towards a Methodology in Early Irish Hagiography', *Peritia* vol. 1 1982, 146–59.

Ó Riain, P (ed) 1985 *Corpus Genealogiarum Sanctorum Hiberniae*. Dublin 1985.

Ó Riain, P 1990 'A misunderstood annal: a hitherto unnoticed *cáin*', *Celtica* 21 (1990), 561–6.

O'Sullivan, J 1994 'Excavation of an early church and a women's cemetery at St Ronan's medieval parish church, Iona', *Proc Soc Antiq Scot* 124 (1994), 327–65.

O'Sullivan, J & Carragain, T O 2007 *Inishmurray – an Irish Monastic and Pilgrimage Landscape: archaeological survey and excavations*. Dublin 2007.

Oakley, G E & Hall, A D 1979 'The Spindle Whorls', in Williams, J H *St Peter's St, Northampton: Excavations 1973–1976* (Northampton Development Corporation archaeological monogr 2), Northampton, 286–9.

Oakley, G E & Webster, L E 1979 'The Copper Alloy Objects' in Williams, J H *St Peter's St, Northampton: excavations 1973–1976* (Northampton Development Corporation Archaeol Monogr no. 2), 248–64. Northampton.

Okasha, E 1985 'The non-ogam inscriptions of Pictland', *Cambridge Medieval Celtic Studies*, 9, 43–69.

Oram, R D 2000 *The Lordship of Galloway*. Edinburgh.

Oram, R D 2005a 'Introduction: an overview of the reign of Alexander II, 1214–49' in Oram 2005b, 1–47.

Oram, R D (ed) 2005b *The Reign of Alexander II, 1214–49*. Brill, Leiden, 2005

Oram, R D & Martin, P 2003 *Inchmarnock: historical evaluation.* Unpublished Headland Archaeology report to client.

Ottaway, P 1992 'Anglo-Scandinavian Ironwork from 16–22 Coppergate', *The Archaeology of York*, Vol. 17/6.

Owen, O A & Lowe, C E 1999 *Kebister: the four-thousand-year-old story of one Shetland township.* (Soc Antiq Scot Monograph 14: 1999).

Parrish, C 1957 *The Notation of Medieval Music. London:* Faber & Faber, 1957.

Parlett, D 1999 *The Oxford History of Board Games*. Oxford: OUP.

Paul, J B 1918 'Saints' Names in Relation to Scottish Fairs', *Proc Soc Antiq Scot* 52 (1917–18), 159–70.

Peers, C R & Radford, C A R 1943 'The Saxon monastery of Whitby', *Archaeologia*, 89 (1943), 27–88.

Pennant's Tour in Scotland and Voyage to the Hebrides, 1772: see Simmons (ed) 1998.

Photos-Jones, E 2005 'Metallurgical Waste', *in* Crone, A & Campbell, E *A Crannog of the 1st Millennium AD. Excavations by Jack Scott at Loch Glashan, Argyll, 1960.* Edinburgh (=Soc Antiq Scot Monograph).

Platt, C & Coleman-Smith, R 1975 *Excavations in Medieval Southampton 1953–1969*, vol 2: The Finds. Leicester.

Pollock, D 1985 'The Lunan Valley Project: Medieval Rural Settlement in Angus', *Proc Soc Antiq Scot* 115 (1985), 357–99.

Plummer, C (ed) 1910 *Vita sanctorum Hiberniae.* (2 volumes). Oxford.

Plummer, C (ed) 1922 *Bethada Naem nErenn, Lives of Irish Saints*, (2 volumes), Oxford 1922.

Price, L 1982 *The Plan of St Gall in Brief.* Berkeley. Los Angeles London.

Pringle, D 2000 'The medieval parish churches of the Isle of Bute: St Blane's, Kingarth, and St Mary's, Rothesay', *Scot Archaeol Review* 22.2 (2000), 123–54.

PSAS 1936 'Donations to the Museum', *Proc Soc Antiq Scot* 71 (1935–36), 13–24.

PSAS 1970 'Donations to and Purchases for the Museum', *Proc Soc Antiq Scot* 102 (1969–70), 295–298.

Quail, G 1979 'Craggan ware', *Scot Pottery Soc News* 4, 39–46.

Radford, C A R 1957 'Excavations at Whithorn (Final Report)'. *Trans Dumfries & Galloway Natural History & Archaeology Society*, 34 (1957), 131–94.

Rahtz, P 1973 'Monasteries as Settlements', *Scot Arch Forum*, 5 (1973), 125–35.

RCAHMS 1971 *Argyll Volume 1: Kintyre.* Edinburgh: HMSO.

RCAHMS 1975 *Argyll Volume 2: Lorn.* Edinburgh: HMSO.

RCAHMS 1980 *Argyll Volume 3: Mull, Tiree, Coll & Northern Argyll (excluding the early medieval and later monuments of Iona).* Edinburgh: HMSO.

RCAHMS 1982 *Argyll Volume 4: Iona.* Edinburgh: HMSO.

RCAHMS 1984 *Argyll Volume 5: Islay, Jura, Colonsay & Oronsay.* Edinburgh: HMSO.

RCAHMS 1988 *Argyll Volume 6: Mid Argyll & Cowal, prehistoric & early historic monuments.* Edinburgh: HMSO.

RCAHMS 1992 *Argyll Volume 7: Mid-Argyll & Cowal, medieval and later monuments.* Edinburgh: HMSO.

Reid, J E 1864 *History of the County of Bute, and families connected therewith.* Glasgow: Thomas Murray & Son.

Rennie, E B 1984 'Excavations at Ardnadam, Cowal, 1964–82', *Glasgow Archaeological Journal*, 11 (1984), 13–39.

Rennie, E B 1999 'Ardnadam, Cowal, Argyll: further thoughts on the origins of the Early Christian Chapel', *Glasgow Archaeological Journal*, 21 (1999), 29–43.

Riddler, I 2007 'The pursuit of *hnefatafl*', in Finkel, I L (ed) *Ancient Board Games in Perspective*, 256–62. London, The British Museum Press.

Ritchie, A 1977 'Excavation of Pictish and Viking-Age farmsteads at Buckquoy, Orkney', *Proc Soc Antiq Scot*, 108 (1976–7), 174–227.

Ritchie, A 1987 'The Picto-Scottish interface in material culture', *in* Small, A (ed) *The Picts: a new look at old problems*, 59–67. Dundee.

Ritchie, A (ed) 1994 *Govan and its Early Medieval Sculpture.*

Ritchie, G (ed) 1997 *The Archaeology of Argyll.* Edinburgh: Edinburgh University Press.

Ritchie, G & Harman, M 1996 *Exploring Scotland's Heritage, Argyll and the Western Isles (RCAHMS).* Edinburgh: HMSO.

Ritchie, P R 1984, 'Soapstone Quarrying in Viking Lands', *in* Fenton, A & Palsson, H (eds), *The Northern and Western isles in the Viking World*, Edinburgh, 59–84.

Rixson, D 1998 *The West Highland Galley.* Edinburgh: Birlinn.

Roberts J 2001 'The Human Bone', *in* C J Moloney 'New evidence for the origins and evolution of Dunbar', *Proc Soc Antiq Scot* 131 (2001), 283–317 (293–303).

Roberts, C and Cox, M 2003 *Health and Disease in Britain from prehistory to the present day*, Sutton.

Robertson, W N 1966 'The game of merelles in Scotland', *Proc Soc Antiq Scot*, 98 (1964–6), 321–3.

Robertson, W N 1974 'Report on Pottery found at Innerpeffray Church, Perthshire', *Glasgow Archaeol Journal 3*, 19–25.

Rodger, N A M 1998 *The Safeguard of the Sea: a naval history of Britain, 660–1649.* London

Ross, A 1994 'Pottery Report', *in* Ballin Smith, B (ed) *Howe: Four millennia of Orkney prehistory, excavations 1978–1982* (Soc Antiq Scot monogr no 9). Edinburgh, 236–57.

Ross, Rev W (ed) 1880 *Blain's History of Bute.* Rothesay.

Ryan, M 1989 'Church metalwork in the eighth and centuries', *in* S Youngs (ed) *'The Work of Angels': Masterpieces of Celtic Metalwork, 6th–9th centuries AD.* British Museum Publications, 1989, 125–30.

Rynne, E 1994 'Drolleries in the Book of Kells', *in* F O'Mahony (ed) *The Book of Kells: Proceedings of a Conference at Trinity College, Dublin, 6–9 September 1992.* Dublin 1994, 311–21.

Sands, R 1997 *Prehistoric woodworking: the analysis and interpretation of Bronze and Iron Age toolmarks.* London: Institute of Archaeology, University College London.

Scheuer, L & Black, S 2000 *Developmental Juvenile Osteology.*

Scott, J E 1970 'Saddell Abbey', *Transactions of the Gaelic Society of Inverness*, xlvi.

Scott, J G 1963 'The rebated cist at Inchmarnock', *Transactions of the Buteshire Natural History Society*, 15, 15–16.

Scott, L 1951 'Corn-drying Kilns', *Antiquity* 20 (1951), 196–208.

Scott, W W 1979 'John of Fordun's description of the Western Isles', *Scottish Studies*, xxiii.

Selmer, C (ed) 1959 *Nauigatio Sancti Brendani Abbatis.* Notre Dame, Indiana, reprinted Dublin.

Sharman, P 1999 'The Steatite', *in* Owen & Lowe 1999, 168–78.

Sharpe, R (ed) 1995 *Life of Columba.* London.

Sharpe, R 2000 'The thriving of Dalriada', *in* S Taylor (ed) *Kings, Clerics and Chronicles in Scotland, 500–1297.* Dublin 2000, 47–61.

Sheridan, J A 2006 'Inchmarnock, Northpark, cist 3'. *Discovery and Excavation in Scotland* 7, 39–40.

Sheridan, J A & Speirs, A (with contributions by J Evans, M Jay, J Montgomery, L Troalen & C Wilkinson) forthcoming *The 'Queen of the Inch': New Research on an Early Bronze Age Aristocrat from Inchmarnock.* Rothesay: Bute Museum.

Shetelig, H (ed) 1954 *Viking Antiquities in Great Britain and Ireland: Volume 6: Civilization of the Viking Settlers in relation to their old and new countries.*

Siggins, G & Carter, S 1993 'The monitoring of an eroding prehistoric site at Achnasavil, Carradale, Kintyre', *Glasgow Archaeological Journal*, 18, 41–48.

Simmons, A (ed) 1998 *A Tour in Scotland and Voyage to the Hebrides 1772, by Thomas Pennant.* Edinburgh: Birlinn, 1998.

Simpson, W G 1972 'A gaming board of Ballinderry-type from Knockanboy, Derrykeighan, Co. Antrim', *Ulster J Archaeol* 35 (1972), 63–4.

Sims-Williams, P 1993 'Some Problems in Deciphering the Early Irish Ogam Alphabet', *Transactions of the Philological Society* 91.2, 133–80.

Sims-Williams, P 2003 *The Celtic Inscriptions of Britain: Phonology and Chronology, c 400–1200*, (Publications of the Philological Society 37). Oxford: Blackwells.

Skene, W F (ed & transl) 1871 *Johannis de Fordun, Chronica Gentis Scotorum.* Edinburgh (reprinted Llanerch, 1993).

Spearman, R M 1997 'The smithy and metalworking debris from Mills Mount', *in* Driscoll, S T & Yeoman, P A (eds), *Excavations within Edinburgh Castle in 1988–91*, 164–8. Edinburgh (=Soc Antiq Scot Monograph Series, 12).

Spiers, A 1996 'The Bute Museum Carved Stone Collection', *Transactions of the Buteshire Natural History Society*, 24, 60–1.

Starley, D 2000 'Metalworking debris', *in* Buxton, K & Howard-Davis, C (eds), *Bremetenacum: Excavations at Roman Ribchester 1980, 1989–1990*, 337–47. Lancaster (=Lancaster Imprints Ser, 9).

Steer, K A & Bannerman, J W M 1977 *Late Medieval Monumental Sculpture in the West Highlands.* Edinburgh: HMSO.

Sterckx, C 1973a 'Les trois damiers de Buckquoy', *Annals de Bretagne*, 80 (1973), 675–89.

Sterckx, C 1973b 'Les jeux de damier celtiques', *Études Celtiques*, 13 (1973), 733–49.

Stevenson, J B 1997 'The Prehistoric Rock Carvings of Argyll', *in* Ritchie 1997, 95–117.

Stirland A J 2000 *Raising the Dead: The skeleton crew of Henry VIII's great ship, the Mary Rose.* Wiley.

Stone, J C 1989 *The Pont Manuscript Maps of Scotland: 16th century origins of a Blaeu atlas.* Map Collector Publications Ltd, Tring, Hertfordshire.

Stokes, W (ed) 1895 *Félire Húi Gormáin* (The Martyrology of Gorman). London.

Stokes, W (ed) 1896 *The Annals of Tigernach* (vol 1). Originally published in *Revue Celtique* 16 & 17. Reprinted 1993 by Llanerch, Felinfach.

Stokes, W & Strachan, J (eds) 1903 *Thesaurus Palaeohibernicus: A collection of Old-Irish glosses, scholia, prose and verse*, vol. ii, Cambridge.

Stratford, N 1997 *The Lewis Chessmen and the enigma of the hoard.* London: The British Museum.

Strecker, K (ed) 1923 *Monumenta Germanica Historica: Poetae Latini Aevae Carolini IV.* Berlin 1923.

Stroud, G & Kemp, R L 1993 *Cemeteries of the Church and Priory of St Andrew, Fishergate.* (=The Archaeology of York, Vol. 12 Fasc 2). CBA.

Stuart, J *et al* (eds) 1878–1908 *The Exchequer Rolls of Scotland.* Edinburgh.

Sutherland, D G 1997 'The Environment of Argyll', *in* Ritchie 1997, 10–24.

Swift, C 1984 *Early ecclesiastical sites on Islay.* Unpublished M Phil dissertation, University of Durham.

Taylor, S forthcoming 'The onomastic landscape of the Gaelic notes', *in* Forsyth, K (ed) *Studies in the Book of Deer: This Splendid Little Book.* Dublin.

Tedeschi, C 2000a, *Contributo allo studio paleografico dei graffiti parietali latini, in Libri, documenti, epigrafi medievali: possibilità di studi comparativi*, Atti del Convegno internazionale dell'Associazione Italiana dei Paleografi e dei Diplomatisti (Bari, 2–5 ottobre 2000), Spoleto.

Tedeschi, C 2000b, 'Graffiti altomedievali del Tempietto sul Clitunno. A proposito della recente edizione di Carola Jäggi', in *Effemeridi graffitologiche I*, ed. C Tedeschi (*Scrittura e civiltà* 24), 413–9.

Tedeschi, C 2005, *Congeries Lapidum. Iscrizioni britanniche dei secoli V-VII*, 2 vols., Pisa, (Pubblicazioni del Centro di Cultura Medievale della Scuola Normale Superiore di Pisa).

Thomson, J M *et al* 1882–1914 (eds) *Registrum Magni Sigilli Regum Scotorum* (Register of the Great Seal). Edinburgh.

Thomson, T & Innes, C 1814–75 (eds) *Acts of the Parliaments of Scotland*. Edinburgh.

Thurneysen, R 1946 *A Grammar of Old Irish*, transl D. A. Binchy and Osborn Bergin, Dublin.

Tipping, R 1994 'The form and fate of Scottish woodlands', *Proc Soc Antiq Scot* 124 (1994), 1–54.

Tipping, R, Tisdall, E & Davies, A 2000 *Palaeoenvironmental Investigations (Inchmarnock), Phase I: Field Reconnaissance and recommendations for further work*. Report to Headland Archaeology Ltd, October 2000.

Tipping, R, Tisdall, E & Davies, A 2001 *Palaeoenvironmental Investigations (Inchmarnock), Phase II: Radiocarbon dating, sampling, analysis and interpretation*. Report to Headland Archaeology Ltd, January 2001.

Tolan-Smith, C 2001 *The Caves of Mid Argyll: an archaeology of human use*. Society of Antiquaries of Scotland Monograph Series Number 20.

Tranter, N 1977 *Argyll and Bute*. London.

Turner, D J & Dunbar, J G 1970 'Breachacha Castle, Coll: Excavations and Field Survey, 1965–8', *Proc Soc Antiq Scot* 102 (1969–70), 155–87.

Velasquez Soriano, I 1988 *Pizarras visigodas, Edición crítica y estudio*. Murcia.

Waddell, J J 1932 'Cross-slabs recently discovered at Fowlis Wester and Millport', *Proc Soc Antiq Scot* 66 (1931–2), 409–12.

Wainwright, F T (ed) 1962 *The Northern Isles*. Edinburgh 1962.

Wakeman, W F 1893 *A Survey of the Antiquarian Remains on the Island of Inishmurray*. Dublin 1893.

Walker, B 2004 'The parallelogram plan: accident or design?', *Yorkshire Buildings 2004* (Yorkshire Vernacular Buildings Study Group, 2004, 52–8). York.

Walker, B, McGregor, C & Stark, G 1996 *Thatch and Thatching Techniques: A Guide to Conserving Scottish Thatching Traditions*. Technical Advice Note no 4, Historic Scotland, Edinburgh 1996.

Walker, G S M (ed) 1970 *Sancti Columbani Opera*. Dublin 1970.

Ward-Perkins J B 1940 *London Museum Medieval Catalogue*. London.

Warren, F E (ed) 1893 *The Antiphonary of Bangor. An Early Irish Manuscript in the Ambrosian Library at Milan*, 2 vols. Part I Facsimile, Part II Amended Text (Henry Bradshaw Society vols 4, 10). London.

Watkins, J G 1987 'The Pottery', Armstrong, P & Ayers, B, *Excavations in High Street and Blackfriargate*, (=East Riding Archaeologist Vol. 8, Hull Old Town Report Series no 5), Hull, 53–181.

Watson, W J 1926 *The History of the Celtic Place-names of Scotland*. Reprinted by Birlinn, Edinburgh 1993.

Watt, D E R (ed) 1969 *Fasti Ecclesiae Scoticanae Medii Aevi ad annum 1638*, 2nd draft, Scottish record Society.

Watt, D E R and Shead, N F (eds) 2001 *The Heads Of Religious Houses in Scotland from Twelfth to Sixteenth Centuries*. Scottish Record Society.

Webb, A 2003 *Inchmarnock Archaeological Research Project; Geophysical Survey*. Report no 1149, Archaeological Services WYAS.

Webster, B (ed) 1976 *Regesta Regum Scotorum*, vi, *The Acts of David II*. Edinburgh.

Whitehead, R 1996 *Buckles 1250–1800*. Chelmsford.

White-Marshall, J & Walsh, C 2005 *Illaunloughan Island: an early medieval monastery in County Kerry*. Wordwell 2005.

Wilson, G & Watson, P M 1998 'Conical gaming pieces', *in* N M Sharples (ed) *Scalloway: a Broch, Late Iron Age Settlement and Medieval Cemetery in Shetland*. Oxbow Monograph 82 (1998), 174–5.

Wilson, W D 1857 'Description of an ancient cross at Kilmory in Argyleshire' *Archaeologica Scotica* 4 (1857), 377–81

Wooding, J 2001 'Biblical narrative and local imagery on the Kilnaruane cross-shaft, Co Cork', *in* Redknap, Edwards, Youngs, Lane & Knight (eds) *Pattern and Purpose in Insular Art: Proceedings of the Fourth International Conference on Insular Art held at the National Museum & Gallery, Cardiff 3–6 September 1998*. Oxbow Books, 253–9.

WEA (Workshop of European Anthropologists) 1980 'Recommendations for age and sex diagnoses of skeletons', *Journal of Human Evolution* 9: 517–49.

Index

Chapter extents are shown in **bold** numbers.
Page numbers in *italics* indicate illustrations or maps.
Sub-entries are in alphabetical order except where *chronological* order is more significant.